TWELVE GREAT PLAYS

TWELVE GREAT PLAYS

Edited by Leonard F. Dean

NEW YORK UNIVERSITY

HARCOURT, BRACE & WORLD, INC.
New York / Chicago / San Francisco / Atlanta

PERFORMING RIGHTS

The OEDIPUS REX of Sophocles, translated by Dudley Fitts and Robert Fitzgerald.

CAUTION: All rights, including professional, amateur, motion picture, recitation, lecturing, public reading, radio broadcasting, and television are strictly reserved. Inquiries on all rights should be addressed to Harcourt, Brace & World, Inc., 757 Third Avenue, New York, New York 10017.

TARTUFFE by Molière, translated by Richard Wilbur.

CAUTION: Professionals and amateurs are hereby warned that this translation, being fully protected under the copyright laws of the United States of America, the British Empire, including the Dominion of Canada, and all other countries which are signatories to the Universal Copyright Convention and the International Copyright Union, is subject to royalty. All rights, including professional, amateur, motion picture, recitation, lecturing, public reading, radio broadcasting, and television, are strictly reserved. Particular emphasis is laid on the question of readings, permission for which must be secured from the author's agent in writing. Inquiries on professional rights (except for amateur rights) should be addressed to Mr. Gilbert Parker, Agency for the Performing Arts, Inc., 120 West 57 Street, New York, New York 10019; inquiries on translation rights should be addressed to Harcourt, Brace & World, Inc., 757 Third Avenue, New York, New York 10017. The amateur acting rights of *Tartuffe* are controlled exclusively by the Dramatists Play Service, Inc., 440 Park Avenue South, New York, New York. No amateur performance of the play may be given without obtaining in advance the written permission of the Dramatists Play Service, Inc., and paying the requisite fee.

ISBN: 0-15-592387-0

Library of Congress Catalog Card Number: 71-103819

Printed in the United States of America

PREFACE

Twelve Great Plays began as a revision of the earlier collection, *Nine Great Plays* (1950, 1956), but it soon turned into a new book, for nine of the present plays were not used before.

Anthologizing, like many other tasks, has its gray side. There is some drudgery. Many contemporary plays are unavailable for a gray mixture of commercial and other reasons. And one can grow gray trying to decide which play to use from Sophocles, Shakespeare, and Jonson.

But anthologizing also has its bright side. Not every day does one get to do something that is potentially profitable, personally rewarding, and socially helpful. I am fascinated by all the plays in this volume, and I enjoyed writing the critical commentaries that follow them. In these commentaries I tried to speak to several audiences, to be helpful and perceptive, and to avoid the language of critical clichés without sounding eccentric or cute. I was also interested in trying once more to understand what I mean by "theatrical" and why I believe there is an essential rightness about the perennial instinct of young people to see and think theatrically.

LEONARD F. DEAN

CONTENTS

TWELVE GREAT PLAYS

AGAMEMNON

Aeschylus

Translated by LOUIS MAC NEICE

CHARACTERS

WATCHMAN	HERALD
CHORUS OF OLD MEN OF THE CITY	AGAMEMNON
	CASSANDRA
CLYTEMNESTRA	AEGISTHUS

SCENE

A space in front of the palace of Agamemnon in Argos. Night. A WATCHMAN *on the roof of the palace.*

WATCHMAN. The gods it is I ask to release me from this watch
A year's length now, spending my nights like a dog,
Watching on my elbow on the roof of the sons of Atreus
So that I have come to know the assembly of the nightly stars
Those which bring storm and those which bring summer to men,
The shining Masters riveted in the sky—
I know the decline and rising of those stars.
And now I am waiting for the sign of the beacon,
The flame of fire that will carry the report from Troy,
News of her taking. Which task has been assigned me
By a woman of sanguine heart but a man's mind.
Yet when I take my restless rest in the soaking dew,
My night not visited with dreams—
For fear stands by me in the place of sleep
That I cannot firmly close my eyes in sleep—
Whenever I think to sing or hum to myself
As an antidote to sleep, then every time I groan
And fall to weeping for the fortunes of this house
Where not as before are things well ordered now.

AGAMEMNON The *Agamemnon* of Aeschylus, translated by Louis MacNeice. Reprinted by permission of Faber and Faber Ltd., Publishers.

But now may a good chance fall, escape from pain,
The good news visible in the midnight fire.

[*Pause. A light appears, gradually increasing, the light of the beacon.*]

Ha! I salute you, torch of the night whose light
Is like the day, an earnest of many dances
In the city of Argos, celebration of Peace.
I call to Agamemnon's wife; quickly to rise
Out of her bed and in the house to raise
Clamour of joy in answer to this torch
For the city of Troy is taken—
Such is the evident message of the beckoning flame.
And I myself will dance my solo first
For I shall count my master's fortune mine
Now that this beacon has thrown me a lucky throw.
And may it be when he comes, the master of this house,
That I grasp his hand in my hand.
As to the rest, I am silent. A great ox, as they say,
Stands on my tongue. The house itself, if it took voice,
Could tell the case most clearly. But I will only speak
To those who know. For the others I remember nothing.

[*Enter* CHORUS OF OLD MEN. *During the following chorus the day begins to dawn.*]

CHORUS. The tenth year it is since Priam's high
Adversary, Menelaus the king
And Agamemnon, the double-throned and sceptred
Yoke of the sons of Atreus
Ruling in fee from God,
From this land gathered an Argive army
On a mission of war a thousand ships,
Their hearts howling in boundless bloodlust
In eagles' fashion who in lonely
Grief for nestlings above their homes hang
Turning in cycles
Beating the air with the oars of their wings,
Now to no purpose
Their love and task of attention.

But above there is One,
Maybe Pan, maybe Zeus or Apollo,
Who hears the harsh cries of the birds
Guests in his kingdom,
Wherefore, though late, in requital
He sends the Avenger.
Thus Zeus our master

Guardian of guest and of host
Sent against Paris the sons of Atreus
For a woman of many men
Many the dog-tired wrestlings
Limbs and knees in the dust pressed—
For both the Greeks and Trojans
An overture of breaking spears.

Things are where they are, will finish
In the manner fated and neither
Fire beneath nor oil above can soothe
The stubborn anger of the unburnt offering.
As for us, our bodies are bankrupt,
The expedition left us behind
And we wait supporting on sticks
Our strength—the strength of a child;
For the marrow that leaps in a boy's body
Is no better than that of the old
For the War God is not in his body;
While the man who is very old
And his leaf withering away
Goes on the three-foot way
No better than a boy, and wanders
A dream in the middle of the day.

But you, daughter of Tyndareus,
Queen Clytemnestra,
What is the news, what is the truth, what have you learnt,
On the strength of whose word have you thus
Sent orders for sacrifice round?
All the gods, the gods of the town,
Of the worlds of Below and Above,
By the door, in the square,
Have their altars ablaze with your gifts,
From here, from there, all sides, all corners,
Sky-high leap the flame-jets fed
By gentle and undeceiving
Persuasion of sacred unguent,
Oil from the royal stores.
Of these things tell
That which you can, that which you may,
Be healer of this our trouble
Which at times torments with evil
Though at times by propitiations
A shining hope repels

The insatiable thought upon grief
Which is eating away our hearts.

Of the omen which powerfully speeded
That voyage of strong men, by God's grace even I
Can tell, my age can still
Be galvanized to breathe the strength of song,
To tell how the kings of all the youth of Greece
Two-throned but one in mind
Were launched with pike and punitive hand
Against the Trojan shore by angry birds.
Kings of the birds to our kings came,
One with a white rump, the other black,
Appearing near the palace on the spear-arm side
Where all could see them,
Tearing a pregnant hare with the unborn young
Foiled of their courses.
   Cry, cry upon Death; but may the good prevail.

But the diligent prophet of the army seeing the sons
Of Atreus twin in temper knew
That the hare-killing birds were the two
Generals, explained it thus—
"In time this expedition sacks the town
Of Troy before whose towers
By Fate's force the public
Wealth will be wasted.
Only let not some spite from the gods benight the bulky battalions,
The bridle of Troy, nor strike them untimely;
For the goddess feels pity, is angry
With the winged dogs of her father
Who killed the cowering hare with her unborn young;
Artemis hates the eagles' feast."
   Cry, cry upon Death; but may the good prevail.

"But though you are so kind, goddess,
To the little cubs of lions
And to all the sucking young of roving beasts
In whom your heart delights,
Fulfil us the signs of these things,
The signs which are good but open to blame,
And I call on Apollo the Healer
That his sister raise not against the Greeks
Unremitting gales to baulk their ships,
Hurrying on another kind of sacrifice, with no feasting,

Barbarous building of hates and disloyalties
Grown on the family. For anger grimly returns
Cunningly haunting the house, avenging the death of a child, never
forgetting its due."
So cried the prophet—evil and good together,
Fate that the birds foretold to the king's house.
In tune with this
Cry, cry upon Death; but may the good prevail.

Zeus, whoever He is, if this
Be a name acceptable,
By this name I will call him.
There is no one comparable
When I reckon all of the case
Excepting Zeus, if ever I am to jettison
The barren care which clogs my heart.

Not He° who formerly was great
With brawling pride and mad for broils
Will even be said to have been.
And He° who was next has met
His match and is seen no more,
But Zeus is the name to cry in your triumph-song
And win the prize for wisdom.

Who setting us on the road
Made this a valid law—
"That men must learn by suffering."
Drop by drop in sleep upon the heart
Falls the laborious memory of pain,
Against one's will comes wisdom;
The grace of the gods is forced on us
Throned inviolably.

So at that time the elder
Chief of the Greek ships
Would not blame any prophet
Nor face the flail of fortune;
For unable to sail, the people
Of Greece were heavy with famine,
Waiting in Aulis where the tides
Flow back, opposite Chalcis.

159. He: Ouranos **162. He:** Cronus

But the winds that blew from the Strymon,°
Bringing delay, hunger, evil harbourage,
Crazing men, rotting ships and cables,
By drawing out the time
Were shredding into nothing the flower of Argos,
When the prophet screamed a new
Cure for that bitter tempest
And heavier still for the chiefs,
Pleading the anger of Artemis so that the sons of Atreus
Beat the ground with their sceptres and shed tears.

Then the elder king found voice and answered:
"Heavy is my fate, not obeying,
And heavy it is if I kill my child, the delight of my house,
And with a virgin's blood upon the altar
Make foul her father's hands.
Either alternative is evil.
How can I betray the fleet
And fail the allied army?
It is right they should passionately cry for the winds to be lulled
By the blood of a girl. So be it. May it be well."
But when he had put on the halter of Necessity
Breathing in his heart a veering wind of evil
Unsanctioned, unholy, from that moment forward
He changed his counsel, would stop at nothing.
For the heart of man is hardened by infatuation,
A faulty adviser, the first link of sorrow.
Whatever the cause, he brought himself to slay
His daughter, an offering to promote the voyage
To a war for a runaway wife.

Her prayers and her cries of father,
Her life of a maiden,
Counted for nothing with those militarists;
But her father, having duly prayed, told the attendants
To lift her, like a goat, above the altar
With her robes falling about her,
To lift her boldly, her spirit fainting,
And hold back with a gag upon her lovely mouth
By the dumb force of a bridle

182. Strymon: modern Struma, a river flowing through southwestern Bulgaria and northern Greece, and formerly the boundary between Macedonia and Thrace. The winds were blowing from the northeast toward Aulis on Euripus Strait in Boeotia, where the Greek fleet was assembled.

The cry which would curse the house.
Then dropping on the ground her saffron dress,
Glancing at each of her appointed
Sacrificers a shaft of pity,
Plain as in a picture she wished
To speak to them by name, for often
At her father's table where men feasted
She had sung in celebration for her father
With a pure voice, affectionately, virginally,
The hymn for happiness at the third libation.
The sequel to this I saw not and tell not
But the crafts of Calchas gained their object.
To learn by suffering is the equation of Justice; the Future
Is known when it comes, let it go till then.
To know in advance is to sorrow in advance.
The facts will appear with the shining of the dawn.
[*Enter* CLYTEMNESTRA.]
But may good, at the least, follow after
As the queen here wishes, who stands
Nearest the throne, the only
Defence of the land of Argos.

LEADER OF THE CHORUS. I have come, Clytemnestra, reverencing your authority.
For it is right to honour our master's wife
When the man's own throne is empty.
But you, if you have heard good news for certain, or if
You sacrifice on the strength of flattering hopes,
I would gladly hear. Though I cannot cavil at silence.

CLYTEMNESTRA. Bearing good news, as the proverb says, may Dawn
Spring from her mother Night.
You will hear something now that was beyond your hopes.
The men of Argos have taken Priam's city.

LEADER OF THE CHORUS. What! I cannot believe it. It escapes me.

CLYTEMNESTRA. Troy in the hands of the Greeks. Do I speak plain?

LEADER OF THE CHORUS. Joy creeps over me, calling out my tears.

CLYTEMNESTRA. Yes. Your eyes proclaim your loyalty.

LEADER OF THE CHORUS. But what are your grounds? Have you a proof of it?

CLYTEMNESTRA. There is proof indeed—unless God has cheated us.

LEADER OF THE CHORUS. Perhaps you believe the inveigling shapes of dreams?

CLYTEMNESTRA. I would not be credited with a dozing brain!

LEADER OF THE CHORUS. Or are you puffed up by Rumour, the wingless flyer?

CLYTEMNESTRA. You mock my common sense as if I were a child.

LEADER OF THE CHORUS. But at what time was the city given to sack?
CLYTEMNESTRA. In this very night that gave birth to this day.
LEADER OF THE CHORUS. What messenger could come so fast?
CLYTEMNESTRA. Hephaestus,° launching a fine flame from Ida,
Beacon forwarding beacon, despatch-riders of fire,
Ida relayed to Hermes' cliff in Lemnos
And the great glow from the island was taken over third
By the height of Athos that belongs to Zeus,
And towering then to straddle over the sea
The might of the running torch joyfully tossed
The gold gleam forward like another sun,
Herald of light to the heights of Mount Macistus,
And he without delay, nor carelessly by sleep
Encumbered, did not shirk his intermediary role,
His farflung ray reached the Euripus' tides
And told Messapion's watchers, who in turn
Sent on the message further
Setting a stack of dried-up heather on fire.
And the strapping flame, not yet enfeebled, leapt
Over the plain of Asopus like a blazing moon
And woke on the crags of Cithaeron
Another relay in the chain of fire.
The light that was sent from far was not declined
By the look-out men, who raised a fiercer yet,
A light which jumped the water of Gorgopis
And to Mount Aegiplanctus duly come
Urged the reveille of the punctual fire.
So then they kindle it squanderingly and launch
A beard of flame big enough to pass
The headland that looks down upon the Saronic gulf,
Blazing and bounding till it reached at length
The Arachnaean steep, our neighbouring heights;
And leaps in the latter end on the roof of the sons of Atreus
Issue and image of the fire on Ida.
Such was the assignment of my torch-racers,
The task of each fulfilled by his successor,
And victor is he who ran both first and last.
Such is the proof I offer you, the sign
My husband sent me out of Troy.
LEADER OF THE CHORUS. To the gods, queen, I shall give thanks presently.

263. Hephaestus: Vulcan, god of fire. The beacons were lighted on Mt. Ida, below Troy, then northwest on the island of Lemnos, on Mt. Athos at the tip of the Acte peninsula in Chalcidice, and so across the Aegean and south on the heights named through Greece to Argos.

But I would like to hear this story further,
To wonder at it in detail from your lips.

CLYTEMNESTRA. The Greeks hold Troy upon this day.
The cries in the town I fancy do not mingle.
Pour oil and vinegar into the same jar,
You would say they stand apart unlovingly;
Of those who are captured and those who have conquered
Distinct are the sounds of their diverse fortunes,
For *these* having flung themselves about the bodies
Of husbands and brothers, or sons upon the bodies
Of aged fathers from a throat no longer
Free, lament the fate of their most loved.
But *those* a night's marauding after battle
Sets hungry to what breakfast the town offers
Not billeted duly in any barracks order
But as each man has drawn his lot of luck.
So in the captive homes of Troy already
They take their lodging, free of the frosts
And dews of the open. Like happy men
They will sleep all night without sentry.
But if they respect duly the city's gods,
Those of the captured land and the sanctuaries of the gods,
They need not, having conquered, fear reconquest.
But let no lust fall first upon the troops
To plunder what is not right, subdued by gain,
For they must still, in order to come home safe,
Get round the second lap of the doubled course.
So if they return without offence to the gods
The grievance of the slain may learn at last
A friendly talk—unless some fresh wrong falls.
Such are the thoughts you hear from me, a woman.
But may the good prevail for all to see.
We have much good. I only ask to enjoy it.

LEADER OF THE CHORUS. Woman, you speak with sense like a prudent man.
I, who have heard your valid proofs, prepare
To give the glory to God.
Fair recompense is brought us for our troubles.

[CLYTEMNESTRA *goes back into the palace.*]

CHORUS. O Zeus our king and Night our friend
Donor of glories,
Night who cast on the towers of Troy
A close-clinging net so that neither the grown
Nor any of the children can pass
The enslaving and huge

Trap of all-taking destruction.
Great Zeus, guardian of host and guest,
I honour who has done his work and taken
A leisured aim at Paris so that neither
Too short nor yet over the stars
  He might shoot to no purpose.

From Zeus is the blow they can tell of,
This at least can be established,
They have fared according to his ruling. For some
Deny that the gods deign to consider those among men
Who trample on the grace of inviolate things;
It is the impious man says this,
For Ruin is revealed the child
Of not to be attempted actions
When men are puffed up unduly
And their houses are stuffed with riches.
Measure is the best. Let danger be distant,
This should suffice a man
With a proper part of wisdom.
  For a man has no protection
  Against the drunkenness of riches
  Once he has spurned from his sight
  The high altar of Justice.

Sombre Persuasion compels him,
Intolerable child of calculating Doom;
All cure is vain, there is no glozing it over
But the mischief shines forth with a deadly light
And like bad coinage
By rubbings and frictions
He stands discoloured and black
Under the test—like a boy
Who chases a winged bird.
He has branded his city for ever.
His prayers are heard by no god.
Who makes such things his practice
The gods destroy him.
  This way came Paris
  To the house of the sons of Atreus
  And outraged the table of friendship
  Stealing the wife of his host.

Leaving to her countrymen clanging of
Shields and of spears and

Launching of warships
And bringing instead of a dowry destruction to Troy
Lightly she was gone through the gates daring
Things undared. Many the groans
Of the palace spokesmen on this theme—
"O the house, the house, and its princes,
O the bed and the imprint of her limbs;
One can see him crouching in silence
Dishonoured and unreviling."
Through desire for her who is overseas, a ghost
Will seem to rule the household.
  And now her husband hates
  The grace of shapely statues;
  In the emptiness of their eyes
  All their appeal is departed.

But appearing in dreams persuasive
Images come bringing a joy that is vain,
Vain for when in fancy he looks to touch her—
Slipping through his hands the vision
Rapidly is gone
Following on wings the walks of sleep.
Such are his griefs in his house on his hearth,
Such as these and worse than these,
But everywhere through the land of Greece which men have left
Are mourning women with enduring hearts
To be seen in all houses; many
Are the thoughts which stab their hearts;
  For those they sent to war
  They know, but in place of men
  That which comes home to them
  Is merely an urn and ashes.

But the money-changer War, changer of bodies,
Holding his balance in the battle
Home from Troy refined by fire
Sends back to friends the dust
That is heavy with tears, stowing
A man's worth of ashes
In an easily handled jar.
And they wail speaking well of the men how that one
Was expert in battle, and one fell well in the carnage—
But for another man's wife.
Muffled and muttered words;
And resentful grief creeps up against the sons

Of Atreus and their cause.
But others there by the wall
Entombed in Trojan ground
Lie, handsome of limb,
Holding and hidden in enemy soil.

Heavy is the murmur of an angry people
Performing the purpose of a public curse;
There is something cowled in the night
That I anxiously wait to hear.
For the gods are not blind to the
Murderers of many and the black
Furies in time
When a man prospers in sin
By erosion of life reduce him to darkness,
Who, once among the lost, can no more
Be helped. Over-great glory
Is a sore burden. The high peak
Is blasted by the eyes of Zeus.
I prefer an unenvied fortune,
Not to be a sacker of cities
Nor to find myself living at another's
Ruling, myself a captive.

AN OLD MAN. From the good news' beacon a swift
Rumour is gone through the town.
Who knows if it be true
Or some deceit of the gods?

ANOTHER OLD MAN. Who is so childish or broken in wit
To kindle his heart at a new-fangled message of flame
And then be downcast
At a change of report?

ANOTHER OLD MAN. It fits the temper of a woman
To give her assent to a story before it is proved.

ANOTHER OLD MAN. The over-credulous passion of women expands
In swift conflagration but swiftly declining is gone
The news that a woman announced.

LEADER OF THE CHORUS. Soon we shall know about the illuminant torches,
The beacons and the fiery relays,
Whether they were true or whether like dreams
That pleasant light came here and hoaxed our wits.
Look: I see, coming from the beach, a herald
Shadowed with olive shoots; the dust upon him,
Mud's thirsty sister and colleague, is my witness
That he will not give dumb news nor news by lighting
A flame of fire with the smoke of mountain timber;

In words he will either corroborate our joy—
But the opposite version I reject with horror.
To the good appeared so far may good be added.

ANOTHER SPEAKER. Whoever makes other prayers for this our city,
May he reap himself the fruits of his wicked heart.

[*Enter the* HERALD, *who kisses the ground before speaking.*]

HERALD. Earth of my fathers, O the earth of Argos,
In the light of the tenth year I reach you thus
After many shattered hopes achieving one,
For never did I dare to think that here in Argive land
I should win a grave in the dearest soil of home;
But now hail, land, and hail, light of the sun,
And Zeus high above the country and the Pythian king—
May he no longer shoot his arrows at us
(Implacable long enough beside Scamander)
But now be saviour to us and be healer,
King Apollo. And all the Assembly's gods
I call upon, and him my patron, Hermes,
The dear herald whom all heralds adore,
And the Heroes who sped our voyage, again with favour
Take back the army that has escaped the spear.
O cherished dwelling, palace of royalty,
O august thrones and gods facing the sun,
If ever before, now with your bright eyes
Gladly receive your king after much time,
Who comes bringing light to you in the night time,
And to all these as well—King Agamemnon.
Give him a good welcome as he deserves,
Who with the axe of judgment-awarding God
Has smashed Troy and levelled the Trojan land;
The altars are destroyed, the seats of the gods,
And the seed of all the land is perished from it.
Having cast this halter round the neck of Troy
The King, the elder son of Atreus, a blessed man,
Comes, the most worthy to have honour of all
Men that are now. Paris nor his guilty city
Can boast that the crime was greater than the atonement.
Convicted in a suit for rape and robbery
He has lost his stolen goods and with consummate ruin
Mowed down the whole country and his father's house.
The sons of Priam have paid their account with interest.

LEADER OF THE CHORUS. Hail and be glad, herald of the Greek army.

HERALD. Yes. Glad indeed! So glad that at the gods' demand
I should no longer hesitate to die.

LEADER OF THE CHORUS. Were you so harrowed by desire for home?

HERALD. Yes. The tears come to my eyes for joy.

LEADER OF THE CHORUS. Sweet then is the fever which afflicts you.

HERALD. What do you mean? Let me learn your drift.

LEADER OF THE CHORUS. Longing for those whose love came back in echo.

HERALD. Meaning the land was homesick for the army?

LEADER OF THE CHORUS. Yes. I would often groan from a darkened heart.

HERALD. This sullen hatred—how did it fasten on you?

LEADER OF THE CHORUS. I cannot say. Silence is my stock prescription.

HERALD. What? In your masters' absence were there some you feared?

LEADER OF THE CHORUS. Yes. In your phrase, death would now be a gratification.

HERALD. Yes, for success is ours. These things have taken time.
Some of them we could say have fallen well,
While some we blame. Yet who except the gods
Is free from pain the whole duration of life?
If I were to tell of our labours, our hard lodging,
The sleeping on crowded decks, the scanty blankets,
Tossing and groaning, rations that never reached us—
And the land too gave matter for more disgust,
For our beds lay under the enemy's walls.
Continuous drizzle from the sky, dews from the marshes,
Rotting our clothes, filling our hair with lice.
And if one were to tell of the bird-destroying winter
Intolerable from the snows of Ida
Or of the heat when the sea slackens at noon
Waveless and dozing in a depressed calm—
But why make these complaints? The weariness is over;
Over indeed for some who never again
Need even trouble to rise.
Why make a computation of the lost?
Why need the living sorrow for the spites of fortune?
I wish to say a long goodbye to disasters.
For us, the remnant of the troops of Argos,
The advantage remains, the pain can not outweigh it;
So we can make our boast to this sun's light,
Flying on words above the land and sea:
"Having taken Troy the Argive expedition
Has nailed up throughout Greece in every temple
These spoils, these ancient trophies."
Those who hear such things must praise the city
And the generals. And the grace of God be honoured
Which brought these things about. You have the whole story.

LEADER OF THE CHORUS. I confess myself convinced by your report.
Old men are always young enough to learn.

[*Enter* CLYTEMNESTRA *from the palace.*]
This news belongs by right first to the house
And Clytemnestra—though I am enriched also.

CLYTEMNESTRA. Long before this I shouted at joy's command
At the coming of the first night-messenger of fire
Announcing the taking and capsizing of Troy.
And people reproached me saying, "Do mere beacons
Persuade you to think that Troy is already down?
Indeed a woman's heart is easily exalted."
Such comments made me seem to be wandering but yet
I began my sacrifices and in the women's fashion
Throughout the town they raised triumphant cries
And in the gods' enclosures
Lulling the fragrant, incense-eating flame.
And now what need is there for you to tell me more?
From the King himself I shall learn the whole story.
But how the best to welcome my honoured lord
I shall take pains when he comes back—For what
Is a kinder light for a woman to see than this,
To open the gates to her man come back from war
When God has saved him? Tell this to my husband,
To come with all speed, the city's darling;
May he returning find a wife as loyal
As when he left her, watchdog of the house,
Good to *him* but fierce to the ill-intentioned,
And in all other things as ever, having destroyed
No seal or pledge at all in the length of time.
I know no pleasure with another man, no scandal,
More than I know how to dye metal red.
Such is my boast, bearing a load of truth,
A boast that need not disgrace a noble wife.
[*Exit.*]

LEADER OF THE CHORUS. Thus has she spoken; if you take her meaning,
Only a specious tale to shrewd interpreters.
But do you, herald, tell me; I ask after Menelaus
Whether he will, returning safe preserved,
Come back with you, our land's loved master.

HERALD. I am not able to speak the lovely falsehood
To profit you, my friends, for any stretch of time.

LEADER OF THE CHORUS. But if only the true tidings could be also good!
It is hard to hide a division of good and true.

HERALD. The prince is vanished out of the Greek fleet,
Himself and ship. I speak no lie.

LEADER OF THE CHORUS. Did he put forth first in the sight of all from
Troy,

Or a storm that troubled all sweep him apart?
HERALD. You have hit the target like a master archer,
Told succinctly a long tale of sorrow.
LEADER OF THE CHORUS. Did the rumours current among the remaining ships
Represent him as alive or dead?
HERALD. No one knows so as to tell for sure
Except the sun who nurses the breeds of earth.
LEADER OF THE CHORUS. Tell me how the storm came on the host of ships
Through the divine anger, and how it ended.
HERALD. Day of good news should not be fouled by tongue
That tells ill news. To each god his season.
When, despair in his face, a messenger brings to a town
The hated news of a fallen army—
One general wound to the city and many men
Outcast, outcursed, from many homes
By the double whip which War is fond of,
Doom with a bloody spear in either hand,
One carrying such a pack of grief could well
Recite this hymn of the Furies at your asking.
But when our cause is saved and a messenger of good
Comes to a city glad with festivity,
How am I to mix good news with bad, recounting
The storm that meant God's anger on the Greeks?
For they swore together, those inveterate enemies,
Fire and sea, and proved their alliance, destroying
The unhappy troops of Argos.
In night arose ill-waved evil,
Ships on each other the blasts from Thrace
Crashed colliding, which butting with horns in the violence
Of big wind and rattle of rain were gone
To nothing, whirled all ways by a wicked shepherd.
But when there came up the shining light of the sun
We saw the Aegean sea flowering with corpses
Of Greek men and their ships' wreckage.
But for us, our ship was not damaged,
Whether someone snatched it away or begged it off,
Some god, not a man, handling the tiller;
And Saving Fortune was willing to sit upon our ship
So that neither at anchor we took the tilt of waves
Nor ran to splinters on the crag-bound coast.
But then having thus escaped death on the sea,
In the white day, not trusting our fortune,
We pastured this new trouble upon our thoughts,
The fleet being battered, the sailors weary,

And now if any of *them* still draw breath,
They are thinking no doubt of us as being lost
And we are thinking of them as being lost.
May the best happen. As for Menelaus
The first guess and most likely is a disaster.
But still—if any ray of sun detects him
Alive, with living eyes, by the plan of Zeus
Not yet resolved to annul the race completely,
There is some hope then that he will return home.
So much you have heard. Know that it is the truth.
[*Exit.*]

CHORUS. Who was it named her thus
In all ways appositely
Unless it was Someone whom we do not see,
Fore-knowing fate
And plying an accurate tongue?
Helen, bride of spears and conflict's
Focus, who as was befitting
Proved a hell to ships and men,
Hell to her country, sailing
Away from delicately-sumptuous curtains,
Away on the wind of a giant Zephyr,
And shielded hunters mustered many
On the vanished track of the oars,
Oars beached on the leafy
Banks of a Trojan river
For the sake of bloody war.

But on Troy was thrust a marring marriage
By the Wrath that working to an end exacts
In time a price from guests
Who dishonoured their host
And dishonoured Zeus of the Hearth,
From those noisy celebrants
Of the wedding hymn which fell
To the brothers of Paris
To sing upon that day.
But learning this, unlearning that,
Priam's ancestral city now
Continually mourns, reviling
Paris the fatal bridegroom.
The city has had much sorrow,
Much desolation in life,
From the pitiful loss of her people.

So in his house a man might rear
A lion's cub caught from the dam
In need of suckling,
In the prelude of its life
Mild, gentle with children,
For old men a playmate,
Often held in the arms
Like a new-born child,
Wheedling the hand,
Fawning at belly's bidding.

But matured by time he showed
The temper of his stock and payed
Thanks for his fostering
With disaster of slaughter of sheep
Making an unbidden banquet
And now the house is a shambles,
Irremediable grief to its people,
Calamitous carnage;
For the pet they had fostered was sent
By God as a priest of Ruin.

So I would say there came
To the city of Troy
A notion of windless calm,
Delicate adornment of riches,
Soft shooting of the eyes and flower
Of desire that stings the fancy.
But swerving aside she achieved
A bitter end to her marriage,
Ill guest and ill companion,
Hurled upon Priam's sons, convoyed
By Zeus, patron of guest and host,
Dark angel dowered with tears.

Long current among men an old saying
Runs that a man's prosperity
When grown to greatness
Comes to the birth, does not die childless—
His good luck breeds for his house
Distress that shall not be appeased.
I only, apart from the others,
Hold that the unrighteous action
Breeds true to its kind,
Leaves its own children behind it.

But the lot of a righteous house
Is a fair offspring always.

Ancient self-glory is accustomed
To bear to light in the evil sort of men
A new self-glory and madness,
Which sometime or sometime finds
The appointed hour for its birth,
And born therewith is the Spirit, intractable, unholy, irresistible,
The reckless lust that brings black Doom upon the house,
A child that is like its parents.

But Honest Dealing is clear
Shining in smoky homes,
Honours the god-fearing life.
Mansions gilded by filth of hands she leaves,
Turns her eyes elsewhere, visits the innocent house,
Not respecting the power
Of wealth mis-stamped with approval,
But guides all to the goal.

[*Enter* AGAMEMNON *and* CASSANDRA *on chariots.*]

CHORUS. Come then my King, stormer of Troy,
Offspring of Atreus,
How shall I hail you, how give you honour
Neither overshooting nor falling short
  Of the measure of homage?
There are many who honour appearance too much
Passing the bounds that are right.
To condole with the unfortunate man
Each one is ready but the bite of the grief
  Never goes through to the heart.
And they join in rejoicing, affecting to share it,
Forcing their face to a smile.
But he who is shrewd to shepherd his sheep
Will fail not to notice the eyes of a man
Which seem to be loyal but lie,
  Fawning with watery friendship.
Even you, in my thought, when you marshalled the troops
For Helen's sake, I will not hide it,
Made a harsh and ugly picture,
Holding badly the tiller of reason,
Paying with the death of men
  Ransom for a willing whore.
But now, not unfriendly, not superficially,
I offer my service, well-doers' welcome.

In time you will learn by inquiry
Who has done rightly, who transgressed
In the work of watching the city.

AGAMEMNON. First to Argos and the country's gods
My fitting salutations, who have aided me
To return and in the justice which I exacted
From Priam's city. Hearing the unspoken case
The gods unanimously had cast their vote
Into the bloody urn for the massacre of Troy;
But to the opposite urn
Hope came, dangled her hand, but did no more.
Smoke marks even now the city's capture.
Whirlwinds of doom are alive, the dying ashes
Spread on the air the fat savour of wealth.
For these things we must pay some memorable return
To Heaven, having exacted enormous vengeance
For wife-rape; for a woman
The Argive monster ground a city to powder,
Sprung from a wooden horse, shield-wielding folk,
Launching a leap at the setting of the Pleiads,
Jumping the ramparts, a ravening lion,
Lapped its fill of the kingly blood.
To the gods I have drawn out this overture
But as for your concerns, I bear them in my mind
And say the same, you have me in agreement.
To few of men does it belong by nature
To congratulate their friends unenviously,
For a sullen poison fastens on the heart,
Doubling the pain of a man with this disease;
He feels the weight of his own griefs and when
He sees another's prosperity he groans.
I speak with knowledge, being well acquainted
With the mirror of comradeship—ghost of a shadow
Were those who seemed to be so loyal to me.
Only Odysseus, who sailed against his will,
Proved, when yoked with me, a ready tracehorse;
I speak of him not knowing if he is alive.
But for what concerns the city and the gods
Appointing public debates in full assembly
We shall consult. That which is well already
We shall take steps to ensure it remain well.
But where there is need of medical remedies,
By applying benevolent cautery or surgery
We shall try to deflect the dangers of disease.
But now, entering the halls where stands my hearth,

First I shall make salutation to the gods
Who sent me a far journey and have brought me back.
And may my victory not leave my side.

[*Enter* CLYTEMNESTRA, *followed by women slaves carrying purple tapestries.*]

CLYTEMNESTRA. Men of the city, you the aged of Argos,
I shall feel no shame to describe to you my love
Towards my husband. Shyness in all of us
Wears thin with time. Here are the facts first hand.
I will tell you of my own unbearable life
I led so long as this man was at Troy.
For first that the woman separate from her man
Should sit alone at home is extreme cruelty,
Hearing so many malignant rumours—First
Comes one, and another comes after, bad news to worse,
Clamour of grief to the house. If Agamemnon
Had had so many wounds as those reported
Which poured home through the pipes of hearsay, then—
Then he would be gashed fuller than a net has holes!
And if only he had died . . . as often as rumour told us,
He would be like the giant in the legend,
Three-bodied. Dying once for every body,
He should have by now three blankets of earth above him—
All that above him; I care not how deep the mattress under!
Such are the malignant rumours thanks to which
They have often seized me against my will and undone
The loop of a rope from my neck.
And this is why our son is not standing here,
The guarantee of your pledges and mine,
As he should be, Orestes. Do not wonder;
He is being brought up by a friendly ally and host,
Strophius the Phocian, who warned me in advance
Of dubious troubles, both your risks at Troy
And the anarchy of shouting mobs that might
Overturn policy, for it is born in men
To kick the man who is down.
This is not a disingenuous excuse.
For me the outrushing wells of weeping are dried up,
There is no drop left in them.
My eyes are sore from sitting late at nights
Weeping for you and for the baffled beacons,
Never lit up. And, when I slept, in dreams
I have been waked by the thin whizz of a buzzing
Gnat, seeing more horrors fasten on you
Than could take place in the mere time of my dream.

Having endured all this, now, with unsorrowed heart
I would hail this man as the watchdog of the farm,
Forestay that saves the ship, pillar that props
The lofty roof, appearance of an only son
To a father or of land to sailors past their hope,
The loveliest day to see after the storm,
Gush of well-water for the thirsty traveller.
Such are the metaphors I think befit him,
But envy be absent. Many misfortunes already
We have endured. But now, dear head, come down
Out of that car, not placing upon the ground
Your foot, O King, the foot that trampled Troy.
Why are you waiting, slaves, to whom the task is assigned
To spread the pavement of his path with tapestries?
At once, at once let his way be strewn with purple
That Justice lead him toward his unexpected home.
The rest a mind, not overcome by sleep
Will arrange rightly, with God's help, as destined.

AGAMEMNON. Daughter of Leda, guardian of my house,
You have spoken in proportion to my absence.
You have drawn your speech out long. Duly to praise me,
That is a duty to be performed by others.
And further—do not by women's methods make me
Effeminate nor in barbarian fashion
Gape ground-grovelling acclamations at me
Nor strewing my path with cloths make it invidious.
It is the gods should be honoured in this way.
But being mortal to tread embroidered beauty
For me is no way without fear.
I tell you to honour me as a man, not god.
Footcloths are very well—Embroidered stuffs
Are stuff for gossip. And not to think unwisely
Is the greatest gift of God. Call happy only him
Who has ended his life in sweet prosperity.
I have spoken. This thing I could not do with confidence.

CLYTEMNESTRA. Tell me now, according to your judgment.

AGAMEMNON. I tell you you shall not override my judgment.

CLYTEMNESTRA. Supposing you had feared something . . .
Could you have vowed to God to do this thing?

AGAMEMNON. Yes. If an expert had prescribed that vow.

CLYTEMNESTRA. And how would Priam have acted in your place?

AGAMEMNON. He would have trod the cloths, I think, for certain.

CLYTEMNESTRA. Then do not flinch before the blame of men.

AGAMEMNON. The voice of the multitude is very strong.

CLYTEMNESTRA. But the man none envy is not enviable.

AGAMEMNON. It is not a woman's part to love disputing.
CLYTEMNESTRA. But it is a conqueror's part to yield upon occasion.
AGAMEMNON. You think such victory worth fighting for?
CLYTEMNESTRA. Give way. Consent to let me have the mastery.
AGAMEMNON. Well, if such is your wish, let someone quickly loose
My vassal sandals, underlings of my feet,
And stepping on these sea-purples may no god
Shoot me from far with the envy of his eye.
Great shame it is to ruin my house and spoil
The wealth of costly weavings with my feet.
But of this matter enough. This stranger woman here
Take in with kindness. The man who is a gentle master
God looks on from far off complacently.
For no one of his will bears the slave's yoke.
This woman, of many riches being the chosen
Flower, gift of the soldiers, has come with me.
But since I have been prevailed on by your words
I will go to my palace home, treading on purples.

[*He dismounts from the chariot and begins to walk up the tapestried path. During the following speech he enters the palace.*]

CLYTEMNESTRA. There is the sea and who shall drain it dry? It breeds
Its wealth in silver of plenty of purple gushing
And ever-renewed, the dyeings of our garments.
The house has its store of these by God's grace, King.
This house is ignorant of poverty
And I would have vowed a pavement of many garments
Had the palace oracle enjoined that vow
Thereby to contrive a ransom for his life.
For while there is root, foliage comes to the house
Spreading a tent of shade against the Dog Star.
So now that you have reached your hearth and home
You prove a miracle—advent of warmth in winter;
And further this—even in the time of heat
When God is fermenting wine from the bitter grape,
Even then it is cool in the house if only
Its master walk at home, a grown man, ripe.
O Zeus the Ripener, ripen these my prayers;
Your part it is to make the ripe fruit fall.

[*She enters the palace.*]

CHORUS. Why, why at the doors
Of my fore-seeing heart
Does this terror keep beating its wings?
And my song play the prophet
Unbidden, unhired—
Which I cannot spit out

Like the enigmas of dreams
Nor plausible confidence
Sit on the throne of my mind?
It is long time since
The cables let down from the stern
Were chafed by the sand when the seafaring army started for Troy.

And I learn with my eyes
And witness myself their return;
But the hymn without lyre goes up,
The dirge of the Avenging Fiend,
In the depths of my self-taught heart
Which has lost its dear
Possession of the strength of hope.
But my guts and my heart
Are not idle which seethe with the waves
Of trouble nearing its hour.
But I pray that these thoughts
May fall out not as I think
And not be fulfilled in the end.

Truly when health grows much
It respects not limit; for disease,
Its neighbour in the next door room,
Presses upon it.
A man's life, crowding sail,
Strikes on the blind reef:
But if caution in advance
Jettison part of the cargo
With the derrick of due proportion,
The whole house does not sink,
Though crammed with a weight of woe
The hull does not go under.
The abundant bounty of God
And his gifts from the year's furrows
Drive the famine back.

But when upon the ground there has fallen once
The black blood of a man's death,
Who shall summon it back by incantations?
Even Asclepius who had the art
To fetch the dead to life, even to him
Zeus put a provident end.
But, if of the heaven-sent fates
One did not check the other,

Cancel the other's advantage,
My heart would outrun my tongue
In pouring out these fears.
But now it mutters in the dark,
Embittered, no way hoping
To unravel a scheme in time
  From a burning mind.

[CLYTEMNESTRA *appears in the door of the palace.*]

CLYTEMNESTRA. Go in too, you; I speak to you, Cassandra,
Since God in his clemency has put you in this house
To share our holy water, standing with many slaves
Beside the altar that protects the house,
Step down from the car there, do not be overproud.
Heracles himself they say was once
Sold, and endured to eat the bread of slavery.
But should such a chance inexorably fall,
There is much advantage in masters who have long been rich.
Those who have reaped a crop they never expected
Are in all things hard on their slaves and overstep the line.
From us you will have the treatment of tradition.

LEADER OF THE CHORUS. You, it is you she has addressed, and clearly.
Caught as you are in these predestined toils
Obey her if you can. But should you disobey . . .

CLYTEMNESTRA. If she has more than the gibberish of the swallow,
An unintelligible barbaric speech,
I hope to read her mind, persuade her reason.

LEADER OF THE CHORUS. As things now stand for you, she says the best.
Obey her; leave that car and follow her.

CLYTEMNESTRA. I have no leisure to waste out here, outside the door.
Before the hearth in the middle of my house
The victims stand already, wait the knife.
You, if you will obey me, waste no time.
But if you cannot understand my language—

[*To* CHORUS LEADER.]

You make it plain to her with the brute and voiceless hand.

LEADER OF THE CHORUS. The stranger seems to need a clear interpreter.
She bears herself like a wild beast newly captured.

CLYTEMNESTRA. The fact is she is mad, she listens to evil thoughts,
Who has come here leaving a city newly captured
Without experience how to bear the bridle
So as not to waste her strength in foam and blood.
I will not spend more words to be ignored.

[*She re-enters the palace.*]

CHORUS. But I, for I pity her, will not be angry.
Obey, unhappy woman. Leave this car.

Yield to your fate. Put on the untried yoke.
CASSANDRA. Apollo! Apollo!
CHORUS. Why do you cry like this upon Apollo?
He is not the kind of god that calls for dirges.
CASSANDRA. Apollo! Apollo!
CHORUS. Once more her funereal cries invoke the god
Who has no place at the scene of lamentation.
CASSANDRA. Apollo! Apollo!
God of the Ways! My destroyer!
Destroyed again—and this time utterly!
CHORUS. She seems about to predict her own misfortunes.
The gift of the god endures, even in a slave's mind.
CASSANDRA. Apollo! Apollo!
God of the Ways! My destroyer!
Where? To what house? Where, where have you brought me?
CHORUS. To the house of the sons of Atreus. If you do not know it,
I will tell you so. You will not find it false.
CASSANDRA. No, no, but to a god-hated, but to an accomplice
In much kin-killing, murdering nooses,
Man-shambles, a floor asperged with blood.
CHORUS. The stranger seems like a hound with a keen scent,
Is picking up a trail that leads to murder.
CASSANDRA. Clues! I have clues! Look! They are these.
These wailing, these children, butchery of children;
Roasted flesh, a father sitting to dinner.
CHORUS. Of your prophetic fame we have heard before
But in this matter prophets are not required.
CASSANDRA. What is she doing? What is she planning?
What is this new great sorrow?
Great crime . . . within here . . . planning
Unendurable to his folk, impossible
Ever to be cured. For help
Stands far distant.
CHORUS. This reference I cannot catch. But the children
I recognized; that refrain is hackneyed.
CASSANDRA. Damned, damned, bringing this work to completion—
Your husband who shared your bed
To bathe him, to cleanse him, and then—
How shall I tell of the end?
Soon, very soon, it will fall.
The end comes hand over hand
Grasping in greed.
CHORUS. Not yet do I understand. After her former riddles
Now I am baffled by these dim pronouncements.
CASSANDRA. Ah God, the vision! God, God, the vision!

A net, is it? Net of Hell!
But herself is the net; shared bed; shares murder.
O let the pack ever-hungering after the family
Howl for the unholy ritual, howl for the victim.
CHORUS. What black Spirit is this you call upon the house—
To raise aloft her cries? Your speech does not lighten me.
Into my heart runs back the blood
Yellow as when for men by the spear fallen
The blood ebbs out with the rays of the setting life
And death strides quickly.
CASSANDRA. Quick! Be on your guard! The bull—
Keep him clear of the cow.
Caught with a trick, the black horn's point,
She strikes. He falls; lies in the water.
Murder; a trick in a bath. I tell what I see.
CHORUS. I would not claim to be expert in oracles
But these, as I deduce, portend disaster.
Do men ever get a good answer from oracles?
No. It is only through disaster
That their garrulous craft brings home
The meaning of the prophet's panic.
CASSANDRA. And for me also, for me, chance ill-destined!
My own now I lament, pour into the cup my own.
Where is this you have brought me in my misery?
Unless to die as well. What else is meant?
CHORUS. You are mad, mad, carried away by the god,
Raising the dirge, the tuneless
Tune, for yourself. Like the tawny
Unsatisfied singer from her luckless heart
Lamenting "Itys, Itys," the nightingale
Lamenting a life luxuriant with grief.
CASSANDRA. Oh the lot of the songful nightingale!
The gods enclosed her in a winged body,
Gave her a sweet and tearless passing.
But for me remains the two-edged cutting blade.
CHORUS. From whence these rushing and God-inflicted
Profitless pains?
Why shape with your sinister crying
The piercing hymn—fear-piercing?
How can you know the evil-worded landmarks
On the prophetic path?
CASSANDRA. Oh the wedding, the wedding of Paris—death to his people!
O river Scamander, water drunk by my fathers!
When I was young, alas, upon your beaches
I was brought up and cared for.

But now it is the River of Wailing and the banks of Hell
That shall hear my prophecy soon.
CHORUS. What is this clear speech, too clear?
A child could understand it.
I am bitten with fangs that draw blood
By the misery of your cries,
Cries harrowing the heart.
CASSANDRA. O trouble on trouble of a city lost, lost utterly!
My father's sacrifices before the towers,
Much killing of cattle and sheep,
No cure—availed not at all
To prevent the coming of what came to Troy,
And I, my brain on fire, shall soon enter the trap.
CHORUS. This speech accords with the former.
What god, malicious, over-heavy, persistently pressing,
Drives you to chant of these lamentable
Griefs with death their burden?
But I cannot see the end.
[CASSANDRA *now steps down from the car.*]
CASSANDRA. The oracle now no longer from behind veils
Will be peeping forth like a newly-wedded bride;
But I can feel it like a fresh wind swoop
And rush in the face of the dawn and, wave-like, wash
Against the sun a vastly greater grief
Than this one. I shall speak no more conundrums.
And bear me witness, pacing me, that I
Am trailing on the scent of ancient wrongs.
For this house here a choir never deserts,
Chanting together ill. For they mean ill,
And to puff up their arrogance they have drunk
Men's blood, this band of revellers that haunts the house,
Hard to be rid of, fiends that attend the family.
Established in its rooms they hymn their hymn
Of that original sin, abhor in turn
The adultery that proved a brother's ruin.
A miss? Or do my arrows hit the mark?
Or am I a quack prophet who knocks at doors, a babbler?
Give me your oath, confess I have the facts,
The ancient history of this house's crimes.
LEADER OF THE CHORUS. And how could an oath's assurance, however finely assured,
Turn out a remedy? I wonder, though, that you
Being brought up overseas, of another tongue,
Should hit on the whole tale as if you had been standing by.
CASSANDRA. Apollo the prophet set me to prophesy.

LEADER OF THE CHORUS. Was he, although a god, struck by desire?
CASSANDRA. Till now I was ashamed to tell that story.
LEADER OF THE CHORUS. Yes. Good fortune keeps us all fastidious.
CASSANDRA. He wrestled hard upon me, panting love.
LEADER OF THE CHORUS. And did you come, as they do, to child-getting?
CASSANDRA. No. I agreed to him. And I cheated him.
LEADER OF THE CHORUS. Were you already possessed by the mystic art?
CASSANDRA. Already I was telling the townsmen all their future suffering.
LEADER OF THE CHORUS. Then how did you escape the doom of Apollo's anger?
CASSANDRA. I did not escape. No one ever believed me.
LEADER OF THE CHORUS. Yet to us your words seem worthy of belief.
CASSANDRA. Oh misery, misery!
Again comes on me the terrible labour of true
Prophecy, dizzying prelude; distracts . . .
Do you see these who sit before the house,
Children, like the shapes of dreams?
Children who seem to have been killed by their kinsfolk,
Filling their hands with meat, flesh of themselves,
Guts and entrails, handfuls of lament—
Clear what they hold—the same their father tasted.
For this I declare someone is plotting vengeance—
A lion? Lion but coward, that lurks in bed,
Good watchdog truly against the lord's return—
My lord, for I must bear the yoke of serfdom.
Leader of the ships, overturner of Troy,
He does not know what plots the accursed hound
With the licking tongue and the pricked-up ear will plan
In the manner of a lurking doom, in an evil hour.
A daring criminal! Female murders male.
What monster could provide her with a title?
An amphisbaena or hag of the sea who dwells
In rocks to ruin sailors—
A raving mother of death who breathes against her folk
War to the finish. Listen to her shout of triumph,
Who shirks no horrors, like men in a rout of battle.
And yet she poses as glad at their return.
If you distrust my words, what does it matter?
That which will come will come. You too will soon stand here
And admit with pity that I spoke too truly.
LEADER OF THE CHORUS. Thyestes' dinner of his children's meat
I understood and shuddered, and fear grips me
To hear the truth, not framed in parables.
But hearing the rest I am thrown out of my course.
CASSANDRA. It is Agamemnon's death I tell you you shall witness.

LEADER OF THE CHORUS. Stop! Provoke no evil. Quiet your mouth!
CASSANDRA. The god who gives me words is here no healer.
LEADER OF THE CHORUS. Not if this shall be so. But may some chance avert it.
CASSANDRA. *You* are praying. But others are busy with murder.
LEADER OF THE CHORUS. What man is he promotes this terrible thing?
CASSANDRA. Indeed you have missed my drift by a wide margin!
LEADER OF THE CHORUS. But I do not understand the assassin's method.
CASSANDRA. And yet too well I know the speech of Greece!
LEADER OF THE CHORUS. So does Delphi but the replies are hard.
CASSANDRA. Ah what a fire it is! It comes upon me.
Apollo, Wolf-Destroyer, pity, pity . . .
It is the two-foot lioness who beds
Beside a wolf, the noble lion away,
It is she will kill me. Brewing a poisoned cup
She will mix my punishment too in the angry draught
And boasts, sharpening the dagger for her husband,
To pay back murder for my bringing here.
Why then do I wear these mockeries of myself,
The wand and the prophet's garland round my neck?
My hour is coming—but you shall perish first.
Destruction! Scattered thus you give me my revenge;
Go and enrich some other woman with ruin.
See: Apollo himself is stripping me
Of my prophetic gear, who has looked on
When in this dress I have been a laughing-stock
To friends and foes alike, and to no purpose;
They called me crazy, like a fortune-teller,
A poor starved beggar-woman—and I bore it.
And now the prophet undoing his prophetess
Has brought me to this final darkness.
Instead of my father's altar the executioner's block
Waits me the victim, red with my hot blood.
But the gods will not ignore me as I die.
One will come after to avenge my death,
A matricide, a murdered father's champion.
Exile and tramp and outlaw he will come back
To gable the family house of fatal crime;
His father's outstretched corpse shall lead him home.
Why need I then lament so pitifully?
For now that I have seen the town of Troy
Treated as she was treated, while her captors
Come to their reckoning thus by the gods' verdict,
I will go in and have the courage to die.
Look, these gates are the gates of Death. I greet them.

And I pray that I may meet a deft and mortal stroke
So that without a struggle I may close
My eyes and my blood ebb in easy death.
LEADER OF THE CHORUS. Oh woman very unhappy and very wise,
Your speech was long. But if in sober truth
You know your fate, why like an ox that the gods
Drive, do you walk so bravely to the altar?
CASSANDRA. There is no escape, strangers. No; not by postponement.
LEADER OF THE CHORUS. But the last moment has the privilege of hope.
CASSANDRA. The day is here. Little should I gain by flight.
LEADER OF THE CHORUS. This patience of yours comes from a brave soul.
CASSANDRA. A happy man is never paid that compliment.
LEADER OF THE CHORUS. But to die with credit graces a mortal man.
CASSANDRA. Oh my father! You and your noble sons!
[*She approaches the door, then suddenly recoils.*]
LEADER OF THE CHORUS. What is it? What is the fear that drives you back?
CASSANDRA. Faugh.
LEADER OF THE CHORUS. Why faugh? Or is this some hallucination?
CASSANDRA. These walls breathe out a death that drips with blood.
LEADER OF THE CHORUS. Not so. It is only the smell of the sacrifice.
CASSANDRA. It is like a breath out of a charnel-house.
LEADER OF THE CHORUS. You think our palace burns odd incense then!
CASSANDRA. But I will go to lament among the dead
My lot and Agamemnon's. Enough of life!
Strangers,
I am not afraid like a bird afraid of a bush
But witness you my words after my death
When a woman dies in return for me a woman
And a man falls for a man with a wicked wife.
I ask this service, being about to die.
LEADER OF THE CHORUS. Alas, I pity you for the death you have foretold.
CASSANDRA. One more speech I have; I do not wish to raise
The dirge for my own self. But to the sun I pray
In face of his last light that my avengers
May make my murderers pay for this my death,
Death of a woman slave, an easy victim.
[*She enters the palace.*]

LEADER OF THE CHORUS. Ah the fortunes of men! When they go well
A shadow sketch would match them, and in ill-fortune
The dab of a wet sponge destroys the drawing.
It is not myself but the life of man I pity.
CHORUS. Prosperity in all men cries
For more prosperity. Even the owner
Of the finger-pointed-at palace never shuts

His door against her, saying "Come no more."
So to our king the blessed gods had granted
To take the town of Priam, and heaven-favoured
He reaches home. But now if for former bloodshed
He must pay blood
And dying for the dead shall cause
Other deaths in atonement
What man could boast he was born
Secure, who heard this story?

AGAMEMNON [*within*]. Oh! I am struck a mortal blow—within!

LEADER OF THE CHORUS. Silence! Listen. Who calls out, wounded with a mortal stroke?

AGAMEMNON. Again—the second blow—I am struck again.

LEADER OF THE CHORUS. You heard the king cry out. I think the deed is done.
Let us see if we can concert some sound proposal.

2ND OLD MAN. Well, I will tell you my opinion—
Raise an alarm, summon the folk to the palace.

3RD OLD MAN. I say burst in with all speed possible,
Convict them of the deed while still the sword is wet.

4TH OLD MAN. And I am partner to some such suggestion.
I am for taking some course. No time to dawdle.

5TH OLD MAN. The case is plain. This is but the beginning.
They are going to set up dictatorship in the state.

6TH OLD MAN. We are wasting time. The assassins tread to earth
The decencies of delay and give their hands no sleep.

7TH OLD MAN. I do not know what plan I could hit on to propose.
The man who acts is in the position to plan.

8TH OLD MAN. So I think, too, for I am at a loss
To raise the dead man up again with words.

9TH OLD MAN. Then to stretch out our life shall we yield thus
To the rule of these profaners of the house?

10TH OLD MAN. It is not to be endured. To die is better.
Death is more comfortable than tyranny.

11TH OLD MAN. And are we on the evidence of groans
Going to give oracle that the prince is dead?

12TH OLD MAN. We must know the facts for sure and *then* be angry.
Guesswork is not the same as certain knowledge.

LEADER OF THE CHORUS. Then all of you back me and approve this plan—
To ascertain how it is with Agamemnon.

[*The doors of the palace open, revealing the bodies of* AGAMEMNON *and* CASSANDRA. CLYTEMNESTRA *stands above them.*]

CLYTEMNESTRA. Much having been said before to fit the moment,
To say the opposite now will not outface me.
How else could one serving hate upon the hated,

Thought to be friends, hang high the nets of doom
To preclude all leaping out?
For me I have long been training for this match,
I tried a fall and won—a victory overdue.
I stand here where I struck, above my victims;
So I contrived it—this I will not deny—
That he could neither fly nor ward off death;
Inextricable like a net for fishes
I cast about him a vicious wealth of raiment
And struck him twice and with two groans he loosed
His limbs beneath him, and upon him fallen
I deal him the third blow to the God beneath the earth,
To the safe keeper of the dead a votive gift,
And with that he spits his life out where he lies
And smartly spouting blood he sprays me with
The sombre drizzle of bloody dew and I
Rejoice no less than in God's gift of rain
The crops are glad when the ear of corn gives birth.
These things being so, you, elders of Argos,
Rejoice if rejoice you will. Mine is the glory.
And if I could pay this corpse his due libation
I should be right to pour it and more than right;
With so many horrors this man mixed and filled
The bowl—and, coming home, has drained the draught himself.

LEADER OF THE CHORUS. Your speech astonishes us. This brazen boast
Above the man who was your king and husband!

CLYTEMNESTRA. You challenge me as a woman without foresight
But I with unflinching heart to you who know
Speak. And you, whether you will praise or blame,
It makes no matter. Here lies Agamemnon,
My husband, dead, the work of this right hand,
An honest workman. There you have the facts.

CHORUS. Woman, what poisoned
Herb of the earth have you tasted
Or potion of the flowing sea
To undertake this killing and the people's curses?
You threw down, you cut off—The people will cast you out,
Black abomination to the town.

CLYTEMNESTRA. Now your verdict—in my case—is exile
And to have the people's hatred, the public curses,
Though then in no way you opposed this man
Who carelessly, as if it were a head of sheep
Out of the abundance of his fleecy flocks,
Sacrificed his own daughter, to me the dearest
Fruit of travail, charm for the Thracian winds.

He was the one to have banished from this land,
Pay off the pollution. But when you hear what I
Have done, you judge severely. But I warn you—
Threaten me on the understanding that I am ready
For two alternatives—Win by force the right
To rule me, but, if God brings about the contrary,
Late in time you will have to learn self-discipline.

CHORUS. You are high in the thoughts,
You speak extravagant things,
After the soiling murder your crazy heart
Fancies your forehead with a smear of blood.
Unhonoured, unfriended, you must
Pay for a blow with a blow.

CLYTEMNESTRA. Listen then to this—the sanction of my oaths:
By the Justice totting up my child's atonement,
By the Avenging Doom and Fiend to whom I killed this man,
For me hope walks not in the rooms of fear
So long as my fire is lit upon my hearth
By Aegisthus, loyal to me as he was before.
The man who outraged me lies here,
The darling of each courtesan at Troy,
And here with him is the prisoner clairvoyant,
The fortune-teller that he took to bed,
Who shares his bed as once his bench on shipboard,
A loyal mistress. Both have their deserts.
He lies so; and she who like a swan
Sang her last dying lament
Lies his lover, and the sight contributes
An appetiser to my own bed's pleasure.

CHORUS. Ah would some quick death come not overpainful,
Not overlong on the sickbed,
Establishing in us the ever-
Lasting unending sleep now that our guardian
Has fallen, the kindest of men,
Who suffering much for a woman
By a woman has lost his life.
O Helen, insane, being one
One to have destroyed so many
And many souls under Troy,
Now is your work complete, blossomed not for oblivion,
Unfading stain of blood. Here now, if in any home,
Is Discord, here is a man's deep-rooted ruin.

CLYTEMNESTRA. Do not pray for the portion of death
Weighed down by these things, do not turn
Your anger on Helen as destroyer of men,

One woman destroyer of many
Lives of Greek men,
A hurt that cannot be healed.

CHORUS. O Evil Spirit, falling on the family,
On the two sons of Atreus and using
Two sisters in heart as your tools,
A power that bites to the heart—
See on the body
Perched like a raven he gloats
Harshly croaking his hymn.

CLYTEMNESTRA. Ah, now you have amended your lips' opinion,
Calling upon this family's three times gorged
Genius—demon who breeds
Blood-hankering lust in the belly:
Before the old sore heals, new pus collects.

CHORUS. It is a great spirit—great—
You tell of, harsh in anger,
A ghastly tale, alas,
Of unsatisfied disaster
Brought by Zeus, by Zeus,
Cause and worker of all.
For without Zeus what comes to pass among us?
Which of these things is outside Providence?
O my king, my king,
How shall I pay you in tears,
Speak my affection in words?
You lie in that spider's web,
In a desecrating death breathe out your life,
Lie ignominiously
Defeated by a crooked death
And the two-edged cleaver's stroke.

CLYTEMNESTRA. You say this is *my* work—mine?
Do not cozen yourself that I am Agamemnon's wife.
Masquerading as the wife
Of the corpse there the old sharp-witted Genius
Of Atreus who gave the cruel banquet
Has paid with a grown man's life
The due for children dead.

CHORUS. That you are not guilty of
This murder who will attest?
No, but you may have been abetted
By some ancestral Spirit of Revenge.
Wading a millrace of the family's blood
The black Manslayer forces a forward path
To make the requital at last

For the eaten children, the blood-clot cold with time.
O my king, my king,
How shall I pay you in tears,
Speak my affection in words?
You lie in that spider's web,
In a desecrating death breathe out your life,
Lie ignominiously
Defeated by a crooked death
And the two-edged cleaver's stroke.

CLYTEMNESTRA. Did he not, too, contrive a crooked
Horror for the house? My child by him,
Shoot that I raised, much-wept-for Iphigeneia,
He treated her like this;
So suffering like this he need not make
Any great brag in Hell having paid with death
Dealt by the sword for work of his own beginning.

CHORUS. I am at a loss for thought, I lack
All nimble counsel as to where
To turn when the house is falling.
I fear the house-collapsing crashing
Blizzard of blood—of which these drops are earnest.
Now is Destiny sharpening her justice
On other whetstones for a new infliction.
O earth, earth, if only you had received me
Before I saw this man lie here as if in bed
In a bath lined with silver.
Who will bury him? Who will keen him?
Will you, having killed your own husband,
Dare now to lament him
And after great wickedness make
Unamending amends to his ghost?
And who above this godlike hero's grave
Pouring praises and tears
Will grieve with a genuine heart?

CLYTEMNESTRA. It is not your business to attend to that.
By my hand he fell low, lies low and dead,
And I shall bury him low down in the earth,
And his household need not weep him
For Iphigeneia his daughter
Tenderly, as is right,
Will meet her father at the rapid ferry of sorrows,
Put her arms round him and kiss him!

CHORUS. Reproach answers reproach,
It is hard to decide,
The catcher is caught, the killer pays for his kill.

But the law abides while Zeus abides enthroned
That the wrongdoer suffers. That is established.
Who could expel from the house the seed of the Curse?
The race is soldered in sockets of Doom and Vengeance.

CLYTEMNESTRA. In this you say what is right and the will of God.
But for my part I am ready to make a contract
With the Evil Genius of the House of Atreus
To accept what has been till now, hard though it is,
But that for the future he shall leave this house
And wear away some other stock with deaths
Imposed among themselves. Of my possessions
A small part will suffice if only I
Can rid these walls of the mad exchange of murder.

[*Enter* AEGISTHUS, *followed by soldiers.*]

AEGISTHUS. O welcome light of a justice-dealing day!
From now on I will say that the gods, avenging men,
Look down from above on the crimes of earth,
Seeing as I do in woven robes of the Furies
This man lying here—a sight to warm my heart—
Paying for the crooked violence of his father.
For his father Atreus, when he ruled the country,
Because his power was challenged, hounded out
From state and home his own brother Thyestes.
My father—let me be plain—was this Thyestes,
Who later came back home a suppliant,
There, miserable, found so much asylum
As not to die on the spot, stain the ancestral floor.
But to show his hospitality godless Atreus
Gave him an eager if not a loving welcome,
Pretending a day of feasting and rich meats
Served my father with his children's flesh.
The hands and feet, fingers and toes, he hid
At the bottom of the dish. My father sitting apart
Took unknowing the unrecognizable portion
And ate of a dish that has proved, as you see, expensive.
But when he knew he had eaten worse than poison
He fell back groaning, vomiting their flesh,
And invoking a hopeless doom on the sons of Pelops
Kicked over the table to confirm his curse—
So may the whole race perish!
Result of this—you see this man lie here.
I stitched this murder together; it was my title.
Me the third son he left, an unweaned infant,
To share the bitterness of my father's exile.
But I grew up and Justice brought me back,

I grappled this man while still beyond his door,
Having pieced together the programme of his ruin.
So now would even death be beautiful to me
Having seen Agamemnon in the nets of Justice.

LEADER OF THE CHORUS. Aegisthus. I cannot respect brutality in distress.
You claim that you deliberately killed this prince
And that you alone planned this pitiful murder.
Be sure that in your turn your head shall not escape
The people's volleyed curses mixed with stones.

AEGISTHUS. Do you speak so who sit at the lower oar
While those on the upper bench control the ship?
Old as you are, you will find it is a heavy load
To go to school when old to learn the lesson of tact.
For old age, too, gaol and hunger are fine
Instructors in wisdom, second-sighted doctors.
You have eyes. Cannot you see?
Do not kick against the pricks. The blow will hurt you.

LEADER OF THE CHORUS. You woman waiting in the house for those who return from battle
While you seduce their wives! Was it you devised
The death of a master of armies?

AEGISTHUS. And these words, too, prepare the way for tears.
Contrast your voice with the voice of Orpheus: he
Led all things after him bewitched with joy, but you
Having stung me with your silly yelps shall be
Led off yourself, to prove more mild when mastered.

LEADER OF THE CHORUS. Indeed! So you are now to be king of Argos,
You who, when you had plotted the king's death,
Did not even dare to do that thing yourself!

AEGISTHUS. No. For the trick of it was clearly woman's work.
I was suspect, an enemy of old.
But now I shall try with Agamemnon's wealth
To rule the people. Any who is disobedient
I will harness in a heavy yoke, no tracehorse work for him
Like barley-fed colt, but hateful hunger lodging
Beside him in the dark will see his temper soften.

LEADER OF THE CHORUS. Why with your cowardly soul did you yourself
Not strike this man but left that work to a woman
Whose presence pollutes our country and its gods?
But Orestes—does he somewhere see the light
That he may come back here by favour of fortune
And kill this pair and prove the final victor?

AEGISTHUS [*summoning his guards*]. Well, if such is your design in deeds and words, you will quickly learn—
Here my friends, here my guards, there is work for you at hand.

LEADER OF THE CHORUS. Come then, hands on hilts, be each and all of us prepared.

[*The old men and the guards threaten each other.*]

AEGISTHUS. Very well! I too am ready to meet death with sword in hand.

LEADER OF THE CHORUS. We are glad you speak of dying. We accept your words for luck.

CLYTEMNESTRA. No, my dearest, do not so. Add no more to the train of wrong.
To reap these many present wrongs is harvest enough of misery.
Enough of misery. Start no more. Our hands are red.
But do you, and you old men, go home and yield to fate in time,
In time before you suffer. We have acted as we had to act.
If only our afflictions now could prove enough, we should agree—
We who have been so hardly mauled in the heavy claws of the evil god.
So stands my word, a woman's, if any man thinks fit to hear. 1611

AEGISTHUS. But to think that these should thus pluck the blooms of an idle tongue
And should throw out words like these, giving the evil god his chance,
And should miss the path of prudence and insult their master so!

LEADER OF THE CHORUS. It is not the Argive way to fawn upon a cowardly man.

AEGISTHUS. Perhaps. But I in later days will take further steps with you.

LEADER OF THE CHORUS. Not if the god who rules the family guides Orestes to his home.

AEGISTHUS. Yes. I know that men in exile feed themselves on barren hopes.

LEADER OF THE CHORUS. Go on, grow fat defiling justice . . . while you have your hour. 1619

AEGISTHUS. Do not think you will not pay me a price for your stupidity.

LEADER OF THE CHORUS. Boast on in your self-assurance, like a cock beside his hen.

CLYTEMNESTRA. Pay no heed, Aegisthus, to these futile barkings. You and I, Masters of this house, from now shall order all things well.

[*They enter the palace.*]

CRITICAL COMMENTARY

Agamemnon is the first of three related plays (the *Oresteia*) that tell a part of the following story. King Atreus banished his brother Thyestes, who had plotted against him and had seduced his wife. Later, pretending to be reconciled, Atreus recalled Thyestes and entertained him at a feast. When Thyestes learned that he was eating the bodies of his own sons he cursed the family of Atreus, and then returned to exile, where he died. One son, Aegisthus, survived to avenge him. Atreus' son, Agamemnon, succeeded to the throne, and he was chosen to lead the forces against Troy to avenge the theft of Helen, the wife of his brother Menelaus. On his way, Agamemnon killed his daughter Iphigenia as a sacrifice in order to gain the help of the gods for the expedition. During Agamemnon's absence, Aegisthus seduced Clytemnestra, Agamemnon's wife, and aided her in killing Agamemnon on his return. They were later killed by Agamemnon's son Orestes.

Thus summarized, this story of lust and violence appears to have little meaning for normal people today. It must be admitted, furthermore, that as sheer narrative *Agamemnon* is inefficient; and for its original spectators it did not even have the elementary attraction of suspense and surprise, since they knew the story in advance.

A second look at the plot, however, reveals a meaningful pattern. Running through the particular circumstances is a sequence of justified wrongs: every evil deed is properly punished, and yet every punishment becomes a new crime demanding fresh vengeance. When the plot is generalized in this fashion, there is no longer any question about its significance. Our impulse, in fact, may now be to turn to the last act and find at once the formula that will release men from the chain of evil duty, from wars-to-end-wars that only breed more violence, from well-meant solutions that only breed more problems. But the meaning of *Agamemnon* and its companion plays is not to be found in a detachable formula at the end of the trilogy; it is available only to the extent that one submits attentively to the symbolic experience through which Aeschylus defines and resolves the great issues of his story. The remarks that follow are an attempt to suggest the deeper meaning of a few illustrative incidents.

The definition of issues is begun in the first speech of the play. The speaker, a watchman, is unnecessary in terms of plot (the beacon signal and the arrival of the army could have been announced in other ways), but his character and his attitude toward events are important. He is a simple man of good heart. The one-year watch has been hard and lonely, yet he has stuck to it like a faithful dog. Filled with natural relief at the sight of the beacon, he puts a good and simple interpretation on the homecoming—now everyone, and especially the queen, will rejoice. Then he checks himself with the dark hint that there is something evil within the palace, but he will say no more, an ox is on his tongue. *He* knows when to be quiet; *he* wasn't born yesterday. We smile at his naive slyness. Whether we know the plot in advance or not, we soon realize that he is certain to be hurt by events that he cannot understand or escape, no matter how small and quiet he may be. We begin to sense that we, too, are watchmen. The great actions of our own time go by too fast, they are dark and ominous, and we hope all will turn out well if we behave ourselves and do not openly name the evil thing. The play, though, will not let us take this role. Its business is to name and exorcise the evil thing. The naming or defining has begun with the characterization of the watchman. Although we like his good-hearted simplicity, we know that it is being turned by Clytemnestra into a part of the facade of national rejoicing behind which she plots her revenge against Agamemnon.

The character of the watchman expands, in the next scene, into the character of the chorus. The members of the chorus are old men, too old for fighting and never able to take clear, positive action. They cannot be Agamemnons; they can only watch and try to understand. In their desperate effort to reduce the danger and mystery of what they are watching, they try to apply the sayings of the wise, and they are eager to hear everyone's explanation. But they always hesitate, even when they stand with Cassandra and hear her true account of the murder that is taking place inside the palace. Apollo had given her the power of prophecy or insight, but because she could not fully submit to him and become one with his divinity, he added the curse that she should never be believed. The chorus act out this curse. They are convinced of her powers, yet they cannot face the truth. Their hesitation suggests that men have better information than that on which they act, that they do not usually live up to their possibilities.

In contrast with the chorus is Agamemnon, who does act. The significance of his choice and manner of action is shown in various ways, and most strikingly in the sacrifice of his daughter and in his homecoming. When Iphigenia is suddenly seized, gagged, carried to the altar, and killed, we are shocked at innocence being thus manhandled. She is not permitted to speak, except with her eyes (after all, who is she, a child, to question an adult decision?), but the destruction of what she represents makes us understand the cost to Agamemnon's personality in his choosing to become an effective man of action. And yet what would we have him do? The rape of Helen must be avenged, and only a hardened leader can take Troy. Again the question is posed: How can one crime be punished without the commission of another?

That Agamemnon is not an instrument of perfect justice is implied by the sacrifice and by the Herald's account of the war; the nature of his imperfection is defined through the way he behaves at his homecoming. Somewhat surprisingly, he is not hard and arrogant, but instead, merely superficial. His complacency and obtuseness are intensified for us by our own awareness of the intrigue that surrounds him and of the moral issues that are at stake. It is appropriate that he should be tricked by a gross appeal to his manliness at the moment when he is least truly a man. His slayer, Clytemnestra, is also deficient in self-knowledge, even though she is his superior in cunning. At the conclusion of the play she asserts that her action has brought the chain of violence to an end, that true order has now been established. The evidence of the play, however, proves that her assertion is wishful thinking and that she has not earned the right to make it. Her motives have always been those of narrow self-interest; she has consequently reduced everything to her own size while at the same time publicly professing to subordinate herself to larger values. A striking example is her speech of welcome to Agamemnon, in which she plays a role that is the opposite of her true character. She begins in the tone of a modest, sheltered woman whose intense emotion overcomes her natural shyness and forces her to open her heart in public. What follows is a remarkably accurate and circumstantial account of how a truly loving wife might feel while her husband was at war, but we are continually reminded (as by her dreams of Agamemnon's death) that it is a diabolical fiction. Her immoral sophistication is in constant contrast with the simplicity of the watchman and the chorus.

Although the basic issues raised by *Agamemnon* have not been resolved at the conclusion, the play is self-contained in the sense that it has defined the form that the resolution must take. The assumptions established by *Agamemnon* demand a conclusion in which the simple heart and the rational mind will be one, in which the letter of the law and the spirit of compassionate understanding will be harmonized, in which a crime is finally punished by a pure avenger. The two plays that follow *Agamemnon* present such a conclusion. Orestes kills his mother not from self-interest but as an instrument of justice. After a period of expiation, he is tried in Athens. The vote of the human jury is a tie; the issue is resolved only by Apollo taking on himself the guilt of every man, and by the union of the merciful wisdom of Athena with the mechanical and traditional justice of the Furies.

Aeschylus, competing in the Athenian dramatic festival for the last time in the year 458 B.C., won the prize with this trilogy, which proposed to his countrymen not a rigid and uncritical defense of the Athenian way of life, but rather a permanent ideal of justice.

Agamemnon always conveys an overpowering sense of the permanence of the human dilemma. How astonishing that a small farming and sea-faring community 2500 years ago should have wrestled with problems that are deeply and startlingly like our own. It may seem even stranger that they should have tried to come to grips with such problems by watching plays rather than by consulting experts. They came to plays that were part of a national spring festival, and they came in large numbers—17,000 spectators in the great open-air theater—open to dawns as ambiguous as in *Agamemnon* or in present-day Greece and America. No one really knows what the audience thought as it watched its familiar legendary stories being shaped into fictions embodying the most central and persistent human issues. What explanation, what language is sufficiently rich and inclusive for the task? *Agamemnon* insists in many theatrical ways that the explanation must at least do justice to the thickness of existence, to the interpenetration of realms of being, of the many modes of consciousness and expression, of past, present, and future. How far can one translate into any lesser language, for example, the meanings and emotions that Clytemnestra, Cassandra, and the chorus act out as they stand together in front of the palace before the murders? What is really meant when the chorus protests that it wants no prophets, or when Clytemnestra attributes Cassandra's silence to stubbornness and the language barrier? What would have to happen before Clytemnestra and Cassandra could communicate? What are prophecy and incoherence and incomprehension? What is communication?

Useful Criticism

Corrigan, Robert W., ed. *Tragedy: Vision & Form.** San Francisco: Chandler, 1965.

Kitto, H. D. F. *Greek Tragedy.** Garden City, N.Y.: Doubleday, 1950.

Lattimore, Richmond. *The Poetry of Greek Tragedy.** New York: Harper & Row, 1966.

Michel, L., and Sewall, R. B., eds. *Tragedy: Modern Essays in Criticism.** Englewood Cliffs, N.J.: Prentice-Hall, 1963.

Swander, Homer D., ed. *Man and the Gods.** New York: Harcourt, Brace & World, 1964.

Thomson, George. *Aeschylus & Athens.* New York: Grosset & Dunlap, 1968.

* Available in paperback.

OEDIPUS REX

Sophocles

An English version by DUDLEY FITTS and ROBERT FITZGERALD

CHARACTERS

OEDIPUS	MESSENGER
A PRIEST	SHEPHERD OF LAÏOS
CREON	SECOND MESSENGER
TEIRESIAS	CHORUS OF THEBAN ELDERS
IOCASTÊ	

THE SCENE

Before the palace of Oedipus, King of Thebes. A central door and two lateral doors open onto a platform which runs the length of the façade. On the platform, right and left, are altars; and three steps lead down into the "orchestra," *or chorus-ground. At the beginning of the action these steps are crowded by suppliants who have brought branches and chaplets of olive leaves and who lie in various attitudes of despair.* OEDIPUS *enters.*

Prologue

OEDIPUS. My children, generations of the living
In the line of Kadmos, nursed at his ancient hearth:
Why have you strewn yourselves before these altars
In supplication, with your boughs and garlands?
The breath of incense rises from the city
With a sound of prayer and lamentation.
Children,
I would not have you speak through messengers,
And therefore I have come myself to hear you—
I, Oedipus, who bear the famous name.

[*To a* PRIEST.]
You, there, since you are eldest in the company,
Speak for them all, tell me what preys upon you,
Whether you come in dread, or crave some blessing:
Tell me, and never doubt that I will help you
In every way I can; I should be heartless
Were I not moved to find you suppliant here.

PRIEST. Great Oedipus, O powerful King of Thebes!
You see how all the ages of our people
Cling to your altar steps: here are boys
Who can barely stand alone, and here are priests
By weight of age, as I am a priest of God,
And young men chosen from those yet unmarried;
As for the others, all that multitude,
They wait with olive chaplets in the squares,
At the two shrines of Pallas, and where Apollo
Speaks in the glowing embers.
Your own eyes
Must tell you: Thebes is in her extremity
And can not lift her head from the surge of death.
A rust consumes the buds and fruits of the earth;
The herds are sick; children die unborn,
And labor is vain. The god of plague and pyre
Raids like detestable lightning through the city,
And all the house of Kadmos is laid waste,
All emptied, and all darkened: Death alone
Battens upon the misery of Thebes.

You are not one of the immortal gods, we know;
Yet we have come to you to make our prayer
As to the man of all men best in adversity
And wisest in the ways of God. You saved us
From the Sphinx, that flinty singer, and the tribute
We paid to her so long; yet you were never
Better informed than we, nor could we teach you:
It was some god breathed in you to set us free.

Therefore, O mighty King, we turn to you:
Find us our safety, find us a remedy,
Whether by counsel of the gods or men.
A king of wisdom tested in the past
Can act in a time of troubles, and act well.
Noblest of men, restore
Life to your city! Think how all men call you

Liberator for your triumph long ago;
Ah, when your years of kingship are remembered,
Let them not say *We rose, but later fell*—
Keep the State from going down in the storm!
Once, years ago, with happy augury,
You brought us fortune; be the same again!
No man questions your power to rule the land:
But rule over men, not over a dead city!
Ships are only hulls, citadels are nothing,
When no life moves in the empty passageways.

OEDIPUS. Poor children! You may be sure I know
All that you longed for in your coming here.
I know that you are deathly sick; and yet,
Sick as you are, not one is as sick as I.
Each of you suffers in himself alone
His anguish, not another's; but my spirit
Groans for the city, for myself, for you.

I was not sleeping, you are not waking me.
No, I have been in tears for a long while
And in my restless thought walked many ways.
In all my search, I found one helpful course,
And that I have taken: I have sent Creon,
Son of Menoikeus, brother of the Queen,
To Delphi, Apollo's place of revelation,
To learn there, if he can,
What act or pledge of mine may save the city.
I have counted the days, and now, this very day,
I am troubled, for he has overstayed his time.
What is he doing? He has been gone too long.
Yet whenever he comes back, I should do ill
To scant whatever hint the god may give.

PRIEST. It is a timely promise. At this instant
They tell me Creon is here.

OEDIPUS. O Lord Apollo!
May his news be fair as his face is radiant!

PRIEST. It could not be otherwise: he is crowned with bay,
The chaplet is thick with berries.

OEDIPUS. We shall soon know;
He is near enough to hear us now.
[*Enter* CREON.]
O Prince:
Brother: son of Menoikeus:
What answer do you bring us from the god?

CREON. It is favorable. I can tell you, great afflictions
Will turn out well, if they are taken well.
OEDIPUS. What was the oracle? These vague words
Leave me still hanging between hope and fear.
CREON. Is it your pleasure to hear me with all these
Gathered around us? I am prepared to speak,
But should we not go in?
OEDIPUS. Let them all hear it.
It is for them I suffer, more than for myself.
CREON. Then I will tell you what I heard at Delphi.

In plain words
The god commands us to expel from the land of Thebes
An old defilement that it seems we shelter.
It is a deathly thing, beyond expiation.
We must not let it feed upon us longer.
OEDIPUS. What defilement? How shall we rid ourselves of it?
CREON. By exile or death, blood for blood. It was
Murder that brought the plague-wind on the city.
OEDIPUS. Murder of whom? Surely the god has named him?
CREON. My lord: long ago Laïos was our king,
Before you came to govern us.
OEDIPUS. I know;
I learned of him from others; I never saw him.
CREON. He was murdered; and Apollo commands us now
To take revenge upon whoever killed him.
OEDIPUS. Upon whom? Where are they? Where shall we find a clue
To solve that crime, after so many years?
CREON. Here in this land, he said.
If we make enquiry,
We may touch things that otherwise escape us.
OEDIPUS. Tell me: Was Laïos murdered in his house,
Or in the fields, or in some foreign country?
CREON. He said he planned to make a pilgrimage.
He did not come home again.
OEDIPUS. And was there no one,
No witness, no companion, to tell what happened?
CREON. They were all killed but one, and he got away
So frightened that he could remember one thing only.
OEDIPUS. What was that one thing? One may be the key
To everything, if we resolve to use it.
CREON. He said that a band of highwaymen attacked them,
Outnumbered them, and overwhelmed the King.
OEDIPUS. Strange, that a highwayman should be so daring—
Unless some faction here bribed him to do it.

CREON. We thought of that. But after Laïos' death
New troubles arose and we had no avenger.
OEDIPUS. What troubles could prevent your hunting down the killers?
CREON. The riddling Sphinx's song
Made us deaf to all mysteries but her own.
OEDIPUS. Then once more I must bring what is dark to light.
It is most fitting that Apollo shows,
As you do, this compunction for the dead.
You shall see how I stand by you, as I should,
To avenge the city and the city's god,
And not as though it were for some distant friend,
But for my own sake, to be rid of evil.
Whoever killed King Laïos might—who knows?—
Decide at any moment to kill me as well.
By avenging the murdered king I protect myself.

Come, then, my children: leave the altar steps,
Lift up your olive boughs!
One of you go
And summon the people of Kadmos to gather here.
I will do all that I can; you may tell them that.
[*Exit a* PAGE.]
So, with the help of God,
We shall be saved—or else indeed we are lost.
PRIEST. Let us rise, children. It was for this we came,
And now the King has promised it himself.
Phoibos has sent us an oracle; may he descend
Himself to save us and drive out the plague.
[*Exeunt* OEDIPUS *and* CREON *into the palace by the central door. The* PRIEST *and the* SUPPLIANTS *disperse R and L. After a short pause the* CHORUS *enters the orchestra.*]

Párodos

CHORUS. What is the god singing in his profound [STROPHE I.]
Delphi of gold and shadow?
What oracle for Thebes, the sunwhipped city?

Fear unjoints me, the roots of my heart tremble.
Now I remember, O Healer, your power, and wonder:
Will you send doom like a sudden cloud, or weave it
Like nightfall of the past?

Ah no: be merciful, issue of holy sound:
Dearest to our expectancy: be tender!

[ANTISTROPHE 1.]

Let me pray to Athenê, the immortal daughter of Zeus,
And to Artemis her sister
Who keeps her famous throne in the market ring,
And to Apollo, bowman at the far butts of heaven—

O gods, descend! Like three streams leap against
The fires of our grief, the fires of darkness;
Be swift to bring us rest!

As in the old time from the brilliant house
Of air you stepped to save us, come again!

Now our afflictions have no end, [STROPHE 2.]
Now all our stricken host lies down
And no man fights off death with his mind;

The noble plowland bears no grain,
And groaning mothers can not bear—

See, how our lives like birds take wing,
Like sparks that fly when a fire soars,
To the shore of the god of evening.

The plague burns on, it is pitiless, [ANTISTROPHE 2.]
Though pallid children laden with death
Lie unwept in the stony ways,

And old gray women by every path
Flock to the strand about the altars

There to strike their breasts and cry
Worship of Zeus in wailing prayers:
Be kind, God's golden child!

There are no swords in this attack by fire, [STROPHE 3.]
No shields, but we are ringed with cries.

Send the besieger plunging from our homes
Into the vast sea-room of the Atlantic
Or into the waves that foam eastward of Thrace—

For the day ravages what the night spares—

Destroy our enemy, lord of the thunder!
Let him be riven by lightning from heaven!

Phoibos Apollo, stretch the sun's bowstring, [ANTISTROPHE 3.]
That golden cord, until it sing for us,
Flashing arrows in heaven!
Artemis, Huntress,
Race with flaring lights upon our mountains!

O scarlet god, O golden-banded brow,
O Theban Bacchos in a storm of Maenads,
[*Enter* OEDIPUS, CHORUS.]
Whirl upon Death, that all the Undying hate!
Come with blinding cressets, come in joy!

Scene 1

OEDIPUS. Is this your prayer? It may be answered. Come,
Listen to me, act as the crisis demands,
And you shall have relief from all these evils.

Until now I was a stranger to this tale,
As I had been a stranger to the crime.
Could I track down the murderer without a clue?
But now, friends,
As one who became a citizen after the murder,
I make this proclamation to all Thebans:
If any man knows by whose hand Laïos, son of Labdakos,
Met his death, I direct that man to tell me everything,
No matter what he fears for having so long withheld it.
Let it stand as promised that no further trouble
Will come to him, but he may leave the land in safety.

Moreover: If anyone knows the murderer to be foreign,
Let him not keep silent: he shall have his reward from me.
However, if he does conceal it; if any man
Fearing for his friend or for himself disobeys this edict,
Hear what I propose to do:

I solemnly forbid the people of this country,
Where power and throne are mine, ever to receive that man
Or speak to him, no matter who he is, or let him
Join in sacrifice, lustration, or in prayer.

I decree that he be driven from every house,
Being, as he is, corruption itself to us: the Delphic
Voice of Zeus has pronounced this revelation.
Thus I associate myself with the oracle
And take the side of the murdered king.

As for the criminal, I pray to God—
Whether it be a lurking thief, or one of a number—
I pray that that man's life be consumed in evil and
wretchedness.
And as for me, this curse applies no less
If it should turn out that the culprit is my guest here,
Sharing my hearth.
You have heard the penalty.
I lay it on you now to attend to this
For my sake, for Apollo's, for the sick
Sterile city that heaven has abandoned.
Suppose the oracle had given you no command:
Should this defilement go uncleansed for ever?
You should have found the murderer: your king,
A noble king, had been destroyed!
Now I,
Having the power that he held before me,
Having his bed, begetting children there
Upon his wife, as he would have, had he lived—
Their son would have been my children's brother,
If Laïos had had luck in fatherhood!
(But surely ill luck rushed upon his reign)—
I say I take the son's part, just as though
I were his son, to press the fight for him
And see it won! I'll find the hand that brought
Death to Labdakos' and Polydoros' child,
Heir of Kadmos' and Agenor's line.
And as for those who fail me,
May the gods deny them the fruit of the earth,
Fruit of the womb, and may they rot utterly!
Let them be wretched as we are wretched, and worse!

For you, for loyal Thebans, and for all
Who find my actions right, I pray the favor
Of justice, and of all the immortal gods.
CHORUS. Since I am under oath, my lord, I swear
I did not do the murder, I can not name
The murderer. Might not the oracle
That has ordained the search tell where to find him?

OEDIPUS. An honest question. But no man in the world
Can make the gods do more than the gods will.
CHORUS. There is one last expedient—
OEDIPUS. Tell me what it is.
Though it seem slight, you must not hold it back.
CHORUS. A lord clairvoyant to the lord Apollo,
As we all know, is the skilled Teiresias.
One might learn much about this from him, Oedipus.
OEDIPUS. I am not wasting time:
Creon spoke of this, and I have sent for him—
Twice, in fact; it is strange that he is not here.
CHORUS. The other matter—that old report—seems useless.
OEDIPUS. Tell me. I am interested in all reports.
CHORUS. The King was said to have been killed by highwaymen.
OEDIPUS. I know. But we have no witnesses to that.
CHORUS. If the killer can feel a particle of dread,
Your curse will bring him out of hiding!
OEDIPUS. No.
The man who dared that act will fear no curse.
[*Enter the blind seer* TEIRESIAS, *led by a* PAGE.]
CHORUS. But there is one man who may detect the criminal.
This is Teiresias, this is the holy prophet
In whom, alone of all men, truth was born.
OEDIPUS. Teiresias: seer: student of mysteries,
Of all that's taught and all that no man tells,
Secrets of Heaven and secrets of the earth:
Blind though you are, you know the city lies
Sick with plague; and from this plague, my lord,
We find that you alone can guard or save us.

Possibly you did not hear the messengers?
Apollo, when we sent to him,
Sent us back word that this great pestilence
Would lift, but only if we established clearly
The identity of those who murdered Laïos.
They must be killed or exiled.
Can you use
Birdflight or any art of divination
To purify yourself, and Thebes, and me
From this contagion? We are in your hands.
There is no fairer duty
Than that of helping others in distress.
TEIRESIAS. How dreadful knowledge of the truth can be
When there's no help in truth! I knew this well,
But did not act on it: else I should not have come.

OEDIPUS. What is troubling you? Why are your eyes so cold?
TEIRESIAS. Let me go home. Bear your own fate, and I'll
Bear mine. It is better so: trust what I say.
OEDIPUS. What you say is ungracious and unhelpful
To your native country. Do not refuse to speak.
TEIRESIAS. When it comes to speech, your own is neither temperate
Nor opportune. I wish to be more prudent.
OEDIPUS. In God's name, we all beg you—
TEIRESIAS. You are all ignorant.
No; I will never tell you what I know.
Now it is my misery; then, it would be yours.
OEDIPUS. What! You do know something, and will not tell us?
You would betray us all and wreck the State?
TEIRESIAS. I do not intend to torture myself, or you.
Why persist in asking? You will not persuade me.
OEDIPUS. What a wicked old man you are! You'd try a stone's
Patience! Out with it! Have you no feeling at all?
TEIRESIAS. You call me unfeeling. If you could only see
The nature of your own feelings . . .
OEDIPUS. Why,
Who would not feel as I do? Who could endure
Your arrogance toward the city?
TEIRESIAS. What does it matter!
Whether I speak or not, it is bound to come.
OEDIPUS. Then, if "it" is bound to come, you are bound to tell me.
TEIRESIAS. No, I will not go on. Rage as you please.
OEDIPUS. Rage? Why not!
And I'll tell you what I think:
You planned it, you had it done, you all but
Killed him with your own hands: if you had eyes,
I'd say the crime was yours, and yours alone.
TEIRESIAS. So? I charge you, then,
Abide by the proclamation you have made:
From this day forth
Never speak again to these men or to me;
You yourself are the pollution of this country.
OEDIPUS. You dare say that! Can you possibly think you have
Some way of going free, after such insolence?
TEIRESIAS. I have gone free. It is the truth sustains me.
OEDIPUS. Who taught you shamelessness? It was not your craft.
TEIRESIAS. You did. You made me speak. I did not want to.
OEDIPUS. Speak what? Let me hear it again more clearly.
TEIRESIAS. Was it not clear before? Are you tempting me?
OEDIPUS. I did not understand it. Say it again.
TEIRESIAS. I say that you are the murderer whom you seek.

OEDIPUS. Now twice you have spat out infamy. You'll pay for it!
TEIRESIAS. Would you care for more? Do you wish to be really angry?
OEDIPUS. Say what you will. Whatever you say is worthless.
TEIRESIAS. I say that you live in hideous love with her
Who is nearest you in blood. You are blind to the evil.
OEDIPUS. It seems you can go on mouthing like this for ever.
TEIRESIAS. I can, if there is power in truth.
OEDIPUS. There is:
But not for you, not for you,
You sightless, witless, senseless, mad old man!
TEIRESIAS. You are the madman. There is no one here
Who will not curse you soon, as you curse me.
OEDIPUS. You child of endless night! You can not hurt me
Or any other man who sees the sun.
TEIRESIAS. True: it is not from me your fate will come.
That lies within Apollo's competence,
As it is his concern.
OEDIPUS. Tell me:
Are you speaking for Creon, or for yourself?
TEIRESIAS. Creon is no threat. You weave your own doom.
OEDIPUS. Wealth, power, craft of statesmanship!
Kingly position, everywhere admired!
What savage envy is stored up against these,
If Creon, whom I trusted, Creon my friend,
For this great office which the city once
Put in my hands unsought—if for this power
Creon desires in secret to destroy me!

He has bought this decrepit fortune-teller, this
Collector of dirty pennies, this prophet fraud—
Why, he is no more clairvoyant than I am!
Tell us:
Has your mystic mummery ever approached the truth?
When that hellcat the Sphinx was performing here,
What help were you to these people?
Her magic was not for the first man who came along:
It demanded a real exorcist. Your birds—
What good were they? or the gods, for the matter of that?
But I came by,
Oedipus, the simple man, who knows nothing—
I thought it out for myself, no birds helped me!
And this is the man you think you can destroy,
That you may be close to Creon when he's king!
Well, you and your friend Creon, it seems to me,
Will suffer most. If you were not an old man,

You would have paid already for your plot.
CHORUS. We can not see that his words or yours
Have been spoken except in anger, Oedipus,
And of anger we have no need. How can God's will
Be accomplished best? That is what most concerns us.
TEIRESIAS. You are a king. But where argument's concerned
I am your man, as much a king as you.
I am not your servant, but Apollo's.
I have no need of Creon to speak for me.

Listen to me. You mock my blindness, do you?
But I say that you, with both your eyes, are blind:
You can not see the wretchedness of your life,
Nor in whose house you live, no, nor with whom.
Who are your father and mother? Can you tell me?
You do not even know the blind wrongs
That you have done them, on earth and in the world below.
But the double lash of your parents' curse will whip you
Out of this land some day, with only night
Upon your precious eyes.
Your cries then—where will they not be heard?
What fastness of Kithairon will not echo them?
And that bridal-descant of yours—you'll know it then,
The song they sang when you came here to Thebes
And found your misguided berthing.
All this, and more, that you can not guess at now,
Will bring you to yourself among your children.
Be angry, then. Curse Creon. Curse my words.
I tell you, no man that walks upon the earth
Shall be rooted out more horribly than you.
OEDIPUS. Am I to bear this from him?—Damnation
Take you! Out of this place! Out of my sight!
TEIRESIAS. I would not have come at all if you had not asked me.
OEDIPUS. Could I have told that you'd talk nonsense, that
You'd come here to make a fool of yourself, and of me?
TEIRESIAS. A fool? Your parents thought me sane enough.
OEDIPUS. My parents again!—Wait: who were my parents?
TEIRESIAS. This day will give you a father, and break your heart.
OEDIPUS. Your infantile riddles! Your damned abracadabra!
TEIRESIAS. You were a great man once at solving riddles.
OEDIPUS. Mock me with that if you like; you will find it true.
TEIRESIAS. It was true enough. It brought about your ruin.
OEDIPUS. But if it saved this town?
[*To the* PAGE.]
TEIRESIAS. Boy, give me your hand.

OEDIPUS. Yes, boy; lead him away.
—While you are here
We can do nothing. Go; leave us in peace.
TEIRESIAS. I will go when I have said what I have to say.
How can you hurt me? And I tell you again:
The man you have been looking for all this time,
The damned man, the murderer of Laïos,
That man is in Thebes. To your mind he is foreign-born,
But it will soon be shown that he is a Theban,
A revelation that will fail to please.
A blind man,
Who has his eyes now; a penniless man, who is rich now;
And he will go tapping the strange earth with his staff.
To the children with whom he lives now he will be
Brother and father—the very same; to her
Who bore him, son and husband—the very same
Who came to his father's bed, wet with his father's blood.
Enough. Go think that over.
If later you find error in what I have said,
You may say that I have no skill in prophecy.
[*Exit* TEIRESIAS, *led by his* PAGE. OEDIPUS *goes into the palace.*]

Ode 1

CHORUS. The Delphic stone of prophecies [STROPHE I.]
Remembers ancient regicide
And a still bloody hand.
That killer's hour of flight has come.
He must be stronger than riderless
Coursers of untiring wind,
For the son of Zeus armed with his father's thunder
Leaps in lightning after him;
And the Furies follow him, the sad Furies.

Holy Parnassos' peak of snow [ANTISTROPHE I.]
Flashes and blinds that secret man,
That all shall hunt him down:
Though he may roam the forest shade
Like a bull gone wild from pasture
To rage through glooms of stone.
Doom comes down on him; flight will not avail him;
For the world's heart calls him desolate,
And the immortal Furies follow, for ever follow.

But now a wilder thing is heard [STROPHE 2.]
From the old man skilled at hearing Fate in the wingbeat of a bird.
Bewildered as a blown bird, my soul hovers and can not find
Foothold in this debate, or any reason or rest of mind.
But no man ever brought—none can bring
Proof of strife between Thebes' royal house,
Labdakos' line, and the son of Polybos;
And never until now has any man brought word
Of Laïos' dark death staining Oedipus the King.

Divine Zeus and Apollo hold [ANTISTROPHE 2.]
Perfect intelligence alone of all tales ever told;
And well though this diviner works, he works in his own night;
No man can judge that rough unknown or trust in second sight,
For wisdom changes hands among the wise.
Shall I believe my great lord criminal
At a raging word that a blind old man let fall?
I saw him, when the carrion woman faced him of old,
Prove his heroic mind! These evil words are lies.

Scene 2

CREON. Men of Thebes:
I am told that heavy accusations
Have been brought against me by King Oedipus.

I am not the kind of man to bear this tamely.

If in these present difficulties
He holds me accountable for any harm to him
Through anything I have said or done—why, then,
I do not value life in this dishonor.
It is not as though this rumor touched upon
Some private indiscretion. The matter is grave.
The fact is that I am being called disloyal
To the State, to my fellow citizens, to my friends.
CHORUS. He may have spoken in anger, not from his mind.
CREON. But did you not hear him say I was the one
Who seduced the old prophet into lying?
CHORUS. The thing was said; I do not know how seriously.
CREON. But you were watching him! Were his eyes steady?
Did he look like a man in his right mind?
CHORUS. I do not know.

I can not judge the behavior of great men.
But here is the King himself.

[*Enter* OEDIPUS.]

OEDIPUS. So you dared come back.
Why? How brazen of you to come to my house,
You murderer!
Do you think I do not know
That you plotted to kill me, plotted to steal my throne?
Tell me, in God's name: am I coward, a fool,
That you should dream you could accomplish this?
A fool who could not see your slippery game?
A coward, not to fight back when I saw it?
You are the fool, Creon, are you not? hoping
Without support or friends to get a throne?
Thrones may be won or bought: you could do neither.

CREON. Now listen to me. You have talked; let me talk, too.
You can not judge unless you know the facts.

OEDIPUS. You speak well: there is one fact; but I find it hard
To learn from the deadliest enemy I have.

CREON. That above all I must dispute with you.

OEDIPUS. That above all I will not hear you deny.

CREON. If you think there is anything good in being stubborn
Against all reason, then I say you are wrong.

OEDIPUS. If you think a man can sin against his own kind
And not be punished for it, I say you are mad.

CREON. I agree. But tell me: what have I done to you?

OEDIPUS. You advised me to send for that wizard, did you not?

CREON. I did. I should do it again.

OEDIPUS. Very well. Now tell me:
How long has it been since Laïos—

CREON. What of Laïos?

OEDIPUS. Since he vanished in that onset by the road?

CREON. It was long ago, a long time.

OEDIPUS. And this prophet,
Was he practicing here then?

CREON. He was; and with honor, as now.

OEDIPUS. Did he speak of me at that time?

CREON. He never did;
At least, not when I was present.

OEDIPUS. But . . . the enquiry?
I suppose you held one?

CREON. We did, but we learned nothing.

OEDIPUS. Why did the prophet not speak against me then?

CREON. I do not know; and I am the kind of man
Who holds his tongue when he has no facts to go on.

OEDIPUS. There's one fact that you know, and you could tell it.
CREON. What fact is that? If I know it, you shall have it.
OEDIPUS. If he were not involved with you, he could not say
That it was I who murdered Laïos.
CREON. If he says that, you are the one that knows it!—
But now it is my turn to question you.
OEDIPUS. Put your questions. I am no murderer.
CREON. First, then: You married my sister?
OEDIPUS. I married your sister.
CREON. And you rule the kingdom equally with her?
OEDIPUS. Everything that she wants she has from me.
CREON. And I am the third, equal to both of you?
OEDIPUS. That is why I call you a bad friend.
CREON. No. Reason it out, as I have done.
Think of this first: Would any sane man prefer
Power, with all a king's anxieties,
To that same power and the grace of sleep?
Certainly not I.
I have never longed for the king's power—only his rights.
Would any wise man differ from me in this?
As matters stand, I have my way in everything
With your consent, and no responsibilities.
If I were king, I should be a slave to policy.
How could I desire a scepter more
Than what is now mine—untroubled influence?
No, I have not gone mad; I need no honors,
Except those with the perquisites I have now.
I am welcome everywhere; every man salutes me,
And those who want your favor seek my ear,
Since I know how to manage what they ask.
Should I exchange this ease for that anxiety?
Besides, no sober mind is treasonable.
I hate anarchy
And never would deal with any man who likes it.

Test what I have said. Go to the priestess
At Delphi, ask if I quoted her correctly.
And as for this other thing: if I am found
Guilty of treason with Teiresias,
Then sentence me to death! You have my word
It is a sentence I should cast my vote for—
But not without evidence!
You do wrong
When you take good men for bad, bad men for good.
A true friend thrown aside—why, life itself

Is not more precious!
In time you will know this well:
For time, and time alone, will show the just man,
Though scoundrels are discovered in a day.
CHORUS. This is well said, and a prudent man would ponder it.
Judgments too quickly formed are dangerous.
OEDIPUS. But is he not quick in his duplicity?
And shall I not be quick to parry him?
Would you have me stand still, hold my peace, and let
This man win everything, through my inaction?
CREON. And you want—what is it, then? To banish me?
OEDIPUS. No, not exile. It is your death I want,
So that all the world may see what treason means.
CREON. You will persist, then? You will not believe me?
OEDIPUS. How can I believe you?
CREON. Then you are a fool.
OEDIPUS. To save myself?
CREON. In justice, think of me.
OEDIPUS. You are evil incarnate.
CREON. But suppose that you are wrong?
OEDIPUS. Still I must rule.
CREON. But not if you rule badly.
OEDIPUS. O city, city!
CREON. It is my city, too!
CHORUS. Now, my lords, be still. I see the Queen,
Iocastê, coming from her palace chambers;
And it is time she came, for the sake of you both.
This dreadful quarrel can be resolved through her.
[*Enter* IOCASTÊ.]
IOCASTÊ. Poor foolish men, what wicked din is this?
With Thebes sick to death, is it not shameful
That you should rake some private quarrel up?
[*To* OEDIPUS.]
Come into the house.
—And you, Creon, go now:
Let us have no more of this tumult over nothing.
CREON. Nothing? No, sister: what your husband plans for me
Is one of two great evils: exile or death.
OEDIPUS. He is right.
Why, woman I have caught him squarely
Plotting against my life.
CREON. No! Let me die
Accurst if ever I have wished you harm!
IOCASTÊ. Ah, believe it, Oedipus!
In the name of the gods, respect this oath of his

For my sake, for the sake of these people here!

[STROPHE I.]

CHORUS. Open your mind to her, my lord. Be ruled by her, I beg you!
OEDIPUS. What would you have me do?
CHORUS. Respect Creon's word. He has never spoken like a fool,
And now he has sworn an oath.
OEDIPUS. You know what you ask?
CHORUS. I do.
OEDIPUS. Speak on, then.
CHORUS. A friend so sworn should not be baited so,
In blind malice, and without final proof.
OEDIPUS. You are aware, I hope, that what you say
Means death for me, or exile at the least.

CHORUS. No, I swear by Helios, first in Heaven! [STROPHE 2.]
May I die friendless and accurst,
The worst of deaths, if ever I meant that!
It is the withering fields
That hurt my sick heart:
Must we bear all these ills,
And now your bad blood as well?
OEDIPUS. Then let him go. And let me die, if I must,
Or be driven by him in shame from the land of Thebes.
It is your unhappiness, and not his talk,
That touches me.
As for him—
Wherever he is, I will hate him as long as I live.
CREON. Ugly in yielding, as you were ugly in rage!
Natures like yours chiefly torment themselves.
OEDIPUS. Can you not go? Can you not leave me?
CREON. I can.
You do not know me; but the city knows me,
And in its eyes I am just, if not in yours.
[*Exit* CREON.]

[ANTISTROPHE I.]

CHORUS. Lady Iocastê, did you not ask the King to go to his chambers?
IOCASTÊ. First tell me what has happened.
CHORUS. There was suspicion without evidence; yet it rankled
As even false charges will.
IOCASTÊ. On both sides?
CHORUS. On both.
IOCASTÊ. But what was said?

CHORUS. Oh let it rest, let it be done with!
Have we not suffered enough?
OEDIPUS. You see to what your decency has brought you:
You have made difficulties where my heart saw none.

[ANTISTROPHE 2.]

CHORUS. Oedipus, it is not once only I have told you—
You must know I should count myself unwise
To the point of madness, should I now forsake you—
You, under whose hand,
In the storm of another time,
Our dear land sailed out free.
But now stand fast at the helm!
IOCASTÊ. In God's name, Oedipus, inform your wife as well:
Why are you so set in this hard anger?
OEDIPUS. I will tell you, for none of these men deserves
My confidence as you do. It is Creon's work,
His treachery, his plotting against me.
IOCASTÊ. Go on, if you can make this clear to me.
OEDIPUS. He charges me with the murder of Laïos.
IOCASTÊ. Has he some knowledge? Or does he speak from hearsay?
OEDIPUS. He would not commit himself to such a charge,
But he has brought in that damnable soothsayer
To tell his story.
IOCASTÊ. Set your mind at rest.
If it is a question of soothsayers, I tell you
That you will find no man whose craft gives knowledge
Of the unknowable.
Here is my proof:

An oracle was reported to Laïos once
(I will not say from Phoibos himself, but from
His appointed ministers, at any rate)
That his doom would be death at the hands of his own son—
His son, born of his flesh and of mine!
Now, you remember the story: Laïos was killed
By marauding strangers where three highways meet;
But his child had not been three days in this world
Before the King had pierced the baby's ankles
And had him left to die on a lonely mountain.

Thus, Apollo never caused that child
To kill his father, and it was not Laïos' fate
To die at the hands of his son, as he had feared.
This is what prophets and prophecies are worth!

Have no dread of them.
It is God himself
Who can show us what he wills, in his own way.
OEDIPUS. How strange a shadowy memory crossed my mind,
Just now while you were speaking; it chilled my heart.
IOCASTÊ. What do you mean? What memory do you speak of?
OEDIPUS. If I understand you, Laïos was killed
At a place where three roads meet.
IOCASTÊ. So it was said;
We have no later story.
OEDIPUS. Where did it happen?
IOCASTÊ. Phokis, it is called: at a place where the Theban Way
Divides into the roads toward Delphi and Daulia.
OEDIPUS. When?
IOCASTÊ. We had the news not long before you came
And proved the right to your succession here.
OEDIPUS. Ah, what net has God been weaving for me?
IOCASTÊ. Oedipus! Why does this trouble you?
OEDIPUS. Do not ask me yet.
First, tell me how Laïos looked, and tell me
How old he was.
IOCASTÊ. He was tall, his hair just touched
With white; his form was not unlike your own.
OEDIPUS. I think that I myself may be accurst
By my own ignorant edict.
IOCASTÊ. You speak strangely.
It makes me tremble to look at you, my King.
OEDIPUS. I am not sure that the blind man can not see.
But I should know better if you were to tell me—
IOCASTÊ. Anything—though I dread to hear you ask it.
OEDIPUS. Was the King lightly escorted, or did he ride
With a large company, as a ruler should?
IOCASTÊ. There were five men with him in all: one was a herald;
And a single chariot, which he was driving.
OEDIPUS. Alas, that makes it plain enough!
But who—
Who told you how it happened?
IOCASTÊ. A household servant,
The only one to escape.
OEDIPUS. And is he still
A servant of ours?
IOCASTÊ. No; for when he came back at last
And found you enthroned in the place of the dead king,
He came to me, touched my hand with his, and begged
That I would send him away to the frontier district

Where only the shepherds go—
As far away from the city as I could send him.
I granted his prayer; for although the man was a slave,
He had earned more than this favor at my hands.

OEDIPUS. Can he be called back quickly?

IOCASTÊ. Easily.
But why?

OEDIPUS. I have taken too much upon myself
Without enquiry; therefore I wish to consult him.

IOCASTÊ. Then he shall come.
But am I not one also
To whom you might confide these fears of yours?

OEDIPUS. That is your right; it will not be denied you,
Now least of all; for I have reached a pitch
Of wild foreboding. Is there anyone
To whom I should sooner speak?

Polybos of Corinth is my father.
My mother is a Dorian: Meropê.
I grew up chief among the men of Corinth
Until a strange thing happened—
Not worth my passion, it may be, but strange.

At a feast, a drunken man maundering in his cups
Cries out that I am not my father's son!

I contained myself that night, though I felt anger
And a sinking heart. The next day I visited
My father and mother, and questioned them. They stormed,
Calling it all the slanderous rant of a fool;
And this relieved me. Yet the suspicion
Remained always aching in my mind;
I knew there was talk; I could not rest;
And finally, saying nothing to my parents,
I went to the shrine at Delphi.

The god dismissed my question without reply;
He spoke of other things.
Some were clear,
Full of wretchedness, dreadful, unbearable:
As, that I should lie with my own mother, breed
Children from whom all men would turn their eyes;
And that I should be my father's murderer.

I heard all this, and fled. And from that day

Corinth to me was only in the stars
Descending in that quarter of the sky,
As I wandered farther and farther on my way
To a land where I should never see the evil
Sung by the oracle. And I came to this country
Where, so you say, King Laïos was killed.

I will tell you all that happened there, my lady.

There were three highways
Coming together at a place I passed;
And there a herald came towards me, and a chariot
Drawn by horses, with a man such as you describe
Seated in it. The groom leading the horses
Forced me off the road at his lord's command;
But as this charioteer lurched over towards me
I struck him in my rage. The old man saw me
And brought his double goad down upon my head
As I came abreast.
He was paid back, and more!
Swinging my club in this right hand I knocked him
Out of his car, and he rolled on the ground.
I killed him.

I killed them all.
Now if that stranger and Laïos were—kin,
Where is a man more miserable than I?
More hated by the gods? Citizen and alien alike
Must never shelter me or speak to me—
I must be shunned by all.
And I myself
Pronounced this malediction upon myself!

Think of it: I have touched you with these hands,
These hands that killed your husband. What defilement!

Am I all evil, then? It must be so,
Since I must flee from Thebes, yet never again
See my own countrymen, my own country,
For fear of joining my mother in marriage
And killing Polybos, my father.
Ah,
If I was created so, born to this fate,
Who could deny the savagery of God?

O holy majesty of heavenly powers!
May I never see that day! Never!
Rather let me vanish from the race of men
Than know the abomination destined me!

CHORUS. We too, my lord, have felt dismay at this.
But there is hope: you have yet to hear the shepherd.

OEDIPUS. Indeed, I fear no other hope is left me.

IOCASTÊ. What do you hope from him when he comes?

OEDIPUS. This much:
If his account of the murder tallies with yours,
Then I am cleared.

IOCASTÊ. What was it that I said
Of such importance?

OEDIPUS. Why, "marauders," you said,
Killed the King, according to this man's story.
If he maintains that still, if there were several,
Clearly the guilt is not mine: I was alone.
But if he says one man, singlehanded, did it,
Then the evidence all points to me.

IOCASTÊ. You may be sure that he said there were several;
And can he call back that story now? He cán not.
The whole city heard it as plainly as I.
But suppose he alters some detail of it:
He can not ever show that Laïos' death
Fulfilled the oracle: for Apollo said
My child was doomed to kill him; and my child—
Poor baby!—it was my child that died first.

No. From now on, where oracles are concerned,
I would not waste a second thought on any.

OEDIPUS. You may be right.
But come: let someone go
For the shepherd at once. This matter must be settled.

IOCASTÊ. I will send for him.
I would not wish to cross you in anything,
And surely not in this.—Let us go in.
[*Exeunt into the palace.*]

Ode 2

CHORUS. Let me be reverent in the ways of right, [STROPHE I.]
Lowly the paths I journey on;
Let all my words and actions keep

The laws of the pure universe
From highest Heaven handed down.
For Heaven is their bright nurse,
Those generations of the realms of light;
Ah, never of mortal kind were they begot,
Nor are they slaves of memory, lost in sleep:
Their Father is greater than Time, and ages not.

The tyrant is a child of Pride [ANTISTROPHE 1.]
Who drinks from his great sickening cup
Recklessness and vanity,
Until from his high crest headlong
He plummets to the dust of hope.
That strong man is not strong.
But let no fair ambition be denied;
May God protect the wrestler for the State
In government, in comely policy,
Who will fear God, and on His ordinance wait.

Haughtiness and the high hand of disdain [STROPHE 2.]
Tempt and outrage God's holy law;
And any mortal who dares hold
No immortal Power in awe
Will be caught up in a net of pain:
The price for which his levity is sold.
Let each man take due earnings, then,
And keep his hands from holy things,
And from blasphemy stand apart—
Else the crackling blast of heaven
Blows on his head, and on his desperate heart;
Though fools will honor impious men,
In their cities no tragic poet sings.

Shall we lose faith in Delphi's obscurities, [ANTISTROPHE 2.]
We who have heard the world's core
Discredited, and the sacred wood
Of Zeus at Elis praised no more?
The deeds and the strange prophecies
Must make a pattern yet to be understood.
Zeus, if indeed you are lord of all,
Throned in light over night and day,
Mirror this in your endless mind:
Our masters call the oracle
Words on the wind, and the Delphic vision blind!

Their hearts no longer know Apollo,
And reverence for the gods has died away.

Scene 3

[*Enter* IOCASTÊ.]

IOCASTÊ. Princes of Thebes, it has occurred to me
To visit the altars of the gods, bearing
These branches as a suppliant, and this incense.
Our King is not himself: his noble soul
Is overwrought with fantasies of dread,
Else he would consider
The new prophecies in the light of the old.
He will listen to any voice that speaks disaster,
And my advice goes for nothing.

[*She approaches the altar, R.*]

To you, then, Apollo,
Lycean lord, since you are nearest, I turn in prayer.
Receive these offerings, and grant us deliverance
From defilement. Our hearts are heavy with fear
When we see our leader distracted, as helpless sailors
Are terrified by the confusion of their helmsman.

[*Enter* MESSENGER.]

MESSENGER. Friends, no doubt you can direct me:
Where shall I find the house of Oedipus,
Or, better still, where is the King himself?

CHORUS. It is this very place, stranger; he is inside.
This is his wife and mother of his children.

MESSENGER. I wish her happiness in a happy house,
Blest in all the fulfillment of her marriage.

IOCASTÊ. I wish as much for you: your courtesy
Deserves a like good fortune. But now, tell me:
Why have you come? What have you to say to us?

MESSENGER. Good news, my lady, for your house and your husband.

IOCASTÊ. What news? Who sent you here?

MESSENGER. I am from Corinth.
The news I bring ought to mean joy for you,
Though it may be you will find some grief in it.

IOCASTÊ. What is it? How can it touch us in both ways?

MESSENGER. The people of Corinth, they say,
Intend to call Oedipus to be their king.

IOCASTÊ. But old Polybos—is he not reigning still?

MESSENGER. No. Death holds him in his sepulchre.
IOCASTÊ. What are you saying? Polybos is dead?
MESSENGER. If I am not telling the truth, may I die myself.
[*To a* MAIDSERVANT.]
IOCASTÊ. Go in, go quickly; tell this to your master.

O riddlers of God's will, where are you now!
This was the man whom Oedipus, long ago,
Feared so, fled so, in dread of destroying him—
But it was another fate by which he died.
[*Enter* OEDIPUS, CHORUS.]
OEDIPUS. Dearest Iocastê, why have you sent for me?
IOCASTÊ. Listen to what this man says, and then tell me
What has become of the solemn prophecies.
OEDIPUS. Who is this man? What is his news for me?
IOCASTÊ. He has come from Corinth to announce your father's death!
OEDIPUS. Is it true, stranger? Tell me in your own words.
MESSENGER. I can not say it more clearly: the King is dead.
OEDIPUS. Was it by treason? Or by an attack of illness?
MESSENGER. A little thing brings old men to their rest.
OEDIPUS. It was sickness, then?
MESSENGER. Yes, and his many years.
OEDIPUS. Ah!
Why should a man respect the Pythian hearth, or
Give heed to the birds that jangle above his head?
They prophesied that I should kill Polybos,
Kill my own father; but he is dead and buried,
And I am here—I never touched him, never,
Unless he died of grief for my departure,
And thus, in a sense, through me. No. Polybos
Has packed the oracles off with him underground.
They are empty words.
IOCASTÊ. Had I not told you so?
OEDIPUS. You had; it was my faint heart that betrayed me.
IOCASTÊ. From now on never think of those things again.
OEDIPUS. And yet—must I not fear my mother's bed?
IOCASTÊ. Why should anyone in this world be afraid,
Since Fate rules us and nothing can be foreseen?
A man should live only for the present day.

Have no more fear of sleeping with your mother:
How many men, in dreams, have lain with their mothers!
No reasonable man is troubled by such things.
OEDIPUS. That is true; only—
If only my mother were not still alive!

But she is alive. I can not help my dread.
IOCASTÊ. Yet this news of your father's death is wonderful.
OEDIPUS. Wonderful. But I fear the living woman.
MESSENGER. Tell me, who is this woman that you fear?
OEDIPUS. It is Meropê, man; the wife of King Polybos.
MESSENGER. Meropê? Why should you be afraid of her?
OEDIPUS. An oracle of the gods, a dreadful saying.
MESSENGER. Can you tell me about it or are you sworn to silence?
OEDIPUS. I can tell you, and I will.
Apollo said through his prophet that I was the man
Who should marry his own mother, shed his father's blood
With his own hands. And so, for all these years
I have kept clear of Corinth, and no harm has come—
Though it would have been sweet to see my parents again.
MESSENGER. And is this the fear that drove you out of Corinth?
OEDIPUS. Would you have me kill my father?
MESSENGER. As for that
You must be reassured by the news I gave you.
OEDIPUS. If you could reassure me, I would reward you.
MESSENGER. I had that in mind, I will confess: I thought
I could count on you when you returned to Corinth.
OEDIPUS. No: I will never go near my parents again.
MESSENGER. Ah, son, you still do not know what you are doing—
OEDIPUS. What do you mean? In the name of God tell me!
MESSENGER. —If these are your reasons for not going home.
OEDIPUS. I tell you, I fear the oracle may come true.
MESSENGER. And guilt may come upon you through your parents?
OEDIPUS. That is the dread that is always in my heart.
MESSENGER. Can you not see that all your fears are groundless?
OEDIPUS. How can you say that? They are my parents, surely?
MESSENGER. Polybos was not your father.
OEDIPUS. Not my father?
MESSENGER. No more your father than the man speaking to you.
OEDIPUS. But you are nothing to me!
MESSENGER. Neither was he.
OEDIPUS. Then why did he call me son?
MESSENGER. I will tell you:
Long ago he had you from my hands, as a gift.
OEDIPUS. Then how could he love me so, if I was not his?
MESSENGER. He had no children, and his heart turned to you.
OEDIPUS. What of you? Did you buy me? Did you find me by chance?
MESSENGER. I came upon you in the crooked pass of Kithairon.
OEDIPUS. And what were you doing there?
MESSENGER. Tending my flocks.
OEDIPUS. A wandering shepherd?

MESSENGER. But your savior, son, that day.
OEDIPUS. From what did you save me?
MESSENGER. Your ankles should tell you that.
OEDIPUS. Ah, stranger, why do you speak of that childhood pain?
MESSENGER. I cut the bonds that tied your ankles together.
OEDIPUS. I have had the mark as long as I can remember.
MESSENGER. That was why you were given the name you bear.
OEDIPUS. God! Was it my father or my mother who did it?
Tell me!
MESSENGER. I do not know. The man who gave you to me
Can tell you better than I.
OEDIPUS. It was not you that found me, but another?
MESSENGER. It was another shepherd gave you to me.
OEDIPUS. Who was he? Can you tell me who he was?
MESSENGER. I think he was said to be one of Laïos' people.
OEDIPUS. You mean the Laïos who was king here years ago?
MESSENGER. Yes; King Laïos; and the man was one of his herdsmen.
OEDIPUS. Is he still alive? Can I see him?
MESSENGER. These men here
Know best about such things.
OEDIPUS. Does anyone here
Know this shepherd that he is talking about?
Have you seen him in the fields, or in the town?
If you have, tell me. It is time things were made plain.
CHORUS. I think the man he means is that same shepherd
You have already asked to see. Iocastê perhaps
Could tell you something.
OEDIPUS. Do you know anything
About him, Lady? Is he the man we have summoned?
Is that the man this shepherd means?
IOCASTÊ. Why think of him?
Forget this herdsman. Forget it all.
This talk is a waste of time.
OEDIPUS. How can you say that,
When the clues to my true birth are in my hands?
IOCASTÊ. For God's love, let us have no more questioning!
Is your life nothing to you?
My own is pain enough for me to bear.
OEDIPUS. You need not worry. Suppose my mother a slave,
And born of slaves: no baseness can touch you.
IOCASTÊ. Listen to me, I beg you: do not this thing!
OEDIPUS. I will not listen; the truth must be made known.
IOCASTÊ. Everything that I say is for your own good!
OEDIPUS. My own good
Snaps my patience, then; I want none of it.

IOCASTÊ. You are fatally wrong! May you never learn who you are!
OEDIPUS. Go, one of you, and bring the shepherd here.
Let us leave this woman to brag of her royal name.
IOCASTÊ. Ah, miserable!
That is the only word I have for you now.
That is the only word I can ever have.
[*Exit into the palace.*]
CHORUS. Why has she left us, Oedipus? Why has she gone
In such a passion of sorrow? I fear this silence:
Something dreadful may come of it.
OEDIPUS. Let it come!
However base my birth, I must know about it.
The Queen, like a woman, is perhaps ashamed
To think of my low origin. But I
Am a child of Luck; I cannot be dishonored.
Luck is my mother; the passing months, my brothers,
Have seen me rich and poor.
If this is so,
How could I wish that I were someone else?
How could I not be glad to know my birth?

Ode 3

CHORUS. If ever the coming time were known [STROPHE.]
To my heart's pondering,
Kithairon, now by Heaven I see the torches
At the festival of the next full moon,
And see the dance, and hear the choir sing
A grace to your gentle shade:
Mountain where Oedipus was found,
O mountain guard of a noble race!
May the god who heals us lend his aid,
And let that glory come to pass
For our king's cradling-ground.

Of the nymphs that flower beyond the years, [ANTISTROPHE.]
Who bore you, royal child,
To Pan of the hills or the timberline Apollo,
Cold in delight where the upland clears,
Or Hermês for whom Kyllenê's heights are piled?
Or flushed as evening cloud,
Great Dionysos, roamer of mountains,
He—was it he who found you there,

And caught you up in his own proud
Arms from the sweet god-ravisher
Who laughed by the Muses' fountains?

Scene 4

OEDIPUS. Sirs: though I do not know the man,
I think I see him coming, this shepherd we want:
He is old, like our friend here, and the men
Bringing him seem to be servants of my house.
But you can tell, if you have ever seen him.
[*Enter* SHEPHERD *escorted by servants.*]
CHORUS. I know him, he was Laïos' man. You can trust him.
OEDIPUS. Tell me first, you from Corinth: is this the shepherd
We were discussing?
MESSENGER. This is the very man.
[*To* SHEPHERD.]
OEDIPUS. Come here. No, look at me. You must answer
Everything I ask.—You belonged to Laïos?
SHEPHERD. Yes: born his slave, brought up in his house.
OEDIPUS. Tell me: what kind of work did you do for him?
SHEPHERD. I was a shepherd of his, most of my life.
OEDIPUS. Where mainly did you go for pasturage?
SHEPHERD. Sometimes Kithairon, sometimes the hills near-by.
OEDIPUS. Do you remember ever seeing this man out there?
SHEPHERD. What would he be doing there? This man?
OEDIPUS. This man standing here. Have you ever seen him before?
SHEPHERD. No. At least, not to my recollection.
MESSENGER. And that is not strange, my lord. But I'll refresh
His memory: he must remember when we two
Spent three whole seasons together, March to September,
On Kithairon or thereabouts. He had two flocks;
I had one. Each autumn I'd drive mine home
And he would go back with his to Laïos' sheepfold.—
Is this not true, just as I have described it?
SHEPHERD. True, yes; but it was all so long ago.
MESSENGER. Well, then: do you remember, back in those days,
That you gave me a baby boy to bring up as my own?
SHEPHERD. What if I did? What are you trying to say?
MESSENGER. King Oedipus was once that little child.
SHEPHERD. Damn you, hold your tongue!
OEDIPUS. No more of that!
It is your tongue needs watching, not this man's.
SHEPHERD. My King, my Master, what is it I have done wrong?

OEDIPUS. You have not answered his question about the boy.
SHEPHERD. He does not know. . . . He is only making trouble. . . .
OEDIPUS. Come, speak plainly, or it will go hard with you.
SHEPHERD. In God's name, do not torture an old man!
OEDIPUS. Come here, one of you; bind his arms behind him.
SHEPHERD. Unhappy king! What more do you wish to learn?
OEDIPUS. Did you give this man the child he speaks of?
SHEPHERD. I did.
And I would to God I had died that very day.
OEDIPUS. You will die now unless you speak the truth.
SHEPHERD. Yet if I speak the truth, I am worse than dead.
OEDIPUS. Very well; since you insist upon delaying—
SHEPHERD. No! I have told you already that I gave him the boy.
OEDIPUS. Where did you get him? From your house? From somewhere else?
SHEPHERD. Not from mine, no. A man gave him to me.
OEDIPUS. Is that man here? Do you know whose slave he was?
SHEPHERD. For God's love, my King, do not ask me any more!
OEDIPUS. You are a dead man if I have to ask you again.
SHEPHERD. Then . . . Then the child was from the palace of Laïos.
OEDIPUS. A slave child? or a child of his own line?
SHEPHERD. Ah, I am on the brink of dreadful speech!
OEDIPUS. And I of dreadful hearing. Yet I must hear.
SHEPHERD. If you must be told, then . . .
They said it was Laïos' child;
But it is your wife who can tell you about that.
OEDIPUS. My wife!—Did she give it to you?
SHEPHERD. My lord, she did.
OEDIPUS. Do you know why?
SHEPHERD. I was told to get rid of it.
OEDIPUS. An unspeakable mother!
SHEPHERD. There had been prophecies . . .
OEDIPUS. Tell me.
SHEPHERD. It was said that the boy would kill his own father.
OEDIPUS. Then why did you give him over to this old man?
SHEPHERD. I pitied the baby, my King,
And I thought that this man would take him far away
To his own country.
He saved him—but for what a fate!
For if you are what this man says you are,
No man living is more wretched than Oedipus.
OEDIPUS. Ah God!
It was true!
All the prophecies!
—Now,

O Light, may I look on you for the last time!
I, Oedipus,
Oedipus, damned in his birth, in his marriage damned,
Damned in the blood he shed with his own hand!
[*He rushes into the palace.*]

Ode 4

CHORUS. Alas for the seed of men. [STROPHE I.]

What measure shall I give these generations
That breathe on the void and are void
And exist and do not exist?

Who bears more weight of joy
Than mass of sunlight shifting in images,
Or who shall make his thoughts stay on
That down time drifts away?

Your splendor is all fallen.

O naked brow of wrath and tears,
O change of Oedipus!
I who saw your days call no man blest—
Your great days like ghósts góne.

That mind was a strong bow. [ANTISTROPHE I.]

Deep, how deep you drew it then, hard archer,
At a dim fearful range,
And brought dear glory down!

You overcame the stranger—
The virgin with her hooking lion claws—
And though death sang, stood like a tower
To make pale Thebes take heart.
Fortress against our sorrow!

Divine king, giver of laws,
Majestic Oedipus!
No prince in Thebes had ever such renown,
No prince won such grace of power.

And now of all men ever known [STROPHE 2.]
Most pitiful is this man's story:
His fortunes are most changed, his state
Fallen to a low slave's
Ground under bitter fate.

O Oedipus, most royal one!
The great door that expelled you to the light
Gave at night—ah, gave night to your glory:
As to the father, to the fathering son.

All understood too late.

How could that queen whom Laïos won,
The garden that he harrowed at his height,
Be silent when that act was done?

But all eyes fail before time's eye, [ANTISTROPHE 2.]
All actions come to justice there.
Though never willed, though far down the deep past,
Your bed, your dread sirings,
Are brought to book at last.

Child by Laïos doomed to die,
Then doomed to lose that fortunate little death,
Would God you never took breath in this air
That with my wailing lips I take to cry:

For I weep the world's outcast.
Blind I was, and can not tell why;
Asleep, for you had given ease of breath;
A fool, while the false years went by.

Éxodos

[*Enter, from the palace,* SECOND MESSENGER.]

2ND MESSENGER. Elders of Thebes, most honored in this land,
What horrors are yours to see and hear, what weight
Of sorrow to be endured, if, true to your birth,
You venerate the line of Labdakos!
I think neither Istros nor Phasis, those great rivers,
Could purify this place of the corruption
It shelters now, or soon must bring to light—

Evil not done unconsciously, but willed.

The greatest griefs are those we cause ourselves.

CHORUS. Surely, friend, we have grief enough already;
What new sorrow do you mean?

2ND MESSENGER.
The Queen is dead.

CHORUS. Iocastê? Dead? But at whose hand?

2ND MESSENGER.
Her own.
The full horror of what happened you cannot know,
For you did not see it; but I, who did, will tell you
As clearly as I can how she met her death.

When she had left us,
In passionate silence, passing through the court,
She ran to her apartment in the house,
Her hair clutched by the fingers of both hands.
She closed the doors behind her; then, by that bed
Where long ago the fatal son was conceived—
That son who should bring about his father's death—
We heard her call upon Laïos, dead so many years,
And heard her wail for the double fruit of her marriage,
A husband by her husband, children by her child.
Exactly how she died I do not know:
For Oedipus burst in moaning and would not let us
Keep vigil to the end: it was by him
As he stormed about the room that our eyes were caught.
From one to another of us he went, begging a sword,
Cursing the wife who was not his wife, the mother
Whose womb had carried his own children and himself.
I do not know: it was none of us aided him,
But surely one of the gods was in control!
For with a dreadful cry
He hurled his weight, as though wrenched out of himself,
At the twin doors: the bolts gave, and he rushed in.
And there we saw her hanging, her body swaying
From the cruel cord she had noosed about her neck.
A great sob broke from him, heartbreaking to hear,
As he loosed the rope and lowered her to the ground.

I would blot out from my mind what happened next!
For the King ripped from her gown the golden brooches
That were her ornament, and raised them, and plunged them down
Straight into his own eyeballs, crying, "No more,

No more shall you look on the misery about me,
The horrors of my own doing! Too long you have known
The faces of those whom I should never have seen,
Too long been blind to those for whom I was searching!
From this hour, go in darkness!" And as he spoke,
He struck at his eyes—not once, but many times;
And the blood spattered his beard,
Bursting from his ruined sockets like red hail.

So from the unhappiness of two this evil has sprung,
A curse on the man and woman alike. The old
Happiness of the house of Labdakos
Was happiness enough: where is it today?
It is all wailing and ruin, disgrace, death—all
The misery of mankind that has a name—
And it is wholly and for ever theirs.

CHORUS. Is he in agony still? Is there no rest for him?

2ND MESSENGER. He is calling for someone to lead him to the gates
So that all the children of Kadmos may look upon
His father's murderer, his mother's—no,
I can not say it!
And then he will leave Thebes,
Self-exiled, in order that the curse
Which he himself pronounced may depart from the house.
He is weak, and there is none to lead him,
So terrible is his suffering.
But you will see:
Look, the doors are opening; in a moment
You will see a thing that would crush a heart of stone.

[*The central door is opened;* OEDIPUS, *blinded, is led in.*]

CHORUS. Dreadful indeed for men to see.
Never have my own eyes
Looked on a sight so full of fear.

Oedipus!
What madness came upon you, what daemon
Leaped on your life with heavier
Punishment than a mortal man can bear?
No; I can not even
Look at you, poor ruined one.
And I would speak, question, ponder,
If I were able. No.
You make me shudder.

OEDIPUS. God. God.
Is there a sorrow greater?
Where shall I find harbor in this world?
My voice is hurled far on a dark wind.
What has God done to me?
CHORUS. Too terrible to think of, or to see.
OEDIPUS. O cloud of night, [STROPHE I.]
Never to be turned away: night coming on,
I can not tell how: night like a shroud!

My fair winds brought me here.
O God. Again
The pain of the spikes where I had sight,
The flooding pain
Of memory, never to be gouged out.
CHORUS. This is not strange.
You suffer it all twice over, remorse in pain,
Pain in remorse.
OEDIPUS. Ah dear friend [ANTISTROPHE I.]
Are you faithful even yet, you alone?
Are you still standing near me, will you stay here,
Patient, to care for the blind?
The blind man!
Yet even blind I know who it is attends me,
By the voice's tone—
Though my new darkness hide the comforter.
CHORUS. Oh fearful act!
What god was it drove you to rake black
Night across your eyes?

OEDIPUS. Apollo. Apollo. Dear [STROPHE 2.]
Children, the god was Apollo.
He brought my sick, sick fate upon me.
But the blinding hand was my own!
How could I bear to see
When all my sight was horror everywhere?
CHORUS. Everywhere; that is true.
OEDIPUS. And now what is left?
Images? Love? A greeting even,
Sweet to the senses? Is there anything?
Ah, no, friends: lead me away.
Lead me away from Thebes.
Lead the great wreck
And hell of Oedipus, whom the gods hate.
CHORUS. Your fate is clear, you are not blind to that.

Would God you had never found it out!

OEDIPUS. Death take the man who unbound [ANTISTROPHE 2.]
My feet on that hillside
And delivered me from death to life! What life?
If only I had died,
This weight of monstrous doom
Could not have dragged me and my darlings down.
CHORUS. I would have wished the same.
OEDIPUS. Oh never to have come here
With my father's blood upon me! Never
To have been the man they call his mother's husband!
Oh accurst! Oh child of evil,
To have entered that wretched bed—
the selfsame one!
More primal than sin itself, this fell to me.
CHORUS. I do not know how I can answer you.
You were better dead than alive and blind.
OEDIPUS. Do not counsel me any more. This punishment
That I have laid upon myself is just.
If I had eyes,
I do not know how I could bear the sight
Of my father, when I came to the house of Death,
Or my mother: for I have sinned against them both
So vilely that I could not make my peace
By strangling my own life.
Or do you think my children,
Born as they were born, would be sweet to my eyes?
Ah never, never! Nor this town with its high walls,
Nor the holy images of the gods.
For I,
Thrice miserable!—Oedipus, noblest of all the line
Of Kadmos, have condemned myself to enjoy
These things no more, by my own malediction
Expelling that man whom the gods declared
To be a defilement in the house of Laïos.
After exposing the rankness of my own guilt,
How could I look men frankly in the eyes?
No, I swear it,
If I could have stifled my hearing at its source,
I would have done it and made all this body
A tight cell of misery, blank to light and sound:
So I should have been safe in a dark agony
Beyond all recollection.
Ah Kithairon!

Why did you shelter me? When I was cast upon you,
Why did I not die? Then I should never
Have shown the world my execrable birth.

Ah Polybos! Corinth, city that I believed
The ancient seat of my ancestors: how fair
I seemed, your child! And all the while this evil
Was cancerous within me!
For I am sick
In my daily life, sick in my origin.

O three roads, dark ravine, woodland and way
Where three roads met: you, drinking my father's blood,
My own blood, spilled by my own hand: can you remember
The unspeakable things I did there, and the things
I went on from there to do?
O marriage, marriage!
The act that engendered me, and again the act
Performed by the son in the same bed—
Ah, the net
Of incest, mingling fathers, brothers, sons,
With brides, wives, mothers: the last evil
That can be known by men: no tongue can say
How evil!
No. For the love of God, conceal me
Somewhere far from Thebes; or kill me; or hurl me
Into the sea, away from men's eyes for ever.

Come, lead me. You need not fear to touch me.
Of all men, I alone can bear this guilt.
[*Enter* CREON.]
CHORUS. We are not the ones to decide; but Creon here
May fitly judge of what you ask. He only
Is left to protect the city in your place.
OEDIPUS. Alas, how can I speak to him? What right have I
To beg his courtesy whom I have deeply wronged?
CREON. I have not come to mock you, Oedipus,
Or to reproach you, either.
[*To* ATTENDANTS.]
—You, standing there:
If you have lost all respect for man's dignity,
At least respect the flame of Lord Helios:
Do not allow this pollution to show itself
Openly here, an affront to the earth
And Heaven's rain and the light of day. No, take him

Into the house as quickly as you can.
For it is proper
That only the close kindred see his grief.

OEDIPUS. I pray you in God's name, since your courtesy
Ignores my dark expectation, visiting
With mercy this man of all men most execrable:
Give me what I ask—for your good, not for mine.

CREON. And what is it that you would have me do?

OEDIPUS. Drive me out of this country as quickly as may be
To a place where no human voice can ever greet me.

CREON. I should have done that before now—only,
God's will had not been wholly revealed to me.

OEDIPUS. But his command is plain: the parricide
Must be destroyed. I am that evil man.

CREON. —That is the sense of it, yes; but as things are,
We had best discover clearly what is to be done.

OEDIPUS. You would learn more about a man like me?

CREON. You are ready now to listen to the god.

OEDIPUS. I will listen. But it is to you
That I must turn for help. I beg you, hear me.

The woman in there—
Give her whatever funeral you think proper:
She is your sister.
—But let me go, Creon!
Let me purge my father's Thebes of the pollution
Of my living here, and go out to the wild hills,
To Kithairon, that has won such fame with me,
The tomb my mother and father appointed for me,
And let me die there, as they willed I should.
And yet I know
Death will not ever come to me through sickness
Or in any natural way: I have been preserved
For some unthinkable fate. But let that be.

As for my sons, you need not care for them.
They are men, they will find some way to live.
But my poor daughters, who have shared my table,
Who never before have been parted from their father—
Take care of them, Creon; do this for me.
And will you let me touch them with my hands
A last time, and let us weep together?
Be kind, my lord,
Great prince, be kind!
Could I but touch them,

They would be mine again, as when I had my eyes.
[*Enter* ANTIGONE *and* ISMENE, *attended.*]
Ah, God!
Is it my dearest children I hear weeping?
Has Creon pitied me and sent my daughters?
CREON. Yes, Oedipus: I knew that they were dear to you
In the old days, and know you must love them still.
OEDIPUS. May God bless you for this—and be a friendlier
Guardian to you than he has been to me!

Children, where are you?
Come quickly to my hands: they are your brother's—
Hands that have brought your father's once clear eyes
To this way of seeing—
Ah dearest ones,
I had neither sight nor knowledge then, your father
By the woman who was the source of his own life!
And I weep for you—having no strength to see you—,
I weep for you when I think of the bitterness
That men will visit upon you all your lives.
What homes, what festivals can you attend
Without being forced to depart again in tears?
And when you come to marriageable age,
Where is the man, my daughters, who would dare
Risk the bane that lies on all my children?
Is there any evil wanting? Your father killed
His father; sowed the womb of her who bore him;
Engendered you at the fount of his own existence!

That is what they will say of you.

Then, whom
Can you ever marry? There are no bridegrooms for you,
And your lives must wither away in sterile dreaming.

O Creon, son of Menoikeus!
You are the only father my daughters have,
Since we, their parents, are both of us gone for ever.
They are your own blood: you will not let them
Fall into beggary and loneliness;
You will keep them from the miseries that are mine!
Take pity on them; see, they are only children,
Friendless except for you. Promise me this,
Great Prince, and give me your hand in token of it.
[CREON *clasps his right hand.*]

Children:
I could say much, if you could understand me,
But as it is, I have only this prayer for you:
Live where you can, be as happy as you can—
Happier, please God, than God has made your father!
CREON. Enough. You have wept enough. Now go within.
OEDIPUS. I must; but it is hard.
CREON. Time eases all things.
OEDIPUS. But you must promise—
CREON. Say what you desire.
OEDIPUS. Send me from Thebes!
CREON. God grant that I may!
OEDIPUS. But since God hates me . . .
CREON. No, he will grant your wish.
OEDIPUS. You promise?
CREON. I can not speak beyond my knowledge.
OEDIPUS. Then lead me in.
CREON. Come now, and leave your children.
OEDIPUS. No! Do not take them from me!
CREON. Think no longer
That you are in command here, but rather think
How, when you were, you served your own destruction.

[*Exeunt into the house all but the* CHORUS; *the* CHORAGOS *chants directly to the audience.*]

CHORUS. Men of Thebes: look upon Oedipus.
This is the king who solved the famous riddle
And towered up, most powerful of men.
No mortal eyes but looked on him with envy,
Yet in the end ruin swept over him.

Let every man in mankind's frailty
Consider his last day; and let none
Presume on his good fortune until he find
Life, at his death, a memory without pain.

CRITICAL COMMENTARY

Sophocles' *Oedipus Rex* is a play of self-discovery. Since the audience knows in advance that Oedipus is the man who has unwittingly killed his father and married his mother, the play on one level is a kind of detective story in which we watch Oedipus discover that he is the criminal. An immediately striking thing about his discovery, however, is that it is made through a series of ironic revelations. For example, the eager attempts of Jocasta and the messenger from Corinth to comfort Oedipus provide unintentionally the very facts that prove his guilt. These recurring ironies make us deeply aware that the play, on another level, is about a discovery that is meaningful to all men who wish to know themselves.

Long before the opening action of the play, Oedipus had come to Thebes and had found that its king, Laius, was dead and that its citizens were being killed by a monster, the Sphinx. She could be conquered only by the person who answered her riddle: What goes on four feet, then on two, and finally on three, yet is weakest when it uses the most feet? When Oedipus gave the correct answer, man, the Sphinx destroyed herself, and Oedipus was awarded the empty throne and the widowed queen of Thebes by the grateful citizens. At the beginning, then, Oedipus is the hero who had saved society by his intelligence. The action that follows this opening is our discovery with Oedipus of the limitation of human reason. The limitation is emphasized through the continuing ironic reversals, which suggest that man's efforts to outwit the logic of events will only reveal his inadequacy. Human intelligence thus constantly defeated takes on the appearance of mere shrewdness that outsmarts itself. Oedipus, for example, becoming rigidly proud of his mental powers, assumes cunningly but wrongly that Creon is motivated by ambition and Jocasta by vanity.

The crucial irony, however, is that Oedipus forces his own exposure. His arrogant treatment of unwilling witnesses and his refusal to let well enough alone suggest an almost obsessive desire to get at the truth. We understand that this man unconsciously intent on his own destruction is also heroically realizing his humanity. Our compassion and admiration, and our knowledge that he has sinned as much through ignorance as through pride or passion, may make us feel that his final ruin is unjust, that the punishment does not fit the crime. This seeming inequity is indeed a central aspect of the theme. Oedipus, in the final analysis, is guilty of being human. His very existence is proof that the nature of things cannot be fundamentally altered. In their desire to control the future and to defeat the prophecy that he would kill his father, his parents had cast away the baby Oedipus to die. But in the warfare between the generations the child is always preserved to usurp his elder's place. From this viewpoint, Oedipus' behavior toward old men like Laius and Teiresias is more than a sign of individual arrogance.

Our feeling that Oedipus' final punishment is excessive may also spring from the modern desire for a psychological solution in which the hero, after various excesses, reaches the happiness of a well-adjusted personality. Such a conclusion, however, would certainly be false to the implications of the whole play, which have never promised that man can be self-sufficient. An end in which the proud man of reason puts out his eyes and thus symbolically admits the inadequacy of his unaided intelligence is the necessary one for the play.

The Greek audience, however, would have understood that Oedipus' savage self-punishment was also the first step in his reconciliation with the gods. That reconciliation is presented in *Oedipus at Colonus,* which was probably written in 406 B.C., when Sophocles was eighty-nine, and when Athens was hard pressed after more than twenty-five years of the Peloponnesian War against Sparta. One of the themes, appropriately, is the ideal of enlightened justice for Athens, which Aeschylus had proposed at the end of his *Oresteia.* The action in Sophocles' later play occurs near Athens, in Colonus, his birthplace, at the grove of the Furies, whose sternness had been harmonized with compassion. This just harmony is represented by the magnanimous Theseus, king of Athens, and it is contrasted with the self-centered disorder of Thebes, where after the banishment of Oedipus, his sons, Eteocles and Polyneices had contended for power with each other and with Creon.

In this later play Oedipus, blind and ragged, enters, led by his daughter Antigone. Before his death, he is visited by Creon and Polyneices. Now that Oedipus is beyond practical good and evil he has become valuable to men of ambition. They have been ordered by the gods to make their peace with him, but to do so sincerely would mean giving up their plots and wars; consequently, they go through the form of things only, professing hypocritically to have come out of concern for Oedipus' welfare. His savage denunciation of them exposes their duplicity and is an index to his hard-won insight into truth. When he has performed the necessary rites, which are now truly symbolic, Oedipus, without a guide, enters the grove and is there taken up by the gods, after first entrusting to Theseus the secret wisdom that transcends reason.

Much recent criticism of *Oedipus Rex* and of Greek tragedy in general has been conscious of the danger of being schoolmasterish, genteel, and narrowly rational; it has therefore stressed the dark underside of the play, whatever in it is communal, mythical, ritualistic, and psychological. It has probed Oedipus for something deeper than misbehavior, for an unconscious fear erupting into anger and marked by a selective memory, "bad hearing," paranoia, and a resistance to self-knowledge comparable to a patient's reluctance to accept therapeutic insights. The general aim, at best, has been to "refresh the simplicity of reason through the complexity of passion, not the other way around." From this premise, William Arrowsmith has urged that,

> the single most pertinent fact of the *Oedipus* was not the hero's flaw, but his refusal to accept a ready-made fate: he wants his own fate, not the gods', and though his personal fate may be cut short by his doom, Oedipus at the close of the play insists upon distinguishing his own responsibility by blinding himself. . . . His anger is anger, neither more nor less; it is not the source of his doom, but the irritant that he exhibits on the road to doom; and if he has a *hamartia,* it is not sin or flaw but the ungovernable tragic ignorance of all men: we do not know who we are or who fathered us but go, blinded by life and hope, toward a wisdom bitter at the gates of hell. (*Tulane Drama Review,* Vol. III, No. 3, 1959)

All this and more brings into question how or in what sense Oedipus overcomes the Sphinx. Does he find out who he is, who man is, by intelligence, by introspection, or by acting? Does he solve the riddle only in the sense that he acts it out as he passes from the abandoned baby on all fours through the upright king to the blind man with a stick, the three-footed exile? Of all the possible Oedipuses, which does Oedipus find himself to be? Is the deepest Oedipus the one whose action seems not attached to character in any fully decipherable sense? When Clytemnestra stands over her victims, she asserts that she did what she had to do. Is Oedipus, as he stands over himself as victim, agent or maker of fate? Does the fact that he spills his own blood rather than that of others distinguish him from Clytemnestra?

The interpenetration of past and present is overpowering in *Oedipus Rex,* perhaps even more so than in *Agamemnon.* This bears on Oedipus' belief that he is the child of chance, of luck, of the mountains. Is he not in fact always the same man, and can his luck ever be the kind that frees him to progress toward a new order of things? The court that acquitted Orestes might also acquit Oedipus, but could it free him from what he has learned through his acting? Oedipus lives "on the edge of humanity," not just because his predicament is so outlandish, but because he is never merely sensible like Creon or even simply human like Jocasta. Does he differ, too, from powerful figures like Clytemnestra or King Claudius in *Hamlet* because he is transparently himself, Oedipus, Swollen-foot, and because his aim is to force truth into the open, to make the fictions of society express rather than hide reality?

Useful Criticism

Bowra, Maurice. *Sophoclean Tragedy.** New York: Oxford University Press, 1965.

Cameron, Alister. *The Identity of Oedipus the King.* New York: New York University Press, 1968.

Kitto, H. D. F. *Greek Tragedy.** Garden City, N.Y.: Doubleday, 1950.

Knox, Bernard. *Oedipus at Thebes.** New Haven: Yale University Press, 1966.

Lattimore, Richmond. *The Poetry of Greek Tragedy.** New York: Harper & Row, 1966.

O'Brien, M. J., ed. *Twentieth Century Interpretations of Oedipus Rex.** Englewood Cliffs, N.J.: Prentice-Hall, 1968.

Waldock, A. J. A. *Sophocles the Dramatist.** New York: Cambridge University Press, 1966.

Woodward, Thomas, ed. *Sophocles** (Twentieth Century Views). Englewood Cliffs, N.J.: Prentice-Hall, 1966.

* Available in paperback.

THE JEW OF MALTA

Christopher Marlowe

CHARACTERS

MACHEVEL, the Prologue
BARABAS, the rich Jew of Malta
2 MERCHANTS
3 JEWS
FERNEZE, Governor of Malta
SELIM-CALYMATH, the Turkish leader
1 BASSO
2 KNIGHTS
2 OFFICERS
1 FRIAR, Jacomo
2 FRIARS, Barnardine
LODOWICK, Ferneze's son
MATHIAS, a young gentleman
MARTIN DEL BOSCO, the Spanish Vice-Admiral
ITHAMORE, Turkish slave to Barabas
ABIGAIL, Barabas' daughter
KATHERINE, mother of Mathias
BELLAMIRA, a courtesan
PILIA-BORZA, Bellamira's pimp
KNIGHTS
BASSOES
NUNS
SLAVES
CARPENTERS

The Prologue

MACHEVEL.

Albeit the world think Machevel is dead,
Yet was his soul but flown beyond the Alps,
And now the Guise° is dead, is come from France
To view this land, and frolic with his friends.
To some perhaps my name is odious,
But such as love me, guard me from their tongues,
And let them know that I am Machevel,
And weigh not men, and therefore not men's words.
Admired I am of those that hate me most.

Prologue 3. Guise: French duke, ringleader in the 1572 St. Bartholomew Massacre of the Protestants. Henry III had him assassinated in 1588.

The Text: This is a corrected and slightly modernized version of the only extant text, the Quarto of 1633, entitled *The Famous Tragedy of the Rich Jew of Malta*. The play was presumably written and first produced in 1589–90, when Marlowe was about 25.

Though some speak openly against my books,
Yet will they read me, and thereby attain
To Peter's chair: and when they cast me off,
Are poisoned by my climbing followers.
I count religion but a childish toy,
And hold there is no sin but ignorance.
Birds of the air will tell of murders past?
I am ashamed to hear such fooleries.
Many will talk of title to a crown.
What right had Caesar to the empery?
Might first made kings, and laws were then most sure
When like the Draco's° they were writ in blood.
Hence comes it, that a strong built citadel
Commands much more than letters can import—
Which maxim had but Phalaris° observed,
H'had never bellowed in a brazen bull
Of great ones' envy. O' the poor petty wits,
Let me be envied and not pitièd!
But whither am I bound? I come not, I,
To read a lecture here in Britanie,
But to present the tragedy of a Jew,
Who smiles to see how full his bags are crammed,
Which money was not got without my means.
I crave but this, grace him as he deserves,
And let him not be entertained the worse
Because he favors me.
[*Exit.*]

ACT I

Scene 1

Enter BARABAS *in his counting-house, with heaps of gold before him*

BARABAS.
So that of thus much that return was made:
And of the third part of the Persian ships,

21. Draco's: Draco was the author of harsh seventh century B.C. Athenian laws. **24. Phalaris:** sixth century B.C. Sicilian tyrant, alleged here to have neglected Machiavellian policy for letter writing, and so ended up in the bull-shaped oven where he had roasted his enemies alive.

There was the venture summed and satisfied.
As for those Samnites, and the men of Uz,
That bought my Spanish oils, and wines of Greece,
Here have I pursed their paltry silverlings.
Fie; what a trouble 'tis to count this trash!
Well fare the Arabians, who so richly pay
The things they traffic for with wedge of gold,
Whereof a man may easily in a day
Tell° that which may maintain him all his life.
The needy groom that never fingered groat,
Would make a miracle of thus much coin:
But he whose steel-barred coffers are crammed full,
And all his life-time hath been tirèd,
Wearying his fingers' ends with telling it,
Would in his age be loath to labor so,
And for a pound to sweat himself to death.
Give me the merchants of the Indian mines,
That trade in metal of the purest mold;
The wealthy Moor, that in the Eastern rocks
Without control can pick his riches up,
And in his house heap pearl like pebble-stones,
Receive them free, and sell them by the weight;
Bags of fiery opals, sapphires, amethysts,
Jacinths, hard topaz, grass-green emeralds,
Beauteous rubies, sparkling diamonds,
And seld-seen costly stones of so great price,
As one of them indifferently° rated,
And of a carat of this quantity,
May serve in peril of calamity
To ransom great kings from captivity.
This is the ware wherein consists my wealth.
And thus methinks should men of judgement frame
Their means of traffic from the vulgar trade,
And as their wealth increaseth, so inclose
Infinite riches in a little room.
But now how stands the wind?
Into what corner peers my halcyon's bill?°
Ha, to the East? Yes. See how stands the vanes?
East and by South: why then I hope my ships
I sent for Egypt and the bordering isles
Are gotten up by Nilus' winding banks;
Mine argosy from Alexandria,

I.1. **11. Tell:** count **29. indifferently:** honestly **39. halcyon's bill:** a dead kingfisher as a weather vane

Loaden with spice and silks, now under sail,
Are smoothly gliding down by Candy° shore
To Malta, through our Mediterranean sea.
But who comes here? How now.
[*Enter a* MERCHANT.]

MERCHANT.
Barabas, thy ships are safe,
Riding in Malta road, and all the merchants
With all their merchandise are safe arrived,
And have sent me to know whether yourself
Will come and custom them.

BARABAS.
The ships are safe thou say'st, and richly fraught?

MERCHANT.
They are.

BARABAS.
Why then go bid them come ashore,
And bring with them their bills of entry.
I hope our credit in the custom-house
Will serve as well as I were present there.
Go send 'em threescore camels, thirty mules,
And twenty wagons to bring up the ware.
But art thou master in a ship of mine,
And is thy credit not enough for that?

MERCHANT.
The very custom barely comes to more
Than many merchants of the town are worth,
And therefore far exceeds my credit, sir.

BARABAS.
Go tell 'em the Jew of Malta sent thee, man!
Tush, who amongst 'em knows not Barabas?

MERCHANT.
I go.

BARABAS.
So then, there's somewhat come.
Sirrah, which of my ships art thou master of?

MERCHANT.
Of the Speranza, sir.

BARABAS.
And saw'st thou not
Mine argosy at Alexandria?
Thou couldst not come from Egypt, or by Caire,
But at the entry there into the sea,

46. Candy: Crete

Where Nilus pays his tribute to the main,
Thou needs must sail by Alexandria.

MERCHANT.
I neither saw them, nor inquired of them.
But this we heard some of our seamen say,
They wondered how you durst with so much wealth
Trust such a crazèd ° vessel, and so far.

BARABAS.
Tush; they are wise, I know her and her strength.
But go, go thou thy ways, discharge thy ship,
And bid my factor bring his loading in.
[*Exit* MERCHANT.]
And yet I wonder at this argosy.
[*Enter a* SECOND MERCHANT.]

2 MERCHANT.
Thine argosy from Alexandria,
Know Barabas, doth ride in Malta road,
Laden with riches, and exceeding store
Of Persian silks, of gold, and orient pearl.

BARABAS.
How chance you came not with those other ships
That sailed by Egypt?

2 MERCHANT.
Sir, we saw 'em not.

BARABAS.
Belike they coasted round by Candy shore
About their oils, or other businesses.
But 'twas ill done of you to come so far
Without the aid or conduct of their ships.

2 MERCHANT.
Sir, we were wafted ° by a Spanish fleet
That never left us till within a league,
That had the galleys of the Turk in chase.

BARABAS.
Oh they were going up to Sicily; well, go
And bid the merchants and my men dispatch
And come ashore, and see the fraught° discharged.

2 MERCHANT.
I go.
[*Exit.*]

BARABAS.
Thus trowls° our fortune in by land and sea,

82. crazèd: rickety **98. wafted:** escorted **103. fraught:** cargo **105. trowls:** flows

And thus are we on every side enriched;
These are the blessings promised to the Jews,
And herein was old Abram's happiness.
What more may heaven do for earthly man
Than thus to pour out plenty in their laps,
Ripping the bowels of the earth for them,
Making the sea their servant, and the winds
To drive their substance with successful blasts?
Who hateth me but for my happiness?
Or who is honored now but for his wealth?
Rather had I a Jew be hated thus,
Than pitied in a Christian poverty.
For I can see no fruits in all their faith,
But malice, falsehood, and excessive pride,
Which methinks fits not their profession.
Haply some hapless man hath conscience,
And for his conscience lives in beggary.
They say we are a scattered nation:
I cannot tell, but we have scambled up°
More wealth by far than those that brag of faith.
There's Kirriah Jairim, the great Jew of Greece,
Obed in Bairseth, Nones in Portugal,
Myself in Malta, some in Italy,
Many in France, and wealthy every one—
Ay, wealthier far than any Christian.
I must confess we come not to be kings:
That's not our fault: alas, our number's few,
And crowns come either by succession
Or urged by force; and nothing violent,
Oft have I heard tell, can be permanent.
Give us a peaceful rule, make Christians kings,
That thirst so much for principality.
I have no charge, nor many children,
But one sole daughter, whom I hold as dear
As Agamemnon did his Iphigen:
And all I have is hers. But who comes here?

[*Enter* THREE JEWS.]

1 JEW.
Tush, tell not me, 'twas done of policy.

2 JEW.
Come, therefore, let us go to Barabas;
For he can counsel best in these affairs;
And here he comes.

124. scambled up: raked together

BARABAS.
Why how now countrymen?
Why flock you thus to me in multitudes?
What accident's betided to the Jews?

1 JEW.
A fleet of warlike galleys, Barabas,
Are come from Turkey, and lie in our road;
And they this day sit in the council-house
To entertain them and their embassy.

BARABAS.
Why let 'em come, so they come not to war;
Or let 'em war, so we be conquerors:
(*Aside.*) Nay, let 'em combat, conquer, and kill all,
So they spare me, my daughter, and my wealth.

1 JEW.
Were it for confirmation of a league,
They would not come in warlike manner thus.

2 JEW.
I fear their coming will afflict us all.

BARABAS.
Fond men, what dream you of their multitudes?
What need they treat of peace that are in league?
The Turks and those of Malta are in league.
Tut, tut, there is some other matter in't.

1 JEW.
Why, Barabas, they come for peace or war.

BARABAS.
Haply for neither, but to pass along
Towards Venice by the Adriatic Sea;
With whom they have attempted ° many times,
But never could effect their stratagem.

3 JEW.
And very wisely said, it may be so.

2 JEW.
But there's a meeting in the senate-house,
And all the Jews in Malta must be there.

BARABAS.
Umh; all the Jews in Malta must be there?
Ay, like enough, why then let every man
Provide him, and be there for fashion-sake.
If any thing shall there concern our state
Assure yourselves I'll look unto (*Aside.*) myself.

167. With . . . attempted: tried to defeat the Venetians

1 JEW.
I know you will; well brethren let us go.
2 JEW.
Let's take our leaves; farewell good Barabas.
BARABAS.
Do so; farewell Zaareth, farewell Temainte.
[*Exeunt the* JEWS.]
And Barabas now search this secret out.
Summon thy senses, call thy wits together:
These silly men mistake the matter clean.
Long to the Turk did Malta contribute;
Which tribute all in policy, I fear,
The Turks have let increase to such a sum
As all the wealth of Malta cannot pay;
And now by that advantage thinks, belike,
To seize upon the town: ay, that he seeks:
Howe'er the world go, I'll make sure for one,
And seek in time to intercept the worst,
Warily guarding that which I ha' got.
Ego mihimet sum semper proximus.°
Why let 'em enter, let 'em take the town.
[*Exit.*]

Scene 2

Enter GOVERNOR *of Malta,* KNIGHTS, *and* OFFICERS, *met by* BASSOES *of the Turk; and* CALYMATH

GOVERNOR.
Now bassoes,° what demand you at our hands?
BASSO.
Know knights of Malta, that we came from Rhodes,
From Cyprus, Candy, and those other isles
That lie betwixt the Mediterranean seas—
GOVERNOR.
What's Cyprus, Candy, and those other isles
To us, or Malta? What at our hands demand ye?
CALYMATH.
The ten years' tribute that remains unpaid.

192. Ego . . . proximus: I always look out for number one.

I.2. **1. bassoes:** bashaws (pashas), Turkish dignitaries

GOVERNOR.
Alas, my lord, the sum is over-great;
I hope your highness will consider us.
CALYMATH.
I wish, grave Governor, 'twere in my power
To favor you, but 'tis my father's cause,
Wherein I may not, nay I dare not dally.
GOVERNOR.
Then give us leave, great Selim-Calymath.
CALYMATH.
Stand all aside, and let the knights determine,
And send to keep our galleys under sail,
For happily we shall not tarry here:
Now Governor, how are you resolved?
GOVERNOR.
Thus: since your hard conditions are such
That you will needs have ten years' tribute past,
We may have time to make collection
Amongst the inhabitants of Malta for't.
BASSO.
That's more than is in our commission.
CALYMATH.
What Callapine, a little courtesy!
Let's know their time, perhaps it is not long;
And 'tis more kingly to obtain by peace
Than to enforce conditions by constraint.
What respite ask you Governor?
GOVERNOR.
But a month.
CALYMATH.
We grant a month, but see you keep your promise.
Now launch our galleys back again to sea,
Where we'll attend the respite you have ta'en,
And for the money send our messenger.
Farewell great Governor, and brave knights of Malta.
[*Exeunt* CALYMATH *and* BASSOES.]
GOVERNOR.
And all good fortune wait on Calymath.
Go one and call those Jews of Malta hither.
Were they not summoned to appear today?
OFFICER.
They were, my lord, and here they come.
[*Enter* BARABAS *and* THREE JEWS.]
1 KNIGHT.
Have you determined what to say to them?

GOVERNOR.
Yes, give me leave, and Hebrews now come near.
From the Emperor of Turkey is arrived
Great Selim-Calymath, his highness' son,
To levy of us ten years' tribute past;
Now then here know that it concerneth us—

BARABAS.
Then good my lord, to keep your quiet still,
Your lordship shall do well to let them have it.

GOVERNOR.
Soft Barabas, there's more 'longs to't than so.
To what this ten years' tribute will amount,
That we have cast,° but cannot compass it
By reason of the wars, that robbed our store;
And therefore are we to request your aid.

BARABAS.
Alas, my lord, we are no soldiers:
And what's our aid against so great a prince?

1 KNIGHT.
Tut, Jew, we know thou art no soldier;
Thou art a merchant, and a moneyed man,
And 'tis thy money, Barabas, we seek.

BARABAS.
How, my lord, my money?

GOVERNOR.
Thine and the rest.
For to be short, amongst you 't must be had.

1 JEW.
Alas, my lord, the most of us are poor!

GOVERNOR.
Then let the rich increase your portions.

BARABAS.
Are strangers with your tribute to be taxed?

2 KNIGHT.
Have strangers leave with us to get their wealth?
Then let them with us contribute.

BARABAS.
How, equally?

GOVERNOR.
No, Jew, like infidels.
For through our sufferance of your hateful lives,
Who stand accursèd in the sight of heaven,
These taxes and afflictions are befallen,

48. cast: calculated

And therefore thus we are determinèd:
Read there the articles of our decrees.

OFFICER (*reads*).

First, the tribute money of the Turks shall all be levied amongst the Jews, and each of them to pay one half of his estate.

BARABAS.

How, half his estate? I hope you mean not mine.

GOVERNOR.

Read on.

OFFICER (*reads*).

Secondly, he that denies to pay, shall straight become a Christian.

BARABAS.

How, a Christian? Hum, what's here to do?

OFFICER (*reads*).

Lastly, he that denies this, shall absolutely lose all he has.

ALL 3 JEWS.

Oh my lord, we will give half.

BARABAS.

Oh earth-metalled villains, and no Hebrews born!
And will you basely thus submit yourselves
To leave your goods to their arbitrement?

GOVERNOR.

Why Barabas wilt thou be christenèd?

BARABAS.

No, Governor, I will be no convertite.

GOVERNOR.

Then pay thy half.

BARABAS.

Why know you what you did by this device?
Half of my substance is a city's wealth.
Governor, it was not got so easily;
Nor will I part so slightly therewithal.

GOVERNOR.

Sir, half is the penalty of our decree,
Either pay that, or we will seize on all.

[*Exeunt* OFFICERS, *on a sign from the* GOVERNOR.]

BARABAS.

Corpi di Dio; stay, you shall have half,
Let me be used but as my brethren are.

GOVERNOR.

No, Jew, thou hast denied the articles,
And now it cannot be recalled.

BARABAS.

Will you then steal my goods?
Is theft the ground of your religion?

GOVERNOR.

No, Jew, we take particularly thine
To save the ruin of a multitude;
And better one want for a common good,
Than many perish for a private man.
Yet Barabas we will not banish thee,
But here in Malta, where thou got'st thy wealth,
Live still; and if thou canst, get more.

BARABAS.

Christians; what, or how can I multiply?
Of nought is nothing made.

1 KNIGHT.

From nought at first thou cam'st to little wealth,
From little unto more, from more to most.
If your first curse fall heavy on thy head,
And make thee poor and scorned of all the world,
'Tis not our fault, but thy inherent sin.

BARABAS.

What? Bring you scripture to confirm your wrongs?
Preach me not out of my possessions.
Some Jews are wicked, as all Christians are;
But say the tribe that I descended of
Were all in general cast away for sin,
Shall I be tried by their transgression?
The man that dealeth righteously shall live:
And which of you can charge me otherwise?

GOVERNOR.

Out, wretched Barabas,
Sham'st thou not thus to justify thyself,
As if we knew not thy profession°?
If thou rely upon thy righteousness,
Be patient and thy riches will increase.
Excess of wealth is cause of covetousness,
And covetousness, oh 'tis a monstrous sin.

BARABAS.

Ay, but theft is worse: tush, take not from me then,
For that is theft; and if you rob me thus,
I must be forced to steal and compass more.

1 KNIGHT.

Grave Governor, list not to his exclaims:
Convert his mansion to a nunnery,
His house will harbor many holy nuns.

123. profession: creed and practice

[*Enter* OFFICERS.]

GOVERNOR.

It shall be so. Now officers, have you done?

OFFICER.

Ay, my lord, we have seized upon the goods
And wares of Barabas, which being valued
Amount to more than all the wealth in Malta.
And of the other we have seizèd half.

GOVERNOR.

Then we'll take order for the residue.

BARABAS.

Well then my lord, say, are you satisfied?
You have my goods, my money, and my wealth,
My ships, my store, and all that I enjoyed;
And having all, you can request no more;
Unless your unrelenting flinty hearts
Suppress all pity in your stony breasts,
And now shall move you to bereave my life.

GOVERNOR.

No, Barabas, to stain our hands with blood
Is far from us and our profession.

BARABAS.

Why, I esteem the injury far less,
To take the lives of miserable men,
Than be the causers of their misery.
You have my wealth, the labor of my life,
The comfort of mine age, my children's hope,
And therefore ne'er distinguish° of the wrong.

GOVERNOR.

Content thee, Barabas, thou hast nought but right.

BARABAS.

Your extreme right does me exceeding wrong:
But take it to you i' the devil's name!

GOVERNOR.

Come, let us in, and gather of these goods
The money for this tribute of the Turk.

1 KNIGHT.

'Tis necessary that be looked unto:
For if we break our day, we break the league,
And that will prove but simple policy.°

[*Exeunt all except* BARABAS *and* JEWS.]

154. distinguish: i.e., between murder and theft **162. simple policy:** foolish management

BARABAS.
Ay, policy; that's their profession,
And not simplicity, as they suggest.
The plagues of Egypt, and the curse of heaven,
Earth's barrenness, and all men's hatred
Inflict upon them, thou great *Primus Motor*.
And here upon my knees, striking the earth,
I ban their souls to everlasting pains
And extreme tortures of the fiery deep,
That thus have dealt with me in my distress.

1 JEW.
Oh yet be patient, gentle Barabas.

BARABAS.
Oh silly brethren, born to see this day!
Why stand you thus unmoved with my laments?
Why weep you not to think upon my wrongs?
Why pine not I, and die in this distress?

1 JEW.
Why, Barabas, as hardly can we brook
The cruel handling of ourselves in this:
Thou seèst they have taken half our goods.

BARABAS.
Why did you yield to their extortion?
You were a multitude, and I but one,
And of me only have they taken all.

1 JEW.
Yet brother Barabas, remember Job.

BARABAS.
What tell you me of Job? I wot his wealth
Was written thus: he had seven thousand sheep,
Three thousand camels, and two hundred yoke
Of laboring oxen, and five hundred
She asses: but for every one of those,
Had they been valued at indifferent rate,
I had at home, and in mine argosy
And other ships that came from Egypt last,
As much as would have bought his beasts and him,
And yet have kept enough to live upon;
So that not he, but I may curse the day,
Thy fatal birth-day, forlorn Barabas;
And henceforth wish for an eternal night,
That clouds of darkness may enclose my flesh,
And hide these extreme sorrows from mine eyes:
For only I have toiled to inherit here

The months of vanity and loss of time
And painful nights have been appointed me.

2 JEW.
Good Barabas, be patient.

BARABAS.
Ay, I pray leave me in my patience.
You that were ne'er possessed of wealth, are pleased with want.
But give him liberty at least to mourn,
That in a field amidst his enemies,
Doth see his soldiers slain, himself disarmed,
And knows no means of his recovery:
Ay, let me sorrow for this sudden chance;
'Tis in the trouble of my spirit I speak;
Great injuries are not so soon forgot.

1 JEW.
Come, let us leave him in his ireful mood,
Our words will but increase his ecstasy.°

2 JEW.
On then: but trust me 'tis a misery
To see a man in such affliction.
Farewell Barabas.
[*Exeunt* JEWS.]

BARABAS.
Ay, fare you well.
See the simplicity of these base slaves,
Who, for the villains have no wit themselves,
Think me to be a senseless lump of clay
That will with every water wash to dirt.
No, Barabas is born to better chance,
And framed of finer mold than common men,
That measure nought but by the present time.
A reaching thought° will search his deepest wits,
And cast with cunning for the time to come:
For evils are apt to happen every day.
But whither wends my beauteous Abigail?
[*Enter* ABIGAIL *the Jew's daughter.*]
Oh what has made my lovely daughter sad?
What? woman, moan not for a little loss.
Thy father has enough in store for thee.

ABIGAIL.
Not for my self, but aged Barabas:
Father, for thee lamenteth Abigail;
But I will learn to leave these fruitless tears,

213. ecstasy: passion **225. reaching thought:** foresighted mind

And urged thereto with my afflictions,
With fierce exclaims run to the senate-house,
And in the senate reprehend them all,
And rent their hearts with tearing of my hair,
Till they reduce the wrongs done to my father.

BARABAS.

No, Abigail, things past recovery
Are hardly cured with exclamations.
Be silent, daughter, sufferance breeds ease,
And time may yield us an occasion,
Which on the sudden cannot serve the turn.
Besides, my girl, think me not all so fond°
As negligently to forgo so much
Without provision for thyself and me.
Ten thousand portagues,° besides great pearls,
Rich costly jewels, and stones infinite,
Fearing the worst of this before it fell,
I closely hid.

ABIGAIL.

Where, father?

BARABAS.

In my house, my girl.

ABIGAIL.

Then shall they ne'er be seen of Barabas,
For they have seized upon thy house and wares.

BARABAS.

But they will give me leave once more, I trow,
To go into my house.

ABIGAIL.

That may they not:
For there I left the Governor placing nuns,
Displacing me; and of thy house they mean
To make a nunnery, where none but their own sect
Must enter in; men generally barred.

BARABAS.

My gold, my gold, and all my wealth is gone.
You partial heavens, have I deserved this plague?
What, will you thus oppose me, luckless stars,
To make me desperate in my poverty?
And knowing me impatient in distress,
Think me so mad as I will hang myself,
That I may vanish o'er the earth in air,
And leave no memory that e'er I was?

245. fond: foolish **248. portagues:** Portuguese gold coins

No, I will live; nor loathe I this my life;
And since you leave me in the ocean thus
To sink or swim, and put me to my shifts,
I'll rouse my senses, and awake myself.
Daughter, I have it: thou perceiv'st the plight
Wherein these Christians have oppressèd me:
Be ruled by me, for in extremity
We ought to make bar of no policy.

ABIGAIL.

Father, whate'er it be to injure them
That have so manifestly wrongèd us,
What will not Abigail attempt?

BARABAS.

Why so;
Then thus: thou told'st me they have turned my house
Into a nunnery, and some nuns are there?

ABIGAIL.

I did.

BARABAS.

Then Abigail, there must my girl
Intreat the abbess to be entertained.

ABIGAIL.

How, as a nun?

BARABAS.

Ay, daughter, for religion
Hides many mischiefs from suspicion.

ABIGAIL.

Ay, but father they will suspect me there.

BARABAS.

Let 'em suspect, but be thou so precise°
As they may think it done of holiness.
Intreat 'em fair, and give them friendly speech,
And seem to them as if thy sins were great,
Till thou hast gotten to be entertained.

ABIGAIL.

Thus, father, shall I much dissemble.

BARABAS.

Tush,
As good dissemble that thou never mean'st
As first mean truth, and then dissemble it;
A counterfeit profession
Is better than unseen hypocrisy.

292. precise: pious

ABIGAIL.
Well father, say I be entertained,
What then shall follow?

BARABAS.
This shall follow then:
There have I hid close underneath the plank
That runs along the upper chamber floor,
The gold and jewels which I kept for thee.
But here they come; be cunning Abigail.

ABIGAIL.
Then father, go with me.

BARABAS.
No, Abigail, in this
It is not necessary I be seen.
For I will seem offended with thee for't.
Be close,° my girl, for this must fetch my gold.
[*Enter* TWO FRIARS, ABBESS, *and* NUN.]

1 FRIAR.
Sisters, we now are almost at the new-made nunnery.

ABBESS.
The better; for we love not to be seen:
'Tis thirty winters long since some of us
Did stray so far amongst the multitude.

1 FRIAR.
But, madam, this house
And waters of this new-made nunnery
Will much delight you.

ABBESS.
It may be so: but who comes here?

ABIGAIL.
Grave abbess, and you happy virgin's guide,
Pity the state of a distressèd maid.

ABBESS.
What art thou daughter?

ABIGAIL.
The hopeless daughter of a hapless Jew,
The Jew of Malta, wretched Barabas;
Sometimes the owner of a goodly house,
Which they have now turned to a nunnery.

ABBESS.
Well, daughter, say, what is thy suit with us?

ABIGAIL.
Fearing the afflictions which my father feels

314. close: cunning

Proceed from sin, or want of faith in us,
I'd pass away my life in penitence,
And be a novice in your nunnery,
To make atonement for my laboring soul.

1 FRIAR.
No doubt, brother, but this proceedeth of the spirit.

2 FRIAR.
Ay, and of a moving spirit too, brother; but come,
Let us intreat she may be entertained.

ABBESS.
Well, daughter, we admit you for a nun.

ABIGAIL.
First let me as a novice learn to frame
My solitary life to your strait laws,
And let me lodge where I was wont to lie;
I do not doubt by your divine precepts
And mine own industry, but to profit much.

BARABAS (*aside*).
As much I hope as all I hid is worth.

ABBESS.
Come daughter, follow us.

BARABAS.
Why how now Abigail,
What mak'st thou amongst these hateful Christians?

1 FRIAR.
Hinder her not, thou man of little faith,
For she has mortified° herself.

BARABAS.
How, mortified!

1 FRIAR.
And is admitted to the sisterhood.

BARABAS.
Child of perdition, and thy father's shame,
What wilt thou do among these hateful fiends?
I charge thee on my blessing that thou leave
These devils, and their damnèd heresy.

ABIGAIL.
Father forgive me—

BARABAS (*whispers to her*).
Nay back, Abigail,
And think upon the jewels and the gold,
The board is marked thus † that covers it.—
Away, accursed, from thy father's sight.

351. mortified: died to the world

1 FRIAR.
Barabas, although thou art in misbelief,
And wilt not see thine own afflictions,
Yet let thy daughter be no longer blind.

BARABAS.
Blind friar, I reck not thy persuasions
(*Aside.*) The board is marked thus † that covers it,
For I had rather die, than see her thus.
Wilt thou forsake me too in my distress,
Seducèd daughter, (*Aside to her.*) Go forget not.—
Becomes it Jews to be so credulous?
(*Aside to her.*) Tomorrow early I'll be at the door.—
No come not at me, if thou wilt be damned,
Forget me, see me not, and so be gone.
(*Aside.*) Farewell. Remember tomorrow morning.—
Out, out thou wretch.

[*Exeunt: on the one side,* BARABAS; *on the other,* FRIARS, ABBESS, NUN, *and* ABIGAIL.]

[*Enter* MATHIAS.]

MATHIAS.
Who's this? Fair Abigail the rich Jew's daughter
Become a nun! Her father's sudden fall
Has humbled her and brought her down to this.
Tut, she were fitter for a tale of love
Than to be tired out with orisons;
And better would she far become a bed
Embracèd in a friendly lover's arms,
Than rise at midnight to a solemn mass.

[*Enter* LODOWICK.]

LODOWICK.
Why how now Don Mathias, in a dump?

MATHIAS.
Believe me, noble Lodowick, I have seen
The strangest sight, in my opinion,
That ever I beheld.

LODOWICK.
What was't, I prithee?

MATHIAS.
A fair young maid scarce fourteen years of age,
The sweetest flower in Cytherea's field,
Cropt from the pleasures of the fruitful earth,
And strangely metamorphosed to a nun.

LODOWICK.
But say, what was she?

MATHIAS.
Why the rich Jew's daughter.

LODOWICK.
What Barabas, whose goods were lately seized?
Is she so fair?

MATHIAS.
And matchless beautiful;
As had you seen her 'twould have moved your heart,
Though countermured° with walls of brass, to love,
Or at the least to pity.

LODOWICK.
And if she be so fair as you report,
'Twere time well spent to go and visit her.
How say you, shall we?

MATHIAS.
I must and will, sir, there's no remedy.

LODOWICK.
And so will I too, or it shall go hard.
Farewell Mathias.

MATHIAS.
Farewell Lodowick.
[*Exeunt.*]

ACT II

Scene 1

Enter BARABAS *with a light*

BARABAS.
Thus like the sad presaging raven that tolls
The sick man's passport in her hollow beak,
And in the shadow of the silent night
Doth shake contagion from her sable wings,
Vexed and tormented runs poor Barabas
With fatal curses towards these Christians.
The incertain pleasures of swift-footed time
Have ta'en their flight, and left me in despair;
And of my former riches rests no more
But bare remembrance; like a soldier's scar,
That has no further comfort for his maim.

399. countermured: double-guarded

Oh thou that with a fiery pillar led'st
The sons of Israel through the dismal shades,
Light Abraham's offspring; and direct the hand
Of Abigail this night; or let the day
Turn to eternal darkness after this.
No sleep can fasten on my watchful eyes,
Nor quiet enter my distempered thoughts,
Till I have answer of my Abigail.
[*Enter* ABIGAIL *above*.]

ABIGAIL.
Now have I happily espied a time
To search the plank my father did appoint;
And here behold (unseen) where I have found
The gold, the pearls, and jewels which he hid.

BARABAS.
Now I remember those old women's words,
Who in my wealth would tell me winter's tales,
And speak of spirits and ghosts that glide by night
About the place where treasure hath been hid:
And now methinks that I am one of those:
For whilst I live, here lives my soul's sole hope,
And when I die, here shall my spirit walk.

ABIGAIL.
Now that my father's fortune were so good
As but to be about this happy place;
'Tis not so happy: yet when we parted last,
He said he would attend me in the morn.
Then, gentle sleep, wheree'er his body rests,
Give charge to Morpheus that he may dream
A golden dream, and of the sudden wake,
Come and receive the treasure I have found.

BARABAS.
Bueno para todos mi ganado no era:°
As good go on, as sit so sadly thus.
But stay, what star shines yonder in the East?
The loadstar of my life, if Abigail.
Who's there?

ABIGAIL.
Who's that?

BARABAS.
Peace, Abigail, 'tis I.

ABIGAIL.
Then father here receive thy happiness.
[*Throws down bags*.]

II.1 39. **Bueno . . . era:** My flock (property) is not for everyone.

BARABAS.
Hast thou't?

ABIGAIL.
Here,
Hast thou't?
There's more, and more, and more.

BARABAS.
Oh my girl,
My gold, my fortune, my felicity;
Strength to my soul, death to mine enemy;
Welcome the first beginner of my bliss.
Oh Abigail, Abigail, that I had thee here too,
Then my desires were fully satisfied—
But I will practise thy enlargement thence.
Oh girl! oh gold! oh beauty! oh my bliss!
[*Hugs his bags.*]

ABIGAIL.
Father, it draweth towards midnight now,
And 'bout this time the nuns begin to wake;
To shun suspicion, therefore, let us part.

BARABAS.
Farewell my joy, and by my fingers take
A kiss from him that sends it from his soul.
[*Exit* ABIGAIL.]
Now Phoebus ope the eye-lids of the day,
And for° the raven wake the morning lark,
That I may hover with her in the air,
Singing o'er these, as she does o'er her young.
Hermoso placer de los dineros.°
[*Exit.*]

Scene 2

Enter GOVERNOR, MARTIN DEL BOSCO, *the* KNIGHTS *and* OFFICERS

GOVERNOR.
Now Captain, tell us whither thou art bound?
Whence is thy ship that anchors in our road?
And why thou cam'st ashore without our leave?

65. for: instead of **68. Hermoso . . . dineros:** the beautiful pleasure of money

BOSCO.

Governor of Malta, hither am I bound;
My ship, the Flying Dragon, is of Spain,
And so am I, Del Bosco is my name;
Vice-admiral unto the Catholic king.

1 KNIGHT.

'Tis true, my lord, therefore intreat him well.

BOSCO.

Our fraught is Grecians, Turks, and Afric Moors,
For late upon the coast of Corsica,
Because we vailed not° to the Turkish fleet,
Their creeping galleys had us in the chase:
But suddenly the wind began to rise,
And then we luffed, and tacked, and fought at ease.
Some have we fired, and many have we sunk;
But one amongst the rest became our prize:
The captain's slain, the rest remains our slaves,
Of whom we would make sale in Malta here.

GOVERNOR.

Martin del Bosco, I have heard of thee;
Welcome to Malta, and to all of us;
But to admit a sale of these thy Turks
We may not, nay we dare not give consent
By reason of a tributary league.

1 KNIGHT.

Del Bosco, as thou lov'st and honour'st us,
Persuade our Governor against the Turk;
This truce we have is but in hope of gold,
And with that sum he craves might we wage war.

BOSCO.

Will Knights of Malta be in league with Turks,
And buy it basely too for sums of gold?
My lord, remember that to Europe's shame,
The Christian isle of Rhodes, from whence you came,
Was lately lost, and you were stated here
To be at deadly enmity with Turks.

GOVERNOR.

Captain we know it, but our force is small.

BOSCO.

What is the sum that Calymath requires?

GOVERNOR.

A hundred thousand crowns.

II.2. **11. vailed not:** did not lower sail in submission **32. stated:** stationed

BOSCO.
My lord and king hath title to this isle,
And he means quickly to expel you hence;
Therefore be ruled by me, and keep the gold:
I'll write unto his Majesty for aid,
And not depart until I see you free.

GOVERNOR.
On this condition shall thy Turks be sold.
Go officers and set them straight in show.
[*Exeunt* OFFICERS.]
Bosco, thou shalt be Malta's general;
We and our warlike knights will follow thee
Against these barbarous misbelieving Turks.

BOSCO.
So shall you imitate those you succeed:
For when their hideous force invironed Rhodes,
Small though the number was that kept the town,
They fought it out, and not a man survived
To bring the hapless news to Christendom.

GOVERNOR.
So will we fight it out; come, let's away.
Proud-daring Calymath, instead of gold,
We'll send thee bullets wrapt in smoke and fire:
Claim tribute where thou wilt, we are resolved:
Honor is bought with blood and not with gold.
[*Exeunt.*]

Scene 3

Enter OFFICERS *with* SLAVES

1 OFFICER.
This is the market-place, here let 'em stand.
Fear not their sale, for they'll be quickly bought.

2 OFFICER.
Every one's price is written on his back,
And so much must they yield or not be sold.
[*Enter* BARABAS.]

1 OFFICER.
Here comes the Jew, had not his goods been seized,
He'd give us present money for them all.

BARABAS.
In spite of these swine-eating Christians

(Unchosen nation, never circumcised;
Such as, poor villains, were ne'er thought upon
Till Titus and Vespasian conquered us),
Am I become as wealthy as I was.
They hoped my daughter would ha' been a nun;
But she's at home, and I have bought a house
As great and fair as is the Governor's;
And there in spite of Malta will I dwell:
Having Ferneze's hand, whose heart I'll have;
Ay, and his son's too, or it shall go hard.
I am not of the tribe of Levy, I,
That can so soon forget an injury.
We Jews can fawn like spaniels when we please;
And when we grin we bite, yet are our looks
As innocent and harmless as a lamb's.
I learned in Florence how to kiss my hand,
Heave up my shoulders when they call me dog,
And duck as low as any bare-foot friar,
Hoping to see them starve upon a stall,
Or else be gathered for° in our synagogue;
That when the offering-basin comes to me,
Even for charity I may spit into't.
Here comes Don Lodowick the Governor's son,
One that I love for his good father's sake.

[*Enter* LODOWICK.]

LODOWICK.

I hear the wealthy Jew walkèd this way;
I'll seek him out, and so insinuate,
That I may have a sight of Abigail;
For Don Mathias tells me she is fair.

BARABAS (*aside*).

Now will I show myself to have more of the serpent than the dove; that is, more knave than fool.

LODOWICK.

Yond walks the Jew, now for fair Abigail.

BABABAS (*aside*).

Ay, ay, no doubt but she's at your command.

LODOWICK.

Barabas, thou know'st I am the Governor's son.

BARABAS.

I would you were his father too, sir, that's all the harm I wish you: (*Aside.*) the slave looks like a hog's cheek new singed.

II.3. **27. gathered for:** i.e., as recipients of charity

LODOWICK.
Whither walk'st thou Barabas?

BARABAS.
No further: 'tis a custom held with us,
That when we speak with Gentiles like to you,
We turn into the air to purge ourselves,
For unto us the promise° doth belong.

LODOWICK.
Well, Barabas, canst help me to a diamond?

BARABAS.
Oh, sir, your father had my diamonds.
Yet I have one left that will serve your turn:
(*Aside.*) I mean my daughter:—but ere he shall have her
I'll sacrifice her on a pile of wood.
I ha' the poison of the city° for him,
And the white° leprosy.

LODOWICK.
What sparkle does it give without a foil?

BARABAS.
The diamond that I talk of, ne'er was foiled:
(*Aside.*) But when he touches it, it will be foiled:—
Lord Lodowick, it sparkles bright and fair.

LODOWICK.
Is it square or pointed, pray let me know.

BARABAS.
Pointed it is, good sir,—(*Aside.*) but not for you.

LODOWICK.
I like it much the better.

BARABAS.
So do I too.

LODOWICK.
How shows it by night?

BARABAS.
Outshines Cynthia's rays:
You'll like it better far a-nights than days.

LODOWICK.
And what's the price?

BARABAS (*aside*).
Your life and if you have it.—O my lord
We will not jar about the price; come to my house
And I will giv't your honor (*Aside.*)—with a vengeance.

47. promise: cf. Romans 4:13–20 **54. poison of the city:** plague **55. white:** scaly (leprosy at its worst)

LODOWICK.
No, Barabas, I will deserve it first.

BARABAS.
Good sir,
Your father has deserved it at my hands,
Who of mere charity and Christian ruth,
To bring me to religious purity,
And as it were in catechizing sort,
To make me mindful of my mortal sins,
Against my will, and whether I would or no,
Seized all I had, and thrust me out-a-doors,
And made my house a place for nuns most chaste.

LODOWICK.
No doubt your soul shall reap the fruit of it.

BARABAS.
Ay, but my lord, the harvest is far off:
And yet I know the prayers of those nuns
And holy friars, having money for their pains,
Are wondrous: (*Aside.*) and indeed do no man good:—
And seeing they are not idle, but still doing,
'Tis likely they in time may reap some fruit,
I mean in fulness of perfection.

LODOWICK.
Good Barabas glance not at our holy nuns.

BARABAS.
No, but I do it through a burning zeal,
(*Aside.*) Hoping ere long to set the house afire;
For though they do awhile increase and multiply,
I'll have a saying to that nunnery.—
As for the diamond, sir, I told you of,
Come home and there's no price shall make us part,
Even for your honorable father's sake.
(*Aside.*) It shall go hard but I will see your death.—
But now I must be gone to buy a slave.

LODOWICK.
And, Barabas, I'll bear thee company.

BARABAS.
Come then, here's the market-place; what's the price of this slave, two hundred crowns? Do the Turks weigh so much?

1 OFFICER.
Sir, that's his price.

BARABAS.
What, can he steal that you demand so much?
Belike he has some new trick for a purse;

And if he has, he is worth three hundred plates,°
So that, being bought, the town-seal might be got
To keep him for his life time from the gallows.
The sessions° day is critical to thieves,
And few or none scape but by being purged.°

LODOWICK.
Ratest thou this Moor but at two hundred plates?

1 OFFICER.
No more, my lord.

BARABAS.
Why should this Turk be dearer than that Moor?

1 OFFICER.
Because he is young and has more qualities.

BARABAS.
What, hast the philosopher's stone?° And thou hast, break my head with it, I'll forgive thee.

SLAVE.
No sir, I can cut and shave.

BARABAS.
Let me see, sirrah, are you not an old shaver?

SLAVE.
Alas, sir, I am a very youth.

BARABAS.
A youth? I'll buy you, and marry you to Lady Vanity, if you do well.

SLAVE.
I will serve you, sir.

BARABAS.
Some wicked trick or other. It may be under color of shaving, thou'lt cut my throat for my goods. Tell me, hast thou thy health well?

SLAVE.
Ay, passing well.

BARABAS.
So much the worse; I must have one that's sickly, and 't be but for sparing vittles: 'tis not a stone° of beef a day will maintain you in these chops;° let me see one that's somewhat leaner.

1 OFFICER.
Here's a leaner, how like you him?

BARABAS.
Where wast thou born?

ITHAMORE.
In Thrace; brought up in Arabia.

104. plates: Spanish silver **107. sessions:** court **108. purged:** hanged **113. stone:** alchemist's substance for changing base metal into gold **125. stone:** 14 pounds **126. chops:** fat jowls

BARABAS.
So much the better, thou art for my turn;
An hundred crowns, I'll have him; there's the coin.

1 OFFICER.
Then mark him, sir, and take him hence.

BARABAS (*aside*).
Ay, mark him, you were best, for this is he
That by my help shall do much villainy.
My lord farewell. Come, sirrah, you are mine.
As for the diamond it shall be yours;
I pray, sir, be no stranger at my house,
All that I have shall be at your command.
[*Enter* MATHIAS *and his* MOTHER.]

MATHIAS (*aside*).
What makes the Jew and Lodowick so private?
I fear me 'tis about fair Abigail.

BARABAS.
Yonder comes Don Mathias, let us stay;
He loves my daughter, and she holds him dear:
But I have sworn to frustrate both their hopes,
And be revenged upon the—(*Aside.*) Governor.
[*Exit* LODOWICK.]

MOTHER.
This Moor is comeliest, is he not? speak, son.

MATHIAS.
No, this is the better, mother, view this well.

BARABAS.
Seem not to know me here before your mother,
Lest she mistrust the match that is in hand.
When you have brought her home, come to my house;
Think of me as thy father; son farewell.

MATHIAS.
But wherefore talked Don Lodowick with you?

BARABAS.
Tush man, we talked of diamonds, not of Abigail.

MOTHER.
Tell me, Mathias, is not that the Jew?

BARABAS.
As for the comment on the Maccabees,
I have it, sir, and 'tis at your command.

MATHIAS.
Yes, madam, and my talk with him was but
About the borrowing of a book or two.

MOTHER.
Converse not with him, he is cast off from heaven.

Thou hast thy crowns, fellow, come let's away.

MATHIAS.

Sirrah, Jew, remember the book.

BARABAS.

Marry will I, sir.

[*Exeunt* MATHIAS *and his* MOTHER, *with a* SLAVE.]

1 OFFICER.

Come, I have made a reasonable market, let's away.

[*Exeunt* OFFICERS *with* SLAVES.]

BARABAS.

Now let me know thy name, and therewithal
Thy birth, condition, and profession.

ITHAMORE.

Faith, sir, my birth is but mean, my name's Ithamore, my profession what you please.

BARABAS.

Hast thou no trade? then listen to my words,
And I will teach thee that shall stick by thee:
First be thou void of these affections,
Compassion, love, vain hope, and heartless fear,
Be moved at nothing, see thou pity none,
But to thyself smile when the Christians moan.

ITHAMORE.

Oh brave, master, I worship your nose for this.

BARABAS.

As for myself, I walk abroad a-nights,
And kill sick people groaning under walls:
Sometimes I go about and poison wells;
And now and then, to cherish Christian thieves,
I am content to lose some of my crowns;
That I may, walking in my gallery,
See 'em go pinioned along by my door.
Being young I studied physic, and began
To practise first upon the Italian;
There I enriched the priests with burials,
And always kept the sexton's arms in ure°
With digging graves and ringing dead men's knells:
And after that was I an engineer,
And in the wars 'twixt France and Germany,
Under pretence of helping Charles the Fifth,
Slew friend and enemy with my stratagems.
Then after that was I an usurer,
And with extorting, cozening, forfeiting,

183. in ure: busy

And tricks belonging unto brokery,
I filled the jails with bankrouts° in a year,
And with young orphans planted hospitals,
And every moon made some or other mad,
And now and then one hang himself for grief,
Pinning upon his breast a long great scroll
How I with interest tormented him.
But mark how I am blest for plaguing them,
I have as much coin as will buy the town.
But tell me now, how hast thou spent thy time?

ITHAMORE.

Faith, master,
In setting Christian villages on fire,
Chaining of eunuchs, binding galley-slaves.
One time I was an hostler in an inn,
And in the night time secretly would I steal
To travellers' chambers, and there cut their throats:
Once at Jerusalem, where the pilgrims kneeled,
I strowèd powder on the marble stones,
And therewithal their knees would rankle, so
That I have laughed a-good to see the cripples
Go limping home to Christendom on stilts.

BARABAS.

Why this is something: make account of me
As of thy fellow; we are villains both:
Both circumcisèd, we hate Christians both.
Be true and secret, thou shalt want no gold.
But stand aside, here comes Don Lodowick.
[*Enter* LODOWICK.]

LODOWICK.

Oh Barabas, well met;
Where is the diamond you told me of?

BARABAS.

I have it for you, sir; please you walk in with me.
What, ho, Abigail; open the door I say.
[*Enter* ABIGAIL.]

ABIGAIL.

In good time, father, here are letters come
From Ormus, and the post stays here within.

BARABAS.

Give me the letters; daughter, do you hear?
Entertain Lodowick the Governors' son
With all the courtesy you can afford;

192. bankrouts: bankrupts

Provided that you keep your maidenhead.
Use him as if he were a (*Aside.*) Philistine.
Dissemble, swear, protest, vow to love him,
He is not of the seed of Abraham.—
I am a little busy, sir, pray pardon me.
Abigail, bid him welcome for my sake.

ABIGAIL.
For your sake and his own he's welcome hither.

BARABAS.
Daughter, a word more; (*Aside.*) kiss him, speak him fair,
And like a cunning Jew so cast about,
That ye be both made sure ere you come out.

ABIGAIL (*aside*).
Oh father, Don Mathias is my love.

BARABAS (*aside*).
I know it: yet I say make love to him;
Do, it is requisite it should be so.—
Nay on my life it is my factor's hand,°
But go you in, I'll think upon the account.
[*Exeunt* ABIGAIL *and* LODOWICK.]
The account is made, for Lodowick dies.
My factor sends me word a merchant's fled
That owes me for a hundred tun of wine:
I weigh it thus much; I have wealth enough.
For now by this has he kissed Abigail;
And she vows love to him, and he to her.
As sure as heaven rained manna for the Jews,
So sure shall he and Don Mathias die:
His father was my chiefest enemy.
[*Enter* MATHIAS.]
Whither goes Don Mathias? Stay a while.

MATHIAS.
Whither but to my fair love Abigail?

BARABAS.
Thou know'st, and heaven can witness it is true,
That I intend my daughter shall be thine.

MATHIAS.
Ay, Barabas, or else thou wrong'st me much.

BARABAS.
Oh heaven forbid I should have such a thought.
Pardon me though I weep; the Governor's son
Will, whether I will or no, have Abigail:
He sends her letters, bracelets, jewels, rings.

239. factor's hand: agent's handwriting

MATHIAS.
Does she receive them?

BARABAS.
She? No, Mathias, no, but sends them back,
And when he comes, she locks herself up fast;
Yet through the key-hole will he talk to her,
While she runs to the window looking out
When you should come and hale him from the door.

MATHIAS.
Oh treacherous Lodowick!

BARABAS.
Even now as I came home, he slipt me in,
And I am sure he is with Abigail.

MATHIAS.
I'll rouse him thence.

BARABAS.
Not for all Malta, therefore sheathe your sword;
If you love me, no quarrels in my house;
But steal you in, and seem to see him not;
I'll give him such a warning ere he goes
As he shall have small hopes of Abigail.
Away, for here they come.
[*Enter* LODOWICK, ABIGAIL.]

MATHIAS.
What hand in hand, I cannot suffer this.

BARABAS.
Mathias, as thou lov'st me, not a word.

MATHIAS.
Well, let it pass, another time shall serve.
[*Exit.*]

LODOWICK.
Barabas, is not that the widow's son?

BARABAS.
Ay, and take heed, for he hath sworn your death.

LODOWICK.
My death? What, is the base-born peasant mad?

BARABAS.
No, no, but happily he stands in fear
Of that which you, I think, ne'er dream upon.
My daughter here, a paltry silly girl—

LODOWICK.
Why, loves she Don Mathias?

BARABAS.
Doth she not with her smiling answer you?

ABIGAIL (*aside*).
He has my heart, I smile against my will.

LODOWICK.
Barabas, thou know'st I have loved thy daughter long.

BARABAS.
And so has she done you, even from a child.

LODOWICK.
And now I can no longer hold my mind.

BARABAS.
Nor I the affection that I bear to you.

LODOWICK.
This is thy diamond, tell me, shall I have it?

BARABAS.
Win it and wear it, it is yet unsoiled.
Oh but I know your lordship would disdain
To marry with the daughter of a Jew:
And yet I'll give her many a golden cross.
With Christian posies round about the ring.

LODOWICK.
'Tis not thy wealth, but her that I esteem,
Yet crave I thy consent.

BARABAS.
And mine you have, yet let me talk to her;
(*Aside.*) This offspring of Cain, this Jebusite
That never tasted of the passover,
Nor e'er shall see the land of Canaan,
Nor our Messias that is yet to come,
This gentle° maggot Lodowick I mean,
Must be deluded. Let him have thy hand,
But keep thy heart till Don Mathias comes.

ABIGAIL (*aside*).
What, shall I be betrothed to Lodowick?

BARABAS (*aside*).
It's no sin to deceive a Christian;
For they themselves hold it a principle,
Faith is not to be held with heretics;
But all are heretics that are not Jews;
This follows well, and therefore daughter fear not.—
I have intreated her, and she will grant.

LODOWICK.
Then gentle Abigail plight thy faith to me.

ABIGAIL.
I cannot choose, seeing my father bids.
Nothing but death shall part my love and me.

LODOWICK.
Now have I that for which my soul hath longed.

304. gentle: aristocratic and gentile

BARABAS (*aside*).
So have not I, but yet I hope I shall.
ABIGAIL (*aside*).
Oh wretched Abigail, what hast thou done?
LODOWICK.
Why on the sudden is your color changed?
ABIGAIL.
I know not, but farewell, I must be gone.
BARABAS.
Stay her, but let her not speak one word more.
LODOWICK.
Mute o' the sudden; here's a sudden change.
BARABAS.
Oh muse not at it, 'tis the Hebrews' guise,
That maidens new betrothed should weep a while.
Trouble her not, sweet Lodowick depart:
She is thy wife, and thou shalt be mine heir.
LODOWICK.
Oh, is't the custom, then I am resolved;
But rather let the brightsome heavens be dim,
And Nature's beauty choke with stifling clouds,
Than my fair Abigail should frown on me.
There comes the villain, now I'll be revenged.
[*Enter* MATHIAS.]
BARABAS.
Be quiet Lodowick, it is enough
That I have made thee sure to Abigail.
LODOWICK.
Well, let him go.
[*Exit.*]
BARABAS.
Well, but for me, as you went in at doors
You had been stabbed, but not a word on't now;
Here must no speeches pass, nor swords be drawn.
MATHIAS.
Suffer me, Barabas, but to follow him.
BARABAS.
No; so shall I, if any hurt be done,
Be made an accessary of your deeds;
Revenge it on him when you meet him next.
MATHIAS.
For this I'll have his heart.
BARABAS.
Do so; lo here I give thee Abigail.

MATHIAS.
What greater gift can poor Mathias have?
Shall Lodowick rob me of so fair a love?
My life is not so dear as Abigail.

BARABAS.
My heart misgives me, that to cross your love,
He's with your mother, therefore after him.

MATHIAS.
What, is he gone unto my mother?

BARABAS.
Nay, if you will, stay till she comes herself.

MATHIAS.
I cannot stay; for if my mother come,
She'll die with grief.
[*Exit.*]

ABIGAIL.
I cannot take my leave of him for tears:
Father, why have you thus incensed them both?

BARABAS.
What's that to thee?

ABIGAIL.
I'll make 'em friends again.

BARABAS.
You'll make 'em friends? Are there not Jews enow in Malta
But thou must dote upon a Christian?

ABIGAIL.
I will have Don Mathias, he is my love.

BARABAS.
Yes, you shall have him. Go put her in.

ITHAMORE.
Ay, I'll put her in.
[*Puts* ABIGAIL *in.*]

BARABAS.
Now tell me, Ithamore, how lik'st thou this?

ITHAMORE.
Faith master, I think by this
You purchase both their lives; is it not so?

BARABAS.
True; and it shall be cunningly performed.

ITHAMORE.
Oh, master, that I might have a hand in this.

BARABAS.
Ay, so thou shalt, 'tis thou must do the deed:
Take this and bear it to Mathias straight,

And tell him that it comes from Lodowick.

ITHAMORE.

'Tis poisoned, is it not?

BARABAS.

No, no, and yet it might be done that way;
It is a challenge feigned from Lodowick.

ITHAMORE.

Fear not, I'll so set his heart afire,
That he shall verily think it comes from him.

BARABAS.

I cannot choose but like thy readiness,
Yet be not rash, but do it cunningly.

ITHAMORE.

As I behave myself in this, employ me hereafter.

BARABAS.

Away then.

[*Exit* ITHAMORE.]

So, now will I go in to Lodowick,
And like a cunning spirit feign some lie,
Till I have set 'em both at enmity.

[*Exit*.]

ACT III

Scene 1

Enter BELLAMIRA

BELLAMIRA.

Since this town was besieged, my gain grows cold.
The time has been, that but for one bare night
A hundred ducats have been freely given,
But now against my will I must be chaste;
And yet I know my beauty doth not fail.
From Venice merchants, and from Padua
Were wont to come rare-witted gentlemen,
Scholars I mean, learned and liberal;
And now, save Pilia-Borza,° comes there none,
And he is very seldom from my house;

III.1. **9. Pilia-Borza:** The name means purse-stealer.

And here he comes.

[*Enter* PILIA-BORZA.]

PILIA-BORZA.

Hold thee, wench, there's something for thee to spend.

[*Shows a bag of silver.*]

BELLAMIRA.

'Tis silver, I disdain it.

PILIA-BORZA.

Ay, but the Jew has gold,
And I will have it or it shall go hard.

BELLAMIRA.

Tell me, how cam'st thou by this?

PILIA-BORZA.

Faith, walking the back lanes through the gardens, I chanced to cast mine eye up to the Jew's counting-house, where I saw some bags of money, and in the night I clambered up with my hooks, and as I was taking my choice, I heard a rumbling in the house; so I took only this, and run my way: but here's the Jew's man. 21

[*Enter* ITHAMORE.]

BELLAMIRA.

Hide the bag.

PILIA-BORZA.

Look not towards him, let's away: zoons what a looking thou keep'st, thou'lt betray's anon.

[*Exeunt* BELLAMIRA *and* PILIA-BORZA.]

ITHAMORE.

O the sweetest face that ever I beheld! I know she is a courtesan by her attire: now would I give a hundred of the Jew's crowns that I had such a concubine. Well, I have delivered the challenge in such sort, As meet they will, and fighting die; brave sport.

[*Exit.*]

Scene 2

Enter MATHIAS, *holding a letter*

MATHIAS.

This is the place, now Abigail shall see
Whether Mathias holds her dear or no.
What, dares the villain write in such base terms?

[*Enter* LODOWICK *reading.*]

LODOWICK.

I did it, and revenge it if thou dar'st.

[*Fight. Enter* BARABAS *above.*]

BARABAS.
Oh bravely fought, and yet they thrust not home.
Now Lodowick, now Mathias, so—
[*Both fall.*]
So, now they have showed themselves to be tall ° fellows.
VOICES (*within*).
Part 'em, part 'em.
BARABAS.
Ay, part 'em now they are dead. Farewell, farewell.
[*Exit.*]
[*Enter* GOVERNOR *and* MATHIAS'S MOTHER, *with* CITIZENS.]
GOVERNOR.
What sight is this? my Lodowick slain!
These arms of mine shall be thy sepulchre.
MOTHER.
Who is this? my son Mathias slain!
GOVERNOR.
Oh Lodowick! had'st thou perished by the Turk,
Wretched Ferneze might have venged thy death.
MOTHER.
Thy son slew mine, and I'll revenge his death.
GOVERNOR.
Look, Katherine, look, thy son gave mine these wounds.
MOTHER.
O leave to grieve me, I am grieved enough.
GOVERNOR.
Oh that my sighs could turn to lively breath;
And these my tears to blood, that he might live.
MOTHER.
Who made them enemies?
GOVERNOR.
I know not, and that grieves me most of all.
MOTHER.
My son loved thine.
GOVERNOR.
And so did Lodowick him.
MOTHER.
Lend me that weapon that did kill my son,
And it shall murder me.
GOVERNOR.
Nay madam stay, that weapon was my son's,
And on that rather should Ferneze die.

III.2. **7. tall:** brave

MOTHER.

Hold, let's inquire the causers of their deaths,
That we may venge their blood upon their heads.

GOVERNOR.

Then take them up, and let them be interred
Within one sacred monument of stone;
Upon which altar I will offer up
My daily sacrifice of sighs and tears,
And with my prayers pierce impartial heavens,
Till they [disclose] the causers of our smarts,
Which forced their hands divide united hearts.
Come, Katherine, our losses equal are,
Then of true grief let us take equal share.
[*Exeunt with the bodies.*]

Scene 3

Enter ITHAMORE

ITHAMORE.

Why, was there ever seen such villainy,
So neatly plotted, and so well performed?
Both held in hand, and flatly both beguiled.
[*Enter* ABIGAIL.]

ABIGAIL.

Why how now Ithamore, why laugh'st thou so?

ITHAMORE.

Oh, mistress, ha ha ha!

ABIGAIL.

Why what ail'st thou?

ITHAMORE.

Oh my master!

ABIGAIL.

Ha?

ITHAMORE.

Oh mistress! I have the bravest, gravest, secret, subtle bottle-nosed knave to my master, that ever gentleman had!

ABIGAIL.

Say, knave, why rail'st upon my father thus?

ITHAMORE.

Oh, my master has the bravest policy.

ABIGAIL.

Wherein?

ITHAMORE.
Why, know you not?

ABIGAIL.
Why no.

ITHAMORE.
Know you not of Mathias' and Don Lodowick's disaster?

ABIGAIL.
No, what was it?

ITHAMORE.
Why the devil invented a challenge, my master writ it, and
I carried it, first to Lodowick, and *imprimis* to Mathias.
And then they met, and as the story says,
In doleful wise they ended both their days.

ABIGAIL.
And was my father furtherer of their deaths?

ITHAMORE.
Am I Ithamore?

ABIGAIL.
Yes.

ITHAMORE.
So sure did your father write, and I carry the challenge.

ABIGAIL.
Well, Ithamore, let me request thee this:
Go to the new-made nunnery, and inquire
For any of the friars of St. Jacques,
And say, I pray them come and speak with me.

ITHAMORE.
I pray, mistress, will you answer me to one question?

ABIGAIL.
Well, sirrah, what is't?

ITHAMORE.
A very feeling one; have not the nuns fine sport with the friars now and then?

ABIGAIL.
Go to, sirrah sauce, is this your question? Get ye gone.

ITHAMORE.
I will forsooth, mistress.
[*Exit.*]

ABIGAIL.
Hard-hearted father, unkind Barabas,
Was this the pursuit of thy policy?
To make me show them favor severally,
That by my favor they should both be slain?
Admit thou lov'dst not Lodowick for his sire,
Yet Don Mathias ne'er offended thee.

But thou wert set upon extreme revenge,
Because the Governor dispossessed thee once,
And couldst not venge it, but upon his son,
Nor on his son, but by Mathias' means,
Nor on Mathias, but by murdering me.
But I perceive there is no love on earth,
Pity in Jews, nor piety in Turks.
But here comes cursed Ithamore with the friar.
[*Enter* ITHAMORE, FRIAR.]

FRIAR.
Virgo, salve.°

ITHAMORE.
When, duck° you?

ABIGAIL.
Welcome grave friar: Ithamore begone.
[*Exit* ITHAMORE.]
Know, holy sir, I am bold to solicit thee.

FRIAR.
Wherein?

ABIGAIL.
To get me be admitted for a nun.

FRIAR.
Why Abigail it is not yet long since
That I did labor thy admission,
And then thou didst not like that holy life.

ABIGAIL.
Then were my thoughts so frail and unconfirmed,
And I was chained to follies of the world;
But now experience, purchasèd with grief,
Has made me see the difference of things.
My sinful soul, alas, hath paced too long
The fatal labyrinth of misbelief,
Far from the sun that gives eternal life.

FRIAR.
Who taught thee this?

ABIGAIL.
The abbess of the house,
Whose zealous admonition I embrace.
Oh therefore, Jacomo, let me be one,
Although unworthy, of that sisterhood.

FRIAR.
Abigail I will, but see thou change no more,
For that will be most heavy to thy soul.

III.3. **50. Virgo, salve:** Virgin, hail **51. duck:** bow and scrape

ABIGAIL.
That was my father's fault.

FRIAR.
Thy father's, how?

ABIGAIL.
Nay, you shall pardon me: (*Aside.*) oh Barabas,
Though thou deservest hardly at my hands,
Yet never shall these lips bewray thy life.

FRIAR.
Come, shall we go?

ABIGAIL.
My duty waits on you.
[*Exeunt.*]

Scene 4

Enter BARABAS *reading a letter*

BARABAS.
What, Abigail become a nun again?
False, and unkind; what, hast thou lost° thy father?
And all unknown, and unconstrained of me,
Art thou again got to the nunnery?
Now here she writes, and wills me to repent.
Repentance? *Spurca:*° what pretendeth this?
I fear she knows ('tis so) of my device
In Don Mathias' and Lodovico's deaths:
If so, 'tis time that it be seen into:
For she that varies from me in belief
Gives great presumption that she loves me not,
Or loving, doth dislike of something done.
But who comes here?
[*Enter* ITHAMORE.]
Oh Ithamore come near;
Come near my love, come near thy master's life,
My trusty servant, nay, my second [self];
For I have now no hope but even in thee;
And on that hope my happiness is built.

III.4. **2. lost:** abandoned **6. Spurca:** dirt

When saw'st thou Abigail?

ITHAMORE.
Today.

BARABAS.
With whom?

ITHAMORE.
A friar.

BARABAS.
A friar? false villain, he hath done the deed.

ITHAMORE.
How sir?

BARABAS.
Why made mine Abigail a nun.

ITHAMORE.
That's no lie, for she sent me for him.

BARABAS.
O unhappy day,
False, credulous, inconstant Abigail!
But let 'em go: and Ithamore, from hence
Ne'er shall she grieve me more with her disgrace;
Ne'er shall she live to inherit aught of mine,
Be blest of me, nor come within my gates,
But perish underneath my bitter curse,
Like Cain by Adam, for his brother's death.

ITHAMORE.
Oh master.

BARABAS.
Ithamore, intreat not for her, I am moved,
And she is hateful to my soul and me.
And 'less thou yield to this that I intreat,
I cannot think but that thou hat'st my life.

ITHAMORE.
Who I, master? Why I'll run to some rock and throw myself headlong into the sea; why I'll do anything for your sweet sake.

BARABAS.
Oh trusty Ithamore; no servant, but my friend;
I here adopt thee for mine only heir,
All that I have is thine when I am dead,
And whilst I live use half; spend as myself;
Here take my keys—I'll give 'em thee anon:
Go buy thee garments: but thou shalt not want.
Only know this, that thus thou art to do—
But first go fetch me in the pot of rice
That for our supper stands upon the fire.

ITHAMORE.
I hold ° my head my master's hungry. I go sir.
[*Exit.*]

BARABAS.
Thus every villain ambles after wealth
Although he ne'er be richer than in hope—
But husht.
[*Enter* ITHAMORE *with the pot.*]

ITHAMORE.
Here 'tis, master.

BARABAS.
Well said, Ithamore; what, hast thou brought the ladle with thee too?

ITHAMORE.
Yes, sir, the proverb says, he that eats with the devil had need of a long spoon, I have brought you a ladle.

BARABAS.
Very well, Ithamore, then now be secret:
And for thy sake, whom I so dearly love,
Now shalt thou see the death of Abigail,
That thou mayst freely live to be my heir.

ITHAMORE.
Why, master, will you poison her with a mess of rice porridge that will preserve life, make her round and plump, and batten more than you are aware?

BARABAS.
Ay, but Ithamore seest thou this?
It is a precious powder that I bought
Of an Italian in Ancona once,
Whose operation is to bind, infect,
And poison deeply: yet not appear
In forty hours after it is ta'en.

ITHAMORE.
How master?

BARABAS.
Thus Ithamore:
This even they use in Malta here ('tis called
Saint Jaques' even) and then I say they use
To send their alms unto the nunneries:
Among the rest bear this, and set it there;
There's a dark entry where they take it in,
Where they must neither see the messenger,
Nor make inquiry who hath sent it them.

50. hold: wager

ITHAMORE.
How so?

BARABAS.
Belike there is some ceremony in't.
There Ithamore must thou go place this pot—
Stay, let me spice it first.

ITHAMORE.
Pray do, and let me help you master. Pray let me taste first.

BARABAS.
Prithee do: what say'st thou now?

ITHAMORE.
Troth master, I'm loath such a pot of pottage should be spoiled.

BARABAS.
Peace, Ithamore, 'tis better so than spared.
Assure thyself thou shalt have broth by the eye.°
My purse, my coffer, and my self is thine.

ITHAMORE.
Well, master, I go.

BARABAS.
Stay, first let me stir it Ithamore.
As fatal be it to her as the draught
Of which great Alexander drunk, and died;
And with her let it work like Borgia's wine,
Whereof his sire, the Pope, was poisonèd.
In few, the blood of Hydra, Lerna's bane,
The juice of hebon, and Cocytus' breath,
And all the poisons of the Stygian pool,
Break from the fiery kingdom; and in this
Vomit your venom, and invenom her
That like a fiend hath left her father thus.

ITHAMORE.
What a blessing has he given't! Was ever pot of rice porridge so sauced? What shall I do with it?

BARABAS.
Oh my sweet Ithamore go set it down
And come again so soon as thou hast done,
For I have other business for thee.

ITHAMORE.
Here's a drench to poison a whole stable of Flanders mares. I'll carry't to the nuns with a powder.

BARABAS.
And the horse pestilence to boot; away.

89. by the eye: in great plenty

ITHAMORE.
I am gone.
Pay me my wages for my work is done.
[*Exit.*]

BARABAS.
I'll pay thee with a vengeance Ithamore.
[*Exit.*]

Scene 5

Enter GOVERNOR, MARTIN DEL BOSCO, KNIGHTS, *meeting a* BASSO

GOVERNOR.
Welcome great Basso, how fares Calymath,
What wind drives you thus into Malta road?

BASSO.
The wind that bloweth all the world besides:
Desire of gold.

GOVERNOR.
Desire of gold, great sir?
That's to be gotten in the Western Ind;
In Malta are no golden minerals.

BASSO.
To you of Malta thus saith Calymath:
The time you took for respite, is at hand,
For the performance of your promise past;
And for the tribute-money I am sent.

GOVERNOR.
Basso, in brief, shalt have no tribute here,
Nor shall the heathens live upon our spoil.
First will we race° the city walls ourselves,
Lay waste the island, hew the temples down,
And shipping off our goods to Sicily,
Open an entrance for the wasteful sea,
Whose billows beating the resistless banks,
Shall overflow it with their refluence.

BASSO.
Well, Governor, since thou hast broke the league
By flat denial of the promised tribute,
Talk not of racing down your city walls,

III.5. **14. race:** raze

You shall not need trouble yourselves so far,
For Selim-Calymath shall come himself,
And with brass bullets batter down your towers,
And turn proud Malta to a wilderness,
For these intolerable wrongs of yours;
And so farewell.
[*Exit.*]

GOVERNOR.
Farewell.
And now you men of Malta look about,
And let's provide to welcome Calymath:
Close your portcullis, charge your basilisks,
And as you profitably take up arms,
So now courageously encounter them;
For by this answer, broken is the league,
And nought is to be looked for now but wars,
And nought to us more welcome is than wars.
[*Exeunt.*]

Scene 6

Enter the TWO FRIARS

1 FRIAR.
Oh brother, brother, all the nuns are sick,
And physic will not help them; they must die.

2 FRIAR.
The abbess sent for me to be confessed.
Oh what a sad confession will there be!

1 FRIAR.
And so did fair Maria send for me.
I'll to her lodging; hereabouts she lies.
[*Exit.*]
[*Enter* ABIGAIL.]

2 FRIAR.
What, all dead save only Abigail?

ABIGAIL.
And I shall die too, for I feel death coming.
Where is the friar that conversed with me?

2 FRIAR.
Oh he is gone to see the other nuns.

ABIGAIL.
I sent for him, but seeing you are come,

Be you my ghostly father; and first know
That in this house I lived religiously,
Chaste, and devout, much sorrowing for my sins;
But ere I came—

2 FRIAR.
What then?

ABIGAIL.
I did offend high heaven so grievously,
As I am almost desperate for my sins:
And one offence torments me more than all.
You knew Mathias and Don Lodowick?

2 FRIAR.
Yes, what of them?

ABIGAIL.
My father did contract me to 'em both:
First to Don Lodowick, him I never loved;
Mathias was the man that I held dear,
And for his sake did I become a nun.

2 FRIAR.
So, say how was their end?

ABIGAIL.
Both jealous of my love, envied each other:
And by my father's practice, which is there
Set down at large, the gallants were both slain.
[*Gives him a paper.*]

2 FRIAR.
Oh monstrous villainy!

ABIGAIL.
To work my peace, this I confess to thee;
Reveal it not, for then my father dies.

2 FRIAR.
Know that confession must not be revealed,
The canon law forbids it, and the priest
That makes it known, being degraded first,
Shall be condemned, and then sent to the fire.

ABIGAIL.
So I have heard; pray therefore keep it close.
Death seizeth on my heart, ah gentle friar
Convert my father that he may be saved,
And witness that I die a Christian.
[*Dies.*]

2 FRIAR.
Ay, and a virgin too, that grieves me most.
But I must to the Jew and exclaim° on him,

III.6. **42. exclaim:** accuse

And make him stand in fear of me.
[*Enter* 1 FRIAR.]

1 FRIAR.
Oh brother, all the nuns are dead, let's bury them.

2 FRIAR.
First help to bury this, then go with me
And help me to exclaim against the Jew.

1 FRIAR.
Why? what has he done?

2 FRIAR.
A thing that makes me tremble to unfold.

1 FRIAR.
What, has he crucified a child?

2 FRIAR.
No, but a worse thing: 'twas told me in shrift;
Thou know'st 'tis death and if it be revealed.
Come let's away.
[*Exeunt with the body.*]

ACT IV

Scene 1

Enter BARABAS, ITHAMORE. *Bells within*

BARABAS.
There is no music to° a Christian's knell!
How sweet the bells ring now the nuns are dead,
That sound at other times like tinkers' pans!
I was afraid the poison had not wrought;
Or though it wrought, it would have done no good,
For every year they swell,° and yet they live;
Now all are dead, not one remains alive.

ITHAMORE.
That's brave, master, but think you it will not be known?

BARABAS.
How can it if we two be secret?

ITHAMORE.
For my part fear you not.

IV.1. **1. to:** equal to **6. swell:** become pregnant

BARABAS.
I'd cut thy throat if I did.
ITHAMORE.
And reason too;
But here's a royal monastery hard by,
Good master let me poison all the monks.
BARABAS.
Thou shalt not need, for now the nuns are dead,
They'll die with grief.
ITHAMORE.
Do you not sorrow for your daughter's death?
BARABAS.
No, but I grieve because she lived so long;
An Hebrew born, and would become a Christian.
Catso, diabole!
[*Enter the* TWO FRIARS.]
ITHAMORE.
Look, look, master, here come two religious caterpillars.°
BARABAS.
I smelt 'em ere they came.
ITHAMORE.
God-a-mercy, nose; come let's begone.
2 FRIAR.
Stay wicked Jew, repent, I say, and stay.
1 FRIAR.
Thou hast offended, therefore must be damned.
BARABAS.
I fear they know we sent the poisoned broth.
ITHAMORE.
And so do I, master, therefore speak 'em fair.
2 FRIAR.
Barabas, thou hast—
1 FRIAR.
Ay, that thou hast—
BARABAS.
True, I have money, what though I have?
2 FRIAR.
Thou art a—
1 FRIAR.
Ay, that thou art, a—
BARABAS.
What needs all this? I know I am a Jew.

21. caterpillars: parasites

2 FRIAR.
Thy daughter—

1 FRIAR.
Ay, thy daughter—

BARABAS.
Oh speak not of her, then I die with grief.

2 FRIAR.
Remember that—

1 FRIAR.
Ay, remember that—

BARABAS.
I must needs say that I have been a great usurer.

2 FRIAR.
Thou hast committed—

BARABAS.
Fornication? but that was in another country: and besides, the wench is dead.

2 FRIAR.
Ay, but Barabas remember Mathias and Don Lodowick.

BARABAS.
Why, what of them?

2 FRIAR.
I will not say that by a forged challenge they met.

BARABAS (*aside to* ITHAMORE).
She has confessed, and we are both undone,
My bosom inmate; but I must dissemble.—
Oh holy friars, the burthen of my sins
Lie heavy on my soul; then pray you tell me,
Is't not too late now to turn Christian?
I have been zealous in the Jewish faith,
Hard-hearted to the poor, a covetous wretch,
That would for lucre's sake have sold my soul.
A hundred for a hundred ° I have ta'en;
And now for store of wealth may I compare
With all the Jews in Malta; but what is wealth?
I am a Jew, and therefore am I lost.
Would penance serve to atone for this my sin,
I could afford to whip myself to death.

ITHAMORE.
And so could I; but penance will not serve.

BARABAS.
To fast, to pray, and wear a shirt of hair,

54. A hundred . . . hundred: 100% interest

And on my knees creep to Jerusalem.
Cellars of wine, and sollars° full of wheat,
Warehouses stuffed with spices and with drugs,
Whole chests of gold, in bullion and in coin,
Besides I know not how much weight in pearl
Orient and round, have I within my house;
At Alexandria, merchandise unsold:
But yesterday two ships went from this town,
Their voyage will be worth ten thousand crowns.
In Florence, Venice, Antwerp, London, Seville,
Frankfort, Lubeck, Moscow, and where not,
Have I debts owing; and in most of these,
Great sums of money lying in the banco;
All this I'll give to some religious house
So I may be baptized and live therein.

1 FRIAR.
Oh good Barabas come to our house.

2 FRIAR.
Oh no, good Barabas come to our house.
And Barabas, you know—

BARABAS.
I know that I have highly sinned,
You shall convert me, you shall have all my wealth.

1 FRIAR.
Oh Barabas, their laws are strict.

BARABAS.
I know they are, and I will be with you.

2 FRIAR.
They wear no shirts, and they go barefoot too.

BARABAS.
Then 'tis not for me; and I am resolved
You shall confess me, and have all my goods.

1 FRIAR.
Good Barabas come to me.

BARABAS.
You see I answer him, and yet he stays;
Rid him away, and go you home with me.

1 FRIAR.
I'll be with you tonight.

BARABAS.
Come to my house at one o'clock this night.

1 FRIAR.
You hear your answer, and you may be gone.

63. sollars: elevated granaries

2 FRIAR.
Why go get you away.
1 FRIAR.
I will not go for thee.
2 FRIAR.
Not, then I'll make thee rogue.
1 FRIAR.
How, dost call me rogue?
[*Fight.*]
ITHAMORE.
Part 'em, master, part 'em.
BARABAS.
This is mere frailty, brethren, be content.
Friar Barnardine go you with Ithamore.
You know my mind, let me alone with him.
1 FRIAR.
Why does he go to thy house, let him begone.
BARABAS.
I'll give him something and so stop his mouth.
[*Exeunt* ITHAMORE *and* 2 FRIAR.]
I never heard of any man but he
Maligned the order of the Jacobins:
But do you think that I believe his words?
Why brother you converted Abigail;
And I am bound in charity to requite it,
And so I will, oh Jacomo, fail not but come.
1 FRIAR.
But Barabas who shall be your godfathers?
For presently you shall be shrived.
BARABAS.
Marry the Turk shall be one of my godfathers,
But not a word to any of your covent.
1 FRIAR.
I warrant thee, Barabas.
[*Exit.*]
BARABAS.
So now the fear is past, and I am safe:
For he that shrived her is within my house.
What if I murdered him ere Jacomo comes?
Now I have such a plot for both their lives,
As never Jew nor Christian knew the like.
One turned my daughter, therefore he shall die;
The other knows enough to have my life,
Therefore 'tis not requisite he should live.
But are not both these wise men to suppose
That I will leave my house, my goods, and all,

To fast and be well whipped; I'll none of that.
Now Friar Barnardine I come to you,
I'll feast you, lodge you, give you fair words,
And after that, I and my trusty Turk—
No more but so: it must and shall be done.
Ithamore, tell me, is the friar asleep?
[*Enter* ITHAMORE.]

ITHAMORE.
Yes; and I know not what the reason is:
Do what I can he will not strip himself,
Nor go to bed, but sleeps in his own clothes;
I fear me he mistrusts what we intend.

BARABAS.
No, 'tis an order which the friars use.
Yet if he knew our meanings, could he scape?

ITHAMORE.
No, none can hear him, cry he ne'er so loud.

BARABAS.
Why true, therefore did I place him there:
The other chambers open towards the street.

ITHAMORE.
You loiter, master, wherefore stay we thus?
Oh how I long to see him shake his heels.

BARABAS.
Come on, sirrah,
Off with your girdle, make a handsome noose;
Friar, awake.

2 FRIAR.
What, do you mean to strangle me?

ITHAMORE.
Yes, 'cause you use to confess.

BARABAS.
Blame not us but the proverb, "confess and be hanged." Pull hard.

2 FRIAR.
What, will you have my life?

BARABAS.
Pull hard, I say, you would have had my goods.

ITHAMORE.
Ay, and our lives too, therefore pull amain.
'Tis neatly done, sir, here's no print at all.

BARABAS.
Then is it as it should be, take him up.

ITHAMORE.
Nay, master, be ruled by me a little; so, let him lean upon his staff; excellent, he stands as if he were begging of bacon.

BARABAS.
Who would not think but that this friar lived?
What time o' night is't now, sweet Ithamore?

ITHAMORE.
Towards one.
[*Enter* 1 FRIAR.]

BARABAS.
Then will not Jacomo be long from hence.
[*Exeunt* BARABAS *and* ITHAMORE.]

1 FRIAR.
This is the hour
Wherein I shall proceed; oh happy hour,
Wherein I shall convert an infidel,
And bring his gold into our treasury.
But soft, is not this Barnardine? It is:
And understanding I should come this way,
Stands here o' purpose, meaning me some wrong,
And intercept my going to the Jew.
Barnardine;
Wilt thou not speak? Thou think'st I see thee not;
Away, I'd wish thee, and let me go by.
No, wilt thou not? Nay then I'll force my way;
And see, a staff stands ready for the purpose.
As thou lik'st that, stop me another time.
[*Strike him, he falls. Enter* BARABAS *and* ITHAMORE.]

BARABAS.
Why how now Jacomo, what hast thou done?

1 FRIAR.
Why stricken him that would have struck at me.

BARABAS.
Who is it? Barnardine? Now out alas, he's slain.

ITHAMORE.
Ay, master, he's slain; look how his brains drop out on's nose.

1 FRIAR.
Good sirs I have done't, but nobody knows it but you two, I may escape.

BARABAS.
So might my man and I hang with you for company.

ITHAMORE.
No, let us bear him to the magistrates.

1 FRIAR.
Good Barabas let me go.

BARABAS.
No, pardon me, the law must have his course.
I must be forced to give in evidence,

That being importuned by this Barnardine
To be a Christian, I shut him out,
And there he sat. Now I to keep my word,
And give my goods and substance to your house,
Was up thus early, with intent to go
Unto your friary because you stayed.

ITHAMORE.
Fie upon 'em, master, will you turn Christian, when holy friars turn devils and murder one another?

BARABAS.
No, for this example I'll remain a Jew:
Heaven bless me; what, a friar a murderer?
When shall you see a Jew commit the like?

ITHAMORE.
Why a Turk could ha' done no more.

BARABAS.
Tomorrow is the sessions; you shall to it.
Come Ithamore, let's help to take him hence.

1 FRIAR.
Villains, I am a sacred person, touch me not.

BARABAS.
The law shall touch you, we'll but lead you, we:
'Las I could weep at your calamity.
Take in the staff too, for that must be shown:
Law wills that each particular be known.
[*Exeunt.*]

Scene 2

Enter BELLAMIRA *and* PILIA-BORZA

BELLAMIRA.
Pilia-Borza, didst thou meet with Ithamore?

PILIA-BORZA.
I did.

BELLAMIRA.
And didst thou deliver my letter?

PILIA-BORZA.
I did.

BELLAMIRA.
And what think'st thou, will he come?

PILIA-BORZA.
I think so, and yet I cannot tell, for at the reading of the letter, he looked like a man of another world.

BELLAMIRA.
Why so?

PILIA-BORZA.
That such a base slave as he should be saluted by such a tall man as I am, from such a beautiful dame as you.

BELLAMIRA.
And what said he?

PILIA-BORZA.
Not a wise word, only gave me a nod, as who should say, Is it even so? And so I left him, being driven to a non-plus at the critical aspect of my terrible countenance.

BELLAMIRA.
And where didst meet him?

PILIA-BORZA.
Upon mine own freehold within forty foot of the gallows, conning his neck-verse° I take it, looking of a friar's execution, whom I saluted with an old hempen° proverb, *Hodie tibi, cras mihi,*° and so I left him to the mercy of the hangman. But the exercise being done, see where he comes.

[*Enter* ITHAMORE.]

ITHAMORE.
I never knew a man take his death so patiently as this friar; he was ready to leap off ere the halter was about his neck: and when the hangman had put on his hempen tippet, he made such haste to his prayers, as if he had had another cure° to serve; well, go whither he will, I'll be none of his followers in haste. And now I think on't, going to the execution, a fellow met me with a muschatoes° like a raven's wing, and a dagger with a hilt like a warming-pan, and he gave me a letter from one Madam Bellamira, saluting me in such sort as if he had meant to make clean my boots with his lips; the effect was, that I should come to her house. I wonder what the reason is; it may be she sees more in me than I can find in myself: for she writes further, that she loves me ever since she saw me, and who would not require such love? Here's her house, and here she comes, and now would I were gone, I am not worthy to look upon her.

PILIA-BORZA.
This is the gentleman you writ to.

ITHAMORE (*aside*).
Gentleman, he flouts me, what gentry can be in a poor Turk of ten pence? I'll be gone.

IV.2. **17. neck-verse:** Latin to test criminals claiming benefit of clergy in an effort to escape hanging. **18. hempen:** hangman's rope **18–19. Hodie . . . mihi:** Today you, tomorrow me **24. cure:** parish **26. muschatoes:** moustache

BELLAMIRA.
Is't not a sweet-faced youth, Pilia-Borza?

ITHAMORE (*aside*).
Again, sweet youth;—Did not you, sir, bring the sweet youth a letter?

PILIA-BORZA.
I did sir, and from this gentlewoman, who as myself, and the rest of the family, stand or fall at your service.

BELLAMIRA.
Though woman's modesty should hale me back,
I can withhold no longer; welcome sweet love.

ITHAMORE (*aside*).
Now am I clean, or rather foully out of the way.

BELLAMIRA.
Whither so soon?

ITHAMORE (*aside*).
I'll go steal some money from my master to make me handsome.—
Pray pardon me, I must go see a ship discharged.

BELLAMIRA.
Canst thou be so unkind to leave me thus?

PILIA-BORZA.
And ye did but know how she loves you, sir—

ITHAMORE.
Nay, I care not how much she loves me; sweet Allamira, would I had my master's wealth for thy sake.

PILIA-BORZA.
And you can have it, sir, and if you please.

ITHAMORE.
If 'twere above ground I could, and would have it; but he hides and buries it up as partridges do their eggs, under the earth.

PILIA-BORZA.
And is't not possible to find it out?

ITHAMORE.
By no means possible.

BELLAMIRA (*aside*).
What shall we do with this base villain then?

PILIA-BORZA (*aside*).
Let me alone, do but you speak him fair:—
But you know some secrets of the Jew, which if they were revealed, would do him harm.

ITHAMORE.
Ay, and such as—Go to, no more, I'll make him send me half he has, and glad he scapes so too. Pen and ink:
I'll write unto him, we'll have money straight.

PILIA-BORZA.
Send for a hundred crowns at least.

ITHAMORE.

Ten hundred thousand crowns. (*He writes.*) 'Master Barabas—'

PILIA-BORZA.

Write not so submissively, but threatening him.

ITHAMORE.

'Sirrah Barabas, send me a hundred crowns.'

PILIA-BORZA.

Put in two hundred at least.

ITHAMORE.

'I charge thee send me three hundred by this bearer, and this shall be your warrant; if you do not, no more but so.'

PILIA-BORZA.

Tell him you will confess.

ITHAMORE.

'Otherwise I'll confess all.' Vanish and return in a twinkle.

PILIA-BORZA.

Let me alone, I'll use him in his kind.

[*Exit.*]

ITHAMORE.

Hang him Jew.

BELLAMIRA.

Now, gentle Ithamore, lie in my lap.
Where are my maids? Provide a running° banquet;
Send to the merchant, bid him bring me silks,
Shall Ithamore my love go in such rags?

ITHAMORE.

And bid the jeweller come hither too.

BELLAMIRA.

I have no husband, sweet, I'll marry thee.

ITHAMORE.

Content, but we will leave this paltry land,
And sail from hence to Greece, to lovely Greece,
I'll be thy Jason, thou my golden fleece!
Where painted carpets o'er the meads are hurled,
And Bacchus' vineyards over-spread the world,
Where woods and forests go in goodly green,
I'll be Adonis, thou shalt be Love's Queen.
The meads, the orchards, and the primrose lanes,
Instead of sedge and reed, bear sugar canes.
Thou in those groves, by Dis° above,
Shalt live with me and be my love.

BELLAMIRA.

Whither will I not go with gentle Ithamore?

76. running: instant **91. Dis:** *Pluto* (actually the god of the underworld)

[*Enter* PILIA-BORZA.]

ITHAMORE.

How now? Hast thou the gold?

PILIA-BORZA.

Yes.

ITHAMORE.

But came it freely, did the cow give down her milk freely?

PILIA-BORZA.

At reading of the letter, he stared and stamped, and turned aside, I took him by the beard, and looked upon him thus; told him he were best to send it, then he hugged and embraced me.

ITHAMORE.

Rather for fear than love.

PILIA-BORZA.

Then like a Jew he laughed and jeered, and told me he loved me for your sake, and said what a faithful servant you had been.

ITHAMORE.

The more villain he to keep me thus: here's goodly 'parel, is there not?

PILIA-BORZA.

To conclude, he gave me ten crowns.

ITHAMORE.

But ten? I'll not leave him worth a grey groat. Give me a ream of paper, we'll have a kingdom of gold for't.

PILIA-BORZA.

Write for five hundred crowns.

ITHAMORE (*writes*).

'Sirrah Jew, as you love your life send me five hundred crowns, and give the bearer a hundred.' Tell him I must have't.

PILIA-BORZA.

I warrant your worship shall have't.

ITHAMORE.

And if he ask why I demand so much, tell him, I scorn to write a line under a hundred crowns.

PILIA-BORZA.

You'd make a rich poet, sir. I am gone.

[*Exit.*]

ITHAMORE.

Take thou the money, spend it for my sake.

BELLAMIRA.

'Tis not thy money, but thy self I weigh:
Thus Bellamira esteems of gold;
[*Throws it aside.*]
But thus of thee.
[*Kisses him.*]

ITHAMORE.

That kiss again, she runs division of° my lips. What an eye she casts on me! It twinkles like a star.

BELLAMIRA.

Come my dear love, let's in and sleep together.

ITHAMORE.

Oh that ten thousand nights were put in one, that we might sleep seven years together afore we wake.

BELLAMIRA.

Come amorous wag, first banquet and then sleep.

[*Exeunt.*]

Scene 3

Enter BARABAS *reading a letter*

BARABAS.

'Barabas send me three hundred crowns.'
Plain Barabas: oh that wicked courtesan!
He was not wont to call me Barabas.
'Or else I will confess': ay, there it goes:
But if I get him, *coupe de gorge* for that.
He sent a shaggy tottered staring slave,
That when he speaks, draws out his grisly beard,
And winds it twice or thrice about his ear;
Whose face has been a grind-stone for men's swords,
His hands are hacked, some fingers cut quite off;
Who when he speaks, grunts like a hog, and looks
Like one that is employed in catzerie,°
And cross-biting,° such a rogue
As is the husband to a hundred whores:
And I by him must send three hundred crowns.
Well, my hope is, he will not stay there still;
And when he comes—Oh that he were but here!

[*Enter* PILIA-BORZA.]

PILIA-BORZA.

Jew, I must ha' more gold.

BARABAS.

Why, want'st thou any of thy tale?°

116. runs divisions of: plays tunes on

IV.3. **12. catzerie:** pimping **13. cross-biting:** cheating **19. tale:** amount

PILIA-BORZA.
No; but three hundred will not serve his turn.

BARABAS.
Not serve his turn, sir?

PILIA-BORZA.
No sir; and therefore I must have five hundred more.

BARABAS.
I'll rather—

PILIA-BORZA.
Oh good words, sir, and send it you were best; see, there's his letter.

BARABAS.
Might he not as well come as send? Pray bid him come and fetch it; what he writes for you, ye shall have straight.

PILIA-BORZA.
Ay, and the rest too, or else—

BARABAS (*aside*).
I must make this villain away:—Please you dine with me, sir, and you shall be most heartily (*Aside.*) poisoned.

PILIA-BORZA.
No, god-a-mercy, shall I have these crowns?

BARABAS.
I cannot do it, I have lost my keys.

PILIA-BORZA.
Oh, if that be all, I can pick ope your locks.

BARABAS.
Or climb up to my counting-house window: you know my meaning.

PILIA-BORZA.
I know enough, and therefore talk not to me of your counting-house; the gold, or know Jew it is in my power to hang thee.

BARABAS (*aside*).
I am betrayed.—
'Tis not five hundred crowns that I esteem,
I am not moved at that: this angers me,
That he who knows I love him as myself
Should write in this imperious vein. Why sir,
You know I have no child, and unto whom
Should I leave all but unto Ithamore?

PILIA-BORZA.
Here's many words but no crowns; the crowns.

BARABAS.
Command me to him, sir, most humbly,
And unto your good mistress as unknown.

PILIA-BORZA.
Speak, shall I have 'em, sir?

BARABAS.
Sir here they are.
(*Aside.*) Oh that I should part with so much gold!—
Here take 'em, fellow, with as good a will—
(*Aside.*) As I would see thee hanged;—oh, love stops my breath:
I never loved man servant as I do Ithamore.

PILIA-BORZA.
I know it, sir.

BARABAS.
Pray when, sir, shall I see you at my house?

PILIA-BORZA.
Soon enough to your cost, sir; fare you well.
[*Exit.*]

BARABAS.
Nay to thine own cost, villain, if thou com'st.
Was ever Jew tormented as I am?
To have a shag-rag knave to come convey
Three hundred crowns, and then five hundred crowns?
Well, I must seek a means to rid 'em all,
And presently: for in his villainy
He will tell all he knows and I shall die for't.
I have it.
I will in some disguise go see the slave,
And how the villain revels with my gold.
[*Exit.*]

Scene 4

Enter BELLAMIRA, ITHAMORE, PILIA-BORZA

BELLAMIRA.
I'll pledge thee, love, and therefore drink it off.

ITHAMORE.
Say'st thou me so? Have at it; and do you hear?
[*Whispers to her.*]

BELLAMIRA.
Go to, it shall be so.

ITHAMORE.
Of that condition I will drink it up. Here's to thee.

BELLAMIRA.
Nay, I'll have all or none.

ITHAMORE.
There, if thou lov'st me do not leave a drop.

BELLAMIRA.
Love thee, fill me three glasses.

ITHAMORE.
Three and fifty dozen, I'll pledge thee.

PILIA-BORZA.
Knavely spoke, and like a knight at arms.

ITHAMORE.
Hey *Rivo Castiliano,* a man's a man.

BELLAMIRA.
Now to the Jew.

ITHAMORE.
Ha! To the Jew, and send me money you were best.

PILIA-BORZA.
What wouldst thou do if he should send thee none?

ITHAMORE.
Do nothing; but I know what I know, he's a murderer.

BELLAMIRA.
I had not thought he had been so brave a man.

ITHAMORE.
You knew Mathias and the Governor's son, he and I killed 'em both, and yet never touched 'em.

PILIA-BORZA.
Oh bravely done.

ITHAMORE.
I carried the broth that poisoned the nuns, and he and I—snicle! hand to! fast!—strangled a friar.

BELLAMIRA.
You two alone.

ITHAMORE.
We two, and 'twas never known, nor never shall be for me.

PILIA-BORZA (*aside*).
This shall with me unto the Governor.

BELLAMIRA (*aside*).
And fit it should: but first let's ha' more gold.
Come gentle Ithamore, lie in my lap.

ITHAMORE.
Love me little, love me long, let music rumble,
Whilst I in thy incony° lap do tumble.

[*Enter* BARABAS *with a lute, disguised.*]

BELLAMIRA.
A French musician, come let's hear your skill?

BARABAS.
Must tuna my lute for sound, twang twang first.

IV.4. **27. incony:** sexy

ITHAMORE.
Wilt drink Frenchman, here's to thee with a—Pox on this drunken hiccup.

BARABAS.
Gramercy, monsieur.

BELLAMIRA.
Prithee, Pilia-Borza, bid the fiddler give me the posy in his hat there.

PILIA-BORZA.
Sirrah, you must give my mistress your posy.

BARABAS.
A vôtre commandement, madame.

BELLAMIRA.
How sweet, my Ithamore, the flowers smell.

ITHAMORE.
Like thy breath, sweetheart, no violet like 'em.

PILIA-BORZA.
Foh, methinks they stink like a hollyhock.

BARABAS (*aside*).
So, now I am revenged upon 'em all.
The scent thereof was death, I poisoned it.

ITHAMORE.
Play, fiddler, or I'll cut your cats' guts into chitterlings.

BARABAS.
Pardonnez moi, be no in tune yet; so now, now all be in.

ITHAMORE.
Give him a crown, and fill me out more wine.

PILIA-BORZA.
There's two crowns for thee, play.

BARABAS (*aside*).
How liberally the villain gives me mine own gold.

PILIA-BORZA.
Methinks he fingers very well.

BARABAS (*aside*).
So did you when you stole my gold.

PILIA-BORZA.
How swift he runs.

BARABAS (*aside*).
You run swifter when you threw my gold out of my window.

BELLAMIRA.
Musician, hast been in Malta long?

BARABAS.
Two, three, four month, madame.

ITHAMORE.
Dost not know a Jew, one Barabas?

BARABAS.

Very mush, monsieur, you no be his man?

PILIA-BORZA.

His man.

ITHAMORE.

I scorn the peasant, tell him so.

BARABAS (*aside*).

He knows it already.

ITHAMORE.

'Tis a strange thing of that Jew, he lives upon pickled grasshoppers, and sauced mushrumbs.

BARABAS (*aside*).

What a slave's this! The Governor feeds not as I do.

ITHAMORE.

He never put on clean shirt since he was circumcised.

BARABAS (*aside*).

Oh rascal! I change myself twice a day.

ITHAMORE.

The hat he wears, Judas left under the elder when he hanged himself.

BARABAS (*aside*).

'Twas sent me for a present from the Great Cham.°

PILIA-BORZA.

A nasty slave he is; whither now, fiddler?

BARABAS.

Pardonnez moi, monsieur, me be no well.

[*Exit.*]

PILIA-BORZA.

Farewell fiddler. One letter more to the Jew.

BELLAMIRA.

Prithee sweet love, one more, and write it sharp.

ITHAMORE.

No, I'll send by word of mouth now; bid him deliver thee a thousand crowns, by the same token, that the nuns loved rice, that Friar Barnardine slept in his own clothes, any of 'em will do it.

PILIA-BORZA.

Let me alone to urge it now I know the meaning.

ITHAMORE.

The meaning has a meaning; come let's in:
To undo a Jew is charity, and not sin.

[*Exeunt.*]

63. Great Cham: Emperor of Tartary

ACT V

Scene 1

Enter GOVERNOR, KNIGHTS, MARTIN DEL BOSCO *and* OFFICERS

GOVERNOR.
Now, gentlemen, betake you to your arms,
And see that Malta be well fortified;
And it behoves you to be resolute;
For Calymath having hovered here so long,
Will win the town, or die before the walls.

KNIGHT.
And die he shall, for we will never yield.
[*Enter* BELLAMIRA, PILIA-BORZA.]

BELLAMIRA.
Oh bring us to the Governor.

GOVERNOR.
Away with her, she is a courtesan.

BELLAMIRA.
Whate'er I am, yet Governor hear me speak;
I bring thee news by whom thy son was slain:
Mathias did it not, it was the Jew.

PILIA-BORZA.
Who, besides the slaughter of these gentlemen,
Poisoned his own daughter and the nuns,
Strangled a friar, and I know not what
Mischief beside.

GOVERNOR.
Had we but proof of this.

BELLAMIRA.
Strong proof, my lord, his man's now at my lodging
That was his agent, he'll confess it all.

GOVERNOR.
Go fetch him straight.
[*Exeunt* OFFICERS.]
I always feared that Jew.
[*Enter* OFFICERS *with* BARABAS *and* ITHAMORE.]

BARABAS.
I'll go alone, dogs do not hale me thus.

ITHAMORE.

Nor me neither, I cannot out-run you constable—Oh my belly.

BARABAS (*aside*).

One dram of powder more had made all sure;
What a damned slave was I!

GOVERNOR.

Make fires, heat irons, let the rack be fetched.

KNIGHT.

Nay stay, my lord, 't may be he will confess.

BARABAS.

Confess; what mean you, lords, who should confess?

GOVERNOR.

Thou and thy Turk; 'twas you that slew my son.

ITHAMORE.

Guilty, my lord, I confess; your son and Mathias
Were both contracted unto Abigail.
'A forged a counterfeit challenge.

BARABAS.

Who carried that challenge?

ITHAMORE.

I carried it, I confess, but who writ it? Marry even he that strangled Barnardine, poisoned the nuns, and his own daughter.

GOVERNOR.

Away with him, his sight is death to me.

BARABAS.

For what? You men of Malta, hear me speak;
She is a courtesan, and he a thief,
And he my bondman, let me have law,
For none of this can prejudice my life.

GOVERNOR.

Once more away with him; you shall have law.

BARABAS.

Devils do your worst, I'll live in spite of you.
As these have spoke so be it to their souls:
(*Aside.*) I hope the poisoned flowers will work anon.

[*Exeunt* OFFICERS *with* BARABAS, ITHAMORE, BELLAMIRA *and* PILIA-BORZA.]

[*Enter* MATHIAS'S MOTHER.]

MOTHER.

Was my Mathias murdered by the Jew?
Ferneze, 'twas thy son that murdered him.

GOVERNOR.

Be patient, gentle madam, it was he,
He forged the daring challenge made them fight.

MOTHER.
Where is the Jew, where is that murderer?

GOVERNOR.
In prison till the law has passed on him.
[*Enter* OFFICER.]

OFFICER.
My lord, the courtesan and her man are dead;
So is the Turk, and Barabas the Jew.

GOVERNOR.
Dead?

OFFICER.
Dead, my lord, and here they bring his body.
[*Enter* OFFICERS, *carrying* BARABAS *as dead.*]

BOSCO.
This sudden death of his is very strange.

GOVERNOR.
Wonder not at it, sir, the heavens are just.
Their deaths were like their lives, then think not of 'em.
Since they are dead, let them be burièd.
For the Jew's body, throw that o'er the walls,
To be a prey for vultures and wild beasts.
So, now away and fortify the town.
[*Exeunt all except* BARABAS.]

BARABAS.
What, all alone? Well fare sleepy drink.
I'll be revenged on this accursèd town;
For by my means Calymath shall enter in.
I'll help to slay their children and their wives,
To fire the churches, pull their houses down,
Take my goods too, and seize upon my lands.
I hope to see the Governor a slave,
And, rowing in a galley, whipped to death.
[*Enter* CALYMATH, BASSOES, TURKS.]

CALYMATH.
Whom have we there, a spy?

BARABAS.
Yes, my good lord, one that can spy a place
Where you may enter, and surprise the town.
My name is Barabas; I am a Jew.

CALYMATH.
Art thou that Jew whose goods we heard were sold
For tribute-money?

BARABAS.
The very same, my lord:
And since that time they have hired a slave, my man,

To accuse me of a thousand villainies.
I was imprisonèd, but scaped their hands.

CALYMATH.
Didst break prison?

BARABAS.
No, no:
I drank of poppy and cold mandrake juice;
And being asleep, belike they thought me dead,
And threw me o'er the walls: so, or how else,
The Jew is here, and rests at your command.

CALYMATH.
'Twas bravely done: but tell me, Barabas,
Canst thou, as thou reportest, make Malta ours?

BARABAS.
Fear not, my lord, for here against the sluice,
The rock is hollow, and of purpose digged,
To make a passage for the running streams
And common channels of the city.
Now whilst you give assault unto the walls,
I'll lead five hundred soldiers through the vault,
And rise with them i' th' middle of the town,
Open the gates for you to enter in,
And by this means the city is your own.

CALYMATH.
If this be true, I'll make thee Governor.

BARABAS.
And if it be not true, then let me die.

CALYMATH.
Thou'st doomed thyself; assault it presently.
[*Exeunt.*]

Scene 2

Alarms. Enter TURKS, BARABAS, *with* GOVERNOR *and* KNIGHTS *prisoners.*

CALYMATH.
Now vail your pride you captive Christians,
And kneel for mercy to your conquering foe.
Now where's the hope you had of haughty Spain?
Ferneze, speak, had it not been much better
T'have kept thy promise than be thus surprised?

GOVERNOR.
What should I say, we are captives and must yield.

CALYMATH.

Ay, villains, you must yield, and under Turkish yokes
Shall groaning bear the burden of our ire;
And Barabas, as erst we promised thee,
For thy desert we make thee Governor;
Use them at thy discretion.

BARABAS.

Thanks, my lord.

GOVERNOR.

Oh fatal day to fall into the hands
Of such a traitor and unhallowed Jew!
What greater misery could heaven inflict?

CALYMATH.

'Tis our command: and Barabas, we give
To guard thy person, these our Janizaries:
Intreat them well, as we have usèd thee.
And now, brave Bassoes, come, we'll walk about
The ruined town, and see the wrack we made.
Farewell brave Jew, farewell great Barabas.

[*Exeunt* CALYMATH *and* BASSOES.]

BARABAS.

May all good fortune follow Calymath.
And now, as entrance to our safety,
To prison with the Governor and these
Captains, his consorts and confederates.

GOVERNOR.

Oh villain, heaven will be revenged on thee.

[*Exeunt all except* BARABAS.]

BARABAS.

Away, no more, let him not trouble me.
Thus hast thou gotten, by thy policy,
No simple place, no small authority.
I now am Governor of Malta; true,
But Malta hates me, and in hating me
My life's in danger, and what boots it thee
Poor Barabas, to be the Governor,
When as thy life shall be at their command?
No, Barabas, this must be looked into;
And since by wrong thou got'st authority,
Maintain it bravely by firm policy,
At least unprofitably lose it not:
For he that liveth in authority,
And neither gets him friends, nor fills his bags,
Lives like the ass that Aesop speaketh of,
That labors with a load of bread and wine,

And leaves it off to snap on thistle tops:
But Barabas will be more circumspect.
Begin betimes, occasion's bald° behind,
Slip not thine opportunity, for fear too late
Thou seek'st for much, but canst not compass it.
Within here!

[*Enter* GOVERNOR *with a* GUARD.]

GOVERNOR.
My lord?

BARABAS.
Ay, lord, thus slaves will learn.
Now Governor—Stand by there, wait within—
[*Exeunt* GUARD.]
This is the reason that I sent for thee;
Thou seest thy life, and Malta's happiness,
Are at my arbitrement; and Barabas
At his discretion may dispose of both.
Now tell me, Governor, and plainly too,
What think'st thou shall become of it and thee?

GOVERNOR.
This, Barabas: since things are in thy power,
I see no reason but of Malta's wrack,
Nor hope of thee but extreme cruelty,
Nor fear I death, nor will I flatter thee.

BARABAS.
Governor, good words, be not so furious;
'Tis not thy life which can avail me aught,
Yet you do live, and live for me you shall;
And as for Malta's ruin, think you not
'Twere slender policy for Barabas
To dispossess himself of such a place?
For sith, as once you said, within this isle
In Malta here, that I have got my goods,
And in this city still have had success,
And now at length am grown your Governor,
Yourselves shall see it shall not be forgot:
For as a friend not known but in distress,
I'll rear up Malta now remediless.

GOVERNOR.
Will Barabas recover Malta's loss?
Will Barabas be good to Christians?

BARABAS.
What wilt thou give me, Governor, to procure

V.2. **45. occasion's bald:** The back of opportunity's head is bald and therefore hard to grasp after it has passed.

A dissolution of the slavish bands
Wherein the Turk hath yoked your land and you?
What will you give me if I render you
The life of Calymath, surprise his men,
And in an out-house of the city shut
His soldiers, till I have consumed 'em all with fire?
What will you give him that procureth this?

GOVERNOR.
Do but bring this to pass which thou pretendest,
Deal truly with us as thou intimatest,
And I will send amongst the citizens
And by my letters privately procure
Great sums of money for thy recompense—
Nay more, do this, and live thou Governor still.

BARABAS.
Nay, do thou this, Ferneze, and be free.
Governor, I enlarge thee, live with me,
Go walk about the city, see thy friends:
Tush, send not letters to 'em, go thyself,
And let me see what money thou canst make;
Here is my hand that I'll set Malta free.
And thus we cast it: to a solemn feast
I will invite young Selim-Calymath,
Where be thou present only to perform
One stratagem that I'll impart to thee,
Wherein no danger shall betide thy life,
And I will warrant Malta free for ever.

GOVERNOR.
Here is my hand, believe me, Barabas,
I will be there, and do as thou desirest.
When is the time?

BARABAS.
Governor, presently.
For Calymath, when he hath viewed the town,
Will take his leave and sail toward Ottoman.

GOVERNOR.
Then will I, Barabas, about this coin,
And bring it with me to thee in the evening.

BARABAS.
Do so, but fail not; now farewell Ferneze.
[*Exit* GOVERNOR.]
And thus far roundly goes the business:
Thus loving neither, will I live with both,
Making a profit of my policy;
And he from whom my most advantage comes,

Shall be my friend.
This is the life we Jews are used to lead;
And reason too, for Christians do the like.
Well, now about effecting this device:
First to surprise great Selim's soldiers,
And then to make provision for the feast,
That at one instant all things may be done.
My policy detests prevention.°
To what event my secret purpose drives,
I know; and they shall witness with their lives.
[*Exit.*]

Scene 3

Enter CALYMATH, BASSOES

CALYMATH.
Thus have we viewed the city, seen the sack,
And caused the ruins to be new repaired,
Which with our bombards' shot and basilisks',
We rent in sunder at our entry:
Two lofty turrets that command the town.
And now I see the situation,
And how secure this conquered island stands
Invironed with the Mediterranean Sea,
Strong countermured with other petty isles;
And toward Calabria backed by Sicily,
Where Syracusian Dionysius reigned;
I wonder how it could be conquered thus.
[*Enter a* MESSENGER.]

MESSENGER.
From Barabas, Malta's Governor, I bring
A message unto mighty Calymath;
Hearing his sovereign was bound for sea,
To sail to Turkey, to great Ottoman,
He humbly would intreat your majesty
To come and see his homely citadel,
And banquet with him ere thou leav'st the isle.

CALYMATH.
To banquet with him in his citadel?
I fear me, messenger, to feast my train
Within a town of war so lately pillaged,

123. prevention: early countermeasures

Will be too costly and too troublesome:
Yet would I gladly visit Barabas,
For well has Barabas deserved of us.

MESSENGER.
Selim, for that, thus saith the Governor,
That he hath in store a pearl so big,
So precious, and withal so orient,
As be it valued but indifferently,
The price thereof will serve to entertain
Selim and all his soldiers for a month;
Therefore he humbly would intreat your highness
Not to depart till he has feasted you.

CALYMATH.
I cannot feast my men in Malta walls,
Except he place his tables in the streets.

MESSENGER.
Know, Selim, that there is a monastery
Which standeth as an out-house to the town;
There will he banquet them, but thee at home,
With all thy bassoes and brave followers.

CALYMATH.
Well, tell the Governor we grant his suit,
We'll in this summer evening feast with him.

MESSENGER.
I shall, my lord.
[*Exit.*]

CALYMATH.
And now, bold bassoes, let us to our tents,
And meditate how we may grace us best
To solemnize our Governor's great feast.
[*Exeunt.*]

Scene 4

Enter GOVERNOR, KNIGHTS, MARTIN DEL BOSCO

GOVERNOR.
In this, my countrymen, be ruled by me,
Have special care that no man sally forth
Till you shall hear a culverin discharged
By him that bears the linstock,° kindled thus;

V.4. **4. linstock:** firing stick

Then issue out and come to rescue me,
For happily I shall be in distress,
Or you releasèd of this servitude.

1 KNIGHT.
Rather than thus to live as Turkish thralls,
What will we not adventure?

GOVERNOR.
On then, begone.

KNIGHTS.
Farewell, grave Governor.
[*Exeunt.*]

Scene 5

Enter BARABAS *with a hammer above, very busy; and* CARPENTERS.

BARABAS.
How stand the cords? How hang these hinges, fast?
Are all the cranes and pulleys sure?

CARPENTER.
All fast.

BARABAS.
Leave nothing loose, all levelled to my mind.
Why now I see that you have art indeed.
There, carpenters, divide that gold amongst you:
Go swill in bowls of sack and muscadine:
Down to the cellar, taste of all my wines.

CARPENTERS.
We shall, my lord, and thank you.
[*Exeunt* CARPENTERS.]

BARABAS.
And if you like them, drink your fill and die:
For so I live, perish may all the world.
Now Selim-Calymath return me word
That thou wilt come, and I am satisfied.
[*Enter* MESSENGER.]
Now sirrah, what, will he come?

MESSENGER.
He will; and has commanded all his men
To come ashore, and march through Malta streets,
That thou mayst feast them in thy citadel.

BARABAS.
Then now are all things as my wish would have 'em,
There wanteth nothing but the Governor's pelf,
And see he brings it.
[*Enter* GOVERNOR.]
Now, Governor, the sum.

GOVERNOR.
With free consent a hundred thousand pounds.

BARABAS.
Pounds, say'st thou, Governor? Well, since it is no more,
I'll satisfy myself with that; nay, keep it still,
For if I keep not promise, trust not me.
And Governor, now partake my policy:
First for his army they are sent before,
Entered the monastery, and underneath
In several places are field-pieces pitched,
Bombards, whole barrels full of gunpowder,
That on the sudden shall dissever it,
And batter all the stones about their ears,
Whence none can possibly escape alive:
Now as for Calymath and his consorts,
Here have I made a dainty gallery,
The floor whereof, this cable being cut,
Doth fall asunder; so that it doth sink
Into a deep pit past recovery.
Here, hold that knife, and when thou seest he comes,
And with his bassoes shall be blithely set,
A warning-piece shall be shot off from the tower,
To give thee knowledge when to cut the cord,
And fire the house; say, will not this be brave?

GOVERNOR.
Oh excellent! Here, hold thee, Barabas,
I trust thy word, take what I promised thee.

BARABAS.
No, Governor, I'll satisfy thee first,
Thou shalt not live in doubt of any thing.
Stand close, for here they come. (GOVERNOR *withdraws.*)
Why, is not this
A kingly kind of trade to purchase towns
By treachery, and sell 'em by deceit?
Now tell me, worldlings, underneath the sun,
If greater falsehood ever has been done.
[*Enter* CALYMATH *and* BASSOES.]

CALYMATH.
Come, my companion bassoes, see I pray

How busy Barabas is there above
To entertain us in his gallery;
Let us salute him. Save thee, Barabas.

BARABAS.
Welcome great Calymath.

GOVERNOR (*Aside*).
How the slave jeers at him!

BARABAS.
Will't please thee, mighty Selim-Calymath,
To ascend our homely stairs?

CALYMATH.
Ay, Barabas, come bassoes, attend.

GOVERNOR (*coming forward*).
Stay, Calymath;
For I will show thee greater courtesy
Than Barabas would have afforded thee.

KNIGHT (*within*).
Sound a charge there.

[*A charge, the cable cut, a cauldron discovered into which* BARABAS *falls.*]

[*Enter* KNIGHTS *and* MARTIN DEL BOSCO.]

CALYMATH.
How now, what means this?

BARABAS.
Help, help me, Christians, help.

GOVERNOR.
See Calymath, this was devised for thee.

CALYMATH.
Treason, treason bassoes, fly.

GOVERNOR.
No, Selim, do not fly;
See his end first, and fly then if thou canst.

BARABAS.
Oh help me, Selim, help me, Christians.
Governor, why stand you all so pitiless?

GOVERNOR.
Should I in pity of thy plaints or thee,
Accursed Barabas, base Jew, relent?
No, thus I'll see thy treachery repaid,
But wish thou hadst behaved thee otherwise.

BARABAS.
You will not help me then?

GOVERNOR.
No, villain, no.

BARABAS.
And villains, know you cannot help me now.
Then Barabas breathe forth thy latest fate,
And in the fury of thy torments, strive
To end thy life with resolution.
Know, Governor, 'twas I that slew thy son;
I framed the challenge that did make them meet.
Know, Calymath, I aimed thy overthrow,
And had I but escaped this stratagem,
I would have brought confusion on you all,
Damned Christians, dogs, and Turkish infidels,
But now begins the extremity of heat
To pinch me with intolerable pangs:
Die life, fly soul, tongue curse thy fill and die.
[*Dies.*]

CALYMATH.
Tell me, you Christians, what doth this portend?

GOVERNOR.
This train° he laid to have intrapped thy life;
Now Selim note the unhallowed deeds of Jews:
Thus he determined to have handled thee,
But I have rather chose to save thy life.

CALYMATH.
Was this the banquet he prepared for us?
Let's hence, lest further mischief be pretended.

GOVERNOR.
Nay, Selim, stay, for since we have thee here,
We will not let thee part so suddenly:
Besides, if we should let thee go, all's one,
For with thy galleys could'st thou not get hence,
Without fresh men to rig and furnish them.

CALYMATH.
Tush, Governor, take thou no care for that,
My men are all aboard,
And do attend my coming there by this.

GOVERNOR.
Why, heard'st thou not the trumpet sound a charge?

CALYMATH.
Yes, what of that?

GOVERNOR.
Why then the house was fired,
Blown up, and all thy soldiers massacred.

V.5. **93. train:** plot

CALYMATH.
Oh monstrous treason!
GOVERNOR.
A Jew's courtesy:
For he that did by treason work our fall,
By treason hath delivered thee to us.
Know therefore, till thy father hath made good
The ruins done to Malta and to us,
Thou canst not part: for Malta shall be freed,
Or Selim ne'er return to Ottoman.
CALYMATH.
Nay rather, Christians, let me go to Turkey,
In person there to mediate your peace;
To keep me here will nought advantage you.
GOVERNOR.
Content thee, Calymath, here thou must stay,
And live in Malta prisoner; for come all the world
To rescue thee, so will we guard us now,
As sooner shall they drink the ocean dry,
Than conquer Malta, or endanger us.
So march away, and let due praise be given
Neither to fate nor fortune, but to heaven.
[*Exeunt.*]

CRITICAL COMMENTARY

The first major dramatist of the second great theatrical era in the West was Christopher Marlowe, who was born some two thousand years after Sophocles. Like Shakespeare he was born in 1564 into a middle-class English family, went through the local schools, got a fellowship to Cambridge to study for the ministry, but in college began writing erotic verse, and upon graduating gave up the church for the London stage. His four major plays (*Tamburlaine, Edward II, Dr. Faustus, The Jew of Malta*) were all different, all unmistakably his, and all highly successful. His career ended abruptly when he was twenty-nine. At the end of a day spent eating, drinking, and talking with companions in a tavern, he was stabbed in the eye. The connections between his life and his genius for the theater are unclear. It was sensed at the time that he had a tough, questioning, unconventional mind; some took comfort in moralizing the manner of his death: See, he got it right in the head! But somehow he had learned to make full use of the big, bare, intimate, flexibly "modern" Elizabethan stage, and he had mastered a rich, wide-ranging theatrical language.

The language tells us how to take the ghost of Machiavelli who introduces *The Jew of Malta.* The tone is wonderfully tricky. Come off it, he says good-naturedly, we all know that I am admired by those who hate me most. And after a few shockers, he concludes with elaborate humility as if in the presence of expert Machiavellians: "I come not, I, to read a lecture here in Britain." The layered tones come through simultaneously—amiable, high-spirited, illusionless, impudent—and prepare us to hear and see what happens next.

The curtains of the inner stage part, and Barabas is discovered in his counting house. Alerted by the Prologue and guided by a voice that is often carelessly over-ample, we sense that Barabas is improvising the role of the big-time international businessman, complete with exotic port names, rare products, and appropriate lingo. As we listen to our affluent, red-wigged, bottle-nosed friend, three small nervous Jews enter with orders to report to the Senate. Now Barabas' roles begin to multiply. Within a single line he patronizes and reassures his second-rate compatriots and clowns out of the corner of his mouth to us. A wink of the eye changes the leader of the Jewish community into the stock victim of comic big-headedness.

The Government is a tricky Christian crowd, but theatrically it is uncomplicated compared to Barabas. Ferneze and the Senators are simply respectable Machiavellians of the stripe implied by the Prologue and described more explicitly and smugly by Barabas:

> For I can see no fruit in all their faith,
> But malice, falsehoods, and excessive pride,
> Which methinks fits not their profession.

It is really not very difficult to see through Ferneze, although debunking a pious fraud always gives one a feeling of heady sophistication; but it is difficult to describe a duplicity that is relatively easy to act. Theatrically, Ferneze is constructed on the elementary principle of never giving the victim a word or act that does not tell against him. He is simply perfect, letter-perfect.

Barabas, on the other hand, is extraordinarily complex theatrically, and his two major roles are logically irreconcilable. On the one hand, he is the traditional Jewish victim of the hypocritical Christian majority; on the other hand, he is a partner with Ferneze in an indivisible military-industrial complex, and this general duplicity overrides the division into Jew, Gentile, and Turk. The discrimination, from this view, is against the whole human race. Barabas appears to fly apart as a character because he is overloaded, but in fact he is never unified as a character. His unity is that of a performer of theatrical assignments, beginning with his portrayal of the Big Businessman. The multiplicity of assignments next explodes into the Farcical Revenger, which has theatrical unity and no character to worry about. He is empty of character because nothing can hurt him. One moment he is beating the ground, he and his only daughter ruined forever; the next moment he is as rich as before, no more harmed than if he had been knocked through a brick wall in an old movie.

The tone of farce controls the emotional effect of Barabas as Revenger. The interlocking acts of violence on the road to vengeance appear as gags. He coaches and rehearses his daughter's two suitors until they run each other through with the split-second precision of a comedy act. His murder of his daughter would be tragic by itself, but a whole convent down the drain with poisoned porridge is hilarious. The two friars, likewise, come through not as victims but as members of a four-man comedy team performing a slapstick routine with broadly satiric overtones. The climax is a Joe Cook special. Barabas has labored on our behalf with incredible energy, setting up one gag after another, improvising with whatever is at hand. The crazy pace accelerates until finally the whole town is rigged like a gigantic Rube Goldberg contraption, with old Barabas high above the stage and hammering like mad, surrounded by cords, hinges, cranes, and pulleys. The gun is fired, the cable cut, and the trap door sprung. Barabas treads water long enough to curse the Establishment, and then the stage recedes, with the great men still jockeying for position and giving "due . . . praise to heaven."

Does it mean anything? Is it terribly serious? Black comedy? Adolescent? Bizarre? Does the increasing speed and complexity of farce generate a kind of significant hysteria? Does the play say something about the moral emptiness of Machiavellian actions, the endlessly repetitive and spasmodic nature of policy? How does Ithamore fit into the play? He starts off as a promising apprentice Machiavellian, but somehow he misses the point and ends up as just an amiable slob. Did he make the mistake of thinking that Machiavellianism is a means to an end, like making money and drinking with the girls, rather than an end in itself?

What happens in class is not what happens on the stage. In class you look at the professor; at the play you look at a red-wigged Jew with an enormous fake nose. Even a modernized Barabas is grossly theatrical: " 'the big extrovert,' 'famous, cosmopolitan, influential, and successful,' 'suavely groomed, the forelock tipped with silver,' " radiating the "assurance and self-satisfaction of the successful tycoon." (James L. Smith, "*The Jew of Malta* in the Theater," *Christopher Marlowe,* Mermaid Commentaries, 1968) What is one to make of this crude insistence on the stereotype of prejudice, the coarse indifference to decent feelings, the vulgar disregard of normal motivation and response? Here are some comments that bear on such questions.

> Barabas . . . is conscious of being hated, and wants to be loved. To be loved—yes, that desire is his secret shame, the tragic weakness of a character whose wickedness is otherwise unflawed. His hatred is the bravado of the outsider whom nobody loves, and his revenges are compensatory efforts to supply people with good reasons for hating him. Poor Barabas, poor old rich man! That he should end by trusting anybody, least of all the one man who wronged him in the beginning! . . . The original miscalculation of Barabas was his failure to reckon with love. Then Abigail, sincerely professing the vows she had taken before out of policy, declared that she had found no love on earth. Having lost her, holding himself apart from the "multitude" of Jews, Barabas must be his own sole friend. . . . Yet he would like to win friends; he needs a confidant; and for a while he views Ithamore, much too trustingly, as his "second self." It is the dilemma of *unus contra mundum,* of the egoist who cannot live with others or without them. Since he conspires against them, they are right to combine against him; but their combinations frequently break down, for each of them is equally self-centered. . . . When every man looks out for himself alone and looks with suspicion on every other man, the ego is

isolated within a vicious circle of mutual distrust. The moral of the drama could be the motto of Melville's *Confidence-Man,* "No Trust." Without trust, sanctions are only invoked to be violated; men live together, not in a commonwealth, but in an acquisitive society, where they behave like wolves to their fellow men. (Harry Levin, *The Overreacher,* 1964, p. 78)

Almost all these trends—the comic exposure of rapacity, the politic abuse of religion, and the assault upon gentile complacency—run in one channel in the play's second scene, a passage that deserves detailed scrutiny, not least for its sharp exposure of the ruinous assumptions that have underlain the history of anti-Semitism: the assumption for instance that the Jews, being alien and accursed, represent a kind of National Deficit Liquidation Fund which can be drawn upon in any crisis; the assumption that their very presence in the community is the cause of ill-fortune, and, conversely, that when a national disaster occurs, it may be traced directly to the activity of the Jews; that Christians, as the chosen people, are the divinely appointed scourge of the wickedness of the rejected people; and that the Jews are collectively accountable for the blood-guilt invoked by their forbears who crucified the Messiah. . . . Part of the scene's mastery resides in the subtle gradations of tone—the elevation of moral sentiment varying directly with the speaker's rapacity, politeness being merely a function of greed, and innocence a preliminary affectation. Ferneze opens with suave urbanity—"Hebrews, now come near"—and expostulates mellifluously—"Soft, Barabas. . . ." The Jew counters with a pretended ignorance of their drift which pierces the euphemistic mist, and the First Knight, enraged by Barabas' feigned belief that they are asking him to fight in the army, explodes, "Tut, Jew, we know thou art no soldier;/ Thou are a merchant, and a money'd man,/And 'tis thy money, Barabas, we seek." The swift transition, from surly contempt to an oily servility before the personification of Mammon, represents dramatic economy of a high order. Barabas' tone undergoes a complementary series of transformations: at first affected innocence ("How, my lord! my money!"), it modulates through mock incredulity to moral indignation ("The man who dealeth righteously shall live"), dying away finally in stoical indifference ("take it to you, i' the devil's name"). Ferneze, on the other hand, preserves a uniformly lofty tone—extortion is no occasion for indecorum. . . . He offers the Jew the kind of supercilious mock-explanation that comes naturally to the consciously impregnable when dealing with a helpless victim. . . . It is the timeless voice of pious dissimulation. (Wilbur Sanders, *The Dramatist and the Received Idea,* 1968, pp. 46–47)

What are we being asked to laugh at? Are we being jollied or educated out of Machiavellianism and into the hope that all will be well when prejudice is removed? Is the play saying that life could be as hilarious, creative, and harmless as farce? Or is the prevailing tone tougher than that, almost as if hope were introduced so that the author could laugh at us when he withdraws it? Or is Marlowe getting us to laugh at A so that we will really laugh at B, as seems to be suggested in this comment:

> The actor who is comically one-down is usually the man we take to our hearts. The little fellow who nervously bows himself out of the queenly presence and backs into a window which he topples out of is profoundly discomfited, and then rewarded by our laughter. And it *is* a reward, because we feel more warmly towards him, perhaps with our less official, more indignity-prone selves, and look forward with fearful joy to his next mishap, with the confidence that fortune will be good to him in the end. This is basically a kindly humour, and there is very little of it in Marlowe. But there is also the actor who is comically one-up; he appeals to our heads —except that the head's approval is usually communicated to the heart, and so we find he has some emotional allegiance too. This is so with Barabas. There is a Marlovian complication here, however, in that what one quick-witted part of the head conspires with the heart to support is exactly what another morally-directed part tells the feelings to condemn. Laughter will by-pass that countering reason and carry our inner allegiance into places where we have no sober intention of their going: hence its importance. (J. B. Steane, *Marlowe,* 1965, pp. 171–72)

Useful Criticism

Leech, Clifford, ed. *Marlowe** (Twentieth Century Views). Englewood Cliffs, N.J.: Prentice-Hall, 1964.

Levin, Harry. *The Overreacher.** Boston: Beacon Press, 1964.

Morris, Brian, ed. *Christopher Marlowe** (Mermaid Critical Commentaries). London: Ernest Benn, 1968.

O'Neill, Judith, ed. *Critics on Marlowe.** London: George Allen and Unwin, 1969.

Sanders, Wilbur. *The Dramatist and the Received Idea: Studies in the Plays of Marlowe and Shakespeare.* New York: Cambridge University Press, 1968.

Steane, J. B. *Marlowe.* New York: Cambridge University Press, 1965.

*Tulane Drama Review** (Marlowe Issue), Vol. VII, No. 4, 1964.

* Available in paperback.

THE FIRST PART OF KING HENRY THE FOURTH

William Shakespeare

CHARACTERS

KING HENRY the Fourth

HENRY, Prince of Wales, } the King's sons

LORD JOHN of Lancaster, } the King's sons

EARL OF WESTMORELAND

SIR WALTER BLUNT

THOMAS PERCY, Earl of Worcester

HENRY PERCY, Earl of Northumberland

HENRY PERCY, "HOTSPUR," his son

EDMUND MORTIMER, Earl of March

ARCHIBALD, Earl of Douglas

OWEN GLENDOWER

SIR RICHARD VERNON

RICHARD SCROOP, Archbishop of York

SIR MICHAEL, a friend of the Archbishop of York

SIR JOHN FALSTAFF

POINS

PETO

BARDOLPH

GADSHILL

LADY PERCY, wife of Hotspur, and sister of Mortimer

LADY MORTIMER, daughter of Glendower, and wife of Mortimer

MISTRESS QUICKLY, hostess of the Boar's Head in Eastcheap

LORDS, OFFICERS, SHERIFF, VINTNER, CHAMBERLAIN, DRAWERS, TWO CARRIERS, OSTLER, MESSENGERS, TRAVELLERS, and ATTENDANTS

SCENE

England and Wales.

ACT I

Scene 1

London. The Palace.

Enter the KING, LORD JOHN OF LANCASTER, EARL OF WESTMORELAND, SIR WALTER BLUNT, *with others.*

KING. So shaken as we are, so wan with care,
Find we a time for frighted peace to pant,
And breathe short-winded accents of new broils
To be commenc'd in stronds° afar remote.
No more the thirsty entrance of this soil
Shall daub her lips with her own children's blood,
No more shall trenching war channel her fields,
Nor bruise her flow'rets with the armed hoofs
Of hostile paces. Those opposed eyes,
Which, like the meteors of a troubled heaven,
All of one nature, of one substance bred,
Did lately meet in the intestine shock°
And furious close of civil butchery,
Shall now, in mutual well-beseeming ranks,
March all one way, and be no more oppos'd
Against acquaintance, kindred, and allies.
The edge of war, like an ill-sheathèd knife,
No more shall cut his master. Therefore, friends,
As far as to the sepulchre of Christ—
Whose soldier now, under whose blessed cross
We are impressed and engag'd to fight—
Forthwith a power of English shall we levy,
Whose arms were molded in their mothers' womb
To chase these pagans in those holy fields
Over whose acres walk'd those blessed feet

The Text: This is a modernized version of the 1598 Quarto, the earliest complete edition of the play. It was presumably written and first acted in 1596–97.

I.1. **4. stronds:** shores, countries. At the end of the preceding play, *Richard II,* Henry had vowed to "make a voyage to the Holy Land/To wash this blood (of murdered Richard) off from my guilty hand." **12. intestine shock:** clash of civil war

Which fourteen hundred years ago were nail'd
For our advantage on the bitter cross.
But this our purpose now is twelve month old,
And bootless 'tis to tell you we will go;
Therefor° we meet not now. Then let me hear
Of you, my gentle cousin Westmoreland,
What yesternight our Council did decree
In forwarding this dear expedience.°

WESTMORELAND. My liege, this haste was hot in question,
And many limits of the charge set down
But yesternight, when all athwart there came
A post from Wales, loaden with heavy news,
Whose worst was that the noble Mortimer,°
Leading the men of Herefordshire to fight
Against the irregular° and wild Glendower,
Was by the rude hands of that Welshman taken,
A thousand of his people butchered,
Upon whose dead corpse there was such misuse,
Such beastly shameless transformation,°
By those Welshwomen done, as may not be
Without much shame retold or spoken of.

KING. It seems then that the tidings of this broil
Brake off our business for the Holy Land.

WESTMORELAND. This match'd with other did, my gracious lord,
For more uneven and unwelcome news
Came from the north, and thus it did import:
On Holy-rood day,° the gallant Hotspur there,
Young Harry Percy, and brave Archibald,
That ever valiant and approved Scot,
At Holmedon met, where they did spend
A sad and bloody hour;
As by discharge of their artillery,
And shape of likelihood, the news was told;
For he that brought them, in the very heat
And pride of their contention did take horse,
Uncertain of the issue any way.

KING. Here is a dear, a true industrious friend,

30. Therefor: for that reason **33. forwarding . . . expedience:** making preparations for this urgent expedition **38. Mortimer:** Shakespeare, following Holinshed's *Chronicles,* confuses Edmund Mortimer, Earl of March, and the legal heir to the throne with his uncle, Sir Edmund Mortimer. The latter, commander of the King's forces in the west and brother of Lady Percy was captured by Glendower on June 22, 1402, and married Glendower's daughter. **40. irregular:** guerrilla **44. transformation:** mutilation **52. Holy-rood day:** September 14 (1402).

Sir Walter Blunt, new lighted from his horse,
Stain'd with the variation of each soil
Betwixt that Holmedon and this seat of ours;
And he hath brought us smooth and welcome news.
The Earl of Douglas is discomfited;
Ten thousand bold Scots, two and twenty knights,
Balk'd° in their own blood, did Sir Walter see
On Holmedon's plains; of prisoners Hotspur took
Mordake, Earl of Fife and eldest son
To beaten Douglas, and the Earl of Athol,
Of Murray, Angus, and Menteith:
And is not this an honorable spoil?
A gallant prize? ha, cousin, is it not?

WESTMORELAND. In faith,
It is a conquest for a prince to boast of.

KING. Yea, there thou mak'st me sad, and mak'st me sin
In envy that my Lord Northumberland
Should be the father to so blest a son;
A son who is the theme of honor's tongue,
Amongst a grove the very straightest plant,
Who is sweet Fortune's minion° and her pride;
Whilst I by looking on the praise of him
See riot and dishonor stain the brow
Of my young Harry. O that it could be prov'd
That some night-tripping fairy had exchang'd
In cradle-clothes our children° where they lay,
And call'd mine Percy, his Plantagenet!
Then would I have his Harry, and he mine—
But let him from my thoughts. What think you, coz,
Of this young Percy's pride? The prisoners°
Which he in this adventure hath surpris'd
To his own use he keeps, and sends me word
I shall have none but Mordake, Earl of Fife.

WESTMORELAND. This is his uncle's teaching, this is Worcester,
Malevolent to you in all aspects,
Which makes him prune° himself, and bristle up
The crest of youth against your dignity.

KING. But I have sent for him to answer this;
And for this cause awhile we must neglect

69. Balk'd: piled in ranks, thwarted **82. minion:** favorite **87. children:** In 1403, Prince Hal was actually 14, Hotspur 39, and King Henry 36. **91. prisoners:** Since Mordake alone had royal blood, Henry was getting only the minimum, the letter of the law. **97. prune:** preen

Our holy purpose to Jerusalem.
Cousin, on Wednesday next our Council we
Will hold at Windsor, so inform the lords;
But come yourself with speed to us again,
For more is to be said and to be done
Than out of anger can be uttered.°

WESTMORELAND. I will, my liege.

[*Exeunt.*]

Scene 2

London. An Apartment of the Prince's.

Enter PRINCE OF WALES *and* SIR JOHN FALSTAFF.

FALSTAFF. Now, Hal, what time of day is it, lad?

PRINCE. Thou are so fat-witted with drinking of old sack,° and unbuttoning thee after supper, and sleeping upon benches after noon, that thou hast forgotten to demand that truly which thou wouldst truly know. What a devil hast thou to do with the time of the day? Unless hours were cups of sack, and minutes capons, and clocks the tongues of bawds, and dials° the signs of leaping-houses,° and the blessed sun himself a fair hot wench in flame-coloured taffeta, I see no reason why thou shouldst be so superfluous to demand the time of the day.

FALSTAFF. Indeed, you come near me now, Hal, for we that take purses go by the moon and the seven stars, and not "by Phœbus,° he, that wand'ring knight so fair"; and I prithee sweet wag, when thou art king, as God save thy Grace—Majesty I should say, for grace° thou wilt have none— 14

PRINCE. What, none?

FALSTAFF. No, by my troth, not so much as will serve to be prologue to an egg and butter.°

PRINCE. Well, how then? Come, roundly, roundly.

FALSTAFF. Marry then sweet wag, when thou art king let not us that are

106. uttered: said in public

I.2. **2. sack:** Spanish white wine **7. dials:** sundials **7. leaping-houses:** brothels **11. Phoebus:** sun (Falstaff apparently sings a line from a ballad.) **13. Grace . . . grace:** punningly used as a royal title, a spiritual condition, and a prayer before food **17. egg and butter:** a small Lenten meal.

squires of the night's body be called thieves of the day's beauty:° let us be Diana's foresters, gentlemen of the shade, minions of the moon; and let men say we be men of good government, being governed as the sea is, by our noble and chaste mistress the moon, under whose countenance° we steal.°

PRINCE. Thou sayest well, and it holds well too, for the fortune of us that are the moon's men doth ebb and flow like the sea, being governed as the sea is, by the moon—as for proof now, a purse of gold most resolutely snatched on Monday night, and most dissolutely spent on Tuesday morning, got with swearing "Lay by!", and spent with crying "Bring in!", now in as low an ebb as the foot of the ladder, and by and by in as high a flow as the ridge of the gallows.

FALSTAFF. By the Lord thou say'st true, lad; and is not my hostess of the tavern a most sweet wench?

PRINCE. As the honey of Hybla, my old lad of the castle;° and is not a buffjerkin a most sweet robe of durance?°

FALSTAFF. How now, how now, mad wag? What, in thy quips and thy quiddities? What a plague have I to do with a buffjerkin?

PRINCE. Why, what a pox have I to do with my hostess of the tavern?

FALSTAFF. Well, thou hast called her to a reckoning many a time and oft.

PRINCE. Did I ever call for thee to pay thy part?

FALSTAFF. No, I'll give thee thy due, thou hast paid all there.

PRINCE. Yea, and elsewhere, so far as my coin would stretch, and where it would not I have used my credit.

FALSTAFF. Yea, and so used it that were it not here apparent that thou art heir apparent—But I prithee sweet wag, shall there be gallows standing in England when thou art king? and resolution thus fubbed° as it is with the rusty curb of old father Antic the law? Do not thou when thou art king hang a thief.

PRINCE. No, thou shalt.

FALSTAFF. Shall I? O rare! By the Lord, I'll be a brave° judge!

PRINCE. Thou judgest false already, I mean thou shalt have the hanging of the thieves, and so become a rare hangman.

FALSTAFF. Well, Hal, well; and in some sort it jumps with my humor, as well as waiting in the court, I can tell you.

PRINCE. For obtaining of suits?°

20. night's . . . beauty: punningly, night's-knight's, beauty-body-bawdy-booty **23. countenance:** face and public support **steal:** rob and creep silently **33. castle:** rascal, name of a London brothel, and Falstaff's name (Oldcastle) in another play **34. jerkin . . . durance:** leather coat worn by police, and play on "durance" meaning durable cloth and imprisonment **45. resolution thus fubbed:** manly firmness thus thwarted **49. brave:** splendid **54. suits:** both a petition for favor and clothes, which were the hangman's perquisites

FALSTAFF. Yea, for obtaining of suits, whereof the hangman hath no lean wardrobe. 'Sblood, I am as melancholy as a gib cat, or a lugged bear.

PRINCE. Or an old lion, or a lover's lute.

FALSTAFF. Yea, or the drone of a Lincolnshire bagpipe.

PRINCE. What sayest thou to a hare, or the melancholy of Moor-ditch?°

FALSTAFF. Thou hast the most unsavory similes, and art indeed the most comparative rascalliest sweet young prince. But Hal, I prithee trouble me no more with vanity. I would to God thou and I knew where a commodity of good names were to be bought. An old lord of the Council rated me the other day in the street about you, sir, but I marked him not, and yet he talked very wisely, but I regarded him not, and yet he talked wisely, and in the street too.

PRINCE. Thou didst well, for wisdom cries out in the streets and no man regards it.°

FALSTAFF. O, thou hast damnable iteration,° and art indeed able to corrupt a saint: thou hast done much harm upon me, Hal, God forgive thee for it. Before I knew thee, Hal, I knew nothing, and now am I, if a man should speak truly, little better than one of the wicked. I must give over this life, and I will give it over; by the Lord, and I do not I am a villain, I'll be damned for never a king's son in Christendom.

PRINCE. Where shall we take a purse tomorrow, Jack?

FALSTAFF. 'Zounds, where thou wilt, lad, I'll make one; an I do not, call me villain and baffle° me.

PRINCE. I see a good amendment of life in thee—from praying to purse-taking.

FALSTAFF. Why, Hal, 'tis my vocation, Hal, 'tis no sin for a man to labor in his vocation.°

[*Enter* POINS.]

Poins! Now shall we know if Gadshill have set a match. O, if men were to be saved by merit,° what hole in hell were hot enough for him? This is the most omnipotent villain that ever cried "Stand!" to a true man.

PRINCE. Good morrow, Ned.

56. gib cat: probably a castrated tom cat **lugged:** tied and baited by dogs **60. Moor-ditch:** London sewage ditch **69. wisdom . . . it:** Cf. Proverbs 1:20–24 **70. damnable iteration:** quoting Scripture for an evil end **79. baffle:** publicly disgrace an unworthy knight by hanging him or his shield upside down **83. vocation:** calling; cf. I Corinthians 7:20 (Geneva Bible): "let every man abide in the same vocation wherein he was called." **84. set a match:** thieves' expression for arranging a holdup **85. merit:** good works rather than grace

POINS. Good morrow, sweet Hal. What says Monsieur Remorse? What says Sir John Sack—and Sugar? Jack! how agrees the devil and thee about thy soul,° that thou soldest him on Good Friday last, for a cup of Madeira and a cold capon's leg?

PRINCE. Sir John stands to his word, the devil shall have his bargain, for he was never yet a breaker of proverbs: he will give the devil his due.

POINS. Then art thou damned for keeping thy word with the devil.

PRINCE. Else he had been damned for cozening° the devil.

POINS. But my lads, my lads, tomorrow morning, by four o'clock early at Gad's Hill,° there are pilgrims going to Canterbury with rich offerings, and traders riding to London with fat purses. I have vizards° for you all; you have horses for yourselves. Gadshill lies tonight in Rochester, I have bespoke supper tomorrow night in Eastcheap. We may do it as secure as sleep. If you will go, I will stuff your purses full of crowns; if you will not, tarry at home and be hanged.

FALSTAFF. Hear ye, Yedward, if I tarry at home and go not, I'll hang you for going.

POINS. You will, chops?°

FALSTAFF. Hal, wilt thou make one?

PRINCE. Who, I rob? I a thief? Not I, by my faith.

FALSTAFF. There's neither honesty, manhood, nor good fellowship in thee, nor thou cam'st not of the blood royal,° if thou darest not stand for° ten shillings.

PRINCE. Well then, once in my days I'll be a madcap.

FALSTAFF. Why, that's well said.

PRINCE. Well, come what will, I'll tarry at home.

FALSTAFF. By the Lord, I'll be a traitor then, when thou art king.

PRINCE. I care not.

POINS. Sir John, I prithee leave the Prince and me alone. I will lay him down such reasons for this adventure that he shall go.

FALSTAFF. Well, God give thee the spirit of persuasion, and him the ears of profiting, that what thou speakest may move, and what he hears may be believed, that the true prince may (for recreation sake) prove a false thief, for the poor abuses of the time want countenance.° Farewell, you shall find me in Eastcheap.

PRINCE. Farewell, the latter spring! Farewell, All-hallown° summer!

[*Exit* FALSTAFF.]

POINS. Now, my good sweet honey lord, ride with us tomorrow. I have a jest to execute that I cannot manage alone. Falstaff, Bardolph, Peto,

91. Sack . . . soul: wine, sackcloth, old age for which wine and sugar is the proper drink **96. cozening:** cheating **98. Gad's Hill:** a stretch of the London road near Rochester frequented by robbers **99. vizards:** masks **106. chops:** fat-face **110. royal, stand for:** punning on "royal," a coin worth 10s. and on "stand for," meaning "valued at" and "stand up and fight." **122. want countenance:** lack public support **124. All-hallown:** November 1, Indian summer

and Gadshill shall rob those men that we have already waylaid—yourself and I will not be there; and when they have the booty, if you and I do not rob them, cut this head off from my shoulders.

PRINCE. How shall we part with them in setting forth?

POINS. Why, we will set forth before or after them, and appoint them a place of meeting, wherein it is at our pleasure to fail; and then will they adventure upon the exploit themselves, which they shall have no sooner achieved but we'll set upon them.

PRINCE. Yea, but 'tis like that they will know us by our horses, by our habits, and by every other appointment to be ourselves.

POINS. Tut, our horses they shall not see, I'll tie them in the wood; our vizards we will change after we leave them; and sirrah, I have cases of buckram for the nonce,° to immask our noted outward garments.

PRINCE. Yea, but I doubt they will be too hard for us.

POINS. Well, for two of them, I know them to be as truebred cowards as ever turned back; and for the third, if he fight longer than he sees reason, I'll forswear arms. The virtue of this jest will be the incomprehensible lies that this same fat rogue will tell us when we meet at supper, how thirty at least he fought with, what wards, what blows, what extremities he endured; and in the reproof of this lives the jest.

PRINCE. Well, I'll go with thee; provide us all things necessary, and meet me tomorrow night in Eastcheap; there I'll sup. Farewell.

POINS. Farewell, my lord.

[*Exit.*]

PRINCE. I know you all, and will awhile uphold
The unyok'd humor of your idleness.
Yet herein will I imitate the sun,
Who doth permit the base contagious clouds
To smother up his beauty from the world,
That, when he please again to be himself,
Being wanted he may be more wonder'd at
By breaking through the foul and ugly mists
Of vapors that did seem to strangle him.
If all the year were playing holidays,
To sport would be as tedious as to work;
But when they seldom come, they wish'd-for come,
And nothing pleaseth but rare accidents:
So when this loose behavior I throw off,
And pay the debt I never promised,
By how much better than my word I am,
By so much shall I falsify men's hopes;
And like bright metal on a sullen ground,°

139. cases . . . nonce: coarse linen cloaks for the occasion
167. sullen ground: dark background

My reformation, glitt'ring o'er my fault,
Shall show more goodly and attract more eyes
Than that which hath no foil to set it off.
I'll so offend to make offence a skill,
Redeeming time when men think least I will.
[*Exit.*]

Scene 3

Windsor. The Council Chamber.

Enter the KING, NORTHUMBERLAND, WORCESTER, HOTSPUR, SIR WALTER BLUNT, *with others.*

KING. My blood hath been too cold and temperate,
Unapt to stir at these indignities,
And you have found me°—for accordingly
You tread upon my patience; but be sure
I will from henceforth rather be myself,
Mighty, and to be fear'd, than my condition,
Which hath been smooth as oil, soft as young down,
And therefore lost that title of respect
Which the proud soul ne'er pays but to the proud.

WORCESTER. Our house, my sovereign liege, little deserves
The scourge of greatness to be us'd on it,
And that same greatness too which our own hands
Have holp to make so portly.°

NORTHUMBERLAND. My lord,—

KING. Worcester, get thee gone, for I do see
Danger and disobedience in thine eye.
O sir, your presence is too bold and peremptory,
And majesty might never yet endure
The moody frontier of a servant brow.
You have good leave to leave us; when we need
Your use and counsel we shall send for you.
[*Exit* WORCESTER.]
(*To* NORTHUMBERLAND.) You were about to speak.

NORTHUMBERLAND. Yea, my good lord.
Those prisoners in your Highness' name demanded,
Which Harry Percy here at Holmedon took,
Were, as he says, not with such strength deny'd
As is deliver'd to your Majesty.

I.3. **3. found me:** found me to be so **13. portly:** stately

Either envy therefore, or misprison,°
Is guilty of this fault, and not my son.

HOTSPUR. My liege, I did deny no prisoners,
But I remember, when the fight was done,
When I was dry with rage, and extreme toil,
Breathless and faint, leaning upon my sword,
Came there a certain lord, neat and trimly dress'd,
Fresh as a bridegroom, and his chin new reap'd
Show'd like a stubble-land at harvest-home.
He was perfumed like a milliner,
And 'twixt his finger and his thumb he held
A pouncet-box,° which ever and anon
He gave his nose, and took't away again—
Who therewith angry, when it next came there,
Took it in snuff—and still he smil'd and talk'd;
And as the soldiers bore dead bodies by,
He call'd them untaught knaves, unmannerly,
To bring a slovenly unhandsome corse
Betwixt the wind and his nobility.
With many holiday and lady terms
He question'd me, amongst the rest demanded
My prisoners in your Majesty's behalf.
I then, all smarting with my wounds being cold,
To be so pester'd with a popinjay,
Out of my grief and my impatience
Answer'd neglectingly, I know not what,
He should, or he should not, for he made me mad
To see him shine so brisk, and smell so sweet,
And talk so like a waiting-gentlewoman
Of guns, and drums, and wounds, God save the mark!
And telling me the sovereignest thing on earth
Was parmacity° for an inward bruise,
And that it was great pity, so it was,
This villainous saltpetre should be digg'd
Out of the bowels of the harmless earth,
Which many a good tall° fellow had destroy'd
So cowardly, and but for these vile guns
He would himself have been a soldier.
This bald unjointed chat of his, my lord,
I answer'd indirectly, as I said,
And I beseech you, let not his report

26. envy . . . misprison: malice . . . mistake **37. pouncet-box:** perforated perfume smelling box **57. parmacity:** spermaceti or whale grease **61. tall:** brave and sturdy

Come current for an accusation
Betwixt my love and your high Majesty.

BLUNT. The circumstance consider'd, good my lord,
Whate'er Lord Harry Percy then had said
To such a person, and in such a place,
At such a time, with all the rest retold,
May reasonably die, and never rise
To do him wrong, or any way impeach
What then he said, so he unsay it now.

KING. Why, yet he doth deny his prisoners,
But with proviso and exception,
That we at our own charge shall ransom straight
His brother-in-law, the foolish Mortimer,
Who, on my soul, hath wilfully betray'd
The lives of those that he did lead to fight
Against that great magician, damn'd Glendower,
Whose daughter, as we hear, the Earl of March
Hath lately marry'd. Shall our coffers then
Be empty'd to redeem a traitor home?
Shall we buy treason, and indent with fears°
When they have lost and forfeited themselves?
No, on the barren mountains let him starve;
For I shall never hold that man my friend
Whose tongue shall ask me for one penny cost
To ransom home revolted Mortimer.

HOTSPUR. Revolted Mortimer!
He never did fall off, my sovereign liege,
But by the chance of war. To prove that true
Needs no more but one tongue for all those wounds,
Those mouthèd wounds, which valiantly he took,
When on the gentle Severn's sedgy bank,
In single opposition hand to hand,
He did confound the best part of an hour
In changing hardiment° with great Glendower.
Three times they breath'd, and three times did they drink
Upon agreement of swift Severn's flood,
Who then affrighted with their bloody looks
Ran fearfully among the trembling reeds,
And hid his crisp° head in the hollow bank,
Bloodstainèd with these valiant combatants.
Never did bare and rotten policy
Color her working with such deadly wounds,

86. indent with fears: do business with cowards **100. changing hardiment:** matching blows and valor **105. crisp:** wavy

Nor never could the noble Mortimer
Receive so many, and all willingly:
Then let not him be slander'd with revolt.

KING. Thou dost belie him, Percy, thou dost belie him,
He never did encounter with Glendower:
I tell thee, he durst as well have met the devil alone
As Owen Glendower for an enemy.
Art thou not asham'd? But sirrah, henceforth
Let me not hear you speak of Mortimer.
Send me your prisoners with the speediest means,
Or you shall hear in such a kind from me
As will displease you. My Lord Northumberland:
We license your departure with your son.
Send us your prisoners, or you will hear of it.
[*Exit* KING *with* BLUNT *and train.*]

HOTSPUR. And if the devil come and roar for them
I will not send them. I will after straight
And tell him so, for I will ease my heart,
Albeit I make a hazard of my head.

NORTHUMBERLAND. What, drunk with choler?° Stay, and pause awhile,
Here comes your uncle.
[*Re-enter* WORCESTER.]

HOTSPUR. Speak of Mortimer?
'Zounds, I will speak of him, and let my soul
Want mercy if I do not join with him.
Yea, on his part I'll empty all these veins,
And shed my dear blood, drop by drop in the dust,
But I will lift the down-trod Mortimer
As high in the air as this unthankful King,
As this ingrate and canker'd Bolingbroke.

NORTHUMBERLAND. Brother, the King hath made your nephew mad.

WORCESTER. Who struck this heat up after I was gone?

HOTSPUR. He will forsooth have all my prisoners,
And when I urg'd the ransom once again
Of my wife's brother, then his cheek look'd pale,
And on my face he turn'd an eye of death,
Trembling even at the name of Mortimer.

WORCESTER. I cannot blame him: was not he proclaim'd,
By Richard that dead is, the next of blood?°

NORTHUMBERLAND. He was, I heard the proclamation;
And then it was, when the unhappy King
(Whose wrongs in us God pardon!) did set forth
Upon his Irish expedition;

127. choler: anger **144. next of blood:** heir to the throne

From whence he, intercepted, did return
To be depos'd, and shortly murdered.

WORCESTER. And for whose death we in the world's wide mouth
Live scandaliz'd and foully spoken of.

HOTSPUR. But soft, I pray you, did King Richard then
Proclaim my brother Edmund Mortimer
Heir to the crown?

NORTHUMBERLAND. He did, myself did hear it.

HOTSPUR. Nay, then I cannot blame his cousin King,
That wish'd him on the barren mountains starve.
But shall it be that you that set the crown
Upon the head of this forgetful man,
And for his sake wear the detested blot
Of murderous subornation—shall it be
That you a world of curses undergo,
Being the agents, or base second means,
The cords, the ladder, or the hangman rather?
—O, pardon me, that I descend so low,
To show the line and the predicament
Wherein you range under this subtle King!
Shall it for shame be spoken in these days,
Or fill up chronicles in time to come,
That men of your nobility and power
Did gage them both in an unjust behalf
(As both of you, God pardon it, have done)
To put down Richard, that sweet lovely rose,
And plant this thorn, this canker° Bolingbroke?
And shall it in more shame be further spoken,
That you are fool'd, discarded, and shook off
By him for whom these shames ye underwent?
No, yet time serves wherein you may redeem
Your banish'd honors, and restore yourselves
Into the good thoughts of the world again.
Revenge the jeering and disdain'd contempt
Of this proud King, who studies day and night
To answer all the debt he owes to you,
Even with the bloody payment of your deaths.
Therefore, I say—

WORCESTER. Peace, cousin, say no more.
And now I will unclasp a secret book,
And to your quick-conceiving discontents
I'll read you matter deep and dangerous,

174. canker: hedgerose, worm, ulcer

As full of peril and adventurous spirit
As to o'er-walk a current roaring loud
On the unsteadfast footing of a spear.

HOTSPUR. If he fall in, good night, or sink, or swim!°
Send danger from the east unto the west,
So honor cross it from the north to south,
And let them grapple. O, the blood more stirs
To rouse a lion than to start a hare!

NORTHUMBERLAND. Imagination of some great exploit
Drives him beyond the bounds of patience.

HOTSPUR. By heaven, methinks it were an easy leap
To pluck bright honor from the pale-fac'd moon,
Or dive into the bottom of the deep,
Where fathom-line could never touch the ground,
And pluck up drownèd honor by the locks,
So he that doth redeem her thence might wear
Without corrival all her dignities—
But out upon this half-fac'd fellowship!

WORCESTER. He apprehends a world of figures° here,
But not the form of what he should attend.
Good cousin, give me audience for a while.

HOTSPUR. I cry you mercy.

WORCESTER. Those same noble Scots
That are your prisoners—

HOTSPUR. I'll keep them all;
By God he shall not have a Scot of them,
No, if a Scot would save his soul he shall not.
I'll keep them, by this hand!

WORCESTER. You start away,
And lend no ear unto my purposes:
Those prisoners you shall keep—

HOTSPUR. Nay, I will: that's flat!
He said he would not ransom Mortimer,
Forbade my tongue to speak of Mortimer,
But I will find him when he lies asleep,
And in his ear I'll holla "Mortimer!"
Nay, I'll have a starling shall be taught to speak
Nothing but "Mortimer", and give it him
To keep his anger still in motion.

WORCESTER. Hear you, cousin, a word.

HOTSPUR. All studies here I solemnly defy,
Save how to gall and pinch this Bolingbroke.

192. sink, or swim: doomed whether he sinks or tries to swim **207. figures:** of speech, empty comparisons

And that same sword-and-buckler° Prince of Wales,
But that I think his father loves him not,
And would be glad he met with some mischance—
I would have him poison'd with a pot of ale!

WORCESTER. Farewell, kinsman: I'll talk to you
When you are better temper'd to attend.

NORTHUMBERLAND. Why, what a wasp-stung and impatient fool
Art thou to break into this woman's mood,
Tying thine ear to no tongue but thine own!

HOTSPUR. Why, look you, I am whipp'd and scourg'd with rods,
Nettled, and stung with pismires,° when I hear
Of this vile politician Bolingbroke.
In Richard's time—what do you call the place?
A plague upon it, it is in Gloucestershire—
'Twas where the mad-cap Duke his uncle kept,
His uncle York—where I first bow'd my knee
Unto this king of smiles, this Bolingbroke,
'Sblood, when you and he came back from Ravenspurgh.

NORTHUMBERLAND. At Berkeley castle.

HOTSPUR. You say true.
Why, what a candy deal of courtesy
This fawning greyhound then did proffer me!
"Look when his infant fortune came to age",
And "gentle Harry Percy", and "kind cousin":
O, the devil take such cozeners!—God forgive me!
Good uncle, tell your tale; I have done.

WORCESTER. Nay, if you have not, to it again,
We will stay your leisure.

HOTSPUR. I have done, i'faith.

WORCESTER. Then once more to your Scottish prisoners;
Deliver them up without their ransom straight,
And make the Douglas' son your only mean
For powers in Scotland, which, for divers reasons
Which I shall send you written, be assur'd
Will easily be granted.—(*To* NORTHUMBERLAND.) You, my lord,
Your son in Scotland being thus employ'd,
Shall secretly into the bosom creep
Of that same noble prelate well-belov'd,
The Archbishop.

HOTSPUR. Of York, is it not?

WORCESTER. True, who bears hard

227. sword-and-buckler: low-class swashbuckler, unknightly **237. pismires:** ants **244. Ravensburgh:** Yorkshire port where Bolingbroke landed in 1399 on returning from exile

His brother's death at Bristow, the Lord Scroop.°
I speak not this in estimation,
As what I think might be, but what I know
Is ruminated, plotted, and set down,
And only stays but to behold the face
Of that occasion that shall bring it on.
HOTSPUR. I smell it. Upon my life it will do well!
NORTHUMBERLAND. Before the game is afoot thou still let'st slip.°
HOTSPUR. Why, it cannot choose but be a noble plot;
And then the power of Scotland, and of York,
To join with Mortimer, ha?
WORCESTER. And so they shall.
HOTSPUR. In faith it is exceedingly well aim'd.
WORCESTER. And 'tis no little reason bids us speed,
To save our heads by raising of a head;°
For, bear ourselves as even as we can,
The King will always think him in our debt,
And think we think ourselves unsatisfy'd,
Till he hath found a time to pay us home:
And see already how he doth begin
To make us strangers to his looks of love.
HOTSPUR. He does, he does, we'll be reveng'd on him.
WORCESTER. Cousin, farewell. No further go in this
Than I by letters shall direct your course.
When time is ripe, which will be suddenly,
I'll steal to Glendower, and Lord Mortimer,
Where you, and Douglas, and our powers at once,
As I will fashion it, shall happily meet,
To bear our fortunes in our own strong arms,
Which now we hold at much uncertainty.
NORTHUMBERLAND. Farewell, good brother; we shall thrive, I trust.
HOTSPUR. Uncle, adieu: O, let the hours be short,
Till fields, and blows, and groans applaud our sport!
[*Exeunt.*]

265. Scroop: executed by Henry in 1399 **272. slip:** loose the hounds **278. head:** army

ACT II

Scene 1

Rochester. An Inn Yard.

Enter a CARRIER *with a lantern in his hand.*

FIRST CARRIER. Heigh-ho! An it be not four by the day° I'll be hanged: Charles' wain° is over the new chimney, and yet our horse not packed. What, ostler!

OSTLER (*within*). Anon, anon.

FIRST CARRIER. I prithee, Tom, beat Cut's saddle, put a few flocks in the point;° poor jade is wrung in the withers out of all cess.

[*Enter another* CARRIER.]

SECOND CARRIER. Peas and beans are as dank here as a dog, and that is the next way to give poor jades the bots.° This house is turned upside down since Robin Ostler died.

FIRST CARRIER. Poor fellow never joyed since the price of oats rose, it was the death of him.

SECOND CARRIER. I think this be the most villainous house in all London road for fleas, I am stung like a tench.°

FIRST CARRIER. Like a tench! By the mass, there is ne'er a king christen could be better bit than I have been since the first cock.

SECOND CARRIER. Why, they will allow us ne'er a jordan,° and then we leak in your chimney,° and your chamber-lye° breeds fleas like a loach.

FIRST CARRIER. What, ostler! Come away, and be hanged, come away!

SECOND CARRIER. I have a gammon of bacon and two razes of ginger to be delivered as far as Charing Cross.

FIRST CARRIER. God's body! The turkeys in my pannier are quite starved. What, ostler! A plague on thee, hast thou never an eye in thy head? canst not hear? And 'twere not as good deed as drink to break the pate on thee, I am a very villain. Come, and be hanged! Hast no faith in thee?

[*Enter* GADSHILL.]

II.1. **1. by the day:** A.M **2. Charles' wain:** Big Dipper **6. flocks in the point:** padding in the pommel **9. bots:** worms **13. tench:** a spotted fish which looks flea-bitten **16. jordan:** chamber pot **17. chimney:** fireplace **chamber-lye:** urine

GADSHILL. Good morrow, carriers, what's o'clock?

FIRST CARRIER. I think it be two o'clock.

GADSHILL. I prithee lend me thy lantern to see my gelding in the stable.

FIRST CARRIER. Nay, by God, soft! I know a trick worth two of that, i'faith.

GADSHILL. I pray thee lend me thine.

SECOND CARRIER. Ay, when? Canst tell? Lend me thy lantern, quoth he! Marry I'll see thee hanged first.

GADSHILL. Sirrah carrier, what time do you mean to come to London?

SECOND CARRIER. Time enough to go to bed with a candle, I warrant thee; come, neighbour Mugs, we'll call up the gentlemen, they will along with company, for they have great charge.°

[*Exeunt* CARRIERS.]

GADSHILL. What ho! Chamberlain!

[*Enter* CHAMBERLAIN.]

CHAMBERLAIN. "At hand, quoth pick-purse."

GADSHILL. That's even as fair as "At hand, quoth the chamberlain": for thou variest no more from picking of purses than giving direction doth from laboring; thou layest the plot how.

CHAMBERLAIN. Good morrow, master Gadshill. It holds current that I told you yesternight: there's a franklin in the Wild of Kent hath brought three hundred marks with him in gold, I heard him tell it to one of his company last night at supper, a kind of auditor, one that hath abundance of charge too, God knows what; they are up already, and call for eggs and butter—they will away presently.

GADSHILL. Sirrah, if they meet not with Saint Nicholas' clerks,° I'll give thee this neck.

CHAMBERLAIN. No, I'll none of it, I pray thee keep that for the hangman, for I know thou worshippest Saint Nicholas, as truly as a man of falsehood may.

GADSHILL. What talkest thou to me of the hangman? If I hang, I'll make a fat pair of gallows, for if I hang, old Sir John hangs with me, and thou knowest he is no starveling. Tut, there are other Troyans° that thou dream'st not of, the which for sport sake are content to do the profession some grace, that would (if matters should be looked into) for their own credit sake make all whole. I am joined with no foot-landrakers,° no long-staff sixpenny strikers,° none of these mad mustachio purple-hued maltworms,° but with nobility and tranquillity, burgomasters and great onyers, such as can hold in,° such as will strike sooner than speak, and speak sooner than drink, and drink sooner

37. charge: goods and baggage **49. Saint Nicholas' clerks:** highwaymen **56. Troyans:** Trojans, boon companions **60. foot-landrakers:** footpads **60. long-staff sixpenny strikers:** petty thieves who would pull you from your horse with a hooked stick for a mere sixpence **61. mustachio . . . maltworms:** big-mustached, purple-faced drunks **62. hold in:** keep their mouths shut

than pray—and yet, 'zounds, I lie, for they pray continually to their saint the commonwealth, or rather not pray to her, but prey on her, for they ride up and down on her, and make her their boots.°

CHAMBERLAIN. What, the commonwealth their boots? Will she hold out water in foul way?

GADSHILL. She will, she will, justice hath liquored° her: we steal as in a castle, cock-sure: we have the receipt of fern-seed, we walk invisible.

CHAMBERLAIN. Nay, by my faith, I think you are more beholding to the night than to fern-seed for your walking invisible.

GADSHILL. Give me thy hand, thou shalt have a share in our purchase,° as I am a true man.

CHAMBERLAIN. Nay, rather let me have it, as you are a false thief.

GADSHILL. Go to, *homo* is a common name to all men. Bid the ostler bring my gelding out of the stable. Farewell, you muddy knave.

[*Exeunt.*]

Scene 2

Gad's Hill. The Highway.

Enter PRINCE, POINS, *and* PETO.

POINS. Come, shelter, shelter! I have removed Falstaff's horse, and he frets° like a gummed velvet.

PRINCE. Stand close!

[*They retire.*]

[*Enter* FALSTAFF.]

FALSTAFF. Poins! Poins, and be hanged! Poins!

PRINCE (*coming forward*). Peace, ye fat-kidneyed rascal, what a brawling dost thou keep!

FALSTAFF. Where's Poins, Hal?

PRINCE. He is walked up to the top of the hill; I'll go seek him.

[*Retires.*]

FALSTAFF. I am accursed to rob in that thief's company; the rascal hath removed my horse and tied him I know not where. If I travel but four foot by the squier° further afoot, I shall break my wind. Well, I doubt not but to die a fair death for all this, if I scape hanging for killing that rogue. I have forsworn his company hourly any time this two and twenty years, and yet I am bewitched with the rogue's com-

66. boots: with a pun on booty **69. liquored:** greased **73. purchase:** loot

II.2. **2. frets:** chafes and complains **11. squier:** square, measuring stick

pany. If the rascal have not given me medicines to make me love him, I'll be hanged. It could not be else, I have drunk medicines. Poins! Hal! A plague upon you both! Bardolph! Peto! I'll starve° ere I'll rob a foot further—and 'twere not as good a deed as drink to turn true man, and to leave these rogues, I am the veriest varlet that ever chewed with a tooth. Eight yards of uneven ground is threescore and ten miles afoot with me, and the stony-hearted villains know it well enough. A plague upon it when thieves cannot be true one to another! (*They whistle.*) Whew! A plague upon you all, give me my horse, you rogues, give me my horse and be hanged!

PRINCE (*coming forward*). Peace, ye fat guts, lie down, lay thine ear close to the ground, and list if thou canst hear the tread of travellers.

FALSTAFF. Have you any levers to lift me up again, being down? 'Sblood, I'll not bear my own flesh so far afoot again for all the coin in thy father's exchequer. What a plague mean ye to colt° me thus?

PRINCE. Thou liest, thou are not colted, thou art uncolted.

FALSTAFF. I prithee good Prince Hal, help me to my horse, good king's son.

PRINCE. Out, ye rogue, shall I be your ostler?

FALSTAFF. Hang thyself in thine own heir-apparent garters! If I be ta'en, I'll peach for this. And I have not ballads made on you all, and sung to filthy tunes, let a cup of sack be my poison. When a jest is so forward, and afoot too, I hate it.

[*Enter* GADSHILL *and* BARDOLPH.]

GADSHILL. Stand!

FALSTAFF. So I do, against my will.

POINS. O, 'tis our setter,° I know his voice. (*Coming forward with* PETO.) Bardolph, what news?

BARDOLPH. Case ye, case ye, on with your vizards, there's money of the King's coming down the hill, 'tis going to the King's exchequer.

FALSTAFF. You lie, ye rogue, 'tis going to the King's tavern.

GADSHILL. There's enough to make us all.

FALSTAFF. To be hanged.

PRINCE. Sirs, you four shall front them in the narrow lane; Ned Poins and I will walk lower—if they scape from your encounter, then they light on us.

PETO. How many be there of them?

GADSHILL. Some eight or ten.

FALSTAFF. 'Zounds, will they not rob us?

PRINCE. What, a coward, Sir John Paunch?

FALSTAFF. Indeed, I am not John of Gaunt your grandfather, but yet no coward, Hal.

PRINCE. Well, we leave that to the proof.

17. starve: die **29. colt:** trick **40. setter:** scout

POINS. Sirrah Jack, thy horse stands behind the hedge; when thou need'st him, there thou shalt find him. Farewell, and stand fast.

FALSTAFF. Now cannot I strike him, if I should be hanged.

PRINCE. Ned, where are our disguises?

POINS. Here, hard by, stand close.

[*Exeunt* PRINCE *and* POINS.]

FALSTAFF. Now, my masters, happy man be his dole, say I—every man to his business.

[*Enter the* TRAVELLERS.]

FIRST TRAVELLER. Come, neighbor, the boy shall lead our horses down the hill; we'll walk afoot awhile and ease our legs.

THIEVES. Stand!

SECOND TRAVELLER. Jesus bless us!

FALSTAFF. Strike, down with them, cut the villains' throats! Ah, whoreson caterpillars,° bacon-fed knaves, they hate us youth! Down with them, fleece them!

FIRST TRAVELLER. O, we are undone, both we and ours for ever!

FALSTAFF. Hang ye, gorbellied° knaves, are ye undone? No, ye fat chuffs,° I would your store were here! On, bacons, on! What, ye knaves! young men must live. You are grandjurors,° are ye? We'll jure ye, faith.

[*Here they rob them and bind them. Exeunt.*]

[*Re-enter the* PRINCE *and* POINS, *disguised.*]

PRINCE. The thieves have bound the true men; now could thou and I rob the thieves, and go merrily to London, it would be argument° for a week, laughter for a month, and a good jest for ever.

POINS. Stand close, I hear them coming.

[*They retire.*]

[*Enter the* THIEVES *again.*]

FALSTAFF. Come, my masters, let us share, and then to horse before day; and the Prince and Poins be not two arrant cowards there's no equity stirring; there's no more valor in that Poins than in a wild duck.

[*As they are sharing, the* PRINCE *and* POINS *set upon them.*]

PRINCE. Your money!

POINS. Villains!

[*They all run away, and* FALSTAFF *after a blow or two runs away too, leaving the booty behind them.*]

PRINCE. Got with much ease. Now merrily to horse.
The thieves are all scatter'd and possess'd with fear
So strongly that they dare not meet each other;
Each takes his fellow for an officer!

69. whoreson caterpillars: miserable social parasites **72. gorbellied:** potbellied **73. chuffs:** tightwads **74. grandjurors:** pillars of society **77. argument:** topic of conversation

Away, good Ned—Falstaff sweats to death,
And lards the lean earth as he walks along.
Were't not for laughing I should pity him.

POINS. How the fat rogue roared.

[*Exeunt.*]

Scene 3

Northumberland. Warwick Castle.

Enter HOTSPUR *solus, reading a letter.*

HOTSPUR. "But, for mine own part, my lord, I could be well contented to be there, in respect of the love I bear your house." He could be contented: why is he not then? In respect of the love he bears our house! He shows in this, he loves his own barn better than he loves our house. Let me see some more. "The purpose you undertake is dangerous"—Why, that's certain; 'tis dangerous to take a cold, to sleep, to drink; but I tell you, my lord fool, out of this nettle, danger, we pluck this flower, safety. "The purpose you undertake is dangerous, the friends you have named uncertain, the time itself unsorted, and your whole plot too light, for the counterpoise of so great an opposition." Say you so, say you so? I say unto you again, you are a shallow cowardly hind,° and you lie. What a lack-brain is this! By the Lord, our plot is a good plot, as ever was laid, our friends true and constant: a good plot, good friends, and full of expectation: an excellent plot, very good friends. What a frosty-spirited rogue is this! Why, my Lord of York commends the plot, and the general course of the action. 'Zounds, and I were now by this rascal I could brain him with his lady's fan. Is there not my father, my uncle, and myself? Lord Edmund Mortimer, my Lord of York, and Owen Glendower? Is there not besides the Douglas? Have I not all their letters to meet me in arms by the ninth of the next month, and are they not some of them set forward already? What a pagan rascal is this, an infidel! Ha! You shall see now in very sincerity of fear and cold heart will he to the King, and lay open all our proceedings! O, I could divide myself, and go to buffets, for moving such a dish of skim milk with so honorable an action! Hang him, let him tell the King, we are prepared. I will set forward tonight.

[*Enter* LADY PERCY.]

How now, Kate? I must leave you within these two hours.

II.3. 12. hind: hick

LADY PERCY. O my good lord, why are you thus alone?
For what offence have I this fortnight been
A banish'd woman from my Harry's bed?
Tell me, sweet lord, what is't that takes from thee
Thy stomach,° pleasure, and thy golden sleep?
Why dost thou bend thine eyes upon the earth,
And start so often when thou sit'st alone?
Why hast thou lost the fresh blood in thy cheeks,
And given my treasures and my rights of thee
To thick-ey'd musing and curst melancholy?
In thy faint slumbers I by thee have watch'd,
And heard thee murmur tales of iron wars,
Speak terms of manage to thy bounding steed,
Cry "Courage! To the field!" And thou hast talk'd
Of sallies, and retires, of trenches, tents,
Of palisadoes,° frontiers, parapets,
Of basilisks, of cannon, culverin,
Of prisoners' ransom, and of soldiers slain,
And all the currents of a heady fight.
Thy spirit within thee hath been so at war,
And thus hath so bestirr'd thee in thy sleep,
That beads of sweat have stood upon thy brow
Like bubbles in a late-disturbed stream,
And in thy face strange motions have appear'd,
Such as we see when men restrain their breath
On some great sudden hest.° O, what portents are these?
Some heavy business hath my lord in hand,
And I must know it, else he loves me not.
HOTSPUR. What ho!
[*Enter a* SERVANT.]
Is Gilliams with the packet gone?
SERVANT. He is, my lord, an hour ago.
HOTSPUR. Hath Butler brought those horses from the sheriff?
SERVANT. One horse, my lord, he brought even now.
HOTSPUR. What horse? A roan, a crop-ear is it not?
SERVANT. It is, my lord.
HOTSPUR. That roan shall be my throne.
Well, I will back him straight. O Esperance!°
Bid Butler lead him forth into the park.
[*Exit* SERVANT.]
LADY PERCY. But hear you, my lord.

33. stomach: desire **44. palisadoes:** iron-pointed stakes **54. hest:** demand, resolve **64. Esperance:** part of the Percy motto and battle cry

HOTSPUR. What say'st thou, my lady?
LADY PERCY. What is it carries you away?
HOTSPUR. Why, my horse, my love, my horse.
LADY PERCY. Out, you mad-headed ape!
A weasel hath not such a deal of spleen
As you are toss'd with. In faith,
I'll know your business, Harry, that I will.
I fear my brother Mortimer doth stir
About his title, and hath sent for you
To line° his enterprise. But if you go—
HOTSPUR. So far afoot I shall be weary, love.
LADY PERCY. Come, come, you paraquito, answer me
Directly unto this question that I ask;
In faith, I'll break thy little finger, Harry,
And if thou wilt not tell me all things true.
HOTSPUR. Away,
Away, you trifler! Love? I love thee not,
I care not for thee, Kate; this is no world
To play with mammets,° and to tilt with lips;
We must have bloody noses, and crack'd crowns,
And pass them current too. God's me! my horse!
What say'st thou, Kate? What wouldst thou have with me?
LADY PERCY. Do you not love me? Do you not indeed?
Well, do not then, for since you love me not
I will not love myself. Do you not love me?
Nay, tell me if you speak in jest or no.
HOTSPUR. Come, wilt thou see me ride?
And when I am a-horseback I will swear
I love thee infinitely. But hark you, Kate,
I must not have you henceforth question me
Whither I go, nor reason whereabout.
Whither I must, I must; and, to conclude,
This evening must I leave you, gentle Kate.
I know you wise, but yet no farther wise
Than Harry Percy's wife; constant you are,
But yet a woman; and for secrecy
No lady closer, for I well believe
Thou wilt not utter what thou dost not know;
And so far will I trust thee, gentle Kate.
LADY PERCY. How? so far?
HOTSPUR. Not an inch further. But hark you, Kate,
Whither I go, thither shall you go too:

75. line: support **84. mammets:** dolls

Today will I set forth, tomorrow you.
Will this content you, Kate?

LADY PERCY. It must, of force.

[*Exeunt.*]

Scene 4

Eastcheap. The Boar's Head Tavern.

Enter PRINCE *and* POINS.

PRINCE. Ned, prithee come out of that fat° room, and lend me thy hand to laugh a little.

POINS. Where hast been, Hal?

PRINCE. With three or four loggerheads,° amongst three or fourscore hogsheads. I have sounded the very basestring of humility. Sirrah, I am sworn brother to a leash of drawers,° and can call them all by their christen names, as Tom, Dick, and Francis. They take it already upon their salvation, that though I be but Prince of Wales, yet I am the king of courtesy, and tell me flatly I am no proud Jack like Falstaff, but a Corinthian, a lad of mettle, a good boy (by the Lord, so they call me!), and when I am King of England I shall command all the good lads in Eastcheap. They call drinking deep "dyeing scarlet", and when you breathe in your watering° they cry "Hem!" and bid you "Play it off!" To conclude, I am so good a proficient in one quarter of an hour that I can drink with any tinker in his own language during my life. I tell thee, Ned, thou hast lost much honor that thou wert not with me in this action; but, sweet Ned—to sweeten which name of Ned I give thee this pennyworth of sugar, clapped even now into my hand by an underskinker,° one that never spake other English in his life than "Eight shillings and sixpence", and "You are welcome", with this shrill addition, "Anon, anon, sir! Score a pint of bastard in the Half-moon",° or so. But Ned, to drive away the time till Falstaff come:—I prithee do thou stand in some by-room, while I question my puny drawer to what end he gave me the sugar, and do thou never leave calling "Francis!", that his tale to me may be nothing but "Anon". Step aside, and I'll show thee a precedent.

[POINS *retires.*]

POINS (*within*). Francis!

PRINCE. Thou art perfect.

POINS (*within*). Francis!

II.4. **1. fat:** vat, hot? **4. loggerheads:** blockheads **6. leash of drawers:** trio of waiters **13. watering:** drinking **19. underskinker:** assistant bartender **22. bastard:** sweet Spanish wine **Half-moon:** name of a room

[*Enter* FRANCIS, *a Drawer.*]

FRANCIS. Anon, anon, sir. Look down into the Pomgarnet, Ralph.

PRINCE. Come hither, Francis.

FRANCIS. My lord?

PRINCE. How long hast thou to serve, Francis?

FRANCIS. Forsooth, five years,° and as much as to—

POINS (*within*). Francis!

FRANCIS. Anon, anon, sir.

PRINCE. Five year! By'r lady, a long lease for the clinking of pewter; but Francis, darest thou be so valiant as to play the coward with thy indenture, and show it a fair pair of heels, and run from it?

FRANCIS. O Lord, sir, I'll be sworn upon all the books in England, I could find in my heart—

POINS (*within*). Francis!

FRANCIS. Anon, sir.

PRINCE. How old art thou, Francis?

FRANCIS. Let me see, about Michaelmas next I shall be—

POINS (*within*). Francis!

FRANCIS. Anon, sir—pray stay a little, my lord.

PRINCE. Nay but hark you, Francis, for the sugar thou gavest me, 'twas a pennyworth, was't not?

FRANCIS. O Lord, I would it had been two!

PRINCE. I will give thee for it a thousand pound—ask me when thou wilt, and thou shalt have it.

POINS (*within*). Francis!

FRANCIS. Anon, anon.

PRINCE. Anon, Francis? No, Francis, but tomorrow, Francis; or, Francis, a-Thursday; or indeed, Francis, when thou wilt. But Francis!

FRANCIS. My lord?

PRINCE. Wilt thou rob this leathern-jerkin, crystal-button, not-pated, agate-ring, puke-stocking, caddis-garter, smooth-tongue Spanish pouch?°

FRANCIS. O Lord, sir, who do you mean?

PRINCE. Why then your brown bastard is your only drink: for look you, Francis, your white canvas doublet will sully. In Barbary, sir, it cannot come to so much.

FRANCIS. What, sir?

POINS (*within*). Francis!

PRINCE. Away, you rogue, dost thou not hear them call?

[*Here they both call him; the* DRAWER *stands amazed, not knowing which way to go.*]

[*Enter* VINTNER.]

34. five years: apprenticeships lasted seven years **58–59. leathern-jerkin . . . pouch:** description of a proper innkeeper or vintner: leather jacket, crystal buttons, short hair, big ring, gray woolen stockings, plain garters, smooth-tongued, Spanish leather change pouch

VINTNER. What, stand'st thou still and hear'st such a calling? Look to the guests within. (*Exit* FRANCIS.) My lord, old Sir John with half-a-dozen more are at the door—shall I let them in?

PRINCE. Let them alone awhile, and then open the door. (*Exit* VINTNER.) Poins!

[*Re-enter* POINS.]

POINS. Anon, anon, sir.

PRINCE. Sirrah, Falstaff and the rest of the thieves are at the door; shall we be merry?

POINS. As merry as crickets, my lad; but hark ye, what cunning match have you made with this jest of the drawer: come, what's the issue?

PRINCE. I am now of all humors that have showed themselves humors since the old days of goodman Adam to the pupil age of this present twelve o'clock at midnight.

[*Re-enter* FRANCIS.]

What's o'clock, Francis?

FRANCIS. Anon, anon, sir.

[*Exit.*]

PRINCE. That ever this fellow should have fewer words than a parrot, and yet the son of a woman! His industry is up-stairs and down-stairs, his eloquence the parcel ° of a reckoning. I am not yet of Percy's mind, the Hotspur of the north, he that kills me some six or seven dozen of Scots at a breakfast, washes his hands, and says to his wife, "Fie upon this quiet life, I want work". "O my sweet Harry", says she, "how many hast thou killed today?" "Give my roan horse a drench", says he, and answers, "Some fourteen", an hour after; "a trifle, a trifle". I prithee call in Falstaff; I'll play Percy, and that damned brawn° shall play Dame Mortimer his wife. *Rivo!* says the drunkard: call in Ribs, call in Tallow.

[*Enter* FALSTAFF, GADSHILL, BARDOLPH, *and* PETO; *followed by* FRANCIS, *with wine.*]

POINS. Welcome, Jack, where hast thou been?

FALSTAFF. A plague of all cowards, I say, and a vengeance too, marry and amen! Give me a cup of sack, boy. Ere I lead this life long, I'll sew nether-stocks,° and mend them and foot them too. A plague of all cowards! Give me a cup of sack, rogue; is there no virtue extant?

[*He drinketh.*]

PRINCE. Didst thou never see Titan° kiss a dish of butter (pitiful-hearted Titan!), that melted at the sweet tale of the sun's? If thou didst, then behold that compound.

FALSTAFF. You rogue, here's lime° in this sack too. There is nothing but roguery to be found in villainous man, yet a coward is worse than

84. parcel: items **90. brawn:** fat boar **96. nether-stocks:** stockings **98. Titan:** the sun **101. lime:** used to doctor wine

a cup of sack with lime in it. A villainous coward! Go thy ways, old Jack, die when thou wilt—if manhood, good manhood, be not forgot upon the face of the earth, then am I a shotten° herring. There lives not three good men unhanged in England, and one of them is fat, and grows old. God help the while, a bad world I say. I would I were a weaver; I could sing psalms, or anything. A plague of all cowards, I say still.

PRINCE. How now, wool-sack, what mutter you?

FALSTAFF. A king's son! If I do not beat thee out of thy kingdom with a dagger of lath, and drive all thy subjects afore thee like a flock of wild geese, I'll never wear hair on my face more. You, Prince of Wales!

PRINCE. Why, you whoreson round man, what's the matter?

FALSTAFF. Are not you a coward? Answer me to that—and Poins there?

POINS. 'Zounds, ye fat paunch, and ye call me coward by the Lord I'll stab thee.

FALSTAFF. I call thee coward? I'll see thee damned ere I call thee coward, but I would give a thousand pound I could run as fast as thou canst. You are straight enough in the shoulders, you care not who sees your back. Call you that backing of your friends? A plague upon such backing, give me them that will face me! Give me a cup of sack; I am a rogue if I drunk today.

PRINCE. O villain! Thy lips are scarce wiped since thou drunk'st last.

FALSTAFF. All is one for that. (*He drinketh.*) A plague of all cowards, still say I.

PRINCE. What's the matter?

FALSTAFF. What's the matter? There be four of us here have ta'en a thousand pound this day morning.

PRINCE. Where is it, Jack, where is it?

FALSTAFF. Where is it? Taken from us it is: a hundred upon poor four of us.

PRINCE. What, a hundred, man?

FALSTAFF. I am a rogue if I were not at half-sword° with a dozen of them two hours together. I have scaped by miracle. I am eight times thrust through the doublet, four through the hose, my buckler cut through and through, my sword hacked like a handsaw—*ecce signum!*° I never dealt better since I was a man—all would not do. A plague of all cowards! Let them speak—if they speak more or less than truth, they are villains, and the sons of darkness.

PRINCE. Speak, sirs, how was it?

GADSHILL. We four set upon some dozen—

FALSTAFF. Sixteen at least, my lord.

GADSHILL. And bound them.

105. shotten: roeless and therefore thin **124. half-sword:** at close quarters
127. ecce signum: behold the evidence

PETO. No, no, they were not bound.

FALSTAFF. You rogue, they were bound, every man of them, or I am a Jew else, an Ebrew Jew.

GADSHILL. As we were sharing, some six or seven fresh men set upon us—

FALSTAFF. And unbound the rest, and then come in the other.

PRINCE. What, fought you with them all?

FALSTAFF. All? I know not what you call all, but if I fought not with fifty of them I am a bunch of radish. If there were not two or three and fifty upon poor old Jack, then am I no two-legg'd creature.

PRINCE. Pray God you have not murdered some of them.

FALSTAFF. Nay, that's past praying for, I have peppered two of them. Two I am sure I have paid, two rogues in buckram suits. I tell thee what, Hal, if I tell thee a lie, spit in my face, call me horse. Thou knowest my old ward°—here I lay, and thus I bore my point. Four rogues in buckram let drive at me—

PRINCE. What, four? Thou saidst but two even now.

FALSTAFF. Four, Hal, I told thee four.

POINS. Ay, ay, he said four.

FALSTAFF. These four came all afront, and mainly thrust at me; I made me no more ado but took all their seven points in my target—thus!

PRINCE. Seven? Why, there were but four even now.

FALSTAFF. In buckram?

POINS. Ay, four, in buckram suits.

FALSTAFF. Seven, by these hilts, or I am a villain else.

PRINCE. Prithee let him alone, we shall have more anon.

FALSTAFF. Dost thou hear me, Hal?

PRINCE. Ay, and mark thee too, Jack.

FALSTAFF. Do so, for it is worth the listening to. These nine in buckram that I told thee of—

PRINCE. So, two more already.

FALSTAFF. Their points° being broken—

POINS. Down fell their hose.

FALSTAFF. Began to give me ground; but I followed me close, came in, foot and hand, and, with a thought, seven of the eleven I paid.

PRINCE. O monstrous! Eleven buckram men grown out of two!

FALSTAFF. But as the devil would have it, three misbegotten knaves in Kendal green came at my back and let drive at me, for it was so dark, Hal, that thou couldst not see thy hand.

PRINCE. These lies are like their father that begets them, gross as a mountain, open, palpable. Why, thou clay-brained guts, thou knotty-pated fool, thou whoreson obscene greasy tallow-catch,—

FALSTAFF. What, art thou mad? art thou mad? Is not the truth the truth?

149. ward: fencing stance **166. points:** of swords and also laces to hold up hose

PRINCE. Why, how couldst thou know these men in Kendal green when it was so dark thou couldst not see thy hand? Come, tell us your reason. What sayest thou to this?

POINS. Come, your reason, Jack, your reason.

FALSTAFF. What, upon compulsion? 'Zounds, and I were at the strappado,° or all the racks in the world, I would not tell you on compulsion. Give you a reason on compulsion? If reasons were as plentiful as blackberries, I would give no man a reason upon compulsion, I.

PRINCE. I'll be no longer guilty of this sin. This sanguine coward, this bed-presser, this horse-back-breaker, this huge hill of flesh,—

FALSTAFF. 'Sblood, you starveling, you eel-skin, you dried neat's°-tongue, you bull's-pizzle,° you stock-fish—O for breath to utter what is like thee!—you tailor's-yard, you sheath, you bow-case, you vile standing tuck!°

PRINCE. Well, breathe awhile, and then to it again, and when thou hast tired thyself in base comparisons hear me speak but this.

POINS. Mark, Jack.

PRINCE. We two saw you four set on four, and bound them and were masters of their wealth—mark now how a plain tale shall put you down. Then did we two set on you four, and, with a word, out-faced you from your prize, and have it, yea, and can show it you here in the house. And Falstaff you carried your guts away as nimbly, with as quick dexterity, and roared for mercy, and still run and roared, as ever I heard bull-calf. What a slave art thou to hack thy sword as thou hast done, and then say it was in fight! What trick, what device, what starting°-hole canst thou now find out, to hide thee from this open and apparent shame?

POINS. Come, let's hear, Jack, what trick hast thou now?

FALSTAFF. By the Lord, I knew ye as well as he that made ye. Why, hear you, my masters, was it for me to kill the heir-apparent? should I turn upon the true prince? Why, thou knowest I am as valiant as Hercules: but beware instinct—the lion will not touch the true prince; instinct is a great matter. I was now a coward on instinct. I shall think the better of myself, and thee, during my life—I for a valiant lion, and thou for a true prince. But by the Lord, lads, I am glad you have the money. Hostess, clap to the doors! Watch tonight, pray tomorrow!—Gallants, lads, boys, hearts of gold, all the titles of good fellowship come to you! What, shall we be merry, shall we have a play extempore?

PRINCE. Content, and the argument shall be thy running away.

FALSTAFF. Ah, no more of that, Hal, and thou lovest me.

[*Enter* HOSTESS.]

HOSTESS. O Jesu, my lord the Prince!

183. strappado: torture device for breaking shoulders **188–189. neat's:** ox **pizzle:** penis **191. tuck:** rapier **202. starting:** hiding

PRINCE. How now, my lady the hostess, what say'st thou to me?

HOSTESS. Marry, my lord, there is a nobleman of the court at door would speak with you. He says he comes from your father.

PRINCE. Give him as much as will make him a royal° man, and send him back again to my mother.

FALSTAFF. What manner of man is he?

HOSTESS. An old man.

FALSTAFF. What doth gravity out of his bed at midnight? Shall I give him his answer?

PRINCE. Prithee do, Jack.

FALSTAFF. Faith, and I'll send him packing.

[*Exit.*]

PRINCE. Now, sirs: by'r lady, you fought fair, so did you, Peto, so did you, Bardolph; you are lions too, you ran away upon instinct, you will not touch the true prince, no, fie!

BARDOLPH. Faith, I ran when I saw others run.

PRINCE. Faith, tell me now in earnest, how came Falstaff's sword so hacked?

PETO. Why, he hacked it with his dagger, and said he would swear truth out of England but he would make you believe it was done in fight, and persuaded us to do the like.

BARDOLPH. Yea, and to tickle our noses with spear-grass, to make them bleed, and then to beslubber our garments with it, and swear it was the blood of true men. I did that I did not this seven year before, I blushed to hear his monstrous devices.

PRINCE. O villain, thou stolest a cup of sack eighteen years ago, and wert taken with the manner, and even since thou hast blushed extempore. Thou hadst fire° and sword on thy side, and yet thou ran'st away—what instinct hadst thou for it?

BARDOLPH. My lord, do you see these meteors? do you behold these exhalations?°

PRINCE. I do.

BARDOLPH. What think you they portend?

PRINCE. Hot livers, and cold purses.

BARDOLPH. Choler, my lord, if rightly taken.

PRINCE. No, if rightly taken, halter.°

[*Re-enter* FALSTAFF.]

Here comes lean Jack, here comes bare-bone. How now, my sweet creature of bombast,° how long is't ago, Jack, since thou sawest thine own knee?

FALSTAFF. My own knee? When I was about thy years, Hal, I was not

221. a royal: ten shillings **244. fire:** red face **246–47. meteors . . . exhalations:** bumps on his face **252. rightly:** punning on rightly (accurately, justly), **taken:** (understood, arrested), **halter:** (choler, collar, noose) **254. bombast:** cotton padding

an eagle's talon in the waist; I could have crept into any alderman's thumb-ring. A plague of sighing and grief, it blows a man up like a bladder. There's villainous news abroad: here was Sir John Bracy from your father; you must to the court in the morning. That same mad fellow of the north, Percy, and he of Wales that gave Amamon the bastinado,° and made Lucifer cuckold, and swore the devil his true liegeman upon the cross of a Welsh hook—what a plague call you him?

POINS. Owen Glendower.

FALSTAFF. Owen, Owen, the same; and his son-in-law Mortimer, and old Northumberland, and that sprightly Scot of Scots, Douglas, that runs a-horseback up a hill perpendicular—

PRINCE. He that rides at high speed, and with his pistol kills a sparrow flying.

FALSTAFF. You have hit it.

PRINCE. So did he never the sparrow.

FALSTAFF. Well, that rascal hath good mettle in him, he will not run.

PRINCE. Why, what a rascal art thou then, to praise him so for running!

FALSTAFF. A-horseback, ye cuckoo, but afoot he will not budge a foot.

PRINCE. Yes, Jack, upon instinct.

FALSTAFF. I grant ye, upon instinct. Well, he is there too, and one Mordake, and a thousand blue-caps° more. Worcester is stolen away tonight; thy father's beard is turned white with the news; you may buy land now as cheap as stinking mackerel.

PRINCE. Why then, it is like if there come a hot June, and this civil buffeting hold, we shall buy maidenheads as they buy hob-nails, by the hundreds.

FALSTAFF. By the mass, lad, thou sayest true, it is like we shall have good trading that way. But tell me, Hal, art not thou horrible afeard? Thou being heir apparent, could the world pick thee out three such enemies again, as that fiend Douglas, that spirit Percy, and that devil Glendower? Art thou not horribly afraid? Doth not thy blood thrill at it?

PRINCE. Not a whit, i'faith, I lack some of thy instinct.

FALSTAFF. Well, thou wilt be horribly chid tomorrow when thou comest to thy father. If thou love me practise an answer.

PRINCE. Do thou stand for my father and examine me upon the particulars of my life.

FALSTAFF. Shall I? Content! This chair shall be my state,° this dagger my sceptre, and this cushion my crown.

PRINCE. Thy state is taken for a joint-stool, thy golden sceptre for a leaden dagger, and thy precious rich crown for a pitiful bald crown.

262. Amamon the bastinado: the devil a beating **278. blue-caps:** Scots **295. state:** throne

FALSTAFF. Well, and the fire of grace be not quite out of thee, now shalt thou be moved. Give me a cup of sack to make my eyes look red, that it may be thought I have wept, for I must speak in passion, and I will do it in King Cambyses' vein.°

PRINCE. Well, here is my leg.°

FALSTAFF. And here is my speech. Stand aside, nobility.

HOSTESS. O Jesu, this is excellent sport, i'faith.

FALSTAFF. Weep not, sweet Queen, for trickling tears are vain.

HOSTESS. O the Father, how he holds his countenance!°

FALSTAFF. For God's sake, lords, convey my tristful Queen,
For tears do stop the floodgates of her eyes.

HOSTESS. O Jesu, he doth it as like one of these harlotry players as ever I see!

FALSTAFF. Peace, good pint-pot, peace, good tickle-brain.—Harry, I do not only marvel where thou spendest thy time, but also how thou art accompanied. For though the camomile, the more it is trodden on the faster it grows, yet youth, the more it is wasted the sooner it wears. That thou art my son I have partly thy mother's word, partly my own opinion, but chiefly a villainous trick of thine eye, and a foolish hanging of thy nether lip, that doth warrant me. If then thou be son to me, here lies the point—why, being son to me, art thou so pointed at? Shall the blessed sun of heaven prove a micher° and eat blackberries? A question not to be asked. Shall the son of England prove a thief, and take purses? A question to be asked. There is a thing, Harry, which thou hast often heard of, and it is known to many in our land by the name of pitch. This pitch (as ancient writers do report) doth defile, so doth the company thou keepest. For, Harry, now I do not speak to thee in drink, but in tears; not in pleasure, but in passion; not in words only, but in woes also. And yet there is a virtuous man whom I have often noted in thy company, but I know not his name.

PRINCE. What manner of man, and it like your Majesty?

FALSTAFF. A goodly portly man, i'faith, and a corpulent; of a cheerful look, a pleasing eye, and a most noble carriage; and, as I think, his age some fifty, or by'r lady inclining to threescore; and now I remember me, his name is Falstaff. If that man should be lewdly given, he deceiveth me; for, Harry, I see virtue in his looks. If then the tree may be known by the fruit, as the fruit by the tree, then peremptorily I speak it, there is virtue in that Falstaff; him keep with, the rest banish. And tell me now, thou naughty varlet, tell me where hast thou been this month?

300. vein: bombastic style of Preston's melodramatic *King Cambyses* (1569) **301. leg:** bow **305. holds his countenance:** keeps his expression of stagy majesty **318. micher:** cadger and truant

PRINCE. Dost thou speak like a king? Do thou stand for me, and I'll play my father.

FALSTAFF. Depose me? If thou dost it half so gravely, so majestically, both in word and matter, hang me up by the heels for a rabbit-sucker° or a poulter's hare.

PRINCE. Well, here I am set.

FALSTAFF. And here I stand. Judge, my masters.

PRINCE. Now, Harry, whence come you?

FALSTAFF. My noble lord, from Eastcheap.

PRINCE. The complaints I hear of thee are grievous.

FALSTAFF. 'Sblood, my lord, they are false—nay, I'll tickle ye for a young prince,° i'faith.

PRINCE. Swearest thou, ungracious boy? Henceforth ne'er look on me. Thou art violently carried away from grace, there is a devil haunts thee in the likeness of an old fat man, a tun of man is thy companion. Why dost thou converse with that trunk of humors,° that bolting-hutch° of beastliness, that swollen parcel of dropsies, that huge bombard° of sack, that stuffed cloak-bag of guts, that roasted Manningtree ox with the pudding° in his belly, that reverend vice, that grey iniquity, that father ruffian, that vanity in years? Wherein is he good, but to taste sack and drink it? wherein neat and cleanly, but to carve a capon and eat it? wherein cunning, but in craft? wherein crafty, but in villainy? wherein villainous, but in all things? wherein worthy, but in nothing?

FALSTAFF. I would your Grace would take me with you. Whom means your Grace?

PRINCE. That villainous abominable misleader of youth, Falstaff, that old white-bearded Satan.

FALSTAFF. My lord, the man I know.

PRINCE. I know thou dost.

FALSTAFF. But to say I know more harm in him than in myself were to say more than I know. That he is old, the more the pity, his white hairs do witness it, but that he is, saving your reverence, a whoremaster, that I utterly deny. If sack and sugar be a fault, God help the wicked! If to be old and merry be a sin, then many an old host that I know is damned. If to be fat be to be hated, then Pharaoh's lean kine are to be loved. No, my good lord: banish Peto, banish Bardolph, banish Poins—but for sweet Jack Falstaff, kind Jack Falstaff, true Jack Falstaff, valiant Jack Falstaff, and therefore more valiant, being as he is old Jack Falstaff, banish not him thy Harry's company, banish not him thy Harry's company, banish plump Jack, and banish all the world.

340. rabbit-sucker: baby rabbit **348. for a young prince:** by my impersonation **352. humors:** body fluids, diseases **353. bolting-hutch:** bin to catch siftings **354. bombard:** big wine skin **355. pudding:** stuffed for barbecuing

PRINCE. I do, I will.

[*A knocking heard. Exeunt* HOSTESS, FRANCIS, *and* BARDOLPH.]

[*Re-enter* BARDOLPH, *running.*]

BARDOLPH. O my lord, my lord, the sheriff with a most monstrous watch is at the door.

FALSTAFF. Out, ye rogue! Play out the play! I have much to say in the behalf of that Falstaff.

[*Re-enter the* HOSTESS.]

HOSTESS. O Jesu, my lord, my lord!

PRINCE. Heigh, heigh, the devil rides upon a fiddle-stick, what's the matter?

HOSTESS. The sheriff and all the watch are at the door; they are come to search the house. Shall I let them in?

FALSTAFF. Dost thou hear, Hal? Never call a true piece of gold a counterfeit: thou art essentially made without seeming so.

PRINCE. And thou a natural coward without instinct.

FALSTAFF. I deny your major.° If you will deny the sheriff, so; if not, let him enter. If I become not a cart as well as another man, a plague on my bringing up! I hope I shall as soon be strangled with a halter as another.

PRINCE. Go hide thee behind the arras,° the rest walk up above. Now, my masters, for a true face, and good conscience.

FALSTAFF. Both which I have had, but their date is out, and therefore I'll hide me.

[*Exeunt all but the* PRINCE *and* PETO.]

PRINCE. Call in the sheriff.

[*Enter* SHERIFF *and the* CARRIER.]

Now, master sheriff, what is your will with me?

SHERIFF. First, pardon me, my lord. A hue and cry
Hath follow'd certain men unto this house.

PRINCE. What men?

SHERIFF. One of them is well known, my gracious lord,
A gross fat man.

CARRIER. As fat as butter.

PRINCE. The man I do assure you is not here,
For I myself at this time have employ'd him;
And sheriff, I will engage my word to thee,
That I will by tomorrow dinner-time
Send him to answer thee, or any man,
For anything he shall be charg'd withal;
And so let me entreat you leave the house.

SHERIFF. I will, my lord: there are two gentlemen
Have in this robbery lost three hundred marks.

391. major: major premise, with a pun on mayor **395. arras:** tapestry hanging

PRINCE. It may be so. If he have robb'd these men
He shall be answerable; and so, farewell.
SHERIFF. Good night, my noble lord.
PRINCE. I think it is good morrow, is it not?
SHERIFF. Indeed, my lord, I think it be two o'clock.
[*Exit, with* CARRIER.]

PRINCE. This oily rascal is known as well as Paul's. Go call him forth.

PETO. Falstaff!—Fast asleep behind the arras, and snorting like a horse.

PRINCE. Hark how hard he fetches breath. Search his pockets. (*He searcheth his pockets, and findeth certain papers.*) What hast thou found?

PETO. Nothing but papers, my lord.

PRINCE. Let's see what they be, read them.

PETO (*Reads*).

Item sauce	4d.
Item sack two gallons	5s. 8d.
Item anchovies and sack after supper	2s. 6d.
Item bread	ob.°

PRINCE. O monstrous! but one halfpennyworth of bread to this intolerable deal of sack? What there is else keep close, we'll read it at more advantage. There let him sleep till day; I'll to the court in the morning. We must all to the wars, and thy place shall be honorable. I'll procure this fat rogue a charge of foot, and I know his death will be a march of twelve score. The money shall be paid back again with advantage. Be with me betimes in the morning; and so, good morrow, Peto.

PETO. Good morrow, good my lord.
[*Exeunt.*]

ACT III

Scene 1

Bangor. The Archdeacon's House.

Enter HOTSPUR, WORCESTER, LORD MORTIMER, OWEN GLENDOWER.

MORTIMER. These promises are fair, the parties sure,
And our induction full of prosperous hope.
HOTSPUR. Lord Mortimer, and cousin Glendower, will you sit down?
And uncle Worcester. A plague upon it!

431. ob: obulus, half-penny

I have forgot the map.
GLENDOWER. No, here it is.
Sit, cousin Percy, sit, good cousin Hotspur;
For by that name as oft as Lancaster doth speak of you
His cheek looks pale, and with a rising sigh
He wisheth you in heaven.
HOTSPUR. And you in hell,
As oft as he hears Owen Glendower spoke of.
GLENDOWER. I cannot blame him; at my nativity
The front of heaven was full of fiery shapes,
Of burning cressets,° and at my birth
The frame and huge foundation of the earth
Shak'd like a coward.
HOTSPUR. Why, so it would have done
At the same season if your mother's cat
Had but kitten'd, though yourself had never been born.
GLENDOWER. I say the earth did shake when I was born.
HOTSPUR. And I say the earth was not of my mind,
If you suppose as fearing you it shook.
GLENDOWER. The heavens were all on fire, the earth did tremble—
HOTSPUR. O, then the earth shook to see the heavens on fire,
And not in fear of your nativity.
Diseasèd nature oftentimes breaks forth
In strange eruptions, oft the teeming earth
Is with a kind of colic pinch'd and vex'd
By the imprisoning of unruly wind
Within her womb, which for enlargement striving
Shakes the old beldam° earth, and topples down
Steeples and moss-grown towers. At your birth
Our grandam earth, having this distemp'rature,
In passion shook.
GLENDOWER. Cousin, of many men
I do not bear these crossings; give me leave
To tell you once again that at my birth
The front of heaven was full of fiery shapes,
The goats ran from the mountains, and the herds
Were strangely clamorous to the frighted fields.
These signs have mark'd me extraordinary,
And all the courses of my life do show
I am not in the roll of common men.
Where is he living, clipp'd in with the sea
That chides the banks of England, Scotland, Wales,
Which calls me pupil or hath read to me?

III.1. **13. cressets:** beacons **29. beldam:** grandmother

And bring him out that is but woman's son
Can trace me in the tedious ways of art,
And hold me pace in deep experiments.
HOTSPUR. I think there's no man speaks better Welsh.
I'll to dinner.
MORTIMER. Peace, cousin Percy, you will make him mad.
GLENDOWER. I can call spirits from the vasty deep.
HOTSPUR. Why, so can I, or so can any man,
But will they come when you do call for them?
GLENDOWER. Why, I can teach you, cousin, to command the devil.
HOTSPUR. And I can teach thee, coz, to shame the devil,
By telling truth; tell truth, and shame the devil.
If thou have power to raise him, bring him hither,
And I'll be sworn I have power to shame him hence.
O, while you live, tell truth, and shame the devil!
MORTIMER. Come, come, no more of this unprofitable chat.
GLENDOWER. Three times hath Henry Bolingbroke made head
Against my power, thrice from the banks of Wye
And sandy-bottom'd Severn have I sent him
Bootless home and weather-beaten back.
HOTSPUR. Home without boots, and in foul weather too!
How scapes he agues, in the devil's name?
GLENDOWER. Come, here is the map, shall we divide our right
According to our threefold order ta'en?
MORTIMER. The Archdeacon hath divided it
Into three limits very equally:
England, from Trent and Severn hitherto,
By south and east is to my part assign'd;
All westward, Wales beyond the Severn shore,
And all the fertile land within that bound,
To Owen Glendower; and, dear coz, to you
The remnant northward lying off from Trent.
And our indentures tripartite are drawn,
Which being sealed interchangeably,
(A business that this night may execute)
Tomorrow, cousin Percy, you and I
And my good Lord of Worcester will set forth
To meet your father and the Scottish power,
As is appointed us, at Shrewsbury.
My father Glendower is not ready yet,
Nor shall we need his help these fourteen days.
To GLENDOWER.) Within that space you may have drawn together
Your tenants, friends, and neighboring gentlemen.
GLENDOWER. A shorter time shall send me to you, lords,
And in my conduct shall your ladies come,

From whom you now must steal and take no leave,
For there will be a world of water shed
Upon the parting of your wives and you.

HOTSPUR. Methinks my moiety,° north from Burton here,
In quantity equals not one of yours.
See how this river comes me cranking in,
And cuts me from the best of all my land
A huge half-moon, a monstrous cantle° out.
I'll have the current in this place damm'd up,
And here the smug and silver Trent shall run
In a new channel fair and evenly;
It shall not wind with such a deep indent,
To rob me of so rich a bottom° here.

GLENDOWER. Not wind? It shall, it must—you see it doth.

MORTIMER. Yea,
But mark how he bears his course, and runs me up
With like advantage on the other side,
Gelding the opposed continent as much
As on the other side it takes from you.

WORCESTER. Yea, but a little charge° will trench him here,
And on this north side win this cape of land,
And then he runs straight and even.

HOTSPUR. I'll have it so, a little charge will do it.

GLENDOWER. I'll not have it alter'd.

HOTSPUR. Will not you?

GLENDOWER. No, nor you shall not.

HOTSPUR. Who shall say me nay?

GLENDOWER. Why, that will I.

HOTSPUR. Let me not understand you then, speak it in Welsh.

GLENDOWER. I can speak English, lord, as well as you,
For I was train'd up in the English court,
Where being but young I framèd to the harp
Many an English ditty lovely well,
And gave the tongue a helpful ornament—
A virtue that was never seen in you.

HOTSPUR. Marry and I am glad of it with all my heart!
I had rather be a kitten and cry "mew"
Than one of these same metre ballad-mongers;
I had rather hear a brazen canstick turn'd,°
Or a dry wheel grate on the axle-tree,
And that would set my teeth nothing on edge,
Nothing so much as mincing poetry—

92. moiety: share **96. cantle:** slice **101. bottom:** river valley **108. charge:** expense **125. canstick turn'd:** candlestick polished on a lathe

'Tis like the forc'd gait of a shuffling nag.
GLENDOWER. Come, you shall have Trent turn'd.
HOTSPUR. I do not care, I'll give thrice so much land
To any well-deserving friend;
But in the way of bargain, mark ye me,
I'll cavil on the ninth part of a hair.
Are the indentures drawn? Shall we be gone?
GLENDOWER. The moon shines fair, you may away by night.
I'll haste the writer, and withal
Break with your wives of your departure hence.
I am afraid my daughter will run mad,
So much she doteth on her Mortimer.
[*Exit.*]
MORTIMER. Fie, cousin Percy, how you cross my father!
HOTSPUR. I cannot choose; sometime he angers me
With telling me of the moldwarp° and the ant,
Of the dreamer Merlin and his prophecies,
And of a dragon and a finless fish,
A clip-wing'd griffin and a moulten raven,
A couching lion and a ramping cat,
And such a deal of skimble-skamble stuff
As puts me from my faith. I tell you what—
He held me last night at least nine hours
In reckoning up the several devils' names
That were his lackeys: I cried "Hum", and "Well, go to!"
But mark'd him not a word. O, he is as tedious
As a tired horse, a railing wife,
Worse than a smoky house. I had rather live
With cheese and garlic in a windmill, far,
Than feed on cates and have him talk to me
In any summer house in Christendom.
MORTIMER. In faith, he is a worthy gentleman,
Exceedingly well read, and profited
In strange concealments,° valiant as a lion,
And wondrous affable, and as bountiful
As mines of India. Shall I tell you, cousin?
He holds your temper in a high respect
And curbs himself even of his natural scope
When you come 'cross his humor, faith he does.
I warrant you that man is not alive
Might so have tempted him as you have done
Without the taste of danger and reproof.
But do not use it oft, let me entreat you.

143. moldwarp: mole **160–61. profited . . . concealments:** expert on magic

WORCESTER. In faith, my lord, you are too wilful-blame,
And since your coming hither have done enough
To put him quite besides his patience;
You must needs learn, lord, to amend this fault.
Though sometimes it shows greatness, courage, blood,
—And that's the dearest grace it renders you—
Yet oftentimes it doth present harsh rage,
Defect of manners, want of government,
Pride, haughtiness, opinion, and disdain,
The least of which haunting a nobleman
Loseth men's hearts and leaves behind a stain
Upon the beauty of all parts besides,
Beguiling them of commendation.

HOTSPUR. Well, I am school'd—good manners be your speed!
Here come our wives, and let us take our leave.

[*Re-enter* GLENDOWER *with the ladies.*]

MORTIMER. This is the deadly spite that angers me,
My wife can speak no English, I no Welsh.

GLENDOWER. My daughter weeps, she'll not part with you,
She'll be a soldier too, she'll to the wars.

MORTIMER. Good father, tell her that she and my aunt Percy
Shall follow in your conduct speedily.

[GLENDOWER *speaks to her in Welsh, and she answers him in the same.*]

GLENDOWER. She is desperate here, a peevish, self-willed harlotry,° one that no persuasion can do good upon.

[*The lady speaks in Welsh.*]

MORTIMER. I understand thy looks, that pretty Welsh
Which thou pourest down from these swelling heavens
I am too perfect in, and but for shame
In such a parley should I answer thee.

[*The lady speaks again in Welsh.*]

I understand thy kisses, and thou mine,
And that's a feeling disputation,
But I will never be a truant, love,
Till I have learnt thy language, for thy tongue
Makes Welsh as sweet as ditties highly penn'd,
Sung by a fair queen in a summer's bow'r
With ravishing division° to her lute.

GLENDOWER. Nay, if you melt, then will she run mad.

[*The lady speaks again in Welsh.*]

192–93. peevish, self-willed harlotry: perverse, silly creature **204. division:** musical variation

MORTIMER. O, I am ignorance itself in this!
GLENDOWER. She bids you on the wanton rushes° lay you down,
And rest your gentle head upon her lap,
And she will sing the song that pleaseth you,
And on your eyelids crown the god of sleep,
Charming your blood with pleasing heaviness,
Making such difference 'twixt wake and sleep
As is the difference betwixt day and night,
The hour before the heavenly-harness'd team
Begins his golden progress in the east.
MORTIMER. With all my heart I'll sit and hear her sing,
By that time will our book I think be drawn.
GLENDOWER. Do so, and those musicians that shall play to you
Hang in the air a thousand leagues from hence,
And straight they shall be here: sit, and attend.
HOTSPUR. Come, Kate, thou art perfect in lying down.
Come, quick, quick, that I may lay my head in thy lap.
LADY PERCY. Go, ye giddy goose.
[*The music plays.*]
HOTSPUR. Now I perceive the devil understands Welsh,
And 'tis no marvel he is so humorous,°
By'r lady, he is a good musician.
LADY PERCY. Then should you be nothing but musical,
For you are altogether govern'd by humors.
Lie still, ye thief, and hear the lady sing in Welsh.
HOTSPUR. I had rather hear Lady my brach° howl in Irish.
LADY PERCY. Wouldst thou have thy head broken?
HOTSPUR. No.
LADY PERCY. Then be still.
HOTSPUR. Neither, 'tis a woman's fault.°
LADY PERCY. Now God help thee!
HOTSPUR. To the Welsh lady's bed.
LADY PERCY. What's that?
HOTSPUR. Peace, she sings.
[*Here the lady sings a Welsh song.*]
Come, Kate, I'll have your song too.
LADY PERCY. Not mine, in good sooth.
HOTSPUR. Not yours, in good sooth! Heart, you swear like a comfit-maker's° wife—"Not you, in good sooth!", and "As true as I live!", and "As God shall mend me!", and "As sure as day!"—

207. wanton rushes: soft floor rushes **225. humorous:** emotional and unpredictable **230. brach:** bitch **234. woman's fault:** womanish, sissy **242. confit-maker's:** confectioner's

And givest such sarcenet° surety for thy oaths
As if thou never walk'st further than Finsbury.°
Swear me, Kate, like a lady as thou art,
A good mouth-filling oath, and leave "In sooth",
And such protest of pepper-gingerbread,°
To velvet-guards and Sunday citizens.°
Come, sing.

LADY PERCY. I will not sing.

HOTSPUR. 'Tis the next way to turn tailor, or be redbreast teacher.° And the indentures be drawn I'll away within these two hours; and so come in when ye will.

[*Exit.*]

GLENDOWER. Come, come, Lord Mortimer, you are as slow
As hot Lord Percy is on fire to go.
By this our book is drawn—we'll but seal,
And then to horse immediately.

MORTIMER. With all my heart.

[*Exeunt.*]

Scene 2

London. The Palace.

Enter the KING, PRINCE OF WALES, *and others.*

KING. Lords, give us leave: the Prince of Wales and I
Must have some private conference; but be near at hand,
For we shall presently have need of you.

[*Exeunt Lords.*]

I know not whether God will have it so
For some displeasing service I have done,
That in his secret doom out of my blood°
He'll breed revengement and a scourge for me;
But thou dost in thy passages of life
Make me believe that thou art only mark'd

244. sarcenet: a kind of silk, and hence soft or delicate **245. Finsbury:** Finsbury Fields where middle class citizens took Sunday walks **248. pepper-gingerbread:** mildly seasoned **249. Sunday citizens:** those who dress up only on Sunday **252. next . . . teacher:** closest thing to being a tailor (who sings at his work) or a teacher of song birds

III.2. **6. blood:** offspring

For the hot vengeance and the rod of heaven,
To punish my mistreadings. Tell me else
Could such inordinate and low desires,
Such poor, such bare, such lewd,° such mean attempts,
Such barren pleasures, rude society,
As thou art match'd withal and grafted to,
Accompany the greatness of thy blood,
And hold their level with thy princely heart?

PRINCE. So please your Majesty, I would I could
Quit all offences with as clear excuse
As well as I am doubtless I can purge
Myself of many I am charg'd withal;
Yet such extenuation let me beg
As, in reproof of many tales devis'd,
Which oft the ear of greatness needs must hear,
By smiling pickthanks and base newsmongers,
I may for some things true, wherein my youth
Hath faulty wander'd and irregular,
Find pardon on my true submission.

KING. God pardon thee! Yet let me wonder, Harry,
At thy affections,° which do hold a wing
Quite from the flight of all thy ancestors.
Thy place in Council thou hast rudely lost,
Which by thy younger brother is supply'd,
And art almost an alien to the hearts
Of all the court and princes of my blood.
The hope and expectation of thy time
Is ruin'd, and the soul of every man
Prophetically do forethink thy fall.
Had I so lavish of my presence been,
So common-hackney'd in the eyes of men,
So stale and cheap to vulgar company,
Opinion,° that did help me to the crown,
Had still kept loyal to possession,
And left me in reputeless banishment,
A fellow of no mark nor likelihood.
By being seldom seen, I could not stir
But like a comet I was wonder'd at,
That men would tell their children, "This is he!"
Others would say, "Where, which is Bolingbroke?"
And then I stole all courtesy from heaven,
And dress'd myself in such humility

13. lewd: base **30. affections:** tastes and impulses **42. Opinion:** public opinion

That I did pluck allegiance from men's hearts,
Loud shouts and salutations from their mouths,
Even in the presence of the crowned King.
Thus did I keep my person fresh and new,
My presence, like a robe pontifical,
Ne'er seen but wonder'd at, and so my state,
Seldom but sumptuous, show'd like a feast,
And won by rareness such solemnity.
The skipping King, he ambled up and down,
With shallow jesters and rash bavin° wits,
Soon kindled and soon burnt, carded° his state,
Mingled his royalty with cap'ring fools,
Had his great name profanèd with their scorns,
And gave his countenance against his name
To laugh at gibing boys, and stand the push
Of every beardless vain comparative,°
Grew a companion to the common streets,
Enfeoff'd° himself to popularity,
That, being daily swallow'd by men's eyes,
They surfeited with honey, and began
To loathe the taste of sweetness, whereof a little
More than a little is by much too much.
So, when he had occasion to be seen,
He was but as the cuckoo is in June,
Heard, not regarded; seen, but with such eyes
As, sick and blunted with community,
Afford no extraordinary gaze,
Such as is bent on sun-like majesty
When it shines seldom in admiring eyes,
But rather drows'd and hung their eyelids down,
Slept in his face, and render'd such aspect
As cloudy men use to their adversaries,
Being with his presence glutted, gorg'd, and full.
And in that very line, Harry, standest thou,
For thou hast lost thy princely privilege
With vile participation. Not an eye
But is a-weary of thy common sight,
Save mine, which hath desir'd to see thee more,
Which now doth that I would not have it do,
Make blind itself with foolish tenderness.

PRINCE. I shall hereafter, my thrice gracious lord,
Be more myself.

61. bavin: kindling **62. carded:** diluted **67. comparative:** wiseacre **69. Enfeoff'd:** sold

KING. For all the world
As thou art to this hour was Richard then
When I from France set foot at Ravenspurgh,
And even as I was then is Percy now.
Now by my sceptre, and my soul to boot,
He hath more worthy interest to the state
Than thou the shadow of succession.
For of no right, nor color like to right,
He doth fill fields with harness in the realm,
Turns head against the lion's armèd jaws,
And being no more in debt to years than thou
Leads ancient lords and reverend bishops on
To bloody battles and to bruising arms.
What never-dying honor hath he got
Against renownèd Douglas! whose high deeds,
Whose hot incursions and great name in arms,
Holds from all soldiers chief majority
And military title capital
Through all the kingdoms that acknowledge Christ.
Thrice hath this Hotspur, Mars in swathling clothes,
This infant warrior, in his enterprises
Discomfited great Douglas, ta'en him once,
Enlarged him, and made a friend of him,
To fill the mouth of deep defiance up,
And shake the peace and safety of our throne.
And what say you to this? Percy, Northumberland,
The Archbishop's Grace of York, Douglas, Mortimer,
Capitulate° against us and are up.
But wherefore do I tell these news to thee?
Why, Harry, do I tell thee of my foes,
Which art my nearest and dearest enemy?
Thou that art like enough, through vassal fear,
Base inclination, and the start of spleen,
To fight against me under Percy's pay,
To dog his heels, and curtsy at his frowns,
To show how much thou art degenerate.
PRINCE. Do not think so, you shall not find it so;
And God forgive them that so much have sway'd
Your Majesty's good thoughts away from me!
I will redeem all this on Percy's head,
And in the closing of some glorious day
Be bold to tell you that I am your son,
When I will wear a garment all of blood,

120. Capitulate: organize

And stain my favors in a bloody mask,
Which, wash'd away, shall scour my shame with it;
And that shall be the day, whene'er it lights,
That this same child of honor and renown,
This gallant Hotspur, this all-praisèd knight,
And your unthought-of Harry chance to meet.
For every honor sitting on his helm,
Would they were multitudes, and on my head
My shames redoubled! For the time will come
That I shall make this northern youth exchange
His glorious deeds for my indignities.
Percy is but my factor,° good my lord,
To engross up glorious deeds on my behalf,
And I will call him to so strict account
That he shall render every glory up,
Yea, even the slightest worship of his time,
Or I will tear the reckoning from his heart.
This in the name of God I promise here,
The which if He be pleas'd I shall perform,
I do beseech your Majesty may salve
The long-grown wounds of my intemperance.
If not, the end of life cancels all bands,°
And I will die a hundred thousand deaths
Ere break the smallest parcel of this vow.

KING. A hundred thousand rebels die in this—
Thou shalt have charge and sovereign trust herein.
[*Enter* BLUNT.]
How now, good Blunt? Thy looks are full of speed.

BLUNT. So hath the business that I come to speak of.
Lord Mortimer of Scotland hath sent word
That Douglas and the English rebels met
The eleventh of this month at Shrewsbury.
A mighty and a fearful head they are,
If promises be kept on every hand,
As ever offer'd foul play in a state.

KING. The Earl of Westmoreland set forth today,
With him my son, Lord John of Lancaster,
For this advertisement is five days old.
On Wednesday next, Harry, you shall set forward,
On Thursday we ourselves will march.
Our meeting is Bridgnorth, and, Harry, you
Shall march through Gloucestershire, by which account,
Our business valued, some twelve days hence

147. factor: purchasing agent **157. bands:** bonds, debts

Our general forces at Bridgnorth shall meet.
Our hands are full of business, let's away,
Advantage feeds him fat while men delay.
[*Exeunt.*]

Scene 3

Eastcheap. The Boar's Head Tavern.

Enter FALSTAFF *and* BARDOLPH.

FALSTAFF. Bardolph, am I not fallen away vilely since this last action? Do I not bate?° Do I not dwindle? Why, my skin hangs about me like an old lady's loose gown. I am withered like an old apple-john.° Well, I'll repent, and that suddenly, while I am in some liking; I shall be out of heart shortly, and then I shall have no strength to repent. And I have not forgotten what the inside of a church is made of, I am a peppercorn, a brewer's horse.° The inside of a church! Company, villainous company, hath been the spoil of me.

BARDOLPH. Sir John, you are so fretful you cannot live long.

FALSTAFF. Why, there is it. Come, sing me a bawdy song, make me merry. I was as virtuously given as a gentleman need to be; virtuous enough; swore little; diced not above seven times—a week; went to a bawdy-house not above once in a quarter—of an hour; paid money that I borrowed—three or four times; lived well, and in good compass; and now I live out of all order, out of all compass.

BARDOLPH. Why, you are so fat, Sir John, that you must needs be out of all compass, out of all reasonable compass, Sir John.

FALSTAFF. Do thou amend thy face, and I'll amend my life. Thou art our admiral,° thou bearest the lantern in the poop, but 'tis in the nose of thee: thou art the Knight of the Burning Lamp.

BARDOLPH. Why, Sir John, my face does you no harm.

FALSTAFF. No, I'll be sworn, I make as good use of it as many a man doth of a death's-head, or a *memento mori.* I never see thy face but I think upon hell-fire, and Dives° that lived in purple: for there he is in his robes, burning, burning. If thou wert any way given to virtue, I would swear by thy face. My oath should be "By this fire, that's God's angel!" But thou art altogether given over; and wert indeed, but for

III.3. **2. bate:** lose weight **3. apple-john:** apple with shriveled skin **7. brewer's horse:** decrepit nag **19. admiral:** flag ship **23. momento mori:** reminder of death, often in the form of a skull **24. Dives:** the rich man in the parable of Lazarus (Luke 16: 19–31) who burned in hell for his lack of charity

the light in thy face, the son of utter darkness. When thou ran'st up Gad's Hill in the night to catch my horse, if I did not think thou hadst been an *ignis fatuus,*° or a ball of wildfire, there's no purchase in money. O, thou art a perpetual triumph, an everlasting bonfire-light! Thou hast saved me a thousand marks in links° and torches, walking with thee in the night betwixt tavern and tavern; but the sack that thou hast drunk me would have bought me lights as good cheap at the dearest chandler's° in Europe. I have maintained that salamander° of yours with fire any time this two and thirty years, God reward me for it!

BARDOLPH. 'Sblood, I would my face were in your belly!

FALSTAFF. God-a-mercy! so should I be sure to be heartburnt.

[*Enter* HOSTESS.]

How now, dame Partlet° the hen, have you enquired yet who picked my pocket?

HOSTESS. Why, Sir John, what do you think, Sir John, do you think I keep thieves in my house? I have searched, I have enquired, so has my husband, man by man, boy by boy, servant by servant—the tithe of a hair was never lost in my house before.

FALSTAFF. Ye lie, hostess. Bardolph was shaved and lost many a hair, and I'll be sworn my pocket was picked. Go to, you are a woman, go.

HOSTESS. Who, I? No, I defy thee. God's light, I was never called so in mine own house before.

FALSTAFF. Go to, I know you well enough.

HOSTESS. No, Sir John, you do not know me, Sir John, I know you, Sir John, you owe me money, Sir John, and now you pick a quarrel to beguile me of it. I bought you a dozen of shirts to your back.

FALSTAFF. Dowlas, filthy dowlas.° I have given them away to bakers' wives; they have made bolters° of them.

HOSTESS. Now as I am a true woman, holland of eight shillings an ell!° You owe money here besides, Sir John, for your diet, and by-drinkings,° and money lent you, four and twenty pound.

FALSTAFF. He had his part of it, let him pay.

HOSTESS. He? Alas, he is poor, he hath nothing.

FALSTAFF. How? Poor? Look upon his face. What call you rich? Let them coin his nose, let them coin his cheeks, I'll not pay a denier. What, will you make a younker° of me? Shall I not take mine ease in

30. ignis fatuus: will o' the wisp **32. links:** flares **35. dearest chandler's:** most expensive candle merchant's **36. salamander:** lizard allegedly able to live in fire **40. Partlet:** clucking, agitated, self-important—from the traditional behavior of a hen **54. dowlas:** coarse linen **55. bolters:** sieves **56. ell:** forty-five inches **58. by-drinkings:** drinks between meals **63. younker:** greenhorn

mine inn but I shall have my pocket picked? I have lost a seal-ring of my grandfather's worth forty mark.

HOSTESS. O Jesu, I have heard the Prince tell him, I know not how oft, that that ring was copper.

FALSTAFF. How? the Prince is a Jack, a sneak-up. 'Sblood, and he were here I would cudgel him like a dog if he would say so.

[*Enter the* PRINCE *marching, with* PETO, *and* FALSTAFF *meets him, playing upon his truncheon° like a fife.*]

How now, lad? Is the wind in that door, i'faith, must we all march?

BARDOLPH. Yea, two and two, Newgate° fashion.

HOSTESS. My lord, I pray you hear me.

PRINCE. What say'st thou, Mistress Quickly? How doth thy husband? I love him well, he is an honest man.

HOSTESS. Good my lord, hear me.

FALSTAFF. Prithee let her alone, and list to me.

PRINCE. What say'st thou, Jack?

FALSTAFF. The other night I fell asleep here, behind the arras, and had my pocket picked. This house is turned bawdy-house, they pick pockets.

PRINCE. What didst thou lose, Jack?

FALSTAFF. Wilt thou believe me, Hal, three or four bonds of forty pound apiece, and a seal-ring of my grandfather's.

PRINCE. A trifle, some eightpenny matter.

HOSTESS. So I told him, my lord, and I said I heard your Grace say so; and, my lord, he speaks most vilely of you, like a foul-mouthed man as he is, and said he would cudgel you.

PRINCE. What! he did not?

HOSTESS. There's neither faith, truth, nor womanhood in me else.

FALSTAFF. There's no more faith in thee than in a stewed prune° nor no more truth in thee than in a drawn fox°—and for womanhood, Maid Marian may be the deputy's wife of the ward to thee.° Go, you thing, go!

HOSTESS. Say, what thing, what thing?

FALSTAFF. What thing? Why, a thing to thank God on.

HOSTESS. I am no thing to thank God on, I would thou shouldst know it, I am an honest man's wife, and setting thy knighthood aside, thou art a knave to call me so.

FALSTAFF. Setting thy womanhood aside, thou art a beast to say otherwise.

s.d. truncheon: cudgel **71. Newgate:** prison **90. stewed prune:** identified with brothels **91. drawn fox:** drawn out of his hole and hence desperately cunning **92. womanhood . . . thee:** compared to you, Maid Marian (a loose character associated with country May games) is as dignified and virtuous as the wife of a city official

HOSTESS. Say, what beast, thou knave, thou?

FALSTAFF. What beast? Why, an otter.

PRINCE. An otter, Sir John? Why an otter?

FALSTAFF. Why? She's neither fish nor flesh, a man knows not where to have her.

HOSTESS. Thou art an unjust man in saying so, thou or any man knows where to have me, thou knave, thou.

PRINCE. Thou say'st true, hostess, and he slanders thee most grossly.

HOSTESS. So he doth you, my lord, and said this other day you ought° him a thousand pound.

PRINCE. Sirrah, do I owe you a thousand pound?

FALSTAFF. A thousand pound, Hal? A million, thy love is worth a million, thou owest me thy love.

HOSTESS. Nay, my lord, he called you Jack, and said he would cudgel you.

FALSTAFF. Did I, Bardolph?

BARDOLPH. Indeed, Sir John, you said so.

FALSTAFF. Yea, if he said my ring was copper.

PRINCE. I say 'tis copper, darest thou be as good as thy word now?

FALSTAFF. Why, Hal, thou knowest as thou art but man I dare, but as thou art prince, I fear thee as I fear the roaring of the lion's whelp.

PRINCE. And why not as the lion?

FALSTAFF. The King himself is to be feared as the lion; dost thou think I'll fear thee as I fear thy father? Nay, and I do, I pray God my girdle break.

PRINCE. O, if it should, how would thy guts fall about thy knees! But sirrah, there's no room for faith, truth, nor honesty in this bosom of thine; it is all filled up with guts and midriff. Charge an honest woman with picking thy pocket? Why, thou whoreson impudent embossed° rascal, if there were anything in thy pocket but tavern reckonings, memorandums of bawdy-houses, and one poor pennyworth of sugar-candy to make thee long-winded, if thy pocket were enriched with any other injuries but these, I am a villian; and yet you will stand to it, you will not pocket up wrong! Art thou not ashamed?

FALSTAFF. Dost thou hear, Hal? Thou knowest in the state of innocency Adam fell, and what should poor Jack Falstaff do in the days of villainy? Thou seest I have more flesh than another man, and therefore more frailty. You confess then, you picked my pocket?

PRINCE. It appears so by the story.

FALSTAFF. Hostess, I forgive thee, go make ready breakfast, love thy husband, look to thy servants, cherish thy guests, thou shalt find me tractable to any honest reason, thou seest I am pacified still, nay prithee be gone. (*Exit* HOSTESS.) Now, Hal, to the news at court—for the robbery, lad, how is that answered?

109. ought: owed **129. embossed:** swollen

PRINCE. O my sweet beef, I must still be good angel to thee: the money is paid back again.

FALSTAFF. O, I do not like that paying back, 'tis a double labor.

PRINCE. I am good friends with my father and may do anything.

FALSTAFF. Rob me the exchequer the first thing thou dost, and do it with unwashed° hands too.

BARDOLPH. Do, my lord.

PRINCE. I have procured thee, Jack, a charge of foot.

FALSTAFF. I would it had been of horse. Where shall I find one that can steal well? O for a fine thief of the age of two and twenty or thereabouts: I am heinously unprovided. Well, God be thanked for these rebels, they offend none but the virtuous; I laud them, I praise them.

PRINCE. Bardolph!

BARDOLPH. My lord?

PRINCE. Go bear this letter to Lord John of Lancaster,
To my brother John, this to my Lord of Westmoreland.
[*Exit* BARDOLPH.]
Go, Peto, to horse, to horse, for thou and I
Have thirty miles to ride yet ere dinner-time.
[*Exit* PETO.]
Jack, meet me tomorrow in the Temple hall
At two o'clock in the afternoon.
There shalt thou know thy charge, and there receive
Money and order for their furniture.
The land is burning, Percy stands on high.
And either we or they must lower lie.
[*Exit.*]

FALSTAFF. Rare words! Brave world! Hostess, my breakfast, come!
O, I could wish this tavern were my drum.°
[*Exit.*]

150. unwashed: without stopping to wash **166. furniture:** equipment **170. drum:** recruiting headquarters

ACT IV

Scene 1

Shrewsbury. The Rebel Camp.

Enter HOTSPUR, WORCESTER, *and* DOUGLAS.

HOTSPUR. Well said, my noble Scot! If speaking truth
In this fine° age were not thought flattery,
Such attribution° should the Douglas have
As not a soldier of this season's stamp°
Should go so general current through the world.
By God, I cannot flatter, I do defy
The tongues of soothers, but a braver place
In my heart's love hath no man than yourself.
Nay, task me to my word, approve° me, lord.
DOUGLAS. Thou art the king of honor:
No man so potent breathes upon the ground
But I will beard him.
HOTSPUR. Do so, and 'tis well.
[*Enter a* MESSENGER *with letters.*]
What letters hast thou there?—I can but thank you.
MESSENGER. These letters come from your father.
HOTSPUR. Letters from him? Why comes he not himself?
MESSENGER. He cannot come, my lord, he is grievous sick.
HOTSPUR. 'Zounds, how has he the leisure to be sick
In such a justling time? Who leads his power?
Under whose government come they along?
MESSENGER. His letters bear his mind, not I, my lord.
WORCESTER. I prithee tell me, doth he keep his bed?
MESSENGER. He did, my lord, four days ere I set forth,
And at the time of my departure thence
He was much fear'd by his physicians.
WORCESTER. I would the state of time had first been whole
Ere he by sickness had been visited;
His health was never better worth than now.
HOTSPUR. Sick now? Droop now? This sickness doth infect
The very life-blood of our enterprise;

IV.1. **2. fine:** over-sophisticated **3. attribution:** recognition **4. stamp:** coinage **9. approve:** put me to the proof

'Tis catching hither, even to our camp.
He writes me here that inward sickness—
And that his friends by deputation could not
So soon be drawn, nor did he think it meet
To lay so dangerous and dear a trust
On any soul remov'd but on his own.
Yet doth he give us bold advertisement
That with our small conjunction° we should on,
To see how fortune is dispos'd to us;
For, as he writes, there is no quailing now,
Because the King is certainly possess'd
Of all our purposes. What say you to it?
WORCESTER. Your father's sickness is a maim to us.
HOTSPUR. A perilous gash, a very limb lopp'd off—
And yet, in faith, it is not! His present want
Seems more than we shall find it. Were it good
To set the exact wealth of all our states
All at one cast? to set so rich a main°
On the nice hazard of one doubtful hour?
It were not good, for therein should we read
The very bottom and the soul of hope,
The very list,° the very utmost bound
Of all our fortunes.
DOUGLAS. Faith, and so we should, where now remains
A sweet reversion;° we may boldly spend
Upon the hope of what is to come in.
A comfort of retirement lives in this.
HOTSPUR. A rendezvous, a home to fly unto,
If that the devil and mischance look big
Upon the maidenhead of our affairs.
WORCESTER. But yet I would your father had been here.
The quality and hair° of our attempt
Brooks no division; it will be thought,
By some that know not why he is away,
That wisdom, loyalty, and mere dislike
Of our proceedings kept the Earl from hence;
And think how such an apprehension
May turn the tide of fearful faction,
And breed a kind of question in our cause.
For well you know we of the off'ring° side
Must keep aloof from strict arbitrement,°

37. conjunction: joint forces **47. main:** stake, army **51. list:** limit **54. reversion:** promise of future addition **61. hair:** nature, character **69. off'ring:** offensive **70. strict arbitrement:** impartial evaluation

And stop all sight-holes, every loop from whence
The eye of reason may pry in upon us.
This absence of your father's draws a curtain
That shows the ignorant a kind of fear
Before not dreamt of.

HOTSPUR. You strain too far.
I rather of his absence make this use:
It lends a lustre and more great opinion,
A larger dare to our great enterprise,
Than if the Earl were here; for men must think
If we without his help can make a head
To push against a kingdom, with his help
We shall o'erturn it topsy-turvy down.
Yet all goes well, yet all our joints are whole.

DOUGLAS. As heart can think: there is not such a word
Spoke of in Scotland as this term of fear.

[*Enter* SIR RICHARD VERNON.]

HOTSPUR. My cousin Vernon! Welcome, by my soul!

VERNON. Pray God my news be worth a welcome, lord.
The Earl of Westmoreland seven thousand strong
Is marching hitherwards, with him Prince John.

HOTSPUR. No harm, what more?

VERNON. And further, I have learn'd,
The King himself in person is set forth,
Or hitherwards intended speedily,
With strong and mighty preparation.

HOTSPUR. He shall be welcome too. Where is his son,
The nimble-footed madcap Prince of Wales,
And his comrades that daft the world aside
And bid it pass?

VERNON. All furnish'd, all in arms;
All plum'd like estridges° that with the wind
Bated,° like eagles having lately bath'd,
Glittering in golden coats like images,
As full of spirit as the month of May,
And gorgeous as the sun at midsummer;
Wanton as youthful goats, wild as young bulls.
I saw young Harry with his beaver° on,
His cushes° on his thighs, gallantly arm'd,
Rise from the ground like feather'd Mercury,
And vaulted with such ease into his seat

98. estridges: ostrich plumes are the emblem of the Prince of Wales **99. Bated:** beat their wings **104. beaver:** helmet face guard **105. cushes:** cuisses, armor

As if an angel dropp'd down from the clouds
To turn and wind° a fiery Pegasus,
And witch the world with noble horsemanship.

HOTSPUR. No more, no more! Worse than the sun in March,
This praise doth nourish agues. Let them come!
They come like sacrifices in their trim,
And to the fire-ey'd maid of smoky war
All hot and bleeding will we offer them.
The mailèd Mars shall on his altar sit
Up to the ears in blood. I am on fire
To hear this rich reprisal° is so nigh,
And yet not ours! Come, let me taste my horse,
Who is to bear me like a thunderbolt
Against the bosom of the Prince of Wales.
Harry to Harry shall, hot horse to horse,
Meet and ne'er part till one drop down a corse.
O that Glendower were come!

VERNON. There is more news:
I learn'd in Worcester as I rode along
He cannot draw his power this fourteen days.

DOUGLAS. That's the worst tidings that I hear of yet.

WORCESTER. Ay, by my faith, that bears a frosty sound.

HOTSPUR. What may the King's whole battle reach unto?

VERNON. To thirty thousand.

HOTSPUR. Forty let it be.
My father and Glendower being both away,
The powers of us may serve so great a day.
Come, let us take a muster speedily—
Doomsday is near; die all, die merrily.

DOUGLAS. Talk not of dying, I am out of fear
Of death or death's hand for this one half year.

[*Exeunt.*]

Scene 2

A public road near Coventry.

Enter FALSTAFF *and* BARDOLPH.

FALSTAFF. Bardolph, get thee before to Coventry; fill me a bottle of sack. Our soldiers shall march through; we'll to Sutton Co'fil' tonight.

109. wind: wheel about **118. reprisal:** prize

BARDOLPH. Will you give me money, captain?

FALSTAFF. Lay out, lay out.

BARDOLPH. This bottle makes an angel.°

FALSTAFF. And if it do, take it for thy labor—and if it make twenty, take them all, I'll answer the coinage. Bid my lieutenant Peto meet me at town's end.

BARDOLPH. I will, captain. Farewell. 9

[*Exit.*]

FALSTAFF. If I be not ashamed of my soldiers, I am a soused gurnet;° I have misused the King's press° damnably. I have got in exchange of a hundred and fifty soldiers three hundred and odd pounds. I press me none but good householders, yeomen's sons, inquire me out contracted bachelors, such as had been asked twice on the banns,° such a commodity of warm slaves as had as lief hear the devil as a drum, such as fear the report of a caliver° worse than a struck fowl or a hurt wild duck. I pressed me none but such toasts-and-butter, with hearts in their bellies no bigger than pins' heads, and they have bought out their services; and now my whole charge consists of ancients,° corporals, lieutenants, gentlemen of companies—slaves as ragged as Lazarus in the painted cloth, where the glutton's dogs licked his sores; and such as indeed were never soldiers, but discarded unjust serving-men, younger sons to younger brothers, revolted tapsters, and ostlers trade-fallen, the cankers of a calm world and a long peace, ten times more dishonorable-ragged than an old fazed ancient;° and such have I to fill up the rooms of them as have bought out their services, that you would think that I had a hundred and fifty tattered prodigals lately come from swine-keeping, from eating draff and husks. A mad fellow met me on the way, and told me I had unloaded all the gibbets and pressed the dead bodies. No eye hath seen such scarecrows. I'll not march through Coventry with them, that's flat; nay, and the villains march wide betwixt the legs as if they had gyves° on, for indeed I had the most of them out of prison. There's not a shirt and a half in all my company, and the half shirt is two napkins tacked together and thrown over the shoulders like a herald's coat without sleeves; and the shirt to say the truth stolen from my host at Saint Albans, or the red-nose innkeeper of Daventry. But that's all one, they'll find linen enough on every hedge.

[*Enter the* PRINCE *and the* LORD OF WESTMORELAND.]

PRINCE. How now, blown Jack?° How now, quilt? 39

FALSTAFF. What, Hal! How now, mad wag? What a devil dost thou in

5. angel: ten shillings **10. soused gurnet:** pickled fish **11. press:** draft **14. banns:** about to be married **16. caliver:** musket **20. ancients:** ensigns, flag bearers **25. fazed ancient:** tattered flag **32. gyves:** leg irons **39. blown Jack:** fat and puffing; a jack is also a soldier's padded jacket

Warwickshire? My good Lord of Westmoreland, I cry you mercy, I thought your honor had already been at Shrewsbury.

WESTMORELAND. Faith, Sir John, 'tis more than time that I were there, and you too, but my powers are there already; the King I can tell you looks for us all, we must away all night.

FALSTAFF. Tut, never fear me, I am as vigilant as a cat to steal cream.

PRINCE. I think, to steal cream indeed, for thy theft hath already made thee butter; but tell me, Jack, whose fellows are these that come after?

FALSTAFF. Mine, Hal, mine.

PRINCE. I did never see such pitiful rascals.

FALSTAFF. Tut, tut, good enough to toss, food for powder, food for powder, they'll fill a pit as well as better; tush, man, mortal men, mortal men.

WESTMORELAND. Ay, but, Sir John, methinks they are exceeding poor and bare, too beggarly.

FALSTAFF. Faith, for their poverty I know not where they had that; and for their bareness I am sure they never learned that of me.

PRINCE. No, I'll be sworn, unless you call three fingers in the ribs bare. But sirrah, make haste; Percy is already in the field.

[*Exit.*]

FALSTAFF. What, is the King encamped?

WESTMORELAND. He is, Sir John, I fear we shall stay too long.

[*Exit.*]

FALSTAFF. Well,
To the latter end of a fray and the beginning of a feast
Fits a dull fighter and a keen guest.

[*Exit.*]

Scene 3

Shrewsbury. The Rebel Camp.

Enter HOTSPUR, WORCESTER, DOUGLAS, VERNON.

HOTSPUR. We'll fight with him tonight.
WORCESTER. It may not be.
DOUGLAS. You give him then advantage.
VERNON. Not a whit.
HOTSPUR. Why say you so, looks he not for supply?
VERNON. So do we.
HOTSPUR. His is certain, ours is doubtful.
WORCESTER. Good cousin, be advis'd, stir not tonight.

VERNON. Do not, my lord.
DOUGLAS. You do not counsel well.
You speak it out of fear and cold heart.
VERNON. Do me no slander, Douglas; by my life,
And I dare well maintain it with my life,
If well-respected honor bid me on,
I hold as little counsel with weak fear
As you, my lord, or any Scot that this day lives;
Let it be seen tomorrow in the battle
Which of us fears.
DOUGLAS. Yea, or tonight.
VERNON. Content.
HOTSPUR. Tonight, say I.
VERNON. Come, come, it may not be. I wonder much,
Being men of such great leading as you are,
That you foresee not what impediments
Drag back our expedition: certain horse
Of my cousin Vernon's are not yet come up,
Your uncle Worcester's horse came but today,
And now their pride and mettle is asleep,
Their courage with hard labor tame and dull,
That not a horse is half the half himself.
HOTSPUR. So are the horses of the enemy
In general journey-bated and brought low.
The better part of ours are full of rest.
WORCESTER. The number of the King exceedeth ours.
For God's sake, cousin, stay till all come in.
[*The trumpet sounds a parley.*]
[*Enter* SIR WALTER BLUNT.]
BLUNT. I come with gracious offers from the King,
If you vouchsafe me hearing and respect.
HOTSPUR. Welcome, Sir Walter Blunt—and would to God
You were of our determination!
Some of us love you well, and even those some
Envy your great deservings and good name,
Because you are not of our quality,
But stand against us like an enemy.
BLUNT. And God defend but still I should stand so,
So long as out of limit and true rule
You stand against anointed majesty.
But to my charge. The King hath sent to know
The nature of your griefs, and whereupon
You conjure from the breast of civil peace
Such bold hostility, teaching his duteous land
Audacious cruelty. If that the King

Have any way your good deserts forgot,
Which he confesseth to be manifold,
He bids you name your griefs, and with all speed
You shall have your desires with interest
And pardon absolute for yourself, and these
Herein misled by your suggestion.

HOTSPUR. The King is kind, and well we know the King
Knows at what time to promise, when to pay.
My father, and my uncle, and myself
Did give him that same royalty he wears,
And when he was not six and twenty strong,
Sick in the world's regard, wretched and low,
A poor unminded outlaw sneaking home,
My father gave him welcome to the shore;
And when he heard him swear and vow to God
He came but to be Duke of Lancaster,
To sue his livery,° and beg his peace
With tears of innocency, and terms of zeal,
My father, in kind heart and pity mov'd,
Swore him assistance, and perform'd it too.
Now when the lords and barons of the realm
Perceiv'd Northumberland did lean to him,
The more and less came in with cap and knee,
Met him in boroughs, cities, villages,
Attended him on bridges, stood in lanes,
Laid gifts before him, proffer'd him their oaths,
Gave him their heirs as pages, follow'd him
Even at the heels in golden multitudes.
He presently, as greatness knows itself,
Steps me a little higher than his vow
Made to my father while his blood was poor
Upon the naked shore at Ravenspurgh;
And now forsooth takes on him to reform
Some certain edicts and some strait decrees
That lie too heavy on the commonwealth;
Cries out upon abuses, seems to weep
Over his country's wrongs; and by this face,
This seeming brow of justice, did he win
The hearts of all that he did angle for;
Proceeded further—cut me off the heads
Of all the favorites that the absent King
In deputation left behind him here,
When he was personal in the Irish war.

IV.3. **62. livery:** his family property, taken by Richard II

BLUNT. Tut, I came not to hear this.
HOTSPUR. Then to the point.
In short time after he depos'd the King,
Soon after that depriv'd him of his life,
And in the neck of that task'd° the whole state;
To make that worse, suffer'd his kinsman March
(Who is, if every owner were well plac'd,
Indeed his King) to be engag'd in Wales,
There without ransom to lie forfeited;
Disgrac'd me in my happy victories,
Sought to entrap me by intelligence,
Rated° mine uncle from the Council-board,
In rage dismiss'd my father from the court,
Broke oath on oath, committed wrong on wrong,
And in conclusion drove us to seek out
This head of safety, and withal to pry
Into his title, the which we find
Too indirect for long continuance.
BLUNT. Shall I return this answer to the King?
HOTSPUR. Not so, Sir Walter. We'll withdraw awhile.
Go to the King, and let there be impawn'd
Some surety for a safe return again,
And in the morning early shall mine uncle
Bring him our purposes—and so, farewell.
BLUNT. I would you would accept of grace and love.
Hotspur. And may be so we shall.
BLUNT. Pray God you do.
[*Exeunt.*]

Scene 4

York. The Archbishop's Palace.

Enter the ARCHBISHOP OF YORK *and* SIR MICHAEL.

ARCHBISHOP. Hie, good Sir Michael, bear this sealed brief
With winged haste to the lord marshal,
This to my cousin Scroop, and all the rest
To whom they are directed. If you knew
How much they do import you would make haste.

92. task'd: taxed **98. rated:** scolded

SIR MICHAEL. My good lord,
I guess their tenor.
ARCHBISHOP. Like enough you do.
Tomorrow, good Sir Michael, is a day
Wherein the fortune of ten thousand men
Must bide the touch; for, sir, at Shrewsbury,
As I am truly given to understand,
The King with mighty and quick-raisèd power
Meets with Lord Harry; and I fear, Sir Michael,
What with the sickness of Northumberland,
Whose power was in the first proportion,
And what with Owen Glendower's absence thence,
Who with them was a rated sinew too,
And comes not in, o'er-rul'd by prophecies,
I fear the power of Percy is too weak
To wage an instant trial with the King.
SIR MICHAEL. Why, my good lord, you need not fear,
There is Douglas, and Lord Mortimer.
ARCHBISHOP. No, Mortimer is not there.
SIR MICHAEL. But there is Mordake, Vernon, Lord Harry Percy,
And there is my Lord of Worcester, and a head
Of gallant warriors, noble gentlemen.
ARCHBISHOP. And so there is, but yet the King hath drawn
The special head of all the land together:
The Prince of Wales, Lord John of Lancaster,
The noble Westmoreland, and warlike Blunt,
And many mo corrivals and dear men
Of estimation and command in arms.
SIR MICHAEL. Doubt not, my lord, they shall be well oppos'd.
ARCHBISHOP. I hope no less, yet needful 'tis to fear;
And to prevent the worst, Sir Michael, speed.
For if Lord Percy thrive not, ere the King
Dismiss his power he means to visit us,
For he hath heard of our confederacy,
And 'tis but wisdom to make strong against him.
Therefore make haste—I must go write again
To other friends; and so, farewell, Sir Michael.
[*Exeunt.*]

ACT V

Scene 1

Shrewsbury. The King's Camp.

Enter the KING, PRINCE OF WALES, LORD JOHN OF LANCASTER, SIR WALTER BLUNT, FALSTAFF.

KING. How bloodily the sun begins to peer
Above yon bulky hill! The day looks pale
At his distemp'rature.
PRINCE. The southern wind
Doth play the trumpet to his purposes,
And by his hollow whistling in the leaves
Foretells a tempest and a blust'ring day.
KING. Then with the losers let it sympathise,
For nothing can seem foul to those that win.
[*The trumpet sounds.*]
[*Enter* WORCESTER *and* VERNON.]
How now, my Lord of Worcester! 'Tis not well
That you and I should meet upon such terms
As now we meet. You have deceiv'd our trust,
And made us doff our robes of peace
To crush our old limbs in ungentle steel.
This is not well, my lord, this is not well.
What say you to it? Will you again unknit
This churlish knot of all-abhorrèd war,
And move in that obedient orb again
Where you did give a fair and natural light,
And be no more an exhal'd meteor,
A prodigy of fear, and a portent
Of broachèd mischief to the unborn times?
WORCESTER. Hear me, my liege:
For mine own part I could be well content
To entertain the lag end of my life
With quiet hours. For I protest
I have not sought the day of this dislike.
KING. You have not sought it? How comes it, then?
FALSTAFF. Rebellion lay in his way, and he found it.

PRINCE. Peace, chewet,° peace!
WORCESTER. It pleas'd your Majesty to turn your looks
Of favor from myself, and all our house,
And yet I must remember you, my lord,
We were the first and dearest of your friends;
For you my staff of office did I break
In Richard's time, and posted day and night
To meet you on the way, and kiss your hand,
When yet you were in place and in account
Nothing so strong and fortunate as I.
It was myself, my brother, and his son,
That brought you home, and boldly did outdare
The dangers of the time. You swore to us,
And you did swear that oath at Doncaster,
That you did nothing purpose 'gainst the state,
Nor claim no further than your new-fall'n right,
The seat of Gaunt, dukedom of Lancaster.
To this we swore our aid; but in short space
It rain'd down fortune show'ring on your head,
And such a flood of greatness fell on you,
What with our help, what with the absent King,
What with the injuries of a wanton time,
The seeming sufferances that you had borne,
And the contrarious winds that held the King
So long in his unlucky Irish wars
That all in England did repute him dead.
And from this swarm of fair advantages
You took occasion to be quickly woo'd
To gripe the general sway into your hand,
Forgot your oath to us at Doncaster,
And being fed by us, you us'd us so
As that ungentle gull the cuckoo's bird
Useth the sparrow—did oppress our nest,
Grew by our feeding to so great a bulk
That even our love durst not come near your sight
For fear of swallowing; but with nimble wing
We were enforc'd for safety sake to fly
Out of your sight, and raise this present head,
Whereby we stand opposèd by such means
As you yourself have forg'd against yourself,
By unkind usage, dangerous countenance,
And violation of all faith and troth

V.1. **29. chewet:** noisy bird, meat pie

Sworn to us in your younger enterprise.
KING. These things indeed you have articulate,
Proclaim'd at market crosses, read in churches,
To face the garment of rebellion
With some fine color that may please the eye
Of fickle changelings and poor discontents,
Which gape and rub the elbow at the news
Of hurlyburly innovation;
And never yet did insurrection want
Such water-colors to impaint his cause,
Nor moody beggars starving for a time
Of pellmell havoc and confusion.
PRINCE. In both your armies there is many a soul
Shall pay full dearly for this encounter
If once they join in trial. Tell your nephew,
The Prince of Wales doth join with all the world
In praise of Henry Percy. By my hopes,
This present enterprise set off his head,°
I do not think a braver gentleman,
More active-valiant or more valiant-young,
More daring or more bold, is now alive
To grace this latter age with noble deeds.
For my part, I may speak it to my shame,
I have a truant been to chivalry,
And so I hear he doth account me too;
Yet this before my father's majesty—
I am content that he shall take the odds
Of his great name and estimation,
And will, to save the blood on either side,
Try fortune with him in a single fight.
KING. And, Prince of Wales, so dare we venture thee,
Albeit, considerations infinite
Do make against it. No, good Worcester, no,
We love our people well, even those we love
That are misled upon your cousin's part,
And will they take the offer of our grace,
Both he, and they, and you, yea, every man
Shall be my friend again, and I'll be his.
So tell your cousin, and bring me word
What he will do. But if he will not yield,
Rebuke and dread correction wait on us,
And they shall do their office. So, be gone;
We will not now be troubled with reply.

88. set . . . head: excepted

We offer fair, take it advisedly.
[*Exit* WORCESTER, *with* VERNON.]

PRINCE. It will not be accepted, on my life;
The Douglas and the Hotspur both together
Are confident against the world in arms.

KING. Hence, therefore, every leader to his charge;
For on their answer will we set on them,
And God befriend us as our cause is just!
[*Exeunt all but the* PRINCE *and* FALSTAFF.]

FALSTAFF. Hal, if thou see me down in the battle and bestride me, so; 'tis a point of friendship.

PRINCE. Nothing but a Colossus can do thee that friendship. Say thy prayers, and farewell.

FALSTAFF. I would 'twere bed-time, Hal, and all well.

PRINCE. Why, thou owest God a death.
[*Exit.*]

FALSTAFF. 'Tis not due yet, I would be loath to pay him before his day—what need I be so forward with him that calls not on me? Well, 'tis no matter, honor pricks me on. Yea, but how if honor prick me off when I come on, how then? Can honor set to a leg? No. Or an arm? No. Or take away the grief of a wound? No. Honor hath no skill in surgery then? No. What is honor? A word. What is in that word honor? What is that honor? Air. A trim reckoning! Who hath it? He that died a-Wednesday. Doth he feel it? No. Doth he hear it? No. 'Tis insensible, then? Yea, to the dead. But will it not live with the living? No. Why? Detraction will not suffer it. Therefore I'll none of it. Honor is a mere scutcheon°—and so ends my catechism.
[*Exit.*]

Scene 2

Shrewsbury. The Rebel Camp.

Enter WORCESTER *and* SIR RICHARD VERNON.

WORCESTER. O no, my nephew must not know, Sir Richard,
The liberal and kind offer of the King.

VERNON. 'Twere best he did.

WORCESTER. Then are we all undone.

130. prick me off: check me off as a casualty **138. scutcheon:** funeral coat of arms

It is not possible, it cannot be,
The King should keep his word in loving us;
He will suspect us still, and find a time
To punish this offence in other faults.
Supposition all our lives shall be stuck full of eyes,°
For treason is but trusted like the fox,
Who, never so tame, so cherish'd and lock'd up,
Will have a wild trick of his ancestors.
Look how we can, or sad or merrily,
Interpretation will misquote our looks,
And we shall feed like oxen at a stall,
The better cherish'd still the nearer death.
My nephew's trespass may be well forgot,
It hath the excuse of youth and heat of blood,
And an adopted name of privilege—
A hare-brain'd Hotspur, govern'd by a spleen:
All his offences live upon my head
And on his father's. We did train him on,
And, his corruption being ta'en from us,
We as the spring of all shall pay for all.
Therefore, good cousin, let not Harry know
In any case the offer of the King.

VERNON. Deliver what you will; I'll say 'tis so.
Here comes your cousin.

[*Enter* HOTSPUR *and* DOUGLAS.]

HOTSPUR. My uncle is return'd;
Deliver up my Lord of Westmoreland.
Uncle, what news?

WORCESTER. The King will bid you battle presently.

DOUGLAS. Defy him by the Lord of Westmoreland.

HOTSPUR. Lord Douglas, go you and tell him so.

DOUGLAS. Marry, and shall, and very willingly.

[*Exit.*]

WORCESTER. There is no seeming mercy in the King.

HOTSPUR. Did you beg any? God forbid!

WORCESTER. I told him gently of our grievances,
Of his oath-breaking; which he mended thus,
By now forswearing that he is forsworn.
He calls us rebels, traitors, and will scourge
With haughty arms this hateful name in us.

[*Re-enter* DOUGLAS.]

DOUGLAS. Arm, gentlemen, to arms! for I have thrown
A brave defiance in King Henry's teeth,

V.2. **8. Supposition . . . eyes:** suspicion will always be spying on us

And Westmoreland that was engag'd° did bear it,
Which cannot choose but bring him quickly on.
WORCESTER. The Prince of Wales stepp'd forth before the King,
And, nephew, challeng'd you to single fight.
HOTSPUR. O, would the quarrel lay upon our heads,
And that no man might draw short breath today
But I and Harry Monmouth! Tell me, tell me,
How show'd his tasking?° Seem'd it in contempt?
VERNON. No, by my soul, I never in my life
Did hear a challenge urg'd more modestly,
Unless a brother should a brother dare
To gentle exercise and proof of arms.
He gave you all the duties of a man,
Trimm'd up your praises with a princely tongue,
Spoke your deservings like a chronicle,
Making you ever better than his praise
By still dispraising praise valu'd with you,
And, which became him like a prince indeed,
He made a blushing cital of himself,
And chid his truant youth with such a grace
As if he master'd there a double spirit
Of teaching and of learning instantly.
There did he pause: but let me tell the world—
If he outlive the envy of this day,
England did never owe so sweet a hope
So much misconstru'd in his wantonness.
HOTSPUR. Cousin, I think thou art enamored
On his follies: never did I hear
Of any prince so wild a liberty.
But be he as he will, yet once ere night
I will embrace him with a soldier's arm,
That he shall shrink under my courtesy.
Arm, arm with speed! And fellows, soldiers, friends,
Better consider what you have to do
Than I that have not well the gift of tongue
Can lift your blood up with persuasion.
[*Enter a* MESSENGER.]
MESSENGER. My lord, here are letters for you.
HOTSPUR. I cannot read them now.
O gentlemen, the time of life is short!
To spend that shortness basely were too long
If life did ride upon a dial's point,
Still ending at the arrival of an hour.

43. engag'd: held as hostage **50. tasking:** challenging

And if we live, we live to tread on kings,
If die, brave death when princes die with us!
Now, for our consciences, the arms are fair
When the intent of bearing them is just.
[*Enter another* MESSENGER.]

MESSENGER. My lord, prepare, the King comes on apace.

HOTSPUR. I thank him that he cuts me from my tale,
For I profess not talking, only this—
Let each man do his best; and here draw I
A sword whose temper I intend to stain
With the best blood that I can meet withal
In the adventure of this perilous day.
Now, Esperance! Percy! and set on,
Sound all the lofty instruments of war,
And by that music let us all embrace,
For, heaven to earth, some of us never shall
A second time do such a courtesy.
[*Here they embrace, the trumpets sound, exeunt.*]

Scene 3

Shrewsbury. The Field of Battle.

The KING *enters with his power. Alarum to the battle. Then enter* DOUGLAS, *and* SIR WALTER BLUNT [*disguised as the* KING].

BLUNT. What is thy name that in the battle thus
Thou crossest me? What honor dost thou seek
Upon my head?

DOUGLAS. Know then my name is Douglas,
And I do haunt thee in the battle thus
Because some tell me that thou art a king.

BLUNT. They tell thee true.

DOUGLAS. The Lord of Stafford dear today hath bought
Thy likeness, for instead of thee, King Harry,
This sword hath ended him; so shall it thee
Unless thou yield thee as my prisoner.

BLUNT. I was not born a yielder, thou proud Scot,
And thou shalt find a king that will revenge
Lord Stafford's death.
[*They fight.* DOUGLAS *kills* BLUNT.]
[*Then enter* HOTSPUR.]

HOTSPUR. O Douglas, hadst thou fought at Holmedon thus
I never had triumph'd upon a Scot.
DOUGLAS. All's done, all's won: here breathless lies the King.
HOTSPUR. Where?
DOUGLAS. Here.
HOTSPUR. This, Douglas? No, I know this face full well,
A gallant knight he was, his name was Blunt,
Semblably furnish'd like the King himself.
DOUGLAS. A fool go with thy soul, whither it goes!
A borrow'd title hast thou bought too dear.
Why didst thou tell me that thou wert a king?
HOTSPUR. The King hath many marching in his coats.
DOUGLAS. Now, by my sword, I will kill all his coats;
I'll murder all his wardrobe, piece by piece,
Until I meet the King.
HOTSPUR. Up and away!
Our soldiers stand full fairly for the day.

[*Exeunt.*]

[*Alarum. Enter* FALSTAFF *solus.*]

FALSTAFF. Though I could scape shot-free° at London, I fear the shot here, here's no scoring° but upon the pate. Soft! who are you? Sir Walter Blunt—there's honor for you! Here's no vanity! I am as hot as molten lead, and as heavy too: God keep lead out of me, I need no more weight than mine own bowels. I have led my ragamuffins where they are peppered; there's not three of my hundred and fifty left alive, and they are for the town's end, to beg during life. But who comes here?

[*Enter the* PRINCE.]

PRINCE. What, stands thou idle here? Lend me thy sword.
Many a nobleman lies stark and stiff
Under the hoofs of vaunting enemies,
Whose deaths are yet unrevenged. I prithee lend me thy sword.

FALSTAFF. O Hal, I prithee give me leave to breathe awhile. Turk Gregory° never did such deeds in arms as I have done this day; I have paid Percy, I have made him sure.

PRINCE. He is indeed, and living to kill thee.
I prithee lend me thy sword.

FALSTAFF. Nay, before God, Hal, if Percy be alive thou gets not my sword, but take my pistol if thou wilt.

PRINCE. Give it me. What, is it in the case!

FALSTAFF. Ay, Hal, 'tis hot, 'tis hot; there's that will sack a city.

V.3. **21. Semblably:** similarly **30. shot-free:** without paying the shot or bill **31. scoring:** cutting, marking up tavern charges **43. Turk Gregory:** Pope Gregory VII, like the Turks, was a byword for cruelty.

[*The* PRINCE *draws it out, and finds it to be a bottle of sack.*]

PRINCE. What, is it a time to jest and dally now?

[*He throws the bottle at him. Exit.*]

FALSTAFF. Well, if Percy be alive, I'll pierce him. If he do come in my way, so; if he do not, if I come in his willingly, let him make a carbonado° of me. I like not such grinning honor as Sir Walter hath. Give me life, which if I can save, so; if not, honor comes unlooked for, and there's an end.

[*Exit.*]

Scene 4

The Same.

Alarum. Excursions. Enter the KING, *the* PRINCE, LORD JOHN OF LANCASTER, EARL OF WESTMORELAND.

KING. I prithee, Harry, withdraw thyself, thou bleed'st too much.
Lord John of Lancaster, go you with him.
LANCASTER. Not I, my lord, unless I did bleed too.
PRINCE. I beseech your Majesty, make up,°
Lest your retirement do amaze your friends.
KING. I will do so. My Lord of Westmoreland,
Lead him to his tent.
WESTMORELAND. Come, my lord, I'll lead you to your tent.
PRINCE. Lead me, my lord? I do not need your help,
And God forbid a shallow scratch should drive
The Prince of Wales from such a field as this,
Where stain'd nobility lies trodden on,
And rebels' arms triumph in massacres!
LANCASTER. We breathe too long. Come, cousin Westmoreland,
Our duty this way lies; for God's sake, come.

[*Exeunt* LANCASTER *and* WESTMORELAND.]

PRINCE. By God, thou hast deceiv'd me, Lancaster,
I did not think thee lord of such a spirit.
Before, I lov'd thee as a brother, John,
But now I do respect thee as my soul.
KING. I saw him hold Lord Percy at the point

54. carbonado: meat cut crosswise for broiling

V.4. 4. make up: go forward

With lustier maintenance than I did look for
Of such an ungrown warrior.

PRINCE. O, this boy
Lends mettle to us all!

[*Exit.*]

[*Enter* DOUGLAS.]

DOUGLAS. Another king! They grow like Hydra's heads.
I am the Douglas, fatal to all those
That wear those colors on them. What art thou
That counterfeit'st the person of a king?

KING. The King himself, who, Douglas, grieves at heart
So many of his shadows thou hast met,
And not the very King. I have two boys
Seek Percy and thyself about the field,
But seeing thou fall'st on me so luckily
I will assay thee, and defend thyself.

DOUGLAS. I fear thou art another counterfeit,
And yet, in faith, thou bearest thee like a king;
But mine I am sure thou art, whoe'er thou be,
And thus I win thee.

[*They fight, the* KING *being in danger.*]

[*Re-enter* PRINCE OF WALES.]

PRINCE. Hold up thy head, vile Scot, or thou art like
Never to hold it up again! The spirits
Of valiant Shirley, Stafford, Blunt are in my arms.
It is the Prince of Wales that threatens thee,
Who never promiseth but he means to pay.

[*They fight:* DOUGLAS *flieth.*]

Cheerly, my lord, how fares your grace?
Sir Nicholas Gawsey hath for succor sent,
And so hath Clifton—I'll to Clifton straight.

KING. Stay and breathe a while.
Thou hast redeem'd thy lost opinion,
And show'd thou mak'st some tender of my life,
In this fair rescue thou hast brought to me.

PRINCE. O God, they did me too much injury
That ever said I hearken'd for your death.
If it were so, I might have let alone
The insulting hand of Douglas over you,
Which would have been as speedy in your end
As all the poisonous potions in the world,
And sav'd the treacherous labor of your son.

KING. Make up to Clifton, I'll to Sir Nicholas Gawsey.

[*Exit.*]

[*Enter* HOTSPUR.]

HOTSPUR. If I mistake not, thou art Harry Monmouth.
PRINCE. Thou speak'st as if I would deny my name.
HOTSPUR. My name is Harry Percy.
PRINCE. Why then I see
A very valiant rebel of the name.
I am the Prince of Wales, and think not, Percy,
To share with me in glory any more.
Two stars keep not their motion in one sphere,
Nor can one England brook a double reign
Of Harry Percy and the Prince of Wales.
HOTSPUR. Nor shall it, Harry, for the hour is come
To end the one of us, and would to God
Thy name in arms were now as great as mine!
PRINCE. I'll make it greater ere I part from thee,
And all the budding honors on thy crest
I'll crop to make a garland for my head.
HOTSPUR. I can no longer brook thy vanities.

[*They fight.*]

[*Enter* FALSTAFF.]

FALSTAFF. Well said, Hal! To it, Hal! Nay, you shall find no boy's play here, I can tell you.

[*Re-enter* DOUGLAS; *he fighteth with* FALSTAFF, *who falls down as if he were dead. Exit* DOUGLAS. *The* PRINCE *mortally wounds* HOTSPUR.]

HOTSPUR. O Harry, thou hast robb'd me of my youth!
I better brook the loss of brittle life
Than those proud titles thou hast won of me;
They wound my thoughts worse than thy sword my flesh.
But thoughts, the slaves of life, and life, time's fool,
And time, that takes survey of all the world,
Must have a stop. O, I could prophesy,
But that the earthy and cold hand of death
Lies on my tongue. No, Percy, thou art dust,
And food for—

[*Dies.*]

PRINCE. For worms, brave Percy. Fare thee well, great heart!
Ill-weav'd ambition, how much art thou shrunk!
When that this body did contain a spirit,
A kingdom for it was too small a bound;
But now two paces of the vilest earth
Is room enough. This earth that bears thee dead
Bears not alive so stout a gentleman.
If thou wert sensible of courtesy
I should not make so dear a show of zeal;

But let my favors° hide thy mangled face,
And even in thy behalf I'll thank myself
For doing these fair rites of tenderness.
Adieu, and take thy praise with thee to heaven!
Thy ignominy sleep with thee in the grave,
But not remember'd in thy epitaph! 100
[*He spieth* FALSTAFF *on the ground.*]
What, old acquaintance, could not all this flesh
Keep in a little life? Poor Jack, farewell!
I could have better spar'd a better man.
O, I should have a heavy miss of thee
If I were much in love with vanity;
Death hath not struck so fat a deer today,
Though many dearer, in this bloody fray.
Embowell'd° will I see thee by and by,
Till then in blood by noble Percy lie. 109
[*Exit.*]
[FALSTAFF *riseth up.*]

FALSTAFF. Embowelled? If thou embowel me today, I'll give you leave to powder° me and eat me too tomorrow. 'Sblood, 'twas time to counterfeit, or that hot termagant° Scot had paid me, scot and lot too. Counterfeit? I lie, I am no counterfeit: to die is to be a counterfeit, for he is but the counterfeit of a man, who hath not the life of a man; but to counterfeit dying, when a man thereby liveth, is to be no counterfeit, but the true and perfect image of life indeed. The better part of valor is discretion, in the which better part I have saved my life. 'Zounds, I am afraid of this gunpowder Percy, though he be dead; how if he should counterfeit too and rise? By my faith, I am afraid he would prove the better counterfeit; therefore I'll make him sure, yea, and I'll swear I killed him. Why may not he rise as well as I? Nothing confutes me but eyes, and nobody sees me: therefore, sirrah (*Stabbing him.*), with a new wound in your thigh, come you along with me. 123
[*He takes up* HOTSPUR *on his back.*]
[*Re-enter* PRINCE *and* LORD JOHN OF LANCASTER.]

PRINCE. Come, brother John, full bravely hast thou flesh'd
Thy maiden sword.

LANCASTER. But soft, whom have we here?
Did you not tell me this fat man was dead?

PRINCE. I did, I saw him dead,
Breathless and bleeding on the ground. Art thou alive?
Or is it fantasy that plays upon our eyesight?

95. favors: probably the plumes from his helmet **108. Embowell'd:** disembowelled for embalming **111. powder:** salt or pickle **112–13. termagant:** brawling, bloodthirsty

I prithee speak, we will not trust our eyes
Without our ears. Thou art not what thou seem'st.

FALSTAFF. No, that's certain, I am not a double-man;° but if I be not Jack Falstaff, then am I a Jack.° There is Percy (*Throwing the body down.*)! If your father will do me any honor, so; if not, let him kill the next Percy himself. I look to be either earl or duke, I can assure you.

PRINCE. Why, Percy I kill'd myself, and saw thee dead.

FALSTAFF. Didst thou? Lord, Lord, how this world is given to lying! I grant you I was down, and out of breath, and so was he, but we rose both at an instant, and fought a long hour by Shrewsbury clock. If I may be believed, so; if not, let them that should reward valor bear the sin upon their own heads. I'll take it upon my death, I gave him this wound in the thigh; if the man were alive, and would deny it, 'zounds, I would make him eat a piece of my sword.

LANCASTER. This is the strangest tale that ever I heard.

PRINCE. This is the strangest fellow, brother John.
Come, bring your luggage nobly on your back.
For my part, if a lie may do thee grace,
I'll gild it with the happiest terms I have.
[*A retreat is sounded.*]
The trumpet sounds retreat, the day is ours.
Come, brother, let us to the highest of the field,
To see what friends are living, who are dead.
[*Exeunt* PRINCE OF WALES *and* LANCASTER.]

FALSTAFF. I'll follow, as they say, for reward. He that rewards me, God reward him! If I do grow great, I'll grow less, for I'll purge, and leave sack, and live cleanly as a nobleman should do.
[*Exit, bearing off the body.*]

Scene 5

The Same.

The trumpets sound. Enter the KING, PRINCE OF WALES, LORD JOHN OF LANCASTER, EARL OF WESTMORELAND, *with* WORCESTER *and* VERNON *prisoners.*

KING. Thus ever did rebellion find rebuke.
Ill-spirited Worcester, did not we send grace,
Pardon, and terms of love to all of you?

132. double-man: wraith, twins **133. Jack:** rascal

And wouldst thou turn our offers contrary?
Misuse the tenor of thy kinsman's trust?
Three knights upon our party slain today,
A noble earl and many a creature else,
Had been alive this hour,
If like a Christian thou hadst truly borne
Betwixt our armies true intelligence.

WORCESTER. What I have done my safety urg'd me to;
And I embrace this fortune patiently,
Since not to be avoided it falls on me.

KING. Bear Worcester to the death, and Vernon too;
Other offenders we will pause upon.
[*Exeunt* WORCESTER *and* VERNON, *guarded.*]
How goes the field?

PRINCE. The noble Scot, Lord Douglas, when he saw
The fortune of the day quite turn'd from him,
The noble Percy slain, and all his men
Upon the foot of fear, fled with the rest,
And falling from a hill, he was so bruis'd
That the pursuers took him. At my tent
The Douglas is; and I beseech your Grace
I may dispose of him.

KING. With all my heart.

PRINCE. Then, brother John of Lancaster, to you
This honorable bounty shall belong;
Go to the Douglas and deliver him
Up to his pleasure, ransomless and free.
His valors shown upon our crests today
Have taught us how to cherish such high deeds,
Even in the bosom of our adversaries.

LANCASTER. I thank your Grace for this high courtesy,
Which I shall give away immediately.

KING. Then this remains, that we divide our power:
You, son John, and my cousin Westmoreland,
Towards York shall bend you with your dearest speed
To meet Northumberland and the prelate Scroop,
Who, as we hear, are busily in arms;
Myself and you, son Harry, will towards Wales,
To fight with Glendower and the Earl of March.
Rebellion in this land shall lose his sway,
Meeting the check of such another day,
And since this business so fair is done,
Let us not leave till all our own be won.
[*Exeunt.*]

CRITICAL COMMENTARY

Who needs to know about the Worcesters and the Westmorelands and the Mortimers and the Battle of Shrewsbury (with its date, 1403), or even about the Wars of the Roses—a whole war and only a few thousand casualties? Answer: Any amateur student of politics and the human enterprise. This is immediately apparent. The play opens with the new king's first speech to the country. The situation would test any speech writer. Henry had got into office by capitalizing, without obviously seeming to, on the real weaknesses of the previous administration of Richard II. Henry had turned out to be a natural political animal, absorbed in the job and able to create a public image that persuaded everyone, finally even himself, that his increasingly aggressive and ruthless efficiency was what the country wanted and needed. His last act was to pressure Richard into confessing his crimes and uncrowning himself in public; later he could be privately liquidated. Now comes the new king's address to the nation. It is a big show. What will the man say? He says what he has to say, which means, of course, that he has to leave a number of things unsaid. Yet the speech is a fine example of its kind, so perfect in fact, as Shakespeare deliberately writes or slightly overwrites it, that it translates easily into the Old Politics of any time and place. We have everything under control now, says Henry. The bloody civil war is over for good. This is a united country. We will all move forward together now against foreign enemies whom every right-thinking person hates, those nasty pagans who committed the atrocities on Christ. Clearly, somebody has to run the country, and obviously Henry wants the job and is able to do the work, and you could hardly expect him to admit that he got in by killing the other so-called nobles or that he has a lot of political debts to pay. Maybe it will work. But of course it does not. There is no rest for the Old Politician. The crowd that put him in, led by Northumberland and Worcester, is already refusing to admit that as king he should get all the loot and prisoners from the military ransom racket. And their young protégé, Hotspur, is a galling reminder to Henry that his own son, Hal, has copped out. The last time Hal had been heard from (at the end of *Richard II*) was in answer to an invitation to his father's first royal tourney. He had sent word from the stews of London that he would be there wearing a whore's handkerchief on his helmet. This cocky behavior was part of the common peoples' idea of New Politics. They had the simple but understandable notion that the court was the last place to look for a hero, and so they reveled in the story that Hal (Henry V) spent his formative years with them in some lucky, nonpolitical, offbeat place like the Boar's Head Tavern. His father, of course, gets it all wrong. He is convinced that the place to learn how to be king is in the office next to his, and that Hal is bumming around with old alcoholics, ruining his health, and losing the conservative vote. Is the King, however, perceptive in wishing that Hal were Hotspur?

As we leave the court after the speech, Henry is busy changing plans, issuing ultimatums, making appointments, and forming committees; then we are with Hal and Falstaff in a very different place. There is a new kind of time here, and plenty of it, and people write their own speeches. The language is for fun, something to kid around and spar with and take off your betters, and you can use all of it because you don't have to be clean or correct or politic. The more you drink, the brighter you are; and hangovers and New Year's resolutions are a joke. When Falstaff decides to reform and then in the next breath eagerly agrees to join a highway robbery, his friends seem to have him cornered—from prayers to purse-taking; but even so he slips out once more with a gag that implies the things that are unsayable at court. "Why, Hal," he says with affected surprise, " 'tis my vocation, Hal. 'Tis no sin for a man to labor in his vocation." The theatrical tone glances at Hal, who as a wayward crown prince is in no position to be critical; at King Henry, a former rebel whose newly-seized royal vocation obliges him to put down more recent rebels; and at the motives behind all the conservative injunctions to keep your place, act your age, and stop rocking the boat.

The gags get rougher and more serious as we follow Falstaff to war. "Thank God for the rebels," he says philosophically, "they offend none but the virtuous"; and he takes full advantage of the fact that wars simplify morality into white for us and black for the enemy. He also catches on to the fact that his old troubles with money are over, that you have no bills once you are in uniform, and that wars are charged. His use of the draft is even more illusionless. Having tapped those who least want to go and are most able to buy their way out, he is caught on the way to the front with a pickup regiment of diseased derelicts. "Tut, tut," he clucks knowingly, "good enough to toss; food for powder, food for powder, they'll fill a pit as well as better. Tush man, mortal men, mortal men." Of course that isn't what is usually said on the recruiting posters, but isn't that what it's all about? Westmoreland is puzzled in his ponderous way: "Ay, but, Sir John, methinks they are exceedingly poor and bare, too beggarly." The sentiment about all men being mortal is vaguely familiar, but Westmoreland is used to hearing it after the victory as we stand on a little knoll with the king and generals, looking over the field strewn with corpses, and philosophizing about life and death. Falstaff finally saves his own skin by playing dead, and then, when no one is looking, stabs the body of Hotspur in the thigh and then lugs him into headquarters, all ready for the medals and the promotion. Isn't that honor—stay alive, get the credit, and don't get caught? But should a Hotspur be treated this way? He was so warm and spontaneous and unguarded, always so innocently himself. Or was he? How should the stabbing of his body be acted?

The hardest role to perform, all actors report, is Hal's. The other roles are largely character parts, but he is open, and he is apparently meant to gain identity by absorbing the virtues but not the failings of the others—Henry's competence and dedication but not his Machiavellianism; Hotspur's gallantry but not his noisy, dated naiveté; Falstaff's comic range, flexibility, and insight but not his irresponsibility. Does the play provide Hal with the scenes and words through which he can act out answers to the hard questions his role implies? Can you cop out and then rejoin the Establishment without losing what you have learned? Can you live with the people without going slumming? Can you command a King's English that is an efficient instrument and at the same time open, rich, and honest? Can you combine tavern and court without being a little more than human and slightly out of the world? Can you be an honorable politician, and an astute innocent? Can you touch pitch and not be defiled?

Falstaff *is* acting: the toady, the boon companion, the glutton, the wino, the suave man of the world, the authoritative householder, the spendthrift, the cadger, the sanctimonious churchgoer, the seducer, the advisor to royalty, the witty commentator, the sleazy entertainer, the tiptoeing coward, the grizzled veteran, the champion of oppressed youth, the aging roué, the heartless farceur, the kindly father and teacher—the roles are almost endless. Do they combine in their myriad ways to generate the twin effects of comedy: disrespect and affection for the human scene? Do they lean toward cynicism or acceptance? Do they counsel debunking or undemanding good fellowship? In what ways and how well does the play combine the dissimilar modes and life styles that Shakespeare undertook to work with: (1) Hal's popular and legendary success story, (2) the gray world of power politics and history as it has to be, and (3) comedy, which loves the thing it criticizes for being all-too-human.

Useful Criticism

Dean, L. F., ed. *Shakespeare: Modern Essays in Criticism.** New York: Oxford University Press, Inc., 1967.

Dorius, R. J., ed. *Discussions of Shakespeare's Histories.** Boston: D. C. Heath & Co., 1964.

Waith, Eugene M., ed. *Shakespeare: The Histories,** (Twentieth Century Views). Englewood Cliffs, N.J.: Prentice-Hall, Inc., 1965.

Young, David P., ed. *Twentieth Century Interpretations of Henry IV, Part Two.** Englewood Cliffs, N.J.: Prentice-Hall, Inc., 1968.

* Available in paperback.

THE ALCHEMIST

Ben Jonson

CHARACTERS

SUBTLE, the alchemist
FACE, the house-keeper
DOL COMMON, their colleague
DAPPER, a lawyer's clerk
DRUGGER, a tobacco-man
LOVEWIT, master of the house
SIR EPICURE MAMMON, a knight
PERTINAX SURLY, a gamester
TRIBULATION WHOLESOME, a pastor of Amsterdam
ANANIAS, a deacon there
KASTRIL, the angry boy
DAME PLIANT, Kastril's sister, a widow
NEIGHBORS
OFFICERS
ATTENDANTS
OTHERS

THE SCENE

London: A room in Lovewit's house. All the action takes place here, or in the street outside the front door. A window opens on the front; a back door leads to a garden, and another door into the laboratory. The action occurs between 9 A.M., *when Dapper, the first visitor, arrives, and about 3* P.M., *when the owner, Lovewit, returns.*

The Argument

T he sickness hot, a master quit, for fear,
H is house in town, and left one servant there.
E ase him corrupted, and gave means to know
A cheater, and his punk; who, now brought low,
L eaving their narrow practice, were become
C ozeners at large; and, only wanting some
H ouse to set up, with him they here contract,
E ach for a share, and all begin to act.
M uch company they draw, and much abuse,
I n casting figures, telling fortunes, news,
S elling of flies, flat bawdry, with the stone:
T ill it, and they, and all in fume are gone.

Prologue

Fortune, that favors fools, these two short hours
We wish away; both for your sakes, and ours,
Judging spectators; and desire in place,
To th'author justice, to ourselves but grace.
Our scene is London, 'cause we would make known,
No country's mirth is better than our own.
No clime breeds better matter, for your whore,
Bawd, squire, imposter, many persons more,
Whose manners, now called humours, feed the stage:
And which have still been subject, for the rage
Or spleen of comic writers. Though this pen
Did never aim to grieve, but better men;
Howe'er the age, he lives in, doth endure
The vices that she breeds, above their cure.
But, when the wholesome remedies are sweet,
And, in their working, gain and profit meet,
He hopes to find no spirit so much diseased,
But will with such fair correctives be pleased.
For here, he doth not fear, who can apply.
If there be any, that will sit so nigh
Unto the stream, to look what it doth run,
They shall find things, they'd think, or wish, were done;
They are so natural follies, but so shown,
As even the doers may see, and yet not own.

ACT I

Scene 1

Enter FACE, SUBTLE, DOL COMMON

FACE.
Believ't, I will.
SUBTLE. Thy worst. I fart at thee.
DOL.
Ha' you your wits? Why gentlemen! For love—

The Text: This is a modernized version of the 1616 Folio edition, which was printed under Jonson's supervision. The play was first acted in 1610.

FACE.
Sirrah, I'll strip you—
SUBTLE. What to do? Lick figs°
Out at my—
FACE. Rogue, rogue, out of all your sleights.
DOL.
Nay, look ye! Sovereign, General, are you madmen?
SUBTLE.
O, let the wild sheep loose. I'll gum your silks
With good strong water,° an' you come.
DOL. Will you have
The neighbours hear you? Will you betray all?
Hark, I hear somebody.
FACE. Sirrah—
SUBTLE. I shall mar
All that the tailor has made, if you approach.
FACE.
You most notorious whelp, you insolent slave,
Dare you do this?
SUBTLE. Yes faith, yes faith.
FACE. Why! Who
Am I, my mongrel? Who am I?
SUBTLE. I'll tell you,
Since you know not yourself—
FACE. Speak lower, rogue.
SUBTLE.
Yes. You were once (time's not long past) the good,
Honest, plain, livery-three-pound-thrum° that kept
Your master's worship's house, here, in the Friars,
For the vacations°—
FACE. Will you be so loud?
SUBTLE.
Since, by my means, translated Suburb-Captain.
FACE.
By your means, Doctor Dog?
SUBTLE. Within man's memory
All this I speak of.
FACE. Why, I pray you, have I

I.1. **3. Lick figs:** see Rabelais, *Pantagruel,* IV.xlv, where a fig is removed by the teeth without using the hands **7. strong water:** Subtle wards off the armed Face with a flask of chemical. **16. livery-three-pound-thrum:** You made three pounds a year and wore a servant's uniform of coarse yarn. **18. vacations:** between court terms

Been countenanced° by you? Or you, by me?
Do but collect, sir, where I met you first.

SUBTLE.
I do not hear well.

FACE. Not of this, I think it.
But I shall put you in mind, sir, at Pie Corner,
Taking your meal of steam in, from cooks' stalls,
Where, like the Father of Hunger, you did walk
Piteously costive,° with your pinched-horn-nose,
And your complexion, of the Roman wash,°
Stuck full of black and melancholic worms,
Like powder corns° shot at th'artillery-yard.

SUBTLE.
I wish you could advance your voice a little.

FACE.
When you went pinned up in the several rags
You'd raked and picked from dunghills before day,
Your feet in mouldy slippers for your kibes,°
A felt of rug,° and a thin threaden cloak,
That scare would cover your no-buttocks—

SUBTLE. So, sir!

FACE.
When all your alchemy, and your algebra,
Your minerals, vegetals, and animals,
Your conjuring, cozening, and your dozen of trades,
Could not relieve your corps,° with so much linen
Would make you tinder but to see a fire;
I ga' you countenance, credit for your coals,
Your stills, your glasses, your materials,
Built you a furnace, drew you customers,
Advanced all your black arts; lent you, beside,
A house to practise in—

SUBTLE. Your master's house?

FACE.
Where you have studied the more thriving skill
Of bawdry since.

SUBTLE. Yes, in your master's house.
You, and the rats, here kept possession.
Make it not strange. I know you're one could keep
The buttery-hatch still locked, and save the chippings,

22. countenanced: favored, elevated **28. costive:** constipated **29. Roman wash:** swarthy, dirty **31. corns:** grains **35. kibes:** ulcerated chilblains **36. felt of rug:** cheap hat **41. corps:** body

Sell the dole-beer° to aqua-vitae-men,°
The which, together with your Christmas vails,°
At post and pair,° your letting out of counters,°
Made you a pretty stock, some twenty marks,
And gave you credit to converse with cobwebs
Here, since your mistress' death hath broke up house.

FACE.
You might talk softlier, rascal.

SUBTLE. No, you scarab,°
I'll thunder you in pieces. I will teach you
How to beware to tempt a Fury again
That carries tempest in his hand, and voice.

FACE.
The place has made you valiant.

SUBTLE. No, your clothes.
Thou vermin, have I ta'en thee out of dung,
So poor, so wretched, when no living thing
Would keep thee company, but a spider, or worse?
Raised thee from brooms, and dust, and watering-pots?
Sublimed thee, and exalted thee, and fixed thee
I'the third region, called our state of grace?
Wrought thee to spirit, to quintessence, with pains
Would twice have won me the philosopher's work?
Put thee in words and fashion? Made thee fit
For more than ordinary fellowships?
Given thee thy oaths, thy quarrelling dimensions?°
Thy rules to cheat at horse-race, cock-pit, cards,
Dice, or whatever gallant tincture else?
Made thee a second in mine own great art?
And have I this for thank? Do you rebel?
Do you fly out,° i' the projection?
Would you be gone, now?

DOL. Gentlemen, what mean you?
Will you mar all?

SUBTLE. Slave, thou hadst had no name—

DOL.
Will you undo yourselves with civil war?

SUBTLE.
Never been known, past *equi clibanum,*°

53. dole-beer: for the poor **aqua-vitae-men:** liquor dealers **54. vails:** tips **55. post and pair:** a card game **counters:** rented to keep score **59. scarab:** dung fly **74. dimensions:** fashionable rules **79. fly out:** blow up **83. equi clibanum:** horse furnace, gentle heat of dung

The heat of horse-dung, under ground, in cellars,
Or an ale-house, darker than deaf John's: been lost
To all mankind, but laundresses and tapsters,
Had not I been.

DOL. Do you know who hears you, Sovereign?

FACE.
Sirrah—

DOL. Nay, General, I thought you were civil—

FACE.
I shall turn desperate, if you grow thus loud.

SUBTLE.
And hang thyself, I care not.

FACE. Hang thee, collier,°
And all thy pots, and pans, in picture I will,
Since thou hast moved me—

DOL. (O, this'll o'erthrow all.)

FACE.
Write thee up bawd in Paul's;° have all thy tricks
Of cozening with a hollow coal,° dust, scrapings,
Searching for things lost with a sieve and shears,°
Erecting figures in your rows of houses°
And taking in of shadows with a glass,
Told in red letters:° and a face cut for thee
Worse than Gamaliel Ratsey's.°

DOL. Are you sound?
Ha' you your senses, masters?

FACE. I will have
A book but barely reckoning thy impostures
Shall prove a true philosopher's stone to printers.

SUBTLE.
Away, you trencher-rascal.

FACE. Out you dog-leech,
The vomit of all prisons—

DOL. Will you be
Your own destructions, gentlemen?

90. collier: black, cheat, devil **91–93. picture . . . Paul's:** People of all kinds frequented St. Paul's to do business, get the news, and look at the advertisements and posters (pictures). **94. cozening . . . coal:** tricking by planting precious metal in a hollowed out piece of charcoal **95. sieve and shears:** a sieve balanced on shears like a divining rod would point toward the thief. **96. Erecting . . . houses:** casting horoscopes **97–98. shadows . . . letters:** reflections cast by a crystal and read by a virgin will tell your fortune **99. Ratsey's:** Ratsey was a highwayman who wore a hideous mask.

FACE. Still spewed out
For lying too heavy o' the basket.°
SUBTLE. Cheater.
FACE.
Bawd.
SUBTLE. Cow-herd.
FACE. Conjurer.
SUBTLE. Cut-purse.
FACE. Witch.
DOL. O me!
We are ruined! Lost! Ha' you no more regard
To your reputations? Where's your judgment? S'light,
Have yet, some care of me, o' your republic—
FACE.
Away this brach.° I'll bring thee, rogue, within
The statute° of sorcery, *tricesimo tertio,*
Of Harry the Eighth: ay, and (perhaps) thy neck
Within a noose for laundering gold and barbing it.
DOL.
You'll bring your head within a coxcomb, will you?
(*She catcheth out* FACE *his sword: and breaks* SUBTLE'*s glass.*)
And you, sir, with your menstrue,° gather it up.
S'death, you abominable pair of stinkards,
Leave off your barking and grow one again,
Or, by the light that shines, I'll cut your throats.
I'll not be made a prey unto the marshal
For ne'er a snarling dog-bolt o' you both.
Ha' you together cozened all this while,
And all the world, and shall it now be said
You've made most courteous shift to cozen yourselves?
You will accuse him? You will bring him in
Within the statute? Who shall take your word?
A whoreson, upstart, apocryphal captain,
Whom not a puritan in Blackfriars will trust
So much as for a feather! And you, too,
Will give the cause, forsooth? You will insult,
And claim a primacy in the divisions?
You must be chief? As if you, only, had
The powder to project with? And the work
Were not begun out of equality?

106. lying . . . basket: being greedy (over-eating on scraps sent in a basket to prisoners) **111. brach:** bitch **112.** statute: of 1541, one of the repeated laws against multiplying gold and silver **114. laundering . . . barbing:** unplating and clipping coins **116. menstrue:** dissolvant

The venture tripartite? All things in common?
Without priority? S'death, you perpetual curs,
Fall to your couples again, and cozen kindly,
And heartily, and lovingly, as you should,
And lose not the beginning of a term,
Or, by this hand, I shall grow factious too,
And take my part and quit you.

FACE. 'Tis his fault,
He ever murmurs, and objects his pains,
And says the weight of all lies upon him.

SUBTLE.
Why, so it does.

DOL. How does it? Do not we
Sustain our parts?

SUBTLE. Yes, but they are not equal.

DOL.
Why, if your part exceed today, I hope
Ours may tomorrow match it.

SUBTLE. Ay, they may.

DOL.
May, murmuring mastiff? Ay, and do. Death on me!
Help me to throttle him.

SUBTLE. Dorothy, mistress Dorothy,
'Ods precious, I'll do anything. What do you mean?

DOL.
Because o' your fermentation and cibation?

SUBTLE.
Not I, by heaven—

DOL. Your Sol and Luna°—help me.

SUBTLE.
Would I were hanged then. I'll conform myself.

DOL.
Will you, sir, do so then, and quickly: swear.

SUBTLE.
What should I swear?

DOL. To leave your faction, sir.
And labor, kindly, in the common work.

SUBTLE.
Let me not breathe if I meant ought beside.
I only used those speeches as a spur
To him.

DOL. I hope we need no spurs, sir. Do we?

152. Sol and Luna: gold and silver

FACE.
'Slid, prove today who shall shark best.
SUBTLE. Agreed.
DOL.
Yes, and work close and friendly.
SUBTLE. 'Slight, the knot
Shall grow the stronger for this breach with me.
DOL.
Why so, my good baboons! Shall we go make
A sort of sober, scurvy, precise° neighbours,
(That scarce have smiled twice since the king came in°)
A feast of laughter at our follies? Rascals
Would run themselves from breath to see me ride.°
Or you t'have but a hole to thrust your heads in,
For which you should pay ear-rent?° No, agree.
And may Don Provost ride a-feasting long
In his old velvet jerkin and stained scarves
(My noble Sovereign and worthy General)
Ere we contribute a new crewel° garter
To his most worsted° worship.
SUBTLE. Royal Dol!
Spoken like Claridiana,° and thyself!
FACE.
For which, at supper, thou shalt sit in triumph,
And not be styled Dol Common, but Dol Proper.
Dol Singular: the longest cut, at night,
Shall draw thee for his Dol Particular.
SUBTLE.
Who's that? One rings. To the window, Dol. Pray heaven,
The master do not trouble us this quarter.
FACE.
O, fear not him. While there dies one a week
O'the plague, he's safe from thinking toward London.
Beside, he's busy at his hop-yards, now:
I had a letter from him. If he do,
He'll send such word for airing o' the house
As you shall have sufficient time to quit it:
Though we break up a fortnight, 'tis no matter.
SUBTLE.
Who is it, Dol?

164. precise: puritanical **165. king came in:** James I in 1603 **167. ride:** whores were carted through town **169. ear-rent:** lose your ears in a pillory **173. crewel:** yarn (and cruel) **174. worsted:** cheap stockings (and baffled) **175. Claridiana:** heroine of *The Mirror of Knighthood*

DOL. A fine young quodling.°

FACE. O,
My lawyer's clerk I lighted on last night,
In Holborn at the Dagger.° He would have
(I told you of him) a familiar,°
To rifle° with at horses, and win cups.

DOL.
O, let him in.

SUBTLE. Stay. Who shall do't?

FACE. Get you
Your robes on. I will meet him, as going out.

DOL.
And what shall I do?

FACE. Not be seen, away.
Seem you very reserved.
[*Exit* DOL.]

SUBTLE. Enough.
[*Exit* SUBTLE.]

FACE. God be w'you, sir.
I pray you, let him know that I was here.
His name is Dapper. I would gladly have stayed, but—

Scene 2

Enter DAPPER, FACE

DAPPER.
Captain, I am here.

FACE. Who's that? He's come, I think, Doctor.
Good faith, sir, I was going away.

DAPPER. In truth,
I am very sorry, Captain.

FACE. But I thought
Sure, I should meet you.

DAPPER. Ay, I am very glad.
I had a scurvy writ, or two, to make,
And I had lent my watch last night, to one
That dines, today, at the sheriff's: and so was robbed

189. quodling: codling, green apple, naive youth **191. Dagger:** an inn **192. familiar:** attendant spirit **193. rifle:** gamble

Of my pass-time.° (*Enter* SUBTLE.) Is this the cunning-man?

FACE.
This is his worship.

DAPPER. Is he a Doctor?

FACE. Yes.

DAPPER.
And ha' you broke with him, Captain?

FACE. Ay.

DAPPER. And how?

FACE.
Faith, he does make the matter, sir, so dainty,
I know not what to say—

DAPPER. Not so, good Captain.

FACE.
Would I were fairly rid on't, believe me.

DAPPER.
Nay, now you grieve me, sir. Why should you wish so?
I dare assure you. I'll not be ungrateful.

FACE.
I cannot think you will, sir. But the law
Is such a thing—and then, he says, Read's matter°
Falling so lately—

DAPPER. Read? He was an ass,
And dealt, sir, with a fool.

FACE. It was a clerk, sir.

DAPPER.
A clerk?

FACE. Nay, hear me, sir, you know the law
Better, I think—

DAPPER. I should, sir, and the danger.
You know I showed the statute to you?

FACE. You did so.

DAPPER.
And will I tell, then? By this hand of flesh
Would it might never write good court-hand more,
If I discover. What do you think of me,
That I am a chouse?

I.2. **8. pass-time:** watch (watches were rare and expensive) **17. Read's matter:** the case of Dr. Simon Read, in trouble from 1602 to 1608 for practicing without a license and for pretending to be able to recover stolen money by the use of spirits **26. chouse:** a con-man, from the case of a Turk in 1607 who cheated the English by pretending to be an official representative, a *chaush,* of the Sultan

FACE. What's that?

DAPPER. The Turk was, here—
As one would say, do you think I am a Turk?

FACE.
I'll tell the Doctor so.

DAPPER. Do, good sweet Captain.

FACE.
Come, noble Doctor, pray thee, let's prevail,
This is the gentleman, and he is no chouse.

SUBTLE.
Captain, I have returned you all my answer.
I would do much, sir, for your love—but this
I neither may, nor can.

FACE. Tut, do not say so.
You deal, now, with a noble fellow, Doctor,
One that will thank you, richly, and he's no chouse:
Let that, sir, move you.

SUBTLE. Pray you, forbear—

FACE. He has
Four angels,° here—

SUBTLE. You do me wrong, good sir.

FACE.
Doctor, wherein? To tempt you with these spirits?

SUBTLE.
To tempt my art, and love, sir, to my peril.
Fore heaven, I scarce can think you are my friend,
That so would draw me to apparent danger.

FACE.
I draw you? A horse draw you, and a halter,°
You, and your flies together—

DAPPER. Nay good Captain.

FACE.
That know no difference of men.

SUBTLE. Good words, sir.

FACE.
Good deeds, sir, Doctor Dogs-meat. 'Slight I bring you
No cheating Clim° o' the Cloughs, or Claribels,°
That look as big as five-and-fifty, and flush,°
And spit out secrets, like hot custard—

DAPPER. Captain.

37. angels: gold coins worth about ten shillings **42. draw . . . halter:** i.e. in a cart to be hanged **46. Clim:** ballad outlaw **Claribels:** big-shot knights (cf. *The Faerie Queene* IV. ix) **47. five-and-fifty and flush:** top cards in Primero

FACE.
Nor any melancholic under-scribe
Shall tell the vicar: but, a special gentle,
That is the heir to forty marks a year,
Consorts with the small poets of the time,
Is the sole hope of his old grandmother,
That knows the law, and writes you six fair hands,
Is a fine clerk, and has his cyphering perfect,
Will take his oath, o' the Greek Xenophon
If need be, in his pocket: and can court
His mistress, out of Ovid.

DAPPER. Nay, dear Captain.

FACE.
Did you not tell me, so?

DAPPER. Yes, but I'd ha' you
Use master Doctor with some more respect.

FACE.
Hang him proud stag, with his broad velvet head.
But, for your sake, I'd choke, ere I would change
An article of breath, with such a puck-fist°—
Come let's be gone.

SUBTLE. Pray you, le' me speak with you.

DAPPER.
His worship calls you, Captain.

FACE. I am sorry,
I e'er embarked myself, in such a business.

DAPPER.
Nay, good sir. He did call you.

FACE. Will he take, then?

SUBTLE.
First, hear me—

FACE. Not a syllable, 'less you take.

SUBTLE.
Pray ye, sir—

FACE. Upon no terms, but an *assumpsit.*°

SUBTLE.
Your humor must be law.
[*He takes the money.*]

FACE. Why now, sir, talk.
Now, I dare hear you with mine honor. Speak.
So may this gentleman too.

SUBTLE. Why, sir—

63. puck-fist: puff-ball, blow-hard **69. assumpsit:** verbal agreement confirmed by a deposit

FACE. No whispering.

SUBTLE.
'Fore heaven, you do not apprehend the loss
You do yourself in this.

FACE. Wherein? For what?

SUBTLE.
Marry, to be so importunate for one,
That, when he has it, will undo you all:
He'll win up all the money i' the town.

FACE.
How!

SUBTLE. Yes. And blow up gamester after gamester,
As they do crackers in a puppet-play.
If I do give him a familiar,
Give you him all you play for; never set° him,
For he will have it.

FACE. You're mistaken, Doctor.
Why, he does ask one but for cups and horses,
A rifling fly: none o' your great familiars.

DAPPER.
Yes, Captain, I would have it for all games.

SUBTLE.
I told you so.

FACE. 'Slight, that's a new business!
I understood you, a tame bird, to fly
Twice in a term, or so; on Friday nights,
When you had left the office, for a nag,
Of forty, or fifty shillings.

DAPPER. Ay, 'tis true, sir,
But I do think, now, I shall leave the law,
And therefore—

FACE. Why, this changes quite the case!
D'you think that I dare move him?

DAPPER. If you please, sir,
All's one to him, I see.

FACE. What! For that money?
I cannot with my conscience. Nor should you
Make the request, methinks.

DAPPER. No, sir, I mean
To add consideration.

FACE. Why then, sir,
I'll try. Say that it were for all games, Doctor?

SUBTLE.
I say, then, not a mouth shall eat for him

81. set: bet against

At any ordinary, but o' the score,°
That is a gaming mouth, conceive me.

FACE. Indeed!

SUBTLE.
He'll draw you all the treasure of the realm,
If it be set him.

FACE. Speak you this from art?

SUBTLE.
Ay, sir, and reason too: the ground of art.
He's o' the only best complexion
The Queen of Fairy loves.

FACE. What! Is he!

SUBTLE. Peace.
He'll overhear you. Sir, should she but see him—

FACE.
What?

SUBTLE. Do not you tell him.

FACE. Will he win at cards too?

SUBTLE.
The spirits of dead Holland, living Isaac,°
You'd swear were in him: such a vigorous luck
As cannot be resisted. 'Slight he'll put
Six o' your gallants, to a cloak,° indeed.

FACE.
A strange success, that some man shall be born to!

SUBTLE.
He hears you, man—

DAPPER. Sir, I'll not be ingrateful.

FACE.
Faith, I have a confidence in his good nature:
You hear, he says he will not be ingrateful.

SUBTLE.
Why, as you please, my venture follows yours.

FACE.
Troth, do it, Doctor. Think him trusty, and make him.
He may make us both happy in an hour:
Win some five thousand pound, and send us two on't.

DAPPER.
Believe it, and I will, sir.

FACE. And you shall, sir.
You have heard all?

99–100. mouth . . . score: i.e. he'll have all the money and others will have to charge their food **109. Holland, living Isaac:** Dutch alchemists **112. to a cloak:** stripped of all but their last garment

DAPPER. No, what was't? Nothing, I, sir.
[FACE *takes him aside.*]

FACE.
Nothing?

DAPPER. A little, sir.

FACE. Well, a rare star
Reigned at your birth.

DAPPER. At mine, sir? No.

FACE. The Doctor
Swears that you are—

SUBTLE. Nay, Captain, you'll tell all now.

FACE.
Allied to the Queen of Fairy.

DAPPER. Who? That I am?
Believe it, no such matter—

FACE. Yes, and that
Yo' were born with a caul o' your head.

DAPPER. Who says so?

FACE. Come.
You know it well enough though you dissemble it.

DAPPER.
I'fac, I do not. You are mistaken.

FACE. How!
Swear by your fac? And in a thing so known
Unto the Doctor? How shall we, sir, trust you
I' the other matter? Can we ever think,
When you have won five, or six thousand pound,
You'll send us shares in't, by this rate?

DAPPER. By Jove, sir,
I'll win ten thousand pound, and send you half.
I'fac's no oath.

SUBTLE. No, no, he did but jest.

FACE.
Go to. Go, thank the Doctor. He's your friend
To take it so.

DAPPER. I thank his worship.

FACE. So?
Another angel.

DAPPER. Must I?

FACE. Must you? 'Slight,
What else is thanks? Will you be trivial? Doctor,
When must he come for his familiar?

DAPPER.
Shall I not ha' it with me?

SUBTLE. O, good sir!
There must a world of ceremonies pass,
You must be bathed and fumigated first;
Besides, the Queen of Fairy does not rise
Till it be noon.

FACE. Not if she danced tonight.

SUBTLE.
And she must bless it.

FACE. Did you never see
Her royal Grace yet?

DAPPER. Whom?

FACE. Your aunt of Fairy?

SUBTLE.
Not since she kissed him in the cradle, Captain,
I can resolve you that.

FACE. Well, see her Grace,
Whate'er it cost you, for a thing that I know!
It will be somewhat hard to compass: but,
How ever, see her. You are made, believe it,
If you can see her. Her Grace is a lone woman,
And very rich, and if she take a fancy,
She will do strange things. See her, at any hand.
'Slid, she may hap to leave you all she has!
It is the Doctor's fear.

DAPPER. How will't be done, then?

FACE.
Let me alone, take you no thought. Do you
But say to me, Captain, I'll see her Grace.

DAPPER.
Captain, I'll see her Grace.

FACE. Enough.
[*One knocks without.*]

SUBTLE. Who's there?
Anon. (Conduct him forth, by the back way)
Sir, against one o'clock prepare yourself.
Till when you must be fasting; only take
Three drops of vinegar in at your nose;
Two at your mouth; and one at either ear;
Then, bathe your fingers' ends; and wash your eyes;
To sharpen your five senses; and cry *hum*
Thrice; and then *buz* as often; and then, come.

FACE.
Can you remember this?

DAPPER. I warrant you.

FACE.
Well, then, away. 'Tis, but your bestowing
Some twenty nobles 'mong her Grace's servants;
And put on a clean shirt: you do not know
What grace her Grace may do you in clean linen.
[*Exeunt.*]

Scene 3

Enter SUBTLE

SUBTLE.
Come in (Good wives, I pray you forbear me now.
Troth I can do you no good till afternoon)
[*Enter* DRUGGER.]
What is your name, say you, Abel Drugger?
DRUGGER. Yes, sir.
SUBTLE.
A seller of tobacco?
DRUGGER. Yes, sir.
SUBTLE. 'Umh.
Free of the grocers?°
DRUGGER. Ay, and't please you.
SUBTLE. Well—
Your business, Abel?
DRUGGER. This, and't please your worship,
I am a young beginner, and am building
Of a new shop, and't like your worship; just
At corner of a street: (here's the plot on't.)
And I would know, by art, sir, of your worship,
Which way I should make my door, by necromancy.
And, where my shelves. And, which should be for boxes.
And, which for pots. I would be glad to thrive, sir.
And, I was wished to your worship by a gentleman,
One Captain Face, that says you know men's planets,
And their good angels, and their bad.
SUBTLE. I do,
If I do see 'em—

I.3. **5. Free of the grocers:** a member in good standing of the Grocers' Company

[*Enter* FACE.]

FACE. What! My honest Abel?
Thou art well met here!

DRUGGER. Troth, sir, I was speaking,
Just as your worship came here, of your worship.
I pray you, speak for me to master Doctor.

FACE.
He shall do anything. Doctor, do you hear?
This is my friend, Abel, an honest fellow,
He lets me have good tobacco, and he does not
Sophisticate° it with sack-lees or oil,
Nor washes it in muscadel and grains,
Nor buries it, in gravel under ground,
Wrapped up in greasy leather or pissed clouts:
But keeps it in fine lily-pots, that opened,
Smell like conserve of roses or French beans.
He has his maple block, his silver tongs,
Winchester pipes, and fire of Juniper.°
A neat, spruce-honest-fellow, and no gold-smith.°

SUBTLE.
He's a fortunate fellow, that I am sure on—

FACE.
Already, sir, ha' you found it? Lo' thee Abel!

SUBTLE.
And, in right way toward riches—

FACE. Sir.

SUBTLE. This summer,
He will be of the clothing of his company:
And, next spring, called to the scarlet.° Spend what he can.

FACE.
What, and so little beard?

SUBTLE. Sir, you must think
He may have a receipt to make hair come.
But he'll be wise, preserve his youth, and fine° for't:
His fortune looks for him another way.

FACE.
'Slid, Doctor, how canst thou know this so soon?
I am amused° at that!

SUBTLE. By a rule, Captain,
In metoposcopy, which I do work by,

24. Sophisticate: ways of moisturizing, and adulterating, dried out and moldy tobacco **30–31. maple . . . Juniper:** equipment for cutting and lighting tobacco **32. gold-smith:** usurer **37. scarlet:** made a sheriff **40. fine:** pay for refusing sheriffship **43. amused:** amazed

A certain star i'the forehead, which you see not.
Your chestnut or your olive-coloured face
Does never fail: and your long ear doth promise.
I knew't by certain spots too in his teeth,
And on the nail of his mercurial finger.

FACE.
Which finger's that?

SUBTLE. His little finger. Look.
You're born upon a Wednesday?

DRUGGER. Yes, indeed, sir.

SUBTLE.
The thumb, in chiromanty, we give Venus;
The forefinger to Jove; the midst, to Saturn;
The ring to Sol; the least, to Mercury:
Who was the lord, sir, of his horoscope,
His house of life being Libra, which foreshowed
He should be a merchant and should trade with balance.

FACE.
Why, this is strange! Is't not, honest Nab?

SUBTLE.
There is a ship now, coming from Ormus,
That shall yield him such a commodity
Of drugs—this is the west, and this the south?

DRUGGER.
Yes, sir.

SUBTLE. And those are your two sides?

DRUGGER. Ay, sir.

SUBTLE.
Make me your door, then, south; your broad side, west:
And, on the east side of your shop, aloft,
Write *Mathlai, Tarmiel,* and *Baraborat*;
Upon the north part, *Rael, Velel, Thiel.*
They are the names of those mercurial spirits,
That do fright flies from boxes.

DRUGGER. Yes, sir.

SUBTLE. And
Beneath your threshold, bury me a loadstone
To draw in gallants that wear spurs: the rest,
They'll seem to follow.

FACE. That's a secret, Nab!

SUBTLE.
And, on your stall, a puppet, with a vice,°

72. puppet . . . vice: mechanical doll

And a court-fucus,° to call city-dames.
You shall deal much with minerals.

DRUGGER. Sir, I have
At home already—

SUBTLE. Ay, I know, you have arsenic,
Vitriol, sal-tartar, argaile, alkali,
Cinoper: I know all. This fellow, Captain,
Will come, in time, to be a great distiller,
And give a say (I will not say directly,
But very fair) at the philosopher's stone.

FACE.
Why, how now, Abel! Is this true?

DRUGGER. Good Captain,
What must I give?

FACE. Nay, I'll not counsel thee.
Thou hear'st what wealth (he says, spend what thou canst)
Th'art like to come to.

DRUGGER. I would gi' him a crown.

FACE.
A crown! And toward such a fortune? Heart,
Thou shalt rather gi' him thy shop. No gold about thee?

DRUGGER.
Yes, I have a portague I ha' kept this half year.

FACE.
Out on thee, Nab; 'Slight, there was such an offer—
Shalt keep't no longer, I'll gi'it him for thee?
Doctor, Nab prays your worship to drink this: and swears
He will appear more grateful as your skill
Does raise him in the world.

DRUGGER. I would entreat
Another favor of his worship.

FACE. What is't, Nab?

DRUGGER.
But to look over, sir, my almanack,
And cross out my ill days, that I may neither
Bargain nor trust upon them.

FACE. That he shall, Nab.
Leave it, it shall be done, 'gainst afternoon.

SUBTLE.
And a direction for his shelves.

FACE. Now, Nab?
Art thou well pleased, Nab?

73. fucus: cosmetic

DRUGGER. Thank, sir, both your worships.
FACE. Away.
[*Exit* DRUGGER.]
Why, now, you smoky persecutor of nature!
Now, do you see, that something's to be done
Beside your beech-coal and your corsive waters,
Your crosslets, crucibles, and cucurbites?
You must have stuff brought home to you to work on?
And, yet, you think, I am at no expense
In searching out these veins, then following 'em,
Then trying 'em out. 'Fore God, my intelligence
Costs me more money than my share oft comes to
In these rare works.
SUBTLE. You are pleasant, sir. How now?

Scene 4

Enter DOL

SUBTLE.
What says my dainty Dolkin?
DOL. Yonder fish-wife
Will not away. And there's your giantess,
The bawd of Lambeth.
SUBTLE. Heart, I cannot speak with 'em.
DOL.
Not afore night I have told 'em, in a voice
Thorough the trunk,° like one of your familiars.
But I have spied Sir Epicure Mammon—
SUBTLE. Where?
DOL.
Coming along, at the far end of the lane,
Slow of his feet, but earnest of his tongue
To one that's with him.
SUBTLE. Face, go you and shift.
Dol, you must presently make ready too—
DOL.
Why, what's the matter?
SUBTLE. O, I did look for him
With the sun's rising: marvel he could sleep!
This is the day I am to perfect for him
The *magisterium,* our great work, the stone;

I.4. **5. trunk:** speaking tube

And yield it, made, into his hands: of which,
He has, this month, talked as he were possessed.
And now he's dealing pieces on't away.
Methinks I see him entering ordinaries,
Dispensing for the pox; and plaguey-houses,
Reaching° his dose; walking Moorfields for lepers;
And offering citizens' wives pomander-bracelets,
As his preservative, made of the elixir;
Searching the spittle,° to make old bawds young;
And the highways for beggars, to make rich:
I see no end of his labors. He will make
Nature ashamed of her long sleep: when art,
Who's but a step-dame, shall do more than she,
In her best love to mankind, ever could.
If his dream last, he'll turn the age to gold.
[*Exeunt.*]

ACT II

Scene 1

Enter MAMMON, SURLY

MAMMON.
Come on, sir. Now you set your foot on shore
In *novo orbe;*° here's the rich Peru:
And there within, sir, are the golden mines,
Great Solomon's Ophir! He was sailing to't
Three years, but we have reached it in ten months.
This is the day, wherein to all my friends
I will pronounce the happy word, be rich.
This day you shall be *spectatissimi.*
You shall no more deal with the hollow die,°
Or the frail card. No more be at charge of keeping
The livery-punk° for the young heir, that must
Seal at all hours in his shirt. No more
If he deny, ha' him beaten to't, as he is
That brings him the commodity. No more

20. Reaching: offering **23. spittle:** hospital, venereal wards

II.1. 2. novo orbe: the New World **9. hollow die:** loaded dice **11. livery-punk:** prostitute, "caught" with the young heir who is blackmailed into signing **(seal)**

Shall thirst of satin, or the covetous hunger
Of velvet entrails for a rude-spun cloak,
To be displayed at Madam Augusta's, make
The sons of sword and hazard fall before
The golden calf, and on their knees, whole nights,
Commit idolatry with wine and trumpets:
Or go a-feasting after drum and ensign.
No more of this. You shall start up young viceroys,
And have your punks and punketees, my Surly.
And unto thee, I speak it first, be rich.
Where is my Subtle, there? Within ho?

FACE. Sir.
[*Within.*]
He'll come to you, by and by.

MAMMON. That's his fire-drake,
His lungs, his Zephyrus, he that puffs his coals,
Till he firk nature up in her own centre.
You are not faithful, sir. This night I'll change
All that is metal in thy house to gold.
And early in the morning will I send
To all the plumbers and the pewterers,
And buy their tin and lead up: and to Lothbury
For all the copper.

SURLY. What, and turn that too?

MAMMON.
Yes, and I'll purchase Devonshire and Cornwall,
And make them perfect Indies! You admire now?

SURLY.
No faith.

MAMMON. But when you see th'effects of the great medicine!
Of which one part projected on a hundred
Of Mercury, or Venus, or the moon,
Shall turn it to as many of the sun;
Nay, to a thousand, so *ad infinitum:*
You will believe me.

SURLY. Yes, when I see't, I will.
But if my eyes do cozen me so (and I
Giving 'em no occasion) sure, I'll have
A whore shall piss 'em out next day.

MAMMON. Ha! Why?
Do you think I fable with you? I assure you,
He that has once the flower of the sun,
The perfect ruby, which we call elixir,
Not only can do that, but by its virtue,
Can confer honor, love, respect, long life,

Give safety, valor: yea, and victory,
To whom he will. In eight and twenty days,
I'll make an old man of fourscore, a child.

SURLY.
No doubt, he's that already.

MAMMON. Nay, I mean
Restore his years, renew him, like an eagle,
To the fifth age; make him get sons and daughters,
Young giants; as our philosophers have done
(The ancient patriarchs afore the flood)
But taking, once a week, on a knive's point,
The quantity of a grain of mustard of it:
Become stout Marses and beget young Cupids.

SURLY.
The decayed Vestals of Pict-Hatch° would thank you,
That keep the fire alive there.

MAMMON. 'Tis the secret
Of nature, naturized 'gainst all infections,
Cures all diseases, coming of all causes,
A month's grief, in a day; a year's in twelve:
And, of what age soever, in a month.
Past all the doses of your drugging Doctors.
I'll undertake, withal, to fright the plague
Out o' the kingdom, in three months.

SURLY. And I'll
Be bound the players shall sing your praises then,
Without their poets.

MAMMON. Sir, I'll do't. Meantime,
I'll give away so much, unto my man,
Shall serve th' whole city with preservative
Weekly, each house his dose, and at the rate—

SURLY.
As he that built the waterwork, does with water?

MAMMON.
You are incredulous.

SURLY. Faith, I have a humor,
I would not willingly be gulled. Your stone
Cannot transmute me.

MAMMON. Pertinax,° Surly,
Will you believe antiquity? Records?
I'll show you a book where Moses and his sister
And Solomon have written of the art;
Ay, and a treatise penned by Adam.

62. Pict-Hatch: red-light district **79. Pertinax:** persistent, stubborn

SURLY. How!

MAMMON.
O' the philosopher's stone, and in High Dutch.°

SURLY.
Did Adam write, sir, in High Dutch?

MAMMON. He did:
Which proves it was the primitive tongue.

SURLY. What paper?

MAMMON.
On cedar board.

SURLY. O that, indeed (they say)
Will last 'gainst worms.

MAMMON. 'Tis like your Irish wood,
'Gainst cobwebs. I have a piece of Jason's fleece, too,
Which was no other than a book of alchemy,
Writ in large sheepskin, a good fat ram-vellum.
Such was Pythagoras' thigh,° Pandora's tub;
And all that fable of Medea's charms,
The manner of our work: the bulls, our furnace,
Still breathing fire; our argent-vive, the dragon:
The dragon's teeth, mercury sublimate,
That keeps the whiteness, hardness, and the biting;
And they are gathered into Jason's helm
(Th' alembic) and then sowed in Mars his field,
And, thence, sublimed so often till they are fixed.
Both this, th' Hesperian garden, Cadmus' story,
Jove's shower, the boon of Midas, Argus' eyes,
Boccace his Demogorgon, thousands more,
All abstract riddles of our stone. How now?

Scene 2

Enter FACE

MAMMON.
Do we succeed? Is our day come? And holds it?

FACE.
The evening will set red upon you, sir;
You have color for it, crimson: the red ferment

84. Dutch: German **89–92. fleece . . . thigh:** both of gold

Has done his office. Three hours hence, prepare you
To see projection.

MAMMON. Pertinax, my Surly,
Again, I say to thee aloud: be rich.
This day thou shalt have ingots: and tomorrow
Give lords th'affront. Is it, my Zephyrus, right?
Blushes the bolt's head?

FACE. Like a wench with child, sir,
That were but now discovered to her master.

MAMMON.
Excellent witty Lungs! My only care is,
Where to get stuff enough now to project on,
This town will not half serve me.

FACE. No, sir? Buy
The covering off o' churches.

MAMMON. That's true.

FACE. Yes.
Let 'em stand bare as do their auditory.
Or cap 'em new with shingles.

MAMMON. No, good thatch:
Thatch will lie light upo' the rafters, Lungs.
Lungs, I will manumit° thee from the furnace;
I will restore thee thy complexion, Puff,
Lost in the embers; and repair this brain,
Hurt wi' the fume o' the metals.

FACE. I have blown, sir,
Hard for your worship; thrown by many a coal
When 'twas not beech; weighed those I put in, just,
To keep your heat, still even; these bleared eyes
Have waked, to read your several colors, sir,
Of the pale citron, the green lion, the crow,
The peacock's tail, the plumed swan.

MAMMON. And, lastly,
Thou hast descried the flower, the *sanguis agni?*

FACE.
Yes, sir.

MAMMON. Where's master?

FACE. At's prayers, sir, he,
Good man, he's doing his devotions,
For the success.

MAMMON. Lungs, I will set a period,
To all thy labors: thou shalt be the master
Of my seraglio.

II.2. 18. manumit: release

FACE. Good, sir.

MAMMON. But do you hear?
I'll geld you, Lungs.

FACE. Yes, sir.

MAMMON. For I do mean
To have a list of wives and concubines,
Equal with Solomon; who had the stone
Alike with me: and I will make me a back
With the elixir that shall be as tough
As Hercules, to encounter fifty a night.
Th'art sure, thou saw'st it blood?

FACE. Both blood and spirit, sir.

MAMMON.
I will have all my beds blown up; not stuffed:
Down is too hard. And then mine oval room
Filled with such pictures as Tiberius took
From Elephantis: and dull Aretine°
But coldly imitated. Then my glasses
Cut in more subtle angles to disperse
And multiply the figures as I walk
Naked between my succubae.° My mists
I'll have of perfume, vapoured 'bout the room
To lose ourselves in; and my baths, like pits
To fall into: from whence, we will come forth
And roll us dry in gossamer and roses.
(Is it arrived at ruby?)—Where I spy
A wealthy citizen or rich lawyer
Have a sublimed pure wife, unto that fellow
I'll send a thousand pound to be my cuckold.

FACE.
And I shall carry it?

MAMMON. No. I'll ha' no bawds
But fathers, and mothers. They will do it best.
Best of all others. And my flatterers
Shall be the pure and gravest of Divines
That I can get for money. My mere fools,
Eloquent burgesses, and then my poets
The same that writ so subtly of the fart,°
Whom I will entertain, still, for that subject.
The few that would give out themselves to be
Court and town stallions, and each-where belie

44. Aretine: Pietro Aretino wrote verses in 1523 for 16 pornographic pictures by Giulio Romano **48. succubae:** concubines **63. fart:** alluding to a popular account of the explosive way a member of Commons said "No"

Ladies, who are known most innocent, for them;
Those will I beg to make me eunuch of:
And they shall fan me with ten ostrich tails
Apiece, made in a plume, to gather wind.
We will be brave, Puff, now we ha' the medicine.
My meat shall all come in in Indian shells,
Dishes of agate, set in gold, and studded
With emeralds, sapphires, hyacinths, and rubies.
The tongues of carps, dormice, and camels' heels,
Boiled i' the spirit of Sol, and dissolved pearl,
(Apicius'° diet, 'gainst the epilepsy)
And I will eat these broths with spoons of amber,
Headed with diamond and carbuncle.
My footboy shall eat pheasants, calvered° salmons,
Knots, godwits,° lampreys: I myself will have
The beards of barbels,° served instead of salads;
Oiled mushrooms; and the swelling unctuous paps
Of a fat pregnant sow, newly cut off,
Dressed with an exquisite and poignant sauce;
For which, I'll say unto my cook, there's gold,
Go forth and be a knight.

FACE. Sir, I'll go look
A little how it heightens.
[*Exit* FACE.]

MAMMON. Do. My shirts
I'll have of taffeta-sarsnet, soft, and light
As cobwebs; and for all my other raiment
It shall be such as might provoke the Persian,
Were he to teach the world riot, anew.
My gloves of fishes', and birds' skins, perfumed
With gums of paradise, and eastern air—

SURLY.
And do you think to have the stone with this?

MAMMON.
No, I do think t' have all this with the stone.

SURLY.
Why, I have heard he must be *homo frugi*,
A pious, holy, and religious man,
One free from mortal sin, a very virgin.

MAMMON.
That° makes it, sir, he is so. But I buy it.
My venture brings it me. He, honest wretch,

77. Apicius': a Roman gourmand **80. calvered:** cut up alive **81. Knots, godwits:** small wildfowl **82. barbels:** "bearded" carp **100. That:** he that

A notable, superstitious, good soul,
Has worn his knees bare, and his slippers bald,
With prayer and fasting for it: and, sir, let him
Do it alone, for me, still. Here he comes,
Not a profane word afore him: 'tis poison.

Scene 3

Enter SUBTLE

MAMMON.
Good morrow, Father.
SUBTLE. Gentle son, good morrow,
And to your friend there. What is he, is with you?
MAMMON.
An heretic that I did bring along
In hope, sir, to convert him.
SUBTLE. Son, I doubt°
You're covetous, that thus you meet your time
I' the just point: prevent° your day at morning.
This argues something worthy of a fear
Of importune and carnal appetite.
Take heed you do not cause the blessing leave you
With your ungoverned haste. I should be sorry
To see my labours, now e'en at perfection,
Got by long watching and large patience,
Not prosper, where my love and zeal hath placed 'em.
Which (heaven I call to witness, with yourself,
To whom, I have poured my thoughts) in all my ends
Have looked no way but unto public good,
To pious uses, and dear charity,
Now grown a prodigy with men. Wherein
If you, my son, should now prevaricate,°
And, to your own particular lusts, employ
So great and catholic a bliss: be sure
A curse will follow, yea, and overtake
Your subtle and most secret ways.
MAMMON. I know, sir,
You shall not need to fear me. I but come

II.3. **4. doubt:** fear **6. prevent:** anticipate **19. prevaricate:** go astray

To ha' you confute this gentleman.

SURLY. Who is,
Indeed, sir, somewhat costive° of belief
Toward your stone: would not be gulled.

SUBTLE. Well, son,
All that I can convince him in is this,
The work is done: bright Sol is in his robe.
We have a medicine of the triple soul,
The glorified spirit. Thanks be to heaven,
And make us worthy of it. Eulenspiegel.

[*Enter* FACE.]

FACE.
Anon, sir.

SUBTLE. Look well to the register,
And let your heat, still, lessen by degrees,
To the aludels.

FACE. Yes, sir.

SUBTLE. Did you look
O' the bolt's head yet?

FACE. Which, on D, sir?

SUBTLE. Ay.
What's the complexion?

FACE. Whitish.

SUBTLE. Infuse vinegar,
To draw his volatile substance, and his tincture:
And let the water in glass E be filtered,
And put into the gripe's egg. Lute him well;
And leave him closed in *balneo*.

FACE. I will, sir.

SURLY.
What a brave language here is? Next to canting?°

SUBTLE.
I have another work; you never saw, son,
That, three days since, passed the philosopher's wheel,
In the lent heat of Athanor; and's become
Sulphur o' nature.

MAMMON. But 'tis for me?

SUBTLE. What need you?
You have enough, in that is perfect.

MAMMON. O, but—

SUBTLE.
Why, this is covetise!

26. costive: constipated, slow **42. canting:** thieves' language

MAMMON. No, I assure you,
I shall employ it all in pious uses,
Founding of colleges and grammar schools,
Marrying young virgins, building hospitals,
And now and then a church.

SUBTLE. How now?

FACE. Sir, please you,
Shall I not change the filter?

SUBTLE. Marry, yes.
And bring me the complexion of glass B.
[*Exit* FACE.]

MAMMON.
Ha' you another?

SUBTLE. Yes, son, were I assured
Your piety were firm, we would not want
The means to glorify it. But I hope the best:
I mean to tinct C in sand-heat tomorrow,
And give him imbibition.

MAMMON. Of white oil?

SUBTLE.
No, sir, of red. F is come over the helm too,
I thank my Maker, in S. Mary's bath,
And shows *lac virginis*. Blessed be heaven.
I sent you of his faeces there, calcined.
Out of that calx, I ha' won the salt of mercury.

MAMMON.
By pouring on your rectified water?

SUBTLE.
Yes, and reverberating an Athanor.
[*Enter* FACE.]
How now? What color says it?

FACE. The ground black, sir.

MAMMON.
That's your crow's head?

SURLY. Your cockscomb's, is't not?

SUBTLE.
No, 'tis not perfect, would it were the crow.
That work wants something.

SURLY. (O, I looked for this.
The hay is a-pitching.°)

SUBTLE. Are you sure you loosed 'em
I' their own menstrue?

FACE. Yes, sir, and then married 'em,

71. hay is a-pitching: rabbit snare is being set

And put 'em in a bolt's head, nipped to digestion,
According as you bade me; when I set
The liquor of Mars to circulation
In the same heat.

SUBTLE. The process, then, was right.

FACE.
Yes, by the token, sir, the retort broke,
And what was saved was put into the pelican,
And signed with Hermes' seal.

SUBTLE. I think 'twas so.
We should have a new amalgama.

SURLY. O, this ferret°
Is rank as any pole-cat.

SUBTLE. But I care not.
Let him e'en die; we have enough beside
In embrion. H has his white shirt on?

FACE. Yes, sir,
He's ripe for inceration: he stands warm
In his ash-fire. I would not you should let
Any die now, if I might counsel, sir,
For luck's sake to the rest. It is not good.

MAMMON.
He says right.

SURLY. Ay, are you bolted?

FACE. Nay, I know't, sir,
I have seen th' ill fortune. What is some three ounces
Of fresh materials?

MAMMON. Is't no more?

FACE. No more, sir,
Of gold, t'amalgam, with some six of mercury.

MAMMON.
Away, here's money. What will serve?

FACE. Ask him, sir.

MAMMON.
How much?

SUBTLE. Give him nine pound: you may gi' him ten.

SURLY.
Yes, twenty, and be cozened, do.

MAMMON. There 'tis.

SUBTLE.
This needs not. But that you will have it, so,
To see conclusions of all. For two
Of our inferior works are at fixation.

80. ferret: to drive (bolt) the rabbit out into the snare

A third is in ascension. Go your ways.
Ha' you set the oil of Luna in kemia?

FACE.
Yes, sir.

SUBTLE. And the philosopher's vinegar?

FACE. Ay.

[*Exit* FACE.]

SURLY.
We shall have a salad.

MAMMON. When do you make projection?

SUBTLE.
Son, be not hasty, I exalt our medicine
By hanging him in *balneo vaporoso;*
And giving him solution; then congeal him;
And then dissolve him; then again congeal him;
For look how oft I iterate the work,
So many times, I add unto his virtue.
As, if at first, one ounce convert a hundred,
After his second loose, he'll turn a thousand;
His third solution, ten; his fourth, a hundred.
After his fifth, a thousand thousand ounces
Of any imperfect metal into pure
Silver, or gold, in all examinations,
As good as any of the natural mine.
Get you your stuff here, against afternoon,
Your brass, your pewter, and your andirons.

MAMMON.
Not those of iron?

SUBTLE. Yes, you may bring them, too.
We'll change all metals.

SURLY. I believe you, in that.

MAMMON.
Then I may send my spits?

SUBTLE. Yes, and your racks.

SURLY.
And dripping pans, and pot-hangers, and hooks?
Shall he not?

SUBTLE. If he please.

SURLY. To be an ass.

SUBTLE.
How, sir!

MAMMON. This gentleman, you must bear withal.
I told you, he had no faith.

SURLY. And little hope, sir,
But, much less charity, should I gull myself.

SUBTLE.
Why, what have you observed, sir, in our art
Seems so impossible?
SURLY. But your whole work, no more.
That you should hatch gold in a furnace, sir,
As they do eggs in Egypt!
SUBTLE. Sir, do you
Believe that eggs are hatched so?
SURLY. If I should?
SUBTLE.
Why, I think that the greater miracle.
No egg, but differs from a chicken, more,
Than metals in themselves.
SURLY. That cannot be.
The egg's ordained by nature to that end:
And is a chicken in *potentia.*
SUBTLE.
The same we say of lead and other metals,
Which would be gold, if they had time.
MAMMON. And that
Our art doth further.
SUBTLE. Ay, for 'twere absurd
To think that nature, in the earth, bred gold
Perfect, i' the instant. Something went before.
There must be remote matter.
SURLY. Ay, what is that?
SUBTLE.
Marry, we say—
MAMMON. Ay, now it heats: stand Father.
Pound him to dust—
SUBTLE. It is, of the one part,
A humid exhalation, which we call
Materia liquida, or the unctuous water;
On th' other part, a certain crass and viscous
Portion of earth; both which, concorporate,
Do make the elementary matter of gold:
Which is not, yet, *propria materia,*
But common to all metals, and all stones.
For, where it is forsaken of that moisture
And hath more dryness, it becomes a stone;
Where it retains more of the humid fatness,
It turns to sulphur or to quicksilver:
Who are the parents of all other metals.
Nor can this remote matter, suddenly,
Progress so from extreme unto extreme,

As to grow gold and leap o'er all the means.
Nature doth, first, beget th' imperfect; then
Proceeds she to the perfect. Of that airy
And oily water, mercury is engendered;
Sulphur o' the fat, and earthy part: the one
(Which is the last) supplying the place of male,
The other of the female, in all metals.
Some do believe hermaphrodeity,
That both do act, and suffer. But, these two
Make the rest ductile, malleable, extensive.
And, even in gold, they are; for we do find
Seeds of them, by our fire, and gold in them:
And can produce the species of each metal
More perfect thence, than nature doth in earth.
Beside, who doth not see, in daily practice,
Art can beget bees, hornets, beetles, wasps,
Out of the carcasses and dung of creatures;
Yea, scorpions of an herb, being rightly placed:
And these are living creatures, far more perfect,
And excellent than metals.

MAMMON. Well said, Father!
Nay, if he take you in hand, sir, with an argument,
He'll bray° you in a mortar.

SURLY. Pray you, sir, stay.
Rather, than I'll be brayed, sir, I'll believe
That alchemy is a pretty kind of game,
Somewhat like tricks o' the cards, to cheat a man
With charming.

SUBTLE. Sir?

SURLY. What else are all your terms,
Whereon no one o' your writers 'grees with other?
Of your elixir, your *lac virginis,*
Your stone, your medicine, and your chrysosperm,
Your sal, your sulphur, and your mercury,
Your oil of height, your tree of life, your blood,
Your marcasite, your tutty, your magnesia,
Your toad, your crow, your dragon, and your panther,
Your sun, your moon, your firmament, your adrop,
Your lato, azoch, zernich, chibrit, autarit,
And then, your red man, and your white woman,
With all your broths, your menstrues, and materials,
Of piss, and eggshells, women's terms, man's blood,
Hair o' the head, burnt clouts, chalk, merds, and clay,

178. bray: pound

Powder of bones, scalings of iron, glass,
And worlds of other strange ingredients,
Would burst a man to name?

SUBTLE. And all these, named
Intending but one thing: which art our writers
Used to obscure their art.

MAMMON. Sir, so I told him,
Because the simple idiot should not learn it,
And make it vulgar.

SUBTLE. Was not all the knowledge
Of the Egyptians writ in mystic symbols?
Speak not the Scriptures, oft, in parables?
Are not the choicest fables of the poets,
That were the fountains and first springs of wisdom,
Wrapped in perplexed allegories?

MAMMON. I urged that,
And cleared to him that Sisyphus was damned
To roll the ceaseless stone only because
He would have made ours common. Who is this?
[DOL. *is seen.*]

SUBTLE.
God's precious—What do you mean? Go in, good lady.
Let me entreat you. Where's this varlet?
[*Enter* FACE.]

FACE. Sir?

SUBTLE.
You very knave! Do you use me thus?

FACE. Wherein, sir?

SUBTLE.
Go in and see you traitor. Go.
[*Exit* FACE.]

MAMMON. Who is it, sir?

SUBTLE.
Nothing, sir. Nothing.

MAMMON. What's the matter? Good, sir!
I have not seen you thus distempered. Who is 't?

SUBTLE.
All arts have still had, sir, their adversaries,
[FACE *returns.*]
But ours the most ignorant. What now?

FACE.
'Twas not my fault, sir, she would speak with you.

SUBTLE.
Would she, sir? Follow me.

MAMMON. Stay, Lungs.

FACE. I dare not, sir.

MAMMON.
How! Pray thee stay.

FACE. She's mad, sir, and sent hither—

MAMMON.
Stay man, what is she?

FACE. A lord's sister, sir.
(He'll be mad too.

MAMMON. I warrant thee.) Why sent hither?

FACE.
Sir, to be cured.

SUBTLE (*within*). Why, rascal!

FACE. Lo you. Here, sir.
[*He goes out.*]

MAMMON.
'Fore God, a Bradamante, a brave piece.

SURLY.
Heart, this is a bawdyhouse! I'll be burnt else.

MAMMON.
O, by this light, no. Do not wrong him. He's
Too scrupulous that way. It is his vice.
No, he's a rare physician, do him right.
An excellent Paracelsian! And has done
Strange cures with mineral physic. He deals all
With spirits, he. He will not hear a word
Of Galen, or his tedious recipes.
[FACE *again.*]
How now, Lungs!

FACE. Softly, sir, speak softly. I meant
To ha' told your worship all. Thus must not hear.

MAMMON.
No, he will not be gulled; let him alone.

FACE.
You're very right, sir, she is a most rare scholar;
And is gone mad, with studying Broughton's° works.
If you but name a word, touching the Hebrew,
She falls into her fit, and will discourse
So learnedly of genealogies,
As you would run mad, too, to hear her, sir.

MAMMON.
How might one do t'have conference with her, Lungs?

FACE.
O, divers have run mad upon the conference.

238. Broughton: a contemporary theologian and rabbinical scholar

I do not know, sir: I am sent in haste
To fetch a vial.

SURLY. Be not gulled, Sir Mammon.

MAMMON.
Wherein? Pray ye, be patient.

SURLY. Yes, as you are.
And trust confederate knaves, and bawds, and whores.

MAMMON.
You are too foul, believe it. Come here, Eulen.
One word.

FACE. I dare not, in good faith.

MAMMON. Stay, knave.

FACE.
He's extreme angry that you saw her, sir.

MAMMON.
Drink that.° What is she, when she's out of her fit?

FACE.
O, the most affablest creature, sir! So merry!
So pleasant! She'll mount you up, like quicksilver,
Over the helm; and circulate, like oil,
A very vegetal: discourse of state,
Of mathematics, bawdry, anything—

MAMMON.
Is she no way accessible? No means,
No trick, to give a man a taste of her—wit—
Or so?

SUBTLE (*within*). Eulen!

FACE. I'll come to you again, sir.
[*Exit* FACE.]

MAMMON.
Surely, I did not think, one o' your breeding
Would traduce personages of worth.

SURLY. Sir Epicure,
Your friend to use: yet, still, loth to be gulled.
I do not like your philosophical bawds.
Their stone is lechery enough to pay for
Without this bait.

MAMMON. Heart, you abuse yourself.
I know the lady, and her friends, and means,
The original of this disaster. Her brother
Has told me all.

SURLY. And yet, you ne'er saw her
Till now?

252. Drink that: money for drink as a bribe

MAMMON. O, yes, but I forgot. I have (believe it)
One of the treacherous'st memories, I do think,
Of all mankind.
SURLY. What call you her, brother?
MAMMON. My lord—
He wi' not have his name known, now I think on't.
SURLY.
A very treacherous memory!
MAMMON. O' my faith—
SURLY.
Tut, if you ha' it not about you, pass it,
Till we meet next.
MAMMON. Nay, by this hand, 'tis true.
He's one I honor, and my noble friend,
And I respect his house.
SURLY. Heart! Can it be,
That a grave sir, a rich, that has no need,
A wise sir, too, at other times, should thus
With his own oaths and arguments make hard means
To gull himself? And this be your elixir,
Your *lapis mineralis,* and your lunary,
Give me your honest trick, yet, at primero
Or gleek;° and take you *lutum sapientis,*
Your *menstruum simplex:* I'll have gold before you,
And with less danger of the quicksilver;
Or the hot sulphur.
[*Enter* FACE.]
FACE. Here's one from Captain Face, sir,
[*To* SURLY.]
Desires you meet him i' the Temple Church,
Some half hour hence, and upon earnest business.
Sir, if you please to quit us now; and come
[*He whispers* MAMMON.]
Again within two hours: you shall have
My master busy examining o' the works;
And I will steal you in, unto the party,
That you may see her converse. [*To* SURLY.]
Sir, shall I say
You'll meet the Captain's worship?
SURLY. Sir, I will.
But, by attorney, and to a second purpose.
Now, I am sure it is a bawdy house;
I'll swear it, were the Marshal here to thank me:

285. gleek: three-handed card game

The naming this Commander doth confirm it.
Don Face! Why, he's the most authentic dealer
I' these commodities! The Superintendent
To all the quainter traffickers in town.
He is their Visitor, and does appoint
Who lies with whom; and at what hour; what price;
Which gown; and in what smock; what fall;° what tire.
Him will I prove by a third person, to find
The subleties of this dark labyrinth:
Which, if I do discover, dear Sir Mammon,
You'll give your poor friend leave, though no philosopher,
To laugh: for you that are, 'tis thought, shall weep.

FACE.
Sir. He does pray you'll not forget.

SURLY. I will not, sir.
Sir Epicure, I shall leave you?
[*Exit* SURLY.]

MAMMON. I follow you straight.

FACE.
But do so, good sir, to avoid suspicion.
This gentleman has a parlous head.

MAMMON. But wilt thou, Eulen,
Be constant to thy promise?

FACE. As my life, sir.

MAMMON.
And wilt thou insinuate what I am? And praise me?
And say I am a noble fellow?

FACE. O, what else, sir?
And, that you'll make her royal with the stone,
An empress; and yourself King of Bantam.°

MAMMON.
Wilt thou do this?

FACE. Will I, sir?

MAMMON. Lungs, my Lungs!
I love thee.

FACE. Send your stuff, sir, that my master
May busy himself, about projection.

MAMMON.
Th'hast witched me, rogue: take, go.

FACE. Your jack and all, sir.

MAMMON.
Thou art a villain—I will send my jack;°

306. fall: flat collar **320. Bantam:** Javanese city, center of Eastern wealth
325. jack: spit, turned by weights and gears

And the weights too. Slave, I could bite thine ear.
Away, thou dost not care for me.

FACE.
Not I, sir?

MAMMON.
Come, I was born to make thee, my good weasel;
Set thee on a bench: and, ha' thee twirl a chain
With the best lord's vermin, of 'em all.

FACE.
Away, sir.

MAMMON.
A count, nay, a count-palatine—

FACE.
Good sir, go.

MAMMON.
Shall not advance thee better: no, nor faster.
[*Exit* MAMMON.]

Scene 4

Enter SUBTLE, DOL

SUBTLE.
Has he bit? Has he bit?

FACE.
And swallowed too, my Subtle.
I ha' given him line, and now he plays, i' faith.

SUBTLE.
And shall we twitch him?

FACE.
Thorough both the gills.
A wench is a rare bait, with which a man
No sooner's taken, but he straight firks mad.

SUBTLE.
Dol, my Lord Wha'ts'hum's sister, you must now
Bear yourself *statelich.*

DOL.
O, let me alone.
I'll not forget my race, I warrant you.
I'll keep my distance, laugh, and talk aloud;
Have all the tricks of a proud scurvy lady,
And be as rude's her woman.

FACE.
Well said, Sanguine.

SUBTLE.
But will he send his andirons?

FACE.
His jack too;
And's iron shoeing horn: I ha' spoke to him. Well,
I must not lose my wary gamester yonder.

SUBTLE.
O Monsieur Caution, that will not be gulled?
FACE.
Ay, if I can strike a fine hook into him, now
The Temple Church, there I have cast mine angle.
Well, pray for me. I'll about it.
SUBTLE. What, more gudgeons!°
[*One knocks.*]
Dol, scout, scout; stay Face, you must go to the door:
Pray God, it be my Anabaptist. Who is't, Dol?
DOL.
I know him not. He looks like a gold-end-man.°
SUBTLE.
Gods so! 'Tis he, he said he would send. What call you him?
The sanctified Elder, that should deal
For Mammon's jack and andirons! Let him in.
Stay, help me off, first, witn my gown. Away
Madam, to your withdrawing chamber. Now,
[*Exit* DOL.]
In a new tune, new gesture, but old language.
This fellow is sent from one negotiates with me
About the stone, too; for the holy Brethren
Of Amsterdam, the exiled Saints:° that hope
To raise their discipline by it. I must use him
In some strange fashion now to make him admire me.

Scene 5

Enter ANANIAS

SUBTLE.
Where is my drudge?
FACE. Sir.
SUBTLE. Take away the recipient,
And rectify your menstrue, from the phlegma.
Then pour it, o' the Sol, in the cucurbite,
And let 'em macerate, together.

II.4. **18. gudgeons:** live bait **21. gold-end-man:** travelling metal buyer
30. exiled Saints: puritans who fled abroad

FACE. Yes, sir.
And save the ground?
SUBTLE. No. *Terra damnata*
Must not have entrance in the work. Who are you?
ANANIAS.
A faithful Brother, if it please you.
SUBTLE. What's that?
A Lullianist? A Ripley?° *Filius artis?*
Can you sublime and dulcify? Calcine?
Know you the *sapor pontic? Sapor styptic?*
Or, what is homogene, or heterogene?
ANANIAS.
I understand no heathen language, truly.
SUBTLE.
Heathen, you Knipperdoling?° Is *Ars sacra,*
Or *chrysopoeia,* or *spagyrica,*
Of the pamphysic, or panarchic knowledge,
A heathen language?
ANANIAS. Heathen Greek, I take it.
SUBTLE.
How? Heathen Greek?
ANANIAS. All's heathen, but the Hebrew.
SUBTLE.
Sirrah, my varlet, stand you forth, and speak to him
Like a philosopher: answer, i' the language.
Name the vexations, and the martyrizations
Of metals in the work.
FACE. Sir, Putrefaction,
Solution, Ablution, Sublimation,
Cohobation, Calcination, Ceration, and
Fixation.
SUBTLE. This is heathen Greek, to you now?
And when comes Vivification?
FACE. After Mortification.
SUBTLE.
What's Cohobation?
FACE. 'Tis the pouring on
Your *Aqua Regis,* and then drawing him off

II.5 8. A Lullianist? A Ripley?: Subtle purposely misunderstands "faithful Brother" to mean not a puritan but a fellow alchemist, perhaps a follower of the Spaniard Raymond Lully (1235–1315) or the Englishman Sir George Ripley (died c. 1490) **13. Knipperdoling:** Bernt Knipperdollinck, a leader in the 1534 German "Kingdom of God" uprising of the Anabaptists, a radical Protestant sect professing holiness and simplicity

To the trine circle of the seven spheres.

SUBTLE.
What's the proper passion of metals?

FACE.
Malleation.

SUBTLE.
What's your *ultimum supplicium auri?*

FACE.
Antimonium.

SUBTLE.
This 's heathen Greek to you? And, what's your mercury?

FACE.
A very fugitive, he will be gone, sir.

SUBTLE.
How know you him?

FACE.
By his viscosity,
His oleosity, and his suscitability.

SUBTLE.
How do you sublime him?

FACE.
With the calce of eggshells,
White marble, talc.

SUBTLE.
Your *magisterium,* now?
What's that?

FACE.
Shifting, sir, your elements,
Dry into cold, cold into moist, moist into
Hot, hot into dry.

SUBTLE.
This 's heathen Greek to you, still?
Your *lapis philosophicus?*

FACE.
'Tis a stone, and not
A stone; a spirit, a soul, and a body:
Which, if you do dissolve, it is dissolved,
If you coagulate, it is coagulated,
If you make it to fly, it flieth.

SUBTLE.
Enough.
[*Exit* FACE.]
This 's heathen Greek to you? What are you, sir?

ANANIAS.
Please you, a servant of the exiled Brethren,
That deal with widows; and with orphans' goods;
And make a just account, unto the Saints:
A Deacon.

SUBTLE.
O, you are sent from master Wholesome,
Your teacher?

ANANIAS.
From Tribulation Wholesome,
Our very zealous Pastor.

SUBTLE.
Good. I have
Some orphans' goods to come here.

ANANIAS. Of what kind, sir?

SUBTLE.
Pewter and brass, andirons, and kitchen ware,
Metals that we must use our medicine on:
Wherein the Brethren may have a penn'orth,
For ready money.

ANANIAS. Were the orphans' parents
Sincere professors?

SUBTLE. Why do you ask?

ANANIAS. Because
We then are to deal justly, and give (in truth)
Their utmost value.

SUBTLE. 'Slid, you'd cozen, else,
And if their parents were not of the faithful?
I will not trust you, now I think on 't,
Till I ha' talked with your Pastor. Ha' you brought money
To buy more coals?

ANANIAS. No, surely.

SUBTLE. No? How so?

ANANIAS.
The Brethren bid me say unto you, sir.
Surely they will not venture any more
Till they may see projection.

SUBTLE. How!

ANANIAS. You've had,
For the instruments, as bricks, and loam, and glasses,
Already thirty pound; and, for materials,
They say, some ninety more: and, they have heard, since,
That one at Heidelberg made it of an egg,
And a small paper of pin-dust.

SUBTLE. What's your name?

ANANIAS.
My name is Ananias.

SUBTLE. Out, the varlet
That cozened the Apostles! Hence, away,
Flee mischief; had your holy Consistory
No name to send me, of another sound,
Than wicked Ananias? Send your Elders
Hither to make atonement for you quickly.
And gi' me satisfaction; or out goes
The fire: and down th' alembics, and the furnace,
Piger Henricus or what not. Thou wretch,
Both Sericon and Bufo shall be lost,
Tell 'em. All hope of rooting out the Bishops,
Or th' Antichristian Hierarchy shall perish

If they stay threescore minutes. The Aqueity,
Terreity, and Sulphureity
Shall run together again, and all be annulled
Thou wicked Ananias. This will fetch 'em,
[*Exit* ANANIAS.]
And make 'em haste towards their gulling more.
A man must deal like a rough nurse, and fright
Those that are froward to an appetite.

Scene 6

Enter DRUGGER, FACE

FACE.
He's busy with his spirits, but we'll upon him.
SUBTLE.
How now! What mates? What Bayards° ha' we here?
FACE.
I told you he would be furious. Sir, here's Nab.
Has brought you another piece of gold to look on:
(We must appease him. Give it me) and prays you
You would devise (what is it Nab?)
DRUGGER. A sign, sir.
FACE.
Ay, a good lucky one, a thriving sign, Doctor.
SUBTLE.
I was devising now.
FACE. ('Slight, do not say so,
He will repent he ga' you any more.)
What say you to his constellation, Doctor?
The Balance?°
SUBTLE. No, that way is stale and common.
A townsman, born in Taurus, gives the bull;
Or the bull's head: in Aries, the ram.
A poor device. No, I will have his name
Formed in some mystic character; whose radii,
Striking the senses of the passers-by,
Shall, by a virtual influence, breed affections,
That may result upon the party owns it:
As thus—

II.6. **2. Bayards:** blind fools, from Charlemagne's legendary blind war horse **11. Balance:** Libra

FACE. Nab!
SUBTLE. He first shall have a bell, that's Abel;
And, by it, standing one whose name is Dee,
In a rug gown; there's D and Rug, that's Drug:
And, right anenst him, a dog snarling Er;
There's Drugger, Abel Drugger. That's his sign.
And here's now mystery, and hieroglyphic!
FACE.
Abel, thou art made.
DRUGGER. Sir, I do thank his worship.
FACE.
Six o' thy legs° more, will not do it, Nab.
He has brought you a pipe of tobacco, Doctor.
DRUGGER. Yes, sir:
I have another thing I would impart—
FACE.
Out with it, Nab.
DRUGGER. Sir, there is lodged, hard by me
A rich young widow—
FACE. Good! *A bona roba?*
DRUGGER.
But nineteen, at the most.
FACE. Very good, Abel.
DRUGGER.
Marry, she's not in fashion, yet; she wears
A hood: but 't stands a cop.°
FACE. No matter, Abel.
DRUGGER.
And, I do now and then give her a fucus—
FACE.
What! Dost thou deal, Nab?
SUBTLE. I did tell you, Captain.
DRUGGER.
And physic too sometimes, sir: for which she trusts me
With all her mind. She's come up here of purpose
To learn the fashion.
FACE. Good (his match too!) on, Nab.
DRUGGER.
And she does strangely long to know her fortune.
FACE.
God's lid, Nab, send her to the Doctor, hither.

26. legs: bowings **33. a cop:** on her head, as a substitute for the more fashionable hat

DRUGGER.
Yes, I have spoken to her of his worship, already:
But she's afraid it will be blown abroad
And hurt her marriage.
FACE. Hurt it? 'Tis the way
To heal it, if 'twere hurt; to make it more
Followed and sought: Nab, thou shalt tell her this.
She'll be more known, more talked of, and your widows
Are ne'er of any price till they be famous;
Their honor is their multitude of suitors:
Send her, it may be thy good fortune. What?
Thou dost not know.
DRUGGER. No, sir, she'll never marry
Under a knight. Her brother has made a vow.
FACE.
What, and dost thou despair, my little Nab,
Knowing what the Doctor has set down for thee,
And seeing so many o' the city, dubbed?
One glass o' thy water° with a Madam I know
Will have it done, Nab. What's her brother? A knight?
DRUGGER.
No, sir, a gentleman, newly warm in his land, sir,
Scarce cold in his one and twenty; that does govern
His sister here: and is a man himself
Of some three thousand a year, and is come up
To learn to quarrel, and to live by his wits,
And will go down again, and die i' the country.
FACE.
How! To quarrel?
DRUGGER. Yes, sir, to carry quarrels,
As gallants do, and manage 'em, by line.°
FACE.
'Slid, Nab! The Doctor is the only man
In Christendom for him. He has made a table,
With mathematical demonstrations,
Touching the art of quarrels. He will give him
An instrument to quarrel by. Go, bring 'em, both:
Him and his sister. And, for thee, with her
The Doctor haply may persuade. Go to.
Shalt give his worship a new damask suit
Upon the premises.
SUBTLE. O, good Captain.
FACE. He shall,

55. water: aphrodisiac? **64. by line:** fashionably

He is the honestest fellow, Doctor. Stay not,
No offers, bring the damask, and the parties.

DRUGGER.
I'll try my power, sir.

FACE. And thy will too, Nab.

SUBTLE.
'Tis good tobacco this! What is't an ounce?

FACE.
He'll send you a pound, Doctor.

SUBTLE. O, no.

FACE. He will do't.
It is the goodest soul. Abel, about it.
(Thou shalt know more anon. Away, be gone.)

[*Exit* DRUGGER.]

A miserable rogue, and lives with cheese,
And has the worms. That was the cause indeed
Why he came now. He dealt with me, in private,
To get a medicine for 'em.

SUBTLE. And shall, sir. This works.

FACE.
A wife, a wife, for one on's, my dear Subtle:
We'll e'en draw lots, and he that fails shall have
The more in goods, the other has in tail.

SUBTLE.
Rather the less. For she may be so light
She may want grains.°

FACE. Ay, or be such a burden
A man would scarce endure her, for the whole.

SUBTLE.
Faith, best let's see her first, and then determine.

FACE.
Content. But Dol must ha' no breath on't.

SUBTLE. Mum.
Away, you to your Surly yonder, catch him.

FACE.
Pray God, I ha' not stayed too long.

SUBTLE. I fear it.

[*Exeunt.*]

89. grain: weight

ACT III

Scene 1

Enter TRIBULATION, ANANIAS

TRIBULATION.
These chastisements are common to the Saints,
And such rebukes we of the Separation
Must bear with willing shoulders, as the trials
Sent forth to tempt our frailties.

ANANIAS. In pure zeal
I do not like the man: he is a heathen.
And speaks the language of Canaan, truly.

TRIBULATION.
I think him a profane person, indeed.

ANANIAS. He bears
The visible mark of the Beast in his forehead.
And for his stone, it is a work of darkness,
And, with philosophy, blinds the eyes of man.

TRIBULATION.
Good Brother, we must bend unto all means
That may give furtherance to the holy cause.

ANANIAS.
Which his cannot: the sanctified cause
Should have a sanctified course.

TRIBULATION. Not always necessary.
The children of perdition are ofttimes
Made instruments even of the greatest works.
Beside, we should give somewhat to man's nature,
The place he lives in, still about the fire,
And fume of metals, that intoxicate
The brain of man, and make him prone to passion.
Where have you greater atheists, than your cooks?
Or more profane or choleric than your glassmen?
More antichristian, than your bellfounders?
What makes the Devil so devilish, I would ask you,
Satan, our common enemy, but his being
Perpetually about the fire, and boiling
Brimstone and arsenic? We must give, I say,
Unto the motives and the stirrers up
Of humours in the blood. It may be so.

When as the work is done, the stone is made,
This heat of his may turn into a zeal,
And stand up for the beauteous discipline
Against the menstruous cloth and rag° of Rome.
We must await his calling, and the coming
Of the good spirit. You did fault t' upbraid him
With the Brethren's blessing of Heidelberg, weighing
What need we have to hasten on the work
For the restoring of the silenced Saints,
Which ne'er will be, but by the philosopher's stone.
And, so a learned Elder, one of Scotland,
Assured me; *aurum potabile* being
The only medicine for the civil magistrate,
T' incline him to a feeling of the cause:
And must be daily used in the disease.

ANANIAS.
I have not edified more, truly, by man;
Not since the beautiful light first shone on me:
And I am sad my zeal hath so offended.

TRIBULATION.
Let us call on him, then.

ANANIAS. The motion's good,
And of the spirit; I will knock first: peace be within.

Scene 2

Enter SUBTLE, TRIBULATION, ANANIAS

SUBTLE.
O, are you come? 'Twas time. Your threescore minutes
Were at the last thread, you see; and down had gone
Furnus acediae, turris circulatorius:
Lembic, bolt's head, retort, and pelican
Had all been cinders. Wicked Ananias!
Art thou returned? Nay then, it goes down yet.

TRIBULATION.
Sir, be appeased, he is come to humble
Himself in spirit, and to ask your patience,
If too much zeal hath carried him aside
From the due path.

SUBTLE. Why, this doth qualify!

III.1. **33. menstruous . . . rag:** derogatory puritan names for the Roman surplice

TRIBULATION.
The Brethren had no purpose, verily,
To give you the least grievance: but are ready
To lend their willing hands to any project
The spirit and you direct.
SUBTLE. This qualifies more!
TRIBULATION.
And, for the orphans' goods, let them be valued,
Or what is needful, else, to the holy work,
It shall be numbered: here, by me, the Saints
Throw down their purse before you.
SUBTLE. This qualifies, most!
Why, thus it should be, now you understand.
Have I discoursed so unto you of our stone?
And of the good that it shall bring your cause?
Showed you, (beside the main of hiring forces
Abroad, drawing the Hollanders, your friends,
From th' Indies, to serve you with all their fleet)
That even the medicinal use shall make you a faction
And party in the realm? As, put the case,
That some great man in state, he have the gout,
Why, you but send three drops of your elixir,
You help him straight: there you have made a friend.
Another has the palsy, or the dropsy,
He takes of your incombustible stuff,
He's young again: there you have made a friend.
A lady, that is past the feat of body,
Though not of mind, and hath her face decayed
Beyond all cure of paintings, you restore
With the oil of talc; there you have made a friend:
And all her friends. A lord that is a leper,
A knight that has the bone-ache,° or a squire
That hath both these, you make 'em smooth, and sound,
With a bare fricace of your medicine: still,
You increase your friends.
TRIBULATION. Ay, 'tis very pregnant.
SUBTLE.
And, then, the turning of this lawyer's pewter
To plate, at Christmas—
ANANIAS. Christ-tide,° I pray you.
SUBTLE.
Yet, Ananias?

III.2. **38. bone-ache:** syphilis **43. Christ-tide:** to avoid the Popish word, **mass**

ANANIAS. I have done.

SUBTLE. Or changing
His parcel gilt to massy° gold. You cannot
But raise you friends. With all, to be of power
To pay an army in the field, to buy
The King of France out of his realms; or Spain
Out of his Indies: what can you not do,
Against lords spiritual, or temporal,
That shall oppone you?

TRIBULATION. Verily, 'tis true.
We may be temporal lords, ourselves, I take it.

SUBTLE.
You may be anything, and leave off to make
Long-winded exercises: or suck up,
Your ha, and hum, in a tune. I not deny,
But such as are not graced, in a state,
May, for their ends, be adverse in religion,
And get a tune to call the flock together:
For (to say sooth) a tune does much with women,
And other phlegmatic people, it is your bell.

ANANIAS.
Bells are profane: a tune may be religious.

SUBTLE.
No warning with you? Then, farewell my patience.
'Slight, it shall down: I will not be thus tortured.

TRIBULATION.
I pray you, sir.

SUBTLE. All shall perish. I have spoke it.

TRIBULATION.
Let me find grace, sir, in your eyes; the man
He stands corrected: neither did his zeal
(But as yourself) allow a tune somewhere.
Which now being toward the stone, we shall not need.

SUBTLE.
No, nor your holy vizard to win widows
To give you legacies; or make zealous wives
To rob their husbands for the common cause:
Nor take the start of bonds broke but one day,
And say they were forfeited by providence.
Nor shall you need o'er night to eat huge meals
To celebrate your next day's fast the better:
The whilst the Brethren, and the Sisters, humbled,
Abate the stiffness of the flesh. Nor cast
Before your hungry hearers, scrupulous bones,

45. parcel . . . massy: plated to solid

As whether a Christian may hawk or hunt;
Or whether matrons of the holy assembly
May lay their hair out or wear doublets:
Or have that idol Starch about their linen.

ANANIAS.
It is, indeed, an idol.

TRIBULATION. Mind him not, sir.
I do command thee, spirit (of zeal, but trouble)
To peace within him. Pray you, sir, go on.

SUBTLE.
Nor shall you need to libel 'gainst the prelates,
And shorten° so your ears, against the hearing
Of the next wire-drawn grace. Nor, of necessity,
Rail against plays, to please the alderman,
Whose daily custard you devour. Nor lie
With zealous rage till you are hoarse. Not one
Of these so singular arts. Nor call yourselves
By names of Tribulation, Persecution,
Restraint, Long-Patience, and such like, affected
By the whole family, or wood° of you,
Only for glory, and to catch the ear
Of the Disciple.

TRIBULATION. Truly, sir, they are
Ways that the godly Brethren have invented,
For propagation of the glorious cause,
As very notable means, and whereby, also,
Themselves grow soon, and profitably famous.

SUBTLE.
O, but the stone, all's idle to it! Nothing!
The art of Angels, nature's miracle,
The divine secret, that doth fly in clouds,
From east to west: and whose tradition
Is not from men, but spirits.

ANANIAS. I hate traditions:
I do not trust 'em—

TRIBULATION. Peace.

ANANIAS. They are popish, all.
I will not peace. I will not—

TRIBULATION. Ananias.

ANANIAS.
Please the profane, to grieve the godly: I may not.

SUBTLE.
Well, Ananias, thou shalt overcome.

87. shorten: clip, as a punishment **95. wood:** crowd

TRIBULATION.
It is an ignorant zeal that haunts him, sir.
But truly, else, a very faithful Brother,
A botcher:° and a man, by revelation,
That hath a competent knowledge of the truth.

SUBTLE.
Has he a competent sum, there, i' the bag,
To buy the goods within? I am made guardian,
And must, for charity and conscience' sake,
Now see the most be made for my poor orphan:
Though I desire the Brethren, too, good gainers.
There they are within. When you have viewed, and bought 'em,
And ta'en the inventory of what they are,
They are ready for projection; there's no more
To do: cast on the medicine, so much silver
As there is tin there, so much gold as brass,
I'll gi' it you in, by weight.

TRIBULATION. But how long time,
Sir, must the Saints expect yet?

SUBTLE. Let me see,
How's the moon now? Eight, nine, ten days hence
He will be silver potate; then, three days,
Before he citronize: some fifteen days
The *magisterium* will be perfected.

ANANIAS.
About the second day, of the third week,
In the ninth month?°

SUBTLE. Yes, my good Ananias.

TRIBULATION.
What will the orphan's goods arise to, think you?

SUBTLE.
Some hundred marks; as much as filled three cars,
Unladed now: you'll make six millions of 'em.
But I must ha' more coals laid in.

TRIBULATION. How!

SUBTLE. Another load,
And then we ha' finished. We must now increase
Our fire to *ignis ardens,* we are past
Fimus equinus, balnei, cineris,
And all those lenter heats. If the holy purse
Should, with this draught, fall low, and that the Saints
Do need a present sum, I have a trick

113. botcher: patcher, tailor **131–32. About . . . month:** He calculates from the beginning of the world in March and avoids Roman calendar names

To melt the pewter you shall buy now instantly,
And, with a tincture, make you as good Dutch dollars
As any are in Holland.

TRIBULATION. Can you so?

SUBTLE.
Ay, and shall bide the third examination.

ANANIAS.
It will be joyful tidings to the Brethren.

SUBTLE.
But you must carry it, secret.

TRIBULATION. Ay, but stay,
This act of coining, is it lawful?

ANANIAS. Lawful?
We know no magistrate. Or, if we did,
This 's foreign coin.

SUBTLE. It is no coining, sir.
It is but casting.

TRIBULATION. Ha? You distinguish well.
Casting of money may be lawful.

ANANIAS. 'Tis, sir.

TRIBULATION.
Truly, I take it so.

SUBTLE. There is no scruple,
Sir, to be made of it; believe Ananias:
This case of conscience he is studied in.

TRIBULATION.
I'll make a question of it to the Brethren.

ANANIAS.
The Brethren shall approve it lawful, doubt not.
Where shall't be done?

SUBTLE. For that we'll talk, anon.
[*Knock without.*]
There's some to speak with me. Go in, I pray you,
And view the parcels. That's the inventory.
[*Exeunt* ANANIAS, TRIBULATION.]
I'll come to you straight. Who is it? Face! Appear.

Scene 3

Enter FACE

SUBTLE.
How now? Good prize?

FACE. Good pox! Yond' costive cheater
Never came on.
SUBTLE. How then?
FACE. I ha' walked the round,
Till now, and no such thing.
SUBTLE. And ha' you quit him?
FACE.
Quit him? And hell would quit him too he were happy.
'Slight would you have me stalk like a mill-jade
All day for one that will not yield us grains?
I know him of old.
SUBTLE. O, but to ha' gulled him
Had been a mastery.
FACE. Let him go, black boy,
And turn thee that some fresh news may possess thee.
A noble count, a don of Spain (my dear
Delicious compeer, and my party-bawd)
Who is come hither, private, for his conscience,
And brought munition with him, six great slops,°
Bigger than three Dutch boys,° beside round trunks,°
Furnished with pistolets, and pieces of eight,
Will straight be here, my rogue, to have thy bath°
(That is the color,) and to make his battery
Upon our Dol, our castle, our Cinque-Port,
Our Dover pier, our what thou wilt. Where is she?
She must prepare perfumes, delicate linen,
The bath in chief, a banquet, and her wit,
For she must milk his epididymis.
Where is the doxy?
SUBTLE. I'll send her to thee:
And but despatch my brace of little John Leydens,
And come again myself.
FACE. Are they within then?
SUBTLE.
Numbering the sum.
FACE. How much?
SUBTLE. A hundred marks, boy.
[*Exit* SUBTLE.]
FACE.
Why, this 's a lucky day! Ten pounds of Mammon!
Three o' my clerk! A portague o' my grocer!

III.3. **13. slops:** wide pants **14. hoys:** boats **round trunks:** padded hose **16. bath:** bagnio, brothel **17. color:** official story

This o' the Brethren! Beside reversions,
And states, to come i' the widow, and my count!
[*Enter* DOL.]
My share, today, will not be bought for forty—

DOL. What?

FACE.
Pounds, dainty Dorothy, art thou so near?

DOL.
Yes, say lord General, how fares our camp?

FACE.
As, with the few that had entrenched themselves
Safe, by their discipline, against a world, Dol:
And laughed within those trenches, and grew fat
With thinking on the booties, Dol, brought in
Daily by their small parties. This dear hour
A doughty don is taken with my Dol;
And thou may'st make his ransom what thou wilt,
My Dousabell: he shall be brought here fettered
With thy fair looks before he sees thee; and thrown
In a downbed, as dark as any dungeon;
Where thou shalt keep him waking, with thy drum;
Thy drum, my Dol; thy drum; till he be tame
As the poor blackbirds were i' the great frost,
Or bees are with a basin:° and so hive him
I' the swanskin coverlid and cambric sheets,
Till he work honey and wax, my little God's-gift.

DOL.
What is he, General?

FACE. An adalantado,
A grandee, girl. Was not my Dapper here, yet?

DOL.
No.

FACE. Nor my Drugger?

DOL. Neither.

FACE. A pox on 'em,
They are so long a-furnishing! Such stinkards
Would not be seen upon these festival days.
[*Enter* SUBTLE.]
How now! Ha' you done?

SUBTLE. Done. They are gone. The sum
Is here in bank, my Face. I would we knew
Another chapman, now, would buy 'em outright.

47. basin: i.e. by tapping on a metal pan

FACE.
'Slid, Nab shall do't, against he ha' the widow,
To furnish household.

SUBTLE. Excellent, well thought on,
Pray God, he come.

FACE. I pray, he keep away
Till our new business be o'erpast.

SUBTLE. But, Face,
How camest thou by this secret don?

FACE. A spirit
Brought me th' intelligence, in a paper, here,
As I was conjuring yonder in my circle
For Surly: I ha' my flies abroad. Your bath
Is famous, Subtle, by my means. Sweet Dol,
You must go tune your virginal, no losing
O' the least time. And, do you hear? Good action.
Firk like a flounder; kiss like a scallop, close:
And tickle him with thy mother-tongue. His great
Verdugoship has not a jot of language:
So much the easier to be cozened, my Dolly.
He will come here in a hired coach, obscure,
And our own coachman, whom I have sent, as guide,
[*One knocks.*]
No creature else. Who's that?

SUBTLE. It i' not he?

FACE.
O no, not yet this hour.

SUBTLE. Who is't?

DOL. Dapper,
Your clerk.

FACE. God's will, then, Queen of Fairy,
On with your tire; and, Doctor, with your robes.
Let's despatch him, for God's sake.

SUBTLE. 'Twill be long.

FACE.
I warrant you, take but the cues I give you,
It shall be brief enough. 'Slight, here are more!
Abel, and I think, the angry boy, the heir,
That fain would quarrel.

SUBTLE. And the widow?

FACE. No,
Not that I see. Away. O sir, you are welcome.
[*Exit* SUBTLE.]

Scene 4

Enter DAPPER

FACE.
The Doctor is within, a-moving for you;
(I have had the most ado to win him to it)
He swears you'll be the darling o' the dice:
He never heard her Highness dote till now (he says.)
Your aunt has given you the most gracious words
That can be thought on.

DAPPER.
Shall I see her Grace?

[*Enter* DRUGGER *and* KASTRIL.]

FACE.
See her, and kiss her, too. What? Honest Nab!
Hast brought the damask?

DRUGGER.
No, sir, here's tobacco.

FACE.
'Tis well done, Nab: thou'lt bring the damask too?

DRUGGER.
Yes, here's the gentleman, Captain, master Kastril,
I have brought to see the Doctor.

FACE.
Where's the widow?

DRUGGER.
Sir, as he likes, his sister (he says) shall come.

FACE.
O, is it so? Good time. Is your name Kastril, sir?

KASTRIL.
Ay, and the best o' the Kastrils, I'd be sorry else,
By fifteen hundred a year. Where is this Doctor?
My mad tobacco-boy, here, tells me of one,
That can do things. Has he any skill?

FACE.
Wherein, sir?

KASTRIL.
To carry a business, manage a quarrel, fairly,
Upon fit terms.

FACE.
It seems sir, you're but young
About the town that can make that a question!

KASTRIL.
Sir, not so young, but I have heard some speech
Of the angry boys, and seen 'em take tobacco;
And in his shop: and I can take it too.
And I would fain be one of 'em, and go down

And practise i' the country.

FACE. Sir, for the *duello,*
The Doctor, I assure you, shall inform you
To the least shadow of a hair: and show you
An instrument he has, of his own making,
Wherewith, no sooner shall you make report
Of any quarrel, but he will take the height on't,
Most instantly; and tell in what degree
Of safety it lies in, or mortality.
And how it may be borne, whether in a right line,
Or a half-circle; or may, else, be cast
Into an angle blunt, if not acute:
All this he will demonstrate. And then, rules
To give and take the lie by.

KASTRIL. How? To take it?

FACE.
Yes, in oblique, he'll show you; or in circle:
But never in diameter. The whole town
Study his theorems, and dispute them, ordinarily,
At the eating academies.

KASTRIL. But, does he teach
Living by the wits, too?

FACE. Anything, whatever.
You cannot think that subtlety but he reads it.
He made me a Captain. I was a stark pimp,
Just o' your standing, 'fore I met with him:
It i' not two months since. I'll tell you his method.
First, he will enter you, at some ordinary.

KASTRIL.
No, I'll not come there. You shall pardon me.

FACE. For why, sir?

KASTRIL.
There's gaming there, and tricks.

FACE. Why, would you be
A gallant, and not game?

KASTRIL. Ay, 'twill spend a man.

FACE.
Spend you? It will repair you when you are spent.
How do they live by their wits, there, that have vented
Six times your fortunes?

KASTRIL. What, three thousand a year!

FACE.
Ay, forty thousand.

KASTRIL. Are there such?

FACE. Ay, sir.

And gallants, yet. Here's a young gentleman,
Is born to nothing, forty marks a year,
Which I count nothing. He's to be initiated,
And have a fly o' the Doctor. He will win you
By unresistable luck, within this fortnight,
Enough to buy a barony. They will set him
Upmost, at the Groom-porter's,° all the Christmas!
And, for the whole year through, at every place
Where there is play, present him with the chair;
The best attendance, the best drink, sometimes
Two glasses of canary, and pay nothing;
The purset linen, and the sharpest knife,
The partridge next his trencher: and, somewhere,
The dainty bed, in private, with the dainty.
You shall ha' your ordinaries bid for him,
As playhouses for a poet; and the master
Pray him, aloud, to name what dish he affects,
Which must be buttered shrimps: and those that drink
To no mouth else will drink to his, as being
The goodly, a president mouth of all the board.

KASTRIL.
Do you not gull one?

FACE. 'Od's my life! Do you think it?
You shall have a cast° commander, (can but get
In credit with a glover, or a spurrier,°
For some two pair of either's ware aforehand)
Will, by most swift posts, dealing with him,
Arrive at competent means to keep himself,
His punk, and naked boy, in excellent fashion.
And be admired for it.

KASTRIL. Will the Doctor teach this?

FACE.
He will do more, sir, when your land is gone,
(As men of spirit hate to keep earth long)
In a vacation, when small money is stirring,
And ordinaries suspended till the term,
He'll show a perspective, where on one side
You shall behold the faces and the persons
Of all sufficient young heirs in town,
Whose bonds are current for commodity;
On th' other side, the merchants' forms, and others
That without help of any second broker

III.4. **61. Groom-porter's:** government gambling regulator **76. cast:** discharged **77. spurrier:** spur maker

(Who would expect a share) will trust such parcels:
In the third square, the very street and sign
Where the commodity dwells, and does but wait
To be delivered, be it pepper, soap,
Hops, or tobacco, oatmeal, woad,° or cheeses.
All which you may so handle to enjoy
To your own use, and never stand obliged.

KASTRIL.
I' faith! Is he such a fellow?

FACE. Why, Nab here knows him.
And then for making matches, for rich widows,
Young gentlewomen, heirs, the fortunat'st man!
He's sent to, far, and near, all over England,
To have his counsel, and to know their fortunes.

KASTRIL.
God's will, my suster shall see him.

FACE. I'll tell you, sir,
What he did tell me of Nab. It's a strange thing!
(By the way you must eat no cheese, Nab, it breeds melancholy:
And that same melancholy breeds worms) but pass it—
He told me, honest Nab, here, was ne'er at tavern,
But once in's life.

DRUGGER. Truth, and no more I was not.

FACE.
And then he was so sick—

DRUGGER. Could he tell you that, too?

FACE.
How should I know it?

DRUGGER. In troth we had been a-shooting,
And had a piece of fat ram-mutton to supper
That lay so heavy o' my stomach—

FACE. And he has no head
To bear any wine; for, what with the noise o' the fiddlers,
And care of his shop, for he dares keep no servants—

DRUGGER.
My head did so ache—

FACE. As he was fain to be brought home,
The Doctor told me. And then, a good old woman—

DRUGGER.
(Yes, faith, she dwells in Sea-coal Lane) did cure me,
With sodden° ale and pellitory° o' the wall:
Cost me but two pence. I had another sickness,
Was worse than that.

97. woad: blue dye **120. sodden:** boiled **pellitory:** medicinal plant

FACE. Ay, that was with the grief
Thou took'st for being 'sessed at eighteen pence
For the water-work.

DRUGGER. In truth, and it was like
T'have cost me almost my life.

FACE. Thy hair went off?

DRUGGER.
Yes, sir, 'twas done for spite.

FACE. Nay, so says the Doctor.

KASTRIL.
Pray thee, tobacco-boy, go fetch my suster,
I'll see this learned boy, before I go:
And so shall she.

FACE. Sir, he is busy now:
But, if you have a sister to fetch hither,
Perhaps your own pains may command her sooner;
And he, by that time, will be free.

KASTRIL. I go.
[*Exit* KASTRIL.]

FACE.
Drugger, she's thine: the damask. (Subtle, and I
[*Exit* DRUGGER.]
Must wrestle for her.) Come on, master Dapper.
You see how I turn clients here away
To give your cause despatch. Ha' you performed
The ceremonies were enjoined you?

DAPPER. Yes, o' the vinegar,
And the clean shirt.

FACE. 'Tis well: that shirt may do you
More worship than you think. Your aunt's afire
But that she will not show it, t'have a sight on you.
Ha' you provided for her Grace's servants?

DAPPER.
Yes, here are six score Edward shillings.

FACE. Good.

DAPPER.
And an old Harry's sovereign.

FACE. Very good.

DAPPER.
And three James shillings, and an Elizabeth groat,
Just twenty nobles.

FACE. O, you are too just.
I would you had had the other noble in Marys.

DAPPER.
I have some Philip, and Marys.

FACE. Ay, those same
Are best of all. Where are they? Hark, the Doctor.

Scene 5

Enter SUBTLE

SUBTLE.
Is yet her Grace's cousin come?
[SUBTLE *disguised like a Priest of Fairy.*]

FACE. He is come.

SUBTLE.
And is he fasting?

FACE. Yes.

SUBTLE. And hath cried *hum?*

FACE.
Thrice, you must answer.

DAPPER. Thrice.

SUBTLE. And as oft *buz?*

FACE.
If you have, say.

DAPPER. I have.

SUBTLE. Then, to her coz,
Hoping, that he hath vinegared his senses,
As he was bid, the Fairy Queen dispenses,
By me, this robe, the petticoat of Fortune;
Which that he straight put on, she doth importune.
And though to Fortune near be her petticoat,
Yet nearer is her smock, the Queen doth note:
And, therefore, even of that a piece she hath sent,
Which, being a child, to wrap him in, was rent;
And prays him, for a scarf he now will wear it
[*They blind him with a rag.*]
(With as much love as then her Grace did tear it)
About his eyes to show he is fortunate.
And, trusting unto her to make his state,
He'll throw away all worldly pelf about him;
Which that he will perform, she doth not doubt him.

FACE.
She need not doubt him, sir. Alas, he has nothing,
But what he will part withall, as willingly,

Upon her Grace's word (throw away your purse)
As she would ask it: (handkerchiefs, and all)
She cannot bid that thing, but he'll obey.
(If you have a ring, about you, cast it off,
Or a silver seal, at your wrist, her Grace will send
[*He throws away, as they bid him.*]
Her fairies here to search you, therefore deal
Directly with her Highness. If they find
That you conceal a mite, you are undone.)

DAPPER.
Truly, there's all.

FACE. All what?

DAPPER. My money, truly.

FACE.
Keep nothing that is transitory about you.
(Bid Dol play music.) Look, the elves are come
[DOL *enters with a cithern: they pinch him.*]
To pinch you, if you tell not truth. Advise you.

DAPPER.
O, I have a paper with a spur-rial° in't.

FACE. *Ti, ti,*
They knew't, they say.

SUBTLE. *Ti, ti, ti, ti,* he has more yet.

FACE.
Ti, ti-ti-ti. I' the t'other pocket?

SUBTLE. *Titi, titi, titi, titi.*
They must pinch him, or he will never confess, they say.

DAPPER.
O, O.

FACE. Nay, pray you hold. He is her Grace's nephew.
Ti, ti, ti? What care you? Good faith, you shall care.
Deal plainly, sir, and shame the fairies. Show
You are an innocent.

DAPPER. By this good light, I ha' nothing.

SUBTLE.
Ti ti, ti ti to ta. He does equivocate, she says:
Ti, ti do ti, ti ti do, ti da. And swears by the light, when he is blinded.

DAPPER.
By this good dark, I ha' nothing but a half crown
Of gold about my wrist that my love gave me;
And a leaden heart I wore, sin' she forsook me.

III.5. **33. spur-rial:** Edward IV noble, worth fifteen shillings

FACE.
I thought 'twas something. And would you incur
Your aunt's displeasure for these trifles? Come,
I had rather you had thrown away twenty half crowns.
You may wear your leaden heart still. How now?

SUBTLE.
What news, Dol?

DOL. Yonder's your knight, sir Mammon.

FACE.
God's lid, we never thought of him till now.
Where is he?

DOL. Here, hard by. He's at the door.

SUBTLE.
And you are not ready now? Dol, get his suit.
He must not be sent back.

FACE. O, by no means.
What shall we do with this same puffin here,
Now he's o' the spit?

SUBTLE. Why, lay him back a while
With some device. *Ti, ti ti, ti ti ti.* Would her Grace speak with me?
I come. Help, Dol.

FACE. Who's there? Sir Epicure;
[*He speaks through the keyhole, the other knocking.*]
My master's i' the way. Please you to walk
Three or four turns, but till his back be turned,
And I am for you. Quickly, Dol.

SUBTLE. Her Grace
Commends her kindly to you, master Dapper.

DAPPER.
I long to see her Grace.

SUBTLE. She now is set
At dinner in her bed; and she has sent you,
From her own private trencher, a dead mouse,
And a piece of gingerbread, to be merry withal,
And stay your stomach, lest you faint with fasting:
Yet, if you could hold out till she saw you (she says)
It would be better for you.

FACE. Sir, he shall
Hold out, and 'twere this two hours, for her Highness;
I can assure you that. We will not lose
All we ha' done—

SUBTLE. He must nor see nor speak
To anybody till then.

FACE. For that, we'll put, sir,
A stay in 's mouth.
SUBTLE. Of what?
FACE. Of gingerbread.
Make you it fit. He that hath pleased her Grace,
Thus far, shall not now crinkle for a little.
Gape sir, and let him fit you.
SUBTLE. Where shall we now
Bestow him?
DOL. I' the privy.
SUBTLE. Come along, sir,
I now must show you Fortune's privy lodgings.
FACE.
Are they perfumed? And his bath ready?
SUBTLE. All.
Only the fumigation's somewhat strong.
FACE.
Sir Epicure, I am yours, sir, by and by.
[*Exeunt.*]

ACT IV

Scene 1

Enter FACE, MAMMON

FACE.
O, sir, you're come i' the only, finest time—
MAMMON.
Where's master?
FACE. Now preparing for projection, sir.
Your stuff will b' all changed shortly.
MAMMON. Into gold?
FACE.
To gold and silver, sir.
MAMMON. Silver I care not for.
FACE.
Yes, sir, a little to give beggars.
MAMMON. Where's the lady?

FACE.
At hand, here. I ha' told her such brave things o' you,
Touching your bounty and your noble spirit—
MAMMON. Hast thou?
FACE.
As she is almost in her fit to see you.
But, good sir, no divinity i' your conference,
For fear of putting her in rage—
MAMMON. I warrant thee.
FACE.
Six men will not hold her down. And, then,
If the old man should hear, or see you—
MAMMON. Fear not.
FACE.
The very house, sir, would run mad. You know it
How scrupulous he is, and violent,
'Gainst the least act of sin. Physic, or mathematics,
Poetry, state, or bawdry (as I told you)
She will endure, and never startle: but
No word of controversy.
MAMMON. I am schooled, good Eulen.
FACE.
And you must praise her house, remember that,
And her nobility.
MAMMON. Let me, alone:
No Herald, no nor Antiquary, Lungs,
Shall do it better. Go.
FACE. Why, this is yet
A kind of modern happiness to have
Dol Common for a great lady.
MAMMON. Now, Epicure,
Heighten thyself, talk to her, all in gold;
Rain her as many showers as Jove did drops
Unto his Danae: show the God a miser,
Compared with Mammon. What? The stone will do't.
She shall feel gold, taste gold, hear gold, sleep gold:
Nay, we will *concumbere*° gold. I will be puissant,
And mighty in my talk to her! Here she comes.
[*Enter* DOL.]
FACE.
To him, Dol, suckle him. This is the noble knight,
I told your ladyship—

IV.1. **30. concumbere:** breed

MAMMON. Madam, with your pardon,
I kiss your vesture.
DOL. Sir, I were uncivil
If I would suffer that, my lip to you, sir.
MAMMON.
I hope my lord your brother be in health, lady?
DOL.
My lord, my brother is, though I no lady, sir.
FACE.
(Well said my Guinea bird.°)
MAMMON. Right noble madam—
FACE.
(O, we shall have most fierce idolatry!)
MAMMON.
'Tis your prerogative.
DOL. Rather your courtesy.
MAMMON.
Were there nought else t'enlarge your virtues, to me
These answers speak your breeding, and your blood.
DOL.
Blood we boast none, sir, a poor baron's daughter.
MAMMON.
Poor! And gat you? Profane not. Had your father
Slept all the happy remnant of his life
After that act, lain but there still, and panted,
He'd done enough, to make himself, his issue,
And his posterity noble.
DOL. Sir, although
We may be said to want the gilt, and trappings,
The dress of honour; yet we strive to keep
The seeds, and the materials.
MAMMON. I do see
The old ingredient, virtue, was not lost,
Nor the drug money, used to make your compound.
There is a strange nobility i' your eye,
This lip, that chin! Methinks you do resemble
One o' the Austriac princes.
FACE. (Very like,
Her father was an Irish costermonger.)
MAMMON.
The house of Valois, just, had such a nose.
And such a forehead, yet, the Medici
Of Florence boast.

38. Guinea bird: prostitute

DOL. Troth, and I have been likened
To all these princes.
FACE. (I'll be sworn, I heard it.)
MAMMON.
I know not how. It is not any one,
But e'en the very choice of all their features.
FACE.
(I'll in, and laugh.)
[*Exit* FACE.]
MAMMON. A certain touch, or air,
That sparkles a divinity, beyond
An earthly beauty!
DOL. O, you play the courtier.
MAMMON.
Good lady, gi' me leave—
DOL. In faith, I may not,
To mock me, sir.
MAMMON. To burn i' this sweet flame:
The Phoenix never knew a nobler death.
DOL.
Nay, now you court the courtier: and destroy
What you would build. This art, sir, i' your words,
Calls your whole faith in question.
MAMMON. By my soul—
DOL.
Nay, oaths are made o' the same air, sir.
MAMMON. Nature
Never bestowed upon mortality
A more unblamed, a more harmonious feature:
She played the stepdame in all faces, else.
Sweet madam, le' me be particular—
DOL.
Particular, sir? I pray you, know your distance.
MAMMON.
In no ill sense, sweet lady, but to ask
How your fair graces pass the hours? I see
You're lodged, here, i' the house of a rare man,
An excellent artist: but, what's that to you?
DOL.
Yes, sir. I study here the mathematics,
And distillation.
MAMMON. O, I cry your pardon.
He's a divine instructor! Can extract
The souls of all things by his art; call all
The virtues, and the miracles of the sun,

Into a temperate furnace: teach dull nature
What her own forces are. A man, the Emperor
Has courted, above Kelley:° sent his medals,
And chains, t' invite him.

DOL. Ay, and for his physic, sir—

MAMMON.
Above the art of Æsculapius,
That drew the envy of the Thunderer!°
I know all this, and more.

DOL. Troth, I am taken, sir,
Whole, with these studies that contemplate nature:

MAMMON.
It is a noble humour. But, this form
Was not intended to so dark a use!
Had you been crooked, foul, of some coarse mould,
A cloister had done well: but, such a feature
That might stand up the glory of a kingdom,
To live recluse! Is a mere solecism,
Though in a nunnery. It must not be.
I muse, my lord your brother will permit it!
You should spend half my land first, were I he.
Does not this diamond better, on my finger,
Than i' the quarry?

DOL. Yes.

MAMMON. Why, you are like it.
You were created, lady, for the light!
Here, you shall wear it; take it, the first pledge
Of what I speak: to bind you, to believe me.

DOL.
In chains of adamant?

MAMMON. Yes, the strongest bands.
And take a secret, too. Here, by your side,
Doth stand, this hour, the happiest man, in Europe.

DOL.
You are contented, sir?

MAMMON. Nay, in true being:
The envy of princes, and the fear of states.

DOL.
Say you so, Sir Epicure!

MAMMON. Yes, and thou shalt prove it,
Daughter of honor. I have cast mine eye

90. Kelley: Edward Kelley (1555–1595), a notorious alchemist who tried to con Rudolph II **93. Thunderer:** Zeus, who struck Aesculapius, god of medicine, with lightning because he restored men to life

Upon thy form, and I will rear this beauty,
Above all styles.

DOL. You mean no treason, sir!

MAMMON.
No, I will take away that jealousy.°
I am the lord of the philosopher's stone,
And thou the lady.

DOL. How sir! Ha' you that?

MAMMON.
I am the master of the mastery.
This day, the good old wretch, here, o' the house
Has made it for us. Now, he's at projection.
Think therefore, thy first wish, now; let me hear it:
And it shall rain into thy lap, no shower,
But floods of gold, whole cataracts, a deluge,
To get a nation on thee!

DOL. You are pleased, sir,
To work on the ambition of our sex.

MAMMON.
I am pleased the glory of her sex should know
This nook, here, of the Friars, is no climate
For her to live obscurely in, to learn
Physic and surgery for the Constable's wife
Of some odd Hundred in Essex; but come forth,
And taste the air of palaces; eat, drink
The toils of empirics, and their boasted practice;
Tincture of pearl, and coral, gold, and amber;
Be seen at feasts, and triumphs; have it asked,
What miracle she is? Set all the eyes
Of court afire, like a burning glass,
And work 'em into cinders; when the jewels
Of twenty states adorn thee; and the light
Strikes out the stars; that, when thy name is mentioned,
Queens may look pale: and, we but showing our love,
Nero's Poppœa may be lost in story!
Thus, will we have it.

DOL. I could well consent, sir.
But, in a monarchy, how will this be?
The Prince will soon take notice; and both seize
You and your stone: it being a wealth unfit
For any private subject.

MAMMON. If he knew it.

DOL.
Yourself to boast it, sir.

119. jealousy: suspicion

MAMMON. To thee, my life.

DOL.
O, but beware, sir! You may come to end
The remnant of your days in a loathed prison
By speaking of it.

MAMMON. 'Tis no idle fear!
We'll therefore go with all, my girl, and live
In a free state; where we will eat our mullets,
Soused in high-country wines, sup pheasants' eggs,
And have our cockles boiled in silver shells,
Our shrimps to swim again, as when they lived,
In a rare butter, made of dolphins' milk,
Whose cream does look like opals: and, with these
Delicate meats, set ourselves high for pleasure,
And take us down again, and then renew
Our youth and strength with drinking the elixir,
And so enjoy a perpetuity
Of life and lust. And, thou shalt ha' thy wardrobe,
Richer than nature's, still, to change thyself,
And vary oftener, for thy pride, than she:
Or art, her wise, and almost equal servant.
[*Enter* FACE.]

FACE.
Sir, you are too loud. I hear you, every word,
Into the laboratory. Some fitter place.
The garden, or great chamber above. How like you her?

MAMMON.
Excellent! Lungs. There's for thee.

FACE. But, do you hear?
Good sir, beware, no mention of the Rabbins.°

MAMMON.
We think not on 'em.
[*Exeunt* DOL, MAMMON.]

FACE. O, it is well, sir. Subtle!

Scene 2

Enter SUBTLE

FACE.
Dost thou not laugh?

174. Rabbins: learned rabbis

SUBTLE. Yes. Are they gone?
FACE. All's clear.
SUBTLE.
The widow is come.
FACE. And your quarrelling disciple?
SUBTLE.
Ay.
FACE. I must to my Captainship again, then.
SUBTLE.
Stay, bring 'em in, first.
FACE. So I meant. What is she?
A bonnibell?
SUBTLE. I know not.
FACE. We'll draw lots,
You'll stand to that?
SUBTLE. What else?
FACE. O, for a suit,
To fall now, like a curtain: flap.°
SUBTLE. To th' door, man.
FACE.
You'll ha' the first kiss, 'cause I am not ready.
[*Exit* FACE.]
SUBTLE.
Yes, and perhaps hit you° through both the nostrils.
FACE (*within*).
Who would you speak with?
KASTRIL (*within*). Where's the Captain?
FACE. Gone, sir.
About some business.
KASTRIL. Gone?
FACE. He'll return straight.
But master Doctor, his lieutenant, is here.
[*Enter* KASTRIL, DAME PLIANT.]
SUBTLE.
Come near, my worshipful boy, my *terrae fili,*°
That is, my boy of land; make thy approaches:
Welcome, I know thy lusts and thy desires,
And I will serve and satisfy 'em.
Charge me from thence, or thence, or in this line;
Here is my centre: ground thy quarrel.
KASTRIL. You lie.

IV.2. **7. fall . . . flap:** a quick change, into his captain's uniform **9. hit you:** put a ring **13. terrae fili:** A nobody as well as a landowner

SUBTLE.
How, child of wrath, and anger! The loud lie?
For what, my sudden boy?
KASTRIL. Nay, that look you to,
I am aforehand.
SUBTLE. O, this 's no true grammar,
And as ill logic! You must render causes, child,
Your first, and second intentions, know your canons,
And your divisions, moods, degrees, and differences,
Your predicaments, substance, and accident,
Series extern, and intern, with their causes
Efficient, material, formal, final,
And ha' your elements perfect—
KASTRIL. What is this!
The angry tongue he talks in?
SUBTLE. That false precept,
Of being aforehand, has deceived a number;
And made 'em enter quarrels, oftentimes,
Before they were aware: and, afterward,
Against their wills.
KASTRIL. How must I do then, sir?
SUBTLE.
I cry this lady mercy. She should, first,
Have been saluted. I do call you lady,
Because you are to be one, ere 't be long,
[*He kisses her.*]
My soft, and buxom widow.
KASTRIL. Is she, i'faith?
SUBTLE.
Yes, or my art is an egregious liar.
KASTRIL.
How know you?
SUBTLE. By inspection, on her forehead,
And subtlety° of her lip, which must be tasted
[*He kisses her again.*]
Often, to make a judgement. 'Slight, she melts
Like a myrobalan!° Here is, yet, a line
In *rivo frontis,*° tells me, he is no knight.
PLIANT.
What is he then, sir?
SUBTLE. Let me see your hand.
O, your *linea Fortunae* makes it plain;

40, 42. subtlety, myrobalan: candy **43. rivo frontis:** vein in the forehead

And *stella* here, in *monte Veneris:*
But, most of all, *iunctura annularis.*
He is a soldier, or a man of art, lady:
But shall have some great honour, shortly.

PLIANT. Brother,
He's a rare man, believe me!

KASTRIL. Hold your peace.

[*Enter* FACE.]

Here comes the tother rare man. Save you Captain.

FACE.
Good master Kastril. Is this your sister?

KASTRIL. Ay, sir.
Please you to kuss her, and be proud to know her?

FACE.
I shall be proud to know you, lady.

PLIANT. Brother,
He calls me lady, too.

KASTRIL. Ay, peace. I heard it.

FACE.
The Count is come.

SUBTLE. Where is he?

FACE. At the door.

SUBTLE.
Why, you must entertain him.

FACE. What'll you do
With these the while?

SUBTLE. Why, have 'em up, and show 'em
Some fustian book, or the dark glass.

FACE. 'Fore God,
She is a delicate dab-chick! I must have her.

[*Exit* FACE.]

SUBTLE.
Must you? Ay, if your fortune will, you must.
Come sir, the Captain will come to us presently.
I'll ha' you to my chamber of demonstrations,
Where I'll show you both the grammar, and logic,
And rhetoric of quarrelling; my whole method,
Drawn out in tables; and my instrument,
That hath the several scale upon't, shall make you
Able to quarrel, at a straw's breadth, by moonlight.
And, lady, I'll have you look in a glass,
Some half an hour, but to clear your eyesight,
Against you see your fortune: which is greater,
Than I may judge upon the sudden, trust me.

[*Exeunt* SUBTLE, KASTRIL, PLIANT.]

Scene 3

Enter FACE

FACE.
Where are you, Doctor?
SUBTLE (*within*). I'll come to you presently.
FACE.
I will ha' this same widow, now I ha' seen her,
On any composition.
[*Enter* SUBTLE.]
SUBTLE. What do you say?
FACE.
Ha' you disposed of them?
SUBTLE. I ha' sent 'em up.
FACE.
Subtle, in troth, I needs must have this widow.
SUBTLE.
Is that the matter?
FACE. Nay, but hear me.
SUBTLE. Go to,
If you rebel once, Dol shall know it all.
Therefore be quiet, and obey your chance.
FACE.
Nay, thou art so violent now—Do but conceive:
Thou art old, and canst not serve—
SUBTLE. Who cannot, I?
'Slight, I will serve her with thee, for a—
FACE. Nay,
But understand: I'll gi' you composition.
SUBTLE.
I will not treat with thee: what, sell my fortune?
'Tis better than my birthright. Do not murmur.
Win her, and carry her. If you grumble, Dol
Knows it directly.
FACE. Well sir, I am silent.
Will you go help to fetch in Don in state?
[*Exit* FACE.]
SUBTLE.
I follow you, sir: we must keep Face in awe,
Or he will overlook us like a tyrant.
[*Enter* FACE, SURLY *like a Spaniard.*]
Brain of a tailor! Who comes here? Don John!

SURLY.
Señores, beso las manos, á vuestras mercedes.°
SUBTLE.
Would you had stooped a little, and kissed our *anos.*
FACE.
Peace Subtle.
SUBTLE. Stab me; I shall never hold, man.
He looks in that deep ruff like a head in a platter,
Served in by a short cloak upon two trestles!
FACE.
Or, what do you say to a collar of brawn, cut down
Beneath the souse, and wriggled° with a knife?
SUBTLE.
'Slud, he does look too fat to be a Spaniard.
FACE.
Perhaps some Fleming, or some Hollander got him
In d'Alva's time: Count Egmont's bastard.
SUBTLE. Don,
Your scurvy, yellow, Madrid face is welcome.
SURLY.
Gratia.
SUBTLE. He speaks, out of a fortification.°
Pray God, he ha' no squibs in those deep sets.
SURLY.
Por Dios, Señores, muy linda casa!°
SUBTLE.
What says he?
FACE. Praises the house, I think,
I know no more but's action.
SUBTLE. Yes, the *casa,*
My precious Diego, will prove fair enough,
To cozen you in. Do you mark? You shall
Be cozened, Diego.
FACE. Cozened, do you see?
My worthy Donzel, cozened.
SURLY. *Entiendo.*°
SUBTLE.
Do you intend it? So do we, dear Don.
Have you brought pistolets? Or portagues?
[*He feels his pockets.*]

IV.3. 21. Señores . . . mercedes: Gentlemen, I kiss your hands. **26–27. collar . . . wriggled:** a pig's neck cut off below the ears and scored **32. fortification:** i.e. his deep ruff **34. Por . . . casa:** Before God, gentlemen, a very fine house **40. Entiendo:** I understand

My solemn Don? Dost thou feel any?

FACE. Full.

SUBTLE.
You shall be emptied, Don; pumped, and drawn,
Dry, as they say.

FACE. Milked, in troth, sweet Don.

SUBTLE.
See all the monsters;° the great lion of all, Don.

SURLY.
Con licencia, se puede ver á esta señora?°

SUBTLE.
What talks he now?

FACE. O' the *Señora.*

SUBTLE. O, Don,
That is the lioness, which you shall see
Also, my Don.

FACE. 'Slid, Subtle, how shall we do?

SUBTLE.
For what?

FACE. Why, Dol's employed, you know.

SUBTLE. That's true!
'Fore heaven I know not: he must stay, that's all.

FACE.
Stay? That he must not by no means.

SUBTLE. No, why?

FACE.
Unless you'll mar all. 'Slight, he'll suspect it.
And then he will not pay, not half so well.
This is a travelled punk-master, and does know
All the delays: a notable hot rascal,
And looks, already, rampant.

SUBTLE. 'Sdeath, and Mammon
Must not be troubled.

FACE. Mammon, in no case!

SUBTLE.
What shall we do then?

FACE Think: you must be sudden.

SURLY.
Entiendo, que la señora es tan hermosa, que codicio tan
á verla, como la bien aventuranza de mi vida.°

46. monsters: i.e. see all the sights, like a tourist, including the lion at the Tower of London **47. Con . . . señora:** May I please see the lady? **61–62. Entiendo . . . vida:** I understand that the lady is so beautiful that I long to see her as the best thing in life.

FACE.
Mi vida? 'Slid, Subtle, he puts me in mind o' the widow.
What dost thou say to draw her to't? Ha?
And tell her, it is her fortune. All our venture
Now lies upon 't. It is but one man more,
Which on's chance to have her: and, beside,
There is no maidenhead to be feared or lost.
What dost thou think on 't, Subtle?

SUBTLE. Who, I? Why—

FACE.
The credit of our house too is engaged.

SUBTLE.
You made me an offer for my share erewhile.
What wilt thou gi' me, i'faith?

FACE. O, by that light,
I'll not by now. You know your doom to me.
E'en take your lot, obey your chance, sir; win her,
And wear her, out for me.

SUBTLE. 'Slight. I'll not work her then.

FACE.
It is the common cause, therefore bethink you.
Dol else must know it, as you said.

SUBTLE. I care not.

SURLY.
Señores, por qué se tarda tanto?°

SUBTLE.
Faith, I am not fit, I am old.

FACE. That's now no reason, sir.

SURLY.
Puede ser, de hacer burla de mi amor?°

FACE.
You hear the Don, too? By this air, I call.
And loose the hinges,° Dol.

SUBTLE. A plague of hell—

FACE.
Will you then do?

SUBTLE. You're a terrible rogue,
I'll think of this: will you, sir, call the widow?

FACE.
Yes, and I'll take her too, with all her faults,
Now I do think on't better.

78. Señores . . . tanto: Gentlemen, why is there such a delay? **80. Puede . . . amor:** Are you trying to make fun of my love? **82. loose the hinges:** break the agreement

SUBTLE. With all my heart, sir,
Am I discharged o' the lot?
FACE. As you please.
SUBTLE. Hands.
FACE.
Remember now, that upon any change,
You never claim her.
SUBTLE. Much good joy and health to you, sir.
Marry a whore? Fate, let me wed a witch first.
SURLY.
Por estas honradas barbas—°
SUBTLE. He swears by his beard.
Despatch, and call the brother too.
[*Exit* FACE.]
SURLY. *Tengo dúda, Señores,*
Que no me hágan alguna traición.°
SUBTLE.
How, issue on? Yes, *presto Señor.* Please you
Enthratha the *chambratha,* worthy Don;
Where if it please the Fates, in your *bathada,*
You shall be soaked, and stroked, and tubbed, and rubbed:
And scrubbed, and fubbed, dear Don, before you go.
You shall, in faith, my scurvy baboon Don:
Be curried,° clawed, and flawed,° and tawed,° indeed.
I will the heartilier go about it now,
And make the widow a punk so much the sooner
To be revenged on this impetuous Face:
The quickly doing of it is the grace.
[*Exit* SUBTLE, SURLY.]

Scene 4

Enter FACE, KASTRIL, DAME PLIANT

FACE.
Come lady: I knew the Doctor would not leave
Till he had found the very nick of her fortune.
KASTRIL.
To be a countess, say you?

91. Por . . . barbas: By this honored beard **92–93. Tengo . . . traición:** I fear, gentlemen, that you are playing tricks on me. **100. curried:** scraped **flawed:** flayed **tawed:** tanned

FACE. A Spanish countess, sir.

PLIANT.
Why? Is that better than an English countess?

FACE.
Better? 'Slight, make you that a question, lady?

KASTRIL.
Nay, she is a fool, Captain, you must pardon her.

FACE.
Ask from your courtier, to your Inns of Court-man,
To your mere milliner: they will tell you all,
Your Spanish jennet is the best horse. Your Spanish
Stoop is the best garb. Your Spanish beard
Is the best cut. Your Spanish ruffs are the best
Wear. Your Spanish pavan the best dance.
Your Spanish titillation in a glove
The best perfume. And, for your Spanish pike,
And Spanish blade, let your poor Captain speak.
Here comes the Doctor.
[*Enter* SUBTLE.]

SUBTLE. My most honoured lady,
(For so I am now to style you, having found
By this my scheme, you are to undergo
An honourable fortune, very shortly.)
What will you say now, if some—

FACE. I ha' told her all, sir.
And her right worshipful brother, here, that she shall be
A countess: do not delay 'em, sir. A Spanish countess.

SUBTLE.
Still, my scarce worshipful Captain, you can keep
No secret. Well, since he has told you, madame,
Do you forgive him, and I do.

KASTRIL. She shall do that, sir.
I'll look to't, 'tis my charge.

SUBTLE. Well then. Nought rests
But that she fit her love, now, to her fortune.

PLIANT.
Truly, I shall never brook a Spaniard.

SUBTLE. No?

PLIANT.
Never, sin' eighty-eight° could I abide 'em,
And that was some three year afore I was born, in truth.

SUBTLE.
Come, you must love him, or be miserable:

IV.4. **29. eighty-eight:** 1588, the year of the Spanish Armada

Choose which you will.
FACE. By this good rush, persuade her,
She will cry strawberries° else, within this twelvemonth.
SUBTLE.
Nay, shads, and mackerel, which is worse.
FACE. Indeed, sir?
KASTRIL.
God's lid, you shall love him, or I'll kick you.
PLIANT. Why?
I'll do as you will ha' me, brother.
KASTRIL. Do,
Or by this hand, I'll maul you.
FACE. Nay, good sir,
Be not so fierce.
SUBTLE. No, my enraged child,
She will be ruled. What, when she come to taste
The pleasures of a countess! To be courted—
FACE.
And kissed, and ruffled!
SUBTLE. Ay, behind the hangings.
FACE.
And then come forth in pomp!
SUBTLE. And know her state!
FACE.
Of keeping all th'idolators o' the chamber
Barer to her than at their prayers!
SUBTLE. Is served
Upon the knee!
FACE. And has her pages, ushers,
Footmen, and coaches—
SUBTLE. Her six mares—
FACE. Nay, eight!
SUBTLE.
To hurry her through London, to th' Exchange,
Bedlam, the China-houses—
FACE. Yes, and have
The citizens gape at her, and praise her tires!°
And my lord's goose-turd bands, that rides with her!
KASTRIL.
Most brave! By this hand, you are not my suster
If you refuse.
PLIANT. I will not refuse, brother.
[*Enter* SURLY.]

33. cry strawberries: become a street vendor **49. tires:** clothes

SURLY.

Qué es esto, Señores, que no se venga?
Esta tradanza me mata!°

FACE. It is the Count come!

The Doctor knew he would be here, by his art.

SUBTLE.

En galanta madama, Don! Galantissima!

SURLY.

Por todos los dioses, la más acabada
Hermosura, que he visto en my vida!°

FACE.

Is't not a gallant language, that they speak?

KASTRIL.

An admirable language! Is't not French?

FACE.

No, Spanish, sir.

KASTRIL. It goes like law-French,

And that, they say, is the courtliest language.

FACE. List, sir.

SURLY.

El sol ha perdido su lumbre, con el
Resplandor, que trae esta dama. Válgame Dios!°

FACE.

He admires your sister.

KASTRIL. Must she not make curtsey?

SUBTLE.

'Ods will, she must go to him, man; and kiss him!
It is the Spanish fashion, for the women
To make first court.

FACE. 'Tis true he tells you, sir:

His art knows all.

SURLY. *Porqué no se acude?*°

KASTRIL.

He speaks to her, I think?

FACE. That he does sir.

SURLY.

Por el amor de Dios, qué es esto, que se tarda?

KASTRIL.

Nay, see: she will not understand him! Gull.
Noddy.

53–54. Qué . . . mata: Why doesn't she come, gentlemen? This delay is killing me! **57–58. Por . . . vida:** By all the gods, the greatest beauty I have ever seen **63–64. El . . . Dios:** The sun is dimmed by the splendor of this lady, so help me! **69. Porqué . . . acude:** Why doesn't she come?

PLIANT. What say you brother?

KASTRIL. Ass, my suster,
Go kuss him, as the cunning man would ha' you,
I'll thrust a pin i' your buttocks else.

FACE. O, no sir.

SURLY.
Señora mía, mi persona muy indigna está
Á llegar á tanta hermosura.°

FACE.
Does he not use her bravely?

KASTRIL. Bravely, i' faith!

FACE.
Nay, he will use her better.

KASTRIL. Do you think so?

SURLY.
Señora, si sera servida, entremos.°
[*Exit* SURLY, DAME PLIANT.]

KASTRIL.
Where does he carry her?

FACE. Into the garden, sir;
Take you no thought: I must interpret for her.

SUBTLE.
Give Dol the word (*Exit* FACE.) Come, my fierce child, advance,
We'll to our quarrelling lesson again.

KASTRIL. Agreed.
I love a Spanish boy with all my heart.

SUBTLE.
Nay, and by this means, sir, you shall be brother
To a great count.

KASTRIL. Ay, I knew that at first.
This match will advance the house of the Kastrils.

SUBTLE.
Pray God, your sister prove but pliant.

KASTRIL. Why,
Her name is so: by her other husband.

SUBTLE. How!

KASTRIL.
The widow Pliant. Knew you not that?

SUBTLE. No faith, sir.
Yet, by erection of her figure, I guessed it.
Come, let's go practice.

76–77. Señora . . . hermosura: My lady, I am quite unworthy to come near such beauty. **80. Señora . . . entremos:** Lady, if you please, let us go in.

KASTRIL. Yes, but do you think, Doctor,
I e'er shall quarrel well?
SUBTLE. I warrant you.
[*Exeunt* SUBTLE, KASTRIL.]

Scene 5

Enter DOL, MAMMON

DOL.
For, after Alexander's death—
[*In her fit of talking.*]
MAMMON. Good lady—
DOL.
That Perdiccas, and Antigonus were slain,
The two that stood, Seleuc', and Ptolomee—°
MAMMON.
Madam.
DOL. Made up the two legs, and the fourth Beast.
That was Gog-north, and Egypt-south: which after
Was called Gog-iron-leg, and South-iron-leg—
MAMMON. Lady—
DOL.
And then Gog-horned. So was Egypt, too.
Then Egypt-clay-leg, and Gog-clay-leg—
MAMMON. Sweet madam.
DOL.
And last Gog-dust, and Egypt-dust, which fall
In the last link of the fourth chain. And these
Be stars in story, which none see, or look at—
MAMMON.
What shall I do?
DOL. For, as he says, except
We call the Rabbins, and the heathen Greeks—
MAMMON.
Dear lady.
DOL. To come from Salem, and from Athens,
And teach the people of Great Britain—
[*Enter* FACE.]

IV.5. 2–3. Perdiccas . . . Ptolomee: Alexander's four generals—taken, with the rest of Dol's fit, from Broughton

FACE. What's the matter, sir?

DOL.
To speak the tongue of Eber, and Javan—

MAMMON. O,
She's in her fit.

DOL. We shall know nothing—

FACE. Death, sir,
We are undone.

DOL. Where, then, a learned linguist
Shall see the ancient used communion
Of vowels, and consonants—

FACE. My master will hear!

DOL.
A wisdom, which Pythagoras held most high—

MAMMON.
Sweet honorable lady.

DOL. To comprise
All sounds of voices, in few marks of letters—

FACE.
Nay, you must never hope to lay her now.
[*They speak together.*]

DOL.
And so we may arrive by Talmud skill,
And profane Greek, to raise the building up
Of Heber's house, against the Ismaelite,
King of Togarmah, and his habergeons
Brimstony, blue, and fiery; and the force
Of King Abaddon, and the Beast of Cittim:
Which Rabbi David Kimchi, Onkelos,
And Aben-Ezra do interpret Rome.

FACE.
How did you put her into't?

MAMMON. Alas I talked
Of a fifth monarchy I would erect,
With the philosopher's stone (by chance) and she
Falls on the other four, straight. FACE. Out of Broughton!
I told you so. 'Slid stop her mouth. MAMMON. Is't best?

FACE.
She'll never leave else. If the old man hear her,
We are but fæces, ashes.

SUBTLE (*within*). What's to do there?

FACE.
O, we are lost. Now she hears him, she is quiet.

[*Upon* SUBTLE'*s entry they disperse.*]

MAMMON.
Where shall I hide me?

SUBTLE. How! What sight is here!
Close deeds of darkness, and that shun the light!
Bring him again. Who is he? What, my son!
O, I have lived too long.
MAMMON. Nay good, dear Father,
There was no unchaste purpose.
SUBTLE. Not? And flee me,
When I come in?
MAMMON. That was my error.
SUBTLE. Error?
Guilt, guilt, my son. Give it the right name. No marvel
If I found check in our great work within,
When such affairs as these were managing!
MAMMON.
Why, have you so?
SUBTLE. It has stood still this half hour:
And all the rest of our less works gone back.
Where is the instrument of wickedness,
My lewd false drudge?
MAMMON. Nay, good sir, blame not him.
Believe me, 'twas against his will or knowledge.
I saw her by chance.
SUBTLE. Will you commit more sin,
T'excuse a varlet?
MAMMON. By my hope, 'tis true, sir.
SUBTLE.
Nay, then I wonder less, if you, for whom
The blessing was prepared, would so tempt heaven:
And lose your fortunes.
MAMMON. Why, sir?
SUBTLE. This'll retard
The work a month at least.
MAMMON. Why, if it do,
What remedy? But think it not, good Father:
Our purposes were honest.
SUBTLE. As they were,
So the reward will prove. How now! Ay me.
[*A great crack and noise within.*]
God, and all saints be good to us. What's that?
[*Enter* FACE.]
FACE.
O sir, we are defeated! All the works
Are flown in *fumo:* every glass is burst.
Furnace, and all rent down! As if a bolt
Of thunder had been driven through the house.

Retorts, receivers, pelicans, boltheads,
All struck in shivers! Help, good sir! Alas,
[SUBTLE *falls down as in a swoon.*]
Coldness and death invades him. Nay, sir Mammon,
Do the fair offices of a man! You stand
As you were readier to depart than he.
Who's there? My lord her brother is come.
[*One knocks.*]

MAMMON. Ha, Lungs?

FACE.
His coach is at the door. Avoid his sight,
For he's as furious as his sister is mad.

MAMMON.
Alas!

FACE. My brain is quite undone with the fume, sir,
I ne'er must hope to be mine own man again.

MAMMON.
Is all lost, Lungs? Will nothing be preserved
Of all our cost?

FACE. Faith, very little, sir.
A peck of coals, or so, which is cold comfort, sir.

MAMMON.
O my voluptuous mind! I am justly punished.

FACE.
And so am I, sir.

MAMMON. Cast from all my hopes—

FACE.
Nay, certainties, sir.

MAMMON. By mine own base affections.

SUBTLE.
O, the curst fruits of vice and lust!
[SUBTLE *seems to come to himself.*]

MAMMON. Good father,
It was my sin. Forgive it.

SUBTLE. Hangs my roof
Over us still, and will not fall, O justice
Upon us, for this wicked man!

FACE. Nay, look, sir,
You grieve him, now, with staying in his sight:
Good sir, the nobleman will come too, and take you,
And that may breed a tragedy.

MAMMON. I'll go.

FACE.
Ay, and repent at home, sir. It may be,
For some good penance you may ha' it yet,

A hundred pound to the box at Bedlam—

MAMMON. Yes.

FACE.
For the restoring such as ha' their wits.

MAMMON. I'll do't.

FACE.
I'll send one to you to receive it.

MAMMON. Do.
Is no projection left?

FACE. All flown, or stinks, sir.

MAMMON.
Will nought be saved that's good for medicine, thinkst thou?

FACE.
I cannot tell, sir. There will be, perhaps,
Something, about the scraping of the shards,
Will cure the itch: though not your itch of mind, sir.
It shall be saved for you, and sent home. Good sir,
This way: for fear the lord should meet you.
[*Exit* MAMMON.]

SUBTLE. Face.

FACE.
Ay.

SUBTLE. Is he gone?

FACE. Yes, and as heavily
As all the gold he hoped for were in his blood.
Let us be light, though.

SUBTLE. Ay, as balls, and bound
And hit our heads against the roof for joy:
There's so much of our care now cast away.

FACE.
Now to our Don.

SUBTLE. Yes, your young widow, by this time
Is made a countess, Face: she's been in travail
Of a young heir for you.

FACE. Good, sir.

SUBTLE. Off with your case,°
And greet her kindly, as a bridegroom should,
After these common hazards.

FACE. Very well, sir.
Will you go fetch Don Diego off the while?

SUBTLE.
And fetch him over too, if you'll be pleased, sir:
Would Dol were in her place, to pick his pockets now.

103. case: disguise, as laboratory assistant

FACE.
Why, you can do it as well, if you would set to't.
I pray you prove your virtue.

SUBTLE. For your sake, sir.
[*Exeunt* SUBTLE *and* FACE.]

Scene 6

Enter SURLY, DAME PLIANT

SURLY.
Lady, you see into what hands you are fallen;
'Mongst what a nest of villains! And how near
Your honor was t'have catched a certain clap
(Through your credulity) had I but been
So punctually forward, as place, time,
And other circumstance would ha' made a man:
For you're a handsome woman: would you're wise, too.
I am a gentleman, come here disguised,
Only to find the knaveries of this citadel,
And where I might have wronged your honor, and have not,
I claim some interest in your love. You are,
They say, a widow, rich: and I am a bachelor,
Worth nought: your fortunes may make me a man,
As mine ha' preserved you a woman. Think upon it,
And whether I have deserved you, or no.

PLIANT. I will, sir.

SURLY.
And for these household-rogues, let me alone,
To treat with them.
[*Enter* SUBTLE.]

SUBTLE. How doth my noble Diego?
And my dear madam, Countess? Hath the Count
Been courteous, lady? Liberal? And open?
Donzell, me thinks you look melancholic,
After your *coitum,* and scurvy! Truly,
I do not like the dulness of your eye:
It hath a heavy cast, 'tis upsee Dutch,
And says you are a lumpish whore-master.
Be lighter, I will make your pockets so.
[*He falls to picking of them.*]

SURLY.
Will you, Don bawd and pickpurse? How now? Reel you?

Stand up sir, you shall find since I am so heavy,
I'll gi' you equal weight.

SUBTLE. Help, murder!

SURLY. No, sir.
There's no such thing intended. A good cart
And a clean whip shall ease you of that fear.
I am the Spanish Don, that should be cozened,
Do you see? Cozened? Where's your Captain Face?
That parcel-broker, and whole-bawd, all rascal.
[*Enter* FACE.]

FACE.
How, Surly!

SURLY. O, make your approach, good Captain.
I have found, from whence your copper rings, and spoons
Come now, wherewith you cheat abroad in taverns.
'Twas here you learned t'anoint your boot with brimstone,
Then rub men's gold on't for a kind of touch,
And say 'twas naught when you had changed the color,
That you might ha't for nothing? And this Doctor,
Your sooty, smoky-bearded compeer, he
Will close you so much gold, in a bolt's head,
And, on a turn, convey (i' the stead) another
With sublimed mercury, that shall burst i' the heat,
And fly out all *in fumo?* Then weeps Mammon:
Then swoons his worship. Or, he is the Faustus,
[FACE *slips out.*]
That casteth figures, and can conjure, cures
Plague, piles, and pox, by the ephemerides,°
And holds intelligence with all the bawds,
And midwives of three shires? While you send in—
Captain, (what is he gone?) damsels with child,
Wives that are barren, or the waiting-maid
With the green sickness? (SUBTLE *attempts to leave.*) Nay, sir, you must tarry
Though he be 'scaped; and answer by the ears, sir.

IV.6. **48. ephemerides:** horoscopes

Scene 7

Enter FACE, KASTRIL, SURLY, SUBTLE

FACE.
Why, now's the time, if ever you will quarrel
Well (as they say) and be a true-born child.
The Doctor and your sister both are abused.

KASTRIL.
Where is he? Which is he? He is a slave
Whate'er he is, and the son of a whore. Are you
The man, sir, I would know?

SURLY.
I should be loath, sir,
To confess so much.

KASTRIL.
Then you lie, i' your throat.

SURLY.
How?

FACE.
A very errant rogue, sir, and a cheater,
Employed here, by another conjurer,
That does not love the Doctor, and would cross him
If he knew how—

SURLY.
Sir, you are abused.

KASTRIL.
You lie:
And 'tis no matter.

FACE.
Well said, sir. He is
The impudentest rascal—

SURLY.
You are indeed. Will you hear me, sir?

FACE.
By no means: bid him be gone.

KASTRIL.
Be gone, sir, quickly.

SURLY.
This's strange! Lady, do you inform your brother.

FACE.
There is not such a foist in all the town,
The Doctor had him, presently: and finds, yet,
The Spanish Count will come here. Bear up, Subtle.

SUBTLE.
Yes, sir, he must appear, within this hour.

FACE.
And yet this rogue, would come, in a disguise,
By the temptation of another spirit,
To trouble our art, though he could not hurt it.

KASTRIL.
Ay,
I know—away, you talk like a foolish mauther.°

SURLY.
Sir, all is truth, she says.

FACE.
Do not believe him, sir:
He is the lyingest swabber! Come your ways, sir.

SURLY.
You are valiant, out of company.

KASTRIL.
Yes, how then, sir?

[*Enter* DRUGGER.]

Nay, here's an honest fellow too, that knows him,
And all his tricks. (Make good what I say, Abel,)
This cheater would ha' cozened thee o' the widow.
He owes this honest Drugger, here, seven pound,
He has had on him, in two-penny 'orths of tobacco.

DRUGGER.
Yes sir. And he's damned himself, three terms, to pay me.

FACE.
And what does he owe for *lotium?*°

DRUGGER.
Thirty shillings, sir:
And for six syringes.

SURLY.
Hydra of villany!

FACE.
Nay, sir, you must quarrel him out o' the house.

KASTRIL.
I will.
Sir, if you get not out o' doors, you lie:
And you are a pimp.

SURLY.
Why, this is madness, sir,
Not valor in you: I must laugh at this.

KASTRIL.
It is my humour: you are a pimp, and a trig,
And an Amadis de Gaul, or a Don Quixote.

DRUGGER.
Or a knight o' the curious coxcomb. Do you see?

[*Enter* ANANIAS.]

ANANIAS.
Peace to the household.

KASTRIL.
I'll keep peace for no man.

ANANIAS.
Casting of dollars is concluded lawful.

KASTRIL.
Is he the constable?

SUBTLE.
Peace, Ananias.

IV.7. **23. mauther:** girl **33. lotium:** stale urine used as hair tonic

FACE. No, sir.

KASTRIL.
Then you are an otter, and a shad, a whit,
A very tim.

SURLY. You'll hear me, sir?

KASTRIL. I will not.

ANANIAS.
What is the motive!

SURLY. Zeal, in the young gentleman,
Against his Spanish slops—

ANANIAS. They are profane,
Lewd, superstitious, and idolatrous breeches.

SURLY.
New rascals!

KASTRIL. Will you be gone, sir?

ANANIAS. Avoid Satan,
Thou art not of the light. That ruff of pride
About thy neck, betrays thee: and is the same
With that, which the unclean birds, in seventy-seven,
Were seen to prank it with on divers coasts.
Thou lookest like Antichrist in that lewd hat.

SURLY.
I must give way.

KASTRIL. Be gone, sir.

SURLY. But I'll take
A course with you—

(ANANIAS. Depart, proud Spanish fiend)

SURLY.
Captain, and Doctor—

ANANIAS. Child of perdition.

KASTRIL. Hence, sir.

[*Exit* SURLY.]

Did I not quarrel bravely?

FACE. Yes, indeed, sir.

KASTRIL.
Nay, and I give my mind to't, I shall do't.

FACE.
O, you must follow, sir, and threaten him tame.
He'll turn again else.

KASTRIL. I'll re-turn him, then.

[*Exit* KASTRIL.]

FACE.
Drugger, this rogue prevented us, for thee:
We had determined that thou shouldst ha' come
In a Spanish suit, and ha' carried her so; and he

A brokerly slave, goes, puts it on himself.
Hast brought the damask?
DRUGGER. Yes sir.
FACE. Thou must borrow
A Spanish suit. Hast thou no credit with the players?
DRUGGER.
Yes, sir, did you never see me play the fool?
FACE.
I know not, Nab: thou shalt, if I can help it.
Hieronymo's° old cloak, ruff, and hat will serve,
I'll tell thee more, when thou bring'st 'em.
[*Exit* DRUGGER.]
ANANIAS. Sir, I know
[SUBTLE *hath whispered with him this while.*]
The Spaniard hates the Brethren, and hath spies
Upon their actions: and that this was one
I make no scruple. But the holy Synod
Have been in prayer, and meditation, for it.
And 'tis revealed no less, to them, than me,
That casting of money is most lawful.
SUBTLE. True.
But here I cannot do it; if the house
Should chance to be suspected, all would out,
And we be locked up in the Tower forever,
To make gold there (for th' state) never come out:
And then are you defeated.
ANANIAS. I will tell
This to the Elders, and the weaker Brethren,
That the whole company of the Separation
May join in humble prayer again.
(SUBTLE. And fasting.)
ANANIAS.
Yea, for some fitter place. The peace of mind
Rest with these walls.
SUBTLE. Thanks, courteous Ananias.
[*Exit* ANANIAS.]
FACE.
What did he come for?
SUBTLE. About casting dollars,
Presently, out of hand. And so I told him
A Spanish minister came here to spy,
Against the faithful—
FACE. I conceive. Come Subtle,

71. Hieronymo's: hero of Kyd's *Spanish Tragedy*

Thou art so down upon the least disaster!
How wouldst th' ha' done, if I had not helped thee out?

SUBTLE.
I thank thee Face, for the angry boy, i' faith.

FACE.
Who would ha' looked, it should ha' been that rascal?
Surly? He had dyed his beard, and all. Well, sir,
Here's damask come to make you a suit.

SUBTLE. Where's Drugger?

FACE.
He is gone to borrow me a Spanish habit,
I'll be the Count now.

SUBTLE. But where's the widow?

FACE.
Within, with my lord's sister: Madam Dol
Is entertaining her.

SUBTLE. By your favor, Face,
Now she is honest, I will stand again.

FACE.
You will not offer it?

SUBTLE. Why?

FACE. Stand to your word,
Or—here comes Dol. She knows—

SUBTLE. You're tyrannous still.

[*Enter* DOL.]

FACE.
Strict for my right. How now, Dol? Hast told her
The Spanish Count will come?

DOL. Yes, but another is come,
You little looked for!

FACE. Who's that?

DOL. Your master:
The master of the house.

SUBTLE. How, Doll!

FACE. She lies.
This is some trick. Come, leave your quiblins, Dorothy.

DOL.
Look out, and see.

SUBTLE. Art thou in earnest?

DOL. 'Slight,
Forty o' the neighbours are about him, talking.

FACE.
'Tis he, by this good day.

DOL. 'Twill prove ill day
For some on us.

FACE. We are undone and taken.

DOL.
Lost, I am afraid.

SUBTLE. You said he would not come,
While there died one a week within the liberties.

FACE.
No: 'twas within the walls.

SUBTLE. Was't so? Cry you mercy:
I thought the liberties. What shall we do now, Face?

FACE.
Be silent: not a word, if he call, or knock.
I'll into mine old shape again and meet him,
Of Jeremy the butler. I' the mean time,
Do you two pack up all the goods and purchase
That we can carry i' the two trunks. I'll keep him
Off for today, if I cannot longer: and then
At night, I'll ship you both away to Ratcliff,
Where we'll meet tomorrow, and there we'll share.
Let Mammon's brass, and pewter keep the cellar:
We'll have another time for that. But, Dol,
Pray thee, go heat a little water, quickly,
Subtle must shave me. All my Captain's beard
Must off, to make me appear smooth Jeremy.
You'll do't?

SUBTLE. Yes, I'll shave you, as well as I can.

FACE.
And not cut my throat, but trim me?

SUBTLE. You shall see, sir.

[*Exeunt* SUBTLE, FACE, DOL.]

ACT V

Scene 1

Enter LOVEWIT, NEIGHBOURS

LOVEWIT.
Has there been such resort, say you?

NEIGHBOUR 1. Daily, sir.

V.1. **6. Pimlico:** a resort, popular for cakes and ale

NEIGHBOUR 2.
And nightly, too.
NEIGHBOUR 3. Ay, some as brave as lords.
NEIGHBOUR 4.
Ladies, and gentlewomen.
NEIGHBOUR 5. Citizens' wives.
NEIGHBOUR 1.
And knights.
NEIGHBOUR 6. In coaches.
NEIGHBOUR 2. Yes, and oyster-women.
NEIGHBOUR 1.
Beside other gallants.
NEIGHBOUR 3. Sailors' wives.
NEIGHBOUR 4. Tobacco-men.
NEIGHBOUR 5.
Another Pimlico!
LOVEWIT. What should my knave advance
To draw this company? He hung out no banners
Of a strange calf with five legs to be seen?
Or a huge lobster with six claws?
NEIGHBOUR 6. No, sir.
NEIGHBOUR 3.
We had gone in then, sir.
LOVEWIT. He has no gift
Of teaching i' the nose, that e'er I knew of!
You saw no bills set up, that promised cure
Of agues, or the toothache?
NEIGHBOUR 2. No such thing, sir.
LOVEWIT.
Nor heard a drum struck, for baboons, or puppets?
NEIGHBOUR 5.
Neither, sir.
LOVEWIT. What device should he bring forth now!
I love a teeming wit, as I love my nourishment.
Pray God he ha' not kept such open house
That he hath sold my hangings and my bedding:
I left him nothing else. If he have eat 'em,
A plague o' the moth, say I. Sure he has got
Some bawdy pictures to call all this ging;
The friar and the nun; or the new motion
Of the knight's courser covering the parson's mare;
The boy of six year old with the great thing:
Or 't may be he has the fleas that run at tilt
Upon a table, or some dog to dance?
When saw you him?

NEIGHBOUR 1. Who sir, Jeremy?

NEIGHBOUR 2. Jeremy butler?
We saw him not this month.

LOVEWIT. How!

NEIGHBOUR 4. Not these five weeks, sir.

NEIGHBOUR 1.
These six weeks, at the least.

LOVEWIT. Y' amaze me, neighbors!

NEIGHBOUR 5.
Sure, if your worship know not wheer he is,
He's slipped away.

NEIGHBOUR 6. Pray God, he be not made away!

LOVEWIT.
[*He knocks.*]
Ha? It's no time to question then.

NEIGHBOUR 6. About
Some three weeks since, I heard a doleful cry,
As I sat up a-mending my wife's stockings.

LOVEWIT.
This's strange! That none will answer! Didst thou hear
A cry, saist thou?

NEIGHBOUR 6. Yes, sir, like unto a man
That had been strangled an hour, and could not speak.

NEIGHBOUR 2.
I heard it too, just this day three weeks, at two o'clock
Next morning.

LOVEWIT. These be miracles, or you make 'em so!
A man an hour strangled, and could not speak,
And both you heard him cry?

NEIGHBOUR 3. Yes, downward, sir.

LOVEWIT.
Thou art a wise fellow: give me thy hand I pray thee.
What trade art thou on?

NEIGHBOUR 3. A smith, and't please your worship.

LOVEWIT.
A smith? Then lend me thy help to get this door open.

NEIGHBOUR 3.
That I will presently, sir, but fetch my tools—
[*Exit* NEIGHBOUR 3.]

NEIGHBOUR 1.
Sir, best to knock again, afore you break it.

Scene 2

LOVEWIT.
I will.
[*Enter* FACE.]
FACE. What mean you, sir?
NEIGHBOURS 1, 2, 4. O, here's Jeremy!
FACE.
Good sir, come from the door.
LOVEWIT. Why! What's the matter?
FACE.
Yet farther, you are too near yet.
LOVEWIT. I'the name of wonder!
What means the fellow?
FACE. The house, sir, has been visited.
LOVEWIT.
What? With the plague? Stand thou then farther.
FACE. *No, sir.*
I had it not.
LOVEWIT. Who had it then? I left
None else but thee i'the house!
FACE. Yes, sir. My fellow,
The cat, that kept the buttery, had it on her
A week before I spied it: but I got her
Conveyed away i'the night. And so I shut
The house up for a month—
LOVEWIT. How!
FACE. Purposing then, sir,
T'have burnt rose-vinegar, treacle, and tar,
And ha' made it sweet, that you should ne'er ha' known it:
Because I knew the news would but afflict you, sir.
LOVEWIT.
Breathe less, and farther off. Why, this is stranger!
The neighbors tell me all, here, that the doors
Have still been open—
FACE. How, sir!
LOVEWIT. Gallants, men, and women,
And of all sorts, tag-rag, been seen to flock here
In threaves, these ten weeks, as to a second Hogsden
In days of Pimlico and Eye-bright!
FACE. Sir,
Their wisdoms will not say so!
LOVEWIT. Today, they speak

Of coaches, and gallants; one in a French hood,
Went in, they tell me: and another was seen
In a velvet gown at the window! Divers more
Pass in and out!

FACE. They did pass through the doors then,
Or walls, I assure their eyesights and their spectacles;
For here, sir, are the keys: and here have been
In this my pocket, now, above twenty days!
And for before, I kept the fort alone there.
But that 'tis yet not deep i'the afternoon,
I should believe my neighbors had seen double
Through the black pot, and made these apparitions!
For, on my faith, to your worship, for these three weeks
And upwards the door has not been opened.

LOVEWIT. Strange!

NEIGHBOUR 1.
Good faith, I think I saw a coach!

NEIGHBOUR 2. And I too,
I'd ha' been sworn!

LOVEWIT. Do you but think it now?
And but one coach?

NEIGHBOUR 4. We cannot tell, sir: Jeremy
Is a very honest fellow.

FACE. Did you see me at all?

NEIGHBOUR 1.
No. That we are sure on.

NEIGHBOUR 2. I'll be sworn o' that.

LOVEWIT.
Fine rogues, to have your testimonies built on!

[*Enter* NEIGHBOUR 3 *with his tools.*]

NEIGHBOUR 3.
Is Jeremy come?

NEIGHBOUR 1. O, yes, you may leave your tools,
We were deceived, he says.

NEIGHBOUR 2. He has had the keys:
And the door has been shut these three weeks.

NEIGHBOUR 3. Like enough.

LOVEWIT.
Peace, and get hence, you changelings.

[*Enter* SURLY *and* MAMMON.]

FACE. Surly come!
And Mammon made acquainted? They'll tell all.
(How shall I beat them off? What shall I do?)
Nothing's more wretched than a guilty conscience.

Scene 3

SURLY.
No, sir, he was a great physician. This,
It was no bawdy-house: but a mere chancel.
You knew the lord and his sister.
MAMMON. Nay, good Surly—
SURLY.
The happy word, 'be rich'—
MAMMON. Play not the tyrant—
SURLY.
Should be today pronounced, to all your friends.
And where be your andirons now? And your brass pots?
That should ha' been golden flagons, and great wedges?
MAMMON.
Let me but breathe. What! They ha' shut their doors,
Me thinks!
[MAMMON *and* SURLY *knock.*]
SURLY. Ay, now 'tis holiday with them.
MAMMON. Rogues,
Cozeners, imposters, bawds.
FACE. What mean you, sir?
MAMMON.
To enter if we can.
FACE. Another man's house?
Here is the owner, sir. Turn you to him,
And speak your business.
MAMMON. Are you, sir, the owner?
LOVEWIT.
Yes, sir.
MAMMON. And are those knaves, within, your cheaters?
LOVEWIT.
What knaves? What cheaters?
MAMMON. Subtle, and his Lungs.
FACE.
The gentleman is distracted, sir! No lungs,
Nor lights ha' been seen here these three weeks, sir,
Within these doors, upon my word!
SURLY. Your word,
Groom arrogant?
FACE. Yes, sir, I am the housekeeper,
And know the keys ha' not been out o' my hands.

SURLY.
This's a new Face?

FACE. You do mistake the house, sir!
What sign was't at?

SURLY. You rascal! This is one
O' the confederacy. Come let's get officers,
And force the door.

LOVEWIT. Pray you stay, gentlemen.

SURLY.
No, sir, we'll come with warrant.

MAMMON. Ay, and then,
We shall ha' your doors open.
[*Exeunt* SURLY, MAMMON.]

LOVEWIT. What means this?

FACE.
I cannot tell, sir!

NEIGHBOUR 1. These are two o' the gallants,
That we do think we saw.

FACE. Two o' the fools?
You talk as idly as they. Good faith, sir,
I think the moon has crazed 'em all!
[*Enter* KASTRIL.]
(O me,
The angry boy come too? He'll make a noise,
And ne'er away till he have betrayed us all.)

KASTRIL.
What rogues, bawds, slaves, you'll open the door anon,
[KASTRIL *knocks.*]
Punk, cockatrice, my suster. By this light
I'll fetch the marshal to you. You are a whore,
To keep your castle—

FACE. Who would you speak with, sir?

KASTRIL.
The bawdy Doctor, and the cozening Captain,
And Puss my suster.

LOVEWIT. This is something, sure!

FACE.
Upon my trust, the doors were never open, sir.

KASTRIL.
I have heard all their tricks, told me twice over,
By the fat knight and the lean gentleman.

LOVEWIT.
Here comes another.
[*Enter* ANANIAS, TRIBULATION.]

FACE. Ananias too?
And his pastor?

TRIBULATION. The doors are shut against us.

ANANIAS.
Come forth, you seed of sulphur, sons of fire,
[*They beat too, at the door.*]
Your stench, it is broke forth: abomination
Is in the house.

KASTRIL. Ay, my suster's there.

ANANIAS. The place,
It is become a cage of unclean birds.

KASTRIL.
Yes, I will fetch the scavenger, and the constable.

TRIBULATION.
You shall do well.

ANANIAS. We'll join, to weed them out.

KASTRIL.
You will not come then? Punk, device, my suster!

ANANIAS.
Call her not sister. She is a harlot, verily.

KASTRIL.
I'll raise the street.

LOVEWIT. Good gentlemen, a word.

ANANIAS.
Satan, avoid, and hinder not our zeal.
[*Exeunt* ANANIAS, TRIBULATION, KASTRIL.]

LOVEWIT.
The world's turned Bedlam.

FACE. These are all broke loose
Out of St. Katherine's where they use to keep
The better sort of mad folks.

NEIGHBOUR 1. All these persons
We saw go in and out here.

NEIGHBOUR 2. Yes, indeed, sir.

NEIGHBOUR 3.
These were the parties.

FACE. Peace, you drunkards. Sir,
I wonder at it! Please you, to give me leave
To touch the door, I'll try and the lock be changed.

LOVEWIT.
It mazes me!

FACE. Good faith, sir, I believe,
There's no such thing. 'Tis all *deceptio visus.*
[DAPPER *cries out within.*]
(Would I could get him away.)

DAPPER. Master Captain, master Doctor.

LOVEWIT.
Who's that?

FACE. (Our clerk within, that I forgot!) I know not, sir.

DAPPER.
For God's sake, when will her Grace be at leisure?

FACE. Ha!
Illusions, some spirit o' the air: (his gag is melted,
And now he sets out the throat.)

DAPPER. I am almost stifled—

FACE.
(Would you were altogether.)

LOVEWIT. 'Tis i' the house.
Ha! List.

FACE. Believe it, sir, i' the air!

LOVEWIT. Peace, you—

DAPPER.
Mine aunt's Grace does not use me well.

SUBTLE (*within*). You fool,
Peace, you'll mar all.

FACE. Or you will else, you rogue.

LOVEWIT.
O, is it so? Then you converse with spirits!
Come sir. No more o' your tricks, good Jeremy,
The truth, the shortest way.

FACE. Dismiss this rabble, sir.
What shall I do? I am catched.

LOVEWIT. Good neighbours,
I thank you all. You may depart.
[*Exeunt* NEIGHBOURS.]
Come sir,
You know that I am an indulgent master:
And therefore, conceal nothing. What's your medicine,
To draw so many several sorts of wild fowl?

FACE.
Sir, you were wont to affect mirth and wit:
(But here's no place to talk on't i' the street.)
Give me but leave to make the best of my fortune,
And only pardon me th'abuse of your house:
It's all I beg. I'll help you to a widow,
In recompense, that you shall gi' me thanks for,
Will make you seven years younger, and a rich one.
'Tis but your putting on a Spanish cloak,
I have her within. You need not fear the house,
It was not visited.

LOVEWIT. But by me, who came
Sooner than you expected.

FACE. It is true, sir.
Pray you forgive me.

LOVEWIT. Well: let's see your widow.

[*Exeunt* LOVEWIT, FACE.]

Scene 4

Enter SUBTLE, DAPPER

SUBTLE.
How! Ha' you eaten your gag?

DAPPER. Yes faith, it crumbled
Away i' my mouth.

SUBTLE. You ha' spoiled all then.

DAPPER. No,
I hope my aunt of Fairy will forgive me.

SUBTLE.
Your aunt's a gracious lady: but in troth
You were to blame.

DAPPER. The fume did overcome me,
And I did do't to stay my stomach. Pray you
So satisfy her Grace. Here comes the Captain.

[*Enter* FACE.]

FACE.
How now! Is his mouth down?

SUBTLE. Ay! He has spoken!

FACE.
(A pox, I heard him, and you too.) He's undone then.
(I have been fain to say the house is haunted
With spirits, to keep churl back.

SUBTLE. And hast thou done it?

FACE.
Sure, for this night.

SUBTLE. Why, then triumph, and sing
Of Face so famous, the precious king
Of present wits.

FACE. Did you not hear the coil
About the door?

SUBTLE. Yes, and I dwindled with it.)

FACE.
Show him his aunt, and let him be dispatched:

I'll send her to you.

[*Exit* FACE.]

SUBTLE. Well sir, your aunt her Grace,
Will give you audience presently, on my suit,
And the Captain's word, that you did not eat your gag
In any contempt of her Highness.

DAPPER. Not I, in troth, sir.

[*Enter* DOL *like the Queen of Fairy.*]

SUBTLE.
Here she is come. Down o' your knees, and wriggle:
She has a stately presence. Good. Yet nearer,
And bid, God save you.

DAPPER. Madam.

SUBTLE. And your aunt.

DAPPER.
And my most gracious aunt, God save your Grace.

DOL.
Nephew, we thought to have been angry with you:
But that sweet face of yours hath turned the tide,
And made it flow with joy that ebbed of love.
Arise, and touch our velvet gown.

SUBTLE. The skirts,
And kiss 'em. So.

DOL. Let me now stroke that head,
Much, nephew, shalt thou win; much shalt thou spend;
Much shalt thou give away: much shalt thou lend.

SUBTLE.
(Ay, much, indeed.) Why do you not thank her Grace?

DAPPER.
I cannot speak, for joy.

SUBTLE. See, the kind wretch!
Your Grace's kinsman right.

DOL. Give me the bird.
Here is your fly in a purse about your neck cousin,
Wear it, and feed it, about this day se'ennight,
On your right wrist—

SUBTLE. Open a vein with a pin
And let it suck but once a week: till then
You must not look on't.

DOL. No. And, kinsman,
Bear yourself worthy of the blood you come on.

SUBTLE.
Her Grace would ha' you eat no more Woolsack° pies,

V.4. 41, 42, 43. Woolsack, Dagger, Heaven and Hell: taverns

Nor Dagger° frumety.

DOL. Nor break his fast
In Heaven and Hell.°

SUBTLE. She's with you everywhere!
Nor play with costermongers, at mum-chance, tray-trip,
God make you rich, (whenas your aunt has done it:)
but keep
The gallantest company, and the best games—

DAPPER. Yes, sir.

SUBTLE.
Gleek and primero: and what you get, be true to us.

DAPPER.
By this hand, I will.

SUBTLE. You may bring's a thousand pound,
Before tomorrow night, (if but three thousand,
Be stirring) and you will.

DAPPER. I swear I will then.

SUBTLE.
Your fly will learn you all games.

FACE (*within*). Ha' you done there?

SUBTLE.
Your grace will command him no more duties?

DOL. No;
But come and see me often. I may chance
To leave him three or four hundred chests of treasure,
And some twelve thousand acres of Fairyland:
If he game well, and comely, with good gamesters.

SUBTLE.
There's a kind aunt! Kiss her departing part.
But you must sell your forty mark a year now:

DAPPER.
Ay, sir, I mean.

SUBTLE. Or, gi't away: pox on't.

DAPPER.
I'll gi't mine aunt. I'll go and fetch the writings.
[*Exit* DAPPER.]

SUBTLE.
'Tis well, away.
[*Enter* FACE.]

FACE. Where's Subtle?

SUBTLE. Here. What news?

FACE.
Drugger is at the door, go take his suit,
And bid him fetch a parson presently:
Say, he shall marry the widow. Thou shalt spend

A hundred pound by the service! (*Exit* SUBTLE.) Now, queen Dol,
Ha' you packed up all?

DOL. Yes.

FACE. And how do you like
The lady Pliant?

DOL. A good dull innocent.

[*Enter* SUBTLE.]

SUBTLE.
Here's your Hieronimo's cloak and hat.

FACE. Give me 'em.

SUBTLE.
And the ruff too?

FACE. Yes, I'll come to you presently.

[*Exit* FACE.]

SUBTLE.
Now, he is gone about his project, Dol,
I told you of, for the widow.

DOL. 'Tis direct
Against our articles.

SUBTLE. Well, we'll fit him, wench.
Hast thou gulled her of her jewels or her bracelets?

DOL.
No, but I will do't.

SUBTLE. Soon at night, my Dolly,
When we are shipped, and all our goods aboard,
Eastward for Ratcliff; we will turn our course
To Brainford, westward, if thou saist the word:
And take our leaves of this o'erweening rascal,
This peremptory Face.

DOL. Content, I am weary of him.

SUBTLE.
Th' hast cause, when the slave will run a-wiving, Dol,
Against the instrument that was drawn between us.

DOL.
I'll pluck his bird as bare as I can.

SUBTLE. Yes, tell her
She must by any means address some present
To th' cunning man; make him amends for wronging
His art with her suspicion; send a ring;
Or chain of pearl; she will be tortured else
Extremely in her sleep, say: and ha' strange things
Come to her. Wilt thou?

DOL. Yes.

SUBTLE. My fine flitter-mouse,

My bird o'the night; we'll tickle it at the Pigeons,°
When we have all, and may unlock the trunks,
And say, this's mine, and thine, and thine, and mine—
[*They kiss.*]
[*Enter* FACE.]

FACE.
What now, a-billing?

SUBTLE. Yes, a little exalted
In the good passage of our stock-affairs.

FACE.
Drugger has brought his parson, take him in, Subtle,
And send Nab back again, to wash his face.

SUBTLE.
I will: and shave himself?

FACE. If you can get him.
[*Exit* SUBTLE.]

DOL.
You are hot upon it, Face, what e'er it is!

FACE.
A trick, that Dol shall spend ten pound a month by.
[*Enter* SUBTLE.]
Is he gone?

SUBTLE. The chaplain waits you i'the hall, sir.

FACE.
I'll go bestow him.
[*Exit* FACE.]

DOL. He'll now marry her, instantly.

SUBTLE.
He cannot, yet, he is not ready. Dear Dol,
Cozen her of all thou canst. To deceive him
Is no deceit, but justice, that would break
Such an inextricable tie as ours was.

DOL.
Let me alone to fit him.
[*Enter* FACE.]

FACE. Come, my venturers,
You ha' packed up all? Where be the trunks? Bring forth.

SUBTLE.
Here.

FACE. Let's see 'em. Where's the money?

SUBTLE. Here,
In this.

FACE. Mammon's ten pound: eight score before.

89. Pigeons: an inn

The Brethren's money, this. Drugger's, and Dapper's.
What paper's that?

DOL. The jewel of the waiting maid's,
That stole it from her lady, to know certain—

FACE.
If she should have precedence of her mistress?

DOL. Yes.

FACE.
What box is that?

SUBTLE. The fish wives' rings, I think:
And th' ale wives' single money. Is't not Dol?

DOL.
Yes: and the whistle that the sailor's wife
Brought to you to know and her husband were with Ward.°

FACE.
We'll wet it tomorrow: and our silver beakers,
And tavern cups. Where be the French petticoats,
And girdles, and hangers?

SUBTLE. Here, i' the trunk,
And the bolts of lawn.

FACE. Is Drugger's damask, there?
And the tobacco?

SUBTLE. Yes.

FACE. Give me the keys.

DOL.
Why you the keys!

SUBTLE. No matter, Dol: because
We shall not open 'em, before he comes.

FACE.
'Tis true, you shall not open them, indeed:
Nor have 'em forth. Do you see? Not forth, Dol.

DOL. No!

FACE.
No, my smock-rampant. The right is, my master
Knows all, has pardoned me, and he will keep 'em.
Doctor, 'tis true (you look) for all your figures:
I sent for him, indeed. Wherefore, good partners,
Both he and she, be satisfied: for here
Determines the indenture tripartite
Twixt Subtle, Dol, and Face. All I can do
Is to help you over the wall, o' the back-side;
Or lend you a sheet to save your velvet gown, Dol.
Here will be officers, presently; bethink you,

116. Ward: a notorious Mediterranean pirate

Of some course suddenly to scape the dock:
For thither you'll come else.
[*Some knock.*]
Hark you, thunder.

SUBTLE.
You are a precious fiend!

OFFICER (*without*). Open the door.

FACE.
Dol, I am sorry for thee i' faith. But hearst thou?
It shall go hard but I will place thee somewhere:
Thou shalt ha' my letter to mistress Amo.

DOL. Hang you—

FACE.
Or madam Cæsarean.

DOL. Pox upon you, rogue,
Would I had but time to beat thee.

FACE. Subtle,
Let's know where you set up next; I'll send you
A customer now and then for old acquaintance:
What new course ha' you?

SUBTLE. Rogue, I'll hang myself:
That I may walk a greater devil than thou,
And haunt thee i' the flock-bed and the buttery.
[*Exeunt* SUBTLE, FACE, DOL.]

Scene 5

Enter LOVEWIT, PARSON

LOVEWIT.
What do you mean, my masters?

MAMMON (*without*). Open your door,
Cheaters, bawds, conjurers.

OFFICER (*without*). Or we'll break it open.

LOVEWIT.
What warrant have you?

OFFICER Warrant enough, sir, doubt not:
If you'll not open it.

LOVEWIT. Is there an officer, there?

OFFICER.
Yes, two or three for failing.°

V.5. **5. for failing:** as a precaution

LOVEWIT. Have but patience,
And I will open it straight.
[*Enter* FACE.]

FACE. Sir, ha' you done?
Is it a marriage? Perfect?

LOVEWIT. Yes, my brain.

FACE.
Off with your ruff and cloak then, be yourself, sir.

SURLY (*without*).
Down with the door.

KASTRIL (*without*). 'Slight, ding it open.

LOVEWIT. Hold.
Hold gentlemen, what means this violence?
[*Enter* MAMMON, SURLY, KASTRIL, ANANIAS, TRIBULATION, OFFICERS.]

MAMMON.
Where is this collier?

SURLY. And my Captain Face?

MAMMON.
These day-owls.

SURLY. That are birding in men's purses.

MAMMON.
Madam Suppository.

KASTRIL. Doxy, my suster.

ANANIAS. Locusts
Of the foul pit.

TRIBULATION. Profane as Bel and the dragon.

ANANIAS.
Worse than the grasshoppers, or the lice of Egypt.

LOVEWIT.
Good gentlemen, hear me. Are you officers,
And cannot stay this violence?

OFFICER. Keep the peace.

LOVEWIT.
Gentlemen, what is the matter? Whom do you seek?

MAMMON.
The chemical cozener.

SURLY. And the Captain pander.

KASTRIL.
The nun my suster.

MAMMON. Madam Rabbi.

ANANIAS. Scorpions,
And caterpillars.

LOVEWIT. Fewer at once, I pray you.

OFFICER.
One after another, gentleman, I charge you,
By virtue of my staff—

ANANIAS. They are the vessels
Of pride, lust, and the cart.

LOVEWIT. Good zeal, lie still
A little while.

TRIBULATION. Peace, deacon Ananias.

LOVEWIT.
The house is mine here, and the doors are open:
If there be any such persons as you seek for,
Use your authority, search on o' God's name.
I am but newly come to town, and finding
This tumult 'bout my door (to tell you true)
It somewhat mazed me; till my man, here, (fearing
My more displeasure) told me he had done
Somewhat an insolent part, let out my house
(Belike, presuming on my known aversion
From any air o' the town, while there was sickness)
To a Doctor and a Captain: who, what they are,
Or where they be, he knows not.

MAMMON. Are they gone?
[*They enter.*]

LOVEWIT.
You may go in and search, sir. Here I find
The empty walls worse than I left 'em, smoked,
A few cracked pots, and glasses, and a furnace,
The ceiling filled with poesies of the candle:
And madam, with a dildo, writ o' the walls.
Only, one gentlewoman, I met here,
That is within, that said she was a widow—

KASTRIL.
Ay, that's my suster. I'll go thump her. Where is she?

LOVEWIT.
And should ha' married a Spanish count, but he,
When he came to't, neglected her so grossly,
That I, a widower, am gone through with her.

SURLY.
How! Have I lost her then?

LOVEWIT. Were you the Don, sir?
Good faith, now, she does blame y'extremely, and says
You swore, and told her you had ta'en the pains
To dye your beard, and umbre o'er your face,
Borrowed a suit, and ruff, all for her love;
And then did nothing. What an oversight,

And want of putting forward, sir, was this!
Well fare an old harquebuzier, yet,
Could prime his powder, and give fire, and hit,
All in a twinkling.

MAMMON. The whole nest are fled!

[MAMMON *comes forth.*]

LOVEWIT.
What sort of birds were they?

MAMMON. A kind of choughs,
Or thievish daws, sir, that have picked my purse
Of eight score and ten pounds within these five weeks,
Beside my first materials; and my goods,
That lie i' the cellar: which I am glad they ha' left.
I may have home yet.

LOVEWIT. Think you so, sir?

MAMMON. Ay.

LOVEWIT.
By order of law, sir, but not otherwise.

MAMMON.
Not mine own stuff?

LOVEWIT. Sir, I can take no knowledge,
That they are yours but by public means.
If you can bring certificate, that you were gulled of 'em,
Or any formal writ, out of a court,
That you did cozen yourself: I will not hold them.

MAMMON.
I'll rather lose 'em.

LOVEWIT. That you shall not, sir,
By me, in troth. Upon these terms they are yours.
What should they ha' been, sir, turned into gold all?

MAMMON. No.
I cannot tell. It may be they should. What then?

LOVEWIT.
What a great loss in hope have you sustained?

MAMMON.
Not I, the Commonwealth has.

FACE. Ay, he would ha' built
The city new; and made a ditch about it
Of silver, should have run with cream from Hogsden:
That, every Sunday in Moorfields, the younkers,
And tits and tomboys should have fed on, *gratis.*

MAMMON.
I will go mount a turnip cart and preach
The end o' the world within these two months. Surly,
What! In a dream?

SURLY. Must I needs cheat myself,
With that same foolish vice of honesty!
Come let us go, and harken out the rogues.
That Face I'll mark for mine, if e'er I meet him.

FACE.
If I can hear of him, sir, I'll bring you word
Unto your lodging: for in troth, they were strangers
To me, I thought 'em honest, as myself, sir.
[*Exeunt* MAMMON, SURLY.]

TRIBULATION.
'Tis well, the Saints shall not lose all yet. Go,
[*They come forth.*]
And get some carts—

LOVEWIT. For what, my zealous friends?

ANANIAS.
To bear away the portion of the righteous,
Out of this den of thieves.

LOVEWIT. What is that portion?

ANANIAS.
The goods, sometimes the orphan's, that the Brethren,
Bought with their silver pence.

LOVEWIT. What, those i' the cellar,
The knight Sir Mammon claims?

ANANIAS. I do defy
The wicked Mammon, so do all the Brethren,
Thou profane man. I ask thee, with what conscience
Thou canst advance that idol against us
That have the seal? Were not the shillings numbered
That made the pounds? Were not the pounds told out,
Upon the second day of the fourth week,
In the eighth month, upon the table dormant,
The year of the last patience of the Saints,
Six hundred and ten.

LOVEWIT. Mine earnest vehement botcher,
And deacon also, I cannot dispute with you,
But, if you get you not away the sooner,
I shall confute you with a cudgel.

ANANIAS. Sir.

TRIBULATION.
Be patient Ananias.

ANANIAS. I am strong,
And will stand up, well girt, against an host,
That threaten Gad in exile.

LOVEWIT. I shall send you
To Amsterdam, to your cellar.

ANANIAS. I will pray there,
Against thy house: may dogs defile thy walls,
And wasps and hornets breed beneath thy roof,
This seat of falsehood, and this cave of cozenage.
[*Exeunt* ANANIAS, TRIBULATION.]
[DRUGGER *enters, and he beats him away*.]

LOVEWIT.
Another too?

DRUGGER. Not I sir, I am no Brother.

LOVEWIT.
Away you Harry Nicholas,° do you talk?
[*Exit* DRUGGER.]

FACE.
No, this was Abel Drugger. Good sir, go,
[*To the* PARSON.]
And satisfy him; tell him, all is done:
He stayed too long a-washing of his face.
The Doctor, he shall hear of him at Westchester;
And of the Captain, tell him at Yarmouth: or
Some good port town else, lying for a wind.
[*Exit* PARSON.]
If you get off the angry child, now, sir—
[*Enter* KASTRIL, DAME PLIANT.]

KASTRIL.
Come on, you ewe, you have matched most sweetly, ha' you not?
[*To his sister*.]
Did not I say I would never ha' you tupped
But by a dubbed boy, to make you a lady tom?
'Slight, you are a mammet! O, I could touse you now.
Death, mun' you marry with a pox?

LOVEWIT. You lie, boy;
As sound as you: and I am aforehand with you.

KASTRIL. Anon?

LOVEWIT.
Come, will you quarrel? I will feeze° you, sirrah.
Why do you not buckle to your tools?

KASTRIL. God's light!
This is a fine old boy, as e'er I saw!

LOVEWIT.
What, do you change your copy now? Proceed,
Here stands my dove: stoop at her, if you dare.

117. Harry Nicholas: another German Anabaptist, leader of the sect called The Family of Love. **131. feeze:** beat

KASTRIL.
'Slight I must love him! I cannot choose, i' faith!
And I should be hanged for't. Suster, I protest,
I honor thee for this match.

LOVEWIT. O, do you so, sir?

KASTRIL.
Yes, and thou canst take tobacco, and drink, old boy,
I'll give her five hundred pound more to her marriage
Than her own state.

LOVEWIT. Fill a pipe-full, Jeremy.

FACE.
Yes, but go in and take it, sir.

LOVEWIT. We will.
I will be ruled by thee in anything, Jeremy.

KASTRIL.
'Slight, thou art not hidebound! Thou art a jovy boy!
Come let's in, I pray thee, and take our whiffs.

LOVEWIT.
Whiff in with your sister, brother boy.
[*Exeunt* KASTRIL, DAME PLIANT.]
That master
That had received such happiness by a servant,
In such a widow, and with so much wealth,
Were very ungrateful, if he would not be
A little indulgent to that servant's wit,
And help his fortune, though with some small strain
Of his own candor.° Therefore, gentlemen,
And kind spectators, if I have outstripped
An old man's gravity, or strict canon, think
What a young wife and a good brain may do:
Stretch age's truth sometimes, and crack it too.
Speak for thyself, knave.

FACE. So I will, sir. Gentlemen,
My part a little fell in this last scene,
Yet 'twas decorum. And though I am clean
Got off from Subtle, Surly, Mammon, Dol,
Hot Ananias, Dapper, Drugger, all
With whom I traded; yet I put myself
On you, that are my country: and this pelf,
Which I have got, if you do quit me, rests
To feast you often, and invite new guests.

152. candor: honor

CRITICAL COMMENTARY

The circumstances behind *The Alchemist* are not uncommon. Empty buildings are always being used for illegal purposes. Few city dwellers would read past the headlines: TRIO OPERATE RACKET IN EMPTY TOWN HOUSE. BUTLER, CON MAN, AND PROSTITUTE TAKE ADVANTAGE OF OWNER'S ABSENCE. REPRESENTATIVES OF LAW, BUSINESS, THE CHURCH, AND SOCIETY AMONG THOSE FLEECED. But this play presents an unusual view of urban crime. Its tone tells us what the facts mean.

Ben Jonson was a man of integrity, and his imagination kept reporting that the whole place is full of junk and that the usual means of handling it are themselves a part of the waste matter. During *The Alchemist* the stage is literally in danger of filling up with junk—cast iron, lead roofing and scrap metal—until it finally explodes along with the plot. The language, too, is as thick and dense with particulars as any swarming city. Much of the thickness of language and objects comes, of course, from the ostensible subject, alchemy, a huge accumulation of ancient metallurgical trade secrets, occult speculations, phony scholarship, dreams of instant wealth and power, and a marvelous technical jargon. People of Johnson's age were attached to alchemy in as many ways as people today are attached to the space age, and alchemy was consequently potential material for many kinds of plays—problem plays, dreamy romances, documentaries, black comedies, tragedies of misused learning, and so on. Jonson chose to mine it for a warmly satiric farce.

We start near the beginning from the inside. Our two male confederates appear to be a captain and a laboratory scientist, but they loudly tell each other, and us, who they really are, neatly and dramatically giving us the initial facts. At the same time we are getting equally important clues about how to take the facts. Instead of seeming sordid and furtive as a cheap racket would, the situation appears almost stage Irish. Face and Subtle obviously enjoy showing off their Terrible Tongues, and Dol, who looks like a prostitute, acts like a mother. Men are still boys; they have to be scolded, stopped from fighting, and comforted before they will go to sleep. In addition to its proverbial noisy warmth, the Irish stage family is typically theatrical and precarious, and so is this one. We live by our wits, by our discipline, which is hard to maintain in this unsteady family "republic," and we are surrounded by enemies. Dol contributes to the precariousness of the situation by the fact that although she is a big, strong, goodhearted girl, she is not as talented as her colleagues. She does, of course, have her own thing, but it is god-given, and she is asked to play parts (the Queen of Faerie, a female scholar subject to spells of depression) that are quite out of character and may be beyond her powers. At such moments Face's encouragement is full of Irish comaraderie—a friendly boost to a fellow artist whose natural talent is narrowly specialized. Give them the old razzmatazz, Dol. But will it work? The precariousness and the staginess bring in the tone of farce with its accelerating series of suddenly assigned parts and the increasing apprehension that too much is happening.

Ben Jonson was born in 1572 (eight years after Marlowe and Shakespeare), the posthumous son of a minister and the stepson of a London bricklayer. After finishing grammar school, he worked at odd jobs, was in and out of the army and jail, got married, lost two young children, continued to educate himself by reading seriously, especially in the classics, and was recognized as a coming playwright by 1598, the date of his comedy, *Every Man in His Humour,* in which Shakespeare played the leading role. He was a professional writer and critic, a master of the masque, the occasional poem, and several kinds of comedy. *The Alchemist* (1610) is the third of his major comedies, following *Volpone* (1601) and *Epicene* (1609) and preceding *Bartholomew Fair* (1614).

The fact that the main racket, alchemy, is hopelessly dated might seem to have a restrictive bearing on the tone and meaning of the play, and it has indeed occasioned a good deal of learned apology. But there is obviously no need to try to save *The Alchemist* by filling the stage with up-to-date laboratory apparatus or by feeling that one must try to think solemnly that it should have been Jonson's version of *Faustus.* The focus is on the human side of science and scholarship, a subject that appears to be timelessly comic.

A good opening example is the encounter between Surly and Subtle (Act II, Scene 3). The Elizabethan Surly has a thoroughly modern opinion of alchemy. He sees clearly what is going on in Lovewit's vacant house—a piece of pseudo-scientific flim-flam with a little prostitution on the side. As we undertake with Subtle to convert this heretic, we find ourselves in familiar surroundings. It is the lecture hall, and Subtle is playing the part of the scientist as patient explainer to the lay public. The tone is wise and fatherly. We lead the understandably doubtful learner by easy steps, helping him along with homely illustrations from his own experience. The indirect object of this comic satire is exposition as brainwashing, a normal stylistic method of the Establishment for diverting attention from the truth to the surface.

Related views of the all-too-human side of science and the learned professions generally are provided by Face. Although as Captain he always seems to be "just leaving," this is simply a part of the surface fiction that a normal activity is going on. His chief role is that of Receptionist, an intermediary between client and expert, and here he is able to suggest that Subtle is (1) completely absorbed in his studies, (2) the pure intellectual, quite indifferent to money except as it is needed for his experiments, and (3) difficult to deal with because he is above average, a distinguished eccentric, and a dedicated ascetic who cannot be appealed to in ordinary human terms. All this, of course, is invented to trick the clients into thinking themselves fortunate to be able to pay more and more for Subtle's services.

The subject is enlarged through Face's role as Laboratory Assistant. Here he appears as an inferior creature from some disadvantaged background, as distinct from a true scientist like Subtle. He has acquired a surprising amount of applied technical information that he can recite like a trained monkey, but this continuous oral examination can never lead to a degree. It is natural that he should be eager to report good news from the laboratory and should look on his master with adoring admiration. Again, all this is to impress the clients. Face as Laboratory Assistant may be a little sooty for our taste, but we could not improve on him as a public relations man and indirectly as an instrument of satire.

More largely, the subject is not alchemy or science, but the middle-class business world. Subtle, Face, and Dol create the impression of being a large, bustling organization, working day and night to please the public, always solicitous and always ready with disinterested expert advice, and prepared to offer any service on a moment's notice.

The human side of alchemy is most comic in what it reveals about the clients. Dapper, a well-named law clerk, is the first to appear. It is soon evident that he is vulnerable. He feels superior to his profession (a "scurvy writ" or two); he is pleased to indicate by a reference to his watch that he dresses above his present place in society; and he is confident that he is a clever enough lawyer to break the law safely. All he wants is a little system for gambling. Subtle's mock fear that this might lead to wrecking the national economy is brushed aside by Face's assurance that Dapper plans only to make an occasional Friday night bet on the horses. Then comes the climatic revelation. "DAPPER. Yes, Captain, I would have it for all games. SUBTLE. I told you so." In a psychological play this might have the painful effect of a sudden intimacy, as if an unsophisticated young person had shown us something secret about himself; in a play of character it might become a step on the road to self-knowledge and maturity; in a problem play it could help to expose the deep sickness of gambling, and so on. But *The Alchemist* is indifferent to such fine feelings and important issues. The focus is on the opportunity for broad character acting. Dapper's initial timorousness is slowly replaced by a look of dawning anticipation, a mixture of surprise at his own daring and increasing firmness leading up to the "Yes, I would have it for all games." He is led away stunned, so nearly in a state of shock at what he has done and what the future holds that he has to be told how to behave: "Go, thank the Doctor." "I thank his Worship," and so on. As he leaves, dazed, he is reminded of his aunt, the Queen of Faerie, and we are in turn reminded that Dol will soon have to undertake this unlikely and difficult role.

The popularity of *The Alchemist* has always been connected with its opportunities for farcically comical acting. An actor named Dogget was described as having a "Farce in his Face" when he played Dapper in 1710. The great Garrick developed the comparable minor role of Drugger, the second client, along similar lines:

> His attitude, his dread of offending the doctor, his saying nothing, his gradual stealing in farther and farther, his impatience to be introduced, his joy to his friend Face, are imitable by none. . . . When he first opens his mouth, the features of his face seem, as it were, to drop upon the tongue; it is all caution; it is timorous, stammering, and inexpressible. When he stands under the conjurer to have his features examined, his teeth, his beard, his little finger, his awkward simplicity, and his concern, mixed with hope and fear, and joy and avarice, and good nature, are above painting. (C. H. Herford and Percy and Evelyn Simpson, eds. *Ben Jonson,* IX, 1950, pp. 229, 233)

Although we laugh at characters who must be acted in this broad fashion, the satire is kindly. The tone asks us to accept the Dappers and the Druggers of the world. To condemn or reform them would destroy their comforting reliability. Good old Dapper and Drugger are always good old Dapper and Drugger.

Sir Epicure Mammon, the third client, would appear to be a very different case. He is certainly far beyond Dapper and Drugger. He is quite at ease with the unlimited possibilities of winning at all games. No more the sordid shifts of the past; this is the new world of instant wealth. Face had to do most of the talking for Dapper and Drugger, but Sir Epicure speaks for himself. His periods roll over Surly's mean-spirited skepticism. The style is ample, affluent, generous. It is the manner to which we were all really born, but of which we have been cheated by bad luck and circumstances. In this moment of splendid aristocratic release, we approve of Face's dazzled and delighted admiration—this is the way white folks should behave, yes, Sir! It is in character for Sir Epicure to have a proprietary attitude toward science. He employs Ph.D.'s, the best money can buy. It pleases him to speak of *our* experiments, to drop a few technical terms, and to back his doctor against the skeptical Surly.

Although Sir Epicure ranges far beyond Dapper and Drugger, he is handled so that he belongs in the same play with them. His weakness appears to be a fondness for women, and in a different kind of play this would again be a serious matter, nasty at best. But in this context he is no more lecherous than W. C. Fields. He is a fine figure of a man, a preview of the Edwardian era, and his lechery is simply an expression of his rich taste and his superior position in life. His inability to distinguish reality from dreams of glory could also be a serious matter, a proper subject for a problem play. Here, however, the emphasis is on the aplomb with which he keeps his form in the face of difficulties that are brought to his attention from the dull world of facts.

The next major clients are the two Puritan churchmen, the Reverend Wholesome Tribulation and his assistant, Deacon Ananias. It is comic but not altogether surprising that they and Subtle should discover themselves to be brothers under the skin. The possibilities of using organized religion as a racket are well known. The Puritans, like our trio, operate from behind a front of impressive jargon and play acting to prey on the gullible. It is Jonson's creative addition to this familiar portrait that maintains the special tone and explains why the religious swindlers are themselves vulnerable. They are exhausted by their own mummery. They allow themselves to be taken in by Subtle because his instant gold frees them from the burden of having to be endlessly hypocritical and fraudulent. This understandable desire for an easy pre-lapsarian short-cut allies them with the other clients and makes them seem good-naturedly human rather than purely reprehensible. Like the other customers, they simply want to be free to be themselves. Why be satisfied with old model iron pots and lead roofing?

Once the victims have been introduced, the plot accelerates as if it had a life of its own. Costumes have to be changed with increasing rapidity, plans have to be altered and roles improvised on a moment's notice, and as the separate actions begin to intersect unexpectedly, the rooms rapidly fill with clients being kept out of sight while newcomers are cared for. The return of Lovewit, as we know from the start, will end the play, but its logical end comes when the plot cannot absorb one more complication without breaking into separate parts and when the accidental collision of characters can no longer produce new comic revelations. There then remain the modulation back to so-called normality and the dramatic assessment of the value of all that has happened. The view of ordinary society as represented by Lovewit's neighbors is unacceptable. It is the biggest thing that has happened on the block and they will talk about it for years, but obviously the neighbors will never really understand what has gone on. Lovewit's view is somewhat better. He forgives Face because he loves a joke and is proud of his witty butler (our man puts on funnier rackets than anyone's). But Lovewit's acceptance of the situation does not equal the experience of the play. Guided by the fertile and inexhaustible Face, we have exercised unexpected talents, experienced an extraordinary range of language, been led through refreshingly novel possibilities and relationships, and been helped to make creative discriminations of tone and meaning. "Humane" may be the best single word to describe the overall tone of the alchemy that takes us in and puts us on in this educational fashion.

Useful Criticism

Barish, Jonas A., ed. *Ben Jonson** (Twentieth Century Views). Englewood Cliffs, N.J.: Prentice-Hall, 1963.

———. *Ben Jonson and the Language of Prose Comedy.* Cambridge, Mass.: Harvard University Press, 1960.

Enck, John J. *Jonson and the Comic Truth.** Madison, Wis.: University of Wisconsin Press, 1966.

Herford, C. H., and Simpson, Percy and Evelyn, eds. *Ben Jonson* (Vols. I, II, IX, X). New York: Oxford University Press, 1925–52.

Kernan, Alvin. *The Cankered Muse.* New Haven, Conn.: Yale University Press, 1959.

Partridge, Edward B. *The Broken Compass.* London: Chatto & Windus, 1958.

* Available in paperback.

TARTUFFE

Molière

Translated by RICHARD WILBUR

CHARACTERS

MME PERNELLE, Orgon's mother
ORGON, Elmire's husband
ELMIRE, Orgon's wife
DAMIS, Orgon's son, Elmire's stepson
MARIANE, Orgon's daughter, Elmire's stepdaughter, in love with Valère
VALÈRE, in love with Mariane
CLÉANTE, Orgon's brother-in-law
TARTUFFE, a hypocrite
DORINE, Mariane's lady's-maid
M. LOYAL, a bailiff
A POLICE OFFICER
FLIPOTE, Mme Pernelle's maid

THE SCENE THROUGHOUT. *Orgon's house in Paris*

ACT I

Scene 1

MADAME PERNELLE *and* FLIPOTE, *her maid,*
ELMIRE, MARIANE, DORINE, DAMIS, CLÉANTE

MADAME PERNELLE.
Come, come, Flipote; it's time I left this place.
ELMIRE.
I can't keep up, you walk at such a pace.
MADAME PERNELLE.
Don't trouble, child; no need to show me out.
It's not your manners I'm concerned about.

ELMIRE.
We merely pay you the respect we owe.
But, Mother, why this hurry? Must you go?

MADAME PERNELLE.
I must. This house appals me. No one in it
Will pay attention for a single minute.
Children, I take my leave much vexed in spirit.
I offer good advice, but you won't hear it.
You all break in and chatter on and on.
It's like a madhouse with the keeper gone.

DORINE.
If . . .

MADAME PERNELLE.
Girl, you talk too much, and I'm afraid
You're far too saucy for a lady's-maid.
You push in everywhere and have your say.

DAMIS.
But . . .

MADAME PERNELLE.
You, boy, grow more foolish every day.
To think my grandson should be such a dunce!
I've said a hundred times, if I've said it once,
That if you keep the course on which you've started,
You'll leave your worthy father broken-hearted.

MARIANE.
I think . . .

MADAME PERNELLE.
And you, his sister, seem so pure,
So shy, so innocent, and so demure.
But you know what they say about still waters.
I pity parents with secretive daughters.

ELMIRE.
Now, Mother . . .

MADAME PERNELLE.
And as for you, child, let me add
That your behavior is extremely bad,
And a poor example for these children, too.
Their dear, dead mother did far better than you.
You're much too free with money, and I'm distressed
To see you so elaborately dressed.
When it's one's husband that one aims to please,
One has no need of costly fripperies.

CLÉANTE.
Oh, Madam, really . . .

MADAME PERNELLE.

You are her brother, Sir,
And I respect and love you; yet if I were
My son, this lady's good and pious spouse,
I wouldn't make you welcome in my house.
You're full of worldly counsels which, I fear,
Aren't suitable for decent folk to hear.
I've spoken bluntly, Sir; but it behooves us
Not to mince words when righteous fervor moves us.

DAMIS.

Your man Tartuffe is full of holy speeches . . .

MADAME PERNELLE.

And practises precisely what he preaches.
He's a fine man, and should be listened to.
I will not hear him mocked by fools like you.

DAMIS.

Good God! Do you expect me to submit
To the tyranny of that carping hypocrite?
Must we forgo all joys and satisfactions
Because that bigot censures all our actions?

DORINE.

To hear him talk—and he talks all the time—
There's nothing one can do that's not a crime.
He rails at everything, your dear Tartuffe.

MADAME PERNELLE.

Whatever he reproves deserves reproof.
He's out to save your souls, and all of you
Must love him, as my son would have you do.

DAMIS.

Ah no, Grandmother, I could never take
To such a rascal, even for my father's sake.
That's how I feel, and I shall not dissemble.
His every action makes me seethe and tremble
With helpless anger, and I have no doubt
That he and I will shortly have it out.

DORINE.

Surely it is a shame and a disgrace
To see this man usurp the master's place—
To see this beggar who, when first he came,
Had not a shoe or shoestring to his name
So far forget himself that he behaves
As if the house were his, and we his slaves.

MADAME PERNELLE.

Well, mark my words, your souls would fare far better

If you obeyed his precepts to the letter.

DORINE.
You see him as a saint. I'm far less awed;
In fact, I see right through him. He's a fraud.

MADAME PERNELLE.
Nonsense!

DORINE. His man Laurent's the same, or worse;
I'd not trust either with a penny purse.

MADAME PERNELLE.
I can't say what his servant's morals may be;
His own great goodness I can guarantee.
You all regard him with distaste and fear
Because he tells you what you're loath to hear,
Condemns your sins, points out your moral flaws,
And humbly strives to further Heaven's cause.

DORINE.
If sin is all that bothers him, why is it
He's so upset when folk drop in to visit?
Is Heaven so outraged by a social call
That he must prophesy against us all?
I'll tell you what I think: if you ask me,
He's jealous of my mistress' company.

MADAME PERNELLE.
Rubbish! (*To* ELMIRE.) He's not alone, child, in complaining
Of all your promiscuous entertaining.
Why, the whole neighborhood's upset, I know,
By all these carriages that come and go,
With crowds of guests parading in and out
And noisy servants loitering about.
In all of this, I'm sure there's nothing vicious;
But why give people cause to be suspicious?

CLÉANTE.
They need no cause; they'll talk in any case.
Madam, this world would be a joyless place
If, fearing what malicious tongues might say,
We locked our doors and turned our friends away.
And even if one did so dreary a thing,
D'you think those tongues would cease their chattering?
One can't fight slander; it's a losing battle;
Let us instead ignore their tittle-tattle.
Let's strive to live by conscience' clear decrees,
And let the gossips gossip as they please.

DORINE.
If there is talk against us, I know the source:
It's Daphne and her little husband, of course.

Those who have greatest cause for guilt and shame
Are quickest to besmirch a neighbor's name.
When there's a chance for libel, they never miss it;
When something can be made to seem illicit
They're off at once to spread the joyous news,
Adding to fact what fantasies they choose.
By talking up their neighbor's indiscretions
They seek to camouflage their own transgressions,
Hoping that others' innocent affairs
Will lend a hue of innocence to theirs,
Or that their own black guilt will come to seem
Part of a general shady color-scheme.

MADAME PERNELLE.
All that is quite irrelevant. I doubt
That anyone's more virtuous and devout
Than dear Orante; and I'm informed that she
Condemns your mode of life most vehemently.

DORINE.
Oh, yes, she's strict, devout, and has no taint
Of worldliness; in short, she seems a saint.
But it was time which taught her that disguise;
She's thus because she can't be otherwise.
So long as her attractions could enthrall,
She flounced and flirted and enjoyed it all,
But now that they're no longer what they were
She quits a world which fast is quitting her,
And wears a veil of virtue to conceal
Her bankrupt beauty and her lost appeal.
That's what becomes of old coquettes today:
Distressed when all their lovers fall away,
They see no recourse but to play the prude,
And so confer a style on solitude.
Thereafter, they're severe with everyone,
Condemning all our actions, pardoning none,
And claiming to be pure, austere, and zealous
When, if the truth were known, they're merely jealous,
And cannot bear to see another know
The pleasures time has forced them to forgo.

MADAME PERNELLE (*initially to* ELMIRE).
That sort of talk is what you like to hear;
Therefore you'd have us all keep still, my dear,
While Madam rattles on the livelong day.
Nevertheless, I mean to have my say.
I tell you that you're blest to have Tartuffe
Dwelling, as my son's guest, beneath this roof;

That Heaven has sent him to forestall its wrath
By leading you, once more, to the true path;
That all he reprehends its reprehensible,
And that you'd better heed him, and be sensible.
These visits, balls, and parties in which you revel
Are nothing but inventions of the Devil.
One never hears a word that's edifying:
Nothing but chaff and foolishness and lying,
As well as vicious gossip in which one's neighbor
Is cut to bits with epee, foil, and saber.
People of sense are driven half-insane
At such affairs, where noise and folly reign
And reputations perish thick and fast.
As a wise preacher said on Sunday last,
Parties are Towers of Babylon, because
The guests all babble on with never a pause;
And then he told a story which, I think . . .
(*To* CLÉANTE)
I heard that laugh, Sir, and I saw that wink!
Go find your silly friends and laugh some more!
Enough; I'm going; don't show me to the door.
I leave this household much dismayed and vexed;
I cannot say when I shall see you next.
(*Slapping* FLIPOTE.)
Wake up, don't stand there gaping into space!
I'll slap some sense into that stupid face.
Move, move, you slut.

Scene 2

CLÉANTE, DORINE

CLÉANTE.
I think I'll stay behind;
I want no further pieces of her mind.
How that old lady . . .

DORINE.
Oh, what wouldn't she say
If she could hear you speak of her that way!
She'd thank you for the *lady,* but I'm sure
She'd find the *old* a little premature.

CLÉANTE.
My, what a scene she made, and what a din!

And how this man Tartuffe has taken her in!

DORINE.

Yes, but her son is even worse deceived;
His folly must be seen to be believed.
In the late troubles, he played an able part
And served his king with wise and loyal heart,
But he's quite lost his senses since he fell
Beneath Tartuffe's infatuating spell.
He calls him brother, and loves him as his life,
Preferring him to mother, child, or wife.
In him and him alone will he confide;
He's made him his confessor and his guide;
He pets and pampers him with love more tender
Than any pretty mistress could engender,
Gives him the place of honor when they dine,
Delights to see him gorging like a swine,
Stuffs him with dainties till his guts distend,
And when he belches, cries "God bless you, friend!"
In short, he's mad; he worships him; he dotes;
His deeds he marvels at, his words he quotes,
Thinking each act a miracle, each word
Oracular as those that Moses heard.
Tartuffe, much pleased to find so easy a victim,
Has in a hundred ways beguiled and tricked him,
Milked him of money, and with his permission
Established here a sort of Inquisition.
Even Laurent, his lackey, dares to give
Us arrogant advice on how to live;
He sermonizes us in thundering tones
And confiscates our ribbons and colognes.
Last week he tore a kerchief into pieces
Because he found it pressed in a *Life of Jesus:*
He said it was a sin to juxtapose
Unholy vanities and holy prose.

Scene 3

ELMIRE, MARIANE, DAMIS, CLÉANTE, DORINE

ELMIRE (*to* CLÉANTE).

You did well not to follow; she stood in the door
And said *verbatim* all she'd said before.
I saw my husband coming. I think I'd best

Go upstairs now, and take a little rest.

CLÉANTE.

I'll wait and greet him here; then I must go.
I've really only time to say hello.

DAMIS.

Sound him about my sister's wedding, please.
I think Tartuffe's against it, and that he's
Been urging Father to withdraw his blessing.
As you well know, I'd find that most distressing.
Unless my sister and Valère can marry,
My hopes to wed *his* sister will miscarry,
And I'm determined . . .

DORINE.

He's coming.

Scene 4

ORGON, CLÉANTE, DORINE

ORGON.

Ah, Brother, good-day.

CLÉANTE.

Well, welcome back. I'm sorry I can't stay.
How was the country? Blooming, I trust, and green?

ORGON.

Excuse me, Brother; just one moment.
(*To* DORINE.)
Dorine . . .
(*To* CLÉANTE.)
To put my mind at rest, I always learn
The household news the moment I return.
(*To* DORINE.)
Has all been well, these two days I've been gone?
How are the family? What's been going on?

DORINE.

You wife, two days ago, had a bad fever,
And a fierce headache which refused to leave her.

ORGON.

Ah. And Tartuffe?

DORINE.

Tartuffe? Why, he's round and red,
Bursting with health, and excellently fed.

ORGON.

Poor fellow!

DORINE.

That night, the mistress was unable
To take a single bite at the dinner-table.
Her headache-pains, she said, were simply hellish.

ORGON.

Ah. And Tartuffe?

DORINE.

He ate his meal with relish,
And zealously devoured in her presence
A leg of mutton and a brace of pheasants.

ORGON.

Poor fellow!

DORINE.

Well, the pains continued strong,
And so she tossed and tossed the whole night long,
Now icy-cold, now burning like a flame.
We sat beside her bed till morning came.

ORGON.

Ah. And Tartuffe?

DORINE.

Why, having eaten, he rose
And sought his room, already in a doze,
Got into his warm bed, and snored away
In perfect peace until the break of day.

ORGON.

Poor fellow!

DORINE.

After much ado, we talked her
Into dispatching someone for the doctor.
He bled her, and the fever quickly fell.

ORGON.

Ah. And Tartuffe?

DORINE.

He bore it very well.
To keep his cheerfulness at any cost,
And make up for the blood *Madame* had lost,
He drank, at lunch, four beakers full of port.

ORGON.

Poor fellow!

DORINE.

Both are doing well, in short.
I'll go and tell *Madame* that you've expressed
Keen sympathy and anxious interest.

Scene 5

ORGON, CLÉANTE

CLÉANTE.

That girl was laughing in your face, and though
I've no wish to offend you, even so
I'm bound to say that she had some excuse.
How can you possibly be such a goose?
Are you so dazed by this man's hocus-pocus
That all the world, save him, is out of focus?
You've given him clothing, shelter, food, and care;
Why must you also . . .

ORGON.

Brother, stop right there.
You do not know the man of whom you speak.

CLÉANTE.

I grant you that. But my judgment's not so weak
That I can't tell, by his effect on others . . .

ORGON.

Ah, when you meet him, you two will be like brothers!
There's been no loftier soul since time began.
He is a man who . . . a man who . . . an excellent man.
To keep his precepts is to be reborn,
And view this dunghill of a world with scorn.
Yes, thanks to him I'm a changed man indeed.
Under his tutelage my soul's been freed
From earthly loves, and every human tie:
My mother, children, brother, and wife could die,
And I'd not feel a single moment's pain.

CLÉANTE.

That's a fine sentiment, Brother; most humane.

ORGON.

Oh, had you seen Tartuffe as I first knew him,
Your heart, like mine, would have surrendered to him.
He used to come into our church each day
And humbly kneel nearby, and start to pray.
He'd draw the eyes of everybody there
By the deep fervor of his heartfelt prayer;
He'd sigh and weep, and sometimes with a sound
Of rapture he would bend and kiss the ground;
And when I rose to go, he'd run before
To offer me holy-water at the door.

His serving-man, no less devout than he,
Informed me of his master's poverty;
I gave him gifts, but in his humbleness
He'd beg me every time to give him less.
"Oh, that's too much," he'd cry, "too much by twice!
I don't deserve it. The half, Sir, would suffice."
And when I wouldn't take it back, he'd share
Half of it with the poor, right then and there.
At length, Heaven prompted me to take him in
To dwell with us, and free our souls from sin.
He guides our lives, and to protect my honor
Stays by my wife, and keeps an eye upon her;
He tells me whom she sees, and all she does,
And seems more jealous than I ever was!
And how austere he is! Why, he can detect
A mortal sin where you would least suspect;
In smallest trifles, he's extremely strict.
Last week, his conscience was severely pricked
Because, while praying, he had caught a flea
And killed it, so he felt, too wrathfully.

CLÉANTE.

Good God, man! Have you lost your common sense—
Or is this all some joke at my expense?
How can you stand there and in all sobriety . . .

ORGON.

Brother, your language savors of impiety.
Too much free-thinking's made your faith unsteady,
And as I've warned you many times already,
'Twill get you into trouble before you're through.

CLÉANTE.

So I've been told before by dupes like you:
Being blind, you'd have all others blind as well;
The clear-eyed man you call an infidel,
And he who sees through humbug and pretense
Is charged, by you, with want of reverence.
Spare me your warnings, Brother; I have no fear
Of speaking out, for you and Heaven to hear,
Against affected zeal and pious knavery.
There's true and false in piety, as in bravery,
And just as those whose courage shines the most
In battle, are the least inclined to boast,
So those whose hearts are truly pure and lowly
Don't make a flashy show of being holy.
There's a vast difference, so it seems to me,
Between true piety and hypocrisy:

How do you fail to see it, may I ask?
Is not a face quite different from a mask?
Cannot sincerity and cunning art,
Reality and semblance, be told apart?
Are scarecrows just like men, and do you hold
That a false coin is just as good as gold?
Ah, Brother, man's a strangely fashioned creature
Who seldom is content to follow Nature,
But recklessly pursues his inclination
Beyond the narrow bounds of moderation,
And often, by transgressing Reason's laws,
Perverts a lofty aim or noble cause.
A passing observation, but it applies.

ORGON.

I see, dear Brother, that you're profoundly wise;
You harbor all the insight of the age.
You are our one clear mind, our only sage,
The era's oracle, its Cato too,
And all mankind are fools compared to you.

CLÉANTE.

Brother, I don't pretend to be a sage,
Nor have I all the wisdom of the age.
There's just one insight I would dare to claim:
I know that true and false are not the same;
And just as there is nothing I more revere
Than a soul whose faith is steadfast and sincere,
Nothing that I more cherish and admire
Than honest zeal and true religious fire,
So there is nothing that I find more base
Than specious piety's dishonest face—
Than these bold mountebanks, these histrios
Whose impious mummeries and hollow shows
Exploit our love of Heaven, and make a jest
Of all that men think holiest and best;
These calculating souls who offer prayers
Not to their Maker, but as public wares,
And seek to buy respect and reputation
With lifted eyes and sighs of exaltation;
These charlatans, I say, whose pilgrim souls
Proceed, by way of Heaven, toward earthly goals,
Who weep and pray and swindle and extort,
Who preach the monkish life, but haunt the court,
Who make their zeal the partner of their vice—
Such men are vengeful, sly, and cold as ice,
And when there is an enemy to defame

They cloak their spite in fair religion's name,
Their private spleen and malice being made
To seem a high and virtuous crusade,
Until, to mankind's reverent applause,
They crucify their foe in Heaven's cause.
Such knaves are all too common; yet, for the wise,
True piety isn't hard to recognize,
And, happily, these present times provide us
With bright examples to instruct and guide us.
Consider Ariston and Périandre;
Look at Oronte, Alcidamas, Clitandre;
Their virtue is acknowledged; who could doubt it?
But you won't hear them beat the drum about it.
They're never ostentatious, never vain,
And their religion's moderate and humane;
It's not their way to criticize and chide:
They think censoriousness a mark of pride,
And therefore, letting others preach and rave,
They show, by deeds, how Christians should behave.
They think no evil of their fellow man,
But judge of him as kindly as they can.
They don't intrigue and wangle and conspire;
To lead a good life is their one desire;
The sinner wakes no rancorous hate in them;
It is the sin alone which they condemn;
Nor do they try to show a fiercer zeal
For Heaven's cause than Heaven itself could feel.
These men I honor, these men I advocate
As models for us all to emulate.
Your man is not their sort at all, I fear:
And, while your praise of him is quite sincere,
I think that you've been dreadfully deluded.

ORGON.
Now then, dear Brother, is your speech concluded?

CLÉANTE.
Why, yes.

ORGON.
Your servant, Sir.
[*He turns to go.*]

CLÉANTE.
No, Brother; wait.
There's one more matter. You agreed of late
That young Valère might have your daughter's hand.

ORGON.
I did.

CLÉANTE.
And set the date, I understand.

ORGON.
Quite so.

CLÉANTE.
You've now postponed it; is that true?

ORGON.
No doubt.

CLÉANTE.
The match no longer pleases you?

ORGON.
Who knows?

CLÉANTE.
D'you mean to go back on your word?

ORGON.
I won't say that.

CLÉANTE.
Has anything occurred
Which might entitle you to break your pledge?

ORGON.
Perhaps.

CLÉANTE.
Why must you hem, and haw, and hedge?
The boy asked me to sound you in this affair . . .

ORGON.
It's been a pleasure.

CLÉANTE.
But what shall I tell Valère?

ORGON.
Whatever you like.

CLÉANTE.
But what have you decided?
What are your plans?

ORGON.
I plan, Sir, to be guided
By Heaven's will.

CLÉANTE.
Come, Brother, don't talk rot.
You've given Valère your word; will you keep it, or not?

ORGON.
Good day.

CLÉANTE.
This looks like poor Valère's undoing;
I'll go and warn him that there's trouble brewing.

ACT II

Scene 1

ORGON, MARIANE

ORGON.
Mariane.

MARIANE.
Yes, Father?

ORGON.
A word with you; come here.

MARIANE.
What are you looking for?

ORGON (*peering into a small closet.*)
Eavesdroppers, dear.
I'm making sure we shan't be overheard.
Someone in there could catch our every word.
Ah, good, we're safe. Now, Mariane, my child,
You're a sweet girl who's tractable and mild,
Whom I hold dear, and think most highly of.

MARIANE.
I'm deeply grateful, Father, for your love.

ORGON.
That's well said, Daughter; and you can repay me
If, in all things, you'll cheerfully obey me.

MARIANE.
To please you, Sir, is what delights me best.

ORGON.
Good, good. Now, what d'you think of Tartuffe, our guest?

MARIANE.
I, Sir?

ORGON.
Yes. Weigh your answer; think it through.

MARIANE.
Oh, dear. I'll say whatever you wish me to.

ORGON.
That's wisely said, my Daughter. Say of him, then,
That he's the very worthiest of men,
And that you're fond of him, and would rejoice
In being his wife, if that should be my choice.
Well?

MARIANE.
What?

ORGON.
What's that?

MARIANE.
I . . .

ORGON.
Well?

MARIANE.
Forgive me, pray.

ORGON.
Did you not hear me?

MARIANE.
Of *whom,* Sir, must I say
That I am fond of him, and would rejoice
In being his wife, if that should be your choice?

ORGON.
Why, of Tartuffe.

MARIANE.
But, Father, that's false, you know.
Why would you have me say what isn't so?

ORGON.
Because I am resolved it shall be true.
That it's my wish should be enough for you.

MARIANE.
You can't mean, Father . . .

ORGON.
Yes, Tartuffe shall be
Allied by marriage to this family,
And he's to be your husband, is that clear?
It's a father's privilege . . .

Scene 2

DORINE, ORGON, MARIANE

ORGON (*to* DORINE).
What are you doing in here?
Is curiosity so fierce a passion
With you, that you must eavesdrop in this fashion?

DORINE.
There's lately been a rumor going about—
Based on some hunch or chance remark, no doubt—

That you mean Mariane to wed Tartuffe.
I've laughed it off, of course, as just a spoof.

ORGON.
You find it so incredible?

DORINE.
Yes, I do.
I won't accept that story, even from you.

ORGON.
Well, you'll believe it when the thing is done.

DORINE.
Yes, yes, of course. Go on and have your fun.

ORGON.
I've never been more serious in my life.

DORINE.
Ha!

ORGON.
Daughter, I mean it; you're to be his wife.

DORINE.
No, don't believe your father; it's all a hoax.

ORGON.
See here, young woman . . .

DORINE.
Come, Sir, no more jokes;
You can't fool us.

ORGON.
How dare you talk that way?

DORINE.
All right, then: we believe you, sad to say.
But how a man like you, who looks so wise
And wears a moustache of such splendid size,
Can be so foolish as to . . .

ORGON.
Silence, please!
My girl, you take too many liberties.
I'm master here, as you must not forget.

DORINE.
Do let's discuss this calmly; don't be upset.
You can't be serious, Sir, about this plan.
What should that bigot want with Mariane?
Praying and fasting ought to keep him busy.
And then, in terms of wealth and rank, what is he?
Why should a man of property like you
Pick out a beggar son-in-law?

ORGON.
That will do.

Speak of his poverty with reverence.
His is a pure and saintly indigence
Which far transcends all worldly pride and pelf.
He lost his fortune, as he says himself,
Because he cared for Heaven alone, and so
Was careless of his interests here below.
I mean to get him out of his present straits
And help him to recover his estates—
Which, in his part of the world, have no small fame.
Poor though he is, he's a gentleman just the same.

DORINE.

Yes, so he tells us; and, Sir, it seems to me
Such pride goes very ill with piety.
A man whose spirit spurns this dungy earth
Ought not to brag of lands and noble birth;
Such worldly arrogance will hardly square
With meek devotion and the life of prayer.
. . . But this approach, I see, has drawn a blank;
Let's speak, then, of his person, not his rank.
Doesn't it seem to you a trifle grim
To give a girl like her to a man like him?
When two are so ill-suited, can't you see
What the sad consequence is bound to be?
A young girl's virtue is imperilled, Sir,
When such a marriage is imposed on her;
For if one's bridegroom isn't to one's taste,
It's hardly an inducement to be chaste,
And many a man with horns upon his brow
Has made his wife the thing that she is now.
It's hard to be a faithful wife, in short,
To certain husbands of a certain sort,
And he who gives his daughter to a man she hates
Must answer for her sins at Heaven's gates.
Think, Sir, before you play so risky a role.

ORGON.

This servant-girl presumes to save my soul!

DORINE.

You would do well to ponder what I've said.

ORGON.

Daughter, we'll disregard this dunderhead.
Just trust your father's judgment. Oh, I'm aware
That I once promised you to young Valère;
But now I hear he gambles, which greatly shocks me;
What's more, I've doubts about his orthodoxy.
His visits to church, I note, are very few.

DORINE.
Would you have him go at the same hours as you,
And kneel nearby, to be sure of being seen?

ORGON.
I can dispense with such remarks, Dorine.
(*To* MARIANE.)
Tartuffe, however, is sure of Heaven's blessing,
And that's the only treasure worth possessing.
This match will bring you joys beyond all measure;
Your cup will overflow with every pleasure;
You two will interchange your faithful loves
Like two sweet cherubs, or two turtle-doves.
No harsh word shall be heard, no frown be seen,
And he shall make you happy as a queen.

DORINE.
And she'll make him a cuckold, just wait and see.

ORGON.
What language!

DORINE.
Oh, he's a man of destiny;
He's *made* for horns, and what the stars demand
Your daughter's virtue surely can't withstand.

ORGON.
Don't interrupt me further. Why can't you learn
That certain things are none of your concern?

DORINE.
It's for your own sake that I interfere.
[*She repeatedly interrupts* ORGON *just as he is turning to speak to his daughter.*]

ORGON.
Most kind of you. Now, hold your tongue, d'you hear?

DORINE.
If I didn't love you . . .

ORGON.
Spare me your affection.

DORINE.
I'll love you, Sir, in spite of your objection.

ORGON.
Blast!

DORINE.
I can't bear, Sir, for your honor's sake,
To let you make this ludicrous mistake.

ORGON.
You mean to go on talking?

DORINE.

If I didn't protest
This sinful marriage, my conscience couldn't rest.

ORGON.

If you don't hold your tongue, you little shrew . . .

DORINE.

What, lost your temper? A pious man like you?

ORGON.

Yes! Yes! You talk and talk. I'm maddened by it.
Once and for all, I tell you to be quiet.

DORINE.

Well, I'll be quiet. But I'll be thinking hard.

ORGON.

Think all you like, but you had better guard
That saucy tongue of yours, or I'll . . .
(*Turning back to* MARIANE.)
Now, child,
I've weighed this matter fully.

DORINE (*aside.*)

It drives me wild
That I can't speak.
[ORGON *turns his head, and she is silent.*]

ORGON.

Tartuffe is no young dandy,
But, still, his person . . .

DORINE (*aside*).

Is as sweet as candy.

ORGON.

Is such that, even if you shouldn't care
For his other merits . . .
[*He turns and stands facing* DORINE, *arms crossed.*]

DORINE (*aside*).

They'll make a lovely pair.
If I were she, no man would marry me
Against my inclination, and go scot-free.
He'd learn, before the wedding-day was over,
How readily a wife can find a lover.

ORGON (*to* DORINE).

It seems you treat my orders as a joke.

DORINE.

Why, what's the matter? 'Twas not to you I spoke.

ORGON.

What *were* you doing?

DORINE.

Talking to myself, that's all.

ORGON.

Ah! (*Aside.*) One more bit of impudence and gall,
And I shall give her a good slap in the face.

(*He puts himself in position to slap her;* DORINE, *whenever he glances at her, stands immobile and silent.*)

Daughter, you shall accept, and with good grace,
The husband I've selected . . . Your wedding-day . . .

(*To* DORINE.)

Why don't you talk to yourself?

DORINE.

I've nothing to say.

ORGON.

Come, just one word.

DORINE.

No thank you, Sir. I pass.

ORGON.

Come, speak; I'm waiting.

DORINE.

I'd not be such an ass.

ORGON (*turning to* MARIANE).

In short, dear Daughter, I mean to be obeyed,
And you must bow to the sound choice I've made.

DORINE (*moving away*).

I'd not wed such a monster, even in jest.

[ORGON *attempts to slap her, but misses.*]

ORGON.

Daughter, that maid of yours is a thorough pest;
She makes me sinfully annoyed and nettled.
I can't speak further; my nerves are too unsettled.
She's so upset me by her insolent talk,
I'll calm myself by going for a walk.

Scene 3

DORINE, MARIANE

DORINE (*returning*).

Well, have you lost your tongue, girl? Must I play
Your part, and say the lines you ought to say?
Faced with a fate so hideous and absurd,
Can you not utter one dissenting word?

MARIANE.

What good would it do? A father's power is great.

DORINE.
Resist him now, or it will be too late.
MARIANE.
But . . .
DORINE.
Tell him one cannot love at a father's whim,
That you shall marry for yourself, not him;
That once it's you who are to be the bride,
It's you, not he, who must be satisfied;
And that if his Tartuffe is so sublime,
He's free to marry him at any time.
MARIANE.
I've bowed so long to Father's strict control,
I couldn't oppose him now, to save my soul.
DORINE.
Come, come, Mariane. Do listen to reason, won't you?
Valère has asked your hand. Do you love him, or don't you?
MARIANE.
Oh, how unjust of you! What can you mean
By asking such a question, dear Dorine?
You know the depth of my affection for him;
I've told you a hundred times how I adore him.
DORINE.
I don't believe in everything I hear;
Who knows if your professions were sincere?
MARIANE.
They were, Dorine, and you do me wrong to doubt it;
Heaven knows that I've been all too frank about it.
DORINE.
You love him, then?
MARIANE.
Oh, more than I can express.
DORINE.
And he, I take it, cares for you no less?
MARIANE.
I think so.
DORINE.
And you both, with equal fire,
Burn to be married?
MARIANE.
That is our one desire.
DORINE.
What of Tartuffe, then? What of your father's plan?
MARIANE.
I'll kill myself, if I'm forced to wed that man.

DORINE.
I hadn't thought of that recourse. How splendid!
Just die, and all your troubles will be ended!
A fine solution. Oh, it maddens me
To hear you talk in that self-pitying key.

MARIANE.
Dorine, how harsh you are! It's most unfair.
You have no sympathy for my despair.

DORINE.
I've none at all for people who talk drivel
And, faced with difficulties, whine and snivel.

MARIANE.
No doubt I'm timid, but it would be wrong . . .

DORINE.
True love requires a heart that's firm and strong.

MARIANE.
I'm strong in my affection for Valère,
But coping with my father is his affair.

DORINE.
But if your father's brain has grown so cracked
Over his dear Tartuffe that he can retract
His blessing, though your wedding-day was named,
It's surely not Valère who's to be blamed.

MARIANE.
If I defied my father, as you suggest,
Would it not seem unmaidenly, at best?
Shall I defend my love at the expense
Of brazenness and disobedience?
Shall I parade my heart's desires, and flaunt . . .

DORINE.
No, I ask nothing of you. Clearly you want
To be Madame Tartuffe, and I feel bound
Not to oppose a wish so very sound.
What right have I to criticize the match?
Indeed, my dear, the man's a brilliant catch.
Monsieur Tartuff! Now, there's a man of weight!
Yes, yes, Monsieur Tartuffe, I'm bound to state,
Is quite a person; that's not to be denied;
'Twill be no little thing to be his bride.
The world already rings with his renown;
He's a great noble—in his native town;
His ears are red, he has a pink complexion,
And all in all, he'll suit you to perfection.

MARIANE.
Dear God!

DORINE.

Oh, how triumphant you will feel
At having caught a husband so ideal!

MARIANE.

Oh, do stop teasing, and use your cleverness
To get me out of this appalling mess.
Advise me, and I'll do whatever you say.

DORINE.

Ah no, a dutiful daughter must obey
Her father, even if he weds her to an ape.
You've a bright future; why struggle to escape?
Tartuffe will take you back where his family lives,
To a small town aswarm with relatives—
Uncles and cousins whom you'll be charmed to meet.
You'll be received at once by the elite,
Calling upon the bailiff's wife, no less—
Even, perhaps, upon the mayoress,
Who'll sit you down in the *best* kitchen chair.
Then, once a year, you'll dance at the village fair
To the drone of bagpipes—two of them, in fact—
And see a puppet-show, or an animal act.
Your husband . . .

MARIANE.

Oh, you turn my blood to ice!
Stop torturing me, and give me your advice.

DORINE (*threatening to go*).

Your servant, Madam.

MARIANE.

Dorine, I beg of you . . .

DORINE.

No, you deserve it; this marriage must go through.

MARIANE.

Dorine!

DORINE.

No.

MARIANE.

Not Tartuffe! You know I think him . . .

DORINE.

Tartuffe's your cup of tea, and you shall drink him.

MARIANE.

I've always told you everything, and relied . . .

DORINE.

No. You deserve to be tartutified.

MARIANE.

Well, since you mock me and refuse to care,

I'll henceforth seek my solace in despair:
Despair shall be my counsellor and friend,
And help me bring my sorrows to an end.
[*She starts to leave.*]

DORINE.
There now, come back; my anger has subsided.
You do deserve some pity, I've decided.

MARIANE.
Dorine, if Father makes me undergo
This dreadful martyrdom, I'll die, I know.

DORINE.
Don't fret; it won't be difficult to discover
Some plan of action . . . But here's Valère, your lover.

Scene 4

VALÈRE, MARIANE, DORINE

VALÈRE.
Madam. I've just received some wondrous news
Regarding which I'd like to hear your views.

MARIANE.
What news?

VALÈRE.
You're marrying Tartuffe.

MARIANE.
I find
That Father does have such a match in mind.

VALÈRE.
Your father, Madam . . .

MARIANE.
. . . has just this minute said
That it's Tartuffe he wishes me to wed.

VALÈRE.
Can he be serious?

MARIANE.
Oh, indeed he can;
He's clearly set his heart upon the plan.

VALÈRE.
And what position do you propose to take,
Madam?

MARIANE.
Why—I don't know.

VALÈRE.
For heaven's sake—
You don't know?

MARIANE.
No.

VALÈRE.
Well, well!

MARIANE.
Advise me, do.

VALÈRE.
Marry the man. That's my advice to you.

MARIANE.
That's your advice?

VALÈRE.
Yes.

MARIANE.
Truly?

VALÈRE.
Oh, absolutely.
You couldn't choose more wisely, more astutely.

MARIANE.
Thanks for this counsel; I'll follow it, of course.

VALÈRE.
Do, do; I'm sure 'twill cost you no remorse.

MARIANE.
To give it didn't cause your heart to break.

VALÈRE.
I gave it, Madam, only for your sake.

MARIANE.
And it's for your sake that I take it, Sir.

DORINE (*withdrawing to the rear of the stage*).
Let's see which fool will prove the stubborner.

VALÈRE.
So! I am nothing to you, and it was flat
Deception when you . . .

MARIANE.
Please, enough of that.
You've told me plainly that I should agree
To wed the man my father's chosen for me,
And since you've deigned to counsel me so wisely,
I promise, Sir, to do as you advise me.

VALÈRE.
Ah, no, 'twas not by me that you were swayed.
No, your decision was already made;
Though now, to save appearances, you protest

That you're betraying me at my behest.

MARIANE.

Just as you say.

VALÈRE.

Quite so. And I now see
That you were never truly in love with me.

MARIANE.

Alas, you're free to think so if you choose.

VALÈRE.

I choose to think so, and here's a bit of news:
You've spurned my hand, but I know where to turn
For kinder treatment, as you shall quickly learn.

MARIANE.

I'm sure you do. Your noble qualities
Inspire affection . . .

VALÈRE.

Forget my qualities, please.
They don't inspire you overmuch, I find.
But there's another lady I have in mind
Whose sweet and generous nature will not scorn
To compensate me for the loss I've borne.

MARIANE.

I'm no great loss, and I'm sure that you'll transfer
Your heart quite painlessly from me to her.

VALÈRE.

I'll do my best to take it in my stride.
The pain I feel at being cast aside
Time and forgetfulness may put an end to.
Or if I can't forget, I shall pretend to.
No self-respecting person is expected
To go on loving once he's been rejected.

MARIANE.

Now, that's a fine, high-minded sentiment.

VALÈRE.

One to which any sane man would assent.
Would you prefer it if I pined away
In hopeless passion till my dying day?
Am I to yield you to a rival's arms
And not console myself with other charms?

MARIANE.

Go then: console yourself; don't hesitate.
I wish you to; indeed, I cannot wait.

VALÈRE.

You wish me to?

MARIANE.

Yes.

VALÈRE.

That's the final straw.
Madam, farewell. Your wish shall be my law.

[*He starts to leave, and then returns: this repeatedly.*]

MARIANE.

Splendid.

VALÈRE (*coming back again*).

This breach, remember, is of your making;
It's you who've driven me to the step I'm taking.

MARIANE.

Of course.

VALÈRE (*coming back again*).

Remember, too, that I am merely
Following your example.

MARIANE.

I see that clearly.

VALÈRE.

Enough. I'll go and do your bidding, then.

MARIANE.

Good.

VALÈRE (*coming back again*).

You shall never see my face again.

MARIANE.

Excellent.

VALÈRE (*walking to the door, then turning about*).

Yes?

MARIANE.

What?

VALÈRE.

What's that? What did you say?

MARIANE.

Nothing. You're dreaming.

VALÈRE.

Ah. Well, I'm on my way.
Farewell, *Madame*.

[*He moves slowly away.*]

MARIANE.

Farewell.

DORINE (*to* MARIANE).

If you ask me,
Both of you are as mad as mad can be.
Do stop this nonsense, now. I've only let you
Squabble so long to see where it would get you.

Whoa there, Monsieure Valère!

[*She goes and seizes* VALÈRE *by the arm; he makes a great show of resistance.*]

VALÈRE.

What's this, Dorine?

DORINE.

Come here.

VALÈRE.

No, no, my hearts too full of spleen.
Don't hold me back; her wish must be obeyed.

DORINE.

Stop!

VALÈRE.

It's too late now; my decision's made.

DORINE.

Oh, pooh!

MARIANE (*aside*).

He hates the sight of me, that's plain.
I'll go, and so deliver him from pain.

DORINE (*leaving* VALÈRE, *running after* MARIANE).

And now *you* run away! Come back.

MARIANE.

No, no.
Nothing you say will keep me here. Let go!

VALÈRE (*aside*).

She cannot bear my presence, I perceive.
To spare her further torment, I shall leave.

DORINE (*leaving* MARIANE, *running after* VALÈRE).

Again! You'll not escape, Sir; don't you try it.
Come here, you two. Stop fussing, and be quiet.

[*She takes* VALÈRE *by the hand, then* MARIANE, *and draws them together.*]

VALÈRE (*to* DORINE).

What do you want of me?

MARIANE (*to* DORINE).

What is the point of this?

DORINE.

We're going to have a little armistice.
(*To* VALÈRE)
Now, weren't you silly to get so overheated?

VALÈRE.

Didn't you see how badly I was treated?

DORINE (*to* MARIANE).

Aren't you a simpleton, to have lost your head?

MARIANE.
Didn't you hear the hateful things he said?
DORINE (*to* VALÈRE).
You're both great fools. Her sole desire, Valère,
Is to be yours in marriage. To that I'll swear.
(*To* MARIANE.)
He loves you only, and he wants no wife
But you, Mariane. On that I'll stake my life.
MARIANE (*to* VALÈRE).
Then why you advised me so, I cannot see.
VALÈRE (*to* MARIANE).
On such a question, why ask advice of *me?*
DORINE.
Oh, you're impossible. Give me your hands, you two.
(*To* VALÈRE.)
Yours first.
VALÈRE (*giving* DORINE *his hand*).
But why?
DORINE (*to* MARIANE).
And now a hand from you.
MARIANE (*also giving* DORINE *her hand*).
What are you doing?
DORINE.
There: a perfect fit.
You suit each other better than you'll admit.
[VALÈRE *and* MARIANE *hold hands for some time without looking at each other.*]
VALÈRE (*turning toward* MARIANE).
Ah, come, don't be so haughty. Give a man
A look of kindness, won't you Mariane?
[MARIANE *turns toward* VALÉRE *and smiles.*]
DORINE.
I tell you, lovers are completely mad!
VALÈRE (*to* MARIANE).
Now come, confess that you were very bad
To hurt my feeling as you did just now.
I have a just complaint, you must allow.
MARIANE.
You must allow that you were most unpleasant . . .
DORINE.
Let's table that discussion for the present;
Your father has a plan which must be stopped.
MARIANE.
Advise us, then; what means must we adopt?

DORINE.
We'll use all manner of means, and all at once.
(*To* MARIANE.)
Your father's addled; he's acting like a dunce.
Therefore you'd better humor the old fossil.
Pretend to yield to him, be sweet and docile,
And then postpone, as often as necessary,
The day on which you have agreed to marry.
You'll thus gain time, and time will turn the trick.
Sometimes, for instance, you'll be taken sick,
And that will seem good reason for delay;
Or some bad omen will make you change the day—
You'll dream of muddy water, or you'll pass
A dead man's hearse, or break a looking-glass.
If all else fails, no man can marry you
Unless you take his ring and say "I do."
But now, let's separate. If they should find
Us talking here, our plot might be divined.
(*To* VALÈRE.)
Go to your friends, and tell them what's occurred,
And have them urge her father to keep his word.
Meanwhile, we'll stir her brother into action,
And get Elmire, as well, to join our faction.
Good- bye.

VALÈRE (*to* MARIANE).
Though each of us will do his best,
It's your true heart on which my hopes shall rest.

MARIANE (*to* VALÈRE).
Regardless of what Father may decide,
None but Valère shall claim me as his bride.

VALÈRE.
Oh, how those words content me! Come what will . . .

DORINE.
Oh, lovers, lovers! Their tongues are never still.
Be off, now.

VALÈRE (*turning to go, then turning back*).
One last word . . .

DORINE.
No time to chat:
You leave by this door; and *you* leave by that.
[DORINE *pushes them, by the shoulders, toward opposing doors.*]

ACT III

Scene 1

DAMIS, DORINE

DAMIS.

May lightning strike me even as I speak,
May all men call me cowardly and weak,
If any fear or scruple holds me back
From settling things, at once, with that great quack!

DORINE.

Now, don't give way to violent emotion.
Your father's merely talked about this notion,
And words and deeds are far from being one.
Much that is talked about is left undone.

DAMIS.

No, I must stop that scoundrel's machinations;
I'll go and tell him off; I'm out of patience.

DORINE.

Do calm down and be practical. I had rather
My mistress dealt with him—and with your father.
She has some influence with Tartuffe, I've noted.
He hangs upon her words, seems most devoted,
And may, indeed, be smitten by her charm.
Pray Heaven it's true! 'Twould do our cause no harm.
She sent for him, just now, to sound him out
On this affair you're so incensed about;
She'll find out where he stands, and tell him, too,
What dreadful strife and trouble will ensue
If he lends countenance to your father's plan.
I couldn't get in to see him, but his man
Says that he's almost finished with his prayers.
Go, now. I'll catch him when he comes downstairs.

DAMIS.

I want to hear this conference, and I will.

DORINE.

No, they must be alone.

DAMIS.

Oh, I'll keep still.

DORINE.

Not you. I know your temper. You'd start a brawl,

And shout and stamp your foot and spoil it all.
Go on.

DAMIS.
I won't; I have a perfect right . . .

DORINE.
Lord, you're a nuisance! He's coming; get out of sight.
[DAMIS *conceals himself in a closet at the rear of the stage.*]

Scene 2

TARTUFFE, DORINE

TARTUFFE (*observing* DORINE, *and calling to his manservant offstage.*)
Hang up my hair-shirt, put my scourge in place,
And pray, Laurent, for Heaven's perpetual grace.
I'm going to the prison now, to share
My last few coins with the poor wretches there.

DORINE (*aside.*)
Dear God, what affectation! What a fake!

TARTUFFE.
You wished to see me?

DORINE.
Yes . . .

TARTUFFE (*taking a handkerchief from his pocket.*)
For mercy's sake,
Please take this handkerchief, before you speak.

DORINE.
What?

TARTUFFE.
Cover that bosom, girl. The flesh is weak,
And unclean thoughts are difficult to control.
Such sights as that can undermine the soul.

DORINE.
Your soul, it seems, has very poor defenses,
And flesh makes quite an impact on your senses.
It's strange that you're so easily excited;
My own desires are not so soon ignited,
And if I saw you naked as a beast,
Not all your hide would tempt me in the least.

TARTUFFE.
Girl, speak more modestly; unless you do,
I shall be forced to take my leave of you.

DORINE.
Oh, no, it's I who must be on my way;
I've just one little message to convey.
Madame is coming down, and begs you, Sir,
To wait and have a word or two with her.

TARTUFFE.
Gladly.

DORINE (*aside.*)
That had a softening effect!
I think my guess about him was correct.

TARTUFFE.
Will she be long?

DORINE.
No: that's her step I hear.
Ah, here she is, and I shall disappear.

Scene 3

ELMIRE, TARTUFFE

TARTUFFE.
May Heaven, whose infinite goodness we adore,
Preserve your body and soul forevermore,
And bless your days, and answer thus the plea
Of one who is its humblest votary.

ELMIRE.
I thank you for that pious wish. But please,
Do take a chair and let's be more at ease.
[*They sit down.*]

TARTUFFE.
I trust that you are once more well and strong?

ELMIRE.
Oh, yes: the fever didn't last for long.

TARTUFFE.
My prayers are too unworthy, I am sure,
To have gained from Heaven this most gracious cure;
But lately, Madam, my every supplication
Has had for object your recuperation.

ELMIRE.
You shouldn't have troubled so. I don't deserve it.

TARTUFFE.
Your health is priceless, Madam, and to preserve it
I'd gladly give my own, in all sincerity.

ELMIRE.
Sir, you outdo us all in Christian charity.
You've been most kind. I count myself your debtor.

TARTUFFE.
'Twas nothing, Madam. I long to serve you better.

ELMIRE.
There's a private matter I'm anxious to discuss.
I'm glad there's no one here to hinder us.

TARTUFFE.
I too am glad; it floods my heart with bliss
To find myself alone with you like this.
For just this chance I've prayed with all my power—
But prayed in vain, until this happy hour.

ELMIRE.
This won't take long, Sir, and I hope you'll be
Entirely frank and unconstrained with me.

TARTUFFE.
Indeed, there's nothing I had rather do
Than bare my inmost heart and soul to you.
First, let me say that what remarks I've made
About the constant visits you are paid
Were prompted not by any mean emotion,
But rather by a pure and deep devotion,
A fervent zeal . . .

ELMIRE.
No need for explanation.
Your sole concern, I'm sure, was my salvation.

TARTUFFE (*taking* ELMIRE'S *hand and pressing her fingertips.*)
Quite so; and such great fervor do I feel . . .

ELMIRE.
Ooh! Please! You're pinching!

TARTUFFE.
'Twas from excess of zeal.
I never meant to cause you pain, I swear.
I'd rather . . .
[*He places his hand on* ELMIRE'S *knee.*]

ELMIRE.
What can your hand be doing there?

TARTUFFE.
Feeling your gown; what soft, fine-woven stuff!

ELMIRE.
Please, I'm extremely ticklish. That's enough.
[*She draws her chair away;* TARTUFFE *pulls his after her.*]

TARTUFFE (*fondling the lace collar of her gown.*)
My, my, what lovely lacework on your dress!

The workmanship's miraculous, no less.
I've not seen anything to equal it.

ELMIRE.

Yes, quite. But let's talk business for a bit.
They say my husband means to break his word
And give his daughter to you, Sir. Had you heard?

TARTUFFE.

He did once mention it. But I confess
I dream of quite a different happiness.
It's elsewhere, Madam, that my eyes discern
The promise of that bliss for which I yearn.

ELMIRE.

I see: you care for nothing here below.

TARTUFFE.

Ah, well—my heart's not made of stone, you know.

ELMIRE.

All your desires mount heavenward, I'm sure,
In scorn of all that's earthly and impure.

TARTUFFE.

A love of heavenly beauty does not preclude
A proper love for earthly pulchritude;
Our senses are quite rightly captivated
By perfect works our Maker has created.
Some glory clings to all that Heaven has made;
In you, all Heaven's marvels are displayed.
On that fair face, such beauties have been lavished.
The eyes are dazzled and the heart is ravished;
How could I look on you, O flawless creature,
And not adore the Author of all Nature,
Feeling a love both passionate and pure
For you, his triumph of self-portraiture?
As first, I trembled lest that love should be
A subtle snare that Hell had laid for me;
I vowed to flee the sight of you, eschewing
A rapture that might prove my soul's undoing;
But soon, fair being, I became aware
That my deep passion could be made to square
With rectitude, and with my bounden duty.
I thereupon surrendered to your beauty.
It is, I know, presumptuous on my part
To bring you this poor offering of my heart,
And it is not my merit, Heaven knows,
But your compassion on which my hopes repose.
You are my peace, my solace, my salvation;

On you depends my bliss—or desolation;
I bide your judgment and, as you think best,
I shall be either miserable or blest.

ELMIRE.

Your declaration is most gallant, Sir,
But don't you think it's out of character?
You'd have done better to restrain your passion
And think before you spoke in such a fashion.
It ill becomes a pious man like you . . .

TARTUFFE.

I may be pious, but I'm human too:
With your celestial charms before his eyes,
A man has not the power to be wise.
I know such words sound strangely, coming from me,
But I'm no angel, nor was meant to be,
And if you blame my passion, you must needs
Reproach as well the charms on which it feeds.
Your loveliness I had no sooner seen
Than you became my soul's unrivalled queen;
Before your seraph glance, divinely sweet,
My heart's defenses crumbled in defeat,
And nothing fasting, prayer, or tears might do
Could stay my spirit from adoring you.
My eyes, my sighs have told you in the past
What now my lips make bold to say at last,
And if, in your great goodness, you will deign
To look upon your slave, and ease his pain,—
If, in compassion for my soul's distress,
You'll stoop to comfort my unworthiness,
I'll raise to you, in thanks for that sweet manna,
An endless hymn, an infinite hosanna.
With me, of course, there need be no anxiety,
No fear of scandal or of notoriety.
These young court gallants, whom all the ladies fancy,
Are vain in speech, in action rash and chancy;
When they succeed in love, the world soon knows it;
No favor's granted them but they disclose it
And by the looseness of their tongues profane
The very altar where their hearts have lain.
Men of my sort, however, love discreetly,
And one may trust our reticence completely.
My keen concern for my good name insures
The absolute security of yours;
In short, I offer you, my dear Elmire,

Love without scandal, pleasure without fear.

ELMIRE.

I've heard your well-turned speeches to the end,
And what you urge I clearly apprehend.
Aren't you afraid that I may take a notion
To tell my husband of your warm devotion,
And that, supposing he were duly told,
His feelings toward you might grow rather cold?

TARTUFFE.

I know, dear lady, that your exceeding charity
Will lead your heart to pardon my temerity;
That you'll excuse my violent affection
As human weakness, human imperfection;
And that—O fairest!—you will bear in mind
That I'm but flesh and blood, and am not blind.

ELMIRE.

Some women might do otherwise, perhaps,
But I shall be discreet about your lapse;
I'll tell my husband nothing of what's occurred
If, in return, you'll give your solemn word
To advocate as forcefully as you can
The marriage of Valère and Mariane,
Renouncing all desires to dispossess
Another of his rightful happiness,
And . . .

Scene 4

DAMIS, ELMIRE, TARTUFFE

DAMIS (*emerging from the closet where he has been hiding.*)

No! We'll not hush up this vile affair;
I heard it all inside that closet there,
Where Heaven, in order to confound the pride
Of this great rascal, prompted me to hide.
Ah, now I have my long-awaited chance
To punish his deceit and arrogance,
And give my father clear and shocking proof
Of the black character of his dear Tartuffe.

ELMIRE.

Ah no, Damis; I'll be content if he
Will study to deserve my leniency.
I've promised silence—don't make me break my word;

To make a scandal would be too absurd.
Good wives laugh off such trifles, and forget them;
Why should they tell their husbands, and upset them?

DAMIS.

You have your reasons for taking such a course,
And I have reasons, too, of equal force.
To spare him now would be insanely wrong.
I've swallowed my just wrath for far too long
And watched this insolent bigot bringing strife
And bitterness into our family life.
Too long he's meddled in my father's affairs,
Thwarting my marriage-hopes, and poor Valère's.
It's high time that my father was undeceived,
And now I've proof that can't be disbelieved—
Proof that was furnished me by Heaven above.
It's too good not to take advantage of.
This is my chance, and I deserve to lose it
If, for one moment, I hesitate to use it.

ELMIRE.

Damis . . .

DAMIS.

No, I must do what I think right.
Madam, my heart is bursting with delight,
And, say whatever you will, I'll not consent
To lose the sweet revenge on which I'm bent.
I'll settle matters without more ado;
And here, most opportunely, is my cue.

Scene 5

ORGON, DAMIS, TARTUFFE, ELMIRE

DAMIS.

Father, I'm glad you've joined us. Let us advise you
Of some fresh news which doubtless will surprise you.
You've just now been repaid with interest
For all your loving-kindness to our guest.
He's proved his warm and grateful feelings toward you;
It's with a pair of horns he would reward you.
Yes, I surprised him with your wife, and heard
His whole adulterous offer, every word.
She, with her all too gentle disposition,
Would not have told you of his proposition;

But I shall not make terms with brazen lechery,
And feel that not to tell you would be treachery.

ELMIRE.

And I hold that one's husband's peace of mind
Should not be spoilt by tattle of this kind.
One's honor doesn't require it: to be proficient
In keeping men at bay is quite sufficient.
These are my sentiments, and I wish, Damis,
That you had heeded me and held your peace.

Scene 6

ORGON, DAMIS, TARTUFFE

ORGON.

Can it be true, this dreadful thing I hear?

TARTUFFE.

Yes, Brother, I'm a wicked man, I fear:
A wretched sinner, all depraved and twisted,
The greatest villain that has ever existed.
My life's one heap of crimes, which grows each minute;
There's naught but foulness and corruption in it;
And I perceive that Heaven, outraged by me,
Has chosen this occasion to mortify me.
Charge me with any deed you wish to name;
I'll not defend myself, but take the blame.
Believe what you are told, and drive Tartuffe
Like some base criminal from beneath your roof;
Yes, drive me hence, and with a parting curse:
I shan't protest, for I deserve far worse.

ORGON (*to* DAMIS.)

Ah, you deceitful boy, how dare you try
To stain his purity with so foul a lie?

DAMIS.

What! Are you taken in by such a bluff?
Did you not hear . . . ?

ORGON.

Enough, you rogue, enough!

TARTUFFE.

Ah, Brother, let him speak: you're being unjust.
Believe his story; the boy deserves your trust.
Why, after all, should you have faith in me?

How can you know what I might do, or be?
Is it on my good actions that you base
Your favor? Do you trust my pious face?
Ah, no, don't be deceived by hollow shows;
I'm far, alas, from being what men suppose;
Though the world takes me for a man of worth,
I'm truly the most worthless man on earth.
(*To* DAMIS.)
Yes, my dear son, speak out now: call me the chief
Of sinners, a wretch, a murderer, a thief;
Load me with all the names men most abhor;
I'll not complain; I've earned them all, and more;
I'll kneel here while you pour them on my head
As a just punishment for the life I've led.

ORGON (*to* TARUFFE.)
This is too much, dear Brother.
(*To* DAMIS.)
Have you no heart?

DAMIS.
Are you so hoodwinked by this rascal's art . . . ?

ORGON.
Be still, you monster.
(*To* TARTUFFE.)
Brother, I pray you, rise.
(*To* DAMIS.)
Villain!

DAMIS.
But . . .

ORGON.
Silence!

DAMIS.
Can't you realize . . . ?

ORGON.
Just one word more, and I'll tear you limb from limb.

TARTUFFE.
In God's name, Brother, don't be harsh with him.
I'd rather far be tortured at the stake
Than see him bear one scratch for my poor sake.

ORGON (*to* DAMIS.)
Ingrate!

TARTUFFE.
If I must beg you, on bended knee,
To pardon him . . .

ORGON (*falling to his knees, addressing* TARTUFFE.)
Such goodness cannot be!

(*To* DAMIS.)
Now, *there's* true charity!

DAMIS.
What, you . . . ?

ORGON.
Villain, be still!
I know your motives; I know you wish him ill:
Yes, all of you—wife, children, servants, all—
Conspire against him and desire his fall,
Employing every shameful trick you can
To alienate me from this saintly man.
Ah, but the more you seek to drive him away,
The more I'll do to keep him. Without delay,
I'll spite this household and confound its pride
By giving him my daughter as his bride.

DAMIS.
You're going to force her to accept his hand?

ORGON.
Yes, and this very night, d'you understand?
I shall defy you all, and make it clear
That I'm the one who gives the orders here.
Come, wretch, kneel down and clasp his blessed feet,
And ask his pardon for your black deceit.

DAMIS.
I ask that swindler's pardon? Why, I'd rather . . .

ORGON.
So! You insult him, and defy your father!
A stick! A stick! (*To* TARTUFFE.) No, no—release me, do.
(*To* DAMIS.)
Out of my house this minute! Be off with you,
And never dare set foot in it again.

DAMIS.
Well, I shall go, but . . .

ORGON.
Well, go quickly, then.
I disinherit you; an empty purse
Is all you'll get from me—except my curse!

Scene 7

ORGON, TARTUFFE

ORGON.
How he blasphemed your goodness! What a son!

TARTUFFE.
Forgive him, Lord, as I've already done.
(*To* ORGON.)
You can't know how it hurts when someone tries
To blacken me in my dear Brother's eyes.

ORGON.
Ahh!

TARTUFFE.
The mere thought of such ingratitude
Plunges my soul into so dark a mood . . .
Such horror grips my heart . . . I gasp for breath,
And cannot speak, and feel myself near death.

ORGON.
[*He runs, in tears, to the door through which he has just driven his son.*]
You blackguard! Why did I spare you? Why did I not
Break you in little pieces on the spot?
Compose yourself, and don't be hurt, dear friend.

TARTUFFE.
These scenes, these dreadful quarrels, have got to end.
I've much upset your household, and I perceive
That the best thing will be for me to leave.

ORGON.
What are you saying!

TARTUFFE.
They're all against me here;
They'd have you think me false and insincere.

ORGON.
Ah, what of that? Have I ceased believing in you?

TARTUFFE.
Their adverse talk will certainly continue,
And charges which you now repudiate
You may find credible at a later date.

ORGON.
No, Brother, never.

TARTUFFE.
Brother, a wife can sway
Her husband's mind in many a subtle way.

ORGON.
No, no.

TARTUFFE.
To leave at once is the solution;
Thus only can I end their persecution.

ORGON.
No, no, I'll not allow it; you shall remain.

TARTUFFE.

Ah, well; 'twill mean much martyrdom and pain,
But if you wish it . . .

ORGON.

Ah!

TARTUFFE.

Enough; so be it.
But one thing must be settled, as I see it.
For your dear honor, and for our friendship's sake,
There's one precaution I feel bound to take.
I shall avoid your wife, and keep away . . .

ORGON.

No, you shall not, whatever they may say.
It pleases me to vex them, and for spite
I'd have them see you with her day and night.
What's more, I'm going to drive them to despair
By making you my only son and heir;
This very day, I'll give to you alone
Clear deed and title to everything I own.
A dear, good friend and son-in-law-to-be
Is more than wife, or child, or kin to me.
Will you accept my offer, dearest son?

TARTUFFE.

In all things, let the will of Heaven be done.

ORGON.

Poor fellow! Come, we'll go draw up the deed.
Then let them burst with disappointed greed!

ACT IV

Scene 1

CLÉANTE, TARTUFFE

CLÉANTE.

Yes, all the town's discussing it, and truly,
Their comments do not flatter you unduly.
I'm glad we've met, Sir, and I'll give my view
Of this sad matter in a word or two.
As for who's guilty, that I shan't discuss;
Let's say it was Damis who caused the fuss;
Assuming, then, that you have been ill-used

By young Damis, and groundlessly accused,
Ought not a Christian to forgive, and ought
He not to stifle every vengeful thought?
Should you stand by and watch a father make
His only son an exile for your sake?
Again I tell you frankly, be advised:
The whole town, high and low, is scandalized;
This quarrel must be mended, and my advice is
Not to push matters to a further crisis.
No, sacrifice your wrath to God above,
And help Damis regain his father's love.

TARTUFFE.

Alas, for my part I should take great joy
In doing so. I've nothing against the boy.
I pardon all, I harbor no resentment;
To serve him would afford me much contentment.
But Heaven's interest will not have it so:
If he comes back, then I shall have to go.
After his conduct—so extreme, so vicious—
Our further intercourse would look suspicious.
God knows what people would think! Why, they'd describe
My goodness to him as a sort of bribe;
They'd say that out of guilt I made pretense
Of loving-kindness and benevolence—
That, fearing my accuser's tongue, I strove
To buy his silence with a show of love.

CLÉANTE.

Your reasoning is badly warped and stretched,
And these excuses, Sir, are most far-fetched.
Why put yourself in charge of Heaven's cause?
Does Heaven need our help to enforce its laws?
Leave vengeance to the Lord, Sir; while we live,
Our duty's not to punish, but forgive;
And what the Lord commands, we should obey
Without regard to what the world may say.
What! Shall the fear of being misunderstood
Prevent our doing what is right and good?
No, no; let's simply do what Heaven ordains,
And let no other thoughts perplex our brains.

TARTUFFE.

Again, Sir, let me say that I've forgiven
Damis, and thus obeyed the laws of Heaven;
But I am not commanded by the Bible
To live with one who smears my name with libel.

CLÉANTE.

Were you commanded, Sir, to indulge the whim
Of poor Orgon, and to encourage him
In suddenly transferring to your name
A large estate to which you have no claim?

TARTUFFE.

'Twould never occur to those who know me best
To think I acted from self-interest.
The treasures of this world I quite despise;
Their specious glitter does not charm my eyes;
And if I have resigned myself to taking
The gift which my dear Brother insists on making,
I do so only, as he well understands,
Lest so much wealth fall into wicked hands,
Lest those to whom it might descend in time
Turn it to purposes of sin and crime,
And not, as I shall do, make use of it
For Heaven's glory and mankind's benefit.

CLÉANTE.

Forget these trumped-up fears. Your argument
Is one the rightful heir might well resent;
It is a moral burden to inherit
Such wealth, but give Damis a chance to bear it.
And would it not be worse to be accused
Of swindling, than to see that wealth misused?
I'm shocked that you allowed Orgon to broach
This matter, and that you feel no self-reproach;
Does true religion teach that lawful heirs
May freely be deprived of what is theirs?
And if the Lord has told you in your heart
That you and young Damis must dwell apart,
Would it not be the decent thing to beat
A generous and honorable retreat,
Rather than let the son of the house be sent,
For your convenience, into banishment?
Sir, if you wish to prove the honesty
Of your intentions . . .

TARTUFFE.

Sir, it is half-past three.
I've certain pious duties to attend to,
And hope my prompt departure won't offend you.

CLÉANTE (*alone*.)

Damn.

Scene 2

ELMIRE, MARIANE, CLÉANTE, DORINE

DORINE.

Stay, Sir, and help Mariane, for Heaven's sake!
She's suffering so, I fear her heart will break.
Her father's plan to marry her off tonight
Has put the poor child in a desperate plight.
I hear him coming. Let's stand together, now,
And see if we can't change his mind, somehow,
About this match we all deplore and fear.

Scene 3

ORGON, ELMIRE, MARIANE, CLÉANTE, DORINE

ORGON.

Hah! Glad to find you all assembled here.
(*To* MARIANE.)
This contract, child, contains your happiness,
And what it says I think your heart can guess.

MARIANE (*falling to her knees.*)

Sir, by that Heaven which sees me here distressed,
And by whatever else can move your breast,
Do not employ a father's power, I pray you,
To crush my heart and force it to obey you,
Nor by your harsh commands oppress me so
That I'll begrudge the duty which I owe—
And do not so embitter and enslave me
That I shall hate the very life you gave me.
If my sweet hopes must perish, if you refuse
To give me to the one I've dared to choose,
Spare me at least—I beg you, I implore—
The pain of wedding one whom I abhor;
And do not, by a heartless use of force,
Drive me to contemplate some desperate course.

ORGON (*feeling himself touched by her.*)

Be firm, my soul. No human weakness, now.

MARIANE.

I don't resent your love for him. Allow

Your heart free rein, Sir; give him your property,
And if that's not enough, take mine from me;
He's welcome to my money; take it, do,
But don't, I pray, include my person too.
Spare me, I beg you; and let me end the tale
Of my sad days behind a convent veil.

ORGON.

A convent! Hah! When crossed in their amours,
All lovesick girls have the same thought as yours.
Get up! The more you loathe the man, and dread him,
The more ennobling it will be to wed him.
Marry Tartuffe, and mortify your flesh!
Enough; don't start that whimpering afresh.

DORINE.

But why . . . ?

ORGON.

Be still, there. Speak when you're spoken to.
Not one more bit of impudence out of you.

CLÉANTE.

If I may offer a word of counsel here . . .

ORGON.

Brother, in counseling you have no peer;
All your advice is forceful, sound, and clever;
I don't propose to follow it, however.

ELMIRE (*to* ORGON).

I am amazed, and don't know what to say;
Your blindness simply takes my breath away.
You are indeed bewitched, to take no warning
From our account of what occurred this morning.

ORGON.

Madam, I know a few plain facts, and one
Is that you're partial to my rascal son;
Hence, when he sought to make Tartuffe the victim
Of a base lie, you dared not contradict him.
Ah, but you underplayed your part, my pet;
You should have looked more angry, more upset.

ELMIRE.

When men make overtures, must we reply
With righteous anger and a battle-cry?
Must we turn back their amorous advances
With sharp reproaches and with fiery glances?
Myself, I find such offers merely amusing,
And make no scenes and fusses in refusing;
My taste is for good-natured rectitude,
And I dislike the savage sort of prude

Who guards her virtue with her teeth and claws,
And tears men's eyes out for the slightest cause:
The Lord preserve me from such honor as that,
Which bites and scratches like an alley-cat!
I've found that a polite and cool rebuff
Discourages a lover quite enough.

ORGON.

I know the facts, and I shall not be shaken.

ELMIRE.

I marvel at your power to be mistaken.
Would it, I wonder, carry weight with you
If I could *show* you that our tale was true?

ORGON.

Show me?

ELMIRE.

Yes.

ORGON.

Rot.

ELMIRE.

Come, what if I found a way
To make you see the facts as plain as day?

ORGON.

Nonsense.

ELMIRE.

Do answer me; don't be absurd.
I'm not now asking you to trust our word.
Suppose that from some hiding-place in here
You learned the whole sad truth by eye and ear—
What would you say of your good friend, after that?

ORGON.

Why, I'd say . . . nothing, by Jehoshaphat!
It can't be true.

ELMIRE.

You've been too long deceived,
And I'm quite tired of being disbelieved.
Come now: let's put my statements to the test,
And you shall see the truth made manifest.

ORGON.

I'll take that challenge. Now do your uttermost.
We'll see how you make good your empty boast.

ELMIRE (*to* DORINE).

Send him to me.

DORINE.

He's crafty; it may be hard

To catch the cunning scoundrel off his guard.

ELMIRE.

No, amorous men are gullible. Their conceit
So blinds them that they're never hard to cheat.
Have him come down (*To* CLÉANTE *and* MARIANE.) Please leave us, for a bit.

Scene 4

ELMIRE, ORGON

ELMIRE.

Pull up this table, and get under it.

ORGON.

What?

ELMIRE.

It's essential that you be well-hidden.

ORGON.

Why there?

ELMIRE.

Oh, Heavens! Just do as you are bidden.
I have my plans; we'll soon see how they fare.
Under the table, now; and once you're there,
Take care that you are neither seen nor heard.

ORGON.

Well, I'll indulge you, since I gave my word
To see you through this infantile charade.

ELMIRE.

Once it is over, you'll be glad we played.
(*To her husband, who is now under the table.*)
I'm going to act quite strangely, now, and you
Must not be shocked at anything I do.
Whatever I may say, you must excuse
As part of that deceit I'm forced to use.
I shall employ sweet speeches in the task
Of making that imposter drop his mask;
I'll give encouragment to his bold desires,
And furnish fuel to his amorous fires.
Since it's for your sake, and for his destruction,
That I shall seem to yield to his seduction,
I'll gladly stop whenever you decide
That all your doubts are fully satisfied.
I'll count on you, as soon as you have seen

What sort of man he is, to intervene,
And not expose me to his odious lust
One moment longer than you feel you must.
Remember: you're to save me from my plight
Whenever . . . He's coming! Hush! Keep out of sight!

Scene 5

TARTUFFE, ELMIRE, ORGON

TARTUFFE.
You wish to have a word with me, I'm told.

ELMIRE.
Yes. I've a little secret to unfold.
Before I speak, however, it would be wise
To close that door, and look about for spies.
[TARTUFFE *goes to the door, closes it, and returns.*]
The very last thing that must happen now
Is a repetition of this morning's row.
I've never been so badly caught off guard.
Oh, how I feared for you! You saw how hard
I tried to make that troublesome Damis
Control his dreadful temper, and hold his peace.
In my confusion, I didn't have the sense
Simply to contradict his evidence;
But as it happened, that was for the best,
And all has worked out in our interest.
This storm has only bettered your position;
My husband doesn't have the least suspicion,
And now, in mockery of those who do,
He bids me be continually with you.
And that is why, quite fearless of reproof,
I now can be alone with my Tartuffe,
And why my heart—perhaps too quick to yield—
Feels free to let its passion be revealed.

TARTUFFE.
Madam, your words confuse me. Not long ago,
You spoke in quite a different style, you know.

ELMIRE.
Ah, Sir, if that refusal made you smart,
It's little that you know of woman's heart,
Or what that heart is trying to convey

When it resists in such a feeble way!
Always, at first, our modesty prevents
The frank avowal of tender sentiments;
However high the passion which inflames us,
Still, to confess its power somehow shames us.
Thus we reluct, at first, yet in a tone
Which tells you that our heart is overthrown,
That what our lips deny, our pulse confesses,
And that, in time, all noes will turn to yesses.
I fear my words are all too frank and free,
And a poor proof of woman's modesty;
But since I'm started, tell me, if you will—
Would I have tried to make Damis be still,
Would I have listened, calm and unoffended,
Until your lengthy offer of love was ended,
And been so very mild in my reaction,
Had your sweet words not given me satisfaction?
And when I tried to force you to undo
The marriage-plans my husband has in view,
What did my urgent pleading signify
If not that I admired you, and that I
Deplored the thought that someone else might own
Part of a heart I wished for mine alone?

TARTUFFE.

Madam, no happiness is so complete
As when, from lips we love, come words so sweet;
Their nectar floods my every sense, and drains
In honeyed rivulets through all my veins.
To please you is my joy, my only goal;
Your love is the restorer of my soul;
And yet I must beg leave, now, to confess
Some lingering doubts as to my happiness.
Might this not be a trick? Might not the catch
Be that you wish me to break off the match
With Mariane, and so have feigned to love me?
I shan't quite trust your fond opinion of me
Until the feelings you've expressed so sweetly
Are demonstrated somewhat more concretely,
And you have shown, by certain kind concessions,
That I may put my faith in your professions.

ELMIRE (*She coughs, to warn her husband.*)

Why be in such a hurry? Must my heart
Exhaust its bounty at the very start?
To make that sweet admission cost me dear,
But you'll not be content, it would appear,

Unless my store of favors is disbursed
To the last farthing, and at the very first.

TARTUFFE.
The less we merit, the less we dare to hope,
And with our doubts, mere words can never cope.
We trust no promised bliss till we receive it;
Not till a joy is ours can we believe it.
I, who so little merit your esteem,
Can't credit this fulfillment of my dream,
And shan't believe it, Madam, until I savor
Some palpable assurance of your favor.

ELMIRE.
My, how tyrannical your love can be,
And how it flusters and perplexes me!
How furiously you take one's heart in hand,
And make your every wish a fierce command!
Come, must you hound and harry me to death?
Will you not give me time to catch my breath?
Can it be right to press me with such force,
Give me no quarter, show me no remorse,
And take advantage, by your stern insistence,
Of the fond feelings which weaken my resistance?

TARTUFFE.
Well, if you look with favor upon my love,
Why, then, begrudge me some clear proof thereof?

ELMIRE.
But how can I consent without offense
To Heaven, toward which you feel such reverence?

TARTUFFE.
If Heaven is all that holds you back, don't worry.
I can remove that hindrance in a hurry.
Nothing of that sort need obstruct our path.

ELMIRE.
Must one not be afraid of Heaven's wrath?

TARTUFFE.
Madam, forget such fears, and be my pupil,
And I shall teach you how to conquer scruple.
Some joys, it's true, are wrong in Heaven's eyes;
Yet Heaven is not averse to compromise;
There is a science, lately formulated,
Whereby one's conscience may be liberated,
And any wrongful act you care to mention
May be redeemed by purity of intention.
I'll teach you, Madam, the secrets of that science;
Meanwhile, just place on me your full reliance.

Assuage my keen desires, and feel no dread:
The sin, if any, shall be on my head.
[ELMIRE *coughs, this time more loudly.*]
You've a bad cough.

ELMIRE.
Yes, yes. It's bad indeed.

TARTUFFE (*producing a little paper bag*).
A bit of licorice may be what you need.

ELMIRE.
No, I've a stubborn cold, it seems. I'm sure it
Will take much more than licorice to cure it.

TARTUFFE.
How aggravating.

ELMIRE.
Oh, more than I can say.

TARTUFFE.
If you're still troubled, think of things this way:
No one shall know our joys, save us alone,
And there's no evil till the act is known;
It's scandal, Madam, which makes it an offense,
And it's no sin to sin in confidence.

ELMIRE (*having coughed once more*).
Well, clearly I must do as you require,
And yield to your importunate desire.
It is apparent, now, that nothing less
Will satisfy you, and so I acquiesce.
To go so far is much against my will;
I'm vexed that it should come to this; but still,
Since you are so determined on it, since you
Will not allow mere language to convince you,
And since you ask for concrete evidence, I
See nothing for it, now, but to comply.
If this is sinful, if I'm wrong to do it,
So much the worse for him who drove me to it.
The fault can surely not be charged to me.

TARTUFFE.
Madam, the fault is mine, if fault there be,
And . . .

ELMIRE.
Open the door a little, and peek out;
I wouldn't want my husband poking about.

TARTUFFE.
Why worry about the man? Each day he grows
More gullible; one can lead him by the nose.
To find us here would fill him with delight,

And if he saw the worst, he'd doubt his sight.

ELMIRE.
Nevertheless, do step out for a minute
Into the hall, and see that no one's in it.

Scene 6

ORGON, ELMIRE

ORGON (*coming out from under the table*).
That man's a perfect monster, I must admit!
I'm simply stunned. I can't get over it.

ELMIRE.
What, coming out so soon? How premature!
Get back in hiding, and wait until you're sure.
Stay till the end, and be convinced completely;
We mustn't stop till things are proved concretely.

ORGON.
Hell never harbored anything so vicious!

ELMIRE.
Tut, don't be hasty. Try to be judicious.
Wait, and be certain that there's no mistake.
No jumping to conclusions, for Heaven's sake!
[*She places* ORGON *behind her, as* TARTUFFE *re-enters.*]

Scene 7

TARTUFFE, ELMIRE, ORGON

TARTUFFE (*not seeing* ORGON).
Madam, all things have worked out to perfection;
I've given the neighboring rooms a full inspection;
No one's about; and now I may at last . . .

ORGON (*intercepting him*).
Hold on, my passionate fellow, not so fast!
I should advise a little more restraint.
Well, so you thought you'd fool me, my dear saint!
How soon you wearied of the saintly life—
Wedding my daughter, and coveting my wife!
I've long suspected you, and had a feeling
That soon I'd catch you at your double-dealing.

Just now, you've given me evidence galore;
It's quite enough; I have no wish for more.

ELMIRE (*to* TARTUFFE).
I'm sorry to have treated you so slyly,
But circumstances forced me to be wily.

TARTUFFE.
Brother, you can't think . . .

ORGON.
No more talk from you;
Just leave this household, without more ado.

TARTUFFE.
What I intended . . .

ORGON.
That seems fairly clear.
Spare me your falsehoods and get out of here.

TARTUFFE.
No, I'm the master, and you're the one to go!
This house belongs to me, I'll have you know,
And I shall show you that you can't hurt *me*
By this contemptible conspiracy,
That those who cross me know not what they do,
And that I've means to expose and punish you,
Avenge offended Heaven, and make you grieve
That ever you dared order me to leave.

Scene 8

ELMIRE, ORGON

ELMIRE.
What was the point of all that angry chatter?

ORGON.
Dear God, I'm worried. This is no laughing matter.

ELMIRE.
How so?

ORGON.
I fear I understood his drift.
I'm much disturbed about that deed of gift.

ELMIRE.
You gave him . . . ?

ORGON.
Yes, it's all been drawn and signed.
But one thing more is weighing on my mind.

ELMIRE.

What's that?

ORGON.

I'll tell you; but first let's see if there's
A certain strong-box in his room upstairs.

ACT V

Scene 1

ORGON, CLÉANTE

CLÉANTE.

Where are you going so fast?

ORGON.

God knows!

CLÉANTE.

Then wait;
Let's have a conference, and deliberate
On how this situation's to be met.

ORGON.

That strong-box has me utterly upset;
This is the worst of many, many shocks.

CLÉANTE.

Is there some fearful mystery in that box?

ORGON.

My poor friend Argas brought that box to me
With his own hands, in utmost secrecy;
'Twas on the very morning of his flight.
It's full of papers which, if they came to light,
Would ruin him—or such is my impression.

CLÉANTE.

Then why did you let it out of your possession?

ORGON.

Those papers vexed my conscience, and it seemed best
To ask the counsel of my pious guest.
The cunning scoundrel got me to agree
To leave the strong-box in his custody,
So that, in case of an investigation,
I could employ a slight equivocation
And swear I didn't have it, and thereby,
At no expense to conscience, tell a lie.

CLÉANTE.

It looks to me as if you're out on a limb.

Trusting him with that box, and offering him
That deed of gift, were actions of a kind
Which scarcely indicate a prudent mind.
With two such weapons, he has the upper hand,
And since you're vulnerable, as matters stand,
You erred once more in bringing him to bay.
You should have acted in some subtler way.

ORGON.

Just think of it: behind that fervent face,
A heart so wicked, and a soul so base!
I took him in, a hungry beggar, and then . . .
Enough, by God! I'm through with pious men:
Henceforth I'll hate the whole false brotherhood,
And persecute them worse than Satan could.

CLÉANTE.

Ah, there you go—extravagant as ever!
Why can you not be rational? You never
Manage to take the middle course, it seems,
But jump, instead, between absurd extremes.
You've recognized your recent grave mistake
In falling victim to a pious fake;
Now, to correct that error, must you embrace
An even greater error in its place,
And judge our worthy neighbors as a whole
By what you've learned of one corrupted soul?
Come, just because one rascal made you swallow
A show of zeal which turned out to be hollow,
Shall you conclude that all men are deceivers,
And that, today, there are no true believers?
Let atheists make that foolish inference;
Learn to distinguish virtue from pretense,
Be cautious in bestowing admiration,
And cultivate a sober moderation.
Don't humor fraud, but also don't asperse
True piety; the latter fault is worse,
And it is best to err, if err one must,
As you have done, upon the side of trust.

Scene 2

DAMIS, ORGON, CLÉANTE

DAMIS.

Father, I hear that scoundrel's uttered threats

Against you; that he pridefully forgets
How, in his need, he was befriended by you,
And means to use your gifts to crucify you.

ORGON.
It's true, my boy. I'm too distressed for tears.

DAMIS.
Leave it to me, Sir; let me trim his ears.
Faced with such insolence, we must not waver.
I shall rejoice in doing you the favor
Of cutting short his life, and your distress.

CLÉANTE.
What a display of young hotheadedness!
Do learn to moderate your fits of rage.
In this just kingdom, this enlightened age,
One does not settle things by violence.

Scene 3

MADAME PERNELLE, MARIANE, ELMIRE, DORINE,
DAMIS, ORGON, CLÉANTE

MADAME PERNELLE.
I hear strange tales of very strange events.

ORGON.
Yes, strange events which these two eyes beheld.
The man's ingratitude is unparalleled.
I save a wretched pauper from starvation,
House him, and treat him like a blood relation,
Shower him every day with my largesse,
Give him my daughter, and all that I possess;
And meanwhile the unconscionable knave
Tries to induce my wife to misbehave;
And not content with such extreme rascality,
Now threatens me with my own liberality,
And aims, by taking base advantage of
The gifts I gave him out of Christian love,
To drive me from my house, a ruined man,
And make me end a pauper, as he began.

DORINE.
Poor fellow!

MADAME PERNELLE.
No, my son, I'll never bring

Myself to think him guilty of such a thing.

ORGON.

How's that?

MADAME PERNELLE.

The righteous always were maligned.

ORGON.

Speak clearly, Mother. Say what's on your mind.

MADAME PERNELLE.

I mean that I can smell a rat, my dear.
You know how everybody hates him, here.

ORGON.

That has no bearing on the case at all.

MADAME PERNELLE.

I told you a hundred times, when you were small,
That virtue in this world is hated ever;
Malicious men may die, but malice never.

ORGON.

No doubt that's true, but how does it apply?

MADAME PERNELLE.

They've turned you against him by a clever lie.

ORGON.

I've told you, I was there and saw it done.

MADAME PERNELLE.

Ah, slanderers will stop at nothing, Son.

ORGON.

Mother, I'll lose my temper . . . For the last time,
I tell you I was witness to the crime.

MADAME PERNELLE.

The tongues of spite are busy night and noon,
And to their venom no man is immune.

ORGON.

You're talking nonsense. Can't you realize
I saw it; saw it; saw it with my eyes?
Saw, do you understand me? Must I shout it
Into your ears before you'll cease to doubt it?

MADAME PERNELLE.

Appearances can deceive, my son. Dear me,
We cannot always judge by what we see.

ORGON.

Drat! Drat!

MADAME PERNELLE.

One often interprets things awry;
Good can seem evil to a suspicious eye.

ORGON.

Was I to see his pawing at Elmire

As an act of charity?

MADAME PERNELLE.

Till his guilt is clear,
A man deserves the benefit of the doubt.
You should have waited, to see how things turned out.

ORGON.

Great God in Heaven, what more proof did I need?
Was I to sit there, watching, until he'd . . .
You drive me to the brink of impropriety.

MADAME PERNELLE.

No, no, a man of such surpassing piety
Could not do such a thing. You cannot shake me.
I don't believe it, and you shall not make me.

ORGON.

You vex me so that, if you weren't my mother,
I'd say to you . . . some dreadful thing or other.

DORINE.

It's your turn now, Sir, not to be listened to;
You'd not trust us, and now she won't trust you.

CLÉANTE.

My friends, we're wasting time which should be spent
In facing up to our predicament.
I fear that scoundrel's threats weren't made in sport.

DAMIS.

Do you think he'd have the nerve to go to court?

ELMIRE.

I'm sure he won't: they'd find it all too crude
A case of swindling and ingratitude.

CLÉANTE.

Don't be too sure. He won't be at a loss
To give his claims a high and righteous gloss;
And clever rogues with far less valid cause
Have trapped their victims in a web of laws.
I say again that to antagonize
A man so strongly armed was most unwise.

ORGON.

I know it; but the man's appalling cheek
Outraged me so, I couldn't control my pique.

CLÉANTE.

I wish to Heaven that we could devise
Some truce between you, or some compromise.

ELMIRE.

If I had known what cards he held, I'd not
Have roused his anger by my little plot.

ORGON (*to* DORINE, *as* M. LOYAL *enters*).
What is that fellow looking for? Who is he?
Go talk to him—and tell him that I'm busy.

Scene 4

MONSIEUR LOYAL, MADAME PERNELLE, ORGON, DAMIS, MARIANE, DORINE, ELMIRE, CLÉANTE

MONSIEUR LOYAL.
Good day, dear sister. Kindly let me see
Your master.

DORINE.
He's involved with company,
And cannot be disturbed just now, I fear.

MONSIEUR LOYAL.
I hate to intrude; but what has brought me here
Will not disturb your master, in any event.
Indeed, my news will make him most content.

DORINE.
Your name?

MONSIEUR LOYAL.
Just say that I bring greetings from
Monsieur Tartuffe, on whose behalf I've come.

DORINE (*to* ORGON).
Sir, he's a very gracious man, and bears
A message from Tartuffe, which he declares,
Will make you most content.

CLÉANTE.
Upon my word,
I think this man had best be seen, and heard.

ORGON.
Perhaps he has some settlement to suggest.
How shall I treat him? What manner would be best?

CLÉANTE.
Control your anger, and if he should mention
Some fair adjustment, give him your full attention.

MONSIEUR LOYAL.
Good health to you, good Sir. May Heaven confound
Your enemies, and may your joys abound.

ORGON (*aside, to* CLÉANTE.)
A gentle salutation: it confirms
My guess that he is here to offer terms.

MONSIEUR LOYAL.
I've always held your family most dear;
I served your father, Sir, for many a year.

ORGON.
Sir, I must ask your pardon; to my shame,
I cannot now recall your face or name.

MONSIEUR LOYAL.
Loyal's my name; I come from Normandy,
And I'm a bailiff, in all modesty.
For forty years, praise God, it's been my boast
To serve with honor in that vital post,
And I am here, Sir, if you will permit
The liberty, to serve you with this writ . . .

ORGON.
To—*what?*

MONSIEUR LOYAL.
Now, please, Sir, let us have no friction:
It's nothing but an order of eviction.
You are to move your goods and family out
And make way for new occupants, without
Deferment or delay, and give the keys . . .

ORGON.
I? Leave this house?

MONSIEUR LOYAL.
Why yes, Sir, if you please.
This house, Sir, from the cellar to the roof,
Belongs now to the good Monsieur Tartuffe,
And he is lord and master of your estate
By virtue of a deed of present date,
Drawn in due form, with clearest legal phrasing . . .

DAMIS.
Your insolence is utterly amazing!

MONSIEUR LOYAL.
Young man, my business here is not with you,
But with your wise and temperate father, who,
Like every worthy citizen, stands in awe
Of justice, and would never obstruct the law.

ORGON.
But . . .

MONSIEUR LOYAL.
Not for a million, Sir, would you rebel
Against authority; I know that well.
You'll not make trouble, Sir, or interfere
With the execution of my duties here.

DAMIS.

Someone may execute a smart tattoo
On that black jacket of yours, before you're through.

MONSIEUR LOYAL.

Sir, bid your son be silent. I'd much regret
Having to mention such a nasty threat
Of violence, in writing my report.

DORINE (*aside.*)

This man Loyal's a most disloyal sort!

MONSIEUR LOYAL.

I love all men of upright character,
And when I agreed to serve these papers, Sir,
It was your feelings that I had in mind.
I couldn't bear to see the case assigned
To someone else, who might esteem you less
And so subject you to unpleasantness.

ORGON.

What's more unpleasant than telling a man to leave
His house and home?

MONSIEUR LOYAL.

You'd like a short reprieve?
If you desire it, Sir, I shall not press you,
But wait until tomorrow to dispossess you.
Splendid. I'll come and spend the night here, then,
Most quietly, with half a score of men.
For form's sake, you might bring me, just before
You go to bed, the keys to the front door.
My men, I promise, will be on their best
Behavior, and will not disturb your rest.
But bright and early, Sir, you must be quick
And move out all your furniture, every stick:
The men I've chosen are both young and strong,
And with their help it shouldn't take you long.
In short, I'll make things pleasant and convenient,
And since I'm being so extremely lenient,
Please show me, Sir, a like consideration,
And give me your entire cooperation.

ORGON (*aside.*)

I may be all but bankrupt, but I vow
I'd give a hundred louis, here and now,
Just for the pleasure of landing one good clout
Right on the end of that complacent snout.

CLÉANTE.

Careful; don't make things worse.

DAMIS.

My bootsole itches
To give that beggar a good kick in the breeches.

DORINE.

Monsieur Loyal, I'd love to hear the whack
Of a stout stick across your fine broad back.

MONSIEUR LOYAL.

Take care: a woman too may go to jail if
She uses threatening language to a bailiff.

CLÉANTE.

Enough, enough, Sir. This must not go on.
Give me that paper, please, and then begone.

MONSIEUR LOYAL.

Well, *au revoir*. God give you all good cheer!

ORGON.

May God confound you, and him who sent you here!

Scene 5

ORGON, CLÉANTE, MARIANE, ELMIRE,
MADAME PERNELLE, DORINE, DAMIS

ORGON.

Now, Mother, was I right or not? This writ
Should change your notion of Tartuffe a bit.
Do you perceive his villainy at last?

MADAME PERNELLE.

I'm thunderstruck. I'm utterly aghast.

DORINE.

Oh, come, be fair. You mustn't take offense
At this new proof of his benevolence.
He's acting out of selfless love, I know.
Material things enslave the soul, and so
He kindly has arranged your liberation
From all that might endanger your salvation.

ORGON.

Will you not ever hold your tongue, you dunce?

CLÉANTE.

Come, you must take some action, and at once.

ELMIRE.

Go tell the world of the low trick he's tried.
The deed of gift is surely nullified

By such behavior, and public rage will not
Permit the wretch to carry out his plot.

Scene 6

VALÈRE, ORGON, CLÉANTE, ELMIRE, MARIANE, MADAME PERNELLE, DAMIS, DORINE

VALÈRE.

Sir, though I hate to bring you more bad news,
Such is the danger that I cannot choose.
A friend who is extremely close to me
And knows my interest in your family
Has, for my sake, presumed to violate
The secrecy that's due to things of state,
And sends me word that you are in a plight
From which your one salvation lies in flight.
That scoundrel who's imposed upon you so
Denounced you to the King an hour ago
And, as supporting evidence, displayed
The strong-box of a certain renegade
Whose secret papers, so he testified,
You had disloyally agreed to hide.
I don't know just what charges may be pressed,
But there's a warrant out for your arrest;
Tartuffe has been instructed, furthermore,
To guide the arresting officer to your door.

CLÉANTE.

He's clearly done this to facilitate
His seizure of your house and your estate.

ORGON.

That man, I must say, is a vicious beast!

VALÈRE.

Quick, Sir; you mustn't tarry in the least.
My carriage is outside, to take you hence;
This thousand louis should cover all expense.
Let's lose no time, or you shall be undone;
The sole defense, in this case, is to run.
I shall go with you all the way, and place you
In a safe refuge to which they'll never trace you.

ORGON.

Alas, dear boy, I wish that I could show you
My gratitude for everything I owe you.

But now is not the time; I pray the Lord
That I may live to give you your reward.
Farewell, my dears; be careful . . .

CLÉANTE.
Brother, hurry.
We shall take care of things; you needn't worry.

Scene 7

THE OFFICER, TARTUFFE, VALÈRE, ORGON, ELMIRE, MARIANE, MADAME PERNELLE, DORINE, CLÉANTE, DAMIS

TARTUFFE.
Gently, Sir, gently; stay right where you are.
No need for haste; your lodging isn't far.
You're off to prison, by order of the Prince.

ORGON.
This is the crowning blow, you wretch; and since
It means my total ruin and defeat,
Your villainy is now at last complete.

TARTUFFE.
You needn't try to provoke me; it's no use.
Those who serve Heaven must expect abuse.

CLÉANTE.
You are indeed most patient, sweet, and blameless.

DORINE.
How he exploits the name of Heaven! It's shameless.

TARTUFFE.
Your taunts and mockeries are all for naught;
To do my duty is my only thought.

MARIANE.
Your love of duty is most meritorious,
And what you've done is little short of glorious.

TARTUFFE.
All deeds are glorious, Madam, which obey
The sovereign prince who sent me here today.

ORGON.
I rescued you when you were destitute;
Have you forgotten that, you thankless brute?

TARTUFFE.
No, no, I well remember everything;
But my first duty is to serve my King.

That obligation is so paramount
That other claims, beside it, do not count;
And for it I would sacrifice my wife,
My family, my friend, or my own life.

ELMIRE.

Hypocrite!

DORINE.

All that we most revere, he uses
To cloak his plots and camouflage his ruses.

CLÉANTE.

If it is true that you are animated
By pure and loyal zeal, as you have stated,
Why was this zeal not roused until you'd sought
To make Orgon a cuckold, and been caught?
Why weren't you moved to give your evidence
Until your outraged host had driven you hence?
I shan't say that the gift of all his treasure
Ought to have damped your zeal in any measure;
But if he is a traitor, as you declare,
How could you condescend to be his heir?

TARTUFFE (*to the* OFFICER.)

Sir, spare me all this clamor; it's growing shrill.
Please carry out your orders, if you will.

OFFICER.

Yes, I've delayed too long, Sir. Thank you kindly.
You're just the proper person to remind me.
Come, you are off to join the other boarders
In the King's prison, according to his orders.

TARTUFFE.

Who? I, Sir?

OFFICER.

Yes.

TARTUFFE.

To prison? This can't be true!

OFFICER.

I owe an explanation, but not to you.
(*To* ORGON.)
Sir, all is well; rest easy, and be grateful.
We serve a Prince to whom all sham is hateful,
A Prince who sees into our inmost hearts,
And can't be fooled by any trickster's arts.
His royal soul, though generous and human,
Views all things with discernment and acumen;
His sovereign reason is not lightly swayed,
And all his judgments are discreetly weighed.

He honors righteous men of every kind,
And yet his zeal for virtue is not blind,
Nor does his love of piety numb his wits
And make him tolerant of hypocrites.
'Twas hardly likely that this man could cozen
A King who's foiled such liars by the dozen.
With one keen glance, the King perceived the whole
Perverseness and corruption of his soul,
And thus high Heaven's justice was displayed:
Betraying you, the rogue stood self-betrayed.
The King soon recognized Tartuffe as one
Notorious by another name, who'd done
So many vicious crimes that one could fill
Ten volumes with them, and be writing still.
But to be brief: our sovereign was appalled
By this man's treachery toward you, which he called
The last, worst villainy of a vile career,
And bade me follow the impostor here
To see how gross his impudence could be,
And force him to restore your property.
Your private papers, by the King's command,
I hereby seize and give into your hand.
The King, by royal order, invalidates
The deed which gave this rascal your estates,
And pardons, furthermore, your grave offense
In harboring an exile's documents.
By these decrees, our Prince rewards you for
Your loyal deeds in the late civil war,
And shows how heartfelt is his satisfaction
In recompensing any worthy action,
How much he prizes merit, and how he makes
More of men's virtues than of their mistakes.

DORINE.
Heaven be praised!

MADAME PERNELLE.
I breathe again, at last.

ELMIRE.
We're safe.

MARIANE.
I can't believe the danger's past.

ORGON (*to* TARTUFFE.)
Well, traitor, now you see . . .

CLÉANTE.
Ah, Brother, please,
Let's not descend to such indignities.

Leave the poor wretch to his unhappy fate,
And don't say anything to aggravate
His present woes; but rather hope that he
Will soon embrace an honest piety,
And mend his ways, and by a true repentance
Move our just King to moderate his sentence.
Meanwhile, go kneel before your sovereign's throne
And thank him for the mercies he has shown.

ORGON.

Well said: let's go at once and, gladly kneeling,
Express the gratitude which all are feeling.
Then, when that first great duty has been done,
We'll turn with pleasure to a second one,
And give Valère, whose love has proven so true,
The wedded happiness which is his due.

CRITICAL COMMENTARY

Molière (Jean Baptiste Poquelin) was born in 1622, six years after the death of Shakespeare and the publication of Jonson's collected plays. He gave up the middle-class security of law school and his father's business for the stage. In 1658 he returned to Paris, an experienced and expert man of the theater after thirteen years of touring the provinces as actor, manager, and playwright. His first production won the approval of Louis XIV, who installed him in the theater of the Palais Royal.

Molière's theater, in contrast to the Elizabethan Globe, was closed to the sky, a box stage within a proscenium arch, ornately decorated, equipped with painted sets, artificial lighting, and a front curtain. Women played the female parts. It was a theater of and for the affluent society, an audience that naturally liked the comfort of traditional comedy with its familiar plot involving young lovers who are temporarily thwarted by adult hang-ups and rigidities but who marry happily in the end with everybody restored to their senses and their property. *Tartuffe* (1669) is obviously based on this old comic plot, the roots of which go back to the classic stage. It offers many secure pleasures, and the familiarity of its formula masks improbabilities and eliminates disturbing perspectives and awkward questions.

You may wonder what Elmire could possibly see in Orgon, but the play does not oblige you to worry about such a youthful and thoughtless question. You have only to cast yourself opposite Elmire, especially when she is confidently played by an attractive actress, and think of yourself as a man of affairs, able to attract and appreciate a mature woman, one who is beautiful and intelligent, intimate yet undemanding, devoted to serving your pleasure and conserving your property. Here is critic Walter Kerr enjoying such thoughts (in *The New York Times*, October 20, 1968) after having watched Martha Henry as Elmire at Stratford, Ontario:

> Perhaps a word about Elmire, the wife Tartuffe so lusts after, is in order. Martha Henry plays her as a woman who cannot be surprised. She is herself reserved, immaculately self-contained, gently delicate. But she is informed. She has a body. She knows precisely its various possible uses, understands without pretence or dismay Tartuffe's crafty designs upon it. She is a good woman but never

> an innocent one. . . . She is too supple and intelligent to engage in affectation. She has told her husband of Tartuffe's lust and her husband has defied her to prove it. "Send him to me" is the line, and it is merely meant to get a servant off and Tartuffe on. "*Send* him to me!" blazes Miss Henry, appalled that any aspersion could be cast on her ability to provoke lust.

This traditionally secure distance or enjoyably dreamy engagement between spectator and play exists also with Orgon, despite his strange fanaticism. Guided by the sensible Cléante and Dorine, you have only to cast yourself as a brilliant psychologist, and Orgon and his mother become comfortably familiar textbook cases. "What these characters want above all," suggests Lionel Grossman,

> is *to be distinguished,* but they refuse to adopt the usual method of social advancement and privilege, since this method offers only a *relative* superiority to others, whereas the superiority they desire is *absolute*. . . . While choosing to be *different* from everybody else, while turning away from what they castigate as the vain ambitions of the world in order to devote themselves to "authentic" values, these characters nevertheless have to believe that they are envied by everybody else. . . . Orgon is bent on using Tartuffe as much as Tartuffe is bent on using him [because] the function of Tartuffe is to guarantee Orgon's superiority to *everybody* else.

And by the time Richard Wilbur is through with him, Orgon is thoroughly domesticated:

> It seems that he, like many another middle-aged man, has been alarmed by a sense of failing powers and failing authority, and that he has compensated by adopting an extreme religious severity. . . . Orgon cherishes Tartuffe because, with the sanction of the latter's austere precepts, he can tyrannize over his family and punish them for possessing what he feels himself to be losing: youth, gaiety, strong natural desires. (Molière, *Tartuffe,* 1963, pp. viii–ix).

Is Tartuffe himself different? He is certainly an outsider, an interloper in the society of the audience and the play. He is crude and vulgar, and we hiss him off the stage after being obliged to participate with him in deplorable pleasures that are properly suppressed in everyday life. One, he gets to put his hand inside the maid's blouse. Two, he makes a complete ass out of a leading citizen and property owner. Three, he obliges proper people to eat their own cant.

Tartuffe also seems more theatrical than anyone else in the play. His first line exhibits a remarkably dramatic fusion of language and acting: "Hang up my hair shirt, put my scourge away." "What a fake!" exclaims

Dorine from her hiding place; and certainly Tartuffe, with his cheap stage properties, is a ridiculous and offensive impostor, ripe for exposure. But with all her irrepressible good sense, Dorine cannot hear and see everything that is being theatrically expressed because she is limited by her role in the play's traditional comic plot. Tartuffe plays his established part in this old plot too, but doesn't he also play over its head to us? "Hang up my hairshirt, put my scourge away." Isn't there a note of weariness here? And why not? Surely, after a hard day of self-flagellation a man may be permitted a moment of human weakness, a touch of self-pity. The relation between the lonely religious ascetic and the tired businessman is hinted at but not insisted upon. One becomes inured to being misunderstood by the world; it is a part of the weariness. Tartuffe is a fake all right, but the dramatic tone asks a tricky question: Is an unconscious fake like you really better than a conscious fake like Tartuffe?

The implications of such a question are made still clearer in Tartuffe's escape from his tightest corner (Act II, Scene 6). Caught by Damis in an attempt to mave love to Elmire, Tartuffe with wonderful aplomb admits his guilt:

> Yes, Brother, I'm a wicked man I fear:
> A wretched sinner, all depraved and twisted,
> The greatest villain that ever existed.

But then he proceeds to enlarge upon his personal guilt until it is lost in the general wickedness of all mankind. Are we not all fallen, all depraved, he asks rhetorically; but of course in this society of propriety and good sense only a person who is temporarily mad like Orgon can think any such thing. There are no Christian fools here. Tartuffe is a theatrical reminder of what is excluded when society is conserved.

Useful Criticism

Fernández, Ramón. *Molière: The Man Seen Through the Plays.** New York: Hill and Wang, 1960.

Grossman, Lionel. *Men and Masks: A Study of Molière.** Baltimore: Johns Hopkins Press, 1969.

Guicharnaud, Jacques, ed. *Molière** (Twentieth Century Views). Englewood Cliffs, N.J.: Prentice-Hall, 1964.

Moore, Will G. *Molière, A New Criticism.* Garden City, N.Y.: Doubleday, 1962.

* Available in paperback.

GHOSTS

Henrik Ibsen

Translated by WILLIAM ARCHER

CHARACTERS

MRS. ALVING, a widow
OSWALD ALVING, her son, an artist
MANDERS, the pastor of the parish
ENGSTRAND, a carpenter
REGINA ENGSTRAND, his daughter, in MRS. ALVING'S service

The action takes place at MRS. ALVING'S *house on one of the larger fjords of western Norway.*

ACT I

SCENE *A large room looking upon a garden. A door in the left-hand wall, and two in the right. In the middle of the room, a round table with chairs set about it, and books, magazines, and newspapers upon it. In the foreground on the left, a window, by which is a small sofa with a work-table in front of it. At the back the room opens into a conservatory rather smaller than the room. From the right-hand side of this a door leads to the garden. Through the large panes of glass that form the outer wall of the conservatory, a gloomy fjord landscape can be discerned, half obscured by steady rain.*

ENGSTRAND *is standing close up to the garden door. His left leg is slightly deformed, and he wears a boot with a clump of wood under the sole.* REGINA, *with an empty garden-syringe in her hand, is trying to prevent his coming in.*

REGINA (*below her breath*). What is it you want? Stay where you are. The rain is dripping off you.

ENGSTRAND. God's good rain, my girl.

REGINA. The Devil's own rain, that's what it is!

ENGSTRAND. Lord, how you talk, Regina. (*Takes a few limping steps forward.*) What I wanted to tell you was this——

REGINA. Don't clump about like that, stupid! The young master is lying asleep upstairs.

ENGSTRAND. Asleep still? In the middle of the day?

REGINA. Well, it's no business of yours.

ENGSTRAND. I was out on the spree last night——

REGINA. I don't doubt it.

ENGSTRAND. Yes, we are poor weak mortals, my girl——

REGINA. We are indeed.

ENGSTRAND. —and the temptations of the world are manifold, you know —but, for all that, here I was at my work at half-past five this morning.

REGINA. Yes, yes, but make yourself scarce now. I am not going to stand here as if I had a rendezvous with you.

ENGSTRAND. As if you had a what?

REGINA. I am not going to have any one find you here: so now you know, and you can go.

ENGSTRAND (*coming a few steps nearer*). Not a bit of it! Not before we have had a little chat. This afternoon I shall have finished my job down at the school house, and I shall be off home to town by to-night's boat.

REGINA (*mutters*). Pleasant journey to you!

ENGSTRAND. Thanks, my girl. To-morrow is the opening of the Orphanage, and I expect there will be a fine kick-up here and plenty of good strong drink, don't you know. And no one shall say of Jacob Engstrand that he can't hold off when temptation comes in his way.

REGINA. Oho!

ENGSTRAND. Yes, because there will be a lot of fine folk here to-morrow. Parson Manders is expected from town, too.

REGINA. What is more, he's coming to-day.

ENGSTRAND. There you are! And I'm going to be precious careful he doesn't have anything to say against me, do you see?

REGINA. Oh, that's your game, is it?

ENGSTRAND. What do you mean?

REGINA (*with a significant look at him*). What is it you want to humbug Mr. Manders out of, this time?

ENGSTRAND. Sh! Sh! Are you crazy? Do you suppose *I* would want to humbug Mr. Manders? No, no—. Mr. Manders has always been too kind a friend for me to do that. But what I wanted to talk to you about, was my going back home to-night.

REGINA. The sooner you go, the better I shall be pleased.

ENGSTRAND. Yes, only I want to take you with me, Regina.

REGINA (*open-mouthed*). You want to take me——? What did you say?

ENGSTRAND. I want to take you home with me, I said.

REGINA (*contemptuously*). You will never get me home with you.

ENGSTRAND. Ah, we shall see about that.

REGINA. Yes, you can be quite certain we *shall* see about that. I, who have been brought up by a lady like Mrs. Alving?—I, who have been treated almost as if I were her own child?—do you suppose I am going home with *you?*—to such a house as yours? Not likely!

ENGSTRAND. What the devil do you mean? Are you setting yourself up against your father, you hussy?

REGINA (*mutters, without looking at him*). You have often told me I was none of yours.

ENGSTRAND. Bah!—why do you want to pay any attention to that?

REGINA. Haven't you many and many a time abused me and called me a ——? For shame!

ENGSTRAND. I'll swear I never used such an ugly word.

REGINA. Oh, it doesn't matter what word you used.

ENGSTRAND. Besides, that was only when I was a bit fuddled—hm! Temptations are manifold in this world, Regina.

REGINA. Ugh!

ENGSTRAND. And it was when your mother was in a nasty temper. I had to find some way of getting my knife into her, my girl. She was always so precious genteel. (*Mimicking her.*) "Let go, Jacob! Let me be! Please to remember that I was three years with the Alvings at Rosenvold, and they were people who went to Court!" (*Laughs.*) Bless my soul, she never could forget that Captain Alving got a Court appointment while she was in service here.

REGINA. Poor mother—you worried her into her grave pretty soon.

ENGSTRAND (*shrugging his shoulders*). Of course, of course; I have got to take the blame for everything.

REGINA (*beneath her breath, as she turns away*). Ugh—that leg, too!

ENGSTRAND. What are you saying, my girl?

REGINA. Pied de mouton.

ENGSTRAND. Is that English?

REGINA. Yes.

ENGSTRAND. You have had a good education out here, and no mistake; and it may stand you in good stead now, Regina.

REGINA (*after a short silence*). And what was it you wanted me to come to town for?

ENGSTRAND. Need you ask why a father wants his only child? Ain't I a poor lonely widower?

REGINA. Oh, don't come to me with that tale. Why do you want me to go?

ENGSTRAND. Well, I must tell you I am thinking of taking up a new line now.

REGINA (*whistles*). You have tried that so often—but it has always proved a fool's errand.

ENGSTRAND. Ah, but this time you will just see, Regina! Strike me dead if——

REGINA (*stamping her feet*). Stop swearing!

ENGSTRAND. Sh! Sh!—you're quite right, my girl, quite right! What I wanted to say was only this, that I have put by a tidy penny out of what I have made by working at this new Orphanage up here.

REGINA. Have you? All the better for you.

ENGSTRAND. What is there for a man to spend his money on, out here in the country?

REGINA. Well, what then?

ENGSTRAND. Well, you see, I thought of putting the money into something that would pay. I thought of some kind of an eating-house for seafaring folk——

REGINA. Heavens!

ENGSTRAND. Oh, a high-class eating-house, of course,—not a pigsty for common sailors. Damn it, no; it would be a place ships' captains and first mates would come to; really good sort of people, you know.

REGINA. And what should I——?

ENGSTRAND. You would help there. But only to make a show, you know. You wouldn't find it hard work, I can promise you, my girl. You should do exactly as you liked.

REGINA. Oh, yes, quite so!

ENGSTRAND. But we must have some women in the house; that is as clear as daylight. Because in the evening we must make the place a little attractive—some singing and dancing, and that sort of thing. Remember they are seafolk—wayfarers on the waters of life! (*Coming nearer to her.*) Now don't be a fool and stand in your own way, Regina. What good are you going to do here? Will this education, that your mistress has paid for, be of any use? You are to look after the children in the new Home, I hear. Is that the sort of work for you? Are you so frightfully anxious to go and wear out your health and strength for the sake of these dirty brats?

REGINA. No, if things were to go as I want them to, then——. Well, it may happen; who knows? It may happen!

ENGSTRAND. What may happen?

REGINA. Never you mind. Is it much that you have put by, up here?

ENGSTRAND. Taking it all round, I should say about forty or fifty pounds.

REGINA. That's not so bad.

ENGSTRAND. It's enough to make a start with, my girl.

REGINA. Don't you mean to give me any of the money?

ENGSTRAND. No, I'm hanged if I do.

REGINA. Don't you mean to send me as much as a dress-length of stuff, just for once?

ENGSTRAND. Come and live in the town with me and you shall have plenty of dresses.

REGINA. Pooh!—I can get that much for myself, if I have a mind to.

ENGSTRAND. But it's far better to have a father's guiding hand, Regina. Just now I can get a nice house in Little Harbour Street. They don't want much money down for it—and we could make it like a sort of seamen's home, don't you know.

REGINA. But I have no intention of living with you! I have nothing whatever to do with you. So now, be off!

ENGSTRAND. You wouldn't be living with me long, my girl. No such luck—not if you knew how to play your cards. Such a fine wench as you have grown this last year or two——

REGINA. Well——?

ENGSTRAND. It wouldn't be very long before some first mate came along —or perhaps a captain.

REGINA. I don't mean to marry a man of that sort. Sailors have no savoir-vivre.

ENGSTRAND. What haven't they got?

REGINA. I know what sailors are, I tell you. They aren't the sort of people to marry.

ENGSTRAND. Well, don't bother about marrying them. You can make it pay just as well. (*More confidentially.*) That fellow—the Englishman —the one with the yacht—he gave seventy pounds, he did; and she wasn't a bit prettier than you.

REGINA (*advancing towards him*). Get out!

ENGSTRAND (*stepping back*). Here! here!—you're not going to hit me, I suppose?

REGINA. Yes! If you talk like that of mother, I *will* hit you. Get out, I tell you! (*Pushes him up to the garden door.*) And don't bang the doors. Young Mr. Alving——

ENGSTRAND. Is asleep—I know. It's funny how anxious you are about young Mr. Alving. (*In a lower tone.*) Oho! is it possible that it is *he* that——?

REGINA. Get out, and be quick about it! Your wits are wandering, my good man. No, don't go that way; Mr. Manders is just coming along. Be off down the kitchen stairs.

ENGSTRAND (*moving towards the right*). Yes, yes—all right. But have a bit of a chat with him that's coming along. He's the chap to tell you what a child owes to its father. For I am your father, anyway, you know. I can prove it by the Register.

[*He goes out through the farther door which* REGINA *has opened. She shuts it after him, looks hastily at herself in the mirror, fans herself with her handkerchief and sets her collar straight, then busies herself with the flowers.* MANDERS *enters the conservatory through the garden door. He wears an overcoat, carries an um-*

brella and has a small travelling-bag slung over his shoulder on a strap.]

MANDERS. Good morning, Miss Engstrand.

REGINA (*turning round with a look of pleased surprise*). Oh, Mr. Manders, good morning. The boat is in, then?

MANDERS. Just in. (*Comes into the room.*) It is most tiresome, this rain every day.

REGINA (*following him in*). It's a splendid rain for the farmers, Mr. Manders.

MANDERS. Yes, you are quite right. We town-folk think so little about that. (*Begins to take off his overcoat.*)

REGINA. Oh, let me help you. That's it. Why, how wet it is. I will hang it up in the hall. Give me your umbrella, too; I will leave it open, so that it will dry.

[*She goes out with the things by the farther door on the right.* MANDERS *lays his bag and his hat down on a chair.* REGINA *re-enters.*]

MANDERS. Ah, it's very pleasant to get indoors. Well, is everything going on well here?

REGINA. Yes, thanks.

MANDERS. Properly busy, though, I expect, getting ready for to-morrow?

REGINA. Oh, yes, there is plenty to do.

MANDERS. And Mrs. Alving is at home, I hope?

REGINA. Yes, she is. She has just gone upstairs to take the young master his chocolate.

MANDERS. Tell me—I heard down at the pier that Oswald had come back.

REGINA. Yes, he came the day before yesterday. We didn't expect him till to-day.

MANDERS. Strong and well, I hope?

REGINA. Yes, thank you, well enough. But dreadfully tired after his journey. He came straight from Paris without a stop—I mean, he came all the way without breaking his journey. I fancy he is having a sleep now, so we must talk a little bit more quietly, if you don't mind.

MANDERS. All right, we will be very quiet.

REGINA (*while she moves an armchair up to the table*). Please sit down, Mr. Manders, and make yourself at home. (*He sits down; she puts a footstool under his feet.*) There! Is that comfortable?

MANDERS. Thank you, thank you. That is most comfortable. (*Looks at her.*) I'll tell you what, Miss Engstrand, I certainly think you have grown since I saw you last.

REGINA. Do you think so? Mrs. Alving says, too, that I have developed.

MANDERS. Developed? Well, perhaps a little—just suitably.

[*A short pause.*]

REGINA. Shall I tell Mrs. Alving you are here?

MANDERS. Thanks, there is no hurry, my dear child.—Now tell me,

Regina my dear, how has your father been getting on here?

REGINA. Thank you, Mr. Manders, he is getting on pretty well.

MANDERS. He came to see me, the last time he was in town.

REGINA. Did he? He is always so glad when he can have a chat with you.

MANDERS. And I suppose you have seen him pretty regularly every day?

REGINA. I? Oh, yes, I do—whenever I have time, that is to say.

MANDERS. Your father has not a very strong character, Miss Engstrand. He sadly needs a guiding hand.

REGINA. Yes, I can quite believe that.

MANDERS. He needs someone with him that he can cling to, someone whose judgment he can rely on. He acknowledged that freely himself, the last time he came up to see me.

REGINA. Yes, he has said something of the same sort to me. But I don't know whether Mrs. Alving could do without me—most of all just now, when we have the new Orphanage to see about. And I should be dreadfully unwilling to leave Mrs. Alving, too; she has always been so good to me.

MANDERS. But a daughter's duty, my good child——. Naturally we should have to get your mistress' consent first.

REGINA. Still I don't know whether it would be quite the thing, at my age, to keep house for a single man.

MANDERS. What!! My dear Miss Engstrand, it is your own father we are speaking of!

REGINA. Yes, I dare say, but still——. Now, if it were in a good house and with a real gentleman——

MANDERS. But, my dear Regina——

REGINA. ——one whom I could feel an affection for, and really feel in the position of a daughter to——

MANDERS. Come, come—my dear good child——

REGINA. I should like very much to live in town. Out here it is terribly lonely; and you know yourself, Mr. Manders, what it is to be alone in the world. And, though I say it, I really am both capable and willing. Don't you know any place that would be suitable for me, Mr. Manders?

MANDERS. I? No, indeed I don't.

REGINA. But, dear Mr. Manders—at any rate don't forget me, in case——

MANDERS (*getting up*). No, I won't forget you, Miss Engstrand.

REGINA. Because, if I——

MANDERS. Perhaps you will be so kind as to let Mrs. Alving know I am here?

REGINA. I will fetch her at once, Mr. Manders.

[*Goes out to the left.* MANDERS *walks up and down the room once or twice, stands for a moment at the farther end of the room with his hands behind his back and looks out into the garden. Then he comes back to the table, takes up a book and looks at the title page, gives a start and looks at some of the others.*]

MANDERS. Hm!—Really!

[MRS. ALVING *comes in by the door on the left. She is followed by* REGINA, *who goes out again at once through the nearer door on the right.*]

MRS. ALVING (*holding out her hand*). I am very glad to see you, Mr. Manders.

MANDERS. How do you do, Mrs. Alving? Here I am, as I promised.

MRS. ALVING. Always punctual!

MANDERS. Indeed, I was hard put to it to get away. What with vestry meetings and committees——

MRS. ALVING. It was all the kinder of you to come in such good time; we can settle our business before dinner. But where is your luggage?

MANDERS (*quickly*). My things are down at the village shop. I am going to sleep there to-night.

MRS. ALVING (*repressing a smile*). Can't I really persuade you to stay the night here this time?

MANDERS. No, no; many thanks all the same; I will put up there, as usual. It is so handy for getting on board the boat again.

MRS. ALVING. Of course you shall do as you please. But it seems to me quite another thing, now we are two old people——

MANDERS. Ha! ha! You will have your joke! And it's natural you should be in high spirits to-day—first of all there is the great event to-morrow, and also you have got Oswald home.

MRS. ALVING. Yes, am I not a lucky woman? It is more than two years since he was home last, and he has promised to stay the whole winter with me.

MANDERS. Has he, really? That is very nice and filial of him, because there must be many more attractions in his life in Rome or in Paris, I should think.

MRS. ALVING. Yes, but he has his mother here, you see. Bless the dear boy, he has got a corner in his heart for his mother still.

MANDERS. Oh, it would be very sad if absence and preoccupation with such a thing as Art were to dull the natural affections.

MRS. ALVING. It would, indeed. But there is no fear of that with him, I am glad to say. I am quite curious to see if you recognize him again. He will be down directly; he is just lying down for a little on the sofa upstairs. But do sit down, my dear friend.

MANDERS. Thank you. You are sure I am not disturbing you?

MRS. ALVING. Of course not. (*She sits down at the table.*)

MANDERS. Good. Then I will show you——. (*He goes to the chair where his bag is lying and takes a packet of papers from it, then sits down at the opposite side of the table and looks for a clear space to put the papers down.*) Now first of all, here is—(*Breaks off*). Tell me, Mrs. Alving, what are these books doing here?

MRS. ALVING. Those books? I am reading them.

MANDERS. Do you read this sort of thing?

MRS. ALVING. Certainly I do.

MANDERS. Do you feel any the better or the happier for reading books of this kind?

MRS. ALVING. I think it makes me, as it were, more self-reliant.

MANDERS. That is remarkable. But why?

MRS. ALVING. Well, they give me an explanation or a confirmation of lots of different ideas that have come into my own mind. But what surprises me, Mr. Manders, is that, properly speaking, there is nothing at all new in these books. There is nothing more in them than what most people think and believe. The only thing is that most people either take no account of it or won't admit it to themselves.

MANDERS. But, good heavens, do you seriously think that most people——?

MRS. ALVING. Yes, indeed, I do.

MANDERS. But not here in the country at any rate? Not here amongst people like ourselves?

MRS. ALVING. Yes, amongst people like ourselves too.

MANDERS. Well, really, I must say——!

MRS. ALVING. But what is the particular objection that you have to these books?

MANDERS. What objection? You surely don't suppose that I take any particular interest in such productions?

MRS. ALVING. In fact, you don't know anything about what you are denouncing?

MANDERS. I have read quite enough about these books to disapprove of them.

MRS. ALVING. Yes, but your own opinion——

MANDERS. My dear Mrs. Alving, there are many occasions in life when one has to rely on the opinion of others. That is the way in this world, and it is quite right that it should be so. What would become of society otherwise?

MRS. ALVING. Well, you may be right.

MANDERS. Apart from that, naturally I don't deny that literature of this kind may have a considerable attraction. And I cannot blame you, either, for wishing to make yourself acquainted with the intellectual tendencies which I am told are at work in the wider world in which you have allowed your son to wander for so long. But——

MRS. ALVING. But——?

MANDERS (*lowering his voice*). But one doesn't talk about it, Mrs. Alving. One certainly is not called upon to account to every one for what one reads or thinks in the privacy of one's own room.

MRS. ALVING. Certainly not. I quite agree with you.

MANDERS. Just think of the consideration you owe to this Orphanage, which you decided to build at a time when your thoughts on such subjects were very different from what they are now—as far as I am able to judge.

MRS. ALVING. Yes, I freely admit that. But it was about the Orphanage——

MANDERS. It was about the Orphanage we were going to talk; quite so. Well—walk warily, dear Mrs. Alving! And now let us turn to the business in hand. (*Opens an envelope and takes out some papers.*) You see these?

MRS. ALVING. The deeds?

MANDERS. Yes, the whole lot—and everything in order. I can tell you it has been no easy matter to get them in time. I had positively to put pressure on the authorities; they are almost painfully conscientious when it is a question of settling property. But here they are at last. (*Turns over the papers.*) Here is the deed of conveyance of that part of the Rosenvold estate known as the Solvik property, together with the buildings newly erected thereon—the school, the masters' houses, and the chapel. And here is the legal sanction for the statutes of the institution. Here, you see—(*reads*) "Statutes for the Captain Alving Orphanage."

MRS. ALVING (*after a long look at the papers*). That seems all in order.

MANDERS. I thought "Captain" was the better title to use, rather than your husband's Court title of "Chamberlain." "Captain" seems less ostentatious.

MRS. ALVING. Yes, yes; just as you think best.

MANDERS. And here is the certificate for the investment of the capital in the bank, the interest being earmarked for the current expenses of the Orphanage.

MRS. ALVING. Many thanks; but I think it will be most convenient if you will kindly take charge of them.

MANDERS. With pleasure. I think it will be best to leave the money in the bank for the present. The interest is not very high, it is true; four per cent at six months' call. Later on, if we can find some good mortgage—of course it must be a first mortgage and on unexceptionable security—we can consider the matter further.

MRS. ALVING. Yes, yes, my dear Mr. Manders, you know best about all that.

MANDERS. I will keep my eye on it, anyway. But there is one thing in connection with it that I have often meant to ask you about.

MRS. ALVING. What is that?

MANDERS. Shall we insure the buildings, or not?

MRS. ALVING. Of course we must insure them.

MANDERS. Ah, but wait a moment, dear lady. Let us look into the matter a little more closely.

MRS. ALVING. Everything of mine is insured—the house and its contents, my livestock—everything.

MANDERS. Naturally. They are your own property. I do exactly the same, of course. But this, you see, is quite a different case. The Orphanage is, so to speak, dedicated to higher uses.

MRS. ALVING. Certainly, but——

MANDERS. As far as I am personally concerned, I can conscientiously say that I don't see the smallest objection to our insuring ourselves against all risks.

MRS. ALVING. That is exactly what I think.

MANDERS. But what about the opinion of the people hereabouts?

MRS. ALVING. Their opinion——?

MANDERS. Is there any considerable body of opinion here—opinion of some account, I mean—that might take exception to it?

MRS. ALVING. What, exactly, do you mean by opinion of some account?

MANDERS. Well, I was thinking particularly of persons of such independent and influential position that one could hardly refuse to attach weight to their opinion.

MRS. ALVING. There are a certain number of such people here, who might perhaps take exception to it if we——

MANDERS. That's just it, you see. In town there are lots of them. All my fellow-clergymen's congregations, for instance! It would be so extremely easy for them to interpret it as meaning that neither you nor I had a proper reliance on Divine protection.

MRS. ALVING. But as far as you are concerned, my dear friend, you have at all events the consciousness that——

MANDERS. Yes, I know, I know; my own mind is quite easy about it, it is true. But we should not be able to prevent a wrong and injurious interpretation of our action. And that sort of thing, moreover, might very easily end in exercising a hampering influence on the work of the Orphanage.

MRS. ALVING. Oh, well, if that is likely to be the effect of it——

MANDERS. Nor can I entirely overlook the difficult—indeed, I may say, painful—position I might possibly be placed in. In the best circles in town the matter of this Orphanage is attracting a great deal of attention. Indeed the Orphanage is to some extent built for the benefit of the town too, and it is to be hoped that it may result in the lowering of our poor-rate by a considerable amount. But as I have been your adviser in the matter and have taken charge of the business side of it, I should be afraid that it would be I that spiteful persons would attack first of all——

MRS. ALVING. Yes, you ought not to expose yourself to that.

MANDERS. Not to mention the attacks that would undoubtedly be made upon me in certain newspapers and reviews——

MRS. ALVING. Say no more about it, dear Mr. Manders; that quite decides it.

MANDERS. Then you don't wish it to be insured?

MRS. ALVING. No, we will give up the idea.

MANDERS (*leaning back in his chair*). But suppose, now, that some accident happened—one can never tell—would you be prepared to make good the damage?

MRS. ALVING. No; I tell you quite plainly I would not do so under any circumstances.

MANDERS. Still, you know, Mrs. Alving—after all, it is a serious responsibility that we are taking upon ourselves.

MRS. ALVING. But do you think we can do otherwise?

MANDERS. No, that's just it. We really can't do otherwise. We ought not to expose ourselves to a mistaken judgment; and we have no right to do anything that will scandalize the community.

MRS. ALVING. You ought not to, as a clergyman, at any rate.

MANDERS. And, what is more, I certainly think that we may count upon our enterprise being attended by good fortune—indeed, that it will be under a special protection.

MRS. ALVING. Let us hope so, Mr. Manders.

MANDERS. Then we will leave it alone?

MRS. ALVING. Certainly.

MANDERS. Very good. As you wish. (*Makes a note.*) No insurance, then.

MRS. ALVING. It's a funny thing that you should just have happened to speak about that to-day——

MANDERS. I have often meant to ask you about it——

MRS. ALVING. ——because yesterday we very nearly had a fire up there.

MANDERS. Do you mean it?

MRS. ALVING. Oh, as a matter of fact it was nothing of any consequence. Some shavings in the carpenter's shop caught fire.

MANDERS. Where Engstrand works?

MRS. ALVING. Yes. They say he is often so careless with matches.

MANDERS. He has so many things on his mind, poor fellow—so many anxieties. Heaven be thanked, I am told he is really making an effort to live a blameless life.

MRS. ALVING. Really? Who told you so?

MANDERS. He assured me himself that it is so. He's a good workman, too.

MRS. ALVING. Oh, yes, when he is sober.

MANDERS. Ah, that sad weakness of his! But the pain in his poor leg often drives him to it, he tells me. The last time he was in town, I was really quite touched by him. He came to my house and thanked me so gratefully for getting him work here, where he could have the chance of being with Regina.

MRS. ALVING. He doesn't see very much of her.

MANDERS. But he assured me that he saw her every day.

MRS. ALVING. Oh, well, perhaps he does.

MANDERS. He feels so strongly that he needs some one who can keep a hold on him when temptations assail him. That is the most winning thing about Jacob Engstrand; he comes to one like a helpless child and accuses himself and confesses his frailty. The last time he came and had a talk with me——. Suppose now, Mrs. Alving, that it were really a necessity of his existence to have Regina at home with him again——

MRS. ALVING (*standing up suddenly*). Regina!

MANDERS. ——you ought not to set yourself against him.

MRS. ALVING. Indeed, I set myself very definitely against that. And, besides, you know Regina is to have a post in the Orphanage.

MANDERS. But consider, after all he is her father——

MRS. ALVING. I know best what sort of father he has been to her. No, she shall never go to him with my consent.

MANDERS. (*getting up*). My dear lady, don't judge so hastily. It is very sad how you misjudge poor Engstrand. One would really think you were afraid——

MRS. ALVING (*more calmly*). That is not the question. I have taken Regina into my charge, and in my charge she remains. (*Listens.*) Hush, dear Mr. Manders, don't say any more about it. (*Her face brightens with pleasure.*) Listen! Oswald is coming downstairs. We will only think about him now.

[OSWALD ALVING, *in a light overcoat, hat in hand and smoking a big meerschaum pipe, comes in by the door on the left.*]

OSWALD (*standing in the doorway*). Oh, I beg your pardon, I thought you were in the office. (*Comes in.*) Good morning, Mr. Manders.

MANDERS (*staring at him*). Well! It's most extraordinary——

MRS. ALVING. Yes, what do you think of him, Mr. Manders?

MANDERS. I—I—no, can it possibly be——?

OSWALD. Yes, it really is the prodigal son, Mr. Manders.

MANDERS. Oh, my dear young friend——

OSWALD. Well, the son come home, then.

MRS. ALVING. Oswald is thinking of the time when you were so opposed to the idea of his being a painter.

MANDERS. We are only fallible, and many steps seem to us hazardous at first, that afterwards—(*Grasps his hand.*) Welcome, welcome! Really, my dear Oswald—may I still call you Oswald?

OSWALD. What else would you think of calling me?

MANDERS. Thank you. What I mean, my dear Oswald, is that you must not imagine that I have any unqualified disapproval of the artist's life. I admit that there are many who, even in that career, can keep the inner man free from harm.

OSWALD. Let us hope so.

MRS. ALVING (*beaming with pleasure*). I know one who has kept both the inner and the outer man free from harm. Just take a look at him, Mr. Manders.

OSWALD (*walks across the room*). Yes, yes, mother dear, of course.

MANDERS. Undoubtedly—no one can deny it. And I hear you have begun to make a name for yourself. I have often seen mention of you in the papers—and extremely favorable mention, too. Although, I must admit, latterly I have not seen your name so often.

OSWALD (*going towards the conservatory*). I haven't done so much painting just lately.

MRS. ALVING. An artist must take a rest sometimes, like other people.

MANDERS. Of course, of course. At those times the artist is preparing and strengthening himself for a greater effort.

OSWALD. Yes. Mother, will dinner soon be ready?

MRS. ALVING. In half an hour. He has a fine appetite, thank goodness.

MANDERS. And a liking for tobacco too.

OSWALD. I found father's pipe in the room upstairs, and——

MANDERS. Ah, that is what it was!

MRS. ALVING. What?

MANDERS. When Oswald came in at that door with the pipe in his mouth, I thought for the moment it was his father in the flesh.

OSWALD. Really?

MRS. ALVING. How can you say so? Oswald takes after me.

MANDERS. Yes, but there is an expression about the corners of his mouth—something about the lips—that reminds me so exactly of Mr. Alving—especially when he smokes.

MRS. ALVING. I don't think so at all. To my mind, Oswald has much more of a clergyman's mouth.

MANDERS. Well, yes—a good many of my colleagues in the church have a similar expression.

MRS. ALVING. But put your pipe down, my dear boy. I don't allow any smoking in here.

OSWALD (*puts down his pipe*). All right, I only wanted to try it, because I smoked it once when I was a child.

MRS. ALVING. You?

OSWALD. Yes, it was when I was quite a little chap. And I can remember going upstairs to father's room one evening when he was in very good spirits.

MRS. ALVING. Oh, you can't remember anything about those days.

OSWALD. Yes, I remember plainly that he took me on his knee and let me smoke his pipe. "Smoke, my boy," he said, "have a good smoke, boy!" And I smoked as hard as I could, until I felt I was turning quite pale, and the perspiration was standing in great drops on my forehead. Then he laughed—such a hearty laugh——

MANDERS. It was an extremely odd thing to do.

MRS. ALVING. Dear Mr. Manders, Oswald only dreamt it.

OSWALD. No indeed, mother, it was no dream. Because—don't you remember—you came into the room and carried me off to the nursery, where I was sick, and I saw that you were crying. Did father often play such tricks?

MANDERS. In his young days he was full of fun——

OSWALD. And, for all that, he did so much with his life—so much that was good and useful, I mean—short as his life was.

MANDERS. Yes, my dear Oswald Alving, you have inherited the name of a man who undoubtedly was both energetic and worthy. Let us hope it will be a spur to your energies——

OSWALD. It ought to be, certainly.

MANDERS. In any case it was nice of you to come home for the day that is to honor his memory.

OSWALD. I could do no less for my father.

MRS. ALVING. And to let me keep him so long here—that's the nicest part of what he has done.

MANDERS. Yes, I hear you are going to spend the winter at home.

OSWALD. I am here for an indefinite time, Mr. Manders.—Oh, it's good to be at home again!

MRS. ALVING (*beaming*). Yes, isn't it?

MANDERS. (*looking sympathetically at him*). You went out into the world very young, my dear Oswald.

OSWALD. I did. Sometimes I wonder if I wasn't too young.

MRS. ALVING. Not a bit of it. It is the best thing for an active boy, and especially for an only child. It's a pity when they are kept at home with their parents and get spoilt.

MANDERS. That is a very debatable question, Mrs. Alving. A child's own home is, and always must be, his proper place.

OSWALD. There I agree entirely with Mr. Manders.

MANDERS. Take the case of your own son. Oh yes, we can talk about it before him. What has the result been in his case? He is six or seven and twenty, and has never yet had the opportunity of learning what a well-regulated home means.

OSWALD. Excuse me, Mr. Manders, you are quite wrong there.

MANDERS. Indeed? I imagined that your life abroad had practically been spent entirely in artistic circles.

OSWALD. So it has.

MANDERS. And chiefly amongst the younger artists.

OSWALD. Certainly.

MANDERS. But I imagined that those gentry, as a rule, had not the means necessary for family life and the support of a home.

OSWALD. There are a considerable number of them who have not the means to marry, Mr. Manders.

MANDERS. That is exactly my point.

OSWALD. But they can have a home of their own, all the same; a good many of them have. And they are very well-regulated and very comfortable homes, too.

[MRS. ALVING, *who has listened to him attentively, nods assent, but says nothing.*]

MANDERS. Oh, but I am not talking of bachelor establishments. By a home I mean family life—the life a man lives with his wife and children.

OSWALD. Exactly, or with his children and his children's mother.

MANDERS. (*starts and clasps his hands*). Good heavens!

OSWALD. What is the matter?

MANDERS. Lives with—with—his children's mother!

OSWALD. Well, would you rather he should repudiate his children's mother?

MANDERS. Then what you are speaking of are those unprincipled conditions known as irregular unions!

OSWALD. I have never noticed anything particularly unprincipled about these people's lives.

MANDERS. But do you mean to say that it is possible for a man of any sort of bringing-up, and a young woman, to reconcile themselves to such a way of living—and to make no secret of it, either?

OSWALD. What else are they to do? A poor artist, and a poor girl—it costs a good deal to get married. What else are they to do?

MANDERS. What are they to do? Well, Mr. Alving, I will tell you what they ought to do. They ought to keep away from each other from the very beginning—that is what they ought to do!

OSWALD. That advice wouldn't have much effect upon hot-blooded young folk who are in love.

MRS. ALVING. No, indeed it wouldn't.

MANDERS (*persistently*). And to think that the authorities tolerate such things! That they are allowed to go on, openly! (*Turns to* MRS. ALVING.) Had I so little reason, then, to be sadly concerned about your son? In circles where open immorality is rampant—where, one may say, it is honored——

OSWALD. Let me tell you this, Mr. Manders. I have been a constant Sunday guest at one or two of these "irregular" households——

MANDERS. On Sunday, too!

OSWALD. Yes, that is the day of leisure. But never have I heard one objectionable word there; still less have I ever seen anything that could be called immoral. No; but do you know when and where I *have* met with immorality in artists' circles?

MANDERS. No, thank heaven, I don't!

OSWALD. Well, then, I shall have the pleasure of telling you. I have met with it when some one or other of your model husbands and fathers have come out there to have a bit of a look around on their own account, and have done the artists the honor of looking them up in their humble quarters. Then we had a chance of learning something, I can tell you. These gentlemen were able to instruct us about places and things that we had never so much as dreamt of.

MANDERS. What? Do you want me to believe that honorable men when they get away from home will——

OSWALD. Have you never, when these same honorable men come home again, heard them deliver themselves on the subject of the prevalence of immorality abroad?

MANDERS. Yes, of course, but——

MRS. ALVING. I have heard them, too.

OSWALD. Well, you take their word for it, unhesitatingly. Some of them are experts in the matter. (*Putting his hands to his head.*) To think that the glorious freedom of the beautiful life over there should be so besmirched!

MRS. ALVING. You musn't get too heated, Oswald; you gain nothing by that.

OSWALD. No, you are quite right, mother. Besides, it isn't good for me. It's because I am so infernally tired, you know. I will go out and take a turn before dinner. I beg your pardon, Mr. Manders. It is impossible for you to realize the feeling; but it takes me that way. (*Goes out by the farther door on the right.*)

MRS. ALVING. My poor boy!

MANDERS. You may well say so. This is what it has brought him to! (MRS. ALVING *looks at him, but does not speak.*) He called himself the prodigal son. It's only too true, alas—only too true! (MRS. ALVING *looks steadily at him.*) And what do you say to all this?

MRS. ALVING. I say that Oswald was right in every single word he said.

MANDERS. Right? Right? To hold such principles as that?

MRS. ALVING. In my loneliness here I have come to just the same opinions as he, Mr. Manders. But I have never presumed to venture upon such topics in conversation. Now there is no need; my boy shall speak for me.

MANDERS. You deserve the deepest pity, Mrs. Alving. It is my duty to say an earnest word to you. It is no longer your business man and adviser, no longer your old friend and your dead husband's old friend, that stands before you now. It is your priest that stands before you, just as he did once at the most critical moment of your life.

MRS. ALVING. And what has my priest to say to me?

MANDERS. First of all I must stir your memory. The moment is well chosen. To-morrow is the tenth anniversary of your husband's death; to-morrow the memorial to the departed will be unveiled; to-morrow I shall speak to the whole assembly that will be met together. But today I want to speak to you alone.

MRS. ALVING. Very well, Mr. Manders, speak!

MANDERS. Have you forgotten that after barely a year of married life you were standing at the very edge of a precipice?—that you forsook your house and home?—and that you ran away from your husband—yes, Mrs. Alving, ran away, ran away—and refused to return to him in spite of his requests and entreaties?

MRS. ALVING. Have you forgotten how unspeakably unhappy I was during that first year?

MANDERS. To crave for happiness in this world is simply to be possessed by a spirit of revolt. What right have we to happiness? No! we must do our duty, Mrs. Alving. And your duty was to cleave to the man you had chosen and to whom you were bound by a sacred bond.

MRS. ALVING. You know quite well what sort of life my husband was living at that time—what excesses he was guilty of.

MANDERS. I know only too well what rumor used to say of him; and I should be the last person to approve of his conduct as a young man, supposing that rumor spoke the truth. But it is not a wife's part to be her husband's judge. You should have considered it your bounden duty humbly to have borne the cross that a higher will had laid upon you. But, instead of that, you rebelliously cast off your cross; you deserted the man whose stumbling footsteps you should have supported; you did what was bound to imperil your good name and reputation, and came very near to imperilling the reputation of others into the bargain.

MRS. ALVING. Of others? Of one other, you mean.

MANDERS. It was the height of imprudence, your seeking refuge with me.

MRS. ALVING. With our priest? With our intimate friend?

MANDERS. All the more on that account. You should thank God that I possessed the necessary strength of mind—that I was able to turn you from your outrageous intention, and that it was vouchsafed to me to succeed in leading you back into the path of duty and back to your lawful husband.

MRS. ALVING. Yes, Mr. Manders, that certainly was your doing.

MANDERS. I was but the humble instrument of a higher power. And is it not true that my having been able to bring you again under the yoke of duty and obedience sowed the seeds of a rich blessing on all the rest of your life? Did things not turn out as I foretold to you? Did not your husband turn from straying in the wrong path as a man should? Did he not, after all, live a life of love and good report with you all his days? Did he not become a benefactor to the neighbourhood? Did he not so raise you up to his level, so that by degrees you became his fellow-worker in all his undertakings—and a noble fellow-worker, too, I know, Mrs. Alving; that praise I will give you.—But now I come to the second serious false step in your life.

MRS. ALVING. What do you mean?

MANDERS. Just as once you forsook your duty as a wife, so, since then, you have forsaken your duty as a mother.

MRS. ALVING. Oh——!

MANDERS. You have been overmastered all your life by a disastrous spirit of wilfulness. All your impulses have led you towards what is undisciplined and lawless. You have never been willing to submit to any restraint. Anything in life that has seemed irksome to you, you have thrown aside recklessly and unscrupulously, as if it were a burden that you were free to rid yourself of if you would. It did not please you to be a wife any longer, and so you left your husband. Your duties as a mother were irksome to you, so you sent your child away among strangers.

MRS. ALVING. Yes, that is true; I did that.

MANDERS. And that is why you have become a stranger to him.

MRS. ALVING. No, no, I am not that!

MANDERS. You are; you must be. And what sort of son is it that you have got back? Think over it seriously, Mrs. Alving. You erred grievously in your husband's case—you acknowledge as much, by erecting this memorial to him. Now you are bound to acknowledge how much you have erred in your son's case; possibly there may still be time to reclaim him from the paths of wickedness. Turn over a new leaf, and set yourself to reform what there may still be that is capable of reformation in him. Because (*With uplifted forefinger.*) in very truth, Mrs. Alving, you are a guilty mother!—That is what I have thought it my duty to say to you. (*A short silence.*)

MRS. ALVING (*speaking slowly and with self-control*). You have had your say, Mr. Manders, and to-morrow you will be making a public speech in memory of my husband. I shall not speak to-morrow. But now I wish to speak to you for a little, just as you have been speaking to me.

MANDERS. By all means; no doubt you wish to bring forward some excuses for your behavior——

MRS. ALVING. No. I only want to tell you something.

MANDERS. Well?

MRS. ALVING. In all that you said just now about me and my husband, and about our life together after you had, as you put it, led me back into the path of duty—there was nothing that you knew at first hand. From that moment you never again set foot in our house—you, who had been our daily companion before that.

MANDERS. Remember that you and your husband moved out of town immediately afterwards.

MRS. ALVING. Yes, and you never once came out here to see us in my husband's lifetime. It was only the business in connection with the Orphanage that obliged you to come and see me.

MANDERS (*in a low and uncertain voice*). Helen—if that is a reproach, I can only beg you to consider——

MRS. ALVING. ——the respect you owed to your calling?—yes. All the more as I was a wife who had tried to run away from her husband. One can never be too careful to have nothing to do with such reckless women.

MANDERS. My dear—Mrs. Alving, you are exaggerating dreadfully——

MRS. ALVING. Yes, yes,—very well. What I mean is this, that when you condemn my conduct as a wife you have nothing more to go upon than ordinary public opinion.

MANDERS. I admit it. What then?

MRS. ALVING. Well—now, Mr. Manders, now I am going to tell you the truth. I had sworn to myself that you should know it one day—you, and you only!

MANDERS. And what may the truth be?

MRS. ALVING. The truth is this, that my husband died just as great a profligate as he had been all his life.

MANDERS (*feeling for a chair*). What are you saying?

MRS. ALVING. After nineteen years of married life, just as profligate—in his desires at all events as he was before you married us.

MANDERS. And can you talk of his youthful indiscretions—his irregularities—his excesses, if you like—as a profligate life?

MRS. ALVING. That was what a the doctor who attended him called it.

MANDERS. I don't understand what you mean.

MRS. ALVING. It is not necessary you should.

MANDERS. It makes my brain reel. To think that your marriage—all the years of wedded life you spent with your husband—were nothing but a hidden abyss of misery.

MRS. ALVING. That and nothing else. Now you know.

MANDERS. This—this bewilders me. I can't understand it! I can't grasp it! How in the world was it possible——? How could such a state of things remain concealed?

MRS. ALVING. That was just what I had to fight for incessantly, day after day. When Oswald was born, I thought I saw a slight improvement. But it didn't last long. And after that I had to fight doubly hard—fight a desperate fight so that no one should know what sort of man my child's father was. You know quite well what an attractive manner he had; it seemed as if people could believe nothing but good of him. He was one of those men whose mode of life seems to have no effect upon their reputations. But at last, Mr. Manders—you must hear this too—at last something happened more abominable than everything else.

MANDERS. More abominable than what you have told me?

MRS. ALVING. I had borne with it all, though I knew only too well what he indulged in in secret, when he was out of the house, But when it came to the point of the scandal coming within our four walls——

MANDERS. Can you mean it? Here?

MRS. ALVING. Yes, here, in our own home. It was in there (*Pointing to the nearer door on the right.*) in the dining-room that I got the first hint of it. I had something to do in there and the door was standing ajar. I heard our maid come up from the garden with water for the flowers in the conservatory.

MANDERS. Well——?

MRS. ALVING. Shortly afterwards I heard my husband come in too. I heard him say something to her in a low voice. And then I heard—(*With a short laugh.*)—oh, it rings in my ears still, with its mixture of what was heartbreaking and what was so ridiculous—I heard my own servant whisper: "Let me go, Mr. Alving! Let me be!"

MANDERS. What unseemly levity on his part! But surely nothing more than levity, Mrs. Alving, believe me.

MRS. ALVING. I soon knew what to believe. My husband had his will of the girl—and that intimacy had consequences, Mr. Manders.

MANDERS (*as if turned to stone*). And all that in this house! In this house!

MRS. ALVING. I have suffered a good deal in this house. To keep him at home in the evening—and at night—I have had to play the part of boon companion in his secret drinking-bouts in his room up there. I have had to sit there alone with him, have had to hobnob and drink with him, have had to listen to his ribald senseless talk, have had to fight with brute force to get him to bed——

MANDERS (*trembling*). And you were able to endure all this!

MRS. ALVING. I had my little boy, and endured it for his sake. But when the crowning insult came—when my own servant—then I made up my mind that there should be an end of it. I took the upper hand in the house, absolutely—both with him and all the others. I had a weapon to use against him, you see; he didn't dare to speak. It was then that Oswald was sent away. He was about seven then, and was beginning to notice things and ask questions as children will. I could endure all that, my friend. It seemed to me that the child would be poisoned if he breathed the air of this polluted house. That was why I sent him away. And now you understand, too, why he never set foot here as long as his father was alive. No one knows what it meant to me.

MANDERS. You have indeed had a pitiable experience.

MRS. ALVING. I could never have gone through with it, if I had not had my work. Indeed, I can boast that I have worked. All the increase in the value of the property, all the improvements, all the useful arrangements that my husband got the honor and glory of—do you suppose that he troubled himself about any of them? He, who used to lie the whole day on the sofa reading old Official Lists! No, you may as well know that too. It was I that kept him up to the mark when he had his lucid intervals; it was I that had to bear the whole burden of it when he began his excesses again or took to whining about his miserable condition.

MANDERS. And this is the man you are building a memorial to!

MRS. ALVING. There you see the power of an uneasy conscience.

MANDERS. An uneasy conscience? What do you mean?

MRS. ALVING. I had always before me the fear that it was impossible that the truth should not come out and be believed. That is why the Orphanage is to exist, to silence all rumors and clear away all doubt.

MANDERS. You certainly have not fallen short of the mark in that, Mrs. Alving.

MRS. ALVING. I had another very good reason. I did not wish Oswald, my own son, to inherit a penny that belonged to his father.

MANDERS. Then it is with Mr. Alving's property——

MRS. ALVING. Yes. The sums of money that, year after year, I have given towards this Orphanage make up the amount of property—I have reckoned it carefully—which in the old days made Lieutenant Alving a catch.

MANDERS. I understand.

MRS. ALVING. That was my purchase money. I don't wish it to pass into Oswald's hands. My son shall have everything from me, I am determined.

[OSWALD *comes in by the farther door on the right. He has left his hat and coat outside.*]

MRS. ALVING. Back again, my own dear boy?

OSWALD. Yes, what can one do outside in this everlasting rain? I hear dinner is nearly ready. That's good!

[REGINA *comes in from the dining-room, carrying a parcel.*]

REGINA. This parcel has come for you, ma'am. (*Gives it to her.*)

MRS ALVING (*glancing at* MANDERS). The ode to be sung to-morrow, I expect.

MANDERS. Hm——!

REGINA. And dinner is ready.

MRS. ALVING. Good. We will come in a moment. I will just—(*Begins to open the parcel.*)

REGINA (*to* OSWALD). Will you drink white or red wine, sir?

OSWALD. Both, Miss Engstrand.

REGINA. Bien—very good, Mr. Alving. (*Goes into the dining-room.*)

OSWALD. I may as well help you to uncork it——. (*Follows her into the dining-room leaving the door ajar after him.*)

MRS. ALVING. Yes, I thought so. Here is the ode, Mr. Manders.

MANDERS (*clasping his hands*). How shall I ever have the courage to-morrow to speak the address that——

MRS. ALVING. Oh, you will get through it.

MANDERS (*in a low voice, fearing to be heard in the dining-room*). Yes, we must raise no suspicions.

MRS. ALVING (*quietly but firmly*). No; and then this long dreadful comedy will be at an end. After to-morrow, I shall feel as if my dead husband had never lived in this house. There will be no one else here then but my boy and his mother.

[*From the dining-room is heard the noise of a chair falling; then* REGINA'S *voice is heard in a loud whisper.*]

REGINA. Oswald! Are you mad? Let me go!

MRS. ALVING (*starting in horror*). Oh——!

[*She stares wildly at the half-open door.* OSWALD *is heard coughing and humming, then the sound of a bottle being uncorked.*]

MANDERS (*in an agitated manner*). What's the matter? What is it, Mrs. Alving?

MRS. ALVING (*hoarsely*). Ghosts. The couple in the conservatory—over again.

MANDERS. What are you saying? Regina——? Is she——?

MRS. ALVING. Yes. Come. Not a word——! (*Grips* MANDERS *by the arm and walks unsteadily with him into the dining-room.*)

ACT II

The same scene. The landscape is still obscured by mist. MANDERS *and* MRS. ALVING *come in from the dining-room.*

MRS. ALVING (*calls into the dining-room from the doorway*). Aren't you coming in here, Oswald?

OSWALD. No, thanks, I think I will go out for a bit.

MRS. ALVING. Yes, do; the weather is clearing a little. (*She shuts the dining-room door, then goes to the hall door and calls.*) Regina!

REGINA (*from without*). Yes, ma'am?

MRS. ALVING. Go down into the laundry and help with the garlands.

REGINA. Yes, ma'am.

[MRS. ALVING *satisfies herself that she has gone, then shuts the door.*]

MANDERS. I suppose he can't hear us?

MRS. ALVING. Not when the door is shut. Besides, he is going out.

MANDERS. I am still quite bewildered. I don't know how I managed to swallow a mouthful of your excellent dinner.

MRS. ALVING (*walking up and down, and trying to control her agitation*). Nor I. But what are we to do?

MANDERS. Yes, what are we to do? Upon my word I don't know; I am so completely unaccustomed to things of this kind.

MRS. ALVING. I am convinced that nothing serious has happened yet.

MANDERS. Heaven forbid! But it is most unseemly behavior, for all that.

MRS. ALVING. It is nothing more than a foolish jest of Oswald's, you may be sure.

MANDERS. Well, of course, as I said, I am quite inexperienced in such matters; but it certainly seems to me——

MRS. ALVING. Out of the house she shall go—and at once. That part of it is as clear as daylight——

MANDERS. Yes, that is quite clear.

MRS. ALVING. But where is she to go? We should not be justified in——

MANDERS. Where to? Home to her father, of course.

MRS. ALVING. To whom, did you say?

MANDERS. To her——. No, of course Engstrand isn't——. But, great heavens, Mrs. Alving, how is such a thing possible? You surely may have been mistaken, in spite of everything.

MRS. ALVING. There was no chance of mistake, more's the pity. Joanna was obliged to confess it to me—and my husband couldn't deny it. So there was nothing else to do but to hush it up.

MANDERS. No, that was the only thing to do.

MRS. ALVING. The girl was sent away at once, and was given a tolerably liberal sum to hold her tongue. She looked after the rest herself when she got to town. She renewed an old acquaintance with the carpenter Engstrand; gave him a hint, I suppose, of how much money she had got, and told him some fairy tale about a foreigner who had been here in his yacht in the summer. So she and Engstrand were married in a great hurry. Why, you married them yourself!

MANDERS. I can't understand it——. I remember clearly Engstrand's coming to arrange about the marriage. He was full of contrition, and accused himself bitterly for the light conduct he and his fiancé had been guilty of.

MRS. ALVING. Of course he had to take the blame on himself.

MANDERS. But the deceitfulness of it! And with me, too! I positively would not have believed it of Jacob Engstrand. I shall most certainly give him a serious talking to.—And the immorality of such a marriage! Simply for the sake of the money——! What sum was it that the girl had?

MRS. ALVING. It was seventy pounds.

MANDERS. Just think of it—for a paltry seventy pounds to let yourself be bound in marriage to a fallen woman!

MRS. ALVING. What about myself, then?—I let myself be bound in marriage to a fallen man.

MANDERS. Heaven forgive you! what are you saying? A fallen man?

MRS. ALVING. Do you suppose my husband was any purer, when I went with him to the altar, than Joanna was when Engstrand agreed to marry her?

MANDERS. The two cases are as different as day from night——

MRS. ALVING. Not so very different, after all. It is true there was a great difference in the price paid, between a paltry seventy pounds and a whole fortune.

MANDERS. How can you compare such totally different things? I presume you consulted your own heart—and your relations.

MRS. ALVING (*looking away from him*). I thought you understood where what you call my heart had strayed to at that time.

MANDERS (*in a constrained voice*). If I had understood anything of the kind, I would not have been a daily guest in your husband's house.

MRS. ALVING. Well, at at any rate this much is certain, that I didn't consult myself in the matter at all.

MANDERS. Still you consulted those nearest to you, as was only right—your mother, your two aunts.

MRS. ALVING. Yes, that is true. The three of them settled the whole matter for me. It seems incredible to me now, how clearly they made out that it would be sheer folly to reject such an offer. If my mother could only see what all that fine prospect has led to!

MANDERS. No one can be responsible for the result of it. Anyway, there is this to be said, that the match was made in complete conformity with law and order.

MRS. ALVING (*going to the window*). Oh, law and order! I often think it is that that is at the bottom of all the misery in the world.

MANDERS. Mrs. Alving, it is very wicked of you to say that.

MRS. ALVING. That may be so; but I don't attach importance to those obligations and considerations any longer. I cannot! I must struggle for my freedom.

MANDERS. What do you mean?

MRS. ALVING (*tapping on the window panes*). I ought never to have concealed what sort of life my husband led. But I had not the courage to do otherwise then—for my own sake, either. I was too much of a coward.

MANDERS. A coward?

MRS. ALVING. If others had known anything of what happened, they would have said: "Poor man, it is natural enough that he should go astray when he has a wife that has run away from him."

MANDERS. They would have had a certain amount of justification for saying so.

MRS. ALVING (*looking fixedly at him*). If I had been the woman I ought, I would have taken Oswald into my confidence and said to him: "Listen, my son, your father was a dissolute man"——

MANDERS. Miserable woman——

MRS. ALVING. ——and I would have told him all I have told you, from beginning to end.

MANDERS. I am almost shocked at you, Mrs. Alving.

MRS. ALVING. I know. I know quite well! I am shocked at myself when I think of it. (*Comes away from the window.*) I am coward enough for that.

MANDERS. Can you call it cowardice that you simply did your duty? Have you forgotten that a child should love and honor his father and mother?

MRS. ALVING. Don't let us talk in such general terms. Suppose we say: "Ought Oswald to love and honor Mr. Alving?"

MANDERS. You are a mother—isn't there a voice in your heart that forbids you to shatter your son's ideals?

MRS. ALVING. And what about the truth?

MANDERS. What about his ideals?

MRS. ALVING. Oh—ideals, ideals! If only I were not such a coward as I am!

MANDERS. Do not spurn ideals, Mrs. Alving—they have a way of avenging themselves cruelly. Take Oswald's own case, now. He hasn't many ideals, more's the pity. But this much I have seen, that his father is something of an ideal to him.

MRS. ALVING. You are right there.

MANDERS. And his conception of his father is what you inspired and encouraged by your letters.

MRS. ALVING. Yes, I was swayed by duty and consideration for others; that was why I lied to my son, year in and year out. Oh, what a coward—what a coward I have been!

MANDERS. You have built up a happy illusion in your son's mind, Mrs. Alving—and that is a thing you certainly ought not to undervalue.

MRS. ALVING. Ah, who knows if that is such a desirable thing after all!—But anyway I don't intend to put up with any goings on with Regina. I am not going to let him get the poor girl into trouble.

MANDERS. Good heavens, no—that would be a frightful thing!

MRS. ALVING. If only I knew whether he meant it seriously, and whether it would mean happiness for him——

MANDERS. In what way? I don't understand.

MRS. ALVING. But that is impossible; Regina is not equal to it, unfortunately.

MANDERS. I don't understand. What do you mean?

MRS. ALVING. If I were not such a miserable coward, I would say to him: "Marry her, or make any arrangement you like with her—only let there be no deceit in the matter."

MANDERS. Heaven forgive you! Are you actually suggesting anything so abominable, so unheard of, as a marriage between them?

MRS. ALVING. Unheard of, do you call it? Tell me honestly, Mr. Manders, don't you suppose there are plenty of married couples out here in the country that are just as nearly related as they are?

MANDERS. I am sure I don't understand you.

MRS. ALVING. Indeed you do.

MANDERS. I suppose you are thinking of cases where possibly——. It is only too true, unfortunately, that family life is not always as stainless as it should be. But as for the sort of thing you hint at—well, it's impossible to tell, at all events with any certainty. Here, on the other hand—for you, a mother, to be willing to allow your——

MRS. ALVING. But I am not willing to allow it. I would not allow it for anything in the world; that is just what I was saying.

MANDERS. No, because you are a coward, as you put it. But, supposing you were not a coward——! Great heavens—such a revolting union!

MRS. ALVING. Well, for the matter of that, we are all descended from a union of that description, so we are told. And who was responsible for this state of things, Mr. Manders?

MANDERS. I can't discuss such questions with you, Mrs. Alving; you are by no means in the right frame of mind for that. But for you to dare to say that it is cowardly of you——!

MRS. ALVING. I will tell you what I mean by that. I am frightened and timid, because I am obsessed by the presence of ghosts that I never can get rid of.

MANDERS. The presence of what?

MRS. ALVING. Ghosts. When I heard Regina and Oswald in there, it was just like seeing ghosts before my eyes. I am half inclined to think we are all ghosts, Mr. Manders. It is not only what we have inherited from our fathers and mothers that exists again in us, but all sorts of old dead ideas and all kinds of old dead beliefs and things of that kind. They are not actually alive in us; but there they are dormant, all the same, and we can never be rid of them. Whenever I take up a newspaper and read it, I fancy I see ghosts creeping between the lines. There must be ghosts all over the world. They must be as countless as the grains of the sands, it seems to me. And we are so miserably afraid of the light, all of us.

MANDERS. Ah!—there we have the outcome of your reading. Fine fruit it has borne—this abominable, subversive, free-thinking literature!

MRS. ALVING. You are wrong there, my friend. You are the one who made me begin to think; and I owe you my best thanks for it.

MANDERS. I?

MRS. ALVING. Yes, by forcing me to submit to what you called my duty and my obligations, by praising as right and just what my whole soul revolted against, as it would against something abominable. That was what led me to examine your teachings critically. I only wanted to unravel one point in them; but as soon as I had got that unravelled, the whole fabric came to pieces. And then I realized that it was only machine-made.

MANDERS (*softly, and with emotion*). Is that all I accomplished by the hardest struggle of my life?

MRS. ALVING. Call it rather the most ignominious defeat of your life.

MANDERS. It was the greatest victory of my life, Helen; victory over myself.

MRS. ALVING. It was a wrong done to both of us.

MANDERS. A wrong?—wrong for me to entreat you as a wife to go back to your lawful husband, when you came to me half distracted and crying: "Here I am, take me!" Was that a wrong?

MRS. ALVING. I think it was.

MANDERS. We two do not understand one another.

MRS. ALVING. Not now, at all events.

MANDERS. Never—even in my most secret thoughts have I for a moment regarded you as anything but the wife of another.

MRS. ALVING. Do you believe what you say?

MANDERS. Helen——!

MRS. ALVING. One so easily forgets one's own feelings.

MANDERS. Not I. I am the same as I always was.

MRS. ALVING. Yes, yes—don't let us talk any more about the old days. You are buried up to your eyes now in committees and all sorts of business; and I am here, fighting with ghosts both without and within me.

MANDERS. I can at all events help you to get the better of those without you. After all that I have been horrified to hear from you to-day, I cannot conscientiously allow a young defenceless girl to remain in your house.

MRS. ALVING. Don't you think it would be best if we could get her settled?—by some suitable marriage, I mean.

MANDERS. Undoubtedly. I think, in any case, it would have been desirable for her. Regina is at an age now that—well, I don't know much about these things, but—

MRS. ALVING. Regina developed very early.

MANDERS. Yes, didn't she? I fancy I remember thinking she was remarkably well developed, bodily, at the time I prepared her for Confirmation. But, for the time being, she must in any case go home. Under her father's care—no, but of course Engstrand is not——. To think that he, of all men, could so conceal the truth from me!

[*A knock is heard at the hall door.*]

MRS. ALVING. Who can that be? Come in!

[ENGSTRAND, *dressed in his Sunday clothes, appears in the doorway.*]

ENGSTRAND. I humbly beg pardon, but——

MANDERS. Aha! Hm!——

MRS. ALVING. Oh, it's you, Engstrand!

ENGSTRAND. There were none of the maids about, so I took the great liberty of knocking.

MRS. ALVING. That's all right. Come in. Do you want to speak to me?

ENGSTRAND (*coming in*). No, thank you very much, ma'am. It was Mr. Manders I wanted to speak to for a moment.

MANDERS (*walking up and down*). Hm!—do you? You want to speak to me, do you?

ENGSTRAND. Yes, sir, I wanted so very much to——

MANDERS (*stopping in front of him*). Well, may I ask what it is you want?

ENGSTRAND. It's this way, Mr. Manders. We are being paid off now. And many thanks to you, Mrs. Alving. And now the work is quite finished, I thought it would be so nice and suitable if all of us, who have worked so honestly together all this time, were to finish up with a few prayers this evening.

MANDERS. Prayers? Up at the Orphanage?

ENGSTRAND. Yes, sir, but if it isn't agreeable to you, then——

MANDERS. Oh, certainly——but—hm!——

ENGSTRAND. I have made a practice of saying a few prayers there myself each evening——

MRS. ALVING. Have you?

ENGSTRAND. Yes, ma'am, now and then—just as a little edification, so to speak. But I am only a poor common man, and haven't rightly the gift, alas—and so I thought that as Mr. Manders happened to be here, perhaps——

MANDERS. Look here, Engstrand. First of all I must ask you a question. Are you in a proper frame of mind for such a thing? Is your conscience free and untroubled?

ENGSTRAND. Heaven have mercy on me a sinner! My conscience isn't worth our speaking about, Mr. Manders.

MANDERS. But it is just what we must speak about. What do you say to my question?

ENGSTRAND. My conscience? Well—it's uneasy sometimes, of course.

MANDERS. Ah, you admit that at all events. Now will you tell me, without any concealment—what is your relationship to Regina?

MRS. ALVING (*hastily*). Mr. Manders!

MANDERS (*calming her*). Leave it to me!

ENGSTRAND. With Regina? Good Lord, how you frightened me! (*Looks at* MRS. ALVING.) There is nothing wrong with Regina, is there?

MANDERS. Let us hope not. What I want to know is, what is your relationship to her? You pass as her father, don't you?

ENGSTRAND (*unsteadily*). Well—hm!—you know, sir, what happened between me and my poor Joanna.

MANDERS. No more distortion of the truth! Your late wife made a full confession to Mrs. Alving, before she left her service.

ENGSTRAND. What!—do you mean to say——? Did she do that after all?

MANDERS. You see it has all come out, Engstrand.

ENGSTRAND. Do you mean to say that she, who gave me her promise and solemn oath——

MANDERS. Did she take an oath?

ENGSTRAND. Well, no—she only gave me her word, but as seriously as a woman could.

MANDERS. And all these years you have been hiding the truth from me —from me, who have had such complete and absolute faith in you.

ENGSTRAND. I am sorry to say I have, sir.

MANDERS. Did I deserve that from you, Engstrand? Haven't I been always ready to help you in word and deed as far as lay in my power? Answer me! Is it not so?

ENGSTRAND. Indeed there's many a time I should have been very badly off without you, sir.

MANDERS. And this is the way you repay me—by causing me to make false entries in the church registers, and afterwards keeping back from me for years the information which you owed it both to me and to your sense of the truth to divulge. Your conduct has been absolutely inexcusable, Engstrand, and from to-day everything is at an end between us.

ENGSTRAND (*with a sigh*). Yes, I can see that's what it means.

MANDERS. Yes, because how can you possibly justify what you did?

ENGSTRAND. Was the poor girl to go and increase her load of shame by talking about it? Just suppose, sir, for a moment that your reverence was in the same predicament as my poor Joanna——

MANDERS. I!

ENGSTRAND. Good Lord, sir, I don't mean the same predicament. I mean, suppose there were something your reverence were ashamed of in the eyes of the world, so to speak. We men oughtn't to judge a poor woman too hardly, Mr. Manders.

MANDERS. But I am not doing so at all. It is you I am blaming.

ENGSTRAND. Will your reverence grant me leave to ask you a small question?

MANDERS. Ask away.

ENGSTRAND. Shouldn't you say it was right for a man to raise up the fallen?

MANDERS. Of course it is.

ENGSTRAND. And isn't a man bound to keep his word of honor?

MANDERS. Certainly he is; but——

ENGSTRAND. At the time when Joanna had her misfortune with this Englishman—or maybe he was an American or a Russian, as they call 'em—well, sir, then she came to town. Poor thing, she had refused me once or twice before; she only had eyes for good-looking men in those days, and I had this crooked leg then. Your reverence will remember how I had ventured up into a dancing-saloon where seafaring men were revelling in drunkenness and intoxication, as they say. And when I tried to exhort them to turn from their evil ways——

MRS. ALVING (*coughs from the window*). Ahem!

MANDERS. I know, Engstrand, I know—the rough brutes threw you downstairs. You have told me about that incident before. The affliction to your leg is a credit to you.

ENGSTRAND. I don't want to claim credit for it, your reverence. But what I wanted to tell you was that she came then and confided in me with tears and gnashing of teeth. I can tell you, sir, it went to my heart to hear her.

MANDERS. Did it, indeed, Engstrand? Well, what then?

ENGSTRAND. Well, then I said to her: "The American is roaming about on the high seas, he is. And you, Joanna," I said, "you have committed a sin and are a fallen woman. But here stands Jacob Engstrand," I said, "on two strong legs"—of course that was only speaking in a kind of metaphor, as it were, your reverence.

MANDERS. I quite understand. Go on.

ENGSTRAND. Well, sir, that was how I rescued her and made her my lawful wife, so that no one should know how recklessly she had carried on with the stranger.

MANDERS. That was all very kindly done. The only thing I cannot justify was your bringing yourself to accept the money——

ENGSTRAND. Money? I? Not a farthing.

MANDERS (*to* MRS. ALVING, *in a questioning tone*). But——

ENGSTRAND. Ah, yes!—wait a bit; I remember now. Joanna did have a trifle of money, you are quite right. But I didn't want to know anything about that. "Fie," I said, "on the mammon of unrighteousness, it's the price of your sin; as for this tainted gold"—or notes, or whatever it was—"we will throw it back in the American's face," I said. But he had gone away and disappeared on the stormy seas, your reverence.

MANDERS. Was that how it was, my good fellow?

ENGSTRAND. It was, sir. So then Joanna and I decided that the money should go towards the child's bringing-up, and that's what became of it; and I can give a faithful account of every single penny of it.

MANDERS. This alters the complexion of the affair very considerably.

ENGSTRAND. That's how it was, your reverence. And I make bold to say that I have been a good father to Regina—as far as was in my power—for I am a poor erring mortal, alas!

MANDERS. There, there, my dear Engstrand——

ENGSTRAND. Yes, I do make bold to say that I brought up the child, and made my poor Joanna a loving and careful husband, as the Bible says we ought. But it never occurred to me to go to your reverence and claim credit for it or boast about it because I had done one good deed in this world. No; when Jacob Engstrand does a thing like that, he holds his tongue about it. Unfortunately it doesn't often happen; I know that only too well. And whenever I do come to see your reverence, I never seem to have anything but trouble and wickedness to talk about. Because, as I said just now—and I say it again—conscience can be very hard on us sometimes.

MANDERS. Give me your hand, Jacob Engstrand.

ENGSTRAND. Oh, sir, I don't like——

MANDERS. No nonsense. (*Grasps his hand.*) That's it!

ENGSTRAND. And may I make bold humbly to beg your reverence's pardon——

MANDERS. You? On the contrary it is for me to beg your pardon——

ENGSTRAND. Oh no, sir.

MANDERS. Yes, certainly it is, and I do it with my whole heart. Forgive me for having so much misjudged you. And I assure you that if I can do anything for you to prove my sincere regret and my goodwill towards you——

ENGSTRAND. Do you mean it, sir?

MANDERS. It would give me the greatest pleasure.

ENGSTRAND. As a matter of fact, sir, you could do it now. I am thinking of using the honest money I have put away out of my wages up here in establishing a sort of Sailors' Home in the town.

MRS. ALVING. You?

ENGSTRAND. Yes, to be a sort of Refuge, as it were. There are such manifold temptations lying in wait for sailor men when they are roaming about on shore. But my idea is that in this house of mine they should have a sort of parental care looking after them.

MANDERS. What do you say to that, Mrs. Alving?

ENGSTRAND. I haven't much to begin such a work with, I know; but Heaven might prosper it, and if I found any helping hand stretched out to me, then——

MANDERS. Quite so; we will talk over the matter further. Your project attracts me enormously. But in the meantime go back to the Orphanage and put everything tidy and light the lights, so that the occasion may seem a little solemn. And then we will spend a little edifying time together, my dear Engstrand, for now I am sure you are in a suitable frame of mind.

ENGSTRAND. I believe I am, sir, truly. Good-bye, then, Mrs. Alving, and thank you for all your kindness; and take good care of Regina for me. (*Wipes a tear from his eye.*) Poor Joanna's child—it is an extraordinary thing, but she seems to have grown into my life and to hold me by the heartstrings. That's how I feel about it, truly. (*Bows and goes out.*)

MANDERS. Now then, what do you think of him, Mrs. Alving? That was quite another explanation that he gave us.

MRS. ALVING. It was, indeed.

MANDERS. There, you see how exceedingly careful we ought to be in condemning our fellow-men. But at the same time it gives one genuine pleasure to find that one was mistaken. Don't you think so?

MRS. ALVING. What I think is that you are, and always will remain, a big baby, Mr. Manders.

MANDERS. I?

MRS. ALVING (*laying her hands on his shoulders*). And I think that I should like very much to give you a good hug.

MANDERS (*drawing back hastily*). No, no, good gracious! What an idea!

MRS. ALVING (*with a smile*). Oh, you needn't be afraid of me.

MANDERS (*standing by the table*). You choose such an extravagant way of expressing yourself sometimes. Now I must get these papers together and put them in my bag. (*Does so.*) That's it. And now good-bye, for the present. Keep your eyes open when Oswald comes back. I will come back and see you again presently.

[*He takes his hat and goes out by the hall door.* MRS. ALVING *sighs, glances out of the window, puts one or two things tidy in the room and turns to go into the dining-room. She stops in the doorway with a stifled cry.*]

MRS. ALVING. Oswald, are you still sitting at table?

OSWALD (*from the dining-room*). I am only finishing my cigar.

MRS. ALVING. I thought you had gone out for a little turn.

OSWALD (*from within the room*). In weather like this? (*A glass is heard clinking.* MRS. ALVING *leaves the door open and sits down with her knitting on the couch by the window.*) Wasn't that Mr. Manders that went out just now?

MRS. ALVING. Yes, he has gone over to the Orphanage.

OSWALD. Oh.

[*The clink of a bottle on a glass is heard again.*]

MRS. ALVING (*with an uneasy expression*). Oswald, dear, you should be careful with that liqueur. It is strong.

OSWALD. It's a good protective against the damp.

MRS. ALVING. Wouldn't you rather come in here?

OSWALD. You know you don't like smoking in there.

MRS. ALVING. You may smoke a cigar in here, certainly.

OSWALD. All right; I will come in, then. Just one drop more. There! (*Comes in, smoking a cigar, and shuts the door after him. A short silence.*) Where has the parson gone?

MRS. ALVING. I told you he had gone over to the Orphanage.

OSWALD. Oh, so you did.

MRS. ALVING. You shouldn't sit so long at table, Oswald.

OSWALD (*holding his cigar behind his back*). But it's so nice and cosy, mother dear. (*Caresses her with one hand.*) Think what it means to me—to have come home; to sit at my mother's own table, in my mother's own room, and to enjoy the charming meals she gives me.

MRS. ALVING. My dear, dear boy!

OSWALD (*a little impatiently, as he walks up and down smoking*). And what else is there for me to do here? I have no occupation——

MRS. ALVING. No occupation?

OSWALD. Not in this ghastly weather, when there isn't a blink of sunshine all day long. (*Walks up and down the floor.*) Not to be able to work, it's——!

MRS. ALVING. I don't believe you were wise to come home.

OSWALD. Yes, mother; I had to.

MRS. ALVING. Because I would ten times rather give up the happiness of having you with me than that you should——

OSWALD (*standing still by the table*). Tell me, mother—is it really such a great happiness for you to have me at home?

MRS. ALVING. Can you ask?

OSWALD (*crumpling up a newspaper*). I should have thought it would have been pretty much the same to you whether I were here or away.

MRS. ALVING. Have you the heart to say that to your mother, Oswald?

OSWALD. But you have been quite happy living without me so far.

MRS. ALVING. Yes, I have lived without you—that is true.

[*A silence. The dusk falls by degrees.* OSWALD *walks restlessly up and down. He has laid aside his cigar.*]

OSWALD (*stopping beside* MRS. ALVING). Mother, may I sit on the couch beside you?

MRS. ALVING. Of course, my dear boy.

OSWALD (*sitting down*). Now I must tell you something mother.

MRS. ALVING (*anxiously*). What?

OSWALD (*staring in front of him*). I can't bear it any longer.

MRS. ALVING. Bear what? What do you mean?

OSWALD (*as before*). I couldn't bring myself to write to you about it; and since I have been at home——

MRS. ALVING (*catching him by the arm*). Oswald, what is it?

OSWALD. Both yesterday and to-day I have tried to push my thoughts away from me—to free myself from them. But I can't.

MRS. ALVING (*getting up*). You must speak plainly, Oswald!

OSWALD (*drawing her down to her seat again*). Sit still, and I will try and tell you. I have made a great deal of the fatigue I felt after my journey——

MRS. ALVING. Well, what of that?

OSWALD. But that isn't what is the matter. It is no ordinary fatigue——

MRS. ALVING (*trying to get up*). You are not ill, Oswald!

OSWALD (*pulling her down again*). Sit still, mother. Do take it quietly. I am not exactly ill—not ill in the usual sense. (*Takes his head in his hands.*) Mother, it's my mind that has broken down—gone to pieces—

I shall never be able to work any more! (*Buries his face in his hands and throws himself at her knees in an outburst of sobs.*)

MRS. ALVING (*pale and trembling*). Oswald! Look at me! No, no, it isn't true!

OSWALD (*looking up with a distracted expression*). Never to be able to work any more! Never—never! A living death! Mother, can you imagine anything so horrible?

MRS. ALVING. My poor unhappy boy! How has this terrible thing happened?

OSWALD (*sitting up again*). That is just what I cannot possibly understand. I have never lived recklessly in any sense. You must believe that of me, mother! I have never done that.

MRS. ALVING. I haven't a doubt of it, Oswald.

OSWALD. And yet this comes upon me all the same!—this terrible disaster!

MRS. ALVING. Oh, but it will all come right again, my dear precious boy. It is nothing but overwork. Believe me, that is so.

OSWALD (*dully*). I thought so too, at first; but it isn't so.

MRS. ALVING. Tell me all about it.

OSWALD. Yes, I will.

MRS. ALVING. When did you first feel anything?

OSWALD. It was just after I had been home last time and had got back to Paris. I began to feel the most violent pains in my head—mostly at the back, I think. It was as if a tight band of iron was pressing on me from my neck upwards.

MRS. ALVING. And then?

OSWALD. At first I thought it was nothing but the headaches I always used to be so much troubled with while I was growing.

MRS. ALVING. Yes, yes——

OSWALD. But it wasn't; I soon saw that. I couldn't work any longer. I would try and start some big new picture; but it seemed as if all my faculties had forsaken me, as if all my strength were paralyzed. I couldn't manage to collect my thoughts; my head seemed to swim—everything went round and round. It was a horrible feeling! At last I sent for a doctor—and from him I learnt the truth.

MRS. ALVING. In what way, do you mean?

OSWALD. He was one of the best doctors there. He made me describe what I felt, and then he began to ask me a whole heap of questions which seemed to me to have nothing to do with the matter. I couldn't see what he was driving at——

MRS. ALVING. Well?

OSWALD. At last he said: "You have had the canker of disease in you practically from your birth"—the actual word he used was "vermoulu." [1]

1. vermoulu: Literally, "worm-eaten."

MRS. ALVING (*anxiously*). What did he mean by that?

OSWALD. I couldn't understand, either—and I asked him for a clearer explanation. And then the old cynic said—(*Clenching his fist.*) Oh——!

MRS. ALVING. What did he say?

OSWALD. He said: "The sins of the fathers are visited on the children."

MRS. ALVING (*getting up slowly*). The sins of the fathers——!

OSWALD. I nearly struck him in the face——

MRS. ALVING (*walking across the room*). The sins of the fathers——!

OSWALD (*smiling sadly*). Yes, just imagine! Naturally I assured him that what he thought was impossible. But do you think he paid any heed to me? No, he persisted in his opinion; and it was only when I got out your letters and translated to him all the passages that referred to my father——

MRS. ALVING. Well, and then?

OSWALD. Well, then of course he had to admit that he was on the wrong tack; and then I learnt the truth—the incomprehensible truth! I ought to have had nothing to do with the joyous happy life I had lived with my comrades. It had been too much for my strength. So it was my own fault!

MRS. ALVING. No, no, Oswald! Don't believe that!

OSWALD. There was no other explanation of it possible, he said. That is the most horrible part of it. My whole life incurably ruined—just because of my own imprudence. All that I wanted to do in the world—not to dare to think of it any more—not to be *able* to think of it! Oh! if only I could live my life over again—if only I could undo what I have done!

[*Throws himself on his face on the couch.* MRS. ALVING *wrings her hand and walks up and down silently fighting with herself.*]

OSWALD. (*Looks up after a while, raising himself on his elbows.*) If only it had been something I had inherited—something I could not help. But, instead of that, to have disgracefully, stupidly, thoughtlessly thrown away one's happiness, one's health, everything in the world—one's future, one's life——

MRS. ALVING. No, no, my darling boy; that is impossible! (*Bending over him.*) Things are not so desperate as you think.

OSWALD. Ah, you don't know——. (*Springs up.*) And to think, mother, that I should bring all this sorrow upon you! Many a time I have almost wished and hoped that you really did not care so very much for me.

MRS. ALVING. I, Oswald? My only son! All that I have in the world! The only thing I care about!

OSWALD (*taking hold of her hands and kissing them*). Yes, yes, I know that is so. When I am at home I know that is true. And that is one of the hardest parts of it to me. But now you know all about it; and now we won't talk any more about it today. I can't stand thinking about it long at a time. (*Walks across the room.*) Let me have something to drink, mother!

MRS. ALVING. To drink? What do you want?

OSWALD. Oh, anything you like. I suppose you have got some punch in the house.

MRS. ALVING. Yes, but my dear Oswald——!

OSWALD. Don't tell me I musn't, mother. Do be nice! I must have something to drown these gnawing thoughts. (*Goes into the conservatory.*) And how—how gloomy it is here! (MRS. ALVING *rings the bell.*) And this incessant rain. It may go on week after week—a whole month. Never a ray of sunshine. I don't remember ever having seen the sun shine once when I have been at home.

MRS. ALVING. Oswald—you are thinking of going away from me!

OSWALD. Hm!—. (*Sighs deeply.*) I am not thinking about anything. I *can't* think about anything! (*In a low voice.*) I have to let that alone.

REGINA (*coming from the dining-room*). Did you ring, ma'am?

MRS. ALVING. Yes, let us have the lamp in.

REGINA. In a moment, ma'am; it is already lit. (*Goes out.*)

MRS. ALVING (*going up to* OSWALD). Oswald, don't keep anything back from me.

OSWALD. I don't, mother. (*Goes to the table.*) It seems to me I have told you a good lot.

[REGINA *brings the lamp and puts it upon the table.*]

MRS. ALVING. Regina, you might bring up a small bottle of champagne.

REGINA. Yes, ma'am. (*Goes out.*)

OSWALD (*taking hold of his mother's face*). That's right. I knew my mother wouldn't let her son go thirsty.

MRS. ALVING. My poor dear boy, how could I refuse you anything now?

OSWALD (*eagerly*). Is that true, mother? Do you mean it?

MRS. ALVING. Mean what?

OSWALD. That you couldn't deny me anything?

MRS. ALVING. My dear Oswald—

OSWALD. Hush!

[REGINA *brings in a tray with a small bottle of champagne and two glasses, which she puts on the table.*]

REGINA. Shall I open the bottle?

OSWALD. No, thank you, I will do it.

[REGINA *goes out.*]

MRS. ALVING (*sitting down at the table*). What did you mean, when you asked if I could refuse you nothing?

OSWALD (*busy opening the bottle*). Let us have a glass first—or two. (*He draws the cork, fills one glass and is going to fill the other.*)

MRS. ALVING (*holding her hand over the second glass*). No, thanks—not for me.

OSWALD. Oh, well, for me then! (*He empties his glass, fills it again and empties it; then sits down at the table.*)

MRS. ALVING (*expectantly*). Now, tell me.

OSWALD (*without looking at her*). Tell me this: I thought you and Mr. Manders seemed so strange—so quiet—at dinner.

MRS. ALVING. Did you notice that?

OSWALD. Yes. Ahem! (*After a short pause.*) Tell me—What do you think of Regina?

MRS. ALVING. What do I think of her?

OSWALD. Yes, isn't she splendid?

MRS. ALVING. Dear Oswald, you don't know her as well as I do—

OSWALD. What of that?

MRS. ALVING. Regina was too long at home, unfortunately. I ought to have taken her under my charge sooner.

OSWALD. Yes, but isn't she splendid to look at mother? (*Fills his glass.*)

MRS. ALVING. Regina has many serious faults——

OSWALD. Yes, but what of that? (*Drinks.*)

MRS. ALVING. But I am fond of her, all the same; and I have made myself responsible for her. I wouldn't for the world she should come to any harm.

OSWALD (*jumping up*). Mother, Regina is my only hope of salvation!

MRS. ALVING (*getting up*). What do you mean?

OSWALD. I can't go on bearing all this agony of mind alone.

MRS. ALVING. Haven't you your mother to help you to bear it?

OSWALD. Yes, I thought so; that was why I came home to you. But it is no use; I see that it isn't. I cannot spend my life here.

MRS. ALVING. Oswald!

OSWALD. I must live a different sort of life, mother, so I shall have to go away from you. I don't want you watching it.

MRS. ALVING. My unhappy boy! But, Oswald, as long as you are ill like this—

OSWALD. If it was only a matter of feeling ill, I would stay with you, mother. You are the best friend I have in the world.

MRS. ALVING. Yes, I am that, Oswald, am I not?

OSWALD (*walking restlessly about*). But all this torment—the regret, the remorse—and the deadly fear. Oh—this horrible fear!

MRS. ALVING (*following him*). Fear? Fear of what? What do you mean?

OSWALD. Oh, don't ask me any more about it. I don't know what it is. I can't put it into words. (MRS. ALVING *crosses the room and rings the bell.*) What do you want?

MRS. ALVING. I want my boy to be happy, that's what I want. He musn't brood over anything. (*To* REGINA, *who has come to the door.*) More champagne—a large bottle.

[REGINA *goes out.*]

OSWALD. Mother!

MRS. ALVING. Do you think we country people don't know how to live?

OSWALD. Isn't she splendid to look at? What a figure! And the picture of health!

MRS. ALVING (*sitting down at the table*). Sit down, Oswald, and let us have a quiet talk.

OSWALD (*sitting down*). You don't know, mother, that I owe Regina a little reparation.

MRS. ALVING. You!

OSWALD. Oh, it was only a little thoughtlessness—call it what you like. Something quite innocent, anyway. The last time I was home——

MRS. ALVING. Yes?

OSWALD. ——she used often to ask me questions about Paris, and I told her one thing and another about the life there. And I remember her saying one day: "Wouldn't you like to go there yourself?"

MRS. ALVING. Well?

OSWALD. I saw her blush, and she said: "Yes, I should like to very much." "All right," I said, "I daresay it might be managed"—or something of that sort.

MRS. ALVING. And then?

OSWALD. I naturally had forgotten all about it; but the day before yesterday I happened to ask her if she was glad I was to be so long at home——

MRS. ALVING. Well?

OSWALD. ——and she looked so queerly at me, and asked: "But what is to become of my trip to Paris?"

MRS. ALVING. Her trip!

OSWALD. And then I got it out of her that she had taken the thing seriously, and had been thinking about me all the time, and had set herself to learn French——

MRS. ALVING. So that was why——

OSWALD. Mother—when I saw this fine, splendid, handsome girl standing there in front of me—I had never paid any attention to her before then—but now, when she stood there as if with open arms ready for me to take her to myself——

MRS. ALVING. Oswald!

OSWALD. ——then I realized that my salvation lay in her, for I saw the joy of life in her.

MRS. ALVING (*starting back*). The joy of life——? Is there salvation in that?

REGINA (*coming in from the dining-room with a bottle of champagne*). Excuse me for being so long, but I had to go to the cellar. (*Puts the bottle down on the table.*)

OSWALD. Bring another glass, too.

REGINA (*looking at him in astonishment*). The mistress's glass is there, sir.

OSWALD. Yes, but fetch one for yourself, Regina. (REGINA *starts, and gives a quick shy glance at* MRS. ALVING.) Well?

REGINA (*in a low and hesitating voice*). Do you wish me to, ma'am?

MRS. ALVING. Fetch the glass, Regina.

[REGINA *goes into the dining-room.*]

OSWALD (*looking after her*). Have you noticed how well she walks?—so firmly and confidently!

MRS. ALVING. It cannot be, Oswald.

OSWALD. It is settled. You must see that. It is no use forbidding it. (REGINA *comes in with a glass, which she holds in her hand.*) Sit down, Regina.

[REGINA *looks questioningly at* MRS. ALVING.]

MRS. ALVING. Sit down. (REGINA *sits down on a chair near the dining-room door, still holding the glass in her hand.*) Oswald, what was it you were saying about the joy of life?

OSWALD. Ah, mother—the joy of life! You don't know very much about that at home here. I shall never realize it here.

MRS. ALVING. Not even when you are with me?

OSWALD. Never at home. But you can't understand that.

MRS. ALVING. Yes, indeed, I almost think I do understand you—now.

OSWALD. That—and the joy of work. They are really the same thing at bottom. But you don't know anything about that either.

MRS. ALVING. Perhaps you are right. Tell me some more about it, Oswald.

OSWALD. Well, all I mean is that here people are brought up to believe that work is a curse and a punishment for sin, and that life is a state of wretchedness and that the sooner we can get out of it the better.

MRS. ALVING. A vale of tears, yes. And we quite conscientiously make it so.

OSWALD. But the people over there will have none of that. There is no one there who really believes doctrines of that kind any longer. Over there the mere fact of being alive is thought to be a matter for exultant happiness. Mother, have you noticed that everything I have painted has turned upon the joy of life?—always upon the joy of life, unfailingly. There is light there, and sunshine, and a holiday feeling—and people's faces beaming with happiness. That is why I am afraid to stay at home here with you.

MRS. ALVING. Afraid? What are you afraid of here, with me?

OSWALD. I am afraid that all these feelings that are so strong in me would degenerate into something ugly here.

MRS. ALVING (*looking steadily at him*). Do you think that is what would happen?

OSWALD. I am certain it would. Even if one lived the same life at home here, as over there—it would never really be the same life.

MRS. ALVING (*who has listened anxiously to him, gets up with a thoughtful expression and says*). Now I see clearly how it all happened.

OSWALD. What do you see?

MRS. ALVING. I see it now for the first time. And now I can speak.

OSWALD (*getting up*). Mother, I don't understand you.

REGINA (*who has got up also*). Perhaps I had better go.

MRS. ALVING. No, stay here. Now I can speak. Now, my son, you shall know the whole truth. Oswald! Regina!

OSWALD. Hush!—here is the parson——

[MANDERS *comes in by the hall door.*]

MANDERS. Well, my friends, we have been spending an edifying time over there.

OSWALD. So have we.

MANDERS. Engstrand must have help with his Sailors' Home. Regina must go home with him and give him her assistance.

REGINA. No, thank you, Mr. Manders.

MANDERS (*perceiving her for the first time*). What——? you in here?—and with a wineglass in your hand!

REGINA (*putting down the glass hastily*). I beg your pardon——!

OSWALD. Regina is going away with me, Mr. Manders.

MANDERS. Going away! With you!

OSWALD. Yes, as my wife—if she insists on that.

MANDERS. But, good heavens——!

REGINA. It is not my fault, Mr. Manders.

OSWALD. Or else she stays here if I stay.

REGINA (*involuntarily*). Here!

MANDERS. I am amazed at you, Mrs. Alving.

MRS. ALVING. Neither of those things will happen, for now I can speak openly.

MANDERS. But you won't do that! No, no, no!

MRS. ALVING. Yes, I can and I will. And without destroying any one's ideals.

OSWALD. Mother, what is it that is being concealed from me?

REGINA (*listening*). Mrs. Alving! Listen! They are shouting outside. (*Goes into the conservatory and looks out.*)

OSWALD (*going to the window on the left*). What can be the matter? Where does that glare come from?

REGINA (*calls out*). The Orphanage is on fire!

MRS. ALVING (*going to the window*). On fire?

MANDERS. On fire? Impossible. I was there just a moment ago.

OSWALD. Where is my hat? Oh, never mind that. Father's Orphanage——! (*Runs out through the garden door.*)

MRS. ALVING. My shawl, Regina! The whole place is in flames.

MANDERS. How terrible! Mrs. Alving, that fire is a judgment on this house of sin!

MRS. ALVING. Quite so. Come, Regina.

[*She and* REGINA *hurry out.*]

MANDERS (*clasping his hands*). And no insurance! (*Follows them out.*)

ACT III

The same scene. All the doors are standing open. The lamp is still burning on the table. It is dark outside, except for a faint glimmer of light seen through the windows at the back. MRS. ALVING, *with a shawl over her head, is standing in the conservatory, looking out.* REGINA, *also wrapped in a shawl, is standing a little behind her.*

MRS. ALVING. Everything burnt—down to the ground.

REGINA. It is burning still in the basement.

MRS. ALVING. I can't think why Oswald doesn't come back. There is no chance of saving anything.

REGINA. Shall I go and take his hat to him?

MRS. ALVING. Hasn't he even got his hat?

REGINA (*pointing to the hall*). No, there it is, hanging up.

MRS. ALVING. Never mind. He is sure to come back soon. I will go and see what he is doing.

[*Goes out by the garden door.* MANDERS *comes in from the hall.*]

MANDERS. Isn't Mrs. Alving here?

REGINA. She has just this moment gone down into the garden.

MANDERS. I have never spent such a terrible night in my life.

REGINA. Isn't it a shocking misfortune, sir!

MANDERS. Oh, don't speak about it. I scarcely dare to think about it.

REGINA. But how can it have happened?

MANDERS. Don't ask me, Miss Engstrand! How should I know? Are you going to suggest too——? Isn't it enough that your father——?

REGINA. What has he done?

MANDERS. He has nearly driven me crazy.

ENGSTRAND (*coming in from the hall*). Mr. Manders——!

MANDERS (*turning round with a start*). Have you even followed me here?

ENGSTRAND. Yes, God help us all——! Great heavens! What a dreadful thing, your reverence!

MANDERS (*walking up and down*). Oh dear, oh dear!

ENGSTRAND. Our little prayer-meeting was the cause of it all, don't you see? (*Aside to* REGINA.) Now we've got the old fool, my girl. (*Aloud.*) And to think it is my fault that Mr. Manders should be the cause of such a thing!

MANDERS. I assure you, Engstrand——

ENGSTRAND. But there was no one else carrying a light there except you, sir.

MANDERS (*standing still*). Yes, so you say. But I have no clear recollection of having had a light in my hand.

ENGSTRAND. But I saw quite distinctly your reverence take a candle and snuff it with your fingers and throw away the burning bit of wick among the shavings.

MANDERS. Did you see that?

ENGSTRAND. Yes, distinctly.

MANDERS. I can't understand it at all. It is never my habit to snuff a candle with my fingers.

ENGSTRAND. Yes, it wasn't like you to do that, sir. But who would have thought it could be such a dangerous thing to do?

MANDERS (*walking restlessly backwards and forwards*). Oh, don't ask me!

ENGSTRAND (*following him about*). And you hadn't insured it either. had you, sir?

MANDERS. No, no, no; you heard me say so.

ENGSTRAND. You hadn't insured it—and then went and set light to the whole place! Good Lord, what bad luck!

MANDERS (*wiping the perspiration from his forehead*). You may well say so, Engstrand.

ENGSTRAND. And that it should happen to a charitable institution that would have been of service both to the town and the country, so to speak! The newspapers won't be very kind to your reverence, I expect.

MANDERS. No, that is just what I am thinking of. It is almost the worst part of the whole thing. The spiteful attacks and accusations—it is horrible to think of!

MRS. ALVING (*coming in from the garden*). I can't get him away from the fire.

MANDERS. Oh, there you are, Mrs. Alving.

MRS. ALVING. You will escape having to make your inaugural address now, at all events, Mr. Manders.

MANDERS. Oh, I would so gladly have——

MRS. ALVING (*in a dull voice*). It is just as well it has happened. This Orphanage would never have come to any good.

MANDERS. Don't you think so?

MRS. ALVING. Do you?

MANDERS. But it is none the less an extraordinary piece of ill luck.

MRS. ALVING. We will discuss it simply as a business matter.—Are you waiting for Mr. Manders, Engstrand?

ENGSTRAND (*at the hall doors*). Yes, I am.

MRS. ALVING. Sit down then, while you are waiting.

ENGSTRAND. Thank you, I would rather stand.

MRS. ALVING (*to* MANDERS). I suppose you are going by the boat?

MANDERS. Yes, It goes in about an hour.

MRS. ALVING. Please take all the documents back with you. I don't want to hear another word about the matter. I have something else to think about now——

MANDERS. Mrs. Alving——

MRS. ALVING. Later on I will send you a power of attorney to deal with it exactly as you please.

MANDERS. I shall be most happy to undertake that. I am afraid the original intention of the bequest will have to be entirely altered now.

MRS. ALVING. Of course.

MANDERS. Provisionally, I should suggest this way of disposing of it. Make over the Solvik property to the parish. The land is undoubtedly not without a certain value; it will always be useful for some purpose or another. And as for the interest on the remaining capital that is on deposit in the bank, possibly I might make suitable use of that in support of some undertaking that promises to be of use to the town.

MRS. ALVING. Do exactly as you please. The whole thing is a matter of indifference to me now.

ENGSTRAND. You will think of my Sailors' Home, Mr. Manders?

MANDERS. Yes, certainly, that is a suggestion. But we must consider the matter carefully.

ENGSTRAND (*aside*). Consider!—devil take it! Oh Lord.

MANDERS (*sighing*). And unfortunately I can't tell how much longer I may have anything to do with the matter—whether public opinion may not force me to retire from it altogether. That depends entirely upon the result of the enquiry into the cause of the fire.

MRS. ALVING. What do you say?

MANDERS. And one cannot in any way reckon upon the result beforehand.

ENGSTRAND (*going nearer to him*). Yes, indeed one can, because here stand I, Jacob Engstrand.

MANDERS. Quite so, but——

ENGSTRAND (*lowering his voice*). And Jacob Engstrand isn't the man to desert a worthy benefactor in the hour of need, as the saying is.

MANDERS. Yes, but, my dear fellow—how——?

ENGSTRAND. You might say Jacob Engstrand is an angel of salvation, so to speak, your reverence.

MANDERS. No, no, I couldn't possibly accept that.

ENGSTRAND. That's how it will be, all the same. I know some one who has taken the blame for some one else on his shoulders before now, I do.

MANDERS. Jacob! (*Grasps his hand.*) You are one in a thousand! You shall have assistance in the matter of your Sailors' Home, you may rely upon that.

[ENGSTRAND *tries to thank him, but is prevented by emotion.*]

MANDERS (*hanging his wallet over his shoulder*). Now we must be off. We will travel together.

ENGSTRAND (*by the dining-room door, says aside to* REGINA). Come with me, you hussy! You shall be as cosy as the yolk in an egg!

REGINA (*tossing her head*). Merci!

[*She goes out into the hall and brings back* MANDERS' *luggage.*]

MANDERS. Good-bye, Mrs. Alving! And may the spirit of order and of what is lawful speedily enter into this house.

MRS. ALVING. Good-bye, Mr. Manders. (*She goes into the conservatory, as she sees* OSWALD *coming in by the garden door.*)

ENGSTRAND (*as he and* REGINA *are helping* MANDERS *on with his coat*). Good-bye, my child. And if anything should happen to you, you know where Jacob Engstrand is to be found. (*Lowering his voice.*) Little Harbour Street, ahem——! (*To* MRS. ALVING *and* OSWALD.) And my house for poor seafaring men shall be called the "Alving Home," it shall. And, if I can carry out my own ideas about it, I shall make bold to hope that it may be worthy of bearing the late Mr. Alving's name.

MANDERS (*at the door*). Ahem—ahem! Come along, my dear Engstrand. Good-bye—good-bye!

[*He and* ENGSTRAND *go out the hall door.*]

OSWALD (*going to the table*). What house was he speaking about?

MRS. ALVING. I believe it is some sort of Home that he and Mr. Manders want to start.

OSWALD. It will be burnt up just like this one.

MRS. ALVING. What makes you think that?

OSWALD. Everything will be burnt up; nothing will be left that is in memory of my father. Here am I being burnt up, too.

[REGINA *looks at him in alarm.*]

MRS. ALVING. Oswald! You should not have stayed so long over there, my poor boy.

OSWALD (*sitting down at the table*). I almost believe you are right.

MRS. ALVING. Let me dry your face, Oswald; you are all wet. (*Wipes his face with her handkerchief.*)

OSWALD (*looking straight before him, with no expression in his eyes*). Thank you, mother.

MRS. ALVING. And aren't you tired, Oswald? Don't you want to go to sleep?

OSWALD (*uneasily*). No, no—not to sleep! I never sleep; I only pretend to. (*Gloomily.*) That will come soon enough.

MRS. ALVING (*looking at him anxiously*). Anyhow, you are really ill, my darling boy.

REGINA (*intently*). Is Mr. Alving ill?

OSWALD (*impatiently*). And do shut all the doors! This deadly fear——

MRS. ALVING. Shut the doors, Regina. (REGINA *shuts the doors and remains standing by the hall door.* MRS. ALVING *takes off her shawl;* REGINA *does the same.* MRS. ALVING *draws up a chair near to* OSWALD'S *and sits down beside him.*) That's it! Now I will sit beside you——

OSWALD. Yes, do. And Regina must stay in here too. Regina must always be near me. You must give me a helping hand, you know, Regina. Won't you do that?

REGINA. I don't understand——

MRS. ALVING. A helping hand?

OSWALD. Yes—when there is need for it.

MRS. ALVING. Oswald, have you not your mother to give you a helping hand?

OSWALD. You? (*Smiles.*) No, mother, you will never give me the kind of helping hand I mean. (*Laughs grimly.*) You? Ha, ha! (*Looks gravely at her.*) After all, you have the best right. (*Impetuously.*) Why don't you call me by my Christian name, Regina? Why don't you say Oswald?

REGINA (*in a low voice*). I did not think Mrs. Alving would like it.

MRS. ALVING. It will not be long before you have the right to do it. Sit down here now beside us, too. (REGINA *sits down quietly and hesitantly at the other side of the table.*) And now, my poor tortured boy, I am going to take the burden off your mind——

OSWALD. You, mother?

MRS. ALVING. ——all that you call remorse and regret and self-reproach.

OSWALD. And you think you can do that?

MRS. ALVING. Yes, now I can, Oswald. A little while ago you were talking about the joy of life, and what you said seemed to shed a new light upon everything in my whole life.

OSWALD (*shaking his head*). I don't in the least understand what you mean.

MRS. ALVING. You should have known your father in his young days in the army. He was full of the joy of life, I can tell you.

OSWALD. Yes, I know.

MRS. ALVING. It gave me a holiday feeling only to look at him, full of irrepressible energy and exuberant spirits.

OSWALD. What then?

MRS. ALVING. Well, then this boy, full of the joy of life—for he was just like a boy, then—had to make his home in a second-rate town which had none of the joy of life to offer him, but only dissipations. He had to come out here and live an aimless life; he had only an official post. He had no work worth devoting his whole mind to; he had nothing more than official routine to attend to. He had not a single companion capable of appreciating what the joy of life meant; nothing but idlers and tipplers——

OSWALD. Mother——!

MRS. ALVING. And so the inevitable happened!

OSWALD. What was the inevitable?

MRS. ALVING. You said yourself this evening what would happen in your case if you stayed at home.

OSWALD. Do you mean that, that father——?

MRS. ALVING. Your poor father never found any outlet for the overmastering joy of life that was in him. And I brought no holiday spirit into his home, either.

OSWALD. You didn't either?

MRS. ALVING. I had been taught about duty, and the sort of thing that I believed in so long here. Everything seemed to turn upon duty—my duty, or his duty—and I am afraid I made your poor father's home unbearable to him, Oswald.

OSWALD. Why did you never say anything about it to me in your letters?

MRS. ALVING. I never looked at it as a thing I could speak of to you, who were his son.

OSWALD. What way did you look at it, then?

MRS. ALVING. I only saw the one fact, that your father was a lost man before ever you were born.

OSWALD (*in a choking voice*). Ah——! (*He gets up and goes to the window.*)

MRS. ALVING. And then I had the one thought in my mind, day and night, that Regina in fact had as good a right in this house—as my own boy had.

OSWALD (*turns round suddenly*). Regina——?

REGINA (*gets up and asks in choking tones*). I——?

MRS. ALVING. Yes, now you both know it.

OSWALD. Regina!

REGINA (*to herself*). So mother was one of that sort too.

MRS. ALVING. Your mother had many good qualities, Regina.

REGINA. Yes, but she was one of that sort too, all the same. I have been thought so myself, sometimes, but——. Then, if you please, Mrs. Alving, may I have permission to leave at once?

MRS. ALVING. Do you really wish to, Regina?

REGINA. Yes, indeed, I certainly wish to.

MRS. ALVING. Of course you shall do as you like, but——

OSWALD (*going to* REGINA). Leave now? This is your home.

REGINA. Merci, Mr. Alving—oh, of course I may say Oswald now, but that is not the way I thought it would become allowable.

MRS. ALVING. Regina, I have not been open with you——

REGINA. No, I can't say you have! If I had known Oswald was ill——. And now that there can never be anything serious between us——. No, I really can't stay here in the country and wear myself out looking after invalids.

OSWALD. Not even for the sake of one who has so near a claim on you?

REGINA. No, indeed I can't. A poor girl must make some use of her youth; otherwise she may easily find herself out in the cold before she knows where she is. And I have got the joy of life in me, too, Mrs. Alving!

MRS. ALVING. Yes, unfortunately; but don't throw yourself away, Regina.

REGINA. Oh, what's going to happen will happen. If Oswald takes after his father, it is just as likely I take after my mother, I expect.——May I ask, Mrs. Alving, whether Mr. Manders knows this about me?

MRS. ALVING. Mr. Manders knows everything.

REGINA (*putting on her shawl*). Oh, well then, the best thing I can do is to get away by the boat as soon as I can. Mr. Manders is such a nice gentleman to deal with; and it certainly seems to me that I have just as much right to some of that money as he—as that horrid carpenter.

MRS. ALVING. You are quite welcome to it, Regina.

REGINA (*looking at her fixedly*). You might as well have brought me up like a gentleman's daughter; it would have been more suitable. (*Tosses her head.*) Oh, well—never mind! (*With a bitter glance at the unopened bottle.*) I daresay some day I shall be drinking champagne with gentlefolk, after all.

MRS. ALVING. If ever you need a home, Regina, come to me.

REGINA. No, thank you, Mrs. Alving. Mr. Manders takes an interest in me, I know. And if things should go very badly with me, I know one house at any rate where I shall feel at home.

MRS. ALVING. Where is that?

REGINA. In the "Alving Home."

MRS. ALVING. Regina—I can see quite well—you are going to your ruin!

REGINA. Pooh!—good-bye. (*She bows to them and goes out through the hall.*)

OSWALD (*standing by the window and looking out*). Has she gone?

MRS. ALVING. Yes

OSWALD (*muttering to himself*). I think it's all wrong.

MRS. ALVING (*going up to him from behind and putting her hands on his shoulders*). Oswald, my dear boy—has it been a great shock to you?

OSWALD (*turning his face towards her*). All this about father, do you mean?

MRS. ALVING. Yes, about your unhappy father. I am so afraid it may have been too much for you.

OSWALD. What makes you think that? Naturally it has taken me entirely by surprise; but, after all I don't know that it matters much to me.

MRS. ALVING (*drawing back her hands*). Doesn't matter?—that your father's life was such a terrible failure?

OSWALD. Of course I can feel sympathy for him, just as I would for anyone else, but——

MRS. ALVING. No more than that! For your own father!

OSWALD (*impatiently*). Father—father! I never knew anything of my father. I don't remember anything else about him except that he once made me sick.

MRS. ALVING. It is dreadful to think of!—But surely a child should feel some affection for his father, whatever happens!

OSWALD. When the child has nothing to thank his father for? When he has never known him? Do you really cling to that antiquated superstition—you, who are so broadminded in other things?

MRS. ALVING. You call it nothing but a superstition!

OSWALD. Yes, and you can see that for yourself quite well, mother. It is one of those beliefs that are put into circulation in the world, and——

MRS. ALVING. Ghosts of beliefs!

OSWALD (*walking across the room*). Yes, you might call them ghosts.

MRS. ALVING (*with an outburst of feeling*). Oswald—then you don't love me either.

OSWALD. You I know, at any rate——

MRS. ALVING. You know me, yes; but is that all?

OSWALD. And I know how fond you are of me, and I ought to be grateful to you for that. Besides, you can be so tremendously useful to me, now that I am ill.

MRS. ALVING. Yes, can't I, Oswald? I could almost bless your illness, as it has driven you home to me. For I see quite well that you are not my very own yet; you must be won.

OSWALD (*impatiently*). Yes, yes, yes; all that is just a way of talking. You must remember I am a sick man, mother. I can't concern myself much with anyone else; I have enough to do, thinking about myself.

MRS. ALVING (*gently*). I will be very good and patient.

OSWALD. And cheerful too, mother!

MRS. ALVING. Yes, my dear boy, you are quite right. (*Goes up to him.*) Now have I taken away all your remorse and self-reproach?

OSWALD. Yes, you have done that. But who will take away the fear?

MRS. ALVING. The fear?

OSWALD (*crossing the room*). Regina would have done it for one kind word.

MRS. ALVING. I don't understand you. What fear do you mean—and what has Regina to do with it?

OSWALD. Is it very late, mother?

MRS. ALVING. It is early morning. (*Looks out through the conservatory windows.*) The dawn is breaking already on the heights. And the sky is clear, Oswald. In a little while you will see the sun.

OSWALD. I am glad of that. After all, there may be many things yet for me to be glad of and to live for——

MRS. ALVING. I should hope so!

OSWALD. Even if I am not able to work——

MRS. ALVING. You will soon find you are able to work again now, my dear boy. You have no longer all those painful depressing thoughts to brood over.

OSWALD. No, it is a good thing that you have been able to rid me of those fancies. If only, now, I could overcome this one thing——. (*Sits down on the couch.*) Let us have a little chat, mother.

MRS. ALVING. Yes, let us. (*Pushes an armchair near to the couch and sits down beside him.*)

OSWALD. The sun is rising—and you know all about it; so I don't feel the fear any longer.

MRS. ALVING. I know all about what?

OSWALD (*without listening to her*). Mother, didn't you say this evening there was nothing in the world you would not do for me if I asked you?

MRS. ALVING. Yes, certainly I said so.

OSWALD. And will you be as good as your word, mother?

MRS. ALVING. You may rely upon that, my own dear boy. I have nothing else to live for, but you.

OSWALD. Yes, yes; well, listen to me, mother. You are very strong-minded, I know. I want you to sit quite quiet when you hear what I am going to tell you.

MRS. ALVING. But what is this dreadful thing——?

OSWALD. You mustn't scream. Do you hear? Will you promise me that? We are going to sit and talk it over quite quietly. Will you promise me that, mother?

MRS. ALVING. Yes, yes, I promise—only tell me what it is.

OSWALD. Well, then, you must know that this fatigue of mine—and my not being able to think about my work—all that is not really the illness itself——

MRS. ALVING. What is the illness itself?

OSWALD. What I am suffering from is hereditary; it— (*Touches his forehead, and speaks very quietly.*)—it lies here.

MRS. ALVING (*almost speechless*). Oswald! No—no!

OSWALD. Don't scream; I can't stand it. Yes, I tell you, it lies here, waiting. And any time, any moment, it may break out.

MRS. ALVING. How horrible——!

OSWALD. Do keep quiet. That is the state I am in——

MRS. ALVING (*springing up*). It isn't true, Oswald! It is impossible! It can't be that!

OSWALD. I had one attack while I was abroad. It passed off quickly. But when I learnt the condition I had been in, then this dreadful haunting fear took possession of me.

MRS. ALVING. That was the fear, then——

OSWALD. Yes, it is so indescribably horrible, you know. If only it had been an ordinary mortal disease——. I am not so much afraid of dying, though, of course, I should like to live as long as I can.

MRS. ALVING. Yes, yes, Oswald, you must!

OSWALD. But this is so appallingly horrible. To become like a helpless child again—to have to be fed, to have to be——. Oh, it's unspeakable!

MRS. ALVING. My child has his mother to tend him.

OSWALD (*jumping up*). No, never; that is just what I won't endure! I dare not think what it would mean to linger on like that for years—to get old and grey like that. And you might die before I did. (*Sits down in* MRS. ALVING's *chair.*) Because it doesn't necessarily have a fatal end quickly, the doctor said. He called it a kind of softening of the brain—or something of that sort. (*Smiles mournfully.*) I think that expression sounds so nice. It always makes me think of cherry-colored velvet curtains—something that is soft to stroke.

MRS. ALVING (*with a scream*). Oswald.

OSWALD (*jumps up and walks about the room*). And now you have taken Regina from me! If I had only had her! She would have given me a helping hand, I know.

MRS. ALVING (*going up to him*). What do you mean, my darling boy? Is there any help in the world I would not be willing to give you?

OSWALD. When I had recovered from the attack I had abroad, the doctor told me that when it recurred—and it will recur—there would be no more hope.

MRS. ALVING. And he was heartless enough to——

OSWALD. I insisted on knowing. I told him I had arrangements to make——. (*Smiles cunningly.*) And so I had. (*Takes a small box from his inner breast-pocket.*) Mother, do you see this?

MRS. ALVING. What is it?

OSWALD. Morphia powders.

MRS. ALVING (*looking at him in terror*). Oswald—my boy!

OSWALD. I have twelve of them saved up——

MRS. ALVING (*snatching at it*). Give me the box, Oswald!

OSWALD. Not yet, mother. (*Puts it back in his pocket.*)

MRS. ALVING. I shall never get over this!

OSWALD. You must. If I had had Regina here now, I would have told her quietly how things stand with me—and asked her to give me this last helping hand. She would have helped me, I am certain.

MRS. ALVING. Never!

OSWALD. If this horrible thing had come upon me and she had seen me lying helpless, like a baby, past help, past saving, past hope—with no chance of recovering——

MRS. ALVING. Never in the world would Regina have done it.

OSWALD. Regina would have done it. Regina was so splendidly light-hearted. And she would very soon have tired of looking after an invalid like me.

MRS. ALVING. Then thank Heaven Regina is not here!

OSWALD. Well, now you have got to give me that helping hand, mother.

MRS. ALVING (*with a loud scream*). I!

OSWALD. Who has a better right than you?

MRS. ALVING. I? Your mother!

OSWALD. Just for that reason.

MRS. ALVING. I, who gave you your life!

OSWALD. I never asked you for life. And what kind of life was it that you gave me? I don't want it! You shall take it back!

MRS. ALVING. Help! Help! (*Runs into the hall.*)

OSWALD (*following her*). Don't leave me! Where are you going?

MRS. ALVING (*in the hall*). To fetch the doctor to you, Oswald! Let me out!

OSWALD (*going into the hall*). You shan't go out. And no one shall come in. (*Turns the key in the lock.*)

MRS. ALVING (*coming in again*). Oswald! Oswald!—my child!

OSWALD (*following her*). Have you a mother's heart—and can bear to see me suffering this unspeakable terror?

MRS. ALVING (*controlling herself, after a moment's silence*). There is my hand on it.

OSWALD. Will you——?

MRS. ALVING. If it becomes necessary. But it shan't become necessary. No, no—it is impossible it should!

OSWALD. Let us hope so. And let us live together as long as we can. Thank you, mother.

[*He sits down in the armchair, which* MRS. ALVING *had moved beside the couch. Day is breaking; the lamp is still burning on the table.*]

MRS. ALVING (*coming cautiously nearer*). Do you feel calmer now?

OSWALD. Yes.

MRS. ALVING (*bending over him*). It has only been a dreadful fancy of yours, Oswald. Nothing but fancy. All this upset has been bad for you. But now you will get some rest, at home with your own mother, my darling boy. You shall have everything you want, just as you did when you were a little child.—There, now. The attack is over. You see how easily it passed off! I knew it would.—And look, Oswald, what a lovely day we are going to have? Brilliant sunshine. Now you will be able to see your home properly.

[*She goes to the table and puts out the lamp. It is sunrise. The glaciers and peaks in the distance are seen bathed in bright morning light.*]

OSWALD (*who has been sitting motionless in the armchair, with his back to the scene outside, suddenly says*). Mother, give me the sun.

MRS. ALVING (*standing at the table, and looking at him in amazement*). What do you say?

OSWALD (*repeats in a dull, toneless voice*). The sun—the sun.

MRS. ALVING (*going up to him*). Oswald, what is the matter with you? (OSWALD *seems to shrink up in the chair; all his muscles relax; his face loses its expression, and his eyes stare stupidly.* MRS. ALVING *is trembling with terror.*) What is it? (*Screams.*) Oswald! What is the matter with you? (*Throws herself on her knees beside him and shakes him.*) Oswald! Oswald! Look at me! Don't you know me?

OSWALD (*in an expressionless voice, as before*). The sun—the sun.

MRS. ALVING. (*Jumps up despairingly, beats her head with her hands, and screams.*) I can't bear it! (*Whispers at though paralyzed with fear.*) I can't bear it! Never! (*Suddenly.*) Where has he got it? (*Passes her hand quickly over his coat.*) Here! (*Draws back a little way and cries:*) No, no, no!—Yes!—no, no!

[*She stands a few steps from him, her hands thrust into her hair, and stares at him in speechless terror.*]

OSWALD (*sitting motionless, as before*). The sun—the sun.

CRITICAL COMMENTARY

It is regularly decided that plays like *Ghosts* are dead or should be, but in fact the kind of drama that includes the problem play appears to be naturally indestructible. It seems to reflect life as it is and to satisfy our compulsion to talk about it. Ibsen himself liked the sweeping pronouncement (small-town life is swinish; Rome is the Forest of Arden; a little fresh air from the prairies of America will blow everything clear; the Ark should have been torpedoed), but by the time of *Ghosts* (1881), when he was 53, he had learned to channel this fondness for the big conclusion into a dramatic form designed to multiply rather than solve problems and to leave the subject open, like life itself, for endless discussion.

The play opens not only with some well-made exposition and planting of clues but also with a thicket of problems. Should Regina help her aging father open a marine restaurant and private whorehouse, or should she stay with the wealthy and cultured Mrs. Alving and her son Oswald and teach in the new orphanage? Can a girl safely rise above her working-class origins? Does education make a person unfit for a life of humble service? Does an occupation like carpentering or the merchant marine inevitably coarsen a man? Can a marriage survive if the husband's work takes him away from home? Are all women romantic daydreamers? Is gentility a sham? And so on.

If this sounds embarrassingly like girl-talk, it can easily be elevated to a more impressive masculine level. "My generation of undergraduates —that of the nineteen thirties," recalls old grad Eric Bentley,

> reserved its greatest contempt for the person who was "only interested in saving his soul" and was therefore neglecting the real task, that of changing the world. We didn't realize to what an appalling extent the motive force of our reforming zeal was fear of the self, a failure to face the self. . . . Consider Mrs. Alving, the individualist as woman. We know that she reads the right books, though Ibsen leaves them unnamed so that each spectator can supply the titles of his own favorites. She belongs to the nineteenth-century Enlightenment. But we find out that she achieves enlightenment in general while keeping herself ignorant in particular of precisely those two or three things which it would do her most

> good to know. . . . When she tells Oswald—at the end—that she shared the blame, because, in her prudishness, her fear of sexuality, she had not welcomed Alving's joy of life, she is also telling herself. Catastrophe, in this story, plays, as it were, the role of psychoanalysis, bringing to consciousness the guilty facts which the protagonist has so zealously kept under. Mrs. Alving, reader of books, has come to know many things; she has not come to know herself. She is not too much an individual, as Manders thinks, but too little. (Rolf Fjelde, ed., *Ibsen* [Twentieth Century Views], 1965, p. 13.)

It is a short step from this to even greater profundities, combining *Ghosts,* life, and a wide range of world masterpieces. "One may see, in *Ghosts,*" with the help of Francis Fergusson,

> behind the surfaces of the savage story, a partially realized tragic form of really poetic scope, the result of Ibsen's more serious and disinterested brooding upon the human condition in general, where it underlies the myopic rebellions and empty clichés of the time. . . . The underlying form of *Ghosts* is that of the tragic rhythm as one finds it in *Oedipus Rex*. . . . As Ibsen was fighting to present his poetic vision within the narrow theater admitted by modern realism, so his protagonist Mrs. Alving is fighting to realize her sense of human life in the blank photograph of her own stuffy parlor. She discovers there no means, no terms, and no nourishment; that is the truncated tragedy which underlies the savage thesis of the play. But she does find her son Oswald, and she makes of him the symbol of all she is seeking: freedom, innocence, joy, and truth. . . . The question of Oswald is at the center. . . . His appearance produces what the Greeks would have called a complex recognition scene, with an implied peripety. . . . It does not have the verbal music of Racine, nor the freedom and sophistication of Hamlet, nor the scope of the Sophoclean chorus. . . . But in the total situation in the Alving parlor . . . it has its own hidden poetry . . . a poetry of the histrionic sensibility. (*The Idea of a Theater,* 1953, pp. 163 ff.)

Either way, girl-talk or masculine profundity, the play itself is no impediment, and it is not meant to be. Although its particulars are localized and dated, they transpose easily into the spectators's own language and interest. Criticism of *Ghosts* and other problem plays ordinarily takes the form of the crib, in which a digest of the play is followed by loosely related speculation. This readily assumes the shape of the formula that stimulated it: a reduction of experience to imperfect twin options, which then double and redouble in all directions. Personality, for example, consists of a public exterior and a private interior. The latter is either hidden evil or repressed good. The former is either a hypocritical mask or an attempt at Spartan character. Girls are either upper class or lower class. If they are the former, their wedding night is a terrible shock; if they are the latter, they become the victims of the frustrated husbands of the wives who have been shocked into frigidity. And so on. But isn't that life for you? Or is it soap opera? And what is wrong with soap opera? Or again, on a more impressive masculine level, isn't the theme of the problem play the same as the recurrent plague in Greek tragedy or the universal "policy" in *The Jew of Malta* or the history-as-usual in *Henry IV*? Or are the tone and context different? At any rate, isn't the problem play more true to life because it excludes abnormal theatrical interlopers like Oedipus or Falstaff or Tartuffe, and unbelievable successes like Hal or Face?

Useful Criticism

Bentley, Eric. *The Playwright as Thinker.** New York: Noonday Press, 1955.

Brustein, Robert. *The Theatre of Revolt.** Boston: Atlantic-Little, Brown, 1964.

Fergusson, Francis. *The Idea of a Theater.** Garden City, N.Y.: Doubleday, 1953.

Fjelde, Rolf, ed. *Ibsen** (Twentieth Century Views). Englewood Cliffs, N.J.: Prentice-Hall, 1965.

* Available in paperback.

THE CHERRY ORCHARD

Anton Chekhov

Translated by JENNIE COVAN

CHARACTERS

LIUBOFF ANDREIEVNA RANEVSKAYA, a landowner

ANYA, her daughter, aged seventeen

VARYA, her adopted daughter, aged twenty-seven

LEONID ANDREIEVITCH GAIEFF, Liuboff Andreievna's brother

YERMOLAI ALEXEIEVITCH LOPAKHIN, a merchant

PETER SERGEIEVITCH TROFIMOFF, a student

BORIS BORISOVITCH SEMYONOFF-PISHCHIK, a landowner

CHARLOTTA IVANOVNA, a governess

SEMYON PANTELEIEVITCH YEPIKHODOFF, a clerk

DUNYASHA (AVDOTYA FYODOROVNA), a maidservant

FIRCE, an old footman, aged eighty-seven

YASHA, a young footman

A TRAMP

A STATION-MASTER

POST-OFFICE CLERK

GUESTS

A SERVANT

SCENE

Mme. Ranevskaya's estate.

ACT I

A room still called the nursery. One of the doors leads into ANYA*'s room. It is almost sunrise of a day in May. The cherry-trees are in bloom, but the chill of early morning is in the garden. The windows are shut.*

[DUNYASHA *enters with a candle, and* LOPAKHIN *with a book in his hand.*]

LOPAKHIN. The train has arrived, thank God. What's the time?

DUNYASHA. It will soon be two. (*Blows out candle.*) It is already light.

LOPAKHIN. How late was the train? At least two hours. (*Yawns and stretches himself.*) I certainly made a fool of myself! I came here on purpose to meet them at the station, and then overslept myself . . . in my chair. It's a pity. I wish you'd called me.

DUNYASHA. I thought you'd gone. (*Listening.*) I think I hear them coming.

LOPAKHIN (*listens*). No . . . They have to collect their baggage and so on. . . . (*Pause.*) Liuboff Andreievna has been living abroad for five years; I don't know what she'll be like now . . . She's a good sort—an easy, simple person. I remember when I was a boy of fifteen, my father, who is dead—he used to keep a shop in the village here—hit me with his fist, and my nose bled . . . We had gone into the yard for something or other, and he was a little drunk. Libuoff Andreievna, as I remember her now, was still young, and very slight, and she took me to the wash-stand here in this very room, the nursery. She said, "Don't cry, my small peasant, all wounds heal at last," (*Pause.*) . . . Small peasant! My father was a peasant, true, but here I am in a white vest and brown shoes . . . like a pearl in an oyster shell. I'm rich now, with lots of money, but just think about it and examine me, and you'll find I'm still a peasant to the core. (*Turns over the pages of his book.*) Here I've been reading this book, but I understand nothing. I read and fell asleep. (*Pause.*)

DUNYASHA. The dogs didn't sleep all night; they feel that their masters are coming.

LOPAKHIN. What's the matter with you, Dunyasha. . . .

DUNYASHA. My hands are shaking. I am going to faint.

LOPAKHIN. You're too sensitive, Dunyasha. You dress just like a lady, and you do your hair like one, too. You shouldn't. You must remember your place in life.

YEPIKHODOFF (*enters with a bouquet. He wears a short jacket and brilliantly polished boots which squeak audibly. He drops the bouquet as he enters, then picks it up*). The gardener sent these; says they're to go into the dining-room. (*Gives the bouquet to* DUNYASHA.)

LOPAKHIN. And you'll bring me some kvass.

DUNYASHA. Yes, sir.

[*Exit.*]

YEPIKHODOFF. There's a frost this morning—three degrees, and the cherry-trees are all in flower. I can't approve of our climate. (*Sighs.*) I can't. Our climate refuses to favor us even this once. And, Yermolai Alexeievitch, allow me to say to you, in addition, that I bought myself a pair of boots two days ago, and I beg to assure you that they squeak in a perfectly intolerable manner. What shall I put on them?

LOPAKHIN. Go away. You bore me.

YEPIKHODOFF. Some misfortune happens to me every day. But I don't complain; I'm used to it, and I even smile at it. (DUNYASHA *comes in and brings* LOPAKHIN *a glass of kvass.*) I am going. (*Knocks over a chair.*) There. . . . (*Triumphantly.*) There, you see, if I may use the word, what circumstances I am in, so to speak. It is simply extraordinary.

[*Exit.*]

DUNYASHA. Let me confess to you, Yermolai Alexeievitch, that Yepikhodoff has proposed to me.

LOPAKHIN. Ah!

DUNYASHA. I don't know what to do about it. He's a nice young man, but every now and then, when he begins talking, you can't understand a word he says. It sounds sincere enough, only I can't understand it. I think I like him. He's madly in love with me. He's an unlucky man; every day something happens to him. We tease him about it. They call him "Two-and-twenty troubles."

LOPAKHIN (*listens*). There they come, I think.

DUNYASHA. They're coming! What's the matter with me? I'm cold all over.

LOPAKHIN. There they are, really. Let's go and meet them. Will she know me? We haven't seen each other for five years.

DUNYASHA (*excited*). I shall faint in a minute. . . . Oh, I'm fainting!

[*Two carriages are heard driving up to the house.* LOPAKHIN *and* DUNYASHA *quickly go out. The stage is empty. There are noises in the adjoining rooms.* FIRCE, *leaning on a stick, walks quickly across the stage; he has just been to meet* LIUBOFF ANDREIEVNA. *He wears an old-fashioned livery and a tall hat. He is saying something to himself, but not a word can be made out. The noise back stage grows louder and louder. A voice is heard: "Let's go in there." Enter* LIUBOFF ANDREIEVNA, ANYA, *and* CHARLOTTA IVANOVNA *leading a little dog on a chain, all dressed in traveling clothes,* VARYA *in a long coat and with a kerchief on her head.* GAIEFF, SEMYONOFF-PISHCHIK, LOPAKHIN, DUNYASHA *with a parcel and an umbrella, and a servant with suitcases—all cross the room.*]

ANYA. Let's go through here. Do you remember this room, mother?

LIUBOFF (*joyfully, through her tears*). The nursery!

VARYA. How cold it is! My hands are quite numb. (*To* LIUBOFF ANDREIEVNA.) Your rooms, the white one and the violet one, are just as they used to be, mother.

LIUBOFF. My dear, beautiful nursery . . . I used to sleep here when I was a baby. (*Kisses her brother, then* VARYA, *then her brother again.*) And Varya is just as she used to be, exactly like a nun. And I recognized Dunyasha. (*Kisses her.*)

GAIEFF. The train was two hours late. There now; how's that for punctuality?

CHARLOTTA (*to* PISHCHIK). My dog eats nuts, too.

PISHCHIK (*astonished*). Just imagine!

[*All leave except* ANYA *and* DUNYASHA.]

DUNYASHA. We did have to wait for you! (*Takes off* ANYA*'s cloak and hat.*)

ANYA. For four nights on the journey I didn't sleep . . . I'm awfully cold.

DUNYASHA. You left during Lent, when it was snowing and frosty, but now? Darling! (*Laughs and kisses her.*) We did have to wait for you, my darling pet! . . . I must tell you at once, I can't wait a minute.

ANYA (*listlessly*). Something else now . . . ?

DUNYASHA. The clerk, Yepikhodoff, proposed to me after Easter.

ANYA. Always the same . . . (*Puts her hair straight.*) I've lost all my hairpins . . . (*She is very tired, and even staggers as she walks.*)

DUNYASHA. I don't know what to think about it. He loves me, he loves me so much!

ANYA (*looks into her room; in a gentle voice*). My room, my windows, as if I'd never left! I'm at home! Tomorrow morning I'll get up and run out into the garden. . . . Oh, if I could only sleep! I didn't sleep the whole journey, I was so restless.

DUNYASHA. Peter Sergeievitch came two days ago.

ANYA. (*joyfully*). Peter!

DUNYASHA. He sleeps in the bath-house, he lives there. He said he was afraid he'd be in the way. (*Looks at her watch.*) I should call him, but Varvara Mihkailovna told me not to. "Don't wake him," she said.

[*Enter* VARYA, *a bunch of keys hanging from her belt.*]

VARYA. Dunyasha, coffee, quick. Mother wishes some.

DUNYASHA. In a moment.

[*Exit.*]

VARYA. Well, you've come, thank God. Home again. (*Caressing her.*) My darling is home again! My pretty one is back at last!

ANYA. I had an awful time, I tell you.

VARYA. I can just imagine it!

ANYA. I went away in Holy Week; it was very cold then. Charlotta talked the whole way and would go on performing her tricks. Why did you force her on me?

VARYA. You couldn't go alone, darling, at seventeen!

ANYA. We went to Paris; it's cold there and snowing. I talk French perfectly dreadfully. My mother lives on the fifth floor. I go to her, and find her there with several Frenchmen, women, an old abbé with a book, and everything wreathed in tobacco smoke and the whole place so uninviting. I suddenly became very sorry for mother—so sorry that I took her head in my arms and hugged her and wouldn't let her go. Then mother started hugging me and crying. . . .

VARYA (*weeping*). Don't say any more, don't say any more . . .

ANYA. She's already sold her villa near Mentone; she has nothing left, nothing. And I haven't a kopeck either; we only just managed to get here. And mother won't understand! We had dinner at a station; she asked for all the expensive things, and tipped the waiters one ruble each. And Charlotta too. Yasha demands a share, too—It is simply awful. Mother has a footman now, Yasha; we've brought him along.

ANYA. How's business? Has the interest been paid?

VARYA. Not much chance of that.

ANYA. Oh God, oh God . . .

VARYA. The place will be sold in August.

ANYA. Oh God . . .

LOPAKHIN (*looks in at the door and moos*). Moo!

[*Exit.*]

VARYA (*through her tears*). I'd like to . . . (*Shakes her fist.*)

ANYA (*embraces* VARYA, *softly*). Varya, has he proposed to you? (VARYA *shakes her head.*) But he loves you. . . . Why don't you decide? Why do you keep on waiting?

VARYA. I'm afraid it will all come to nothing. He's a busy man. I'm not his sort . . . he pays no attention to me. Bless the man, I don't wish to see him. . . . But everybody talks about our marriage, everybody congratulates me, and there's nothing in it at all, it's all like a dream. (*A different voice.*) You have a brooch that looks like a bee.

ANYA (*wistfully*). Mother bought it. (*Goes into her room, and talks lightly, like a child.*) In Paris I went up in a balloon!

VARYA. My darling has come back, my pretty one is home again! (DUNYASHA *has already returned with the coffee-pot and is making coffee.*) I go about all day, looking after the house, and I think all the time, if only you could marry a rich man, I'd be happy and would go away somewhere by myself, perhaps to Kieff . . . or to Moscow, and so on, from one holy place to another. I'd tramp and tramp. That would be splendid!

ANYA. The birds are singing in the garden. What time is it now?

VARYA. It must be getting on towards three. It's time you went to sleep. darling. (*Goes into* ANYA*'s room.*) Splendid!

[*Enter* YASHA *with a plaid shawl and a traveling bag.*]

YASHA (*crossing the stage; politely*). May I go this way?

DUNYASHA. I hardly recognized you, Yasha. You have changed abroad.

YASHA. Hm . . . and who are you?

DUNYASHA. When you went away I was only so high. (*Showing with her hand.*) I'm Dunyasha, the daughter of Fyodor Kozoyedoff. You don't remember?

YASHA. Oh, you small cucumber! (*Looks round and embraces her. She screams and drops a saucer.* YASHA *goes out quickly.*)

VARYA (*in the doorway, in an angry voice*). What's that?

DUNYASHA (*through her tears*). I've broken a saucer.

VARYA. It may bring luck.

ANYA (*coming out of her room*). We must tell mother that Peter's here.

VARYA. I told them not to call him.

ANYA (*thoughtfully*). Father died six years ago, and a month later my brother Grisha was drowned in the river—such a dear little boy of seven! Mother couldn't bear it; she went away, away, without looking round. . . . (*Shudders.*) How I understand her; if only she knew! (*Pause.*) And Peter Trofimoff was Grisha's tutor, he might remind her. . . .

[*Enter* FIRCE *in a short jacket and white vest. Goes to the coffee-pot.*]

FIRCE. Madame is going to have a bite here. (*He is preoccupied, putting on white gloves.*) Is the coffee ready? (*To* DUNYASHA, *severely.*) You!

DUNYASHA. Oh, dear me . . . ! (*Leaving hurriedly.*)

FIRCE (*fussing round the coffee-pot*). Oh, you bungler . . . (*Murmurs to himself.*) Back from Paris. . . . the master went to Paris once . . . in a carriage . . . (*Laughs.*)

VARYA. What are you mumbling, Firce?

FIRCE. I beg your pardon? (*Joyfully.*) The mistress is home again. I've lived to see her! I don't care if I die now . . . (*Weeps with joy.*)

[*Enter* LIUBOFF ANDREIEVNA, GAIEFF, LOPAKHIN, *and* SEMYONOFF-PISHCHIK, *the latter in a long jacket of thin cloth and loose trousers.* GAIEFF, *coming in, moves his arms and body about as if he were playing billiards.*]

LIUBOFF. Let me remember now. Red into the corner! Twice into the center!

GAIEFF. Right into the pocket! Once upon a time you and I, sister, both slept in this room, and now I'm fifty-one; it does seem strange.

LOPAKHIN. Yes, time does fly!

GAIEFF. What?

LOPAKHIN. I said that time does fly.

GAIEFF. It smells of patchouli here.

ANYA. I'm going to bed. Good-night, mother. (*Kisses her.*)

LIUBOFF. My dear little child. (*Kisses her hand.*) Glad to be at home? I can't get over it.

ANYA. Good-night, uncle.

GAIEFF (*kisses her face and hands*). God be with you. How you do resemble your mother! (*To his sister.*) You were just like her at her age, Liuba.

[ANYA *gives her hand to* LOPAKHIN *and* PISHCHIK *and goes out shutting the door behind her.*]

LIUBOFF. She's awfully tired.

PISHCHIK. It's a very long journey.

VARYA (*to* LOPAKHIN *and* PISHCHIK). Well, gentlemen, it's getting on toward three. High time to retire.

LIUBOFF (*laughs*). You're just the same as ever, Varya. (*Draws her close and kisses her.*) I'll have some coffee now; then we'll all go. (FIRCE *lays a cushion under her feet.*) Thank you, dear. I'm used to coffee. I drink it day and night. Thank you, dear old man. (*Kisses* FIRCE.)

VARYA. I'll go and see whether they've brought in all the luggage.

[*Exit.*]

LIUBOFF. Is it really I who am sitting here? (*Laughs.*) I feel like jumping about and waving my arms. (*Covers her face with her hands.*) But suppose I'm dreaming! God knows I love my own country, I love it dearly; I couldn't look out of the railway carriage, I cried so much. (*Through her tears.*) Still, I must have my coffee. Thank you, Firce. Thank you, dear old man. I'm so glad you're still with us.

FIRCE. The day before yesterday.

GAIEFF. He doesn't hear well.

LOPAKHIN. I have to go to Kharkoff by the five o'clock train. I'm awfully sorry! I should like to have a look at you, to gossip a little. You're as fine-looking as ever.

PISHCHIK (*breathes heavily*). Even finer-looking . . . dressed in Paris fashion . . . confound it all.

LOPAKHIN. Your brother, Leonid Andreievitch, says I'm a snob, a usurer, but that is absolutely nothing to me. Let him talk. Only I do wish you would believe in me as you once did, that your wonderful, touching eyes would look at me as they used to. Merciful God! My father was the serf of your grandfather and your own father, but you—more than anybody else—did so much for me once upon a time that I've forgotten everything and love you as if you were one of my own family . . . and even more.

LIUBOFF. I can't sit still, I can't! (*Jumps up and walks about in great excitement.*) I'll never survive this happiness. . . . You can laugh at me; I'm a silly woman . . . My dear little cupboard. (*Kisses cupboard.*) My little table.

GAIEFF. Nurse died during your absence.

LIUBOFF (*sits and drinks coffee*). Yes, God rest her soul. I heard by letter.

GAIEFF. And Anastasia died, too. Peter Kosoy has left me and now lives in town with the Commissioner of Police. (*Takes a box of candy out of his pocket and sucks a piece.*)

PISHCHIK. My daughter, Dashenka, sends her love.

LOPAKHIN. I wish to say something very pleasant, very delightful, to you. (*Looks at his watch.*) I'm going away at once, I haven't much time . . . but I'll tell you all about it in two or three words. As you already know, your cherry orchard is to be sold to pay your debts, and the sale is arranged for August 22; but you needn't be alarmed, dear madam, you may sleep in peace; there's a way out. Here's my plan. Please listen carefully! Your estate is only thirteen miles from town, the railway runs past it and if the cherry orchard and the land by the river are broken up into building parcels and are then leased as villa sites, you'll have at least twenty-five thousand rubles a year income.

GAIEFF. How utterly absurd!

LIUBOFF. I don't understand you at all, Yermolai Alexeievitch.

LOPAKHIN. You will get twenty-five rubles a year for each dessiatine from the leaseholders at the very least, and if you advertise now, I'm willing to bet that you won't have a vacant parcel left by the autumn; they'll all go. In a word, you're saved. I congratulate you. Only, of course, you'll have to straighten things out carefully . . . For instance, you'll have to pull down all the old buildings, this house, which is of no use to anybody now, and cut down the old cherry orchard. . . .

LIUBOFF. Cut it down? My dear man, you must forgive me, but you don't understand anything at all. If there's anything interesting or remarkable in the whole province, it's this cherry orchard of ours.

LOPAKHIN. The only remarkable thing about the orchard is its great size. It bears fruit only every other year, and even then you don't know what to do with the cherries; nobody buys any.

GAIEFF. This orchard is mentioned in the "Encyclopaedia."

LOPAKHIN (*looks at his watch*). If we can't think of anything and don't make up our minds, then on August 22 both the cherry orchard and the whole estate will be sold at auction. Make up your mind! I swear there's no other way out. You may believe me!

FIRCE. In the old days, forty or fifty years ago, they dried the cherries, soaked them and pickled them, and made jam, and it used to happen that . . .

GAIEFF. Be quiet, Firce.

FIRCE. And then we'd send the dried cherries in carts to Moscow and Kharkoff. And money! And the dried cherries were soft, juicy, sweet, and fragrant. They knew the way. . . .

LIUBOFF. How was it done?

FIRCE. They've forgotten. Nobody remembers.

PISHCHIK (*to* LIUBOFF ANDREIEVNA). What about Paris? Eh? Did you eat frogs?

LIUBOFF. I ate crocodiles.

PISHCHIK. Just imagine!

LOPAKHIN. Formerly there were only the gentry and the laborers, in the villages, and now the people who live in villas have arrived. All towns now, even small ones, are surrounded by villas. And it's safe to say that in twenty years' time the villa residents will have increased tremendously. At present they sit on their balconies, and drink tea, but it may well happen that they'll commence to cultivate their patches of land, and then your cherry orchard will be happy, rich, glorious.

GAIEFF (*angry*). What nonsense!

[*Enter* VARYA *and* YASHA.]

VARYA. There are two telegrams for you, mother dear. (*Picks out a key and noisily unlocks an antique cupboard.*) Here they are.

LIUBOFF. They're from Paris . . . (*Tears them up without reading them.*) I'm through with Paris.

GAIEFF. And do you know, Liuba, how old this cupboard is? A week ago I pulled out the bottom drawer; I looked and saw numbers carved in it. That cupboard was made exactly a hundred years ago. What do you think of that? What? We could celebrate its jubilee. It hasn't a soul of its own, but still, say what you will, it's a fine piece of furniture.

PISHCHIK (*astonished*). A hundred years . . . Just imagine!

GAIEFF. Yes . . . it's a genuine thing. (*Examining it.*) My dear and honored cupboard! I congratulate you on your career, which has for more than a hundred years been devoted to the noble ideals of good and justice; your silent call to productive labor has not decreased in the hundred years (*Weeping.*) during which you have inspired in our generation virtue and courage and faith for a better future, holding before our eyes lofty ideals and the knowledge of a common consciousness. (*Pause.*)

LOPAKHIN. Yes.

LIUBOFF. You're just the same as ever, Leon.

GAIEFF (*a little confused*). Off the white on the right, into the corner pocket. Red ball goes into the center pocket!

LOPAKHIN (*looks at his watch*). It's time I went.

YASHA (*giving* LIUBOFF ANDREIEVNA *her medicine*). Will you take your pills now?

PISHCHIK. You shouldn't take medicines, dearest; they do you neither harm nor good . . . Give them to me, dearest. (*Takes the pills, turns them out into the palm of his hand, blows on them, puts them into his mouth, and drinks some kvass.*) There!

LIUBOFF (*frightened*). You're mad!

PISHCHIK. I've swallowed all the pills.

LOPAKHIN. You greedy man! (*All laugh.*)

FIRCE. They were here in Easter week and ate half a pailful of cucumbers . . . (*Mumbles.*)

LIUBOFF. What does he mean?

VARYA. He's been mumbling away for three years. We're used to that.

YASHA. Senile decay.

[CHARLOTTA IVANOVNA *crosses the stage, dressed in white; she is very thin and tightly laced; she has a lorgnette at her waist.*]

LOPAKHIN. Excuse me, Charlotta Ivanovna, I haven't bidden you welcome yet. (*Tries to kiss her hand.*)

CHARLOTTA (*Takes her hand away*). If you let people kiss your hand, then they'll want your elbow, then your shoulder, and then . . .

LOPAKHIN. I'm out of luck today! (*All laugh.*) Show us a trick, Charlotta Ivanovna!

LIUBOFF. Charlotta, do a trick for us!

CHARLOTTA. It's not necessary. I must go to bed.

[*Exit.*]

LOPAKHIN. We shall see each other in three weeks. (*Kisses* LIUBOFF ANDREIEVNA'*s hand.*) Now, good-bye. It's time I went. (*To* GAIEFF.) See you again. (*Kisses* PISHCHIK.) Au revoir. (*Gives his hand to* VARYA, *then to* FIRCE *and to* YASHA.) I don't want to go away. (*To* LIUBOFF ANDREIEVNA.) If you think about the villas and come to a decision, just let me know, and I'll raise a loan of 50,000 rubles at once. Think about it seriously.

VARYA (*angrily*). Do go, now!

LOPAKHIN. I'm going, I'm going. . . .

[*Exit.*]

GAIEFF. Snob. Still, I beg pardon . . . Varya's going to marry him, he's Varya's young man.

VARYA. Don't talk too much, uncle.

LIUBOFF. Why not, Varya? I should be glad of it. He's a good man.

PISHCHIK. To speak the honest truth . . . he's a worthy man . . . And my Dashenka . . . also says that . . . she says lots of things. (*Snores, but wakes up again at once.*) But still, dear madam, if you could lend me . . . 240 rubles . . . to pay the interest on my mortgage tomorrow . . .

VARYA (*frightened*). We haven't it, we haven't it!

LIUBOFF. It's quite true. I've nothing at all.

PISHCHIK. You'll manage somehow. (*Laughs.*) I never lose hope. I used to think, "Everything's lost now. I'm a dead man," when, lo and behold, a railway was built across my land . . . and they paid me for it. And something else will happen today or tomorrow. Dashenka may win 20,000 rubles . . . she's got a lottery ticket.

LIUBOFF. The coffee's all gone, we can go to bed.

FIRCE (*brushing* GAIEFF'*s trousers; in an insistent tone*). You are wearing the wrong trousers again. What am I to do with you?

VARYA (*quietly*). Anya's asleep. (*Opens window quietly.*) The sun has risen already; it isn't cold. Look, mother, dear; what lovely trees! And the air! The starlings are singing!

GAIEFF (*opens the other window*). The whole garden is white. You haven't forgotten, Liuba? There's that long avenue going straight, straight, like an arrow; it shines on moonlight nights. Do you remember? You haven't forgotten?

LIUBOFF (*looks into the garden*). Oh, my childhood, days of my innocence! In this nursery I used to sleep; I used to look out from here into the orchard. Happiness used to wake with me every morning, and then it was just as it is now; nothing has changed. (*Laughs with joy.*) It's all, all white! Oh, my orchard! After the dreary autumns and the cold winters, you're young again, full of happiness, the angels of heaven haven't left you . . . If only I could take this strong burden from my breast and shoulders, if I could forget my past!

GAIEFF. Yes, and they'll sell this orchard to pay off the debts. How strange it seems!

LIUBOFF. Look, there's my dead mother walking in the orchard . . . dressed in white! (*Laughs with joy.*) That's she.

GAIEFF. Where?

VARYA. God be with you, mother dear!

LIUBOFF. Nobody is there; I thought I saw somebody. On the right, at the turning by the summer-house, a little white tree bent down, resembling a woman. (*Enter* TROFIMOFF *in a worn student uniform and spectacles.*) What a marvelous garden! White masses of flowers, the blue sky. . . .

TROFIMOFF. Liuboff Andreievna! (*She looks round at him.*) I only wish to pay my respects to you, and I'll go away. (*Kisses her hand warmly.*) I was told to wait till the morning, but I didn't have the patience. (LIUBOFF ANDREIEVNA *looks surprised.*)

VARYA (*crying*). It's Peter Trofimoff.

TROFIMOFF. Peter Trofimoff, once the tutor of your Grisha . . . Have I changed so much? (LIUBOFF ANDREIEVNA *embraces him and cries softly.*)

GAIEFF (*confused*). That's enough, that's enough, Liuba.

VARYA (*weeps*). But I told you, Peter, to wait till tomorrow.

LIUBOFF. My Grisha . . . my boy . . . Grisha . . . my son.

VARYA. What are we to do, dear mother? It's the will of God.

TROFIMOFF (*softly, through his tears*). It's all right, it's all right.

LIUBOFF (*still weeping*). My boy's dead; he was drowned. Why? Why, my friend? (*Softly.*) Anya's asleep in there. I am speaking so loudly, making so much noise . . . Well, Peter? What's made you look so bad? Why have you grown so old?

TROFIMOFF. In the train an old woman called me a decayed gentleman.

LIUBOFF. You were quite a boy then, a jolly little student, and now your hair has grown thin and you wear spectacles. Are you really still a student? (*Goes to the door.*)

TROFIMOFF. I suppose I shall always be a student.

LIUBOFF (*kisses her brother, then* VARYA). Well, let's go to bed . . . And you've grown older, Leonid.

PISHCHIK (*follows her*). Yes, we must go to bed . . . Oh, my gout! I'll stay the night here. If only, Liuboff Andreievna, my dear, you could get me 240 rubles tomorrow morning—

GAIEFF. Still the same story.

PISHCHIK. Two hundred and forty rubles . . . to pay the interest on the mortgage.

LIUBOFF. I haven't any money, dear man.

PISHCHIK. I'll give it back . . . it's a small sum . . .

LIUBOFF. Well then, Leonid will give it to you . . . Let him have it, Leonid.

GAIEFF. By all means; hold out your hand.

LIUBOFF. Why not? He wants it; he'll give it back.

[LIUBOFF ANDREIEVNA, TROFIMOFF, PISHCHIK *and* FIRCE *go out.* GAIEFF, VARYA, *and* YASHA *remain.*]

GAIEFF. My sister hasn't lost the habit of throwing money away. (*To* YASHA.) Don't come near me: you smell like a chicken-coop!

YASHA (*grins*). You are just the same as ever, Leonid Andreievitch.

GAIEFF. Really? (*To* VARYA.) What's he saying?

VARYA (*to* YASHA). Your mother has come from the village; she's been sitting in the servants' room since yesterday, and wishes to see you . . .

YASHA. Bless the woman!

VARYA. Shameless man.

YASHA. A lot of use there is in her coming. She might just as well have come tomorrow.

[*Exit.*]

VARYA. Mother hasn't altered a bit, she's just as she always was. She'd give away everything, if the idea only entered her head.

GAIEFF. Yes . . . (*Pause.*) If there's any illness for which people have a remedy of remedies, you may be sure that particular illness is incurable. I work my brains as hard as I can. I've several remedies, very many, and that really means I've none at all. It would be nice to inherit a fortune from somebody, it would be nice to marry off our Anya to a rich man, it would be nice to go to Yaroslavl and try my luck with my aunt the Countess. My aunt is very, very rich.

VARYA (*weeps*). If only God would help us.

GAIEFF. Don't cry. My aunt's very rich, but she doesn't like us. My sister, in the first place, married a lawyer, not an aristocrat . . . (ANYA *appears in the doorway.*) She not only married a man who was not an aristocrat, but she behaved in a way which cannot be described as proper. She's nice and kind and charming and I'm very fond of her, but say what you will in her favor and you still have to admit that she's bad; you can feel it in her slightest movements.

VARYA (*whispers*). Anya's in the doorway.

GAIEFF. Really? (*Pause.*) It's curious, something's blown into my right eye . . . I can't see out of it properly. And on Thursday, when I was at the District Court . . .

[*Enter* ANYA.]

VARYA. Why aren't you in bed, Anya?

ANYA. I can't sleep. It's no use.

GAIEFF. My darling. (*Kisses* ANYA'*s face and hands.*) My child. (*Crying.*) You're not my niece, you're my angel, you're my all . . . Believe in me, believe . . . .

ANYA. I do believe you, uncle. Everybody loves and respects you . . .

but, uncle dear, you should say nothing, no more than that. What were you saying just now about my mother, about your own sister! Why did you say such things?

GAIEFF. Yes, yes. (*Covers his face with her hand.*) Yes, really, it was terrible. Save me, my God! And only just now I made a speech before a cupboard . . . it's so silly! And only when I'd finished I knew how silly it was.

VARYA. Yes, uncle dear, you really should say less. Keep quiet, that's all.

ANYA. You'd be so much happier if you only kept quiet.

GAIEFF. All right, I'll be quiet. (*Kisses their hands.*) I'll be quiet. But let's talk business. On Thursday I was in the District Court, and a lot of us met there and we began to talk of this, that, and the other, and now I think I can arrange a loan to pay the interest to the bank.

VARYA. If only God would help us!

GAIEFF. I'll go on Tuesday. I'll talk to you about it again. (*To* VARYA.) Don't cry. (*To* ANYA.) Your mother will have a talk with Lopakhin; he, of course, won't refuse . . . And when you've rested you'll go to Yaroslavl to the Countess, your grandmother. So you see, we shall have three irons in the fire, and we shall be safe. We'll pay the interest. I'm certain. (*Puts some candy in his mouth.*) I swear on my honor, on anything you wish, that the estate will not be sold! (*Excitedly.*) I swear on my happiness! Here's my hand on it! You may call me a dishonorable sinner if I let it be sold at auction! I swear by all I am!

ANYA (*calm again and happy*). How good and clever you are, uncle. (*Embraces him.*) I'm happy now! I'm happy! All's well!

[*Enter* FIRCE.]

FIRCE (*reproachfully*). Leonid Andreievitch, don't you fear God? When are you going to bed?

GAIEFF. Soon, soon. You go away, Firce! I'll undress myself. Well, children, au revoir . . . ! I'll tell you the details tomorrow, but let's go to bed now. (*Kisses* ANYA *and* VARYA.) I'm a man of the eighties . . . People don't praise those years much, but I can still say that I've suffered for my beliefs. The peasants don't love me for nothing, I assure you. We have to learn how to understand the peasants! We should learn how . . .

ANYA. You're doing it again, uncle!

VARYA. Be quiet, uncle!

FIRCE (*angrily*). Leonid Andreievitch!

GAIEFF. I'm coming, I'm coming . . . Go to bed now. Off two cushions into the center! I turn over a new leaf . . .

[*Exit.* FIRCE *goes out after him.*]

ANYA. I'm more quiet now. I don't wish to go to Yaroslavl, I don't like grandmother; but I'm calm now, thanks to uncle. (*Sits down.*)

VARYA. It's time to go to sleep. I'll go. There have been amazing things happening here during your absence. In the old servants' quarter of the house, as you know, only the old people live—little old Yefim and Polya and Yevstigny, and Karp as well. They commenced letting tramps or the like spend the night there—I said nothing. Then I heard that they were saying I had ordered them to be fed on peas and nothing else; from meanness, you see . . . And it was all Yevstigny's doing. Very well, I thought, if that's what the matter is, just you wait. So I call Yevstigny . . . (*Yawns.*) He comes. "What's this," I say. "Yevstigny, you old fool" . . . (*Looks at* ANYA.) Anya dear! (*Pause.*) She's dozed off . . . (*Takes* ANYA'S *arm.*) Let's go to bed . . . Come along! . . . (*Leads her.*) My darling's gone to sleep! Come on . . . (*They go. In the distance, the other side of the orchard, a shepherd plays his pipe.* TROFIMOFF *crosses the stage and stops when he sees* VARYA *and* ANYA.) Sh! She's asleep, asleep. Come on, dear.

ANYA (*quietly, half-asleep*). I'm so tired . . . I hear bells . . . uncle, dear! Mother and uncle!

VARYA. Come on, dear, come on! (*They go into* ANYA'*s room.*)

TROFIMOFF (*deeply moved*). Sunshine! Springtime of my life!

ACT II

A field. An old, tumble-down shrine, which has been long abandoned; near it a well and large stones, which apparently are old tombstones, and an old garden seat. The road to Gaieff's estate is seen. On one side dark poplars rise, behind them the cherry orchard begins. In the distance is a row of telegraph poles, and on the far horizon are the indistinct signs of a large town, which can be seen only on the finest and clearest days. It is near sunset.

[CHARLOTTA, YASHA, *and* DUNYASHA *are sitting on a bench.* YEPIKHODOFF *stands nearby playing on a guitar; all seem thoughtful.* CHARLOTTA *wears a man's old peaked cap; she has unslung a rifle from her shoulders and is straightening the strap-buckle.*]

CHARLOTTA (thoughtfully). I haven't a real passport. I don't know how old I am, but I think I'm young. When I was a little girl my father and mother used to travel from fair to fair and give very good performances, and I used to do the somersault and various little things. And when papa and mamma died, a German lady took me to her home and brought me up. I liked it. I grew up and became a governess. And where I came from and who I am, I don't know . . . Who my parents were—perhaps they weren't married—I don't know. (*Takes a cucumber from her pocket and eats.*) I don't know anything. (*Pause.*) I do wish to talk, but I haven't anybody to talk to . . . I haven't anybody at all.

YEPIKHODOFF (*plays on the guitar and sings*).

"What do I care for this noisy earth?
What do I care for friend and foe?"

I like playing on the mandolin!

DUNYASHA. That's a guitar, not a mandolin. (*Looks at herself in a little pocket mirror and powders herself.*)

YEPIKHODOFF. For a lovelorn lunatic, this constitutes a mandolin. (*Sings.*)

"Oh would the fire of love
Warm my pitiful heart!"

[YASHA *sings, too.*]

CHARLOTTA. These people sing so badly. . . . Bah! Like jackals.

DUNYASHA (*to* YASHA). Still it must be nice to live abroad.

YASHA. Yes, it is. I can't differ from you there. (*Yawns and lights a cigar.*)

YEPIKHODOFF. That is perfectly natural. Abroad everything is in such complete harmony.

YASHA. That goes without saying.

YEPIKHODOFF. I'm an educated man, I read various remarkable books, but I cannot understand where I want to go, myself—whether to keep on living or to shoot myself, as it were. So at any rate, I always carry a revolver about with me. Here it is. (*Shows a revolver.*)

CHARLOTTA. I've finished. Now I'll go. (*Slings the rifle over her shoulder.*) You, Yepikhodoff, are a very clever man and very frightful; women must be madly in love with you. Brrr! (*Going.*) These wise people are all so stupid. I've nobody to talk to. I'm always alone, alone; I've nobody at all . . . and I don't know who I am or why I live.

[*Exit slowly.*]

YEPIKHODOFF. As a matter of fact, independently of everything else, I must express my conviction, among other things, that fate has been as merciless in her dealings with me as a storm is to a small ship. Suppose, let us grant, I am wrong; then why did I wake up this morning, for example, and behold an enormous spider on my chest as big as this? (*Shows with both hands.*) And if I do drink kvass, why must I always find in the glass such an unsociable animal as a cockroach! (*Pause.*) Have you read Buckle? (*Pause.*) May I have a few words with you, Avdotya Fyodorovna?

DUNYASHA. Go on!

YEPIKHODOFF. I should prefer to be alone with you. (*Sighs.*)

DUNYASHA (*shy*). Very well, only please bring me my cloak first. . . . It's by the cupboard. It's a little damp here.

YEPIKHODOFF. Very well. . . . I'll bring it. . . . Now I know what to do with my revolver.

[*Takes guitar and exit, strumming.*]

YASHA. Two-and-twenty troubles! A foolish man, between you and me and the gatepost. (*Yawns.*)

DUNYASHA (*pause*). I hope to goodness he won't shoot himself. (*Pause.*) I'm so nervous, so worried. I entered service when I was quite a little girl, and now I'm not used to common life, and my hands are as white as a lady's. I'm so tender and so delicate now, respectable and afraid of everything. . . . I'm so frightened. And I don't know what will happen to my nerves if you deceive me, Yasha.

YASHA (*kisses her*). Tiny cucumber! Of course, every girl must respect herself; there's nothing I dislike more than a badly behaved girl.

DUNYASHA. I'm so much in love with you; you're educated, you can talk about everything. (*Pause.*)

YASHA (*yawns*). Yes, I think that if a girl loves anybody, it means she's immoral. (*Pause.*) It's nice to smoke a cigar out in the open air. . . . (*Listens.*) Somebody's coming. It's the mistress, and the people with her. (DUNYASHA *embraces him suddenly.*) Go to the house, as if you'd been bathing in the river; go by this path, or they'll run across you and will think I've been meeting you. I can't stand that sort of thing.

DUNYASHA (*coughs quietly*). Your cigar has given me a headache.

[*Exit.* YASHA *remains, sitting by the shrine. Enter* LIUBOFF ANDREIEVNA, GAIEFF, *and* LOPAKHIN.]

LOPAKHIN. You must make up your mind definitely—there's no time to waste. The question is perfectly simple. Are you willing to let the land for villas or no? Just one word, yes or no? Just one word!

LIUBOFF. Who's smoking bad cigars here? (*Sits.*)

GAIEFF. They built that railway; that's made this place very convenient. (*Sits.*) Went to town and had lunch . . . red in the center! I'd like to go to the house now and have just one game.

LIUBOFF. You'll have time.

LOPAKHIN. Just one word! (*Imploringly.*) Give me an answer!

GAIEFF (*yawns*). Really!

LIUBOFF (*looks in her purse*). I had a lot of money yesterday, but there's very little left today. My poor Varya feeds everybody on milk soup to save money; in the kitchen the old people get peas only; and I spend recklessly. (*Drops the purse, scattering gold coins.*) There, money all over the place.

YASHA. Permit me to pick them up. (*Collects the coins.*)

LIUBOFF. Please do, Yasha. And why did I go and lunch there? . . . A terrible restaurant with a band and tablecloths smelling of soap. . . . Why do you drink so much, Leon? Why do you eat so much? Why do you talk so much? You talked too much again today in the restaurant, and it wasn't at all to the point—about the seventies and about decadents. And to whom? Talking to the waiters about decadents! Imagine!

LOPAKHIN. Yes.

GAIEFF (*waves his hand*). I can't be cured, that's obvious. . . . (*Irritably to* YASHA.) What's the matter? Why do you always manage to keep in front of me?

YASHA (*laughs*). I can't listen to your voice without laughing.

GAIEFF (*to his sister*). Either he or I . . .

LIUBOFF. Go away, Yasha! Go!

YASHA (*gives purse to* LIUBOFF ANDREIEVNA). I'll go at once. (*Hardly able to keep from laughing.*) This minute. . . .

[*Exit.*]

LOPAKHIN. That rich man Deriganoff is preparing to buy your estate. They say he'll attend the sale in person.

LIUBOFF. Where did you hear that?

LOPAKHIN. They say so in town.

GAIEFF. Our aunt in Yaroslavl promised to send something, but I don't know when or how much.

LOPAKHIN. How much will she send? A hundred thousand rubles? Or two, perhaps?

LIUBOFF. I'd be glad if we get ten or fifteen thousand.

LOPAKHIN. You must excuse my saying so, but I've never met such frivolous people as you before, or anybody so unbusinesslike and peculiar. Here I am telling you in plain language that your estate will be sold, and you don't seem to understand.

LIUBOFF. What are we to do? Tell us, what?

LOPAKHIN. I tell you every day. Every day I say the same thing. Both the cherry orchard and the land must be leased for villas and at once, —the auction is staring you in the face: Understand! Once you definitely make up your minds to the villas, you'll have as much money as you wish and you'll be saved.

LIUBOFF. Villas and villa residents—it's so vulgar, pardon me.

GAIEFF. I agree with you entirely.

LOPAKHIN. I must cry or yell or faint. I can't! You're too much for me! (*To* GAIEFF.) You old woman!

GAIEFF. Really!

LOPAKHIN. Old woman!

[*Going out.*]

LIUBOFF (*frightened.*) No, don't go away, stop; be a dear. Please. Perhaps we'll find some way out!

LOPAKHIN. There is nothing to think about.

LIUBOFF. Please don't go. It's nicer when you're here. . . . (*Pause.*) I keep on waiting for something to happen, as if the house were going to collapse over our heads.

GAIEFF (*thinking deeply*). Double in the corner . . . across the center.

LIUBOFF. We have been too sinful. . . .

LOPAKHIN. What sins have you been guilty of?

GAIEFF (*puts candy in his mouth*). They say that I've wasted all my money in buying candy. (*Laughs.*)

LIUBOFF. Oh, my sins . . . I've always scattered money about without being able to control myself, like a madwoman, and I married a man who made nothing but debts. My husband died of champagne—he drank terribly—and to my misfortune, I fell in love with another man and went off with him, and just at that time—it was my first punishment, a blow that struck me squarely on the head—here, in the river . . . my boy was drowned, and I went away, abroad, never to return, never to see this river again. . . . I closed my eyes and ran without thinking, but he ran after me . . . without mercy, without respect. I bought a villa near Mentone because he fell ill there, and for three years I knew no rest, day or night; the sick man wore me out, and my soul dried up. And last year, when they had sold the villa to pay my debts, I went to Paris, and there he robbed me of all I had and threw me over and went off with another woman. I tried to poison myself. . . . It was so silly, so shameful . . . And suddenly I longed to go back to Russia, my own country, with my little daughter . . . (*Wipes her tears.*) Lord, Lord be merciful to me, forgive my sins! Punish me no more! (*Takes a telegram from her pocket.*) I had this today from Paris. . . . He begs my forgiveness, he implores me to return . . . (*Tears it up.*) Don't I hear music? (*Listens.*)

GAIEFF. That is our famous Jewish band. You remember—four violins, a flute, and a double-bass.

LIUBOFF. So it still exists? It would be nice if they came some evening.

LOPAKHIN (*listens*). I can't hear. . . . (*Sings quietly.*) "For money will the Germans make a Frenchman of a Russian." (*Laughs.*) I saw such an awfully funny thing at the theatre last night.

LIUBOFF. I'm quite sure there wasn't anything funny at all. You shouldn't go and see plays, you ought to go and look at yourself. What a drab life you lead! What a lot of unnecessary things you say!

LOPAKHIN. It's true. To speak the honest truth, we live a silly life. (*Pause.*) My father was a peasant, an idiot, he understood nothing, he didn't teach me, he was always drunk, and always beat me. As a matter of fact, I'm a fool and an idiot, too. I've never learned anything, my handwriting is bad, I write so that I'm quite ashamed before people, like a pig!

LIUBOFF. You should marry, my friend.

LOPAKHIN. Yes . . . that's true.

LIUBOFF. Why not our Varya? She's a nice girl.

LOPAKHIN. Yes.

LIUBOFF. She's a simple, unaffected girl, works all day, and, what matters most, she's in love with you. And you've liked her for a long time.

LOPAKHIN. Well? I don't mind . . . She's a nice girl. (*Pause.*)

GAIEFF. I'm offered a place in a bank. Six thousand rubles a year . . . Did you hear?

LIUBOFF. What's the matter with you! Stay where you are . . .

[*Enter* FIRCE *with an overcoat.*]

FIRCE (*to* GAIEFF). Please sir, put this on, it's damp.

GAIEFF (*putting it on*). You're a nuisance, old man.

FIRCE. It's all very well. . . . You went away this morning without telling me. (*Examining* GAIEFF.)

LIUBOFF. How old you've grown, Firce!

FIRCE. I beg your pardon?

LOPAKHIN. She says you've grown very old!

FIRCE. I've lived a long time. They were getting ready to marry me before your father was born . . . (*Laughs.*) And when the Emancipation came I was already first valet. Only I didn't agree with the Emancipation and remained with my masters . . . (*Pause.*) I remember everybody was happy, but they didn't know why.

LOPAKHIN. It was very good for them in the old days. At any rate, they beat them formerly.

FIRCE (*not hearing*). Rather. The peasants kept their distance from the masters and the masters kept their distance from the peasants, but now everything is in a muddle, and you can't make head or tail of anything.

GAIEFF. Be quiet, Firce. I have to go to town tomorrow. I have the promise of an introduction to a General who may lend me money on a note.

LOPAKHIN. Nothing will come of it. And you won't pay your interest, don't you worry.

LIUBOFF. He's out of his head. There's no General at all.

[*Enter* TROFIMOFF, ANYA, *and* VARYA.]

GAIEFF. Here, come on, folks!

ANYA. Mother's sitting down here.

LIUBOFF (*tenderly*). Come, come, my dears . . . (*Embracing* ANYA *and* VARYA.) If you two only knew how much I love you. Sit down next to me, like that. (*All sit down.*)

LOPAKHIN. Our eternal student is always with the ladies.

TROFIMOFF. That's none of your business.

LOPAKHIN. He'll soon be fifty, and he's still a student.

TROFIMOFF. Stop your silly jokes!

LOPAKHIN. Getting angry, eh, silly?

TROFIMOFF. Shut up, can't you?

LOPAKHIN (*laughs*). I wonder what you think of me?

TROFIMOFF. I think, Yermolai Alexeievitch, that you're rich, and you'll soon be a millionaire. Just as the wild beast which eats everything it finds is needed to make certain changes in cosmic matter, so you are needed too. (*All laugh.*)

VARYA. Better tell us something about the planets, Peter.

LIUBOFF. No, let's continue yesteday's discussion.

TROFIMOFF. What was it about?

GAIEFF. About the proud man.

TROFIMOFF. Yesterday we talked for a long time, but we arrived at no conclusion. In your opinion there's something mystic in pride. Perhaps you are right from your point of view, but if you look at the matter sanely, without complicating it, then what pride can there be, what logic in a man who is imperfectly made, physiologically speaking, and who in the vast majority of cases is coarse and stupid and profoundly unhappy? We must stop admiring one another. We must work, nothing more.

GAIEFF. You'll die, all the same.

TROFIMOFF. Who knows? And what does it mean—you'll die? Perhaps a man has a hundred senses, and when he dies only the five known to us are destroyed and the remaining ninety-five are left alive.

LIUBOFF. How clever of you, Peter!

LOPAKHIN (*ironically*). Oh, awfully!

TROFIMOFF. The human race progresses, perfecting its powers. Everything that is unattainable now will some day be near and intelligible, but we must work, we must help with all our energy, those who seek to know the truth. Meanwhile in Russia only a very few of us work. The vast majority of those intellectuals whom I know seek for nothing, do nothing, and are at present incapable of hard work. They call themselves intellectuals, but they use "thou" and "thee" to their servants, they treat the peasants like animals, they learn slowly, they read nothing with discernment, they do absolutely nothing, they gabble on about science, about art they understand little. They are all serious, they all have severe faces, they all talk about important things. They philosophize, and at the same time, the vast majority of us, ninety-nine out of a hundred, live like savages, fighting and cursing on the slightest excuse, have filthy table manners, sleep in the dirt, in stuffiness among fleas, stinks, smells, moral stench, and so on. . . . And it's obvious that all our nice talk is only carried on to delude ourselves and others. Tell me, where are those crèches we hear so much of? And where are those reading-rooms? People only write novels about them; they don't really exist. Only dirt, coarseness, and Asiatic barbarism really exist. . . . I'm afraid; and I don't like serious faces at all. I don't like serious conversation. Let's say no more about it.

LOPAKHIN. You know, I get up at five every morning, I work till evening, I am always dealing with money—my own and other people's—and I see what others are like. You have only to start doing anything at all, and you'll find out how few honest, honorable people there are. Sometimes, when I can't sleep, I think: "Oh Lord, you've given us huge forests, infinite fields, and endless horizons, and we, living here, ought really to be giants."

LIUBOFF. You want giants, do you? . . . They're only good in stories, and even there they frighten one. (YEPIKHODOFF *enters at the back of the stage playing his guitar.* LIUBOFF ANDREIEVNA *speaks thoughtfully.*) Yepikhodoff has come.

ANYA (*thoughtfully*). Yepikhodoff has come.

GAIEFF. The sun's set.

TROFIMOFF. Yes.

GAIEFF (*not loudly, as if declaiming*). Oh, Nature, thou art wonderful, thou shinest with eternal radiance! Oh, beautiful and lofty one, thou whom we call mother, thou containest in thyself life and death, thou livest and destroyest. . . .

VARYA (*entreatingly*). Uncle, dear!

ANYA. Uncle, you're doing it again!

TROFIMOFF. You'd better double the yellow into the center.

GAIEFF. I'll be quiet, I'll be quiet.

[*They all sit thoughtfully. It is quiet. Only the mumbling of* FIRCE *is heard. Suddenly a distant sound comes as if from the sky, the sound of a breaking string, which dies away sadly.*]

LIUBOFF. What's that?

LOPAKHIN. I don't know. Perhaps a bucket fell, down a well somewhere. But it's a long way off.

GAIEFF. Or perhaps it's some bird . . . like a heron.

TROFIMOFF. Or an owl.

LIUBOFF (*shudders*). It's unpleasant, somehow. (*A pause.*)

FIRCE. Before the catastrophe the same thing happened. An owl screamed and the samovar hummed without stopping.

GAIEFF. Before what catastrophe?

FIRCE. Before the Emancipation. (*A pause.*)

LIUBOFF. You know, my friends, let's go in; it's evening now. (*To* ANYA.) You've tears in your eyes. . . . What is it, little girl? (*Embraces her.*)

ANYA. It's nothing, mother.

TROFIMOFF. Some one's coming.

[*Enter a* TRAMP *in an old white peaked cap and overcoat. He is slightly drunk.*]

TRAMP. Excuse me, may I go this way straight through to the station?

GAIEFF. You may. Go along this path. . . .

TRAMP. I thank you with all my heart. (*Hiccoughs.*) Lovely weather. . . . (*Declaims.*) My brother, my suffering brother. . . . Come out on the Volga, you whose groans . . . (*To* VARYA.) Mademoiselle, please give a hungry Russian thirty kopecks. . . .

[VARYA *screams, frightened.*]

LOPAKHIN (*angrily*). Everybody should have some sort of manners!

LIUBOFF (*with a start*). Take this . . . here you are . . . (*Feels in her purse.*) There's no silver . . . It doesn't matter, here's gold.

TRAMP. I am very grateful to you!

[*Exit. Laughter.*]

VARYA (*frightened*). I'm going. I'm going. . . . Oh, mother dear, at home there's nothing for the servants to eat, and yet you gave him gold.

LIUBOFF. What is to be done with such a fool as I am! At home, I'll give you everything I have. Yermolai Alexeievitch, lend me some more! . . .

LOPAKHIN. Very well.

LIUBOFF. Let's go, it's time. And Varya, we've settled your affairs; I congratulate you.

VARYA (*crying*). You shouldn't joke about this, mother.

LOPAKHIN. Ophelia! Get thee to a nunnery.

GAIEFF. My hands are trembling; I haven't played billiards for a long time.

LOPAKHIN. Ophelia! Nymph! Remember me in thine orisons!

LIUBOFF. Come along; it'll soon be suppertime.

VARYA. He frightened me. My heart is beating fast.

LOPAKHIN. Let me remind you, ladies and gentlemen, on August 22nd, the cherry orchard will be sold. Think of that! . . . Think of that! . . . (*All go out except* TROFIMOFF *and* ANYA.)

ANYA (*laughs*). Thanks to the tramp who frightened Varya, we're alone now.

TROFIMOFF. Varya's afraid that we may fall in love with each other and won't leave us alone for days on end. Her narrow mind won't permit her to understand that we are above love. To escape all the petty and deceptive things which prevent our being happy and free, such is the aim and object of our lives. Forward! We go irresistibly on to that bright star which burns there, in the distance! Don't lag behind, friends!

ANYA (*clapping her hands*). How beautifully you talk! (*Pause.*) It is glorious here today!

TROFIMOFF. Yes, the weather is wonderful.

ANYA. What have you done to me, Peter? I don't love the cherry orchard as I used to. I loved it so tenderly, I thought there was no better place in the world than our orchard.

TROFIMOFF. All Russia is our orchard. The land is great and beautiful, there are many glorious places in it. (*Pause.*) Think, Anya, your grandfather, your great-grandfather, and all your ancestors were serf-owners, they owned human beings; and now, doesn't something human look at you from every cherry in the orchard, every leaf and every branch? Don't you hear voices . . . ? Oh, it's awful, your orchard is frightful; and when in the evening or at night you walk through the orchard, then the old bark on the trees sheds a dim light and the old cherry-trees seem to dream of all that happened a hundred, two hundred years ago, and are burdened with their heavy visions. Still, we've left those two hundred years behind us. So far we've gained nothing at all—we don't yet know what the past will bring us—we only philosophize, we complain that we are dull, or we drink vodka. For it's so clear that to begin to live in the present we must first redeem the past, and that can be done only by suffering, by strenuous, uninterrupted work. Understand that, Anya.

ANYA. The house in which we live has long ceased to be our house; I shall go away, I give you my word.

TROFIMOFF. If you have the keys of the household, throw them down the well and go away. Be as free as the wind.

ANYA (*enthusiastically*). How beautifully you said that!

TROFIMOFF. Believe me, Anya, believe me! I'm not thirty yet, I'm young, I'm still a student, but I have gone through so much already! I'm as hungry as the winter, I'm ill, I'm shaken. I'm as poor as a beggar, and where haven't I been—fate has tossed me everywhere! But my soul is always my own; every minute of the day and the night it is filled with glorious and dim visions. I feel that happiness is coming, Anya, I see it already. . . .

ANYA (*thoughtful*). The moon is rising.

[YEPIKHODOFF *is heard playing the same sad song on his guitar. The moon rises. Somewhere near the poplars* VARYA *is looking for* ANYA *and calling, "Anya, where are you?"*]

TROFIMOFF. Yes, the moon has risen. (*Pause.*) There is happiness, there it comes; it comes nearer and nearer; I hear its footsteps already. And if we do not see it, we shall not know it, but what does that matter? Others will see it!

VARYA'S VOICE. Anya! Where are you?

TROFIMOFF. That's Varya again! (*Angry.*) Disgraceful!

ANYA. Never mind. Let's go to the river. It's nice there.

TROFIMOFF. Let's go. (*They leave.*)

VARYA'S VOICE. Anya! Anya!

ACT III

A reception-room, separated by an arch from a drawing-room. Lighted chandelier. A Jewish band, the one referred to in Act II, is heard playing in another room. Evening. In the drawing-room the cotillion is being danced.

[*Voice of* SEMYONOFF PISHCHIK, *"Promenade à une paire!" Dancers come into the reception-room; the first pair are* PISHCHIK *and* CHARLOTTA IVANOVNA; *the second* TROFIMOFF *and* LIUBOFF ANDREIEVNA; *the third* ANYA *and the* POST OFFICE CLERK; *the fourth* VARYA *and the* STATION-MASTER, *and so on.* VARYA *is crying gently and dries her eyes as she dances.* DUNYASHA *is in the last pair. They go off into the drawing-room, shouting, "Grand rond, balancez:" and "Les cavaliers à genoux et remerciez vos dames!"* FIRCE, *in a dress-coat, carries a tray with seltzer-water across the stage. Enter* PISHCHIK *and* TROFIMOFF *from the drawing-room.*]

PISHCHIK. I'm full-blooded and already I've had two strokes; it's hard for me to dance, but, as they say, if you're in Rome, you must do as the Romans do. I've the constitution of a horse. My late father, who liked a joke, peace to his ashes, used to say, talking of our ancestors, that the ancient stock of the Semyonoff Pishchiks was descended from the identical horse that Caligula appointed senator. . . . (*Sits.*) But the trouble is, I've no money! A hungry dog believes only in meat. (*Drops off to sleep and wakes up again immediately.*) So I . . . believe only in money. . . .

TROFIMOFF. Yes. There is something horsy about your figure.

PISHCHIK. Well . . . a horse is a valuable animal . . . you can sell a horse.

[*The sound of billiard playing comes from the next room,* VARYA *appears under the arch.*]

TROFIMOFF (*Teasing*). Madame Lopakhin! Madame Lopakhin!

VARYA (*Angry*). Decayed gentleman!

TROFIMOFF. Yes, I am a decayed gentleman, and I'm proud of it!

VARYA (*Bitterly*). We've hired the musicians, but how are they to be paid? [*Exit.*]

TROFIMOFF (*To* PISHCHIK). If you would put to better use the energy which you are wasting day by day, in looking for money to pay interest, I believe you'd finally succeed in moving heaven and earth.

PISHCHIK. Nietzsche . . . a philosopher . . . a very great and famous man . . . a man of enormous brain, says in his books that you can forge bank-notes.

TROFIMOFF. And have you read Nietzsche?

PISHCHIK. Well . . . Dashenka told me. Now I'm in such a position, I wouldn't mind making counterfeit money . . . I have to pay 310 rubles day after tomorrow . . . I've obtained 130 already . . . (*Feels his pockets, nervously.*) I've lost the money! The money's gone! (*Crying.*) Where's the money? (*Joyfully.*) Here it is in the lining. . . . Why I was in a cold sweat!

[*Enter* LIUBOFF ANDREIEVNA *and* CHARLOTTA IVANOVNA.]

LIUBOFF (*humming a Caucasian dance song*). What is keeping Leonid so long? What's he doing in town? (*To* DUNYASHA.) Dunyasha, give the musicians some tea.

TROFIMOFF. The business is off, I suppose.

LIUBOFF. And the musicians needn't have come, and we needn't have arranged this ball. . . . Well, never mind. . . . (*Sits and sings softly.*)

CHARLOTTA (*gives a pack of cards to* PISHCHIK). Here's a deck of cards, think of any card you like.

PISHCHIK. I've thought of one.

CHARLOTTA. Now shuffle. All right, now. Pass them over, my dear Mr. Pishchik. Eins, zwei, drei! Now look and you'll find it in your hind pocket.

PISHCHIK (*takes a card out of his hind pocket*). Eight of spades, quite right! (*Surprised.*) Just imagine!

CHARLOTTA (*holds the deck of cards in the palm of her hand. To* TROFIMOFF). Now tell me quickly. What's the top card?

TROFIMOFF. Well, the queen of spades.

CHARLOTTA. Right! (*To* PISHCHIK.) And now? What card's on top?

PISHCHIK. Ace of hearts.

CHARLOTTA. Right! (*Clasps her hands, the deck of cards vanishes.*) How lovely the weather is today. (*A mysterious woman's voice answers her, as if from under the floor, "Oh yes, it's lovely weather, Madam."*) You are so beautiful, you are my ideal. (*Voice, "You, Madam, please me very much, too."*)

STATION-MASTER (*applauds*). Madame the ventriloquist, bravo!

PISHCHIK (*surprised*). Just imagine! Delightful, Charlotta Ivanovna . . . I'm simply in love. . . .

CHARLOTTA. In love? (*Shrugging her shoulders.*) Can you love? Guter Mensch aber schlechter Musikant.

TROFIMOFF (*slaps* PISHCHIK *on the shoulder*). Oh, you horse!

CHARLOTTA. Attention, please, here's another trick. (*Takes a shawl from a chair.*) Here's a very nice plaid shawl. I'm going to sell it. . . . (*Shakes it.*) Won't somebody buy it?

PISHCHIK (*astonished*). Just imagine!

CHARLOTTA. Eins, zwei, drei. (*She quickly lifts up the shawl, which is hanging down.* ANYA *appears behind it; she bows and runs to her mother, hugs her and runs back to the drawing-room amid general applause.*)

LIUBOFF (*applauds*). Bravo, bravo!

CHARLOTTA. Once again! Eins, zwei, drei! (*Lifts the shawl.* VARYA *appears behind it and bows.*)

PISHCHIK (*astonished*). Just imagine!

CHARLOTTA. The end! (*Throws the shawl at* PISHCHIK, *curtseys and runs into the drawing-room.*)

PISHCHIK (*Runs after her*). Little witch! . . . What? Would you?

[*Exit.*]

LIUBOFF. Leonid hasn't come yet. I don't understand what is keeping him so long in town! Everything must be over by now. The estate must be sold; or, if the sale never came off, then why does he stay away so long?

VARYA (*tries to soothe her*). Uncle has bought it. I'm certain of it.

TROFIMOFF (*sarcastically*). Oh, yes!

VARYA. Grandmother sent him her authority to buy it in her name and transfer the debt to her. She's doing it for Anya. And I'm certain that God will help us and that uncle will buy it.

LIUBOFF. Grandmother sent fifteen thousand rubles from Yaroslavl to buy the property in her name—she won't trust us—and that wasn't even enough to pay the interest. (*Covers her face with her hands.*) My fate will be settled today, my fate. . . .

TROFIMOFF (*teasing* VARYA). Madame Lopakhin!

VARYA (*angry*). Eternal student? He's been expelled from the university, twice already.

LIUBOFF. Why are you growing angry, Varya? He's teasing you about Lopakhin. Well, what of it? You can marry Lopakhin if you wish. He's a good, interesting man. . . . You needn't if you don't wish to; nobody is going to force you against your will, my darling.

VARYA. I look at the matter seriously, mother dear, to be quite frank. He's a good man, and I like him.

LIUBOFF. Then marry him. I don't understand what you're waiting for.

VARYA. I can't propose to him myself, mother dear. People have been talking about him to me for two years now, but he either says nothing, or jokes about it. I understand. He's getting rich, he's busy, he can't bother about me. If I had some money, even a little, even only a hundred rubles, I'd throw up everything and go away. I'd go into a convent.

TROFIMOFF. What bliss!

VARYA (*to* TROFIMOFF). A student should have common sense! (*Gently, in tears.*) How ugly you are now, Peter, how old you've grown! (*To* LIUBOFF ANDREIEVNA, *no longer crying.*) But I can't go on without working, mother dear. I'm eager to be doing something every minute.

[*Enter* YASHA.]

YASHA (*nearly laughing*). Yepikhodoff's broken a billiard cue!

[*Exit.*]

VARYA. Why is Yepikhodoff here? Who said he could play billiards? I don't understand these people.

[*Exit.*]

LIUBOFF. Don't tease her, Peter, you see that she's unhappy enough without it.

TROFIMOFF. She undertakes too much herself; she is continually interfering in other people's business. The whole summer she gave Anya and me not a moment's peace. She's afraid we'll have a romance all to ourselves. What concern of hers is it? As if I'd ever given her grounds to believe I'd stoop to such vulgarity! We are above love.

LIUBOFF. Then I suppose I must be beneath love. (*In agitation.*) Why isn't Leonid here? If I only knew whether the estate is sold or not! The catastrophe seems to me so unbelievable that I don't know what to think, I'm all at sea . . . I may scream . . . or do something foolish. Save me, Peter. Say something, say something.

TROFIMOFF. Isn't it all the same whether the estate is sold today or not? For a long time it's been a foregone conclusion that it would be sold. There's no turning back, the path is obliterated. Be calm, dear, you shouldn't deceive yourself; for once in your life, at any rate, you must look the truth straight in the eyes.

LIUBOFF. What truth? You see where truth is, and where falsehood is, but I seem to have lost my sight and see nothing. You settle all important questions boldly, but tell me, dear, isn't it because you're young, because you have not as yet had time to suffer in settling any one of these questions? You look forward boldly, but isn't it because you neither feel nor expect anything terrible, because so far life has been hidden from your young eyes? You are bolder, more honest, deeper than we are, but only think, be just a little magnanimous, and have pity on me. I was born here, my father and mother lived here, my grandfather, too. I love this house. I couldn't understand my life without that cherry orchard, and if it really must be sold, sell me with it! (*Embraces* TROFIMOFF, *kisses his forehead.*) My son was drowned here . . . (*Weeps.*) Have pity on me, good, kind man.

TROFIMOFF. You know that I sympathize with all my heart.

LIUBOFF. Yes, but it should be said differently. . . . (*Takes another handkerchief, a telegram falls on the floor.*) I'm so sick at heart today, you can't imagine. Here it's so noisy, my soul trembles at every sound. I shake all over, and I can't go away by myself, I'm afraid of the silence. Don't judge me harshly, Peter. . . . I love you, as if you belonged to the family. I'd gladly let Anya marry you, I swear it, only dear, you ought to work to finish your studies. You don't do anything, only fate tosses you about from place to place, it's so strange. . . . Isn't it true? Yes? And you ought to do something to your beard to make it grow better. (*Laughs.*) You are funny!

TROFIMOFF (*picking up telegram*). I don't wish to be a Beau Brummell.

LIUBOFF. This telegram's from Paris. I receive one every day. Yesterday and today. That wild man is ill again, he's bad again. . . . He begs for forgiveness, and implores me to come, and I really should go to Paris to be near him. You look severe, Peter, but what can I do, my dear, what can I do? He's ill, he's alone, unhappy, and who's to look after him, who's to keep him out of harm's way, to give him his medicine punctually? And why should I conceal it and say nothing about it? I love him, that's plain, I love him, I love him. . . . That love is a stone round my neck; I shall sink with it to the bottom, but I love that stone and can't live without it. (*Squeezes* TROFIMOFF's *hand.*) Don't think harshly of me, Peter, don't say anything to me, don't say . . .

TROFIMOFF (*weeping*). For God's sake forgive my speaking candidly, but that man has robbed you!

LIUBOFF. No, no, you should not say that! (*Stops her ears.*)

TROFIMOFF. But he's a scoundrel, you alone don't know it! He's a petty thief, a nobody. . . .

LIUBOFF (*angry, but restrained*). You're twenty-six or twenty-seven, and still a school-boy of the second grade!

TROFIMOFF. Why not?

LIUBOFF. You should be a man, at your age you should be able to understand those who love. And you should be in love yourself, you must fall in love! (*Angry.*) Yes, yes! You aren't pure, you're just a freak, a queer fellow, a funny fungus.

TROFIMOFF (*in horror*). What is she saying?

LIUBOFF. "I'm above love!" You're not above love, you're just what our Firce calls a bungler. Not to have a mistress at your age!

TROFIMOFF (*in horror*). This is terrible! What is she saying? (*Goes quickly into the drawing-room, seizing his head with both his hands.*) It's awful . . . I can't stand it. I'll go away. (*Exit, but returns at once.*) All is over between us!

[*Exit.*]

LIUBOFF (*shouts after him*). Peter, wait! Silly boy, I was joking! Peter! (*Somebody is heard going out and falling downstairs noisily.* ANYA *and* VARYA *scream; laughter is heard immediately.*) What's that? (ANYA *comes running in, laughing.*)

ANYA. Peter's fallen downstairs!

[*Runs out again.*]

LIUBOFF. This Peter's a funny creature!

[*The* STATION-MASTER *stands in the middle of the drawing-room and recites "The Magdalen" by Tolstoy. They listen to him, but he has delivered only a few lines when a waltz is heard from the front room, and the recitation is stopped. Everybody dances,* TROFIMOFF, ANYA, VARYA, *and* LIUBOFF ANDREIEVNA *come in from the front room.*]

LIUBOFF. Well, Peter . . . you pure soul . . . I beg your pardon. . . . Let's dance.

[*She dances with* PETER. ANYA *and* VARYA *dance.* FIRCE *enters and leans his stick against a side door.* YASHA *has also come in and watches the dance.*]

YASHA. Well, grandfather?

FIRCE. I'm not well. At our balls some time ago, generals and barons and admirals used to dance, and now we send for post-office clerks and the station-master, and even they come reluctantly. I'm very weak. The dead master, the grandfather, used to give everybody sealing-wax when anything was wrong. I've taken sealing-wax every day for twenty years, and more; possibly that's why I am still alive.

YASHA. I'm tired of you, grandfather. (*Yawns.*) If you'd only hurry up and kick the bucket.

FIRCE (*muttering*). Oh, you . . . bungler!

[TROFIMOFF *and* LIUBOFF ANDREIEVNA *dance in the reception-room, then into the sitting-room.*]

LIUBOFF. Merci. I'll sit down. (*Sits.*) I'm tired.

[*Enter* ANYA.]

ANYA (*excited*). Somebody in the kitchen was saying just now that the cherry orchard was sold today.

LIUBOFF. Sold to whom?

ANYA. He didn't say to whom. He went away. (*Dances out into the reception-room with* TROFIMOFF.)

YASHA. Some old man was chattering about it a long time ago. A stranger!

FIRCE. And Leonid Andreievitch isn't here yet, he hasn't come. He's wearing a light autumn overcoat. He'll catch cold. Oh, these young fellows.

LIUBOFF. I'll die of this. Go and find out, Yasha, to whom it's sold.

YASHA. Oh, but he's been gone a long time, the old man. (*Laughs.*)

LIUBOFF (*slightly vexed*). Why do you laugh? What are you so happy about?

YASHA. Yepikhodoff's too funny. He's a foolish man. Two-and-twenty troubles.

LIUBOFF. Firce, if the estate is sold, where will you go?

FIRCE. I'll go wherever you command me to go.

LIUBOFF. Why do you look like that? Are you ill? I think you should go to bed. . . .

FIRCE. Yes . . . (*With a smile.*) I'll go to bed, and who'll hand things round and give orders without me? I've the whole house on my shoulders.

YASHA (*to* LIUBOFF ANDREIEVNA). Liuboff Andreievna! I wish to ask a favor of you, if you'll be so kind! If you go to Paris again, take me along. I beg of you! It's absolutely impossible for me to remain here. (*Looking round; in an undertone.*) What's the good of talking about it? You see for yourself that this is an uncivilized country, with an immoral population, and it's so dull. The food in the kitchen is wretched, and here's this Firce walking about mumbling all kinds of inappropriate things. Take me with you. Please!

[*Enter* PISHCHIK.]

PISHCHIK. May I have the pleasure of a little waltz, dear lady . . . ? (LIUBOFF ANDREIEVNA *goes to him.*) But all the same, you wonderful woman, I must have 180 little rubles from you. . . . I must. . . . (*They dance.*) 180 little rubles. . . .

[*They go through into the drawing-room.*]

YASHA (*sings softly*).

"Oh, will you understand
My soul's deep restlessness?"

[*In the drawing-room a figure in a gray top-hat and in baggy check trousers is waving its hands; and there are cries of "Bravo, Charlotta Ivanovna!"*]

DUNYASHA (*stops to powder her face*). The young mistress tells me to dance—there are lots of gentlemen, but few ladies—and my head whirls when I dance, and my heart beats, Firce Nikolaievitch; the Post-office clerk told me something just now that almost took my breath away.

[*The music grows faint.*]

FIRCE. What did he tell you?

DUNYASHA. He says, "You're like a little flower."

YASHA (*yawns*). Impolite. . . .

[*Exit.*]

DUNYASHA. Like a little flower. I'm such a delicate girl; I simply love tender words.

FIRCE. You'll lose your head.

[*Enter* YEPIKHODOFF.]

YEPIKHODOFF. You, Avdotya Fyodorovna, are about as anxious to see me as if I were some insect. (*Sighs.*) Oh, life!

DUNYASHA. What do you wish?

YEPIKHODOFF. Perhaps, doubtless, you may be right. (*Sighs.*) But, certainly, if you consider the matter in that light, then you, if I may say so, and you must excuse my candidness, have absolutely reduced me to the state of mind in which I find myself. I know my fate. Every day something unfortunate happens to me, and I've grown used to it a long time ago. I never look at my fate with a smile. You gave me your word, and though I. . . .

DUNYASHA. Please, we'll talk later on, but leave me alone now. I'm thinking now. (*Fans herself.*)

YEPIKHODOFF. Every day something unfortunate happens to me, and I, if I may so express myself, only smile, and even laugh.

[VARYA *enters from the drawing-room.*]

VARYA. Haven't you gone yet, Semyon? You really have no respect for anybody. (*To* DUNYASHA.) Go away, Dunyasha. (*To* YEPIKHODOFF.) You play billiards and break a cue, and stroll about the drawing-room as if you were a visitor!

YEPIKHODOFF. You cannot, if I may say so, call me to order.

VARYA. I'm not calling you to order, I'm only telling you. You just walk about from place to place and never do your work. Goodness only knows why we keep a clerk.

YEPIKHODOFF (*offended*). Whether I work, or walk about, or eat, or play billiards, is only a matter to be settled by people of understanding and my elders.

VARYA. You dare talk to me like that! (*Furious.*) You dare? You mean to insinuate that I know nothing? Go away! This minute!

YEPIKHODOFF (*nervous*). I must ask you to express yourself more delicately.

VARYA (*beside herself*). Get out this minute. Get out! (*He goes to the door, she follows.*) Two-and-twenty troubles! Not another sign of you here! I don't wish to set eyes on you again! (YEPIKHODOFF *has gone out; his voice can be heard outside: "I'll make a complaint against you."*) What, coming back? (*Snatches up the stick left by* FIRCE *near the door.*) Go . . . go . . . go. I'll show you . . . Are you going? Are you going? Well, then take that. (*She lashes out with the stick as* LOPAKHIN *enters.*)

LOPAKHIN. Much obliged.

VARYA (*angry but amused*). I'm sorry.

LOPAKHIN. Never mind. I thank you for the pleasant reception you gave me!

VARYA. It isn't worthy of thanks. (*Walks away, then looks back and asks gently.*) I didn't hurt you, did I?

LOPAKHIN. No, not at all. There'll be a huge bump, no more.

VOICES FROM THE DRAWING-ROOM. Lopakhin's returned! Yermolai Alexeievitch!

PISHCHIK. Now we'll see what there is to see and hear what there is to hear. . . . (*Kisses* LOPAKHIN.) You smell of brandy, my dashing soul. And we're all enjoying ourselves.

[*Enter* LIUBOFF ANDREIEVNA.]

LIUBOFF. Is that you, Yermolai Alexeievitch? Why were you so long? Where's Leonid?

LOPAKHIN. Leonid Andreievitch returned with me, he's coming. . . .

LIUBOFF (*excited*). Well, what? Is it sold? Tell me?

LOPAKHIN (*confused, afraid to show his pleasure*). The sale was over at four o'clock. . . . We missed the train, and had to wait till half-past nine. (*Sighs heavily.*) Ooh! My head's swimming a little.

[*Enter* GAIEFF; *in his right hand he carries things that he has brought, with his left he dries his eyes.*]

LIUBOFF. Leon, what's happened? Leon, well? (*Impatiently, in tears.*) Quick, for the love of God. . . .

GAIEFF (*says nothing to her, only waves his hand; to* FIRCE, *weeping*). Here, take this . . . Here are anchovies, herrings from Kertch. . . . I've had no food today. . . . I have had a time! (*The door from the billiard-room is open; the clicking of the balls is heard, and* YASHA'*s voice, "Seven, eighteen!"* GAIEFF'*s expression changes, he no longer cries.*) I'm awfully tired. Let me change my clothes, Firce. (*Goes out through the drawing-room;* FIRCE *following him.*)

PISHCHIK. What happened? Come on, tell us!

LIUBOFF. Is the cherry orchard sold?

LOPAKHIN. It is sold.

LIUBOFF. Who bought it?

LOPAKHIN. I bought it. (*Pause.* LIUBOFF ANDREIEVNA *is overwhelmed; she would fall if she were not leaning against an armchair and a table.* VARYA *takes her keys off her belt, throws them on the floor into the middle of the room and goes out.*) I bought it! Wait, ladies and gentlemen, please, my head's going round, I can't talk. . . . (*Laughing.*) When we reached the sale, Deriganoff was there already. Leonid Andreievitch had only fifteen thousand rubles, and Deriganoff offered thirty thousand on top of the mortgage to begin with. I saw how matters stood, so I went right after him and bid forty. He raised his bid to forty-five, I offered fifty-five. That means he went up by fives and I went up by tens. . . . Well, it came to an end at last, I bid ninety more than the mortgage; and it stayed with me. The cherry orchard is mine now, mine! (*Roars with laughter.*) My God, my God, the cherry orchard's mine! Tell me I'm drunk, or crazy, or dreaming. . . . (*Stamps his feet.*) Don't laugh at me! If my father and grandfather rose from their graves and looked at the whole affair, and saw how their Yermolai, their whipped and illiterate Yermolai, who used to run barefoot in the winter, how that very Yermolai has bought an estate, the most beautiful spot in the world! I've bought the estate where my grandfather and my father were slaves, where they weren't even allowed to enter the kitchen. I'm asleep, it's only a dream, an illusion. . . . It's the fruit of imagination, wrapped in the fog of the unknown. . . . (*Picks up the keys, gaily smiling.*) She threw down the keys, she wished to show that she was no longer mistress here. . . . (*Jingles keys.*) Well, it's all one! (*Hears the band tuning up.*) Eh, musicians, play, I wish to hear you! Come and look at Yermolai Lopakhin swinging his ax against the cherry orchard, come and look at the trees falling! We'll build villas here, and our grandsons and great-grandsons will see a new life here. . . . Play on, music. (*The band plays.* LIUBOFF ANDREIEVNA *sinks into a chair and weeps bitterly.* LOPAKHIN *continues reproachfully.*) Why then, why didn't you take my advice? My poor, dear woman, you can't go back now. (*Weeps.*) Oh, if only the whole thing were finished, if only our uneven, unhappy lives were changed!

PISHCHIK (*takes his arm; in an undertone*). She's crying. Let's go into the drawing-room and leave her by herself . . . come on . . .

[*Takes his arm and leads him out.*]

LOPAKHIN. What's that? Bandsmen, play up! Go on, do just as I wish you to! (*Ironically.*) The new owner, the owner of the cherry orchard is coming! (*He accidentally knocks up against a little table and nearly upsets the candelabra.*) I can pay for everything now!

[*Exit with* PISHCHIK.]

[*In the reception-room and the drawing-room nobody remains except* LIUBOFF ANDREIEVNA, *who sits huddled up and weeping bitterly. The band plays softly.* ANYA *and* TROFIMOFF *come in quickly.* ANYA *goes up to her mother and kneels in front of her.* TROFIMOFF *stands at the drawing-room entrance.*]

ANYA. Mother! Mother, are you crying? My dear, kind, good mother, my beautiful mother, I love you! Bless you! The cherry orchard is sold. We own it no longer, it's true. But don't cry, mother, you still have your life before you, you've still your beautiful pure soul. . . . Come with me, come, dear, away from here, come! We'll plant a new orchard more beautiful than this, and you'll see it, and you'll understand, and deep soothing joy will enfold your soul, like the evening sun, and you'll smile, mother! Come, dear, let's go!

ACT IV

Same as Act I. There are no curtains on the windows, no pictures; only a few pieces of furniture are left piled up in a corner as if for sale. The emptiness is apparent. There are bags and suitcases by the door that leads out of the house and at the back of the stage.

[*The door at the left is open; the voices of* VARYA *and* ANYA *can be heard through it.* LOPAKHIN *stands and waits.* YASHA *holds a tray with little glasses of champagne. Outside,* YEPIKHODOFF *is tying up a box. Voices are heard behind the stage. The peasants have come to say good-bye. The voice of* GAIEFF *is heard; "Thank you, brothers, thank you."*]

YASHA. The peasants have come to say good-bye. I am of the opinion, Yermolai Alexeievitch, that they're good people, but they don't understand very much.

[*The voices die away.* LIUBOFF ANDREIEVNA *and* GAIEFF *enter. She is not crying but is pale, and her face twitches; she can hardly speak.*]

GAIEFF. You gave them your purse, Liuba. You can't go on like that, you can't!

LIUBOFF. I couldn't help myself, I couldn't!

[*They go out.*]

LOPAKHIN (*in the doorway, looking after them*). Please, I ask you most humbly! Just a little glass for farewell. I didn't remember to bring any from town and I found only one bottle at the station. Please, do!

(*Pause.*) Won't you really have any? (*Goes away from the door.*) If I only knew—I wouldn't have bought any. Well, I shan't drink any, either. (YASHA *carefully puts the tray on a chair.*) You have a drink, Yasha, at any rate.

YASHA. To those departing! And good luck to those who stay behind! (*Drinks.*) I can assure you that this isn't real champagne.

LOPAKHIN. Eight rubles a bottle. (*Pause.*) It's frightfully cold here.

YASHA. We made no fire today, since we're going away. (*Laughs.*)

LOPAKHIN. What's the matter with you?

YASHA. I'm happy—that's all!

LOPAKHIN. It's October, but it's as sunny and quiet as if it were summer. Good for building. (*Looking at his watch and speaking through the door.*) Ladies and gentlemen, please remember that it's only forty-seven minutes till train time! You must leave for the station in twenty minutes. Hurry up.

[TROFIMOFF, *in an overcoat, enters from the outside.*]

TROFIMOFF. I think it's time we went. The carriages are waiting. Where the devil are my rubbers? They're lost. (*Through the door.*) Anya, I can't find my rubbers! I can't!

LOPAKHIN. I have to go to Kharkoff. I'm going on the same train as you. I'm going to spend the whole winter in Kharkoff. I've been hanging around with you people. I am tired of doing nothing. I must have something to do with my hands; they seem to belong to a different person if I don't use them.

TROFIMOFF. We'll go away now and then you'll start again on your useful occupations!

LOPAKHIN. Have a glass?

TROFIMOFF. No—thanks!

LOPAKHIN. So you're off to Moscow now?

TROFIMOFF. Yes. I'll see them into town and tomorrow I'm going to Moscow.

LOPAKHIN. Yes . . . I suppose the professors aren't lecturing yet; they're waiting till you turn up!

TROFIMOFF. That does not concern you.

LOPAKHIN. How many years have you been going to the university?

TROFIMOFF. Think of something new! This is old and trite! (*Looking for his rubbers.*) You know, we may not meet again, so just let me give you a parting bit of advice: Don't wave your hands about! Get rid of that habit of waving them about. And then, building villas and reckoning on their residents becoming freeholders in time—that's the same thing; it's all a matter of waving your hands . . . I like you in spite of everything . . . You've slender, delicate fingers, like those of an artist, and you've a gentle, refined soul. . . .

LOPAKHIN (*embraces him*). Good-bye, dear fellow. Thanks for all you've said. If you need money for the journey, let me give you some.

TROFIMOFF. What for? I don't need any.

LOPAKHIN. But you've nothing!

TROFIMOFF. Yes, I have, thank you; I received some for a translation. Here it is in my pocket. (*Nervously.*) But I can't find my rubbers!

VARYA (*from the other room*). Take your rubbish away! (*Throws a pair of rubbers on stage.*)

TROFIMOFF. Why are you angry, Varya? H'm! These aren't my rubbers!

LOPAKHIN. In the spring I sowed three thousand acres of poppies, and now I've netted forty thousand rubles profit. Why turn up your nose at it? I'm just a simple peasant. . . . And when my poppies were in bloom, what a picture it was! So, as I was saying, I made forty thousand rubles, and I mean I'd like to lend you some, because I can afford it.

TROFIMOFF. Your father was a peasant, mine was a druggist, and that means nothing at all. (LOPAKHIN *takes out his pocketbook.*) No, no . . . Even if you gave me twenty thousand I should refuse. I'm a free man. And everything that rich and poor alike value so highly carries no more weight with me than thistledown in a wind. I can do without, you, I can pass you by. I'm strong and proud. Mankind goes on to the highest possible truths and happiness on earth, and I march in the front ranks!

LOPAKHIN. Will you reach there?

TROFIMOFF. I shall! (*Pause.*) I'll reach there and show the way to others.

[*Axes cutting the trees are heard in the distance.*]

LOPAKHIN. Well, good-bye, old man. It's time to go. Here we stand pulling one another's noses, but life goes its own way all the while. When I work for a long stretch tirelessly, my thoughts become clearer and it seems to me that I understand the reasons for existence. But think, brother, how many people live in Russia without knowing why—? But all this is beside the point. Leonid Andreievitch, they say, has accepted a post in a bank; he will get six thousand rubles a year . . . But he won't stand it; he's very lazy.

ANYA (*at the door*). Mother asks if you will stop them cutting down the orchard until she has gone away.

TROFIMOFF. Yes, really, you ought to have enough tact not to do that.

[*Exit.*]

LOPAKHIN. All right, all right . . . What funny people!

[*Exit.*]

ANYA. Has Firce been sent to the hospital?

YASHA. I gave the order this morning. I suppose they've sent him.

ANYA (*to* YEPIKHODOFF, *who crosses the room*). Semyon Panteleievitch, please make inquiries if Firce has been sent to the hospital.

YASHA (*offended*). I told Yegor this morning. What's the use of asking ten times?

YEPIKHODOFF. That old Firce, in my conclusive opinion, isn't worth mending; he had better join his ancestors. I only envy him. (*Puts a trunk on a hat-box and squashes it.*) Well, of course. I thought so!

[*Exit.*]

YASHA (*grinning*). Two-and-twenty troubles.

VARYA (*behind the door*). Has Firce been taken away to the hospital?

ANYA. Yes.

VARYA. Why didn't they take the letter to the doctor?

ANYA. It'll have to be sent after him.

[*Exit.*]

VARYA (*in the next room*). Where's Yasha? Tell him his mother has come and wishes to say good-bye to him.

YASHA (*waving his hand*). She'll make me lose all patience!

[DUNYASHA *meanwhile has been busying herself with the bags; now that* YASHA *is left alone, she goes to him.*]

DUNYASHA. If you would only look at me once, Yasha. You're going away, leaving me behind . . . (*Weeps and hugs him.*)

YASHA. What's the use of crying? (*Drinks champagne.*) In six days I'll be back again in Paris. Tomorrow we get into the express and off we go. I can hardly believe it. Vive la France! It doesn't suit me here, I can't live here . . . it's no good. Well, I've seen the uncivilized world; I have had enough of it. (*Drinks champagne.*) What are you crying for? Behave decently and then you'll have no cause for tears!

DUNYASHA (*powders herself, looking in the mirror*). Write me from Paris! I loved you so much, Yasha, so much! I am a delicate girl, Yasha.

YASHA. Somebody's coming.

[*He bustles around the baggage, singing softly. Enter* LIUBOFF ANDREIEVNA, GAIEFF, ANYA, *and* CHARLOTTA IVANOVNA.]

GAIEFF. We'd better be off. There's no time to lose. (*Looks at* YASHA.) Somebody smells of herring!

LIUBOFF. We needn't get into our carriages for ten minutes. (*Looks round the room.*) Good-bye, dear house, old grandfather. The winter will pass, the spring will come, and then you'll be here no more. You'll be pulled down. How much these walls have seen! (*Passionately kisses her daughter.*) My treasure, you're radiant, your eyes flash like two jewels! Are you happy? Very?

ANYA. Very! A new life is beginning, mother!

GAIEFF (*gaily*). Yes, really, everything's all right now. Before the cherry orchard was sold we all were excited and worried, and then, when the question was solved once and for all, we all calmed down, and even became cheerful. I'm a bank official now, and a financier . . . red in the center; and you, Liuba, look better for some reason or other, there's no doubt about it.

LIUBOFF. Yes. My nerves are better, it's true. (*She puts on her coat and hat.*) I sleep well. Take my baggage out, Yasha. It's time. (*To* ANYA.) My little girl, we'll soon see each other again . . . I'm off to Paris. I'll live there on the money your grandmother from Yaroslavl sent to buy the estate—bless her!—though it won't last long.

ANYA. You'll come back soon, soon, mother, won't you? I'll get ready, and pass the examination at the High School, and then I'll work and help you. We'll read all sorts of books together, won't we? (*Kisses her mother's hands.*) We'll read in the autumn evenings; we'll read many books, and a beautiful new world will open up before us . . . (*Thoughtfully.*) You'll come, mother. . . .

LIUBOFF. I'll come, my darling. (*Embraces her.*)

[*Enter* LOPAKHIN. CHARLOTTA *is singing to herself.*]

GAIEFF. Charlotta is happy; she's singing!

CHARLOTTA. (*takes a bundle, looking like a wrapped-up baby*). My little baby, bye-bye. (*The baby seems to answer, "Oua, oua!"*) Hush, my nice little boy. (*"Oua! Oua!"*) I'm so sorry for you! (*Throws the bundle back.*) So please find me a new place. I can't go on like this.

LOPAKHIN. We'll find one, Charlotta Ivanovna, don't you be afraid.

GAIEFF. Everybody's leaving us. Varya's going away . . . we've suddenly become unnecessary.

CHARLOTTA. I've nowhere to live in town. I must go away. (*Hums.*) Never mind.

[*Enter* PISHCHIK.]

LOPAKHIN. The miracle of nature!

PISHCHIK (*puffing*). Oh, let me get my breath again. I'm fagged . . . My honorable friends, give me some water . . .

GAIEFF. Come for money did you? I'm your humble servant, and I'm going out of the way of temptation.

[*Exit.*]

PISHCHIK. I haven't been here for ever so long . . . dear madam. (*To* LOPAKHIN.) You here? Glad to see you . . . man of tremendous brain . . . take this . . . take it . . . (*Gives* LOPAKHIN *money.*) Four hundred rubles . . . that leaves 841—

LOPAKHIN (*shrugs his shoulders in surprise*). It's like a dream. Where did you get this?

PISHCHIK. Stop . . . it's hot . . . A most unexpected thing happened. A group of Englishmen came along and found some white clay on my land. . . . (*To* LIUBOFF ANDREIEVNA.) And here's four hundred for you . . . beautiful lady . . . (*Gives her money.*) Give you the rest later . . . (*Drinks water.*) Just now a young man in the train was saying that some great philosopher advises us all to jump from the roofs. "Jump!" he says, and that's all. (*Astonished.*) Just imagine! More water!

LOPAKHIN. Who were these Englishmen?

PISHCHIK. I've leased the land with the clay to them for twenty-four years . . . Now, excuse me, I've no time. I must hurry or—I'll go to Gnoikoff—to Kardamanoff—I owe everybody—(*Drinks.*) Good-bye—I'll drop in Thursday.

LIUBOFF. We're just starting off to town, and tomorrow I go abroad.

PISHCHIK (*agitated*). What? Why to town? I see furniture . . . trunks . . . Well, never mind. (*Crying.*) Never mind. These Englishmen are men of tremendous intellect . . . Never mind . . . Be happy . . . God will help you . . . Never mind . . . Everything in this world comes to an end . . . (*Kisses* LIUBOFF ANDREIEVNA*'s hand.*) And if you should happen to hear that my end has come, just remember this old . . . horse and say: "There used to be a certain fellow called Semyonoff-Pishchik, God bless his soul. . . ." Wonderful weather . . . yes . . . (*Exit deeply moved, but returns at once and says in the door.*) Dashenka sent her love!

[*Exit.*]

LIUBOFF. Now we can go. I've two worries, though. The first is poor Firce. (*Looks at her watch.*) We've still five minutes . . .

ANYA. Mother, Firce has already been sent to the hospital. Yasha sent him off this morning.

LIUBOFF. The second is Varya. She's used to getting up early and to work, and now she has no work to do, she's like a fish out of water. She's grown thin and pale, and she cries, poor thing. . . . (*Pause.*) You know very well, Yermolai Alexeievitch, that I hoped formerly to marry her to you, and I suppose you are going to marry somebody? (*Whispers to* ANYA, *who nods to* CHARLOTTA, *and they both go out.*) She loves you, she's your sort, and I don't understand, I really don't, why you seem to be keeping away from each other. I don't understand!

LOPAKHIN. To tell the truth, I don't understand it myself. It's all so strange. . . . If there's still time, I'll be ready at once. Let's get it over, once and for all; I don't feel as if I could ever propose to her without you.

LIUBOFF. Excellent. It'll take only a minute. I'll call her.

LOPAKHIN. The champagne comes in very handy. (*Looking at the glass.*) They're empty, somebody's drunk them already. (YASHA *coughs.*) I call that licking it up. . . .

LIUBOFF (*animated*). Excellent. We'll go out. Yasha, *allez.* I'll call her . . . (*At the door.*) Varya, leave that and come here. Come!

[*Exit with* YASHA.]

LOPAKHIN (*looks at his watch*). Yes . . . (*Pause.*)

[*There is a restrained laugh behind the door, a whisper, then* VARYA *comes in. She examines the luggage at length.*]

VARYA. I can't seem to find it . . .

LOPAKHIN. What are you looking for?

VARYA. I packed it myself and I don't remember. (*Pause.*)

LOPAKHIN. Where are you going now, Varvara Mikhailovna?

VARYA. I? To the Ragulins . . . I've accepted a position, to look after their household . . . housekeeper or something.

LOPAKHIN. Is that at Yashnevo? It's about fifty miles. (*Pause.*) So life in this house is finished now. . . .

VARYA (*looking at the baggage*). Where is it? . . . perhaps I've put it away in the trunk . . . Yes, there'll be no more life in this house . . .

LOPAKHIN. And I'm off to Kharkoff at once . . . by this train. I've a lot of business on hand. I'm leaving Yepikhodoff here . . . I've hired him.

VARYA. Well, well!

LOPAKHIN. Last year at this time the snow was already falling, if you remember, and now it's nice and sunny. Only it's rather cold . . . There's three degrees of frost.

VARYA. I didn't look. (*Pause.*) And our thermometer's broken. . . . (*Pause.*)

VOICE AT THE DOOR. Yermolai Alexeievitch!

LOPAKHIN (*As if he has long been waiting to be called.*) Just a minute.

[*Exit quickly.* VARYA, *sitting on the floor, puts her face against a bundle of clothes and weeps gently. The door opens.* LIUBOFF ANDREIEVNA *enters carefully.*]

LIUBOFF. Well? (*Pause.*) We must go.

VARYA (*not crying now, wipes her eyes*). Yes, it's quite time, dear mother. I'll get to the Ragulins today, if I don't miss the train. . . .

LIUBOFF (*at the door*). Anya, put on your things. (*Enter* ANYA, *then* GAIEFF, *and* CHARLOTTA IVANOVNA. GAIEFF *wears a warm overcoat with a cape. A servant and drivers come in.* YEPIKHODOFF *bustles around the baggage.*) Now we can go away.

ANYA (*joyfully*). Away!

GAIEFF. My friends, my dear friends! Can I be silent, in leaving this house forever?—can I restrain myself, in saying farewell, from expressing those feelings which now fill all my soul?

ANYA (*imploringly*). Uncle!

VARYA. Uncle, you shouldn't!

GAIEFF (*stupidly*). Double the red into the center . . . I'll be quiet.

[*Enter* TROFIMOFF, *then* LOPAKHIN.]

TROFIMOFF. Well, it's time to go!

LOPAKHIN. Yepikhodoff, my coat!

LIUBOFF. I'll sit here one minute more. It's as if I'd never really noticed what the walls and ceilings of this house were like, and now I look at them greedily, with such tender love. . . .

GAIEFF. I remember, when I was six years old, on Trinity Sunday, I sat at this window and looked and watched my father go to church. . . .

LIUBOFF. Have all the things been taken away?

LOPAKHIN. Yes, all, I think. (*To* YEPIKHODOFF, *putting on his coat.*) You see that everything's quite straight, Yepikhodoff.

YEPIKHODOFF (*hoarsely*). You may depend upon me, Yermolai Alexeievitch!

LOPAKHIN. What's the matter with your voice?

YEPIKHODOFF. I swallowed something just now; I was taking a drink of water.

YASHA (*suspiciously*). What manners . . .

LIUBOFF. We go away, and not a soul remains behind.

LOPAKHIN. Till the spring.

VARYA (*drags an umbrella out of a bundle, and seems to be waving it about.* LOPAKHIN *appears to be frightened*). What are you doing? . . . I never thought . . .

TROFIMOFF. Come along, let's take our seats . . . it's time! The train will be in presently.

VARYA. Peter, here they are, your rubbers, by that trunk. (*In tears.*) And how old and dirty they are . . .

TROFIMOFF (*putting them on*). Come on!

GAIEFF (*deeply moved, nearly crying*). The train . . . the station . . . Cross in the center, a white double in the corner. . . .

LIUBOFF. Let's go!

LOPAKHIN. Are you all here? There's nobody else? (*Locks the side-door on the left.*) There's a lot of things in there. I must lock them up. Come!

ANYA. Good-bye, home! Good-bye, old life!

TROFIMOFF. Welcome, new life. (*Exit with* ANYA. VARYA *looks round the room and goes out slowly.* YASHA *and* CHARLOTTA, *with her little dog, go out.*)

LOPAKHIN. Till the spring then! Come on . . . till we meet again!

[*Exit.*]

[LIUBOFF ANDREIEVNA *and* GAIEFF *are left alone. They seem to have been waiting for this moment. They fall into each other's arms and sob restrainedly and quietly, fearing that somebody might hear them.*]

GAIEFF (*in despair*). My sister, my sister . . .

LIUBOFF. My dear, my gentle, beautiful orchard! My life, my youth, my happiness, good-bye! Good-bye!

ANYA'S VOICE (*gaily*). Mother!

TROFIMOFF'S VOICE (*gaily, excited*). Coo-ee!

LIUBOFF. To look at the walls and the windows for the last time . . . My late mother used to like to walk about this room . . .

GAIEFF. My sister, my sister!

ANYA'S VOICE. Mother!

TROFIMOFF'S VOICE (*gaily, excited*). Coo-ee!

LIUBOFF. We're coming! (*They go out. The stage is empty. The sound of keys turned in the locks is heard, and then the noise of the carriages driving off. It is quiet. Then the sound of an ax against the trees is heard in the silence sadly and staccato. Footsteps are heard.* FIRCE *comes in from the door on the right. He is dressed as usual, in a short jacket and white vest, with slippers on his feet. He is ill. He goes to the door and tries the handle.*)

FIRCE. It's locked. They've left. (*Sits on sofa.*) They've forgotten me. . . . Never mind, I'll sit here . . . And Leonid Andreievitch has probably gone in a light overcoat instead of putting on his fur coat . . . (*Sighs anxiously.*) I didn't see. . . . Oh, these young people! (*Mumbles something unintelligible.*) Life's gone on as if I'd never lived. (*Lying down.*) I'll lie down. . . . You've no strength left in you, nothing left at all. . . . Oh, you . . . bungler! (*He lies motionless. The distant sound is heard, as if from the sky, of a string breaking, dying away morosely. Silence follows it, and only the sound somewhere in the distance, of the ax falling on the trees, is audible.*)

CRITICAL COMMENTARY

It is pretty well understood that *The Cherry Orchard* is too hard for the average person. This is because the average person is a crude, pushy know-it-all; whereas a proper spectator of *The Cherry Orchard* has got to be a more sensitive type, sensitive enough to realize that life is such a can of worms that you might as well see it as it is and try to enjoy it. Since "can of worms" is a rather crude critical term, the play is ordinarily described by critics in language more like this: "a drama of 'pathetic motivation,' a theater-poem of the suffering of change . . . a mode of action and awareness . . . much closer to the skeptical basis of modern realism . . . direct perception before predication is always true . . . drama neither as a vehicle for individualistic self-realization (Ibsen) nor a means of exorcistic self-expression (Strindberg) but rather as a form for depicting that fluid world beyond the self, with the author functioning only as an impartial witness."

Chekhov himself did not like to talk about his plays in this way and always changed the subject, generally by saying that he was just a doctor, although not the kind who read only the monthly medical journal and diagnosed everything as catarrh. Occasionally he did become exercised enough to blurt out statements like the following (in a letter of October, 1889):

> I am afraid of those who look for a tendency between the lines, and who are determined to regard me as a liberal or as a conservative. I am not a liberal, not a conservative, not a believer in gradual progress, not a monk, not an indifferentist. I should like to be a free artist and nothing more. . . . That is why I have no preference either for gendarmes, or for butchers, or for scientists, or for writers, or for the younger generation. I regard trade-marks and labels as a superstition. My holy of holies is the human body, health, intelligence, talent, inspiration, love, and the most absolute freedom—freedom from violence and lying, whatever forms they take.

He also went so far as to make some rather fey efforts to prevent the Moscow Art Theater from taking *The Cherry Orchard* too solemnly, as they rehearsed it during the fall of 1903: "Why do you say in your telegram that there are many tearful people in the play? Where are they? . . . There is no cemetery in Act II . . . The play [is] not a drama, but a comedy, in parts even a farce. . . ." Stanislavsky, the director, replied that they were doing their best to get the halftones, but that the play made him cry like a woman. Chekhov was apparently trying to keep a balance so that the play would say what the can of worms is really like and how he felt about it. "What is important is that there should be a play and that the author should be felt in it. In the modern plays one has to read there is no author, as though they were all made in the same factory by one machine. . . ." (from a letter of September 2, 1903). He explained that he called the play *The Cherry Orchard* because it sounded good, and he presumably decided on the content of the play because it seemed a good sample of life as he saw it and felt it: a dozen second-rate Russians standing around watching a defunct country estate being subdivided into building lots.

Attempts to clarify Chekhov's tone and feelings (elusive, passionate, honest, detached, amused, tolerant, good-natured, illusionless) by translating them into nondramatic terms always seem to end up as overstatements or simplifications. The sense of comedy in the play, for example, obviously has something to do with our distance from the characters and the action. But where exactly are we? It also seems to come from what the play does to time, what it asks us to feel about the meaning of change, how past, present, and future go together. It is clearly not the gray or pugnacious feeling we get from the morning paper or from the problem play. It is also related to the fact that just as we get a character analyzed and typed he does something human and then, being human, turns into being not quite with it or talking in non sequiturs. Is it possible that the characters do have in common, at least, a preoccupation with self, human separateness in the absence of any unifying value, an inability to hear and say important things, a proneness to linguistic accidents—and all intensified or undercut by the irrelevant busyness of everyday life? Or is that too solemn a way to put it? At any rate, both dialogue and incidents flow through patterns that are related to the extra-logical nature and form of comedy.

Stanislavsky describes how, with Chekhov's permission, the Moscow Art Theater cut a scene from the end of Act II.

> There takes place a meeting of two lonely people [Fiers and Charlotta]. They have nothing to speak about, but they so want to speak, for a human being must speak to some one. Charlotta begins to tell Fiers of how she worked in her youth in a circus and performed the *salto mortale,* in those very words, which, in our version she says in the beginning of the act. . . . In answer to her story, Fiers talks at length and randomly about something that cannot be understood that happened in the days of his youth, when somebody was taken

> somewhere in a wagon accompanied by sounds of squeaking and crying, and Fiers interprets these sounds with the words "cling-clang." Charlotta does not understand anything in his story, but catches up his cue so that the one common moment in the lives of these two lonely people may not be disturbed. They cry "Cling-Clang" to each other and both laugh very sincerely. This was the way Chekhov ended the act. (Herbert Goldstone, ed., *A Casebook on The Cherry Orchard,* 1965, pp. 68–69)

Stanislavsky goes on to explain that such a "lyric ending lowered the atmosphere of the act" and they could not lift it again. Lyric? Lowered? Or too harsh, intense, modern? Or should it have been kept?

Useful Criticism

Brustein, Robert. *The Theater of Revolt.** Boston: Atlantic-Little, Brown, 1964.

Fergusson, Francis. *The Idea of a Theater.** Garden City, N.Y.: Doubleday, 1953.

Goldstone, Herbert, ed. *A Casebook on The Cherry Orchard.** Boston: Allyn and Bacon, 1965.

Hingley, Ronald. *Chekhov: A Biographical and Critical Study.** New York: Barnes & Noble, 1966.

Jackson, Robert Louis, ed. *Chekhov** (Twentieth Century Views). Englewood Cliffs, N.J.: Prentice-Hall, 1967.

Simmons, Ernest J. *Chekhov: A Biography.** Boston: Atlantic-Little, Brown, 1962.

* Available in paperback.

SIX CHARACTERS IN SEARCH OF AN AUTHOR

(*Sei personaggi in cerca d'autore*)

A COMEDY IN THE MAKING

Luigi Pirandello

English version by EDWARD STORER

ACTORS OF THE COMPANY

THE MANAGER	OTHER ACTORS AND ACTRESSES
LEADING LADY	PROPERTY MAN
LEADING MAN	PROMPTER
SECOND LADY	MACHINIST
LEAD	MANAGER'S SECRETARY
L'INGÉNUE	DOOR-KEEPER
JUVENILE LEAD	SCENE-SHIFTERS

Daytime. The Stage of a Theatre

N. B. The Comedy is without acts or scenes. The performance is interrupted once, without the curtain being lowered, when the manager and the chief characters withdraw to arrange the scenario. A second interruption of the action takes place when, by mistake, the stage hands let the curtain down.

ACT I

The spectators will find the curtain raised and the stage as it usually is during the day time. It will be half dark, and empty, so that from the

---

beginning the public may have the impression of an impromptu performance.

Prompter's box and a small table and chair for the manager.

Two other small tables and several chairs scattered about as during rehearsals.

The ACTORS *and* ACTRESSES *of the company enter from the back of the stage:*
first one, then another, then two together; nine or ten in all. They are about to rehearse a Pirandello play: Mixing It Up.[1] *Some of the company move off towards their dressing rooms. The* PROMPTER *who has the "book" under his arm, is waiting for the manager in order to begin the rehearsal.*

The ACTORS *and* ACTRESSES, *some standing, some sitting, chat and smoke. One perhaps reads a paper; another cons his part.*

Finally, THE MANAGER *enters and goes to the table prepared for him. His* SECRETARY *brings him his mail, through which he glances. The* PROMPTER *takes his seat, turns on a light, and opens the "book."*

THE MANAGER (*throwing a letter down on the table*). I can't see (*To* PROPERTY MAN.) Let's have a little light, please!

PROPERTY MAN. Yes sir, yes, at once. (*A light comes down on to the stage.*)

THE MANAGER (*clapping his hands*). Come along! Come along! Second act of "Mixing It Up." (*Sits down.*)

[*The* ACTORS *and* ACTRESSES *go from the front of the stage to the wings, all except the three who are to begin the rehearsal.*]

PROMPTER (*reading the "book"*). "Leo Gala's house. A curious room serving as dining-room and study."

THE MANAGER (*to* PROPERTY MAN). Fix up the old red room.

PROPERTY MAN (*noting it down*). Red set. All right!

PROMPTER (*continuing to read from the "book"*). "Table already laid and writing desk with books and papers. Book-shelves. Exit rear to Leo's bedroom. Exit left to kitchen. Principal exit to right."

THE MANAGER (*energetically*). Well, you understand: The principal exit over there; here, the kitchen. (*Turning to* ACTOR *who is to play the part of* SOCRATES.) You make your entrances and exits here. (*To* PROPERTY MAN.) The baize doors at the rear, and curtains.

PROPERTY MAN (*noting it down*). Right!

PROMPTER (*reading as before*). "When the curtain rises, Leo Gala, dressed in cook's cap and apron is busy beating an egg in a cup. Philip, also dressed as a cook, is beating another egg. Guido Venanzi is seated and listening."

LEADING MAN (*to* MANAGER). Excuse me, but must I absolutely wear a cook's cap?

[1] i.e. *Il giuoco delle parti.*

THE MANAGER (*annoyed*). I imagine so. It says so there anyway. (*Pointing to the "book."*)

LEADING MAN. But it's ridiculous!

THE MANAGER (*jumping up in a rage*). Ridiculous? Ridiculous? Is it my fault if France won't send us any more good comedies, and we are reduced to putting on Pirandello's works, where nobody understands anything, and where the author plays the fool with us all? (*The* ACTORS *grin. The* MANAGER *goes to* LEADING MAN *and shouts.*) Yes sir, you put on the cook's cap and beat eggs. Do you suppose that with all this egg-beating business you are on an ordinary stage? Get that out of your head. You represent the shell of the eggs you are beating! (*Laughter and comments among the* ACTORS.) Silence! and listen to my explanations, please! (*To* LEADING MAN.) "The empty form of reason without the fullness of instinct, which is blind."—You stand for reason, your wife is instinct. It's a mixing up of the parts, according to which you who act your own part become the puppet of yourself. Do you understand?

LEADING MAN. I'm hanged if I do.

THE MANAGER. Neither do I. But let's get on with it. It's sure to be a glorious failure anyway. (*Confidentially.*) But I say, please face three-quarters. Otherwise, what with the abstruseness of the dialogue, and the public that won't be able to hear you, the whole thing will go to hell. Come on! come on!

PROMPTER. Pardon sir, may I get into my box? There's a bit of a draught.

THE MANAGER. Yes, yes, of course!

At this point, the DOOR-KEEPER *has entered from the stage door and advances towards the manager's table, taking off his braided cap. During this manoeuvre, the* SIX CHARACTERS *enter, and stop by the door at back of stage, so that when the* DOOR-KEEPER *is about to announce their coming to the* MANAGER, *they are already on the stage. A tenuous light surrounds them, almost as if irradiated by them—the faint breath of their fantastic reality.*

This light will disappear when they come forward towards the actors. They preserve, however, something of the dream lightness in which they seem almost suspended; but this does not detract from the essential reality of their forms and expressions.

He who is known as THE FATHER *is a man of about 50: hair, reddish in colour, thin at the temples; he is not bald, however; thick moustaches, falling over his still fresh mouth, which often opens in an empty and uncertain smile. He is fattish, pale; with an especially wide forehead. He has blue, oval-shaped eyes, very clear and piercing. Wears light trousers and a dark jacket. He is alternatively mellifluous and violent in his manner.*

THE MOTHER *seems crushed and terrified as if by an intolerable weight of shame and abasement. She is dressed in modest black and wears a thick widow's veil of crêpe. When she lifts this, she reveals a wax-like face. She always keeps her eyes downcast.*

THE STEP-DAUGHTER, *is dashing, almost impudent, beautiful. She wears mourning too, but with great elegance. She shows contempt for the timid half-frightened manner of the wretched* BOY *(14 years old, and also dressed in black); on the other hand, she displays a lively tenderness for her little sister,* THE CHILD *(about four), who is dressed in white, with a black silk sash at the waist.*

THE SON *(22) tall, severe in his attitude of contempt for* THE FATHER, *supercilious and indifferent to* THE MOTHER. *He looks as if he had come on the stage against his will.*

DOOR-KEEPER (*cap in hand*). Excuse me, sir . . .

THE MANAGER (*rudely*). Eh? What is it?

DOOR-KEEPER (*timidly*). These people are asking for you, sir.

THE MANAGER (*furious*). I am rehearsing, and you know perfectly well no one's allowed to come in during rehearsals! (*Turning to the* CHARACTERS.) Who are you, please? What do you want?

THE FATHER (*coming forward a little, followed by the others who seem embarrassed*). As a matter of fact . . . we have come here in search of an author . . .

THE MANAGER (*half angry, half amazed*). An author? What author?

THE FATHER. Any author, sir.

THE MANAGER. But there's no author here. We are not rehearsing a new piece.

THE STEP-DAUGHTER (*vivaciously*). So much the better, so much the better! We can be your new piece.

AN ACTOR (*coming forward from the others*). Oh, do you hear that?

THE FATHER (*to* STEP-DAUGHTER). Yes, but if the author isn't here . . . (*To* MANAGER.) unless you would be willing . . .

THE MANAGER. You are trying to be funny.

THE FATHER. No, for Heaven's sake, what are you saying? We bring you a drama, sir.

THE STEP-DAUGHTER. We may be your fortune.

THE MANAGER. Will you oblige me by going away? We haven't time to waste with mad people.

THE FATHER (*mellifluously*). Oh sir, you know well that life is full of infinite absurdities, which, strangely enough, do not even need to appear plausible, since they are true.

THE MANAGER. What the devil is he talking about?

THE FATHER. I say that to reverse the ordinary process may well be considered a madness: that is, to create credible situations, in order that they may appear true. But permit me to observe that if this be madness, it is the sole *raison d'être* of your profession, gentlemen. (*The* ACTORS *look hurt and perplexed.*)

THE MANAGER (*getting up and looking at him*). So our profession seems to you one worthy of madmen then?

THE FATHER. Well, to make seem true that which isn't true . . . without any need . . . for a joke as it were . . . Isn't that your mission, gentlemen: to give life to fantastic characters on the stage?

THE MANAGER (*interpreting the rising anger of the* COMPANY). But I would beg you to believe, my dear sir, that the profession of the comedian is a noble one. If today, as things go, the playwrights give us stupid comedies to play and puppets to represent instead of men, remember we are proud to have given life to immortal works here on these very boards! (*The* ACTORS, *satisfied, applaud their* MANAGER.)

THE FATHER (*interrupting furiously*). Exactly, perfectly, to living beings more alive than those who breathe and wear clothes: beings less real perhaps, but truer! I agree with you entirely. (*The* ACTORS *look at one another in amazement.*)

THE MANAGER. But what do you mean? Before, you said . . .

THE FATHER. No, excuse me, I meant it for you, sir, who were crying out that you had no time to lose with madmen, while no one better than yourself knows that nature uses the instrument of human fantasy in order to pursue her high creative purpose.

THE MANAGER. Very well,—but where does all this take us?

THE FATHER. Nowhere! It is merely to show you that one is born to life in many forms, in many shapes, as tree, or as stone, as water, as butterfly, or as woman. So one may also be born a character in a play.

THE MANAGER (*with feigned comic dismay*). So you and these other friends of yours have been born characters?

THE FATHER. Exactly, and alive as you see! (MANAGER *and* ACTORS *burst out laughing.*)

THE FATHER (*hurt*). I am sorry you laugh, because we carry in us a drama, as you can guess from this woman here veiled in black.

THE MANAGER (*losing patience at last and almost indignant*). Oh, chuck it! Get away please! Clear out of here! (*To* PROPERTY MAN.) For Heaven's sake, turn them out!

THE FATHER (*resisting*). No, no, look here, we . . .

THE MANAGER (*roaring*). We come here to work, you know.

LEADING ACTOR. One cannot let oneself be made such a fool of.

THE FATHER (*determined, coming forward*). I marvel at your incredulity, gentlemen. Are you not accustomed to see the characters created by an author spring to life in yourselves and face each other? Just because there is no "book" (*Pointing to the* PROMPTER'*s box.*) which contains us, you refuse to believe . . .

THE STEP-DAUGHTER (*advances towards* MANAGER, *smiling and coquettish*). Believe me, we are really six most interesting characters, sir; side-tracked however.

THE FATHER. Yes, that is the word! (*To* MANAGER *all at once.*) In the sense, that is, that the author who created us alive no longer wished, or was no longer able, materially to put us into a work of art. And this was a real crime, sir; because he who has had the luck to be born a character can laugh even at death. He cannot die. The man, the writer, the instrument of the creation will die, but his creation does not die. And to live for ever, it does not need to have extraordinary gifts or to be able to work wonders. Who was Sancho Panza? Who was Don Abbondio? Yet they live eternally because—live germs as they were—they had the fortune to find a fecundating matrix, a fantasy which could raise and nourish them: make them live for ever!

THE MANAGER. That is quite all right. But what do you want here, all of you?

THE FATHER. We want to live.

THE MANAGER (*ironically*). For Eternity?

THE FATHER. No, sir, only for a moment . . . in you.

AN ACTOR. Just listen to him!

LEADING LADY. They want to live, in us . . . !

JUVENILE LEAD (*pointing to the* STEP-DAUGHTER). I've no objection, as far as that one is concerned!

THE FATHER. Look here! look here! The comedy has to be made. (*To the* MANAGER.) But if you and your actors are willing, we can soon concert it among ourselves.

THE MANAGER (*annoyed*). But what do you want to concert? We don't go in for concerts here. Here we play dramas and comedies!

THE FATHER. Exactly! That is just why we have come to you.

THE MANAGER. And where is the "book"?

THE FATHER. It is in us! (*The* ACTORS *laugh.*) The drama is in us, and we are the drama. We are impatient to play it. Our inner passion drives us on to this.

THE STEP-DAUGHTER (*disdainful, alluring, treacherous, full of impudence*). My passion, sir! Ah, if you only knew! My passion for him! (*Points to* THE FATHER *and makes a pretence of embracing him. Then she breaks out into a loud laugh.*)

THE FATHER (*angrily*). Behave yourself! And please don't laugh in that fashion.

THE STEP-DAUGHTER. With your permission, gentlemen, I, who am a two months' orphan, will show you how I can dance and sing. (*Sings and then dances* Prenez garde à Tchou-Tchin-Tchou.)

Les chinois sont un peuple malin,
De Shangaî à Pekin,
Ils ont mis des écriteaux partout:
Prenez garde à Tchou-Tchin-Tchou.

ACTORS AND ACTRESSES. Bravo! Well done! Tip-top!

THE MANAGER. Silence! This isn't a café concert, you know! (*Turning to the* FATHER *in consternation.*) Is she mad?

THE FATHER. Mad? No, she's worse than mad.

THE STEP-DAUGHTER (*to* MANAGER). Worse? Worse? Listen! Stage this drama for us at once! Then you will see that at a certain moment I . . . when this little darling here . . . (*Takes the* CHILD *by the hand and leads her to the* MANAGER.) Isn't she a dear? (*Takes her up and kisses her.*) Darling! Darling! (*Puts her down again and adds feelingly.*) Well, when God suddenly takes this dear little child away from that poor mother there; and this imbecile here (*Seizing hold of the* BOY *roughly and pushing him forward.*) does the stupidest things, like the fool he is, you will see me run away. Yes, gentlemen, I shall be off. But the moment hasn't arrived yet. After what has taken place between him and me (*Indicates the* FATHER *with a horrible wink.*) I can't remain any longer in this society, to have to witness the anguish of this mother here for that fool . . . (*Indicates the* SON.) Look at him! Look at him! See how indifferent, how frigid he is, because he is the legitimate son. He despises me, despises him (*Pointing to the* BOY.), despises this baby here; because . . . we are bastards. (*Goes to the* MOTHER *and embraces her.*) And he doesn't want to recognize her as his mother—she who is the common mother of us all. He looks down upon her as if she were only the mother of us three bastards. Wretch! (*She says all this very rapidly, excitedly. At the word "bastards" she raises her voice, and almost spits out the final "Wretch!"*)

THE MOTHER (*to the* MANAGER, *in anguish*). In the name of these two little children, I beg you . . . (*She grows faint and is about to fall.*) Oh God!

THE FATHER (*coming forward to support her as do some of the* ACTORS). Quick, a chair, a chair for this poor widow!

THE ACTORS. Is it true? Has she really fainted?

THE MANAGER. Quick, a chair! Here!

[*One of the* ACTORS *brings a chair, the* OTHERS *proffer assistance. The* MOTHER *tries to prevent the* FATHER *from lifting the veil which covers her face.*]

THE FATHER. Look at her! Look at her!

THE MOTHER. No, no; stop it please!

THE FATHER (*raising her veil*). Let them see you!

THE MOTHER (*rising and covering her face with her hands, in desperation*). I beg you, sir, to prevent this man from carrying out his plan which is loathsome to me.

THE MANAGER (*dumbfounded*). I don't understand at all. What is the situation? Is this lady your wife? (*To the* FATHER.)

THE FATHER. Yes, gentlemen: my wife!

THE MANAGER. But how can she be a widow if you are alive? (*The* ACTORS *find relief for their astonishment in a loud laugh.*)

THE FATHER. Don't laugh! Don't laugh like that, for Heaven's sake. Her drama lies just here in this: she has had a lover, a man who ought to be here.

THE MOTHER (*with a cry*). No! No!

THE STEP-DAUGHTER. Fortunately for her, he is dead. Two months ago as I said. We are in mourning, as you see.

THE FATHER. He isn't here you see, not because he is dead. He isn't here —look at her a moment and you will understand—because her drama isn't a drama of the love of two men for whom she was incapable of feeling anything except possibly a little gratitude—gratitude not for me but for the other. She isn't a woman, she is a mother, and her drama—powerful sir, I assure you—lies, as a matter of fact, all in these four children she has had by two men.

THE MOTHER. I had them? Have you got the courage to say that I wanted them? (*To the* COMPANY.) It was his doing. It was he who gave me that other man, who forced me to go away with him.

THE STEP-DAUGHTER. It isn't true.

THE MOTHER (*startled*). Not true, isn't it?

THE STEP-DAUGHTER. No, it isn't true, it just isn't true.

THE MOTHER. And what can you know about it?

THE STEP-DAUGHTER. It isn't true. Don't believe it. (*To* MANAGER.) Do you know why she says so? For that fellow there. (*Indicates the* SON.) She tortures herself, destroys herself on account of the neglect of that son there; and she wants him to believe that if she abandoned him when he was only two years old, it was because he (*Indicates the* FATHER.) made her do so.

THE MOTHER (*vigorously*). He forced me to it, and I call God to witness it. (*To the* MANAGER.) Ask him (*Indicates* HUSBAND.) if it isn't true. Let him speak. You (*To* DAUGHTER.) are not in a position to know anything about it.

THE STEP-DAUGHTER. I know you lived in peace and happiness with my father while he lived. Can you deny it?

THE MOTHER. No, I don't deny it . . .

THE STEP-DAUGHTER. He was always full of affection and kindness for you. (*To the* BOY, *angrily.*) It's true, isn't it? Tell them! Why don't you speak, you little fool?

THE MOTHER. Leave the poor boy alone. Why do you want to make me appear ungrateful, daughter? I don't want to offend your father. I have answered him that I didn't abandon my house and my son through any fault of mine, nor from any wilful passion.

THE FATHER. It is true. It was my doing.

LEADING MAN (*to the* COMPANY). What a spectacle!

LEADING LADY. We are the audience this time.

JUVENILE LEAD. For once, in a way.

THE MANAGER (*beginning to get really interested*). Let's hear them out. Listen!

THE SON. Oh yes, you're going to hear a fine bit now. He will talk to you of the Demon of Experiment.

THE FATHER. You are a cynical imbecile. I've told you so already a hundred times. (*To the* MANAGER.) He tries to make fun of me on account of this expression which I have found to excuse myself with.

THE SON (*with disgust*). Yes, phrases! phrases!

THE FATHER. Phrases! Isn't everyone consoled when faced with a trouble or fact he doesn't understand, by a word, some simple word, which tells us nothing and yet calms us?

THE STEP-DAUGHTER. Even in the case of remorse. In fact, especially then.

THE FATHER. Remorse? No, that isn't true. I've done more than use words to quieten the remorse in me.

THE STEP-DAUGHTER. Yes, there was a bit of money too. Yes, yes, a bit of money. There were the hundred lire he was about to offer me in payment, gentlemen . . . (*Sensation of horror among the* ACTORS.)

THE SON (*to the* STEP-DAUGHTER). This is vile.

THE STEP-DAUGHTER. Vile? There they were in a pale blue envelope on a little mahogany table in the back of Madame Pace's shop. You know Madame Pace—one of those ladies who attract poor girls of good family into their ateliers, under the pretext of their selling *robes et manteaux*.

THE SON. And he thinks he has bought the right to tyrannize over us all with those hundred lire he was going to pay; but which, fortunately—note this, gentlemen—he had no chance of paying.

THE STEP-DAUGHTER. It was a near thing, though, you know! (*Laughs ironically.*)

THE MOTHER (*protesting*). Shame, my daughter, shame!

THE STEP-DAUGHTER. Shame indeed! This is my revenge! I am dying to live that scene . . . The room . . . I see it . . . Here is the window with the mantles exposed, there the divan, the looking-glass, a screen, there in front of the window the little mahogany table with the blue envelope containing one hundred lire. I see it. I see it. I could take hold of it . . . But you, gentlemen, you ought to turn your backs now: I am almost nude, you know. But I don't blush: I leave that to him. (*Indicating* FATHER.)

THE MANAGER. I don't understand this at all.

THE FATHER. Naturally enough. I would ask you, sir, to exercise your authority a little here, and let me speak before you believe all she is trying to blame me with. Let me explain.

THE STEP-DAUGHTER. Ah yes, explain it in your own way.

THE FATHER. But don't you see that the whole trouble lies here. In words, words. Each one of us has within him a whole world of things, each man of us his own special world, and how can we ever come to an understanding if I put in the words I utter the sense and value of things as I see them; while you who listen to me must inevitably translate them according to the conception of things each one of you has within himself. We think we understand each other, but we never really do. Look here! This woman (*Indicating the* MOTHER.) takes all my pity for her as a special ferocious form of cruelty.

THE MOTHER. But you drove me away.

THE FATHER. Do you hear her? I drove her away! She believes I really sent her away.

THE MOTHER. You know how to talk, and I don't; but, believe me, sir (*To* MANAGER.), after he had married me . . . who knows why? . . . I was a poor insignificant woman . . .

THE FATHER. But, good Heavens! it was just for your humility that I married you. I loved this simplicity in you. (*He stops when he sees she makes signs to contradict him, opens his arms wide in sign of desperation, seeing how hopeless it is to make himself understood.*) You see she denies it. Her mental deafness, believe me, is phenomenal, the limit: (*Touches his forehead.*) deaf, deaf, mentally deaf! She has plenty of feeling. Oh yes, a good heart for the children; but the brain—deaf, to the point of desperation——!

THE STEP-DAUGHTER. Yes, but ask him how his intelligence has helped us.

THE FATHER. If we could see all the evil that may spring from good, what should we do? (*At this point the* LEADING LADY *who is biting her lips with rage at seeing the* LEADING MAN *flirting with the* STEP-DAUGHTER, *comes forward and says to the* MANAGER.)

LEADING LADY. Excuse me, but are we going to rehearse today?

THE MANAGER. Of course, of course; but let's hear them out.

JUVENILE LEAD. This is something quite new.

L'INGÉNUE. Most interesting!

LEADING LADY. Yes, for the people who like that kind of thing. (*Casts a glance at* LEADING MAN.)

THE MANAGER (*to* FATHER). You must please explain yourself quite clearly. (*Sits down.*)

THE FATHER. Very well then: listen! I had in my service a poor man, a clerk, a secretary of mine, full of devotion, who became friends with her. (*Indicating the* MOTHER.) They understood one another, were kindred souls in fact, without, however, the least suspicion of any evil existing. They were incapable even of thinking of it.

THE STEP-DAUGHTER. So he thought of it—for them!

THE FATHER. That's not true. I meant to do good to them—and to myself, I confess, at the same time. Things had come to the point that I could not say a word to either of them without their making a mute appeal, one to the other, with their eyes. I could see them silently asking each other how I was to be kept in countenance, how I was to be kept quiet. And this, believe me, was just about enough of itself to keep me in a constant rage, to exasperate me beyond measure.

THE MANAGER. And why didn't you send him away then—this secretary of yours?

THE FATHER. Precisely what I did, sir. And then I had to watch this poor woman drifting forlornly about the house like an animal without a master, like an animal one has taken in out of pity.

THE MOTHER. Ah yes . . . !

THE FATHER (*suddenly turning to the* MOTHER). It's true about the son anyway, isn't it?

THE MOTHER. He took my son away from me first of all.

THE FATHER. But not from cruelty. I did it so that he should grow up healthy and strong by living in the country.

THE STEP-DAUGHTER (*pointing to him ironically*). As one can see.

THE FATHER (*quickly*). Is it my fault if he has grown up like this? I sent him to a wet nurse in the country, a peasant, as *she* did not seem to me strong enough, though she is of humble origin. That was, anyway, the reason I married her. Unpleasant all this may be, but how can it be helped? My mistake possibly, but there we are! All my life I have had these confounded aspirations towards a certain moral sanity. (*At this point the* STEP-DAUGHTER *bursts into a noisy laugh.*) Oh, stop it! Stop it! I can't stand it.

THE MANAGER. Yes, please stop it, for Heaven's sake.

THE STEP-DAUGHTER. But imagine moral sanity from him, if you please—the client of certain ateliers like that of Madame Pace!

THE FATHER. Fool! That is the proof that I am a man! This seeming contradiction, gentlemen, is the strongest proof that I stand here a live man before you. Why, it is just for this very incongruity in my nature that I have had to suffer what I have. I could not live by the side of that woman (*Indicating the* MOTHER.) any longer; but not so much for the boredom she inspired me with as for the pity I felt for her.

THE MOTHER. And so he turned me out—.

THE FATHER. —well provided for! Yes, I sent her to that man, gentlemen . . . to let her go free of me.

THE MOTHER. And to free himself.

THE FATHER. Yes, I admit it. It was also a liberation for me. But great evil has come of it. I meant well when I did it; and I did it more for her sake than mine. I swear it. (*Crosses his arms on his chest; then turns suddenly to the* MOTHER.) Did I ever lose sight of you until that other man carried you off to another town, like the angry fool he was? And on account of my pure interest in you . . . my pure interest, I repeat, that had no base motive in it . . . I watched with the tenderest concern the new family that grew up around her. She can bear witness to this. (*Points to the* STEP-DAUGHTER.)

THE STEP-DAUGHTER. Oh yes, that's true enough. When I was a kiddie, so so high, you know, with plaits over my shoulders and knickers longer than my skirts, I used to see him waiting outside the school for me to come out. He came to see how I was growing up.

THE FATHER. This is infamous, shameful!

THE STEP-DAUGHTER. No. Why?

THE FATHER. Infamous! infamous! (*Then excitedly to* MANAGER *explaining.*) After she (*Indicating* MOTHER.) went away, my house seemed suddenly empty. She was my incubus, but she filled my house. I was like a dazed fly alone in the empty rooms. This boy here (*Indicating the* SON.) was educated away from home, and when he came back, he seemed to me to be no more mine. With no mother to stand between him and me, he grew up entirely for himself, on his own, apart, with no tie of intellect or affection binding him to me. And then—strange but true—I was driven, by curiosity at first and then by some tender sentiment, towards her family, which had come into being through my will. The thought of her began gradually to fill up the emptiness I felt all around me. I wanted to know if she were happy in living out the simple daily duties of life. I wanted to think of her as fortunate and happy because far away from the complicated torments of my spirit. And so, to have proof of this, I used to watch that child coming out of school.

THE STEP-DAUGHTER. Yes, yes. True. He used to follow me in the street and smiled at me, waved his hand, like this. I would look at him with interest, wondering who he might be. I told my mother, who guessed at once. (*The* MOTHER *agrees with a nod.*) Then she didn't want to send me to school for some days; and when I finally went back, there he was again—looking so ridiculous—with a paper parcel in his hands. He came close to me, caressed me, and drew out a fine straw hat from the parcel, with a bouquet of flowers—all for me!

THE MANAGER. A bit discursive this, you know!

THE SON (*contemptuously*). Literature! Literature!

THE FATHER. Literature indeed! This is life, this is passion!

THE MANAGER. It may be, but it won't act.

THE FATHER. I agree. This is only the part leading up. I don't suggest this should be staged. She (*Pointing to the* STEP-DAUGHTER.), as you see, is no longer the flapper with plaits down her back—.

THE STEP-DAUGHTER. —and the knickers showing below the skirt!

THE FATHER. The drama is coming now, sir; something new, complex, most interesting.

THE STEP-DAUGHTER. As soon as my father died . . .

THE FATHER. —there was absolute misery for them. They came back here, unknown to me. Through her stupidity! (*Pointing to the* MOTHER.) It is true she can barely write her own name; but she could anyhow have got her daughter to write to me that they were in need . . .

THE MOTHER. And how was I to divine all this sentiment in him?

THE FATHER. That is exactly your mistake, never to have guessed any of my sentiments.

THE MOTHER. After so many years apart, and all that had happened . . .

THE FATHER. Was it my fault if that fellow carried you away? It happened quite suddenly; for after he had obtained some job or other, I could find no trace of them; and so, not unnaturally, my interest in them dwindled. But the drama culminated unforeseen and violent on their return, when I was impelled by my miserable flesh that still lives . . . Ah! what misery, what wretchedness is that of the man who is alone and disdains debasing *liaisons!* Not old enough to do without women, and not young enough to go and look for one without shame. Misery? It's worse than misery; it's a horror; for no woman can any longer give him love; and when a man feels this . . . One ought to do without, you say? Yes, yes, I know. Each of us when he appears before his fellows is clothed in a certain dignity. But every man knows what unconfessable things pass within the secrecy of his own heart. One gives way to the temptation, only to rise from it again, afterwards, with a great eagerness to re-establish one's dignity, as if it were a tombstone to place on the grave of one's shame, and a monument to hide and sign the memory of our weaknesses. Everybody's in the same case. Some folks haven't the courage to say certain things, that's all!

THE STEP-DAUGHTER. All appear to have the courage to do them though.

THE FATHER. Yes, but in secret. Therefore, you want more courage to say these things. Let a man but speak these things out, and folks at once label him a cynic. But it isn't true. He is like all the others, better indeed, because he isn't afraid to reveal with the light of the intelligence the red shame of human bestiality on which most men close their eyes so as not to see it.

Woman—for example, look at her case! She turns tantalizing inviting glances on you. You seize her. No sooner does she feel herself in your grasp than she closes her eyes. It is the sign of her mission, the sign by which she says to man: "Blind yourself, for I am blind."

THE STEP-DAUGHTER. Sometimes she can close them no more: when she no longer feels the need of hiding her shame to herself, but dry-eyed and dispassionately, sees only that of the man who has blinded himself without love. Oh, all these intellectual complications make me sick, disgust me—all this philosophy that uncovers the beast in man, and then seeks to save him, excuse him . . . I can't stand it, sir. When a man seeks to "simplify" life bestially, throwing aside every relic of humanity, every chaste aspiration, every pure feeling, all sense of ideality, duty, modesty, shame . . . then nothing is more revolting and nauseous than a certain kind of remorse—crocodiles' tears, that's what it is.

THE MANAGER. Let's come to the point. This is only discussion.

THE FATHER. Very good, sir! But a fact is like a sack which won't stand up when it is empty. In order that it may stand up, one has to put into it the reason and sentiment which have caused it to exist. I couldn't possibly know that after the death of that man, they had decided to return here, that they were in misery, and that she (*Pointing to the* MOTHER.) had gone to work as a modiste, and at a shop of the type of that of Madame Pace.

THE STEP-DAUGHTER. A real high-class modiste, you must know, gentlemen. In appearance, she works for the leaders of the best society; but she arranges matters so that these elegant ladies serve her purpose . . . without prejudice to other ladies who are . . . well . . . only so so.

THE MOTHER. You will believe me, gentlemen, that it never entered my mind that the old hag offered me work because she had her eyes on my daughter.

THE STEP-DAUGHTER. Poor mamma! Do you know, sir, what that woman did when I brought her back the work my mother had finished? She would point out to me that I had torn one of my frocks, and she would give it back to my mother to mend. It was I who paid for it, always I; while this poor creature here believed she was sacrificing herself for me and these two children here, sitting up at night sewing Madame Pace's robes.

THE MANAGER. And one day you met there . . .

THE STEP-DAUGHTER. Him, him. Yes sir, an old client. There's a scene for you to play! Superb!

THE FATHER. She, the Mother arrived just then . . .

THE STEP-DAUGHTER (*treacherously*). Almost in time!

THE FATHER (*crying out*). No, in time! in time! Fortunately I recognized her . . . in time. And I took them back home with me to my house. You can imagine now her position and mine; she, as you see her; and I who cannot look her in the face.

THE STEP-DAUGHTER. Absurd! How can I possibly be expected—after that—to be a modest young miss, a fit person to go with his confounded aspirations for "a solid moral sanity"?

THE FATHER. For the drama lies all in this—in the conscience that I have, that each one of us has. We believe this conscience to be a single thing, but it is manysided. There is one for this person, and another for that. Diverse consciences. So we have this illusion of being one person for all, of having a personality that is unique in all our acts. But it isn't true. We perceive this when, tragically perhaps, in something we do, we are as it were, suspended, caught up in the air on a kind of hook. Then we perceive that all of us was not in that act, and that it would be an atrocious injustice to judge us by that action alone, as if all our existence were summed up in that one deed. Now do you understand the perfidy of this girl? She surprised me in a place, where she ought not to have known me, just as I could not exist for her; and she now seeks to attach to me a reality such as I could never suppose I should have to assume for her in a shameful and fleeting moment of my life. I feel this above all else. And the drama, you will see, acquires a tremendous value from this point. Then there is the position of the others . . . his . . . (*Indicating the* SON.)

THE SON (*shrugging his shoulders scornfully*). Leave me alone! I don't come into this.

THE FATHER. What? You don't come into this?

THE SON. I've got nothing to do with it, and don't want to have; because you know well enough I wasn't made to be mixed up in all this with the rest of you.

THE STEP-DAUGHTER. We are only vulgar folk! He is the fine gentleman. You may have noticed, Mr. Manager, that I fix him now and again with a look of scorn while he lowers his eyes—for he knows the evil he has done me.

THE SON (*scarcely looking at her*). I?

THE STEP-DAUGHTER. You! you! I owe my life on the streets to you. Did you or did you not deny us, with your behaviour, I won't say the intimacy of home, but even that mere hospitality which makes guests feel at their ease? We were intruders who had come to disturb the kingdom of your legitimacy. I should like to have you witness, Mr. Manager, certain scenes between him and me. He says I have tyrannized over everyone. But it was just his behaviour which made me insist on the reason for which I had come into the house,—this reason he calls "vile"—into his house, with my mother who is his mother too. And I came as mistress of the house.

THE SON. It's easy for them to put me always in the wrong. But imagine, gentlemen, the position of a son, whose fate it is to see arrive one day at his home a young woman of impudent bearing, a young woman who inquires for his father, with whom who knows what business she has. This young man has then to witness her return bolder than ever, accompanied by that child there. He is obliged to watch her treat his father in an equivocal and confidential manner. She asks money of him in a way that lets one suppose he must give it her, *must*, do you understand, because he has every obligation to do so.

THE FATHER. But I have, as a matter of fact, this obligation. I owe it to your mother.

THE SON. How should I know? When had I ever seen or heard of her? One day there arrive with her (*Indicating* STEP-DAUGHTER.) that lad and this baby here. I am told: "This is your mother too, you know." I divine from her manner (*Indicating* STEP-DAUGHTER *again.*) why it is they have come home. I had rather not say what I feel and think about it. I shouldn't even care to confess to myself. No action can therefore be hoped for from me in this affair. Believe me, Mr. Manager, I am an "unrealized" character, dramatically speaking; and I find myself not at all at ease in their company. Leave me out of it, I beg you.

THE FATHER. What? It is just because you are so that . . .

THE SON. How do you know what I am like? When did you ever bother your head about me?

THE FATHER. I admit it. I admit it. But isn't that a situation in itself? This aloofness of yours which is so cruel to me and to your mother, who returns home and sees you almost for the first time grown up, who doesn't recognize you but knows you are her son . . . (*Pointing out the* MOTHER *to the* MANAGER.) See, she's crying!

THE STEP-DAUGHTER (*angrily, stamping her foot*). Like a fool!

THE FATHER (*indicating* STEP-DAUGHTER). She can't stand him you know. (*Then referring again to the* SON.) He says he doesn't come into the affair, whereas he is really the hinge of the whole action. Look at that lad who is always clinging to his mother, frightened and humiliated. It is on account of this fellow here. Possibly his situation is the most painful of all. He feels himself a stranger more than the others. The poor little chap feels mortified, humiliated at being brought into a home out of charity as it were. (*In confidence.*) He is the image of his father. Hardly talks at all. Humble and quiet.

THE MANAGER. Oh, we'll cut him out. You've no notion what a nuisance boys are on the stage . . .

THE FATHER. He disappears soon, you know. And the baby too. She is the first to vanish from the scene. The drama consists finally in this: when that mother re-enters my house, her family born outside of it, and shall we say superimposed on the original, ends with the death of the little girl, the tragedy of the boy and the flight of the elder daughter. It cannot go on, because it is foreign to its surroundings. So after much torment, we three remain: I, the mother, that son. Then, owing to the disappearance of that extraneous family, we too find ourselves strange to one another. We find we are living in an atmosphere of mortal desolation which is the revenge, as he (*Indicating* SON.) scornfully said of the Demon of Experiment, that unfortunately hides in me. Thus, sir, you see when faith is lacking, it becomes impossible to create certain states of happiness, for we lack the necessary humility. Vaingloriously, we try to substitute ourselves for this faith, creating thus for the rest of the world a reality which we believe after their fashion, while, actually, it doesn't exist. For each one of us has his own reality to be respected before God, even when it is harmful to one's very self.

THE MANAGER. There is something in what you say. I assure you all this interests me very much. I begin to think there's the stuff for a drama in all this, and not a bad drama either.

THE STEP-DAUGHTER (*coming forward*). When you've got a character like me.

THE FATHER (*shutting her up, all excited to learn the decision of the* MANAGER). You be quiet!

THE MANAGER (*reflecting, heedless of interruption*). It's new . . . hem . . . yes . . .

THE FATHER. Absolutely new!

THE MANAGER. You've got a nerve though, I must say, to come here and fling it at me like this . . .

THE FATHER. You will understand, sir, born as we are for the stage . . .

THE MANAGER. Are you amateur actors then?

THE FATHER. No. I say born for the stage, because . . .

THE MANAGER. Oh, nonsense. You're an old hand, you know.

THE FATHER. No sir, no. We act that rôle for which we have been cast, that rôle which we are given in life. And in my own case, passion itself, as usually happens, becomes a trifle theatrical when it is exalted.

THE MANAGER. Well, well, that will do. But you see, without an author . . . I could give you the address of an author if you like . . .

THE FATHER. No, no. Look here! You must be the author.

THE MANAGER. I? What are you talking about?

THE FATHER. Yes, you, you! Why not?

THE MANAGER. Because I have never been an author: that's why.

THE FATHER. Then why not turn author now? Everybody does it. You don't want any special qualities. Your task is made much easier by the fact that we are all here alive before you . . .

THE MANAGER. It won't do.

THE FATHER. What? When you see us live our drama . . .

THE MANAGER. Yes, that's all right. But you want someone to write it.

THE FATHER. No, no. Someone to take it down, possibly, while we play it, scene by scene! It will be enough to sketch it out at first, and then try it over.

THE MANAGER. Well . . . I am almost tempted. It's a bit of an idea. One might have a shot at it.

THE FATHER. Of course. You'll see what scenes will come out of it. I can give you one, at once . . .

THE MANAGER. By Jove, it tempts me. I'd like to have a go at it. Let's try it out. Come with me to my office. (*Turning to the* ACTORS.) You are at liberty for a bit, but don't step out of the theatre for long. In a quarter of an hour, twenty minutes, all back here again! (*To the* FATHER.) We'll see what can be done. Who knows if we don't get something really extraordinary out of it?

THE FATHER. There's no doubt about it. They (*Indicating the* CHARACTERS.) had better come with us too, hadn't they?

THE MANAGER. Yes, yes. Come on! come on! (*Moves away and then turning to the* ACTORS.) *Be punctual, please!* (MANAGER *and the* SIX CHARACTERS *cross the stage and go off. The other* ACTORS *remain, looking at one another in astonishment.*)

LEADING MAN. Is he serious? What the devil does he want to do?

JUVENILE LEAD. This is rank madness.

THIRD ACTOR. Does he expect to knock up a drama in five minutes?

JUVENILE LEAD. Like the improvisers!

LEADING LADY. If he thinks I'm going to take part in a joke like this . . .

JUVENILE LEAD. I'm out of it anyway.

FOURTH ACTOR. I should like to know who they are. (*Alludes to* CHARACTERS).

THIRD ACTOR. What do you suppose? Madmen or rascals!

JUVENILE LEAD. And he takes them seriously!

L'INGÉNUE. Vanity! He fancies himself as an author now.

LEADING MAN. It's absolutely unheard of. If the stage has come to this . . . well I'm . . .

FIFTH ACTOR. It's rather a joke.

THIRD ACTOR. Well, we'll see what's going to happen next.

[*Thus talking, the* ACTORS *leave the stage; some going out by the little door at the back; others retiring to their dressing-rooms. The curtain remains up. The action of the play is suspended for twenty minutes.*]

ACT II

The stage call-bells ring to warn the company that the play is about to begin again.

The STEP-DAUGHTER *comes out of the* MANAGER's *office along with the* CHILD *and the* BOY. *As she comes out of the office, she cries:—*

Nonsense! nonsense! Do it yourselves! I'm not going to mix myself up in this mess. (*Turning to the* CHILD *and coming quickly with her on to the stage.*) Come on, Rosetta, let's run!

[*The* BOY *follows them slowly, remaining a little behind and seeming perplexed.*]

THE STEP-DAUGHTER (*stops, bends over the* CHILD *and takes the latter's face between her hands*). My little darling! You're frightened, aren't you? You don't know where we are, do you? (*Pretending to reply to a question of the* CHILD.) What is the stage? It's a place, baby, you know, where people play at being serious, a place where they act comedies. We've got to act a comedy now, dead serious, you know; and you're in it also, little one. (*Embraces her, pressing the little head *to her breast, and rocking the* CHILD *for a moment.*) Oh darling, darling, what a horrid comedy you've got to play! What a wretched part they've found for you! A garden . . . a fountain . . . look . . . just suppose, kiddie, it's here. Where, you say? Why, right here in the middle. It's all pretence you know. That's the trouble, my pet: it's all make-believe here. It's better to imagine it though, because if they fix it up for you, it'll only be painted cardboard, painted cardboard for the rockery, the water, the plants . . . Ah, but I think a baby like this one would sooner have a make-believe fountain than a real one, so she could play with it. What a joke it'll be for the others! But for you, alas! not quite such a joke: you who are real, baby dear, and really play by a real fountain that is big and green and beautiful, with ever so many bamboos around it that are reflected in the water, and a whole lot of little ducks swimming about . . . No, Rosetta, no, your mother doesn't bother about you on account of that wretch of a son there. I'm in the devil of a temper, and as for that lad . . . (*Seizes* BOY *by the arm to force him to take one of his hands out of his pockets.*) What have you got there? What are you hiding? (*Pulls his hand out of his pocket, looks into it and catches the glint of a revolver.*) Ah! where did you get this? (*The* BOY, *very pale in the face, looks at her, but does not answer.*) Idiot! If I'd been in your place, instead of killing myself, I'd have shot one of those two, or both of them: father and son.

[*The* FATHER *enters from the office, all excited from his work. The* MANAGER *follows him.*]

THE FATHER. Come on, come on dear! Come here for a minute! We've arranged everything. It's all fixed up.

THE MANAGER (*also excited*). If you please, young lady, there are one or two points to settle still. Will you come along?

THE STEP-DAUGHTER (*following him towards the office*). Ouff! what's the good, if you've arranged everything.

[*The* FATHER, MANAGER *and* STEP-DAUGHTER *go back into the office again* (*off*) *for a moment. At the same time, the* SON *followed by the* MOTHER, *comes out.*]

THE SON (*looking at the three entering office*). Oh this is fine, fine! And to think I can't even get away!

[*The* MOTHER *attempts to look at him, but lowers her eyes immediately when* HE *turns away from her.* SHE *then sits down. The* BOY *and the* CHILD *approach her.* SHE *casts a glance again at the* SON, *and speaks with humble tones, trying to draw him into conversation.*]

THE MOTHER. And isn't my punishment the worst of all? (*Then seeing from the* SON'*s manner that he will not bother himself about her.*) My God! Why are you so cruel? Isn't it enough for one person to support all this torment? Must you then insist on others seeing it also?

THE SON (*half to himself, meaning the* MOTHER *to hear, however*). And they want to put it on the stage! If there was at least a reason for it! He thinks he has got at the meaning of it all. Just as if each one of us in every circumstance of life couldn't find his own explanation of it! (*Pauses.*) He complains he was discovered in a place where he ought not to have been seen, in a moment of his life which ought to have remained hidden and kept out of the reach of that convention which he has to maintain for other people. And what about my case? Haven't I had to reveal what no son ought ever to reveal: how father and mother live and are man and wife for themselves quite apart from that idea of father and mother which we give them? When this idea is revealed, our life is then linked at one point only to that man and that woman; and as such it should shame them, shouldn't it?

[*The* MOTHER *hides her face in her hands. From the dressing-rooms and the little door at the back of the stage the* ACTORS *and* STAGE MANAGER *return, followed by the* PROPERTY MAN, *and the* PROMPTER. *At the same moment, the* MANAGER *comes out of his office, accompanied by the* FATHER *and the* STEP-DAUGHTER.]

THE MANAGER. Come on, come on, ladies and gentlemen! Heh! you there, machinist!

MACHINIST. Yes sir?

THE MANAGER. Fix up the white parlor with the floral decorations. Two wings and a drop with a door will do. Hurry up!

[*The* MACHINIST *runs off at once to prepare the scene, and arranges it while the* MANAGER *talks with the* STAGE MANAGER, *the* PROPERTY MAN, *and the* PROMPTER *on matters of detail.*]

THE MANAGER (*to* PROPERTY MAN). Just have a look, and see if there isn't a sofa or divan in the wardrobe . . .

PROPERTY MAN. There's the green one.

THE STEP-DAUGHTER. No no! Green won't do. It was yellow, ornamented with flowers—very large! and most comfortable!

PROPERTY MAN. There isn't one like that.

THE MANAGER. It doesn't matter. Use the one we've got.

THE STEP-DAUGHTER. Doesn't matter? It's most important!

THE MANAGER. We're only trying it now. Please don't interfere. (*To* PROPERTY MAN.) See if we've got a shop window—long and narrowish.

THE STEP-DAUGHTER. And the little table! The little mahogany table for the pale blue envelope!

PROPERTY MAN (*to* MANAGER). There's that little gilt one.

THE MANAGER. That'll do fine.

THE FATHER. A mirror.

THE STEP-DAUGHTER. And the screen! We must have a screen. Otherwise how can I manage?

PROPERTY MAN. That's all right, Miss. We've got any amount of them.

THE MANAGER (*to the* STEP-DAUGHTER). We want some clothes pegs too, don't we?

THE STEP-DAUGHTER. Yes, several, several!

THE MANAGER. See how many we've got and bring them all.

PROPERTY MAN. All right!

[*The* PROPERTY MAN *hurries off to obey his orders. While he is putting the things in their places, the* MANAGER *talks to the* PROMPTER *and then with the* CHARACTERS *and the* ACTORS.]

THE MANAGER (*to* PROMPTER). Take your seat. Look here: this is the outline of the scenes, act by act. (*Hands him some sheets of paper.*) And now I'm going to ask you to do something out of the ordinary.

PROMPTER. Take it down in shorthand?

THE MANAGER (*pleasantly surprised*). Exactly! Can you do shorthand?

PROMPTER. Yes, a little.

THE MANAGER. Good! (*Turning to a* STAGE HAND.) Go and get some paper from my office, plenty, as much as you can find.

[*The* STAGE HAND *goes off, and soon returns with a handful of paper which he gives to the* PROMPTER.]

THE MANAGER (*to* PROMPTER). You follow the scenes as we play them, and try and get the points down, at any rate the most important ones. (*Then addressing the* ACTORS.) Clear the stage, ladies and gentlemen! Come over here (*Pointing to the left.*) and listen attentively.

LEADING LADY. But, excuse me, we . . .

THE MANAGER (*guessing her thought*). Don't worry! You won't have to improvise.

LEADING MAN. What have we to do then?

THE MANAGER. Nothing. For the moment you just watch and listen. Everybody will get his part written out afterwards. At present we're going to try the thing as best we can. They're going to act now.

THE FATHER (*as if fallen from the clouds into the confusion of the stage*). We? What do you mean, if you please, by a rehearsal?

THE MANAGER. A rehearsal for them. (*Points to the* ACTORS.)

THE FATHER. But since we are the characters . . .

THE MANAGER. All right: "characters" then, if you insist on calling yourselves such. But here, my dear sir, the characters don't act. Here the actors do the acting. The characters are there, in the "book" (*Pointing towards* PROMPTER'*s box.*)—when there is a "book"!

THE FATHER. I won't contradict you; but excuse me, the actors aren't the characters. They want to be, they pretend to be, don't they? Now if these gentlemen here are fortunate enough to have us alive before them . . .

THE MANAGER. Oh this is grand! You want to come before the public yourselves then?

THE FATHER. As we are . . .

THE MANAGER. I can assure you it would be a magnificent spectacle!

LEADING MAN. What's the use of us here anyway then?

THE MANAGER. You're not going to pretend that you can act? It makes me laugh! (*The* ACTORS *laugh.*) There, you see, they are laughing at the notion. But, by the way, I must cast the parts. That won't be difficult. They cast themselves. (*To the* SECOND LADY LEAD.) You play the Mother. (*To the* FATHER.) We must find her a name.

THE FATHER. Amalia, sir.

THE MANAGER. But that is the real name of your wife. We don't want to call her by her real name.

THE FATHER. Why ever not, if it is her name? . . . Still, perhaps, if that lady must . . . (*Makes a slight motion of the hand to indicate the* SECOND LADY LEAD.) I see this woman here (*Means the* MOTHER.) as Amalia. But do as you like. (*Gets more and more confused.*) I don't know what to say to you. Already, I begin to hear my own words ring false, as if they had another sound . . .

THE MANAGER. Don't you worry about it. It'll be our job to find the right tones. And as for her name, if you want her Amalia, Amalia it shall be; and if you don't like it, we'll find another! For the moment though, we'll call the characters in this way: (*To* JUVENILE LEAD.) You are the Son. (*To the* LEADING LADY.) You naturally are the Step-Daughter . . .

THE STEP-DAUGHTER (*excitedly*). What? what? I, that woman there? (*Bursts out laughing.*)

THE MANAGER (*angry*). What is there to laugh at?

LEADING LADY (*indignant*). Nobody has ever dared to laugh at me. I insist on being treated with respect; otherwise I go away.

THE STEP-DAUGHTER. No, no, excuse me . . . I am not laughing at you . . .

THE MANAGER (*to* STEP-DAUGHTER). You ought to feel honored to be played by . . .

LEADING LADY (*at once, contemptuously*). "That woman there" . . .

THE STEP-DAUGHTER. But I wasn't speaking of you you know. I was speaking of myself—whom I can't see at all in you! That is all. I don't know . . . but . . . you . . . aren't in the least like me . . .

THE FATHER. True. Here's the point. Look here, sir, our temperaments, our souls . . .

THE MANAGER. Temperament, soul, be hanged! Do you suppose the spirit of the piece is in you? Nothing of the kind!

THE FATHER. What, haven't we our own temperaments, our own souls?

THE MANAGER. Not at all. Your soul or whatever you like to call it takes shape here. The actors give body and form to it, voice and gesture. And my actors—I may tell you—have given expression to much more lofty material than this little drama of yours, which may or may not hold up on the stage. But if it does, the merit of it, believe me, will be due to my actors.

THE FATHER. I don't dare contradict you, sir; but, believe me, it is a terrible suffering for us who are as we are, with these bodies of ours, these features to see . . .

THE MANAGER (*cutting him short and out of patience*). Good heavens! The make-up will remedy all that, man, the make-up . . .

THE FATHER. Maybe. But the voice, the gestures . . .

THE MANAGER. Now, look here! On the stage, you as yourself, cannot exist. The actor here acts you, and that's an end to it!

THE FATHER. I understand. And now I think I see why our author who conceived us as we are, all alive, didn't want to put us on the stage after all. I haven't the least desire to offend your actors. Far from it! But when I think that I am to be acted by . . . I don't know by whom . . .

LEADING MAN (*on his dignity*). By me, if you've no objection!

THE FATHER (*humbly, mellifluously*). Honored, I assure you, sir. (*Bows.*) Still, I must say that try as this gentleman may, with all his good will and wonderful art, to absorb me into himself . . .

LEADING MAN. Oh chuck it! "Wonderful art!" Withdraw that, please!

THE FATHER. The performance he will give, even doing his best with make-up to look like me . . .

LEADING MAN. It will certainly be a bit difficult! (*The* ACTORS *laugh.*)

THE FATHER. Exactly! It will be difficult to act me as I really am. The effect will be rather—apart from the make-up—according as to how he supposes I am, as he senses me—if he does sense me—and not as I inside of myself feel myself to be. It seems to me then that account should be taken of this by everyone whose duty it may become to criticize us . . .

THE MANAGER. Heavens! The man's starting to think about the critics now! Let them say what they like. It's up to us to put on the play if we can. (*Looking around.*) Come on! come on! Is the stage set? (*To the* ACTORS *and* CHARACTERS.) Stand back—stand back! Let me see, and don't let's lose any more time! (*To the* STEP-DAUGHTER.) Is it all right as it is now?

THE STEP-DAUGHTER. Well, to tell the truth, I don't recognize the scene.

THE MANAGER. My dear lady, you can't possibly suppose that we can construct that shop of Madame Pace piece by piece here? (*To the* FATHER.) You said a white room with flowered wall paper, didn't you?

THE FATHER. Yes.

THE MANAGER. Well then. We've got the furniture right more or less. Bring that little table a bit further forward. (*The* STAGE HANDS *obey the order. To* PROPERTY MAN.) You go and find an envelope, if possible, a pale blue one; and give it to that gentleman. (*Indicates* FATHER.)

PROPERTY MAN. An ordinary envelope?

MANAGER *and* FATHER. Yes, yes, an ordinary envelope.

PROPERTY MAN. At once, sir. (*Exit.*)

THE MANAGER. Ready, everyone! First scene—the Young Lady. (*The* LEADING LADY *comes forward.*) No, no, you must wait. I meant her (*Indicating the* STEP-DAUGHTER.) You just watch—

THE STEP-DAUGHTER (*adding at once*). How I shall play it, how I shall live it! . . .

LEADING LADY (*offended*). I shall live it also, you may be sure, as soon as I begin!

THE MANAGER (*with his hands to his head*). Ladies and gentlemen, if you please! No more useless discussions! Scene I: the young lady with Madame Pace: Oh! (*Looks around as if lost.*) And this Madame Pace, where is she?

THE FATHER. She isn't with us, sir.

THE MANAGER. Then what the devil's to be done?

THE FATHER. But she is alive too.

THE MANAGER. Yes, but where is she?

THE FATHER. One minute. Let me speak! (*Turning to the* ACTRESSES.) If these ladies would be so good as to give me their hats for a moment . . .

THE ACTRESSES (*half surprised, half laughing, in chorus*). What?
Why?
Our hats?
What does he say?

THE MANAGER. What are you going to do with the ladies' hats? (*The* ACTORS *laugh.*)

THE FATHER. Oh nothing. I just want to put them on these pegs for a moment. And one of the ladies will be so kind as to take off her mantle . . .

THE ACTORS. Oh, what d'you think of that?
Only the mantle?
He must be mad.

SOME ACTRESSES. But why?
Mantles as well?

THE FATHER. To hang them up here for a moment. Please be so kind, will you?

THE ACTRESSES (*taking off their hats, one or two also their cloaks, and going to hang them on the racks*). After all, why not?
There you are!
This is really funny.
We've got to put them on show.

THE FATHER. Exactly; just like that, on show.

THE MANAGER. May we know why?

THE FATHER. I'll tell you. Who knows if, by arranging the stage for her, she does not come here herself, attracted by the very articles of her trade? (*Inviting the* ACTORS *to look towards the exit at back of stage.*) Look! Look!

[*The door at the back of stage opens and* MADAME PACE *enters and takes a few steps forward. She is a fat, oldish woman with puffy oxygenated hair. She is rouged and powdered, dressed with a comical elegance in black silk. Round her waist is a long silver chain from which hangs a pair of scissors. The* STEP-DAUGHTER *runs over to her at once amid the stupor of the actors.*]

THE STEP-DAUGHTER (*turning towards her*). There she is! There she is!

THE FATHER (*radiant*). It's she! I said so, didn't I? There she is!

THE MANAGER (*conquering his surprise, and then becoming indignant*). What sort of a trick is this?

LEADING MAN (*almost at the same time*). What's going to happen next?

JUVENILE LEAD. Where does *she* come from?

L'INGÉNUE. They've been holding her in reserve, I guess.

LEADING LADY. A vulgar trick!

THE FATHER (*dominating the protests*). Excuse me, all of you! Why are you so anxious to destroy in the name of a vulgar, commonplace sense of truth, this reality which comes to birth attracted and formed by the magic of the stage itself, which has indeed more right to live here than you, since it is much truer than you—if you don't mind my saying so? Which is the actress among you who is to play Madame Pace? Well, here is Madame Pace herself. And you will allow, I fancy, that the actress who acts her will be less true than this woman here, who is herself in person. You see my daughter recognized her and went over to her at once. Now you're going to witness the scene!

[*But the scene between the* STEP-DAUGHTER *and* MADAME PACE *has already begun despite the protest of the actors and the reply of the* FATHER. *It has begun quietly, naturally, in a manner impossible for the stage. So when the actors, called to attention by the* FATHER, *turn round and see* MADAME PACE, *who has placed one hand under the* STEP-DAUGHTER'*s chin to raise her head, they observe her at first with great attention, but hearing her speak in an unintelligible manner their interest begins to wane.*]

THE MANAGER. Well? well?

LEADING MAN. What does she say?

LEADING LADY. One can't hear a word.

JUVENILE LEAD. Louder! Louder please!

THE STEP-DAUGHTER (*leaving* MADAME PACE, *who smiles a Sphinx-like smile, and advancing towards the* ACTORS). Louder? Louder? What are you talking about? These aren't matters which can be shouted at the top of one's voice. If I have spoken them out loud, it was to shame him and have my revenge. (*Indicates* FATHER.) But for Madame it's quite a different matter.

THE MANAGER. Indeed? indeed? But here, you know, people have got to make themselves heard, my dear. Even we who are on the stage can't hear you. What will it be when the public's in the theatre? And anyway, you can very well speak up now among yourselves, since we shan't be present to listen to you as we are now. You've got to pretend to be alone in a room at the back of a shop where no one can hear you.

[*The* STEP-DAUGHTER *coquettishly and with a touch of malice makes a sign of disagreement two or three times with her finger.*]

THE MANAGER. What do you mean by no?

THE STEP-DAUGHTER (*sotto voce, mysteriously*). There's someone who will hear us if she (*Indicating* MADAME PACE.) speaks out loud.

THE MANAGER (*in consternation*). What? Have you got someone else to spring on us now? (*The* ACTORS *burst out laughing.*)

THE FATHER. No, no sir. She is alluding to me. I've got to be here—there behind that door, in waiting; and Madame Pace knows it. In fact, if you will allow me, I'll go there at once, so I can be quite ready. (*Moves away.*)

THE MANAGER (*stopping him*). No! Wait! wait! We must observe the conventions of the theatre. Before you are ready . . .

THE STEP-DAUGHTER (*interrupting him*). No, get on with it at once! I'm just dying, I tell you, to act this scene. If he's ready, I'm more than ready.

THE MANAGER (*shouting*). But, my dear young lady, first of all, we must have the scene between you and this lady . . . (*Indicates* MADAME PACE.) Do you understand? . . .

THE STEP-DAUGHTER. Good Heavens! She's been telling me what you know already: that mamma's work is badly done again, that the material's ruined; and that if I want her to continue to help us in our misery I must be patient . . .

MADAME PACE (*coming forward with an air of great importance*). Yes indeed, sir, I no wanta take advantage of her, I no wanta be hard . . .

[*Note.* MADAME PACE *is supposed to talk in a jargon half Italian, half English.*]

THE MANAGER (*alarmed*). What? What? She talks like that? (*The* ACTORS *burst out laughing again.*)

THE STEP-DAUGHTER (*also laughing*). Yes yes, that's the way she talks, half English, half Italian! Most comical it is!

MADAME PACE. Itta seem not verra polite gentlemen laugha atta me eef I trya best speaka English.

THE MANAGER. *Diamine!* Of course! Of course! Let her talk like that! Just what we want. Talk just like that, Madame, if you please! The effect will be certain. Exactly what was wanted to put a little comic relief into the crudity of the situation. Of course she talks like that! Magnificent!

THE STEP-DAUGHTER. Magnificent? Certainly! When certain suggestions are made to one in language of that kind, the effect is certain, since it seems almost a joke. One feels inclined to laugh when one hears her talk about an "old signore" "who wanta talka nicely with you." Nice old signore, eh, Madame?

MADAME PACE. Not so old my dear, not so old! And even if you no lika him, he won't make any scandal!

THE MOTHER (*jumping up amid the amazement and consternation of the* ACTORS *who had not been noticing her. They move to restrain her*). You old devil! You murderess!

THE STEP-DAUGHTER (*running over to calm her* MOTHER). Calm yourself, Mother, calm yourself! Please don't . . .

THE FATHER (*going to her also at the same time*). Calm yourself! Don't get excited! Sit down now!

THE MOTHER. Well then, take that woman away out of my sight!

THE STEP-DAUGHTER (*to* MANAGER). It is impossible for my mother to remain here.

THE FATHER (*to* MANAGER). They can't be here together. And for this reason, you see: that woman there was not with us when we came . . . If they are on together, the whole thing is given away inevitably, as you see.

THE MANAGER. It doesn't matter. This is only a first rough sketch—just to get an idea of the various points of the scene, even confusedly . . . (*Turning to the* MOTHER *and leading her to her chair.*) Come along, my dear lady, sit down now, and let's get on with the scene . . .

[*Meanwhile, the* STEP-DAUGHTER, *coming forward again, turns to* MADAME PACE.]

THE STEP-DAUGHTER. Come on, Madame, come on!

MADAME PACE (*offended*). No, no, *grazie*. I not do anything witha your mother present.

THE STEP-DAUGHTER. Nonsense! Introduce this "old signore" who wants to talk nicely to me. (*Addressing the* COMPANY *imperiously.*) We've got to do this scene one way or another, haven't we? Come on! (*To* MADAME PACE.) You can go!

MADAME PACE. Ah yes! I go'way! I go'way! Certainly! (*Exits furious.*)

THE STEP-DAUGHTER (*to the* FATHER). Now you make your entry. No, you needn't go over here. Come here. Let's suppose you've already come in. Like that, yes! I'm here with bowed head, modest like. Come on! Out with your voice! Say "Good morning, Miss" in that peculiar tone, that special tone . . .

THE MANAGER. Excuse me, but are you the Manager, or am I? (*To the* FATHER, *who looks undecided and perplexed.*) Get on with it, man! Go down there to the back of the stage. You needn't go off. Then come right forward here.

[*The* FATHER *does as he is told, looking troubled and perplexed at first. But as soon as he begins to move, the reality of the action affects him, and he begins to smile and to be more natural. The* ACTORS *watch intently.*]

THE MANAGER (*sotto voce, quickly to the* PROMPTER *in his box*). Ready! ready? Get ready to write now.

THE FATHER (*coming forward and speaking in a different tone*). Good afternoon, Miss!

THE STEP-DAUGHTER (*head bowed down slightly, with restrained disgust*). Good afternoon!

THE FATHER (*looks under her hat which partly covers her face. Perceiving she is very young, he makes an exclamation, partly of surprise, partly of fear lest he compromise himself in a risky adventure*). Ah . . . but . . . ah . . . I say . . . this is not the first time that you have come here, is it?

THE STEP-DAUGHTER (*modestly*). No sir.

THE FATHER. You've been here before, eh? (*Then seeing her nod agreement.*) More than once? (*Waits for her to answer, looks under her hat, smiles, and then says.*) Well then, there's no need to be so shy, is there? May I take off your hat?

THE STEP-DAUGHTER (*anticipating him and with veiled disgust*). No sir . . . I'll do it myself. (*Takes it off quickly.*)

[*The* MOTHER, *who watches the progress of the scene with the* SON *and the other two children who cling to her, is on thorns; and follows with varying expressions of sorrow, indignation, anxiety, and horror the words and actions of the other two. From time to time she hides her face in her hands and sobs.*]

THE MOTHER. Oh, my God, my God!

THE FATHER (*playing his part with a touch of gallantry*). Give it to me! I'll put it down. (*Takes hat from her hands.*) But a dear little head like yours ought to have a smarter hat. Come and help me choose one from the stock, won't you?

L'INGÉNUE (*interrupting*). I say . . . those are our hats you know.

THE MANAGER (*furious*). Silence! silence! Don't try and be funny, if you please . . . We're playing the scene now I'd have you notice. (*To the* STEP-DAUGHTER.) Begin again, please!

THE STEP-DAUGHTER (*continuing*). No thank you, sir.

THE FATHER. Oh, come now. Don't talk like that. You must take it. I shall be upset if you don't. There are some lovely little hats here; and then—Madame will be pleased. She expects it, anyway, you know.

THE STEP-DAUGHTER. No, no! I couldn't wear it!

THE FATHER. Oh, you're thinking about what they'd say at home if they saw you come in with a new hat? My dear girl, there's always a way round these little matters, you know.

THE STEP-DAUGHTER (*all keyed up*). No, it's not that. I couldn't wear it because I am . . . as you see . . . you might have noticed . . . (*Showing her black dress.*)

THE FATHER. . . . in mourning! Of course: I beg your pardon: I'm frightfully sorry . . .

THE STEP-DAUGHTER (*forcing herself to conquer her indignation and nausea*). Stop! Stop! It's I who must thank you. There's no need for you to feel mortified or specially sorry. Don't think any more of what I've said. (*Tries to smile.*) I must forget that I am dressed so . . . .

THE MANAGER (*interrupting and turning to the* PROMPTER). Stop a minute! Stop! Don't write that down. Cut out that last bit. (*Then to the* FATHER *and* STEP-DAUGHTER.) Fine! it's going fine! (*To the* FATHER *only.*) And now you can go on as we arranged. (*To the* ACTORS.) Pretty good that scene, where he offers her the hat, eh?

THE STEP-DAUGHTER. The best's coming now. Why can't we go on?

THE MANAGER. Have a little patience! (*To the* ACTORS.) Of course, it must be treated rather lightly.

LEADING MAN. Still, with a bit of go in it!

LEADING LADY. Of course! It's easy enough! (*To* LEADING MAN.) Shall you and I try it now?

LEADING MAN. Why, yes! I'll prepare my entrance. (*Exit in order to make his entrance.*)

THE MANAGER (*to* LEADING LADY). See here! The scene between you and Madame Pace is finished. I'll have it written out properly after. You remain here . . . oh, where are you going?

LEADING LADY. One minute. I want to put my hat on again (*Goes over to hat-rack and puts her hat on her head.*)

THE MANAGER. Good! You stay here with your head bowed down a bit.

THE STEP-DAUGHTER. But she isn't dressed in black.

LEADING LADY. But I shall be, and much more effectively than you.

THE MANAGER (*to* STEP-DAUGHTER). Be quiet please, and watch! You'll be able to learn something. (*Clapping his hands.*) Come on! come on! Entrance, please!

[*The door at rear of stage opens, and the* LEADING MAN *enters with the lively manner of an old gallant. The rendering of the scene by the* ACTORS *from the very first words is seen to be quite a different thing, though it has not in any way the air of a parody. Naturally, the* STEP-DAUGHTER *and the* FATHER, *not being able to recognize themselves in the* LEADING LADY *and the* LEADING MAN, *who deliver their words in different tones and with a different psychology, express, sometimes with smiles, sometimes with gestures, the impression they receive.*]

LEADING MAN. Good afternoon, Miss . . .

THE FATHER (*at once unable to contain himself*). No! no!

[*The* STEP-DAUGHTER *noticing the way the* LEADING MAN *enters, bursts out laughing.*]

THE MANAGER (*furious*). Silence! And you please just stop that laughing. If we go on like this, we shall never finish.

THE STEP-DAUGHTER. Forgive me, sir, but it's natural enough. This lady (*Indicating* LEADING LADY.) stands there still; but if she is supposed to be me, I can assure you that if I heard anyone say "Good afternoon" in that manner and in that tone, I should burst out laughing as I did.

THE FATHER. Yes, yes, the manner, the tone . . .

THE MANAGER. Nonsense! Rubbish! Stand aside and let me see the action.

LEADING MAN. If I've got to represent an old fellow who's coming into a house of an equivocal character . . .

THE MANAGER. Don't listen to them, for Heaven's sake! Do it again! It goes fine. (*Waiting for the* ACTORS *to begin again.*) Well?

LEADING MAN. Good afternoon, Miss.

LEADING LADY. Good afternoon.

LEADING MAN (*imitating the gesture of the* FATHER *when he looked under the hat, and then expressing quite clearly first satisfaction and then fear*). Ah, but . . . I say . . . this is not the first time that you have come here, is it?

THE MANAGER. Good, but not quite so heavily. Like this. (*Acts himself.*) "This isn't the first time that you have come here" . . . (*To* LEADING LADY.) And you say: "No, sir."

LEADING LADY. No, sir.

LEADING MAN. You've been here before, more than once.

THE MANAGER. No, no, stop! Let her nod "yes" first. "You've been here before, eh?" (*The* LEADING LADY *lifts up her head slightly and closes her eyes as though in disgust. Then she inclines her head twice.*)

THE STEP-DAUGHTER (*unable to contain herself*). Oh my God! (*Puts a hand to her mouth to prevent herself from laughing.*)

THE MANAGER (*turning round*). What's the matter?

THE STEP-DAUGHTER. Nothing, nothing!

THE MANAGER (*to* LEADING MAN). Go on!

LEADING MAN. You've been here before, eh? Well then, there's no need to be so shy, is there? May I take off your hat?

[*The* LEADING MAN *says this last speech in such a tone and with such gestures that the* STEP-DAUGHTER, *though she has her hand to her mouth, cannot keep from laughing.*]

LEADING LADY (*indignant*). I'm not going to stop here to be made a fool of by that woman there.

LEADING MAN. Neither am I! I'm through with it!

THE MANAGER (*shouting to* STEP-DAUGHTER). Silence! for once and all, I tell you!

THE STEP-DAUGHTER. Forgive me! forgive me!

THE MANAGER. You haven't any manners: that's what it is! You go too far.

THE FATHER (*endeavoring to intervene*). Yes, it's true, but excuse her . . .

THE MANAGER. Excuse what? It's absolutely disgusting.

THE FATHER. Yes, sir, but believe me, it has such a strange effect when . . .

THE MANAGER. Strange? Why strange? Where is it strange?

THE FATHER. No, sir; I admire your actors—this gentleman here, this lady; but they are certainly not us!

THE MANAGER. I should hope not. Evidently they cannot be you, if they are actors.

THE FATHER. Just so: actors! Both of them act our parts exceedingly well. But, believe me, it produces quite a different effect on us. They want to be us, but they aren't, all the same.

THE MANAGER. What is it then anyway?

THE FATHER. Something that is . . . that is theirs—and no longer ours . . .

THE MANAGER. But naturally, inevitably. I've told you so already.

THE FATHER. Yes, I understand . . . I understand . . .

THE MANAGER. Well then, let's have no more of it! (*Turning to the* ACTORS.) We'll have the rehearsals by ourselves, afterwards, in the ordinary way. I never could stand rehearsing with the author present. He's never satisfied! (*Turning to* FATHER *and* STEP-DAUGHTER.) Come on! Let's get on with it again; and try and see if you can't keep from laughing.

THE STEP-DAUGHTER. Oh, I shan't laugh any more. There's a nice little bit coming for me now: you'll see.

THE MANAGER. Well then: when she says "Don't think any more of what I've said. I must forget, etc.," you (*Addressing the* FATHER.) come in sharp with "I understand, I understand"; and then you ask her . . .

THE STEP-DAUGHTER (*interrupting*). What?

THE MANAGER. Why she is in mourning.

THE STEP-DAUGHTER. Not at all! See here: when I told him that it was useless for me to be thinking about my wearing mourning, do you know how he answered me? "Ah well," he said, "then let's take off this little frock."

THE MANAGER. Great! Just what we want, to make a riot in the theatre!

THE STEP-DAUGHTER. But it's the truth!

THE MANAGER. What does that matter? Acting is our business here. Truth up to a certain point, but no further.

THE STEP-DAUGHTER. What do you want to do then?

THE MANAGER. You'll see, you'll see! Leave it to me.

THE STEP-DAUGHTER. No sir! What you want to do is to piece together a little romantic sentimental scene out of my disgust, out of all the reasons, each more cruel and viler than the other, why I am what I am. He is to ask me why I'm in mourning; and I'm to answer with tears in my eyes, that it is just two months since papa died. No sir, no! He's got to say to me; as he did say: "Well, let's take off this little dress at once." And I; with my two months' mourning in my heart, went there behind that screen, and with these fingers tingling with shame . . .

THE MANAGER (*running his hands through his hair*). For Heaven's sake! What are you saying?

THE STEP-DAUGHTER (*crying out excitedly*). The truth! The truth!

THE MANAGER. It may be. I don't deny it, and I can understand all your horror; but you must surely see that you can't have this kind of thing on the stage. It won't go.

THE STEP-DAUGHTER. Not possible, eh? Very well! I'm much obliged to you—but I'm off!

THE MANAGER. Now be reasonable. Don't lose your temper!

THE STEP-DAUGHTER. I won't stop here! I won't! I can see you've fixed it all up with him in your office. All this talk about what is possible for the stage . . . I understand! He wants to get at his complicated "cerebral drama," to have his famous remorses and torments acted; but I want to act my part, *my part!*

THE MANAGER (*annoyed, shaking his shoulders*). Ah! Just *your* part! But, if you will pardon me, there are other parts than yours: His (*Indicating the* FATHER.) and hers. (*Indicating the* MOTHER.) On the stage you can't have a character becoming too prominent and overshadowing all the others. The thing is to pack them all into a neat little framework and then act what is actable. I am aware of the fact that everyone has his own interior life which he wants very much to put forward. But the difficulty lies in this fact: to set out just so much as is necessary for the stage, taking the other characters into consideration, and at the same time hint at the unrevealed interior life of each. I am willing to admit, my dear young lady, that from your point of view it would be a fine idea if each character could tell the public all his troubles in a nice monologue or a regular one hour lecture. (*Good humoredly.*) You must restrain yourself, my dear, and in your own interest, too; because this fury of yours, this exaggerated disgust you show, may make a bad impression, you know. After you have confessed to me that there were others before him at Madame Pace's and more than once . . .

THE STEP-DAUGHTER (*bowing her head, impressed*). It's true. But remember those others mean him for me all the same.

THE MANAGER (*not understanding*). What? The others? What do you mean?

THE STEP-DAUGHTER. For one who has gone wrong, sir, he who was responsible for the first fault is responsible for all that follow. He is responsible for my faults, was, even before I was born. Look at him, and see if it isn't true!

THE MANAGER. Well, well! And does the weight of so much responsibility seem nothing to you? Give him a chance to act it, to get it over!

THE STEP-DAUGHTER. How? How can he act all his "noble remorses," all his "moral torments," if you want to spare him the horror of being discovered one day—after he had asked her what he did ask her—in the arms of her, that already fallen woman, that child, sir, that child he used to watch come out of school? (*She is moved.*)

[*The* MOTHER *at this point is overcome with emotion, and breaks out into a fit of crying. All are touched. A long pause.*]

THE STEP-DAUGHTER (*as soon as the* MOTHER *becomes a little quieter, adds resolutely and gravely*). At present, we are unknown to the public. Tomorrow, you will act us as you wish, treating us in your own manner. But do you really want to see drama, do you want to see it flash out as it really did?

THE MANAGER. Of course! That's just what I do want, so I can use as much of it as is possible.

THE STEP-DAUGHTER. Well then, ask that Mother there to leave us.

THE MOTHER (*changing her low plaint into a sharp cry*). No! No! Don't permit it, sir, don't permit it!

THE MANAGER. But it's only to try it.

THE MOTHER. I can't bear it. I can't.

THE MANAGER. But since it has happened already . . . I don't understand!

THE MOTHER. It's taking place now. It happens all the time. My torment isn't a pretended one. I live and feel every minute of my torture. Those two children there—have you heard them speak? They can't speak any more. They cling to me to keep up my torment actual and vivid for me. But for themselves, they do not exist, they aren't any more. And she (*Indicating the* STEP-DAUGHTER.) has run away, she has left me, and is lost. If I now see her here before me, it is only to renew for me the tortures I have suffered for her too.

THE FATHER. The eternal moment! She (*Indicating the* STEP-DAUGHTER.) is here to catch me, fix me, and hold me eternally in the stocks for that one fleeting and shameful moment of my life. She can't give it up! And you sir, cannot either fairly spare me it.

THE MANAGER. I never said I didn't want to act it. It will form, as a matter of fact, the nucleus of the whole first act right up to her surprise. (*Indicates the* MOTHER.)

THE FATHER. Just so! This is my punishment: the passion in all of us that must culminate in her final cry.

THE STEP-DAUGHTER. I can hear it still in my ears. It's driven me mad, that cry!—You can put me on as you like; it doesn't matter. Fully dressed, if you like—provided I have at least the arm bare; because, standing like this (*She goes close to the* FATHER *and leans her head on his breast.*) with my head so, and my arms round his neck, I saw a vein pulsing in my arm here; and then, as if that live vein had awakened disgust in me, I closed my eyes like this, and let my head sink on his breast. (*Turning to the* MOTHER.) Cry out mother! Cry out! (*Buries head in* FATHER*'s breast, and with her shoulders raised as if to prevent her hearing the cry, adds in tones of intense emotion.*) Cry out as you did then!

THE MOTHER (*coming forward to separate them*). No! My daughter, my daughter! (*And after having pulled her away from him.*) You brute! you brute! She is my daughter! Don't you see she's my daughter?

THE MANAGER (*walking backwards towards footlights*). Fine! fine! Damned good! And then, of course—curtain!

THE FATHER (*going towards him excitedly*). Yes, of course, because that's the way it really happened.

THE MANAGER (*convinced and pleased*). Oh, yes, no doubt about it. Curtain here, curtain!

[*At the reiterated cry of the* MANAGER, *the* MACHINIST *lets the curtain down, leaving the* MANAGER *and the* FATHER *in front of it before the footlights.*]

THE MANAGER. The darned idiot! I said "curtain" to show the act should end there, and he goes and lets it down in earnest. (*To the* FATHER, *while he pulls the curtain back to go on to the stage again.*) Yes, yes, it's all right. Effect curtain! That's the right ending. I'll guarantee the first act at any rate.

ACT III

When the curtain goes up again, it is seen that the stage hands have shifted the bit of scenery used in the last part, and have rigged up instead at the back of the stage a drop, with some trees, and one or two wings. A portion of a fountain basin is visible. The MOTHER *is sitting on the right with the two children by her side. The* SON *is on the same side, but away from the others. He seems bored, angry, and full of shame. The* FATHER *and the* STEP-DAUGHTER *are also seated towards the right front. On the other side (left) are the* ACTORS, *much in the positions they occupied before the curtain was lowered. Only the* MANAGER *is standing up in the middle of the stage, with his hand closed over his mouth in the act of meditating.*

THE MANAGER (*shaking his shoulders after a brief pause*). Ah yes: the second act! Leave it to me, leave it all to me as we arranged, and you'll see! It'll go fine!

THE STEP-DAUGHTER. Our entry into his house (*Indicates* FATHER.) in spite of him . . . (*Indicates the* SON.)

THE MANAGER (*out of patience*). Leave it to me, I tell you!

THE STEP-DAUGHTER. Do let it be clear, at any rate, that it is in spite of my wishes.

THE MOTHER (*from her corner, shaking her head*). For all the good that's come of it . . .

THE STEP-DAUGHTER (*turning towards her quickly*). It doesn't matter. The more harm done us, the more remorse for him.

THE MANAGER (*impatiently*). I understand! Good Heavens! I understand! I'm taking it into account.

THE MOTHER (*supplicatingly*). I beg you, sir, to let it appear quite plain that for conscience' sake I did try in every way . . .

THE STEP-DAUGHTER (*interrupting indignantly and continuing for the* MOTHER). . . . to pacify me, to dissuade me from spiting him. (*To* MANAGER.) Do as she wants: satisfy her, because it is true! I enjoy it immensely. Anyhow, as you can see, the meeker she is, the more she tries to get at his heart, the more distant and aloof does he become.

THE MANAGER. Are we going to begin this second act or not?

THE STEP-DAUGHTER. I'm not going to talk any more now. But I must tell you this: you can't have the whole action take place in the garden, as you suggest. It isn't possible!

THE MANAGER. Why not?

THE STEP-DAUGHTER. Because he (*Indicates the* SON *again.*) is always shut up alone in his room. And then there's all the part of that poor dazed-looking boy there which takes place indoors.

THE MANAGER. Maybe! On the other hand, you will understand—we can't change scenes three or four times in one act.

THE LEADING MAN. They used to once.

THE MANAGER. Yes, when the public was up to the level of that child there.

THE LEADING LADY. It makes the illusion easier.

THE FATHER (*irritated*). The illusion! For Heaven's sake, don't say illusion. Please don't use that word, which is particularly painful for us.

THE MANAGER (*astounded*). And why, if you please?

THE FATHER. It's painful, cruel, really cruel; and you ought to understand that.

THE MANAGER. But why? What ought we to say then? The illusion, I tell you, sir, which we've got to create for the audience . . .

THE LEADING MAN. With our acting.

THE MANAGER. The illusion of a reality.

THE FATHER. I understand; but you, perhaps, do not understand us. Forgive me! You see . . . here for you and your actors, the thing is only—and rightly so . . . a kind of game . . .

THE LEADING LADY (*interrupting indignantly*). A game! We're not children here, if you please! We are serious actors.

THE FATHER. I don't deny it. What I mean is the game, or play, of your art, which has to give, as the gentleman says, a perfect illusion of reality.

THE MANAGER. Precisely—!

THE FATHER. Now, if you consider the fact that we (*Indicates himself and the other five* CHARACTERS.), as we are, have no other reality outside of this illusion . . .

THE MANAGER (*astonished, looking at his* ACTORS, *who are also amazed*). And what does that mean?

THE FATHER (*after watching them for a moment with a wan smile*). As I say, sir, that which is a game of art for you is our sole reality. (*Brief pause. He goes a step or two nearer the* MANAGER *and adds.*) But not only for us, you know, by the way. Just you think it over well. (*Looks him in the eyes.*) Can you tell me who you are?

THE MANAGER (*perplexed, half smiling*). What? Who am I? I am myself.

THE FATHER. And if I were to tell you that that isn't true, because you and I . . . ?

THE MANAGER. I should say you were mad—! (*The* ACTORS *laugh.*)

THE FATHER. You're quite right to laugh: because we are all making believe here. (*To* MANAGER.) And you can therefore object that it's only for a joke that that gentleman there (*Indicates the* LEADING MAN.), who naturally is himself, has to be me, who am on the contrary myself—this thing you see here. You see I've caught you in a trap! (*The* ACTORS *laugh.*)

THE MANAGER (*annoyed*). But we've had all this over once before. Do you want to begin again?

THE FATHER. No, no! That wasn't my meaning! In fact, I should like to request you to abandon this game of art (*Looking at the* LEADING LADY *as if anticipating her.*) which you are accustomed to play here with your actors, and to ask you seriously once again: who are you?

THE MANAGER (*astonished and irritated, turning to his* ACTORS). If this fellow here hasn't got a nerve! A man who calls himself a character comes and asks me who I am!

THE FATHER (*with dignity, but not offended*). A character, sir, may always ask a man who he is. Because a character has really a life of his own, marked with his especial characteristics; for which reason he is always "somebody." But a man—I'm not speaking of you now—may very well be "nobody."

THE MANAGER. Yes, but you are asking these questions of me, the boss, the manager! Do you understand?

THE FATHER. But only in order to know if you, as you really are now, see yourself as you once were with all the illusions that were yours then, with all the things both inside and outside of you as they seemed to you—as they were then indeed for you. Well, sir, if you think of all those illusions that mean nothing to you now, of all those things which don't even *seem* to you to exist any more, while once they *were* for you, don't you feel that—I won't say these boards—but the very earth under your feet is sinking away from you when you reflect that in the same way this *you* as you feel it today—all this present reality of yours—is fated to seem a mere illusion to you tomorrow?

THE MANAGER (*without having understood much, but astonished by the specious argument*). Well, well! And where does all this take us anyway?

THE FATHER. Oh, nowhere! It's only to show you that if we (*Indicating the* CHARACTERS.) have no other reality beyond the illusion, you too must not count overmuch on your reality as you feel it today, since, like that of yesterday, it may prove an illusion for you tomorrow.

THE MANAGER (*determining to make fun of him*). Ah, excellent! Then you'll be saying next that you, with this comedy of yours that you brought here to act, are truer and more real than I am.

THE FATHER (*with the greatest seriousness*). But of course; without doubt!

THE MANAGER. Ah, really?

THE FATHER. Why, I thought you'd understand that from the beginning.

THE MANAGER. More real than I?

THE FATHER. If your reality can change from one day to another . . .

THE MANAGER. But everyone knows it can change. It is always changing, the same as anyone else's.

THE FATHER (*with a cry*). No, sir, not ours! Look here! That is the very difference! Our reality doesn't change: it can't change! It can't be other than what it is, because it is already fixed for ever. It's terrible. Ours is an immutable reality which should make you shudder when you approach us if you are really conscious of the fact that your reality is a mere transitory and fleeting illusion, taking this form today and that tomorrow, according to the conditions, according to your will, your sentiments, which in turn are controlled by an intellect that shows them to you today in one manner and tomorrow . . . who knows how? . . . Illusions of reality represented in this fatuous comedy of life that never ends, nor can ever end! Because if tomorrow it were to end . . . then why, all would be finished.

THE MANAGER. Oh for God's sake, will you *at least* finish with this philosophizing and let us try and shape this comedy which you yourself have brought me here? You argue and philosophize a bit too much, my dear sir. You know you seem to me almost, almost . . . (*Stops and looks him over from head to foot.*) Ah, by the way, I think you introduced yourself to me as a—what shall . . . we say—a "character," created by an author who did not afterward care to make a drama of his own creations.

THE FATHER. It is the simple truth, sir.

THE MANAGER. Nonsense! Cut that out, please! None of us believes it isn't a thing, as you must recognize yourself, which one can believe seriously. If you want to know, it seems to me you are trying to imitate the manner of a certain author whom I heartily detest—I warn you—although I have unfortunately bound myself to put on one of his works. As a matter of fact, I was just starting to rehearse it, when you arrived. (*Turning to the* ACTORS.) And this is what we've gained—out of the frying-pan into the fire!

THE FATHER. I don't know to what author you may be alluding, but believe me I feel what I think; and I seem to be philosophizing only for those who do not think what they feel, because they blind themselves with their own sentiment. I know that for many people this self-blinding seems much more "human"; but the contrary is really true. For man never reasons so much and becomes so introspective as when he suffers; since he is anxious to get at the cause of his sufferings, to learn who has produced them, and whether it is just or unjust that he should have to bear them. On the other hand, when he is happy, he takes his happiness as it comes and doesn't analyze it, just as if happiness were his right. The animals suffer without reasoning about their sufferings. But take the case of a man who suffers and begins to reason about it. Oh, no! it can't be allowed! Let him suffer like an animal, and then—ah yet, he is "human"!

THE MANAGER. Look here! Look here! You're off again, philosophizing worse than ever.

THE FATHER. Because I suffer, sir! I'm not philosophizing: I'm crying aloud the reason of my sufferings.

THE MANAGER (*makes brusque movement as he is taken with a new idea*). I should like to know if anyone has ever heard of a character who gets right out of his part and perorates and speechifies as you do. Have you ever heard of a case? I haven't.

THE FATHER. You have never met such a case, sir, because authors, as a rule, hide the labour of their creations. When the characters are really alive before their author, the latter does nothing but follow them in their action, in their words, in the situations which they suggest to him; and he has to will them the way they will themselves—for there's trouble if he doesn't. When a character is born, he acquires at once such an independence, even of his own author, that he can be imagined by everybody even in many other situations where the author never dreamed of placing him; and so he acquires for himself a meaning which the author never thought of giving him.

THE MANAGER. Yes, yes, I know this.

THE FATHER. What is there then to marvel at in us? Imagine such a misfortune for characters as I have described to you: to be born of an author's fantasy, and be denied life by him; and then answer me if these characters left alive, and yet without life, weren't right in doing what they did do and are doing now, after they have attempted everything in their power to persuade him to give them their stage life. We've all tried him in turn, I, see (*Indicating the* STEP-DAUGHTER.) and she. (*Indicating the* MOTHER.)

THE STEP-DAUGHTER. It's true. I too have sought to tempt him, many, many times, when he has been sitting at his writing table, feeling a bit melancholy, at the twilight hour. He would sit in his armchair too lazy to switch on the light, and all the shadows that crept into his room were full of our presence coming to tempt him. (*As if she saw herself still there by the writing table, and was annoyed by the presence of the* ACTORS.) Oh, if you would only go away, go away and leave us alone —mother here with that son of hers—I with that Child—that Boy there always alone—and then I with him (*Just hints at the* FATHER.)— and then I alone, alone . . . in those shadows! (*Makes a sudden movement as if in the vision she has of herself illuminating those shadows she wanted to seize hold of herself.*) Ah! my life! my life! Oh, what scenes we proposed to him—and I tempted him more than any of the others!

THE FATHER. Maybe. But perhaps it was your fault that he refused to give us life: because you were too insistent, too troublesome.

THE STEP-DAUGHTER. Nonsense! Didn't he make me so himself? (*Goes close to the* MANAGER *to tell him as if in confidence.*) In my opinion he abandoned us in a fit of depression, of disgust for the ordinary theatre as the public knows it and likes it.

THE SON. Exactly what it was, sir; exactly that!

THE FATHER. Not at all! Don't believe it for a minute. Listen to me! You'll be doing quite right to modify, as you suggest, the excesses both of this girl here, who wants to do too much, and of this young man, who won't do anything at all.

THE SON. No, nothing!

THE MANAGER. You too get over the mark occasionally, my dear sir, if I may say so.

THE FATHER. I? When? Where?

THE MANAGER. Always! Continuously! Then there's this insistence of yours in trying to make us believe you are a character. And then too, you must really argue and philosophize less, you know, much less.

THE FATHER. Well, if you want to take away from me the possibility of representing the torment of my spirit which never gives me peace, you will be suppressing me: that's all. Every true man, sir, who is a little above the level of the beasts and plants does not live for the sake of living, without knowing how to live; but he lives so as to give a meaning and a value of his own to life. For me this is *everything*. I cannot give up this, just to represent a mere fact as she (*Indicating the* STEP-DAUGHTER.) wants. It's all very well for her, since her "vendetta" lies in the "fact." I'm not going to do it. It destroys my *raison d'être*.

THE MANAGER. Your *raison d'être!* Oh, we're going ahead fine! First she starts off, and then you jump in. At this rate, we'll never finish.

THE FATHER. Now, don't be offended! Have it your own way—provided, however, that within the limits of the parts you assign us each one's sacrifice isn't too great.

THE MANAGER. You've got to understand that you can't go on arguing at your own pleasure. Drama is action, sir, action and not confounded philosophy.

THE FATHER. All right. I'll do just as much arguing and philosophizing as everybody does when he is considering his own torments.

THE MANAGER. If the drama permits! But for Heaven's sake, man, let's get along and come to the scene.

THE STEP-DAUGHTER. It seems to me we've got too much action with our coming into his house. (*Indicating* FATHER.) You said, before, you couldn't change the scene every five minutes.

THE MANAGER. Of course not. What we've got to do is to combine and group up all the facts in one simultaneous, close-knit, action. We can't have it as you want, with your little brother wandering like a ghost from room to room, hiding behind doors and meditating a project which—what did you say it did to him?

THE STEP-DAUGHTER. Consumes him, sir, wastes him away!

THE MANAGER. Well, it may be. And then at the same time, you want the little girl there to be playing in the garden . . . one in the house, and the other in the garden: isn't that it?

THE STEP-DAUGHTER. Yes, in the sun, in the sun! That is my only pleasure: to see her happy and careless in the garden after the misery and squalor of the horrible room where we all four slept together. And I had to sleep with her—I, do you understand?—with my vile contaminated body next to hers; with her folding me fast in her loving little arms. In the garden, whenever she spied me, she would run to take me by the hand. She didn't care for the big flowers, only the little ones; and she loved to show me them and pet me.

THE MANAGER. Well then, we'll have it in the garden. Everything shall happen in the garden; and we'll group the other scenes there. (*Calls a* STAGE HAND.) Here, a backcloth with trees and something to do as a fountain basin. (*Turning round to look at the back of the stage.*) Ah, you've fixed it up. Good! (*To* STEP-DAUGHTER.) This is just to give an idea, of course. The Boy, instead of hiding behind the doors, will wander about here in the garden, hiding behind the trees. But it's going to be rather difficult to find a child to do that scene with you where she shows you the flowers. (*Turning to the* BOY.) Come forward a little, will you please? Let's try it now! Come along! come along!

(*Then seeing him come shyly forward, full of fear and looking lost.*) It's a nice business, this lad here. What's the matter with him? We'll have to give him a word or two to say. (*Goes close to him, puts a hand on his shoulders, and leads him behind one of the trees.*) Come on! come on! Let me see you a little! Hide here . . . yes, like that. Try and show your head just a little as if you were looking for someone . . . (*Goes back to observe the effect, when the* BOY *at once goes through the action.*) *Excellent! fine!* (*Turning to* STEP-DAUGHTER.) Suppose the little girl there were to surprise him as he looks round, and run over to him, so we could give him a word or two to say?

THE STEP-DAUGHTER. It's useless to hope he will speak, as long as that fellow there is here . . . (*Indicates the* SON.) You must send him away first.

THE SON (*jumping up*). Delighted! Delighted! I don't ask for anything better. (*Begins to move away.*)

THE MANAGER (*at once stopping him*). No! No! Where are you going? Wait a bit!

[*The* MOTHER *gets up alarmed and terrified at the thought that he is really about to go away. Instinctively she lifts her arms to prevent him, without, however, leaving her seat.*]

THE SON (*to* MANAGER *who stops him*). I've got nothing to do with this affair. Let me go please! Let me go!

THE MANAGER. What do you mean by saying you've got nothing to do with this?

THE STEP-DAUGHTER (*calmly, with irony*). Don't bother to stop him: he won't go away.

THE FATHER. He has to act the terrible scene in the garden with his mother.

THE SON (*suddenly resolute and with dignity*). I shall act nothing at all. I've said so from the very beginning. (*To the* MANAGER.) Let me go!

THE STEP-DAUGHTER (*going over to the* MANAGER). Allow me? (*Puts down the* MANAGER*'s arm which is restraining the* SON.) Well, go away then, if you want to! (*The* SON *looks at her with contempt and hatred. She laughs and says.*) You see, he can't, he can't go away! He is obliged to stay here, indissolubly bound to the chain. If I, who fly off when that happens which has to happen, because I can't bear him—if I am still here and support that face and expression of his, you can well imagine that he is unable to move. He has to remain here, has to stop with that nice father of his, and that mother whose only son he is. (*Turning to the* MOTHER.) Come on, mother, come along! (*Turning to* MANAGER *to indicate her.*) You see, she was getting up to keep him back. (*To the* MOTHER, *beckoning her with her hand.*) Come on! come on! (*Then to* MANAGER.) You can imagine how little she wants to show these actors of yours what she really feels; but so eager is she to get near him that . . . There, you see? She is willing to act her part.

(*And in fact, the* MOTHER *approaches him; and as soon as the* STEP-DAUGHTER *has finished speaking, opens her arms to signify that she consents.*)

THE SON (*suddenly*). No! no! If I can't go away, then I'll stop here; but I repeat: I act nothing!

THE FATHER (*to* MANAGER *excitedly*). You can force him, sir.

THE SON. Nobody can force me.

THE FATHER. I can.

THE STEP-DAUGHTER. Wait a minute, wait . . . First of all, the baby has to go to the fountain . . . (*Runs to take the* CHILD *and leads her to the fountain.*)

THE MANAGER. Yes, yes of course; that's it. Both at the same time.

[*The second* LADY LEAD *and the* JUVENILE LEAD *at this point separate themselves from the group of* ACTORS. *One watches the* MOTHER *attentively; the other moves about studying the movements and manner of the* SON *whom he will have to act.*]

THE SON (*to* MANAGER). What do you mean by both at the same time? It isn't right. There was no scene between me and her. (*Indicates the* MOTHER.) Ask her how it was!

THE MOTHER. Yes, it's true. I had come into his room . . .

THE SON. Into my room, do you understand? Nothing to do with the garden.

THE MANAGER. It doesn't matter. Haven't I told you we've got to group the action?

THE SON (*observing the* JUVENILE LEAD *studying him*). What do you want?

THE JUVENILE LEAD. Nothing! I was just looking at you.

THE SON (*turning towards the* SECOND LADY LEAD). Ah! she's at it too: to re-act her part! (*Indicating the* MOTHER.)

THE MANAGER. Exactly! And it seems to me that you ought to be grateful to them for their interest.

THE SON. Yes, but haven't you yet perceived that it isn't possible to live in front of a mirror which not only freezes us with the image of ourselves, but throws our likeness back at us with a horrible grimace?

THE FATHER. That is true, absolutely true. You must see that.

THE MANAGER (*to* SECOND LADY LEAD *and* JUVENILE LEAD). He's right! Move away from them!

THE SON. Do as you like. I'm out of this!

THE MANAGER. Be quiet, you, will you? And let me hear your mother! (*To* MOTHER.) You were saying you had entered . . .

THE MOTHER. Yes, into his room, because I couldn't stand it any longer. I went to empty my heart to him of all the anguish that tortures me . . . But as soon as he saw me come in . . .

THE SON. Nothing happened! There was no scene. I went away, that's all! I don't care for scenes!

THE MOTHER. It's true, true. That's how it was.

THE MANAGER. Well now, we've got to do this bit between you and him. It's indispensable.

THE MOTHER. I'm ready . . . when you are ready. If you could only find a chance for me to tell him what I feel here in my heart.

THE FATHER (*going to* SON *in a great rage*). You'll do this for your mother, for your mother, do you understand?

THE SON (*quite determined*). I do nothing!

THE FATHER (*taking hold of him and shaking him*). For God's sake, do as I tell you! Don't you hear your mother asking you for a favor? Haven't you even got the guts to be a son?

THE SON (*taking hold of the* FATHER). No! No! And for God's sake stop it, or else . . . (*General agitation. The* MOTHER, *frightened, tries to separate them.*)

THE MOTHER (*pleading*). Please! please!

THE FATHER (*not leaving hold of the* SON). You've got to obey, do you hear?

THE SON (*almost crying from rage*). What does it mean, this madness you've got? (*They separate.*) Have you no decency, that you insist on showing everyone our shame? I won't do it! I won't! And I stand for the will of our author in this. He didn't want to put us on the stage, after all!

THE MANAGER. Man alive! You came here . . .

THE SON (*indicating* FATHER). *He* did! I didn't!

THE MANAGER. Aren't you here now?

THE SON. It was his wish, and he dragged us along with him. He's told you not only the things that did happen, but also things that have never happened at all.

THE MANAGER. Well, tell me then what did happen. You went out of your room without saying a word?

THE SON. Without a word, so as to avoid a scene!

THE MANAGER. And then what did you do?

THE SON. Nothing . . . walking in the garden . . . (*Hesitates for a moment with expression of gloom.*)

THE MANAGER (*coming closer to him, interested by his extraordinary reserve*). Well, well . . . walking in the garden . . .

THE SON (*exasperated*). Why on earth do you insist? It's horrible! (*The* MOTHER *trembles, sobs, and looks towards the fountain.*)

THE MANAGER (*slowly observing the glance and turning towards the* SON *with increasing apprehension*). The baby?

THE SON. There in the fountain . . .

THE FATHER (*pointing with tender pity to the* MOTHER). She was following him at the moment . . .

THE MANAGER (*to the* SON *anxiously*). And then you . . .

THE SON. I ran over to her; I was jumping in to drag her out when I saw something that froze my blood . . . the boy standing stock still, with eyes like a madman's, watching his little drowned sister, in the fountain! (*The* STEP-DAUGHTER *bends over the fountain to hide the* CHILD. *She sobs.*) Then . . . (*A revolver shot rings out behind the trees where the* BOY *is hidden.*)

THE MOTHER (*with a cry of terror runs over in that direction together with several of the* ACTORS *amid general confusion*). My son! My son! (*Then amid the cries and exclamations one hears her voice.*) Help! Help!

THE MANAGER (*pushing the* ACTORS *aside while they lift up the* BOY *and carry him off.*) Is he really wounded?

SOME ACTORS. He's dead! dead!

OTHER ACTORS. No, no, it's only make believe, it's only pretence!

THE FATHER (*with a terrible cry*). Pretence? Reality, sir, reality!

THE MANAGER. Pretence? Reality? To hell with it all! Never in my life has such a thing happened to me. I've lost a whole day over these people, a whole day!

CRITICAL COMMENTARY

Six Characters in Search of an Author, through a mixture of Freudianism, esthetics, and show business, generates problems about identity in a theatrically schizophrenic world, and it is therefore with some reason thought of as being typically modern. It may be useful at the outset, however, to compare it with an older play, *The Alchemist.* An identity, on second thought, is even more desirable than instant wealth; and a discussion of identity in the context of a scientific mystery like schizophrenia becomes as rigorously circular and self-contained as the jargon about alchemy. When all this is combined with the built-in double identity of the theater and with the oscillations arising from the situation of six characters searching for identity in a dramatic fiction, the result has been compared, understandably, to cubist art.

Attempts to interpret and clarify *Six Characters* by summarizing its plot seem to show that its cubist obscurities are somehow unlike the planted clues in *Ghosts.* Is this merely because a narrative summary cannot represent the cubist interplay of planes of reality in *Six Characters,* or is it because Ibsen's ideas about character and identity are actually simpler than Pirandello's?

Although *Six Characters* may not be an Ibsenite problem play, it spawns more problems than Ibsen dreamed of. Or do they simply seem more numerous because they seem more modern and compelling? Here is just a sampling of Pirandellian problems, mostly from the first few hundred lines of the play: What is the relation of the theater to reality? How is an answer affected by our sight of the theater off-guard, an unbuttoned rehearsal on a bare stage with the curtain up and the air full of professional in-jokes, including jibes at Pirandello's obscurity? In what sense is a fiction truer than life? What is the relation between the invented credibility of fictional situations and the absurd situations in real life that are credible merely because they have happened? What is the relation between characters and their fiction, the "fecundating matrix" that the Father asserts some famous characters have been lucky enough to find? Why do these characters want to find a fiction? In order to exist? What does that mean? To find out who they are? To reveal what they have been? To us? Or to themselves so that they can understand themselves? Why do the characters have only generic names? Because they have not yet been given proper names in a particular fiction? Or because they represent primal and basic types? What is the relation between a specific father, Mr. Smith, and Father? Why does this Father talk in such an old-fashioned theatrical way? What is going on between him and Step-Daughter? Will we find out that these wandering, fictive, fictionless characters are really real? Do they become less real when they are acted conventionally by real actors? Are they representations of real people who feel compelled to buttonhole everyone and tell their story? Don't the characters get their time schemes mixed up? Are they saying, in effect, that time is blurred and repetitive because we are determined or fated by basic fictions assigned to us? Assigned how and by whom? By the fact that we are not men and women but fathers and mothers and sons and daughters? Can verbal fictions really enable people to break out of their private identities and communicate with one another? (Is this comparable to the question of separateness raised by *The Cherry Orchard*?) What is signified by a character asking a real person to say who he is outside of his theatrical role as Manager or Actor? Is an unchanging fictional character more real than a changing real person? Is the play really a perpetual cinema, and can it end only accidentally by a momentary blunder like a curtain drop? Once the play has evoked questions of this sort, does one have to be deeply engaged with it? Do the questions follow a pattern from which one can go on endlessly inventing similar questions?

Pirandello's ideal human being has been described as one "who has enough psychological and moral agility to mold every minute of his life into a form, assume full consciousness thereof, and then renounce the form right away, in order to resume contact with life in the following minute . . . the only truth resides in this psychological actualism." (Glauco Cambon, ed., *Pirandello* [Twentieth Century Views], 1967, p. 138) At a glance that seems to be a fair description of Falstaff and even Face as they flow from part to part, but are their rapid impersonations the same as the fluid theatricality of *Six Characters*?

The theatricality of life is an ancient conception, and has taken many forms for many purposes. The theatrical duplicity of the Machiavellians in *The Jew of Malta* is one example. Is this like or unlike the mixture of acting and reality in *Six Characters*?

The search for identity is also ancient. Is Hal's movement toward being himself based on the assumptions about the nature of identity that underlie *Six Characters*? Does Hal learn who he is by learning to play many roles under Falstaff's tutelage or by learning that he is not a person but a generic King?

It is fashionable now to merge the audience and the actors. Is this related to Pirandello's manipulation of apparent reality and real appearances? Here is a comment on the subject:

> In a widespread practice (for instance in the Pirandello theater and the "happening") audience and cast, actors and characters they

> represent, stage and theater, drama and life are merged. We seem to have a choice only between listening to a lecture and a drunken carouse. . . . Though complete surrender to the show seems naive, and the rejection of the differentiation of art and life "sophisticated," the two really come together. For the assimilation of cast and characters, of pit and stage, in effect reduces everyone to the position of the simple-minded theatergoer who from Elizabethan times has been laughed at for his taking stage transactions as actualities. When the whole audience is confused about boundaries, then underdistancing has paradoxically done the work of overdistancing, for the theatergoer becomes, not the possessor of an experience, but the asker of questions and the seeker of answers. (Robert B. Heilman, *Tragedy and Melodrama,* 1968, pp. 247–48)

If one develops a comparison between *Six Characters* and *The Alchemist,* differences in tone and point of view become apparent. What are they, and what do they imply? Is there any relation between the secret and common selves revealed by the philosopher's stone and the half-buried Freudian selves of the six characters?

Useful Criticism

Bentley, Eric. *The Playwright as Thinker.** New York: Noonday Press, 1955.

Brustein, Robert. *The Theater of Revolt.** Boston: Atlantic-Little, Brown, 1964.

Cambon, Glauco, ed. *Pirandello** (Twentieth Century Views). Englewood Cliffs, N.J.: Prentice-Hall, 1967.

Fergusson, Francis. *The Idea of a Theater.** Garden City, N.Y.: Doubleday, 1953.

Starkie, Walter. *Luigi Pirandello,* 3rd ed.* Berkeley: University of California Press, 1965.

Vittorini, Domenico. *The Drama of Luigi Pirandello.* New York: Dover Books, 1935.

* Available in paperback.

THE CAUCASIAN CHALK CIRCLE

Bertolt Brecht

Revised English version by ERIC BENTLEY

CHARACTERS

OLD MAN on the right
PEASANT WOMAN on the right
YOUNG PEASANT
A VERY YOUNG WORKER
OLD MAN on the left
PEASANT WOMAN on the left
AGRICULTURIST KATO
GIRL TRACTORIST
WOUNDED SOLDIER
THE DELEGATE from the capital
THE SINGER
GEORGI ABASHWILI, the Governor
NATELLA, the Governor's wife
MICHAEL, their son
SHALVA, an adjutant
ARSEN KAZBEKI, a fat prince
MESSENGER from the capital
NIKO MIKADZE and MIKA LOLADZE, doctors
SIMON SHASHAVA, a soldier
GRUSHA VASHNADZE, a kitchen maid
OLD PEASANT with the milk
CORPORAL and PRIVATE
PEASANT and his wife
LAVRENTI VASHNADZE, Grusha's brother
ANIKO, his wife
PEASANT WOMAN, for a while Grusha's mother-in-law
JUSSUP, her son
MONK
AZDAK, village recorder
SHAUWA, a policeman
GRAND DUKE
DOCTOR
INVALID
LIMPING MAN
BLACKMAILER
LUDOVICA
INNKEEPER, her father-in-law
STABLEBOY
POOR OLD PEASANT WOMAN
IRAKLI, her brother-in-law, a bandit
THREE WEALTHY FARMERS
ILLO SHUBOLADZE and SANDRO OBOLADZE, lawyers
OLD MARRIED COUPLE

SOLDIERS, SERVANTS, PEASANTS, BEGGARS, MUSICIANS, MERCHANTS, NOBLES, ARCHITECTS

The time and the place: After a prologue, set in 1945, we move back perhaps 1000 years.

The action of The Caucasian Chalk Circle *centers on Nuka (or Nukha), a town in Azerbaijan. However, the capital referred to in the prologue is not Baku (capital of Soviet Azerbaijan) but Tiflis (or Tbilisi), capital of Georgia. When Azdak, later, refers to "the capital" he means Nuka itself, though whether Nuka was ever capital of Georgia I do not know: in what reading I have done on the subject I have only found Nuka to be the capital of a Nuka Khanate.*

The word "Georgia" has not been used in this English version because of its American associations; instead, the alternative name "Grusinia" (in Russian, Gruziya) has been used.

The reasons for resettling the old Chinese story in Transcaucasia are not far to seek. The play was written when the Soviet chief of state, Joseph Stalin, was a Georgian, as was his favorite poet, cited in the Prologue, Mayakovsky. And surely there is a point in having this story acted out at the place where Europe and Asia meet, a place incomparably rich in legend and history. Here Jason found the Golden Fleece. Here Noah's Ark touched ground. Here the armies of both Genghis Khan and Tamerlane wrought havoc.

—E.B.

Prologue

Summer, 1945.

Among the ruins of a war-ravaged Caucasian village the members of two Kolkhoz villages, mostly women and older men, are sitting in a circle, smoking and drinking wine. With them is a DELEGATE *of the State Reconstruction Commission from Nuka.*

PEASANT WOMAN, *left* (*pointing*). In those hills over there we stopped three Nazi tanks, but the apple orchard was already destroyed.

OLD MAN, *right.* Our beautiful dairy farm: a ruin.

GIRL TRACTORIST. I laid the fire, Comrade.

[*Pause.*]

DELEGATE. Nuka, Azerbaijan S.S.R. Delegation received from the goat-breeding Kolkhoz "Rosa Luxemburg." This is a collective farm which moved eastwards on orders from the authorities at the approach of Hitler's armies. They are now planning to return. Their delegates have looked at the village and the land and found a lot of destruction. (*Delegates on the right nod.*) But the neighboring fruit farm—Kolkhoz (*To the left.*) "Galinsk"—proposes to use the former grazing land of

Kolkhoz "Rosa Luxemburg" for orchards and vineyards. This land lies in a valley where grass doesn't grow very well. As a delegate of the Reconstruction Commission in Nuka I request that the two Kolkhoz villages decide between themselves whether Kolkhoz "Rosa Luxemburg" shall return or not.

OLD MAN, *right*. First of all, I want to protest against the time limit on discussion. We of Kolkhoz "Rosa Luxemburg" have spent three days and three nights getting here. And now discussion is limited to half a day.

WOUNDED SOLDIER, *left*. Comrade, we haven't as many villages as we used to have. We haven't as many hands. We haven't as much time.

GIRL TRACTORIST. All pleasures have to be rationed. Tobacco is rationed, and wine. Discussion should be rationed.

OLD MAN, *right* (*sighing*). Death to the fascists! But I will come to the point and explain why we want our valley back. There are a great many reasons, but I'll begin with one of the simplest. Makinä Abakidze, unpack the goat cheese. (*A peasant woman from right takes from a basket an enormous cheese wrapped in a cloth. Applause and laughter.*) Help yourselves, Comrades, start in!

OLD MAN, *left* (*suspiciously*). Is this a way of influencing us?

OLD MAN, *right* (*amid laughter*). How could it be a way of influencing you, Surab, you valley-thief? Everyone knows you'll take the cheese and the valley, too. (*Laughter.*) All I expect from you is an honest answer. Do you like the cheese?

OLD MAN, *left*. The answer is: yes.

OLD MAN, *right*. Really. (*Bitterly.*) I ought to have known you know nothing about cheese.

OLD MAN, *left*. Why not? When I tell you I like it?

OLD MAN, *right*. Because you can't like it. Because it's not what it was in the old days. And why not? Because our goats don't like the new grass as they did the old. Cheese is not cheese because grass is not grass, that's the thing. Please put that in your report.

OLD MAN, *left*. But your cheese is excellent.

OLD MAN, *right*. It isn't excellent. It's just passable. The new grazing land is no good, whatever the young people may say. One can't live there. It doesn't even smell of morning in the morning. (*Several people laugh.*)

DELEGATE. Don't mind their laughing: they understand you. Comrades, why does one love one's country? Because the bread tastes better there, the air smells better, voices sound stronger, the sky is higher, the ground is easier to walk on. Isn't that so?

OLD MAN, *right*. The valley has belonged to us from all eternity.

SOLDIER, *left*. What does *that* mean—from all eternity? Nothing belongs to anyone from all eternity. When you were young you didn't even belong to yourself. You belonged to the Kazbeki princes.

OLD MAN, *right.* Doesn't it make a difference, though, what kind of trees stand next to the house you are born in? Or what kind of neighbors you have? Doesn't that make a difference? We want to go back just to have you as our neighbors, valley-thieves! Now you can all laugh again.

OLD MAN, *left* (*laughing*). Then why don't you listen to what your neighbor, Kato Wachtang, our agriculturist, has to say about the valley?

PEASANT WOMAN, *right.* We've not said all we have to say about our valley. By no means. Not all the houses are destroyed. As for the dairy farm, at least the foundation wall is still standing.

DELEGATE. You can claim State support—here and there—you know that. I have suggestions here in my pocket.

PEASANT WOMAN, *right.* Comrade Specialist, we haven't come here to haggle. I can't take your cap and hand you another, and say "This one's better." The other one might *be* better, but you *like* yours better.

GIRL TRACTORIST. A piece of land is not a cap—not in our country, Comrade.

DELEGATE. Don't get mad. It's true we have to consider a piece of land as a tool to produce something useful, but it's also true that we must recognize love for a particular piece of land. As far as I'm concerned, I'd like to find out more exactly what you (*To those on the left.*) want to do with the valley.

OTHERS. Yes, let Kato speak.

KATO (*rising; she's in military uniform*). Comrades, last winter, while we were fighting in these hills here as Partisans, we discussed how, once the Germans were expelled, we could build up our fruit culture to ten times its original size. I've prepared a plan for an irrigation project. By means of a cofferdam on our mountain lake, 300 hectares of unfertile land can be irrigated. Our Kolkhoz could not only cultivate more fruit, but also have vineyards. The project, however, would pay only if the disputed valley of Kolkhoz "Rosa Luxemburg" were also included. Here are the calculations. (*She hands* DELEGATE *a briefcase.*)

OLD MAN, *right.* Write into the report that our Kolkhoz plans to start a new stud farm.

GIRL TRACTORIST. Comrades, the project was conceived during days and nights when we had to take cover in the mountains. We were often without ammunition for our half-dozen rifles. Even finding a pencil was difficult. (*Applause from both sides.*)

OLD MAN, *right.* Our thanks to the Comrades of Kolkhoz "Galinsk" and all those who've defended our country! (*They shake hands and embrace.*)

PEASANT WOMAN, *left.* In doing this our thought was that our soldiers—both your men and our men—should return to a still more productive homeland.

GIRL TRACTORIST. As the poet Mayakovsky said: "The home of the Soviet people shall also be the home of Reason"!

[*The delegates excluding the* OLD MAN *have got up, and with the* DELEGATE *specified proceed to study the Agriculturist's drawings. Exclamations such as:* "Why is the altitude of fall 22 meters?"—"This rock will have to be blown up"—"Actually, all they need is cement and dynamite"—"They force the water to come down here, that's clever!"]

A VERY YOUNG WORKER, *right* (*to* OLD MAN, *right*). They're going to irrigate all the fields between the hills, look at that, Aleko!

OLD MAN, *right.* I'm not going to look. I knew the project would be good. I won't have a pistol pointed at me!

DELEGATE. But they only want to point a pencil at you!

[*Laughter.*]

OLD MAN, *right* (*gets up gloomily, and walks over to look at the drawings*). These valley-thieves know only too well that we in this country are suckers for machines and projects.

PEASANT WOMAN, *right.* Aleko Bereshwili, you have a weakness for new projects. That's well known.

DELEGATE. What about my report? May I write that you will all support the cession of your old valley in the interests of this project when you get back to your Kolkhoz?

PEASANT WOMAN, *right.* I will. What about you, Aleko?

OLD MAN, *right* (*bent over drawings*). I suggest that you give us copies of the drawings to take along.

PEASANT WOMAN, *right.* Then we can sit down and eat. Once he has the drawings and he's ready to discuss them, the matter is settled. I know him. And it will be the same with the rest of us.

[*Delegates laughingly embrace again.*]

OLD MAN, *left.* Long live the Kolkhoz "Rosa Luxemburg" and much luck to your horse-breeding project!

PEASANT WOMAN, *left.* In honor of the visit of the delegates from Kolkhoz "Rosa Luxemburg" and of the Specialist, the plan is that we all hear a presentation of the Singer Arkadi Tscheidse.

[*Applause.* GIRL TRACTORIST *has gone off to bring the* SINGER.]

PEASANT WOMAN, *right.* Comrades, your entertainment had better be good. It's going to cost us a valley.

PEASANT WOMAN, *left.* Arkadi Tscheidse knows about our discussion. He's promised to perform something that has a bearing on the problem.

KATO. We wired Tiflis three times. The whole thing nearly fell through at the last minute because his driver had a cold.

PEASANT WOMAN, *left.* Arkadi Tscheidse knows 21,000 lines of verse.

OLD MAN, *left.* He's hard to get. You and the Planning Commission should persuade him to come north more often, Comrade.

DELEGATE. We are more interested in economics, I'm afraid.

OLD MAN, *left* (*smiling*). You arrange the redistribution of vines and tractors, why not songs?

[*Enter the* SINGER *Arkadi Tscheidse, led by* GIRL TRACTORIST. *He is a well-built man of simple manners, accompanied by* FOUR MUSICIANS *with their instruments. The artists are greeted with applause.*]

GIRL TRACTORIST. This is the Comrade Specialist, Arkadi.

[*The* SINGER *greets them all.*]

DELEGATE. Honored to make your acquaintance. I heard about your songs when I was a boy at school. Will it be one of the old legends?

SINGER. A very old one. It's called "The Chalk Circle" and comes from the Chinese. But we'll do it, of course, in a changed version. Comrades, it's an honor for me to entertain you after a difficult debate. We hope you will find that the voice of the old poet also sounds well in the shadow of Soviet tractors. It may be a mistake to mix different wines, but old and new wisdom mix admirably. Now I hope we'll get something to eat before the performance begins—it would certainly help.

VOICES. Surely. Everyone into the Club House!

[*While everyone begins to move,* DELEGATE *turns to* GIRL TRACTORIST.]

DELEGATE. I hope it won't take long. I've got to get back tonight.

GIRL TRACTORIST. How long will it last, Arkadi? The Comrade Specialist must get back to Tiflis tonight.

SINGER (*casually*). It's actually two stories. An hour or two.

GIRL TRACTORIST (*confidentially*). Couldn't you make it shorter?

SINGER. No.

VOICE. Arkadi Tscheidse's performance will take place here in the square after the meal.

[*And they all go happily to eat.*]

ACT I

The Noble Child

As the lights go up, the SINGER *is seen sitting on the floor, a black sheepskin cloak round his shoulders, and a little, well-thumbed notebook in his hand. A small group of listeners—the chorus—sits with him. The manner of his recitation makes it clear that he has told his story over and over again. He mechanically fingers the pages, seldom looking at them. With appropriate gestures, he gives the signal for each scene to begin.*

SINGER.

In olden times, in a bloody time,
There ruled in a Caucasian city—
Men called it City of the Damned—
A Governor.
His name was Georgi Abashwili.
He was rich as Croesus
He had a beautiful wife
He had a healthy baby.
No other governor in Grusinia
Had so many horses in his stable
So many beggars on his doorstep
So many soldiers in his service
So many petitioners in his courtyard.
Georgi Abashwili—how shall I describe him to you?
He enjoyed his life.
On the morning of Easter Sunday
The Governor and his family went to church.

[*At the left a large doorway, at the right an even larger gateway.* BEGGARS *and* PETITIONERS *pour from the gateway, holding up thin* CHILDREN, *crutches, and petitions. They are followed by* IRONSHIRTS, *and then, expensively dressed, the* GOVERNOR'*s* FAMILY.]

BEGGARS AND PETITIONERS.

—Mercy! Mercy, Your Grace! The taxes are too high.

—I lost my leg in the Persian War, where can I get . . .

—My brother is innocent, Your Grace, a misunderstanding . . .

—The child is starving in my arms!

—Our petition is for our son's discharge from the army, our last remaining son!

—Please, Your Grace, the water inspector takes bribes.

[*One servant collects the petitions. Another distributes coins from a purse. Soldiers push the crowd back, lashing at them with thick leather whips.*]

SOLDIER. Get back! Clear the church door!

[*Behind the* GOVERNOR, *his* WIFE, *and the* ADJUTANT, *the* GOVERNOR'*s* CHILD *is brought through the gateway in an ornate carriage.*]

CROWD.

—The baby!

—I can't see it, don't shove so hard!

—God bless the child, Your Grace!

SINGER (*while the crowd is driven back with whips*).

For the first time on that Easter Sunday, the people saw the Governor's heir.

Two doctors never moved from the noble child, apple of the Governor's eye.

Even the mighty Prince Kazbeki bows before him at the church door.

[*The* FAT PRINCE *steps forwards and greets the* FAMILY.]

FAT PRINCE. Happy Easter, Natella Abashwili! What a day! When it was raining last night, I thought to myself, gloomy holidays! But this morning the sky was gay. I love a gay sky, a simple heart, Natella Abashwili. And little Michael is a governor from head to foot! Tititi! (*He tickles the* CHILD.)

GOVERNOR'S WIFE. What do you think, Arsen, at last Georgi has decided to start building the east wing. All those wretched slums are to be torn down to make room for the garden.

FAT PRINCE. Good news after so much bad! What's the latest on the war, Brother Georgi? (*The* GOVERNOR *indicates a lack of interest.*) Strategical retreat, I hear. Well, minor reverses are to be expected. Sometimes things go well, sometimes not. Such is war. Doesn't mean a thing, does it?

GOVERNOR'S WIFE. He's coughing. Georgi, did you hear? (*She speaks sharply to the* DOCTORS, *two dignified men standing close to the little carriage.*) He's coughing!

FIRST DOCTOR (*to the* SECOND). May I remind you, Niko Mikadze, that I was against the lukewarm bath? (*To the* GOVERNOR'S WIFE.) There's been a little error over warming the bath water, Your Grace.

SECOND DOCTOR (*equally polite*). Mika Loladze, I'm afraid I can't agree with you. The temperature of the bath water was exactly what our great, beloved Mishiko Oboladze prescribed. More likely a slight draft during the night, Your Grace.

GOVERNOR'S WIFE. But do pay more attention to him. He looks feverish, Georgi.

FIRST DOCTOR (*bending over the* CHILD). No cause for alarm, Your Grace. The bath water will be warmer. It won't occur again.

SECOND DOCTOR (*with a venomous glance at the* FIRST). I won't forget that, my dear Mika Loladze. No cause for concern, Your Grace.

FAT PRINCE. Well, well, well! I always say: "A pain in my liver? Then the doctor gets fifty strokes on the soles of his feet." We live in a decadent age. In the old days one said: "Off with his head!"

GOVERNOR'S WIFE. Let's go into church. Very likely it's the draft here.

[*The procession of* FAMILY *and* SERVANTS *turns into the doorway. The* FAT PRINCE *follows, but the* GOVERNOR *is kept back by the* ADJUTANT, *a handsome young man. When the crowd of* PETITIONERS *has been driven off, a young dust-stained* RIDER, *his arm in a sling, remains behind.*]

ADJUTANT (*pointing at the* RIDER, *who steps forward*). Won't you hear the messenger from the capital, Your Excellency? He arrived this morning. With confidential papers.

GOVERNOR. Not before Service, Shalva. But did you hear Brother Kazbeki wish me a happy Easter? Which is all very well, but I don't believe it did rain last night.

ADJUTANT (*nodding*). We must investigate.

GOVERNOR. Yes, at once. Tomorrow.

[*They pass through the doorway. The* RIDER, *who has waited in vain for an audience, turns sharply round and, muttering a curse, goes off. Only one of the palace guards*—SIMON SHASHAVA—*remains at the door.*]

SINGER.

The city is still.
Pigeons strut in the church square.
A soldier of the Palace Guard
Is joking with a kitchen maid
As she comes up from the river with a bundle.

[*A girl*—GRUSHA VASHNADZE—*comes through the gateway with a bundle made of large green leaves under her arm.*]

SIMON. What, the young lady is not in church? Shirking?

GRUSHA. I was dressed to go. But they needed another goose for the banquet. And they asked me to get it. I know about geese.

SIMON. A goose? (*He feigns suspicion.*) I'd like to see that goose. (GRUSHA *does not understand.*) One must be on one's guard with women. "I only went for a fish," they tell you, but it turns out to be something else.

GRUSHA (*walking resolutely toward him and showing him the goose*). There! If it isn't a fifteen-pound goose stuffed full of corn, I'll eat the feathers.

SIMON. A queen of a goose! The Governor himself will eat it. So the young lady has been down to the river again?

GRUSHA. Yes, at the poultry farm.

SIMON. Really? At the poultry farm, down by the river . . . not higher up maybe? Near those willows?

GRUSHA. I only go to the willows to wash the linen.

SIMON (*insinuatingly*). Exactly.

GRUSHA. Exactly what?

SIMON (*winking*). Exactly that.

GRUSHA. Why shouldn't I wash the linen by the willows?

SIMON (*with exaggerated laughter*). "Why shouldn't I wash the linen by the willows!" That's good, really good!

GRUSHA. I don't understand the soldier. What's so good about it?

SIMON (*slyly*). "If something I know someone learns, she'll grow hot and cold by turns!"

GRUSHA. I don't know what I could learn about those willows.

SIMON. Not even if there was a bush opposite? That one could see everything from? Everything that goes on there when a certain person is—"washing linen"?

GRUSHA. What does go on? Won't the soldier say what he means and have done?

SIMON. Something goes on. Something can be seen.

GRUSHA. Could the soldier mean I dip my toes in the water when it's hot? There's nothing else.

SIMON. There's more. Your toes. And more.

GRUSHA. More what? At most my foot?

SIMON. Your foot. And a little more. (*He laughs heartily.*)

GRUSHA (*angrily*). Simon Shashava, you ought to be ashamed of yourself! To sit in a bush on a hot day and wait till a girl comes and dips her legs in the river! And I bet you bring a friend along too! (*She runs off.*)

SIMON (*shouting after her*). I didn't bring any friend along!

[*As the* SINGER *resumes his tale, the* SOLDIER *steps into the doorway as though to listen to the service.*]

SINGER.

The city lies still
But why are there armed men?
The Governor's palace is at peace
But why is it a fortress?
And the Governor returned to his palace
And the fortress was a trap
And the goose was plucked and roasted
But the goose was not eaten this time
And noon was no longer the hour to eat:
Noon was the hour to die.

[*From the doorway at the left the* FAT PRINCE *quickly appears, stands still, looks around. Before the gateway at the right two* IRONSHIRTS *are squatting and playing dice. The* FAT PRINCE *sees them, walks slowly past, making a sign to them. They rise: one goes through the gateway, the other goes off at the right. Muffled voices are heard from various directions in the rear:* "To your posts!" *The palace is surrounded. The* FAT PRINCE *quickly goes off. Church bells in the distance. Enter, through the doorway, the Governor's family and procession, returning from church.*]

GOVERNOR'S WIFE (*passing the* ADJUTANT). It's impossible to live in such a slum. But Georgi, of course, will only build for his little Michael. Never for me! Michael is all! All for Michael!

[*The procession turns into the gateway. Again the* ADJUTANT *lingers behind. He waits. Enter the wounded* RIDER *from the doorway. Two* IRONSHIRTS *of the Palace Guard have taken up positions by the gateway.*]

ADJUTANT (*to the* RIDER). The Governor does not wish to receive military news before dinner—especially if it's depressing, as I assume. In the afternoon His Excellency will confer with prominent architects. They're coming to dinner too. And here they are! (*Enter three gentlemen through the doorway.*) Go to the kitchen and eat, my friend. (*As the* RIDER *goes, the* ADJUTANT *greets the* ARCHITECTS.) Gentlemen, His Excellency expects you at dinner. He will devote all his time to you and your great new plans. Come!

ONE OF THE ARCHITECTS. We marvel that His Excellency intends to build. There are disquieting rumors that the war in Persia has taken a turn for the worse.

ADJUTANT. All the more reason to build! There's nothing to those rumors anyway. Persia is a long way off, and the garrison here would let itself be hacked to bits for its Governor. (*Noise from the palace. The shrill scream of a woman. Someone is shouting orders. Dumbfounded, the* ADJUTANT *moves toward the gateway. An* IRONSHIRT *steps out, points his lance at him.*) What's this? Put down that lance, you dog.

ONE OF THE ARCHITECTS. It's the Princes! Don't you know the Princes met last night in the capital? And they're against the Grand Duke and his Governors? Gentlemen, we'd better make ourselves scarce. (*They rush off. The* ADJUTANT *remains helplessly behind.*)

ADJUTANT (*furiously to the Palace Guard*). Down with those lances! Don't you see the Governor's life is threatened?

[*The* IRONSHIRTS *of the Palace Guard refuse to obey. They stare coldly and indifferently at the* ADJUTANT *and follow the next events without interest.*]

SINGER.

O blindness of the great!
They go their way like gods,
Great over bent backs,
Sure of hired fists,
Trusting in the power
Which has lasted so long.
But long is not forever.
O change from age to age!
Thou hope of the people!

[*Enter the* GOVERNOR, *through the gateway, between two* SOLDIERS *armed to the teeth. He is in chains. His face is gray.*]

Up, great sir, deign to walk upright!
From your palace the eyes of many foes follow you!
And now you don't need an architect, a carpenter will do.
You won't be moving into a new palace
But into a little hole in the ground.
Look about you once more, blind man!

[*The arrested man looks round.*]

Does all you had please you?
Between the Easter Mass and the Easter meal
You are walking to a place whence no one returns.

[*The* GOVERNOR *is led off. A horn sounds an alarm. Noise behind the gateway.*]

When the house of a great one collapses
Many little ones are slain.
Those who had no share in the *good* fortunes of the mighty
Often have a share in their *mis*fortunes.
The plunging wagon
Drags the sweating oxen down with it
Into the abyss.

[*The* SERVANTS *come rushing through the gateway in panic.*]

SERVANTS (*among themselves*).

—The baskets!

—Take them all into the third courtyard! Food for five days!

—The mistress has fainted! Someone must carry her down.

—She must get away.

—What about us? We'll be slaughtered like chickens, as always.

—Goodness, what'll happen? There's bloodshed already in the city, they say.

—Nonsense, the Governor has just been asked to appear at a Princes' meeting. All very correct. Everything'll be ironed out. I heard this on the best authority . . .

[*The two* DOCTORS *rush into the courtyard.*]

FIRST DOCTOR (*trying to restrain the other*). Niko Mikadze, it is your duty as a doctor to attend Natella Abashwili.

SECOND DOCTOR. My duty! It's yours!

FIRST DOCTOR. Whose turn is it to look after the child today, Niko Mikadze, yours or mine?

SECOND DOCTOR. Do you really think, Mika Loladze, I'm going to stay a minute longer in this accursed house on that little brat's account? (*They start fighting. All one hears is:* "You neglect your duty!" *and* "Duty, my foot!" *Then the* SECOND DOCTOR *knocks the* FIRST *down.*) Go to hell! (*Exit.*)

[*Enter the soldier,* SIMON SHASHAVA. *He searches in the crowd for* GRUSHA.]

SIMON. Grusha! There you are at last! What are you going to do?

GRUSHA. Nothing. If worst comes to worst, I've a brother in the mountains. How about you?

SIMON. Forget about me. (*Formally again.*) Grusha Vashnadze, your wish to know my plans fills me with satisfaction. I've been ordered to accompany Madam Abashwili as her guard.

GRUSHA. But hasn't the Palace Guard mutinied?

SIMON (*seriously*). That's a fact.

GRUSHA. Isn't it dangerous to go with her?

SIMON. In Tiflis, they say: Isn't the stabbing dangerous for the knife?

GRUSHA. You're not a knife, you're a man, Simon Shashava, what has that woman to do with you?

SIMON. That woman has nothing to do with me. I have my orders, and I go.

GRUSHA. The soldier is pigheaded: he is running into danger for nothing —nothing at all. I must get into the third courtyard, I'm in a hurry.

SIMON. Since we're both in a hurry we shouldn't quarrel. You need time for a good quarrel. May I ask if the young lady still has parents?

GRUSHA. No, just a brother.

SIMON. As time is short—my second question is this: Is the young lady as healthy as a fish in water?

GRUSHA. I may have a pain in the right shoulder once in a while. Otherwise I'm strong enough for my job. No one has complained. So far.

SIMON. That's well known. When it's Easter Sunday, and the question arises who'll run for the goose all the same, she'll be the one. My third question is this: Is the young lady impatient? Does she want apples in winter?

GRUSHA. Impatient? No. But if a man goes to war without any reason and then no message comes—that's bad.

SIMON. A message will come. And now my final question . . .

GRUSHA. Simon Shashava, I must get to the third courtyard at once. My answer is yes.

SIMON (*very embarrassed*). Haste, they say, is the wind that blows down the scaffolding. But they also say: The rich don't know what haste is. I'm from . . .

GRUSHA. Kutsk . . .

SIMON. The young lady has been inquiring about me? I'm healthy, I have no dependents, I make ten piasters a month, as paymaster twenty piasters, and I'm asking—very sincerely—for your hand.

GRUSHA. Simon Shashava, it suits me well.

SIMON (*taking from his neck a thin chain with a little cross on it*). My mother gave me this cross, Grusha Vashnadze. The chain is silver. Please wear it.

GRUSHA. Many thanks, Simon.

SIMON (*hangs it round her neck*). It would be better to go to the third courtyard now. Or there'll be difficulties. Anyway, I must harness the horses. The young lady will understand?

GRUSHA. Yes, Simon.

[*They stand undecided.*]

SIMON. I'll just take the mistress to the troops that have stayed loyal. When the war's over, I'll be back. In two weeks. Or three. I hope my intended won't get tired, awaiting my return.

GRUSHA.

Simon Shashava, I shall wait for you.
Go calmly into battle, soldier
The bloody battle, the bitter battle
From which not everyone returns:
When you return I shall be there.
I shall be waiting for you under the green elm
I shall be waiting for you under the bare elm
I shall wait until the last soldier has returned
And longer
When you come back from the battle
No boots will stand at my door
The pillow beside mine will be empty
And my mouth will be unkissed.
When you return, when you return
You will be able to say: It is just as it was.

SIMON. I thank you, Grusha Vashnadze. And good-bye!

[*He bows low before her. She does the same before him. Then she runs quickly off without looking round. Enter the* ADJUTANT *from the gateway.*]

ADJUTANT (*harshly*). Harness the horses to the carriage! Don't stand there doing nothing, scum!

[SIMON SHASHAVA *stands to attention and goes off. Two* SERVANTS *crowd from the gateway, bent low under huge trunks. Behind them, supported by her women, stumbles* NATELLA ABASHWILI. *She is followed by a* WOMAN *carrying the* CHILD.]

GOVERNOR'S WIFE. I hardly know if my head's still on. Where's Michael? Don't hold him so clumsily. Pile the trunks onto the carriage. No news from the city, Shalva?

ADJUTANT. None. All's quiet so far, but there's not a minute to lose. No room for all those trunks in the carriage. Pick out what you need. (*Exit quickly.*)

GOVERNOR'S WIFE. Only essentials! Quick, open the trunks! I'll tell you what I need. (*The trunks are lowered and opened. She points at some brocade dresses.*) The green one! And, of course, the one with the fur trimming. Where are Niko Mikadze and Mika Loladze? I've suddenly got the most terrible migraine again. It always starts in the temples. (*Enter* GRUSHA.) Taking your time, eh? Go and get the hot water bottles this minute! (GRUSHA *runs off, returns later with hot water bottles; the* GOVERNOR'S WIFE *orders her about by signs.*) Don't tear the sleeves.

A YOUNG WOMAN. Pardon, madam, no harm has come to the dress.

GOVERNOR'S WIFE. Because I stopped you. I've been watching you for a long time. Nothing in your head but making eyes at Shalva Tzereteli. I'll kill you, you bitch! (*She beats the* YOUNG WOMAN.)

ADJUTANT (*appearing in the gateway*). Please make haste, Natella Abashwili. Firing has broken out in the city. (*Exit.*)

GOVERNOR'S WIFE (*letting go of the* YOUNG WOMAN). Oh dear, do you think they'll lay hands on us? Why should they? Why? (*She herself begins to rummage in the trunks.*) How's Michael? Asleep?

WOMAN WITH THE CHILD. Yes, madam.

GOVERNOR'S WIFE. Then put him down a moment and get my little saffron-colored boots from the bedroom. I need them for the green dress. (*The* WOMAN *puts down the* CHILD *and goes off.*) Just look how these things have been packed! No love! No understanding! If you don't give them every order yourself . . . At such moments you realize what kind of servants you have! They gorge themselves at your expense, and never a word of gratitude! I'll remember this.

ADJUTANT (*entering, very excited*). Natella, you must leave at once!

GOVERNOR'S WIFE. Why? I've got to take this silver dress—it cost a thousand piasters. And that one there, and where's the wine-colored one?

ADJUTANT (*trying to pull her away*). Riots have broken out! We must leave at once. Where's the baby?

GOVERNOR'S WIFE (*calling to the* YOUNG WOMAN *who was holding the baby*). Maro, get the baby ready! Where on earth are you?

ADJUTANT (*leaving*). We'll probably have to leave the carriage behind and go ahead on horseback.

[*The* GOVERNOR'*s* WIFE *rummages again among her dresses, throws some onto the heap of chosen clothes, then takes them off again. Noises, drums are heard. The* YOUNG WOMAN *who was beaten creeps away. The sky begins to grow red.*]

GOVERNOR'S WIFE (*rummaging desperately*). I simply cannot find the wine-colored dress. Take the whole pile to the carriage. Where's Asja? And why hasn't Maro come back? Have you all gone crazy?

ADJUTANT (*returning*). Quick! Quick!

GOVERNOR'S WIFE (*to the* FIRST WOMAN). Run! Just throw them into the carriage!

ADJUTANT. We're not taking the carriage. And if you don't come now, I'll ride off on my own.

GOVERNOR'S WIFE (*as the* FIRST WOMAN *can't carry everything*). Where's that bitch Asja? (*The* ADJUTANT *pulls her away.*) Maro, bring the baby! (*To the* FIRST WOMAN.) Go and look for Masha. No, first take the dresses to the carriage. Such nonsense! I wouldn't dream of going on horseback!

[*Turning round, she sees the red sky, and starts back rigid. The fire burns. She is pulled out by the* ADJUTANT. *Shaking, the* FIRST WOMAN *follows with the dresses.*]

MARO (*from the doorway with the boots*). Madam! (*She sees the trunks and dresses and runs toward the* CHILD, *picks it up, and holds it a moment.*) They left it behind, the beasts. (*She hands it to* GRUSHA.) Hold it a moment. (*She runs off, following the* GOVERNOR'S WIFE.)

[*Enter* SERVANTS *from the gateway.*]

COOK. Well, so they've actually gone. Without the food wagons, and not a minute too early. It's time for us to clear out.

GROOM. This'll be an unhealthy neighborhood for quite a while. (*To one of the* WOMEN.) Suliko, take a few blankets and wait for me in the foal stables.

GRUSHA. What have they done with the Governor?

GROOM (*gesturing throat cutting*). Ffffft.

A FAT WOMAN (*seeing the gesture and becoming hysterical*). Oh dear, oh dear, oh dear, oh dear! Our master Georgi Abashwili! A picture of health he was, at the morning Mass—and now! Oh, take me away, we're all lost, we must die in sin like our master, Georgi Abashwili!

OTHER WOMAN (*soothing her*). Calm down, Nina! You'll be taken to safety. You've never hurt a fly.

FAT WOMAN (*being led out*). Oh dear, oh dear, oh dear! Quick! Let's all get out before they come, before they come!

A YOUNG WOMAN. Nina takes it more to heart than the mistress, that's a fact. They even have to have their weeping done for them.

COOK. We'd better get out, all of us.

ANOTHER WOMAN (*glancing back*). That must be the East Gate burning.

YOUNG WOMAN (*seeing the* CHILD *in* GRUSHA'*s arms*). The baby! What are you doing with it?

GRUSHA. It got left behind.

YOUNG WOMAN. She simply left it there. Michael, who was kept out of all the drafts!

[*The* SERVANTS *gather round the* CHILD.]

GRUSHA. He's waking up.

GROOM. Better put him down, I tell you. I'd rather not think what'd happen to anybody who was found with that baby.

COOK. That's right. Once they get started, they'll kill each other off, whole families at a time. Let's go.

[*Exeunt all but* GRUSHA, *with the* CHILD *on her arm, and* TWO WOMEN.]

TWO WOMEN. Didn't you hear? Better put him down.

GRUSHA. The nurse asked me to hold him a moment.

OLDER WOMAN. She's not coming back, you simpleton.

YOUNGER WOMAN. Keep your hands off it.

OLDER WOMAN (*amiably*). Grusha, you're a good soul, but you're not very bright, and you know it. I tell you, if he had the plague he couldn't be more dangerous.

GRUSHA (*stubbornly*). He hasn't got the plague. He looks at me! He's human!

OLDER WOMAN. Don't look at *him.* You're a fool—the kind that always gets put upon. A person need only say, "Run for the salad, you have the longest legs," and you run. My husband has an ox cart—you can come with us if you hurry! Lord, by now the whole neighborhood must be in flames.

[*Both women leave, sighing. After some hesitation,* GRUSHA *puts the sleeping* CHILD *down, looks at it for a moment, then takes a brocade blanket from the heap of clothes and covers it. Then both women return, dragging bundles.* GRUSHA *starts guiltily away from the* CHILD *and walks a few steps to one side.*]

YOUNGER WOMAN. Haven't you packed anything yet? There isn't much time, you know. The Ironshirts will be here from the barracks.

GRUSHA. Coming!

[*She runs through the doorway. Both women go to the gateway and wait. The sound of horses is heard. They flee, screaming. Enter the* FAT PRINCE *with drunken* IRONSHIRTS. *One of them carries the* GOVERNOR*'s head on a lance.*]

FAT PRINCE. Here! In the middle! (*One soldier climbs onto the other's back, takes the head, holds it tentatively over the door.*) That's not the middle. Farther to the right. That's it. What I do, my friends, I do well. (*While with hammer and nail, the soldier fastens the head to the wall by its hair.*) This morning at the church door I said to Georgi Abashwili: "I love a gay sky." Actually, I prefer the lightning that comes out of a gay sky. Yes, indeed. It's a pity they took the brat along, though, I need him, urgently.

[*Exit with* IRONSHIRTS *through the gateway. Trampling of horses again. Enter* GRUSHA *through the doorway looking cautiously about her. Clearly she has waited for the* IRONSHIRTS *to go. Carrying a bundle, she walks toward the gateway. At the last moment, she turns to see if the* CHILD *is still there. Catching sight of the head over the doorway, she screams. Horrified, she picks up her bundle again, and is about to leave when the* SINGER *starts to speak. She stands rooted to the spot.*]

SINGER.

As she was standing between courtyard and gate,
She heard or she thought she heard a low voice calling.
The child called to her,
Not whining, but calling quite sensibly,
Or so it seemed to her.
"Woman," it said, "help me."
And it went on, not whining, but saying quite sensibly:
"Know, woman, he who hears not a cry for help
But passes by with troubled ears will never hear
The gentle call of a lover nor the blackbird at dawn

Nor the happy sigh of the tired grape-picker as the Angelus rings."

[*She walks a few steps toward the* CHILD *and bends over it.*]

Hearing this she went back for one more look at the child:
Only to sit with him for a moment or two,
Only till someone should come,
His mother, or anyone.

[*Leaning on a trunk, she sits facing the* CHILD.]

Only till she would have to leave, for the danger was too great,
The city was full of flame and crying.

[*The light grows dimmer, as though evening and night were coming on.*]

Fearful is the seductive power of goodness!

[GRUSHA *now settles down to watch over the* CHILD *through the night. Once, she lights a small lamp to look at it. Once, she tucks it in with a coat. From time to time she listens and looks to see whether someone is coming.*]

And she sat with the child a long time,
Till evening came, till night came, till dawn came.
She sat too long, too long she saw
The soft breathing, the small clenched fists,
Till toward morning the seduction was complete
And she rose, and bent down and, sighing, took the child
And carried it away.

[*She does what the* SINGER *says as he describes it.*]

As if it was stolen goods she picked it up.
As if she was a thief she crept away.

ACT II

The Flight into the Northern Mountains

SINGER.

When Grusha Vashnadze left the city
On the Grusinian highway
On the way to the Northern Mountains
She sang a song, she bought some milk.

CHORUS.

How will this human child escape
The bloodhounds, the trap-setters?
Into the deserted mountains she journeyed

Along the Grusinian highway she journeyed
She sang a song, she bought some milk.

[GRUSHA VASHNADZE *walks on. On her back she carries the* CHILD *in a sack, in one hand is a large stick, in the other a bundle. She sings.*]

The Song of the Four Generals

Four generals
Set out for Iran.
With the first one, war did not agree.
The second never won a victory.
For the third the weather never was right.
For the fourth the men would never fight.
Four generals
And not a single man!
Sosso Robakidse
Went marching to Iran
With him the war did so agree
He soon had won a victory.
For him the weather was always right.
For him the men would always fight.
Sosso Robakidse,
He is our man!

[*A peasant's cottage appears.*]

GRUSHA (*to the* CHILD). Noontime is meal time. Now we'll sit hopefully in the grass, while the good Grusha goes and buys a little pitcher of milk. (*She lays the* CHILD *down and knocks at the cottage door. An* OLD MAN *opens it.*) Grandfather, could I have a little pitcher of milk? And a corn cake, maybe?

OLD MAN. Milk? We have no milk. The soldiers from the city have our goats. Go to the soldiers if you want milk.

GRUSHA. But grandfather, you must have a little pitcher of milk for a baby?

OLD MAN. And for a God-bless-you, eh?

GRUSHA. Who said anything about a God-bless-you? (*She shows her purse.*) We'll pay like princes. "Head in the clouds, backside in the water." (*The peasant goes off, grumbling, for milk.*) How much for the milk?

OLD MAN. Three piasters. Milk has gone up.

GRUSHA. Three piasters for this little drop? (*Without a word the* OLD MAN *shuts the door in her face.*) Michael, did you hear that? Three piasters! We can't afford it! (*She goes back, sits down again, and gives the* CHILD *her breast.*) Suck. Think of the three piasters. There's nothing there, but you *think* you're drinking, and that's something. (*Shaking her head, she sees that the* CHILD *isn't sucking any more. She gets up, walks back to the door, and knocks again.*) Open, grandfather, we'll pay. (*Softly.*) May lightning strike you! (*When the* OLD MAN *appears.*) I thought it would be half a piaster. But the baby must be fed. How about one piaster for that little drop?

OLD MAN. Two.

GRUSHA. Don't shut the door again. (*She fishes a long time in her bag.*) Here are two piasters. The milk better be good. I still have two days' journey ahead of me. It's a murderous business you have here—and sinful, too!

OLD MAN. Kill the soldiers if you want milk.

GRUSHA (*giving the* CHILD *some milk*). This is an expensive joke. Take a sip, Michael, it's a week's pay. Around here they think we earned our money just sitting on our behinds. Oh, Michael, Michael, you're a nice little load for a girl to take on! (*Uneasy, she gets up, puts the* CHILD *on her back, and walks on. The* OLD MAN, *grumbling, picks up the pitcher and looks after her unmoved.*)

SINGER.

As Grusha Vashnadze went northward
The Princes' Ironshirts went after her.

CHORUS.

How will the barefoot girl escape the Ironshirts,
The bloodhounds, the trap-setters?
They hunt even by night.
Pursuers never tire.
Butchers sleep little.

[*Two* IRONSHIRTS *are trudging along the highway.*]

CORPORAL. You'll never amount to anything, blockhead, your heart's not in it. Your senior officer sees this in little things. Yesterday, when I made the fat gal, yes, you grabbed her husband as I commanded, and you did kick him in the belly, at my request, but did you *enjoy* it, like a loyal Private, or were you just doing your duty? I've kept an eye on you blockhead, you're a hollow reed and a tinkling cymbal, you won't get promoted. (*They walk a while in silence.*) Don't think I've forgotten how insubordinate you are, either. Stop limping! I forbid you to limp! You limp because I sold the horses, and I sold the horses because I'd never have got that price again. You limp to show me you don't like marching. I know you. It won't help. You wait. Sing!

TWO IRONSHIRTS (*singing*).

Sadly to war I went my way
Leaving my loved one at her door.
My friends will keep her honor safe
Till from the war I'm back once more.

CORPORAL. Louder!

TWO IRONSHIRTS (*singing*).

When 'neath a headstone I shall be
My love a little earth will bring:
"Here rest the feet that oft would run to me
And here the arms that oft to me would cling."

[*They begin to walk again in silence.*]

CORPORAL. A good soldier has his heart and soul in it. When he receives an order, he gets a hard-on, and when he drives his lance into the enemy's guts, he comes. (*He shouts for joy.*) He lets himself be torn to bits for his superior officer, and as he lies dying he takes note that his corporal is nodding approval, and that is reward enough, it's his dearest wish. *You* won't get any nod of approval, but you'll croak all right. Christ, how'm I to get my hands on the Governor's bastard with the help of a fool like you! (*They stay on stage behind.*)

SINGER.

When Grusha Vashnadze came to the River Sirra
Flight grew too much for her, the helpless child too heavy.
In the cornfields the rosy dawn
Is cold to the sleepless one, only cold.
The gay clatter of the milk cans in the farmyard where the smoke rises
Is only a threat to the fugitive.
She who carries the child feels its weight and little more.

[GRUSHA *stops in front of a farm. A fat* PEASANT WOMAN *is carrying a milk can through the door.* GRUSHA *waits until she has gone in, then approaches the house cautiously.*]

GRUSHA (*to the* CHILD). Now you've wet yourself again, and you know I've no linen. Michael, this is where we part company. It's far enough from the city. They wouldn't want you *so* much that they'd follow you all *this* way, little good-for-nothing. The peasant woman is kind, and can't you just smell the milk? (*She bends down to lay the* CHILD *on the threshold.*) So farewell, Michael, I'll forget how you kicked me in the back all night to make me walk faster. And you can forget the meager fare—it was meant well. I'd like to have kept you—your nose is so tiny—but it can't be. I'd have shown you your first rabbit, I'd have trained you to keep dry, but now I must turn around. My sweetheart the soldier might be back soon, and suppose he didn't find me? You can't ask that, can you? (*She creeps up to the door and lays the* CHILD *on the threshold. Then, hiding behind a tree, she waits until the* PEASANT WOMAN *opens the door and sees the bundle.*)

PEASANT WOMAN. Good heavens, what's this? Husband!

PEASANT. What is it? Let me finish my soup.

PEASANT WOMAN (*to the* CHILD). Where's your mother then? Haven't you got one? It's a boy. Fine linen. He's from a good family, you can see that. And they just leave him on our doorstep. Oh, these are times!

PEASANT. If they think we're going to feed it, they're wrong. You can take it to the priest in the village. That's the best we can do.

PEASANT WOMAN. What'll the priest do with him? He needs a mother. There, he's waking up. Don't you think we could keep him, though?

PEASANT (*shouting*). No!

PEASANT WOMAN. I could lay him in the corner by the armchair. All I need is a crib. I can take him into the fields with me. See him laughing? Husband, we have a roof over our heads. We can do it. Not another word out of you!

[*She carries the* CHILD *into the house. The* PEASANT *follows protesting.* GRUSHA *steps out from behind the tree, laughs, and hurries off in the opposite direction.*]

SINGER.

Why so cheerful, making for home?

CHORUS.

Because the child has won new parents with a laugh,
Because I'm rid of the little one, I'm cheerful.

SINGER.

And why so sad?

CHORUS.

Because I'm single and free, I'm sad
Like someone who's been robbed
Someone who's newly poor.

[*She walks for a short while, then meets the two* IRONSHIRTS *who point their lances at her.*]

CORPORAL. Lady, you are running straight into the arms of the Armed Forces. Where are you coming from? And when? Are you having illicit relations with the enemy? Where is he hiding? What movements is he making in your rear? How about the hills? How about the valleys? How are your stockings held in position? (GRUSHA *stands there frightened.*) Don't be scared, we always withdraw, if necessary . . . what, blockhead? I always withdraw. In that respect at least, I can be relied on. Why are you staring like that at my lance? In the field no soldier drops his lance, that's a rule. Learn it by heart, blockhead. Now, lady, where are you headed?

GRUSHA. To meet my intended, one Simon Shashava, of the Palace Guard in Nuka.

CORPORAL. Simon Shashava? Sure, I know him. He gave me the key so I could look you up once in a while. Blockhead, we are getting to be unpopular. We must make her realize we have honorable intentions. Lady, behind apparent frivolity I conceal a serious nature, so let me tell you officially: I want a child from you. (GRUSHA *utters a little scream.*) Blockhead, she understands me. Uh-huh, isn't it a sweet shock? "Then first I must take the noodles out of the oven, Officer. Then first I must change my torn shirt, Colonel." But away with jokes, away with my lance! We are looking for a baby. A baby from a good family. Have you heard of such a baby, from the city, dressed in fine linen, and suddenly turning up here?

GRUSHA. No, I haven't heard a thing. (*Suddenly she turns round and runs back, panic-stricken. The* IRONSHIRTS *glance at each other, then follow her, cursing.*)

SINGER.

Run, kind girl! The killers are coming!
Help the helpless babe, helpless girl!
And so she runs!

CHORUS.

In the bloodiest times
There are kind people.

[*As* GRUSHA *rushes into the cottage, the* PEASANT WOMAN *is bending over the* CHILD*'s crib.*]

GRUSHA. Hide him. Quick! The Ironshirts are coming! I laid him on your doorstep. But he isn't mine. He's from a good family.

PEASANT WOMAN. Who's coming? What Ironshirts?

GRUSHA. Don't ask questions. The Ironshirts that are looking for it.

PEASANT WOMAN. They've no business in my house. But I must have a little talk with you, it seems.

GRUSHA. Take off the fine linen. It'll give us away.

PEASANT WOMAN. Linen, my foot! In this house I make the decisions! "*You* can't vomit in *my* room!" Why did you abandon it? It's a sin.

GRUSHA (*looking out the window*). Look, they're coming out from behind those trees! I shouldn't have run away, it made them angry. Oh, what shall I do?

PEASANT WOMAN (*looking out the window and suddenly starting with fear*). Gracious! Ironshirts!

GRUSHA. They're after the baby.

PEASANT WOMAN. Suppose they come in!

GRUSHA. You mustn't give him to them. Say he's yours.

PEASANT WOMAN. Yes.

GRUSHA. They'll run him through if you hand him over.

PEASANT WOMAN. But suppose they ask for it? The silver for the harvest is in the house.

GRUSHA. If you let them have him, they'll run him through, right here in this room! You've got to say he's yours!

PEASANT WOMAN. Yes. But what if they don't believe me?

GRUSHA. You must be firm.

PEASANT WOMAN. They'll burn the roof over our heads.

GRUSHA. That's why you must say he's yours. His name's Michael. But I shouldn't have told you. (*The* PEASANT WOMAN *nods.*) Don't nod like that. And don't tremble—they'll notice.

PEASANT WOMAN. Yes.

GRUSHA. And stop saying yes, I can't stand it. (*She shakes the* WOMAN.) Don't you have any children?

PEASANT WOMAN (*muttering*). He's in the war.

GRUSHA. Then maybe *he's* an Ironshirt? Do you want *him* to run children through with a lance? You'd bawl him out. "No fooling with lances in my house!" you'd shout, "is that what I've reared you for? Wash your neck before you speak to your mother!"

PEASANT WOMAN. That's true, he couldn't get away with anything around here!

GRUSHA. So you'll say he's yours?

PEASANT WOMAN. Yes.

GRUSHA. Look! They're coming!

[*There is a knocking at the door. The women don't answer. Enter* IRONSHIRTS. *The* PEASANT WOMAN *bows low.*]

CORPORAL. Well, here she is. What did I tell you? What a nose I have! I *smelt* her. Lady, I have a question for you. Why did you run away? What did you think I would do to you? I'll bet it was something unchaste. Confess!

GRUSHA (*while the* PEASANT WOMAN *bows again and again*). I'd left some milk on the stove, and I suddenly remembered it.

CORPORAL. Or maybe you imagined I looked at you unchastely? Like there could be something between us? A carnal glance, know what I mean?

GRUSHA. I didn't see it.

CORPORAL. But it's possible, huh? You admit that much. After all, I might be a pig. I'll be frank with you: I could think of all sorts of things if we were alone. (*To the* PEASANT WOMAN.) Shouldn't you be busy in the yard? Feeding the hens?

PEASANT WOMAN (*falling suddenly to her knees*). Soldier, I didn't know a thing about it. Please don't burn the roof over our heads.

CORPORAL. What are you talking about?

PEASANT WOMAN. I had nothing to do with it. She left it on my doorstep, I swear it!

CORPORAL (*suddenly seeing the* CHILD *and whistling*). Ah, so there's a little something in the crib! Blockhead, I smell a thousand piasters. Take the old girl outside and hold on to her. It looks like I have a little cross-examining to do. (*The* PEASANT WOMAN *lets herself be led out by the* PRIVATE, *without a word.*) So, you've *got* the child I wanted from you! (*He walks toward the crib.*)

GRUSHA. Officer, he's mine. He's not the one you're after.

CORPORAL. I'll just take a look. (*He bends over the crib.*)

[GRUSHA *looks round in despair.*]

GRUSHA. He's mine! He's mine!

CORPORAL. Fine linen!

[GRUSHA *dashes at him to pull him away. He throws her off and again bends over the crib. Again looking round in despair, she sees a log of wood, seizes it, and hits the* CORPORAL *over the head from behind. The* CORPORAL *collapses. She quickly picks up the* CHILD *and rushes off.*]

SINGER.

And in her flight from the Ironshirts
After twenty-two days of journeying
At the foot of the Janga-Tau Glacier
Grusha Vashnadze decided to adopt the child.

CHORUS.

The helpless girl adopted the helpless child.

[GRUSHA *squats over a half-frozen stream to get the* CHILD *water in the hollow of her hand.*]

GRUSHA.

Since no one else will take you, son,
I must take you.
Since no one else will take you, son,
You must take me.
O black day in a lean, lean year,
The trip was long, the milk was dear,
My legs are tired, my feet are sore:
But I wouldn't be without you any more.
I'll throw your silken shirt away
And wrap you in rags and tatters.
I'll wash you, son, and christen you in glacier water.
We'll see it through together.

[*She has taken off the child's fine linen and wrapped it in a rag.*]

SINGER.

When Grusha Vashnadze
Pursued by the Ironshirts
Came to the bridge on the glacier
Leading to the villages of the Eastern Slope
She sang the Song of the Rotten Bridge
And risked two lives.

[*A wind has risen. The bridge on the glacier is visible in the dark. One rope is broken and half the bridge is hanging down the abyss.* MERCHANTS, *two men and a woman, stand undecided before the bridge as* GRUSHA *and the* CHILD *arrive. One man is trying to catch the hanging rope with a stick.*]

FIRST MAN. Take your time, young woman. You won't get across here anyway.

GRUSHA. But I *have* to get the baby to the east side. To my brother's place.

MERCHANT WOMAN. Have to? How d'you mean, "have to"? I have to get there, too—because I have to buy carpets in Atum—carpets a woman had to sell because her husband had to die. But can *I* do what I have to? Can she? Andrei's been fishing for that rope for hours. And I ask you, how are we going to fasten it, even if he gets it up?

FIRST MAN (*listening*). Hush, I think I hear something.

GRUSHA. The bridge isn't quite rotted through. I think I'll try it.

MERCHANT WOMAN. *I* wouldn't—if the devil himself were after me. It's suicide.

FIRST MAN (*shouting*). Hi!

GRUSHA. Don't shout! (*To the* MERCHANT WOMAN.) Tell him not to shout.

FIRST MAN. But there's someone down there calling. Maybe they've lost their way.

MERCHANT WOMAN. Why shouldn't he shout? Is there something funny about you? Are they after you?

GRUSHA. All right, I'll tell. The Ironshirts are after me. I knocked one down.

SECOND MAN. Hide our merchandise!

[*The* WOMAN *hides a sack behind a rock.*]

FIRST MAN. Why didn't you say so right away? (*To the others.*) If they catch her they'll make mincemeat out of her!

GRUSHA. Get out of my way. I've got to cross that bridge.

SECOND MAN. You can't. The precipice is two thousand feet deep.

FIRST MAN. Even with the rope it'd be no use. We could hold it up with our hands. But then we'd have to do the same for the Ironshirts.

GRUSHA. Go away.

[*There are calls from the distance:* "Hi, up there!"]

MERCHANT WOMAN. They're getting near. But you can't take the child on that bridge. It's sure to break. And look!

[GRUSHA *looks down into the abyss. The* IRONSHIRTS *are heard calling again from below.*]

SECOND MAN. Two thousand feet!

GRUSHA. But those men are worse.

FIRST MAN. You can't do it. Think of the baby. Risk your life but not a child's.

SECOND MAN. With the child she's that much heavier!

MERCHANT WOMAN. Maybe she's *really* got to get across. Give *me* the baby. I'll hide it. Cross the bridge alone!

GRUSHA. I won't. We belong together. (*To the* CHILD.) "Live together, die together." (*She sings.*)

The Song of the Rotten Bridge

Deep is the abyss, son,
I see the weak bridge sway
But it's not for us, son,
To choose the way.

The way I know
Is the one you must tread,
And all you will eat
Is my bit of bread.

Of every four pieces
You shall have three.
Would that I knew
How big they will be!

Get out of my way, I'll try it without the rope.

MERCHANT WOMAN. You are tempting God!

[*There are shouts from below.*]

GRUSHA. Please, throw that stick away, or they'll get the rope and follow me. (*Pressing the* CHILD *to her, she steps onto the swaying bridge. The* MERCHANT WOMAN *screams when it looks as though the bridge is about to collapse. But* GRUSHA *walks on and reaches the far side.*)

FIRST MAN. She made it!

MERCHANT WOMAN (*who has fallen on her knees and begun to pray, angrily*). I still think it was a sin.

[*The* IRONSHIRTS *appear; the* CORPORAL*'s head is bandaged.*]

CORPORAL. Seen a woman with a child?

FIRST MAN (*while the* SECOND MAN *throws the stick into the abyss*). Yes, there! But the bridge won't carry you!

CORPORAL. You'll pay for this, blockhead!

[GRUSHA, *from the far bank, laughs and shows the* CHILD *to the* IRONSHIRTS. *She walks on. The wind blows.*]

GRUSHA (*turning to the* CHILD). You mustn't be afraid of the wind. He's a poor thing too. He has to push the clouds along and he gets quite cold doing it. (*Snow starts falling.*) And the snow isn't so bad, either, Michael. It covers the little fir trees so they won't die in winter. Let me sing you a little song. (*She sings.*)

The Song of the Child

Your father is a bandit
A harlot the mother who bore you.
Yet honorable men
Shall kneel down before you.
Food to the baby horses
The tiger's son will take.
The mothers will get milk
From the son of the snake.

ACT III

In the Northern Mountains

SINGER.

Seven days the sister, Grusha Vashnadze,
Journeyed across the glacier
And down the slopes she journeyed.
"When I enter my brother's house," she thought,
"He will rise and embrace me."
"Is that you, sister?" he will say,
"I have long expected you.
This is my dear wife,
And this is my farm, come to me by marriage,
With eleven horses and thirty-one cows. Sit down.
Sit down with your child at our table and eat."
The brother's house was in a lovely valley.
When the sister came to the brother,
She was ill from walking.
The brother rose from the table.

[*A fat peasant couple rise from the table.* LAVRENTI VASHNADZE *still has a napkin round his neck, as* GRUSHA, *pale and supported by a* SERVANT, *enters with the* CHILD.]

LAVRENTI. Where've *you* come from, Grusha?

GRUSHA (*feebly*). Across the Janga-Tu Pass, Lavrenti.

SERVANT. I found her in front of the hay barn. She has a baby with her.

SISTER-IN-LAW. Go and groom the mare.

[*Exit the* SERVANT.]

LAVRENTI. This is my wife Aniko.

SISTER-IN-LAW. I thought you were in service in Nuka.

GRUSHA (*barely able to stand*). Yes, I was.

SISTER-IN-LAW. Wasn't it a good job? We were told it was.

GRUSHA. The Governor got killed.

LAVRENTI. Yes, we heard there were riots. Your aunt told us. Remember, Aniko?

SISTER-IN-LAW. Here with us, it's very quiet. City people always want something going on. (*She walks toward the door, calling.*) Sosso, Sosso, don't take the cake out of the oven yet, d'you hear? Where on earth are you? (*Exit, calling.*)

LAVRENTI (*quietly, quickly*). Is there a father? (*As she shakes her head.*) I thought not. We must think up something. She's religious.

SISTER-IN-LAW (*returning*). Those servants! (*To* GRUSHA.) You have a child.

GRUSHA. It's mine. (*She collapses.* LAVRENTI *rushes to her assistance.*)

SISTER-IN-LAW. Heavens, she's ill—what are we going to do?

LAVRENTI (*escorting her to a bench near the stove*). Sit down, sit. I think it's just weakness, Aniko.

SISTER-IN-LAW. As long as it's not scarlet fever!

LAVRENTI. She'd have spots if it was. It's only weakness. Don't worry, Aniko. (*To* GRUSHA.) Better, sitting down?

SISTER-IN-LAW. Is the child hers?

GRUSHA. Yes, mine.

LAVRENTI. She's on her way to her husband.

SISTER-IN-LAW. I see. Your meat's getting cold. (LAVRENTI *sits down and begins to eat.*) Cold food's not good for you, the fat mustn't get cold, you know your stomach's your weak spot. (*To* GRUSHA.) If your husband's not in the city, where is he?

LAVRENTI. She got married on the other side of the mountain, she says.

SISTER-IN-LAW. On the other side of the mountain. I see. (*She also sits down to eat.*)

GRUSHA. I think I should lie down somewhere, Lavrenti.

SISTER-IN-LAW. If it's consumption we'll all get it. (*She goes on cross-examining her.*) Has your husband got a farm?

GRUSHA. He's a soldier.

LAVRENTI. But he's coming into a farm—a small one—from his father.

SISTER-IN-LAW. Isn't he in the war? Why not?

GRUSHA (*with effort*). Yes, he's in the war.

SISTER-IN-LAW. Then why d'you want to go to the farm?

LAVRENTI. When he comes back from the war, he'll return to his farm.

SISTER-IN-LAW. But you're going there now?

LAVRENTI. Yes, to wait for him.

SISTER-IN-LAW (*calling shrilly*). Sosso, the cake!

GRUSHA (*murmuring feverishly*). A farm—a soldier—waiting—sit down, eat.

SISTER-IN-LAW. It's scarlet fever.

GRUSHA (*starting up*). Yes, he's got a farm!

LAVRENTI. I think it's just weakness, Aniko. Would you look after the cake yourself, dear?

SISTER-IN-LAW. But when will he come back if war's broken out again as people say? (*She waddles off, shouting.*) Sosso! Where on earth are you? Sosso!

LAVRENTI (*getting up quickly and going to* GRUSHA). You'll get a bed in a minute. She has a good heart. But wait till after supper.

GRUSHA (*holding out the* CHILD *to him*). Take him.

LAVRENTI (*taking it and looking around*). But you can't stay here long with the child. She's religious, you see.

[GRUSHA *collapses.* LAVRENTI *catches her.*]

SINGER.

The sister was so ill,
The cowardly brother had to give her shelter.
Summer departed, winter came.
The winter was long, the winter was short.
People mustn't know anything.
Rats mustn't bite.
Spring mustn't come.

[GRUSHA *sits over the weaving loom in a workroom. She and the* CHILD, *who is squatting on the floor, are wrapped in blankets. She sings.*]

The Song of the Center

And the lover started to leave
And his betrothed ran pleading after him
Pleading and weeping, weeping and teaching:
"Dearest mine, dearest mine
When you go to war as now you do
When you fight the foe as soon you will
Don't lead with the front line
And don't push with the rear line
At the front is red fire
In the rear is red smoke
Stay in the war's center
Stay near the standard bearer
The first always die
The last are also hit
Those in the center come home."

Michael, we must be clever. If we make ourselves as small as cockroaches, the sister-in-law will forget we're in the house, and then we can stay till the snow melts.

[*Enter* LAVRENTI. *He sits down beside his sister.*]

LAVRENTI. Why are you sitting there muffled up like coachmen, you two? Is it too cold in the room?

GRUSHA (*hastily removing one shawl*). It's not too cold, Lavrenti.

LAVRENTI. If it's too cold, you shouldn't be sitting here with the child. Aniko would never forgive herself! (*Pause.*) I hope our priest didn't question you about the child?

GRUSHA. He did, but I didn't tell him anything.

LAVRENTI. That's good. I wanted to speak to you about Aniko. She has a good heart but she's very, very sensitive. People need only mention our farm and she's worried. She takes everything hard, you see. One time our milkmaid went to church with a hole in her stocking. Ever since, Aniko has worn two pairs of stockings in church. It's the old family in her. (*He listens.*) Are you sure there are no rats around? If there are rats, you couldn't live here. (*There are sounds as of dripping from the roof.*) What's that, dripping?

GRUSHA. It must be a barrel leaking.

LAVRENTI. Yes, it must be a barrel. You've been here six months, haven't you? Was I talking about Aniko? (*They listen again to the snow melting.*) You can't imagine how worried she gets about your soldier-husband. "Suppose he comes back and can't find her!" she says and lies awake. "He can't come before the spring," I tell her. The dear woman! (*The drops begin to fall faster.*) When d'you think he'll come? What do *you* think? (GRUSHA *is silent.*) Not before the spring, you agree? (GRUSHA *is silent.*) You don't believe he'll come at all? (GRUSHA *is silent.*) But when the spring comes and the snow melts here and on the passes, you can't stay on. They may come and look for you. There's already talk of an illegitimate child. (*The "glockenspiel" of the falling drops has grown faster and steadier.*) Grusha, the snow is melting on the roof. Spring is here.

GRUSHA. Yes.

LAVRENTI (*eagerly*). I'll tell you what we'll do. You need a place to go, and, because of the child (*He sighs.*), you have to have a husband, so people won't talk. Now I've made cautious inquiries to see if we can find you a husband. Grusha, I *have* one. I talked to a peasant woman who has a son. Just the other side of the mountain. A small farm. And she's willing.

GRUSHA. But I *can't* marry! I must wait for Simon Shashava.

LAVRENTI. Of course. That's all been taken care of. You don't need a man in bed—you need a man on paper. And I've found you one. The son of this peasant woman is going to die. Isn't that wonderful? He's at his last gasp. And all in line with our story—a husband from the other side of the mountain! And when you met him he was at the last gasp. So you're a widow. What do you say?

GRUSHA. It's true I could use a document with stamps on it for Michael.

LAVRENTI. Stamps make all the difference. Without something in writing the Shah couldn't prove he's a Shah. And you'll have a place to live.

GRUSHA. How much does the peasant woman want?

LAVRENTI. Four hundred piasters.

GRUSHA. Where will you find it?

LAVRENTI (*guiltily*). Aniko's milk money.

GRUSHA. No one would know us there. I'll do it.

LAVRENTI (*getting up*). I'll let the peasant woman know.

[*Quick exit.*]

GRUSHA. Michael, you make a lot of work. I came by you as the pear tree comes by sparrows. And because a Christian bends down and picks up a crust of bread so nothing will go to waste. Michael, it would have been better had I walked quickly away on that Easter Sunday in Nuka in the second courtyard. Now I *am* a fool.

SINGER.

The bridegroom was on his deathbed when the bride arrived.
The bridegroom's mother was waiting at the door, telling her to hurry.
The bride brought a child along.
The witness hid it during the wedding.

[*On one side the bed. Under the mosquito net lies a very sick man.* GRUSHA *is pulled in at a run by her future mother-in-law. They are followed by* LAVRENTI *and the* CHILD.]

MOTHER-IN-LAW. Quick! Quick! Or he'll die on us before the wedding. (*To* LAVRENTI.) I was never told she had a child already.

LAVRENTI. What difference does it make? (*Pointing toward the dying man.*) It can't matter to him—in his condition.

MOTHER-IN-LAW. To him? But I'll never survive the shame! We are honest people. (*She begins to weep.*) My Jussup doesn't have to marry a girl with a child!

LAVRENTI. All right, make it another two hundred piasters. You'll have it in writing that the farm will go to you: but she'll have the right to live here for two years.

MOTHER-IN-LAW (*drying her tears*). It'll hardly cover the funeral expenses. I hope she'll really lend a hand with the work. And what's happened to the monk? He must have slipped out through the kitchen window. We'll have the whole village on our necks when they hear Jussup's end is come! Oh dear! I'll go get the monk. But he mustn't see the child!

LAVRENTI. I'll take care he doesn't. But why only a monk? Why not a priest?

MOTHER-IN-LAW. Oh, he's just as good. I only made one mistake: I paid half his fee in advance. Enough to send him to the tavern. I only hope . . . (*She runs off.*)

LAVRENTI. She saved on the priest, the wretch! Hired a cheap monk.

GRUSHA. You *will* send Simon Shashava to see me if he turns up after all?

LAVRENTI. Yes. (*Pointing at the* SICK PEASANT.) Won't you take a look at him? (GRUSHA, *taking* MICHAEL *to her, shakes her head.*) He's not moving an eyelid. I hope we aren't too late.

[*They listen. On the opposite side enter neighbors who look around and take up positions against the walls, thus forming another wall near the bed, yet leaving an opening so that the bed can be seen. They start murmuring prayers. Enter the* MOTHER-IN-LAW *with a* MONK. *Showing some annoyance and surprise, she bows to the guests.*]

MOTHER-IN-LAW. I hope you won't mind waiting a few moments? My son's bride has just arrived from the city. An emergency wedding is about to be celebrated. (*To the* MONK *in the bedroom.*) I might have known you couldn't keep your trap shut. (*To* GRUSHA.) The wedding can take place at once. Here's the license. Me and the bride's brother (LAVRENTI *tries to hide in the background, after having quietly taken* MICHAEL *back from* GRUSHA. *The* MOTHER-IN-LAW *waves him away.*) are the witnesses.

[GRUSHA *has bowed to the* MONK. *They go to the bed. The* MOTHER-IN-LAW *lifts the mosquito net. The* MONK *starts reeling off the marriage ceremony in Latin. Meanwhile the* MOTHER-IN-LAW *beckons to* LAVRENTI *to get rid of the* CHILD, *but fearing that it will cry he draws its attention to the ceremony,* GRUSHA *glances once at the* CHILD, *and* LAVRENTI *waves the* CHILD'*s hand in a greeting.*]

MONK. Are you prepared to be a faithful, obedient, and good wife to this man, and to cleave to him until death you do part?

GRUSHA (*looking at the* CHILD). I am.

MONK (*to the* SICK PEASANT). Are you prepared to be a good and loving husband to your wife until death you do part? (*As the* SICK PEASANT *does not answer, the* MONK *looks inquiringly around.*)

MOTHER-IN-LAW. Of course he is! Didn't you hear him say yes?

MONK. All right. We declare the marriage contracted! How about extreme unction?

MOTHER-IN-LAW. Nothing doing! The wedding cost quite enough. Now I must take care of the mourners. (*To* LAVRENTI.) Did we say seven hundred?

LAVRENTI. Six hundred. (*He pays.*) Now I don't want to sit with the guests and get to know people. So farewell, Grusha, and if my widowed sister comes to visit me, she'll get a welcome from my wife, or I'll show my teeth. (*Nods, gives the* CHILD *to* GRUSHA, *and leaves. The mourners glance after him without interest.*)

MONK. May one ask where this child comes from?

MOTHER-IN-LAW. Is there a child? I don't see a child. And you don't see a child either—you understand? Or it may turn out I saw all sorts of things in the tavern! Now come on.

[*After* GRUSHA *has put the* CHILD *down and told him to be quiet, they move over left,* GRUSHA *is introduced to the neighbors.*]

This is my daughter-in-law. She arrived just in time to find dear Jussup still alive.

ONE WOMAN. He's been ill now a whole year, hasn't he? When our Vassili was drafted he was there to say good-bye.

ANOTHER WOMAN. Such things are terrible for a farm. The corn all ripe and the farmer in bed! It'll really be a blessing if he doesn't suffer too long, I say.

FIRST WOMAN (*confidentially*). You know why we thought he'd taken to his bed? Because of the draft! And now his end is come!

MOTHER-IN-LAW. Sit yourselves down, please! And have some cakes!

[*She beckons to* GRUSHA *and both women go into the bedroom, where they pick up the cake pans off the floor. The guests, among them the* MONK, *sit on the floor and begin conversing in subdued voices.*]

ONE PEASANT (*to whom the* MONK *has handed the bottle which he has taken from his soutane*). There's a child, you say! How can that have happened to Jussup?

A WOMAN. She was certainly lucky to get herself married, with him so sick!

MOTHER-IN-LAW. They're gossiping already. And wolfing down the funeral cakes at the same time! If he doesn't die today, I'll have to bake some more tomorrow!

GRUSHA. I'll bake them for you.

MOTHER-IN-LAW. Yesterday some horsemen rode by, and I went out to see who it was. When I came in again he was lying there like a corpse! So I sent for you. It can't take much longer. (*She listens.*)

MONK. Dear wedding and funeral guests! Deeply touched, we stand before a bed of death and marriage. The bride gets a veil; the groom, a shroud: how varied, my children, are the fates of men! Alas! One man dies and has a roof over his head, and the other is married and the flesh turns to dust from which it was made. Amen.

MOTHER-IN-LAW. He's getting his own back. I shouldn't have hired such a cheap one. It's what you'd expect. A more expensive monk would behave himself. In Sura there's one with a real air of sanctity about him, but of course he charges a fortune. A fifty piaster monk like that has no dignity, and as for piety, just fifty piasters' worth and no more! When I came to get him in the tavern he'd just made a speech, and he was shouting: "The war is over, beware of the peace!" We must go in.

GRUSHA (*giving* MICHAEL *a cake*). Eat this cake, and keep nice and still, Michael.

[*The two women offer cakes to the guests. The dying man sits up in bed. He puts his head out from under the mosquito net, stares at the two women, then sinks back again. The* MONK *takes two bottles from his soutane and offers them to the peasant beside him. Enter three* MUSICIANS *who are greeted with a sly wink by the* MONK.]

MOTHER-IN-LAW (*to the* MUSICIANS). What are you doing here? With instruments?

ONE MUSICIAN. Brother Anastasius here (*Pointing at the* MONK.) told us there was a wedding on.

MOTHER-IN-LAW. What? You brought them? Three more on my neck! Don't you know there's a dying man in the next room?

MONK. A very tempting assignment for a musician: something that could be either a subdued Wedding March or a spirited Funeral Dance.

MOTHER-IN-LAW. Well, you might as well play. Nobody can stop you eating in any case.

[*The musicians play a potpourri. The women serve cakes.*]

MONK. The trumpet sounds like a whining baby. And you, little drum, what have you got to tell the world?

DRUNKEN PEASANT (*beside the* MONK, *sings*).

There was a young woman who said:
I thought I'd be happier, wed.
But my husband is old
And remarkably cold
So I sleep with a candle instead.

[*The* MOTHER-IN-LAW *throws the* DRUNKEN PEASANT *out. The music stops. The guests are embarrassed.*]

GUESTS (*loudly*).

—Have you heard? The Grand Duke is back! But the Princes are against him.

—They say the Shah of Persia has lent him a great army to restore order in Grusinia.

—But how is that possible? The Shah of Persia is the enemy . . .

—The enemy of Grusinia, you donkey, not the enemy of the Grand Duke!

—In any case, the war's over, so our soldiers are coming back.

[GRUSHA *drops a cake pan.* GUESTS *help her pick up the cake.*]

AN OLD WOMAN (*to* GRUSHA). Are you feeling bad? It's just excitement about dear Jussup. Sit down and rest a while, my dear. (GRUSHA *staggers.*)

GUESTS. Now everything'll be the way it was. Only the taxes'll go up because now we'll have to pay for the war.

GRUSHA (*weakly*). Did someone say the soldiers are back?

A MAN. I did.

GRUSHA. It can't be true.

FIRST MAN (*to a woman*). Show her the shawl. We bought it from a soldier. It's from Persia.

GRUSHA (*looking at the shawl*). They are here. (*She gets up, takes a step, kneels down in prayer, takes the silver cross and chain out of her blouse, and kisses it.*)

MOTHER-IN-LAW (*while the guests silently watch* GRUSHA). What's the matter with you? Aren't you going to look after our guests? What's all this city nonsense got to do with us?

GUESTS (*resuming conversation while* GRUSHA *remains in prayer*).

—You can buy Persian saddles from the soldiers too. Though many want crutches in exchange for them.

—The leaders on one side can win a war, the soldiers on both sides lose it.

—Anyway, the war's over. It's something they can't draft you any more.

[The dying man sits bolt upright in bed. He listens.]

—What we need is two weeks of good weather.

—Our pear trees are hardly bearing a thing this year.

MOTHER-IN-LAW (*offering cakes*). Have some more cakes and welcome! There are more!

[The MOTHER-IN-LAW *goes to the bedroom with the empty cake pans. Unaware of the dying man, she is bending down to pick up another tray when he begins to talk in a hoarse voice.]*

PEASANT. How many more cakes are you going to stuff down their throats? D'you think I can shit money?

[The MOTHER-IN-LAW *starts, stares at him aghast, while he climbs out from behind the mosquito net.]*

FIRST WOMAN (*talking kindly to* GRUSHA *in the next room*). Has the young wife got someone at the front?

A MAN. It's good news that they're on their way home, huh?

PEASANT. Don't stare at me like that! Where's this wife you've saddled me with?

[Receiving no answer, he climbs out of bed and in his nightshirt staggers into the other room. Trembling, she follows him with the cake pan.]

GUESTS (*seeing him and shrieking*). Good God! Jussup!

[Everyone leaps up in alarm. The women rush to the door. GRUSHA, *still on her knees, turns round and stares at the man.]*

PEASANT. A funeral supper! You'd enjoy that, wouldn't you? Get out before I throw you out! (*As the guests stampede from the house, gloomily to* GRUSHA.) I've upset the apple cart, huh? (*Receiving no answer, he turns round and takes a cake from the pan which his mother is holding.*)

SINGER.

O confusion! The wife discovers she has a husband.
By day there's the child, by night there's the husband.
The lover is on his way both day and night.
Husband and wife look at each other.
The bedroom is small.

[Near the bed the PEASANT *is sitting in a high wooden bathtub, naked, the* MOTHER-IN-LAW *is pouring water from a pitcher. Opposite* GRUSHA *cowers with* MICHAEL, *who is playing at mending straw mats.]*

PEASANT (*to his mother*). That's her work, not yours. Where's she hiding out now?

MOTHER-IN-LAW (*calling*). Grusha! The peasant wants you!

GRUSHA (*to* MICHAEL). There are still two holes to mend.

PEASANT (*when* GRUSHA *approaches*). Scrub my back!

GRUSHA. Can't the peasant do it himself?

PEASANT. "Can't the peasant do it himself?" Get the brush! To hell with you! Are you the wife here? Or are you a visitor? (*To the* MOTHER-IN-LAW.) It's too cold!

MOTHER-IN-LAW. I'll run for hot water.

GRUSHA. Let me go.

PEASANT. You stay here. (*The* MOTHER-IN-LAW *exits.*) Rub harder. And no shirking. You've seen a naked fellow before. That child didn't come out of thin air.

GRUSHA. The child was not conceived in joy, if that's what the peasant means.

PEASANT (*turning and grinning*). You don't look the type. (GRUSHA *stops scrubbing him, starts back. Enter the* MOTHER-IN-LAW.)

PEASANT. A nice thing you've saddled me with! A simpleton for a wife!

MOTHER-IN-LAW. She just isn't cooperative.

PEASANT. Pour—but go easy! Ow! Go easy, I said. (*To* GRUSHA.) Maybe you did something wrong in the city . . . I wouldn't be surprised. Why else should you be here? But I won't talk about that. I've not said a word about the illegitimate object you brought into my house either. But my patience has limits! It's against nature. (*To the* MOTHER-IN-LAW.) More! (*To* GRUSHA.) And even if your soldier does come back, you're married.

GRUSHA. Yes.

PEASANT. But your soldier won't come back. Don't you believe it.

GRUSHA. No.

PEASANT. You're cheating me. You're my wife and you're not my wife. Where you lie, nothing lies, and yet no other woman can lie there. When I go to work in the morning I'm tired—when I lie down at night I'm awake as the devil. God has given you sex—and what d'you do? I don't have ten piasters to buy myself a woman in the city. Besides, it's a long way. Woman weeds the fields and opens up her legs, that's what our calendar says. D'you hear?

GRUSHA (*quietly*). Yes. I didn't mean to cheat you out of it.

PEASANT. She didn't mean to cheat me out of it! Pour some more water! (*The* MOTHER-IN-LAW *pours.*) Ow!

SINGER.

As she sat by the stream to wash the linen
She saw his image in the water
And his face grew dimmer with the passing moons.
As she raised herself to wring the linen
She heard his voice from the murmuring maple
And his voice grew fainter with the passing moons.
Evasions and sighs grew more numerous,
Tears and sweat flowed.
With the passing moons the child grew up.

[GRUSHA *sits by a stream, dipping linen into the water. In the rear, a few children are standing.*]

GRUSHA (*to* MICHAEL). You can play with them, Michael, but don't let them boss you around just because you're the littlest. (MICHAEL *nods and joins the children. They start playing.*)

BIGGEST BOY. Today it's the Heads-Off Game. (*To a* FAT BOY.) You're the Prince and you laugh. (*To* MICHAEL.) You're the Governor. (*To a* GIRL.) You're the Governor's wife and you cry when his head's cut off. And I do the cutting. (*He shows his wooden sword.*) With this. First, they lead the Governor into the yard. The Prince walks in front. The Governor's wife comes last.

[*They form a procession. The* FAT BOY *is first and laughs. Then comes* MICHAEL, *then the* BIGGEST BOY, *and then the* GIRL, *who weeps.*]

MICHAEL (*standing still*). Me cut off head!

BIGGEST BOY. That's my job. You're the littlest. The Governor's the easy part. All you do is kneel down and get your head cut off—simple.

MICHAEL. Me want sword!

BIGGEST BOY. It's mine! (*He gives* MICHAEL *a kick.*)

GIRL (*shouting to* GRUSHA). He won't play his part!

GRUSHA (*laughing*). Even the little duck is a swimmer, they say.

BIGGEST BOY. You can be the Prince if you can laugh. (MICHAEL *shakes his head.*)

FAT BOY. I laugh best. Let him cut off the head just once. Then you do it, then me.

[*Reluctantly, the* BIGGEST BOY *hands* MICHAEL *the wooden sword and kneels down. The* FAT BOY *sits down, slaps his thigh, and laughs with all his might. The* GIRL *weeps loudly.* MICHAEL *swings the big sword and "cuts off" the head. In doing so, he topples over.*]

BIGGEST BOY. Hey! I'll show you how to cut heads off!

[MICHAEL *runs away. The children run after him.* GRUSHA *laughs, following them with her eyes. On looking back, she sees* SIMON SHASHAVA *standing on the opposite bank. He wears a shabby uniform.*]

GRUSHA. Simon!

SIMON. Is that Grusha Vashnadze?

GRUSHA. Simon!

SIMON (*formally*). A good morning to the young lady. I hope she is well.

GRUSHA (*getting up gaily and bowing low*). A good morning to the soldier. God be thanked he has returned in good health.

SIMON. They found better fish, so they didn't eat me, said the haddock.

GRUSHA. Courage, said the kitchen boy. Good luck, said the hero.

SIMON. How are things here? Was the winter bearable? The neighbor considerate?

GRUSHA. The winter was a trifle rough, the neighbor as usual, Simon.

SIMON. May one ask if a certain person still dips her toes in the water when rinsing the linen?

GRUSHA. The answer is no. Because of the eyes in the bushes.

SIMON. The young lady is speaking of soldiers. Here stands a paymaster.

GRUSHA. A job worth twenty piasters?

SIMON. And lodgings.

GRUSHA (*with tears in her eyes*). Behind the barracks under the date trees.

SIMON. Yes, there. A certain person has kept her eyes open.

GRUSHA. She has, Simon.

SIMON. And has not forgotten? (GRUSHA *shakes her head.*) So the door is still on its hinges as they say? (GRUSHA *looks at him in silence and shakes her head again.*) What's this? Is anything not as it should be?

GRUSHA. Simon Shashava, I can never return to Nuka. Something has happened.

SIMON. What can have happened?

GRUSHA. For one thing, I knocked an Ironshirt down.

SIMON. Grusha Vashnadze must have had her reasons for that.

GRUSHA. Simon Shashava, I am no longer called what I used to be called.

SIMON (*after a pause*). I do not understand.

GRUSHA. When do women change their names, Simon? Let me explain. Nothing stands between us. Everything is just as it was. You must believe that.

SIMON. Nothing stands between us and yet there's something?

GRUSHA. How can I explain it so fast and with the stream between us? Couldn't you cross the bridge there?

SIMON. Maybe it's no longer necessary.

GRUSHA. It is very necessary. Come over on this side, Simon. Quick!

SIMON. Does the young lady wish to say someone has come too late?

[GRUSHA *looks up at him in despair, her face streaming with tears.* SIMON *stares before him. He picks up a piece of wood and starts cutting it.*]

SINGER.

So many words are said, so many left unsaid.
The soldier has come.
Where he comes from, he does not say.
Hear what he thought and did not say:
"The battle began, gray at dawn, grew bloody at noon.
The first man fell in front of me, the second behind me, the third at my side.
I trod on the first, left the second behind, the third was run through by the captain.
One of my brothers died by steel, the other by smoke.

My neck caught fire, my hands froze in my gloves, my toes in my socks.
I fed on aspen buds, I drank maple juice, I slept on stone, in water."

SIMON. I see a cap in the grass. Is there a little one already?

GRUSHA. There is, Simon. There's no keeping *that* from you. But please don't worry, it is not mine.

SIMON. When the wind once starts to blow, they say, it blows through every cranny. The wife need say no more. (GRUSHA *looks into her lap and is silent.*)

SINGER.

There was yearning but there was no waiting.
The oath is broken. Neither could say why.
Hear what she thought but did not say:
"While you fought in the battle, soldier,
The bloody battle, the bitter battle
I found a helpless infant
I had not the heart to destroy him
I had to care for a creature that was lost
I had to stoop for breadcrumbs on the floor
I had to break myself for that which was not mine
That which was other people's.
Someone must help!
For the little tree needs water
The lamb loses its way when the shepherd is asleep
And its cry is unheard!"

SIMON. Give me back the cross I gave you. Better still, throw it in the stream. (*He turns to go.*)

GRUSHA (*getting up*). Simon Shashava, don't go away! He isn't mine! He isn't mine! (*She hears the children calling.*) What's the matter, children?

VOICES. Soldiers! And they're taking Michael away!

[GRUSHA *stands aghast as two* IRONSHIRTS, *with* MICHAEL *between them, come toward her.*]

ONE OF THE IRONSHIRTS. Are you Grusha? (*She nods.*) Is this your child?

GRUSHA. Yes. (SIMON *goes.*) Simon!

IRONSHIRT. We have orders, in the name of the law, to take this child, found in your custody, back to the city. It is suspected that the child is Michael Abashwili, son and heir of the late Governor Georgi Abashwili, and his wife, Natella Abashwili. Here is the document and the seal. (*They lead the* CHILD *away.*)

GRUSHA (*running after them, shouting*). Leave him here. Please! He's mine!

SINGER.

The Ironshirts took the child, the beloved child.

The unhappy girl followed them to the city, the dreaded city.
She who had borne him demanded the child.
She who had raised him faced trial.
Who will decide the case?
To whom will the child be assigned?
Who will the judge be? A good judge? A bad?
The city was in flames.
In the judge's seat sat Azdak.[1]

ACT IV

The Story of the Judge

SINGER.

Hear the story of the judge
How he turned judge, how he passed judgment, what kind of judge he was.
On that Easter Sunday of the great revolt, when the Grand Duke was overthrown
And his Governor Abashwili, father of our child, lost his head
The Village Scrivener Azdak found a fugitive in the woods and hid him in his hut.

[AZDAK, *in rags and slightly drunk, is helping an old beggar into his cottage.*]

AZDAK. Stop snorting, you're not a horse. And it won't do you any good with the police to run like a snotty nose in April. Stand still, I say. (*He catches the* OLD MAN, *who has marched into the cottage as if he'd like to go through the walls.*) Sit down. Feed. Here's a hunk of cheese. (*From under some rags, in a chest, he fishes out some cheese, and the* OLD MAN *greedily begins to eat.*) Haven't eaten in a long time, huh? (*The* OLD MAN *growls.*) Why were you running like that, asshole? The cop wouldn't even have seen you.

OLD MAN. Had to! Had to!

AZDAK. Blue funk? (*The* OLD MAN *stares, uncomprehending.*) Cold feet? Panic? Don't lick your chops like a Grand Duke. Or an old sow. I can't stand it. We have to accept respectable stinkers as God made them, but not you! I once heard of a senior judge who farted at a public dinner to show an independent spirit! Watching you eat like that gives me the most awful ideas. Why don't you say something? (*Sharply.*) Show me your hand. Can't you hear? (*The* OLD MAN *slowly puts out his hand.*)

[1] The name Azdak should be accented on the second syllable.—E. B.

White! So you're not a beggar at all! A fraud, a walking swindle! And I'm hiding you from the cops like you were an honest man! Why were you running like that if you're a landowner? For that's what you are. Don't deny it! I see it in your guilty face! (*He gets up.*) Get out! (*The* OLD MAN *looks at him uncertainly.*) What are you waiting for, peasant-flogger?

OLD MAN. Pursued. Need undivided attention. Make proposition . . .

AZDAK. Make what? A proposition? Well, if that isn't the height of insolence. He's making me a proposition! The bitten man scratches his fingers bloody, and the leech that's biting him makes him a proposition! Get out, I tell you!

OLD MAN. Understand point of view! Persuasion! Pay hundred thousand piasters one night! Yes?

AZDAK. What, you think you can buy me? For a hundred thousand piasters? Let's say a hundred and fifty thousand. Where are they?

OLD MAN. Have not them here. Of course. Will be sent. Hope do not doubt.

AZDAK. Doubt very much. Get out!

[*The* OLD MAN *gets up, waddles to the door. A* VOICE *is heard offstage.*]

VOICE. Azdak!

[*The* OLD MAN *turns, waddles to the opposite corner, stands still.*]

AZDAK (*calling out*). I'm not in! (*He walks to door.*) So *you're* sniffing around here again, Shauwa?

SHAUWA (*reproachfully*). You caught another rabbit, Azdak. And you'd promised me it wouldn't happen again!

AZDAK (*severely*). Shauwa, don't talk about things you don't understand. The rabbit is a dangerous and destructive beast. It feeds on plants, especially on the species of plants known as weeds. It must therefore be exterminated.

SHAUWA. Azdak, don't be so hard on me. I'll lose my job if I don't arrest you. I know you have a good heart.

AZDAK. I do not have a good heart! How often must I tell you I'm a man of intellect?

SHAUWA (*slyly*). I know, Azdak. You're a superior person. You say so yourself. I'm just a Christian and an ignoramus. So I ask you: When one of the Prince's rabbits is stolen, and I'm a policeman, what should I do with the offending party?

AZDAK. Shauwa, Shauwa, shame on you. You stand and ask me a question, than which nothing could be more seductive. It's like you were a woman—let's say that bad girl Nunowna, and you showed me your thigh—Nunowna's thigh, that would be—and asked me: "What shall I do with my thigh, it itches?" Is she as innocent as she pretends? Of course not. I catch a rabbit, but you catch a man. Man is made in God's image. Not so a rabbit, you know that. I'm a rabbit-eater, but you're a man-eater, Shauwa. And God will pass judgment on you. Shauwa, go home and repent. No, stop, there's something . . . (*He looks at the* OLD MAN *who stands trembling in the corner.*) No, it's nothing. Go home and repent. (*He slams the door behind* SHAUWA.) Now you're surprised, huh? Surprised I didn't hand you over? I couldn't hand over a bedbug to that animal. It goes against the grain. Now don't tremble because of a cop! So old and still so scared? Finish your cheese, but eat it like a poor man, or else they'll still catch you. Must I even explain how a poor man behaves? (*He pushes him down, and then gives him back the cheese.*) That box is the table. Lay your elbows on the table. Now, encircle the cheese on the plate like it might be snatched from you at any moment—what right have you to be safe, huh?—now, hold your knife like an undersized sickle, and give your cheese a troubled look because, like all beautiful things, it's already fading away. (AZDAK *watches him.*) They're after you, which speaks in your favor, but how can we be sure they're not mistaken about you? In Tiflis one time they hanged a landowner, a Turk, who could prove he quartered his peasants instead of merely cutting them in half, as is the custom, and he squeezed twice the usual amount of taxes out of them, his zeal was above suspicion. And yet they hanged him like a common criminal—because he was a Turk—a thing he couldn't do much about. What injustice! He got onto the gallows by a sheer fluke. In short, I don't trust you.

SINGER.

Thus Azdak gave the old beggar a bed,
And learned that old beggar was the old butcher, the Grand Duke himself,
And was ashamed.
He denounced himself and ordered the policeman to take him to Nuka, to court, to be judged.

[*In the court of justice three* IRONSHIRTS *sit drinking. From a beam hangs a man in judge's robes. Enter* AZDAK, *in chains, dragging* SHAUWA *behind him.*]

AZDAK (*shouting*). I've helped the Grand Duke, the Grand Thief, the Grand Butcher, to escape! In the name of justice I ask to be severely judged in public trial!

FIRST IRONSHIRT. Who's this queer bird?

SHAUWA. That's our Village Scrivener, Azdak.

AZDAK. I am contemptible! I am a traitor! A branded criminal! Tell them, flatfoot, how I insisted on being tied up and brought to the capital. Because I sheltered the Grand Duke, the Grand Swindler, by mistake. And how I found out afterwards. See the marked man denounce himself! Tell them how I forced you to walk half the night with me to clear the whole thing up.

SHAUWA. And all by threats. That wasn't nice of you, Azdak.

AZDAK. Shut your mouth, Shauwa. You don't understand. A new age is upon us! It'll go thundering over you. You're finished. The police will be wiped out—poof! Everything will be gone into, everything will be brought into the open. The guilty will give themselves up. Why? They couldn't escape the people in any case. (*To* SHAUWA.) Tell them how I shouted all along Shoemaker Street (*With big gestures, looking at the* IRONSHIRTS.) "In my ignorance I let the Grand Swindler escape! So tear me to pieces, brothers!" I wanted to get it in first.

FIRST IRONSHIRT. And what did your brothers answer?

SHAUWA. They comforted him in Butcher Street, and they laughed themselves sick in Shoemaker Street. That's all.

AZDAK. But with you it's different. I can see you're men of iron. Brothers, where's the judge? I must be tried.

FIRST IRONSHIRT (*pointing at the hanged man*). There's the judge. And please stop "brothering" us. It's rather a sore spot this evening.

AZDAK. "There's the judge." An answer never heard in Grusinia before. Townsman, where's His Excellency the Governor? (*Pointing to the ground.*) There's His Excellency, stranger. Where's the Chief Tax Collector? Where's the official Recruiting Officer? The Patriarch? The Chief of Police? There, there, there—all there. Brothers, I expected no less of you.

SECOND IRONSHIRT. What? *What* was it you expected, funny man?

AZDAK. What happened in Persia, brother, what happened in Persia?

SECOND IRONSHIRT. What did happen in Persia?

AZDAK. Everybody was hanged. Viziers, tax collectors. Everybody. Forty years ago now. My grandfather, a remarkable man by the way, saw it all. For three whole days. Everywhere.

SECOND IRONSHIRT. And who ruled when the Vizier was hanged?

AZDAK. A peasant ruled when the Vizier was hanged.

SECOND IRONSHIRT. And who commanded the army?

AZDAK. A soldier, a soldier.

SECOND IRONSHIRT. And who paid the wages?

AZDAK. A dyer. A dyer paid the wages.

SECOND IRONSHIRT. Wasn't it a weaver, maybe?

FIRST IRONSHIRT. And why did all this happen, Persian?

AZDAK. Why did all this happen? Must there be a special reason? Why do you scratch yourself, brother? War! Too long a war! And no justice! My grandfather brought back a song that tells how it was. I will sing it for you. With my friend the policeman. (*To* SHAUWA.) And hold the rope tight. It's very suitable. (*He sings, with* SHAUWA *holding the rope tight around him.*)

The Song of Injustice in Persia

Why don't our sons bleed any more? Why don't our
daughters weep?

Why do only the slaughterhouse cattle have blood in their veins?
Why do only the willows shed tears on Lake Urmia?
The king must have a new province, the peasant must give up his savings.
That the roof of the world might be conquered, the roof of the cottage is torn down.
Our men are carried to the ends of the earth, so that great ones can eat at home.
The soldiers kill each other, the marshals salute each other.
They bite the widow's tax money to see if it's good, their swords break.
The battle was lost, the helmets were paid for.
Refrain: Is it so? Is it so?

SHAUWA (*refrain*). Yes, yes, yes, yes, yes it's so.
AZDAK. Want to hear the rest of it? (*The* FIRST IRONSHIRT *nods.*)
SECOND IRONSHIRT (*to* SHAUWA). Did he teach you that song?
SHAUWA. Yes, only my voice isn't very good.
SECOND IRONSHIRT. No. (*To* AZDAK.) Go on singing.
AZDAK. The second verse is about the peace. (*He sings.*)

The offices are packed, the streets overflow with officials.
The rivers jump their banks and ravage the fields.
Those who cannot let down their own trousers rule countries.
They can't count up to four, but they devour eight courses.
The corn farmers, looking round for buyers, see only the starving.
The weavers go home from their looms in rags.
Refrain: Is it so? Is it so?

SHAUWA (*refrain*). Yes, yes, yes, yes, yes it's so.
AZDAK.

That's why our sons don't bleed any more, that's why our daughters don't weep.
That's why only the slaughterhouse cattle have blood in their veins,
And only the willows shed tears by Lake Urmia toward morning.

FIRST IRONSHIRT. Are you going to sing that song here in town?
AZDAK. Sure. What's wrong with it?
FIRST IRONSHIRT. Have you noticed that the sky's getting red? (*Turning round,* AZDAK *sees the sky red with fire.*) It's the people's quarters on the outskirts of town. The carpet weavers have caught the "Persian Sickness," too. And they've been asking if Prince Kazbeki isn't eating too many courses. This morning they strung up the city judge. As for us we beat them to pulp. We were paid one hundred piasters per man, you understand?
AZDAK (*after a pause*). I understand. (*He glances shyly round and, creeping away, sits down in a corner, his head in his hands.*)

IRONSHIRTS (*to each other*). If there ever was a troublemaker it's him. —He must've come to the capital to fish in the troubled waters.

SHAUWA. Oh, I don't think he's a really bad character, gentlemen. Steals a few chickens here and there. And maybe a rabbit.

SECOND IRONSHIRT (*approaching* AZDAK). Came to fish in the troubled waters, huh?

AZDAK (*looking up*). I don't know why I came.

SECOND IRONSHIRT. Are you in with the carpet weavers maybe? (AZDAK *shakes his head.*) How about that song?

AZDAK. From my grandfather. A silly and ignorant man.

SECOND IRONSHIRT. Right. And how about the dyer who paid the wages?

AZDAK (*muttering*). That was in Persia.

FIRST IRONSHIRT. And this denouncing of yourself? Because you didn't hang the Grand Duke with your own hands?

AZDAK. Didn't I tell you I let him run? (*He creeps farther away and sits on the floor.*)

SHAUWA. I can swear to that: he let him run.

[*The* IRONSHIRTS *burst out laughing and slap* SHAUWA *on the back.* AZDAK *laughs loudest. They slap* AZDAK *too, and unchain him. They all start drinking as the* FAT PRINCE *enters with a young man.*]

FIRST IRONSHIRT (*to* AZDAK, *pointing at the* FAT PRINCE). There's your "new age" for you! (*More laughter.*)

FAT PRINCE. Well, my friends, what is there to laugh about? Permit me a serious word. Yesterday morning the Princess of Grusinia overthrew the warmongering government of the Grand Duke and did away with his Governors. Unfortunately the Grand Duke himself escaped. In this fateful hour our carpet weavers, those eternal troublemakers, had the effrontery to stir up a rebellion and hang the universally loved city judge, our dear Illo Orbeliani. Ts—ts—ts. My friends, we need peace, peace, peace in Grusinia! And justice! So I've brought along my dear nephew Bizergan Kazbeki. He'll be the new judge, hm? A very gifted fellow. What do you say? I want your opinion. Let the people decide!

SECOND IRONSHIRT. Does this mean *we* elect the judge?

FAT PRINCE. Precisely. Let the people propose some very gifted fellow! Confer among yourselves, my friends. (*The* IRONSHIRTS *confer.*) Don't worry, my little fox. The job's yours. And when we catch the Grand Duke we won't have to kiss this rabble's ass any longer.

IRONSHIRTS (*among themselves*).

—Very funny: they're wetting their pants because they haven't caught the Grand Duke.

—When the outlook isn't so bright, they say: "My friends!" and "Let the people decide!"

—Now he even wants justice for Grusinia! But fun is fun as long as it lasts! (*Pointing at* AZDAK.) *He* knows all about justice. Hey, rascal, would you like this nephew fellow to be the judge?

AZDAK. Are you asking me? You're not asking *me?!*

FIRST IRONSHIRT. Why not? Anything for a laugh!

AZDAK. You'd like to test him to the marrow, correct? Have you a criminal on hand? An experienced one? So the candidate can show what he knows?

SECOND IRONSHIRT. Let's see. We do have a couple of doctors downstairs. Let's use them.

AZDAK. Oh, no, that's no good, we can't take real criminals till we're sure the judge will be appointed. He may be dumb, but he must be appointed, or the law is violated. And the law is a sensitive organ. It's like the spleen, you mustn't hit it—that would be fatal. Of course you can hang those two without violating the law, because there was no judge in the vicinity. But judgment, when pronounced, must be pronounced with absolute gravity—it's all such nonsense. Suppose, for instance, a judge jails a woman—let's say she's stolen a corn cake to feed her child—and this judge isn't wearing his robes—or maybe he's scratching himself while passing sentence and half his body is uncovered—a man's thigh *will* itch once in a while—the sentence this judge passes is a disgrace and the law is violated. In short it would be easier for a judge's robe and a judge's hat to pass judgment than for a man with no robe and no hat. If you don't treat it with respect, the law just disappears on you. Now you don't try out a bottle of wine by offering it to a dog; you'd only lose your wine.

FIRST IRONSHIRT. Then what do you suggest, hairsplitter?

AZDAK. I'll be the defendant.

FIRST IRONSHIRT. You? (*He bursts out laughing.*)

FAT PRINCE. What have you decided?

FIRST IRONSHIRT. We've decided to stage a rehearsal. Our friend here will be the defendant. Let the candidate be the judge and sit there.

FAT PRINCE. It isn't customary, but why not? (*To the* NEPHEW.) A mere formality, my little fox. What have I taught you? Who got there first—the slow runner or the fast?

NEPHEW. The silent runner, Uncle Arsen.

[*The* NEPHEW *takes the chair. The* IRONSHIRTS *and the* FAT PRINCE *sit on the steps. Enter* AZDAK, *mimicking the gait of the Grand Duke.*]

AZDAK (*in the Grand Duke's accent*). Is any here knows me? Am Grand Duke.

IRONSHIRTS.

—*What* is he?

—The Grand Duke. He knows him, too.

—Fine. So get on with the trial.

AZDAK. Listen! Am accused instigating war? Ridiculous! Am saying ridiculous! That enough? If not, have brought lawyers. Believe five hundred. (*He points behind him, pretending to be surrounded by lawyers.*) Requisition all available seats for lawyers! (*The* IRONSHIRTS *laugh; the* FAT PRINCE *joins in.*)

NEPHEW (*to the* IRONSHIRTS). You really wish me to try this case? I find it rather unusual. From the taste angle, I mean.

FIRST IRONSHIRT. Let's go!

FAT PRINCE (*smiling*). Let him have it, my little fox!

NEPHEW. All right. People of Grusinia versus Grand Duke. Defendant, what have you got to say for yourself?

AZDAK. Plenty. Naturally, have read war lost. Only started on the advice of patriots. Like Uncle Arsen Kazbeki. Call Uncle Arsen as witness.

FAT PRINCE (*to the* IRONSHIRTS, *delightedly*). What a madcap!

NEPHEW. Motion rejected. One cannot be arraigned for declaring a war, which every ruler has to do once in a while, but only for running a war badly.

AZDAK. Rubbish! Did not run it at all! Had it run! Had it run by Princes! Naturally, they messed it up.

NEPHEW. Do you by any chance deny having been commander-in-chief?

AZDAK. Not at all! Always *was* commander-in-chief. At birth shouted at wet nurse. Was trained drop turds in toilet, grew accustomed to command. Always commanded officials rob my cash box. Officers flog soldiers only on command. Landowners sleep with peasants' wives only on strictest command. Uncle Arsen here grew his belly at *my* command!

IRONSHIRTS (*clapping*). He's good! Long live the Grand Duke!

FAT PRINCE. Answer him, my little fox: I'm with you.

NEPHEW. I shall answer him according to the dignity of the law. Defendant, preserve the dignity of the law!

AZDAK. Agreed. Command you proceed with trial!

NEPHEW. It is not your place to command me. You claim that the Princes forced you to declare war. How can you claim, then, that they—er—"messed it up"?

AZDAK. Did not send enough people. Embezzled funds. Sent sick horses. During attack, drinking in whorehouse. Call Uncle Arsen as witness.

NEPHEW. Are you making the outrageous suggestion that the Princes of this country did not fight?

AZDAK. No. Princes fought. Fought for war contracts.

FAT PRINCE (*jumping up*). That's too much! This man talks like a carpet weaver!

AZDAK. Really? Told nothing but truth.

FAT PRINCE. Hang him! Hang him!

FIRST IRONSHIRT (*pulling the* PRINCE *down*). Keep quiet! Go on, Excellency!

NEPHEW. Quiet! I now render a verdict: You must be hanged! By the neck! Having lost war!

AZDAK. Young man, seriously advise not fall publicly into jerky clipped speech. Cannot be watchdog if howl like wolf. Got it? If people realize Princes speak same language as Grand Duke, may hang Grand Duke *and Princes,* huh? By the way, must overrule verdict. Reason? War lost, but not for Princes. Princes won their war. Got 3,863,000 piasters for horses not delivered, 8,240,000 piasters for food supplies not produced. Are therefore victors. War lost only for Grusinia, which is not present in this court.

FAT PRINCE. I think that will do, my friends. (*To* AZDAK.) You can withdraw, funny man. (*To the* IRONSHIRTS.) You may now ratify the new judge's appointment, my friends.

FIRST IRONSHIRT. Yes, we can. Take down the judge's gown. (*One* IRONSHIRT *climbs on the back of the other, pulls the gown off the hanged man.*) (*To the* NEPHEW.) Now you run away so the right ass can get on the right chair. (*To* AZDAK.) Step forward! Go to the judge's seat! Now sit in it! (AZDAK *steps up, bows, and sits down.*) The judge was always a rascal! Now the rascal shall be a judge! (*The judge's gown is placed round his shoulders, the hat on his head.*) And what a judge!

SINGER.

And there was civil war in the land.
The mighty were not safe.
And Azdak was made a judge by the Ironshirts.
And Azdak remained a judge for two years.

SINGER AND CHORUS.

When the towns were set afire
And rivers of blood rose higher and higher,
Cockroaches crawled out of every crack.
And the court was full of schemers
And the church of foul blasphemers.
In the judge's cassock sat Azdak.

[AZDAK *sits in the judge's chair, peeling an apple.* SHAUWA *is sweeping out the hall. On one side an* INVALID *in a wheelchair. Opposite, a young man accused of blackmail. An* IRONSHIRT *stands guard, holding the Ironshirts' banner.*]

AZDAK. In consideration of the large number of cases, the Court today will hear two cases at a time. Before I open the proceedings, a short announcement—I accept. (*He stretches out his hand. The* BLACKMAILER *is the only one to produce any money. He hands it to* AZDAK.) I reserve the right to punish one of the parties for contempt of court. (*He glances at the* INVALID.) You (*To the* DOCTOR.) are a doctor, and you (*To the* INVALID.) are bringing a complaint against him. Is the doctor responsible for your condition?

INVALID. Yes. I had a stroke on his account.

AZDAK. That would be professional negligence.

INVALID. Worse than negligence. I gave this man money for his studies. So far, he hasn't paid me back a cent. It was when I heard he was treating a patient free that I had my stroke.

AZDAK. Rightly. (*To a* LIMPING MAN.) And what are *you* doing here?

LIMPING MAN. I'm the patient, Your Honor.

AZDAK. He treated your leg for nothing?

LIMPING MAN. The wrong leg! My rheumatism was in the left leg, he operated on the right. That's why I limp.

AZDAK. And you were treated free?

INVALID. A five-hundred-piaster operation free! For nothing! For a God-bless-you! And I paid for this man's studies! (*To the* DOCTOR.) Did they teach you to operate free?

DOCTOR. Your Honor, it is the custom to demand the fee before the operation, as the patient is more willing to pay before an operation than after. Which is only human. In the case in question I was convinced, when I started the operation, that my servant had already received the fee. In this I was mistaken.

INVALID. He was mistaken! A good doctor doesn't make mistakes! He examines before he operates!

AZDAK. That's right: (*To* SHAUWA.) Public Prosecutor, what's the other case about?

SHAUWA (*busily sweeping*). Blackmail.

BLACKMAILER. High Court of Justice, I'm innocent. I only wanted to find out from the landowner concerned if he really *had* raped his niece. He informed me very politely that this was not the case, and gave me the money only so I could pay for my uncle's studies.

AZDAK. Hm. (*To the* DOCTOR.) You, on the other hand, can cite no extenuating circumstances for your offense, huh?

DOCTOR. Except that to err is human.

AZDAK. And you are aware that in money matters a good doctor is a highly responsible person? I once heard of a doctor who got a thousand piasters for a sprained finger by remarking that sprains have something to do with blood circulation, which after all a less good doctor might have overlooked, and who, on another occasion made a real gold mine out of a somewhat disordered gall bladder, he treated it with such loving care. You have no excuse, Doctor. The corn merchant Uxu had his son study medicine to get some knowledge of trade, our medical schools are so good. (*To the* BLACKMAILER.) What's the landowner's name?

SHAUWA. He doesn't want it mentioned.

AZDAK. In that case I will pass judgment. The Court considers the blackmail proved. And you (*To the* INVALID.) are sentenced to a fine of one thousand piasters. If you have a second stroke, the doctor will have to treat you free. Even if he has to amputate. (*To the* LIMPING MAN.) As compensation, you will receive a bottle of rubbing alcohol. (*To the* BLACKMAILER.) You are sentenced to hand over half the proceeds of your deal to the Public Prosecutor to keep the landowner's name secret. You are advised, moreover, to study medicine—you seem well suited to that calling. (*To the* DOCTOR.) You have perpetrated an unpardonable error in the practice of your profession: you are acquitted. Next cases!

SINGER AND CHORUS.

Men won't do much for a shilling.
For a pound they may be willing.
For twenty pounds the verdict's in the sack.
As for the many, all too many,
Those who've only got a penny—
They've one single, sole recourse: Azdak.

[*Enter* AZDAK *from the caravansary on the highroad, followed by an old bearded* INNKEEPER. *The judge's chair is carried by a stableman and* SHAUWA. *An* IRONSHIRT, *with a banner, takes up his position.*]

AZDAK. Put me down. Then we'll get some air, maybe even a good stiff breeze from the lemon grove there. It does justice good to be done in the open: the wind blows her skirts up and you can see what she's got. Shauwa, we've been eating too much. These official journeys are exhausting. (*To the* INNKEEPER.) It's a question of your daughter-in-law?

INNKEEPER. Your Worship, it's a question of the family honor. I wish to bring an action on behalf of my son, who's away on business on the other side the mountain. This is the offending stableman, and here's my daughter-in-law.

[*Enter the* DAUGHTER-IN-LAW, *a voluptuous wench. She is veiled.*]

AZDAK (*sitting down*). I accept. (*Sighing, the* INNKEEPER *hands him some money.*) Good. Now the formalities are disposed of. This is a case of rape?

INNKEEPER. Your Honor, I caught the fellow in the act. Ludovica was in the straw on the stable floor.

AZDAK. Quite right, the stable. Lovely horses! I specially liked the little roan.

INNKEEPER. The first thing I did, of course, was to question Ludovica. On my son's behalf.

AZDAK (*seriously*). I said I specially liked the little roan.

INNKEEPER (*coldly*). Really? Ludovica confessed the stableman took her against her will.

AZDAK. Take your veil off, Ludovica. (*She does so.*) Ludovica, you please the Court. Tell us how it happened.

LUDOVICA (*well schooled*). When I entered the stable to see the new foal the stableman said to me on his own accord: "It's hot today!" and laid his hand on my left breast. I said to him: "Don't do that!" But he continued to handle me indecently, which provoked my anger. Before I realized his sinful intentions, he got much closer. It was all over when my father-in-law entered and accidently trod on me.

INNKEEPER (*explaining*). On my son's behalf.

AZDAK (*to the* STABLEMAN). You admit you started it?

STABLEMAN. Yes.

AZDAK. Ludovica, you like to eat sweet things?

LUDOVICA. Yes, sunflower seeds!

AZDAK. You like to lie a long time in the bathtub?

LUDOVICA. Half an hour or so.

AZDAK. Public Prosecutor, drop your knife—there on the ground. (SHAUWA *does so.*) Ludovica, pick up that knife. (LUDOVICA, *swaying her hips, does so.*) See that? (*He points at her.*) The way it moves? The rape is now proven. By eating too much—sweet things, especially—by lying too long in warm water, by laziness and too soft a skin, you have raped that unfortunate man. Think you can run around with a behind like that and get away with it in court? This is a case of intentional assault with a dangerous weapon! You are sentenced to hand over to the Court the little roan which your father liked to ride "on his son's behalf." And now, come with me to the stables, so the Court can inspect the scene of the crime, Ludovica.

SINGER AND CHORUS.

When the sharks the sharks devour
Little fishes have their hour.
For a while the load is off their back.
On Grusinia's highways faring
Fixed-up scales of justice bearing
Strode the poor man's magistrate: Azdak.

And he gave to the forsaken
All that from the rich he'd taken.
And a bodyguard of roughnecks was Azdak's,
And our good and evil man, he
Smiled upon Grusinia's Granny.
His emblem was a tear in sealing wax.

All mankind should love each other
But when visiting your brother
Take an ax along and hold it fast.
Not in theory but in practice
Miracles are wrought with axes
And the age of miracles is not past.

[AZDAK'*s judge's chair is in a tavern. Three rich* FARMERS *stand before* AZDAK. SHAUWA *brings him wine. In a corner stands an*

OLD PEASANT WOMAN. *In the open doorway, and outside, stand villagers looking on. An* IRONSHIRT *stands guard with a banner.*]

AZDAK. The Public Prosecutor has the floor.

SHAUWA. It concerns a cow. For five weeks, the defendant has had a cow in her stable, the property of the farmer Suru. She was also found to be in possession of a stolen ham, and a number of cows belonging to Shutoff were killed after he asked the defendant to pay the rent on a piece of land.

FARMERS.
—It's a matter of my ham, Your Honor.
—It's a matter of my cow, Your Honor.
—It's a matter of my land, Your Honor.

AZDAK. Well, Granny, what have *you* got to say to all this?

OLD WOMAN. Your Honor, one night toward morning, five weeks ago, there was a knock at my door, and outside stood a bearded man with a cow. "My dear woman," he said, "I am the miracle-working Saint Banditus and because your son has been killed in the war, I bring you this cow as a souvenir. Take good care of it."

FARMERS.
—The robber, Irakli, Your Honor!
—Her brother-in-law, Your Honor!
—The cow-thief!
—The incendiary!
—He must be beheaded!

[*Outside, a woman screams. The crowd grows restless, retreats. Enter the* BANDIT *Irakli with a huge ax.*]

BANDIT. A very good evening, dear friends! A glass of vodka!

FARMERS (*crossing themselves*). Irakli!

AZDAK. Public Prosecutor, a glass of vodka for our guest. And who are you?

BANDIT. I'm a wandering hermit, Your Honor. Thanks for the gracious gift. (*He empties the glass which* SHAUWA *has brought.*) Another!

AZDAK. I am Azdak. (*He gets up and bows. The* BANDIT *also bows.*) The Court welcomes the foreign hermit. Go on with your story, Granny.

OLD WOMAN. Your Honor, that first night I didn't yet know Saint Banditus could work miracles, it was only the cow. But one night, a few days later, the farmer's servants came to take the cow away again. Then they turned round in front of my door and went off without the cow. And bumps as big as a fist sprouted on their heads. So I knew that Saint Banditus had changed their hearts and turned them into friendly people.

[*The* BANDIT *roars with laughter.*]

FIRST FARMER. I know what changed them.

AZDAK. That's fine. You can tell us later. Continue.

OLD WOMAN. Your Honor, the next one to become a good man was the farmer Shutoff—a devil, as everyone knows. But Saint Banditus arranged it so he let me off the rent on the little piece of land.

SECOND FARMER. Because my cows were killed in the field.

[*The* BANDIT *laughs.*]

OLD WOMAN (*answering* AZDAK'*s sign to continue*). Then one morning the ham came flying in at my window. It hit me in the small of the back. I'm still lame, Your Honor, look. (*She limps a few steps. The* BANDIT *laughs.*) Your Honor, was there ever a time when a poor old woman could get a ham *without* a miracle?

[*The* BANDIT *starts sobbing.*]

AZDAK (*rising from his chair*). Granny, that's a question that strikes straight at the Court's heart. Be so kind as to sit here. (*The* OLD WOMAN, *hesitating, sits in the judge's chair.*)

AZDAK (*sits on the floor, glass in hand, reciting*).

Granny
We could almost call you Granny Grusinia
The Woebegone
The Bereaved Mother
Whose sons have gone to war.
Receiving the present of a cow
She bursts out crying.
When she is beaten
She remains hopeful.
When she's not beaten
She's surprised.
On us
Who are already damned
May you render a merciful verdict
Granny Grusinia!

(*Bellowing at the* FARMERS.) Admit you don't believe in miracles, you atheists! Each of you is sentenced to pay five hundred piasters! For godlessness! Get out! (*The* FARMERS *slink out.*) And you Granny, and you (*To the* BANDIT.) pious man, empty a pitcher of wine with the Public Prosecutor and Azdak!

SINGER AND CHORUS.

And he broke the rules to save them.
Broken law like bread he gave them,
Brought them to shore upon his crooked back.
At long last the poor and lowly
Had someone who was not too holy
To be bribed by empty hands: Azdak.

For two years it was his pleasure
To give the beasts of prey short measure:
He became a wolf to fight the pack.

From All Hallows to All Hallows
On his chair beside the gallows
Dispensing justice in his fashion sat Azdak.

SINGER.

But the era of disorder came to an end.
The Grand Duke returned.
The Governor's wife returned.
A trial was held.
Many died.
The people's quarters burned anew.
And fear seized Azdak.

[AZDAK'*s judge's chair stands again in the court of justice.* AZDAK *sits on the floor, shaving and talking to* SHAUWA. *Noises outside. In the rear the* FAT PRINCE'*s head is carried by on a lance.*]

AZDAK. Shauwa, the days of your slavery are numbered, maybe even the minutes. For a long time now I have held you in the iron curb of reason, and it has torn your mouth till it bleeds. I have lashed you with reasonable arguments, I have manhandled you with logic. You are by nature a weak man, and if one slyly throws an argument in your path, you *have* to snap it up, you can't resist. It is your nature to lick the hand of some superior being. But superior beings can be of very different kinds. And now, with your liberation, you will soon be able to follow your natural inclinations, which are low. You will be able to follow your infallible instinct, which teaches you to plant your fat heel on the faces of men. Gone is the era of confusion and disorder, which I find described in the Song of Chaos. Let us now sing that song together in memory of those terrible days. Sit down and don't do violence to the music. Don't be afraid. It sounds all right. And it has a fine refrain. (*He sings.*)

The Song of Chaos

Sister, hide your face! Brother, take your knife!
The times are out of joint!
Big men are full of complaint
And small men full of joy.
The city says:
"Let us drive the mighty from our midst!"
Offices are raided. Lists of serfs are destroyed.
They have set Master's nose to the grindstone.
They who lived in the dark have seen the light.
The ebony poor box is broken.
Sesnem[2] wood is sawed up for beds.

[2] I do not know what kind of wood this is, so I have left the word exactly as it stands in the German original. The song is based on an Egyptian papyrus which Brecht cites as such in his essay, "Five Difficulties in the Writing of the Truth."

Who had no bread have full barns.
Who begged for alms of corn now mete it out.

SHAUWA (*refrain*). Oh, oh, oh, oh.
AZDAK (*refrain*).
Where are you, General, where are you?
Please, please, please, restore order!

The nobleman's son can no longer be recognized;
The lady's child becomes the son of her slave-girl
The councilors meet in a shed.
Once, this man was barely allowed to sleep on the wall;
Now, he stretches his limbs in a bed.
Once, this man rowed a boat; now, he owns ships.
Their owner looks for them, but they're his no longer.
Five men are sent on a journey by their master.
"Go yourself," they say, "we have arrived."

SHAUWA (*refrain*). Oh, oh, oh, oh.
AZDAK (*refrain*).
Where are you, General, where are you?
Please, please, please, restore order!

Yes, so it might have been, had order been neglected much longer. But now the Grand Duke has returned to the capital, and the Persians have lent him an army to restore order with. The people's quarters are already aflame. Go and get me the big book I always sit on. (SHAUWA *brings the big book from the judge's chair.* AZDAK *opens it.*) This is the Statute Book and I've always used it, as you can testify. Now I'd better look in this book and see what they can do to me. I've let the down-and-outs get away with murder, and I'll have to pay for it. I helped poverty onto its skinny legs, so they'll hang me for drunkenness. I peeped into the rich man's pocket, which is bad taste. And I can't hide anywhere—everybody knows me because I've helped everybody.

SHAUWA. Someone's coming!

AZDAK (*in panic, he walks trembling to the chair*). It's the end. And now they'd enjoy seeing what a Great Man I am. I'll deprive them of that pleasure. I'll beg on my knees for mercy. Spittle will slobber down my chin. The fear of death is in me.

[*Enter Natella Abashwili, the* GOVERNOR'S WIFE, *followed by the* ADJUTANT *and an* IRONSHIRT.]

GOVERNOR'S WIFE. What sort of a creature is that, Shalva?

AZDAK. A willing one, Your Highness, a man ready to oblige.

I should think he must have come across it in Adolf Erman's *Die Literatur der Aegypter,* 1923, p. 130 ff. Erman too gives the word as Sesnem. The same papyrus is quoted in Karl Jaspers' *Man in the Modern Age* (Anchor edition, pp. 18–19) but without the sentence about the Sesnem wood.—E.B.

ADJUTANT. Natella Abashwili, wife of the late Governor, has just returned. She is looking for her two-year-old son, Michael. She has been informed that the child was carried off to the mountains by a former servant.

AZDAK. The child will be brought back, Your Highness, at your service.

ADJUTANT. They say that the person in question is passing it off as her own.

AZDAK. She will be beheaded, Your Highness, at your service.

ADJUTANT. That is all.

GOVERNOR'S WIFE (*leaving*). I don't like that man.

AZDAK (*following her to door, bowing*). At your service, Your Highness, it will all be arranged.

ACT V

The Chalk Circle

SINGER.

Hear now the story of the trial
Concerning Governor Abashwili's child
And the determination of the true mother
By the famous test of the Chalk Circle.

[*Law court in Nuka.* IRONSHIRTS *lead* MICHAEL *across stage and out at the back.* IRONSHIRTS *hold* GRUSHA *back with their lances under the gateway until the child has been led through. Then she is admitted. She is accompanied by the former* GOVERNOR'S COOK. *Distant noises and a fire-red sky.*]

GRUSHA (*trying to hide*). He's brave, he can wash himself now.

COOK. You're lucky. It's not a real judge. It's Azdak, a drunk who doesn't know what he's doing. The biggest thieves have got by through him. Because he gets everything mixed up and the rich never offer him big enough bribes, the like of us sometimes do pretty well.

GRUSHA. I *need* luck right now.

COOK. Touch wood. (*She crosses herself.*) I'd better offer up another prayer that the judge may be drunk. (*She prays with motionless lips, while* GRUSHA *looks around, in vain, for the child.*) Why must you hold on to it at any price if it isn't yours? In days like these?

GRUSHA. He's mine. I brought him up.

COOK. Have you never thought what'd happen when she came back?

GRUSHA. At first I thought I'd give him to her. Then I thought she wouldn't come back.

COOK. And even a borrowed coat keeps a man warm, hm? (GRUSHA *nods.*) I'll swear to anything for you. You're a decent girl. (*She sees the soldier* SIMON SHASHAVA *approaching.*) You've done wrong by Simon, though. I've been talking with him. He just can't understand.

GRUSHA (*unaware of* SIMON'*s presence*). Right now I can't be bothered whether he understands or not!

COOK. He knows the child isn't yours, but you married and not free "till death you do part"—he can't understand *that.*

[GRUSHA *sees* SIMON *and greets him.*]

SIMON (*gloomily*). I wish the lady to know I will swear I am the father of the child.

GRUSHA (*low*). Thank you, Simon.

SIMON. At the same time I wish the lady to know my hands are not tied —nor are hers.

COOK. You needn't have said that. You know she's married.

SIMON. And it needs no rubbing in.

[*Enter an* IRONSHIRT.]

IRONSHIRT. Where's the judge? Has anyone seen the judge?

ANOTHER IRONSHIRT (*stepping forward*). The judge isn't here yet. Nothing but a bed and a pitcher in the whole house!

[*Exeunt* IRONSHIRTS.]

COOK. I hope nothing has happened to him. With any other judge you'd have as much chance as a chicken has teeth.

GRUSHA (*who has turned away and covered her face*). Stand in front of me. I shouldn't have come to Nuka. If I run into the Ironshirt, the one I hit over the head . . .

[*She screams. An* IRONSHIRT *had stopped and, turning his back, had been listening to her. He now wheels around. It is the* CORPORAL, *and he has a huge scar across his face.*]

IRONSHIRT (*in the gateway*). What's the matter, Shotta? Do you know her?

CORPORAL (*after staring for some time*). No.

IRONSHIRT. She's the one who stole the Abashwili child, or so they say. If you know anything about it you can make some money, Shotta.

[*Exit the* CORPORAL, *cursing.*]

COOK. Was it him? (GRUSHA *nods.*) I think he'll keep his mouth shut, or he'd be admitting he was after the child.

GRUSHA. I'd almost forgotten him.

[*Enter the* GOVERNOR'S WIFE, *followed by the* ADJUTANT *and two* LAWYERS.]

GOVERNOR'S WIFE. At least there are no common people here, thank God. I can't stand their smell. It always gives me migraine.

FIRST LAWYER. Madam, I must ask you to be careful what you say until we have another judge.

GOVERNOR'S WIFE. But I didn't say anything, Illo Shuboladze. I love the people with their simple straightforward minds. It's only that their smell brings on my migraine.

SECOND LAWYER. There won't be many spectators. The whole population is sitting at home behind locked doors because of the riots in the people's quarters.

GOVERNOR'S WIFE (*looking at* GRUSHA). Is that the creature?

FIRST LAWYER. Please, most gracious Natella Abashwili, abstain from invective until it is certain the Grand Duke has appointed a new judge and we're rid of the present one, who's about the lowest fellow ever seen in judge's gown. Things are all set to move, you see.

[*Enter* IRONSHIRTS *from the courtyard.*]

COOK. Her Grace would pull your hair out on the spot if she didn't know Azdak is for the poor. He goes by the face.

[IRONSHIRTS *begin fastening a rope to a beam.* AZDAK, *in chains, is led in, followed by* SHAUWA, *also in chains. The three* FARMERS *bring up the rear.*]

AN IRONSHIRT. Trying to run away, were you? (*He strikes* AZDAK.)

ONE FARMER. Off with his judge's gown before we string him up!

[IRONSHIRTS *and* FARMERS *tear off* AZDAK'S *gown. His torn underwear is visible. Then someone kicks him.*]

AN IRONSHIRT (*pushing him into someone else*). Want a load of justice? Here it is!

[*Accompanied by shouts of* "You take it!" *and* "Let me have him, Brother!" *they throw* AZDAK *back and forth until he collapses. Then he is lifted up and dragged under the noose.*]

GOVERNOR'S WIFE (*who, during this "ballgame," has clapped her hands hysterically*). I disliked that man from the moment I first saw him.

AZDAK (*covered with blood, panting*). I can't see. Give me a rag.

AN IRONSHIRT. What is it you want to see?

AZDAK. You, you dogs! (*He wipes the blood out of his eyes with his shirt.*) Good morning, dogs! How goes it, dogs! How's the dog world? Does it smell good? Got another boot for me to lick? Are you back at each other's throats, dogs?

[*Accompanied by a* CORPORAL, *a dust-covered* RIDER *enters. He takes some documents from a leather case, looks at them, then interrupts.*]

RIDER. Stop! I bring a dispatch from the Grand Duke, containing the latest appointments.

CORPORAL (*bellowing*). Atten—shun!

RIDER. Of the new judge it says: "We appoint a man whom we have to thank for saving a life indispensable to the country's welfare—a certain Azdak of Nuka." Which is he?

SHAUWA (*pointing*). That's him, Your Excellency.

CORPORAL (*bellowing*). What's going on here?

AN IRONSHIRT. I beg to report that His Honor Azdak was already His

Honor Azdak, but on these farmers' denunciation was pronounced the Grand Duke's enemy.

CORPORAL (*pointing at the* FARMERS). March them off! (*They are marched off. They bow all the time.*) See to it that His Honor Azdak is exposed to no more violence.

[*Exeunt* RIDER *and* CORPORAL.]

COOK (*to* SHAUWA). She clapped her hands! I hope he saw it!

FIRST LAWYER. It's a catastrophe.

[AZDAK *has fainted. Coming to, he is dressed again in judge's robes. He walks, swaying, toward the* IRONSHIRTS.]

AN IRONSHIRT. What does Your Honor desire?

AZDAK. Nothing, fellow dogs, or just an occasional boot to lick. (*To* SHAUWA.) I pardon you. (*He is unchained.*) Get me some red wine, the sweet kind. (SHAUWA *stumbles off.*) Get out of here, I've got to judge a case. (*Exeunt* IRONSHIRTS. SHAUWA *returns with a pitcher of wine.* AZDAK *gulps it down.*) Something for my backside. (SHAUWA *brings the Statute Book, puts it on the judge's chair.* AZDAK *sits on it.*) I accept.

[*The Prosecutors, among whom a worried council has been held, smile with relief. They whisper.*]

COOK. Oh dear!

SIMON. A well can't be filled with dew, they say.

LAWYERS (*approaching* AZDAK, *who stands up, expectantly*). A quite ridiculous case, Your Honor. The accused has abducted a child and refuses to hand it over.

AZDAK (*stretching out his hand, glancing at* GRUSHA). A most attractive person. (*He fingers the money, then sits down, satisfied.*) I declare the proceedings open and demand the whole truth. (*To* GRUSHA.) Especially from you.

FIRST LAWYER. High Court of Justice! Blood, as the popular saying goes, is thicker than water. This old adage . . .

AZDAK (*interrupting*). The Court wants to know the lawyers' fee.

FIRST LAWYER (*surprised*). I beg your pardon? (AZDAK, *smiling, rubs his thumb and index finger.*) Oh, I see. Five hundred piasters, Your Honor, to answer the Court's somewhat unusual question.

AZDAK. Did you hear? The question is unusual. I ask it because I listen in quite a different way when I know you're good.

FIRST LAWYER (*bowing*). Thank you, Your Honor. High Court of Justice, of all ties the ties of blood are strongest. Mother and child—is there a more intimate relationship? Can one tear a child from its mother? High Court of Justice, she has conceived it in the holy ecstasies of love. She has carried it in her womb. She has fed it with her blood. She has borne it with pain. High Court of Justice, it has been observed that the wild tigress, robbed of her young, roams restless through the mountains, shrunk to a shadow. Nature herself . . .

AZDAK (*interrupting, to* GRUSHA). What's your answer to all this and anything else that lawyer might have to say?

GRUSHA. He's mine.

AZDAK. Is that all? I hope you can prove it. Why should I assign the child to you in any case?

GRUSHA. I brought him up like the priest says "according to my best knowledge and conscience." I always found him something to eat. Most of the time he had a roof over his head. And I went to such trouble for him. I had expenses too. I didn't look out for my own comfort. I brought the child up to be friendly with everyone, and from the beginning taught him to work. As well as he could, that is. He's still very little.

FIRST LAWYER. Your Honor, it is significant that the girl herself doesn't claim any tie of blood between her and the child.

AZDAK. The Court takes note of that.

FIRST LAWYER. Thank you, Your Honor. And now permit a woman bowed in sorrow—who has already lost her husband and now has also to fear the loss of her child—to address a few words to you. The gracious Natella Abashwili is . . .

GOVERNOR'S WIFE (*quietly*). A most cruel fate, sir, forces me to describe to you the tortures of a bereaved mother's soul, the anxiety, the sleepless nights, the . . .

SECOND LAWYER (*bursting out*). It's outrageous the way this woman is being treated! Her husband's palace is closed to her! The revenue of her estates is blocked, and she is cold-bloodedly told that it's tied to the heir. She can't do a thing without that child. She can't even pay her lawyers! ! (*To the* FIRST LAWYER, *who, desperate about this outburst, makes frantic gestures to keep him from speaking.*) Dear Illo Shuboladze, surely it can be divulged now that the Abashwili estates are at stake?

FIRST LAWYER. Please, Honored Sandro Oboladze! We agreed . . . (*To* AZDAK.) Of course it is correct that the trial will also decide if our noble client can take over the Abashwili estates, which are rather extensive. I say "also" advisedly, for in the foreground stands the human tragedy of a mother, as Natella Abashwili very properly explained in the first words of her moving statement. Even if Michael Abashwili were not heir to the estates, he would still be the dearly beloved child of my client.

AZDAK. Stop! The Court is touched by the mention of estates. It's a proof of human feeling.

SECOND LAWYER. Thanks, Your Honor. Dear Illo Shuboladze, we can prove in any case that the woman who took the child is not the child's mother. Permit me to lay before the Court the bare facts. High Court of Justice, by an unfortunate chain of circumstances, Michael Abashwili was left behind on that Easter Sunday while his mother was making her escape. Grusha, a palace kitchen maid, was seen with the baby . . .

COOK. All her mistress was thinking of was what dresses she'd take along!

SECOND LAWYER (*unmoved*). Nearly a year later Grusha turned up in a mountain village with a baby and there entered into the state of matrimony with . . .

AZDAK. How'd you get to that mountain village?

GRUSHA. On foot, Your Honor. And he was mine.

SIMON. I'm the father, Your Honor.

COOK. I used to look after it for them, Your Honor. For five piasters.

SECOND LAWYER. This man is engaged to Grusha, High Court of Justice: his testimony is suspect.

AZDAK. Are you the man she married in the mountain village?

AZDAK (*to* GRUSHA). Why? (*Pointing at* SIMON.) Is he no good in bed? Tell the truth.

GRUSHA. We didn't get that far. I married because of the baby. So he'd have a roof over his head. (*Pointing at* SIMON.) He was in the war, Your Honor.

AZDAK. And now he wants you back again, huh?

SIMON. I wish to state in evidence . . .

GRUSHA (*angrily*). I am no longer free, Your Honor.

AZDAK. And the child, you claim, comes from whoring? (GRUSHA *doesn't answer.*) I'm going to ask you a question: What kind of child is he? A ragged little bastard? Or from a good family?

GRUSHA (*angrily*). He's an ordinary child.

AZDAK. I mean—did he have refined features from the beginning?

GRUSHA. He had a nose on his face.

AZDAK. A very significant comment! It has been said of me that I went out one time and sniffed at a rosebush before rendering a verdict—tricks like that are needed nowadays. Well, I'll make it short, and not listen to any more lies. (*To* GRUSHA.) Especially not yours. (*To all the accused.*) I can imagine what you've cooked up to cheat me! I know you people. You're swindlers.

GRUSHA (*suddenly*). I can understand your wanting to cut it short, now I've seen what you accepted!

AZDAK. Shut up! Did I accept anything from you?

GRUSHA (*while the* COOK *tries to restrain her*). I haven't got anything.

AZDAK. True. Quite true. From starvelings I never get a thing. I might just as well starve, myself. You want justice, but do you want to pay for it, hm? When you go to a butcher you know you have to pay, but you people go to a judge as if you were off to a funeral supper.

SIMON (*loudly*). When the horse was shod, the horsefly held out its leg, as the saying is.

AZDAK (*eagerly accepting the challenge*). Better a treasure in manure than a stone in a mountain stream.

SIMON. A fine day. Let's go fishing, said the angler to the worm.

AZDAK. I'm my own master, said the servant, and cut off his foot.

SIMON. I love you as a father, said the Czar to the peasants, and had the Czarevitch's head chopped off.

AZDAK. A fool's worst enemy is himself.

SIMON. However, a fart has no nose.

AZDAK. Fined ten piasters for indecent language in court! That'll teach you what justice is.

GRUSHA (*furiously*). A fine kind of justice! You play fast and loose with us because we don't talk as refined as that crowd with their lawyers.

AZDAK. That's true. You people are too dumb. It's only right you should get it in the neck.

GRUSHA. You want to hand the child over to her, and she wouldn't even know how to keep it dry, she's so "refined"! You know about as much about justice as I do!

AZDAK. There's something in that. I'm an ignorant man. Haven't even a decent pair of pants on under this gown. Look! With me, everything goes on food and drink—I was educated in a convent. Incidentally, I'll fine you ten piasters for contempt of court. And you're a very silly girl, to turn me against you, instead of making eyes at me and wiggling your backside a little to keep me in a good temper. Twenty piasters!

GRUSHA. Even if it was thirty, I'd tell you what I think of your justice, you drunken onion! (*Incoherently.*) How dare you talk to me like the cracked Isaiah on the church window? As if you were somebody? For you weren't born to this. You weren't born to rap your own mother on the knuckles if she swipes a little bowl of salt someplace. Aren't you ashamed of yourself when you see how I tremble before you? You've made yourself their servant so no one will take their houses from them—houses they had stolen! Since when have houses belonged to the bedbugs? But you're on the watch, or they couldn't drag our men into their wars! You bribetaker!

[AZDAK *half gets up, starts beaming. With his little hammer he halfheartedly knocks on the table as if to get silence. As* GRUSHA'*s scolding continues, he only beats time with his hammer.*]

I've no respect for you. No more than for a thief or a bandit with a knife! You can do what you want. You can take the child away from me, a hundred against one, but I tell you one thing: only extortioners should be chosen for a profession like yours, and men who rape children! As punishment! Yes, let *them* sit in judgment on their fellow creatures. It is worse than to hang from the gallows.

AZDAK (*sitting down*). Now it'll be thirty! And I won't go on squabbling with you—we're not in a tavern. What'd happen to my dignity as a judge? Anyway, I've lost interest in your case. Where's the couple who wanted a divorce? (*To* SHAUWA.) Bring 'em in. This case is adjourned for fifteen minutes.

FIRST LAWYER (*to the* GOVERNOR'S WIFE). Even without using the rest of the evidence, Madam, we have the verdict in the bag.

COOK (*to* GRUSHA). You've gone and spoiled your chances with him. You won't get the child now.

GOVERNOR'S WIFE. Shalva, my smelling salts!

[*Enter a very old couple.*]

AZDAK. I accept. (*The old couple don't understand.*) I hear you want to be divorced. How long have you been together?

OLD WOMAN. Forty years, Your Honor.

AZDAK. And why do you want a divorce?

OLD MAN. We don't like each other, Your Honor.

AZDAK. Since when?

OLD WOMAN. Oh, from the very beginning, Your Honor.

AZDAK. I'll think about your request and render my verdict when I'm through with the other case. (SHAUWA *leads them back.*) I need the child. (*He beckons* GRUSHA *to him and bends not unkindly toward her.*) I've noticed you have a soft spot for justice. I don't believe he's your child, but if he *were* yours, woman, wouldn't you want him to be rich? You'd only have to say he wasn't yours, and he'd have a palace and many horses in his stable and many beggars on his doorstep and many soldiers in his service and many petitioners in his courtyard, wouldn't he? What do you say—don't you want him to be rich?

[GRUSHA *is silent.*]

SINGER.

Hear now what the angry girl thought but did not say:

Had he golden shoes to wear
He'd be cruel as a bear
Evil would his life disgrace.
He'd laugh in my face.

Carrying a heart of flint
Is too troublesome a stint.
Being powerful and bad
Is hard on a lad.

Then let hunger be his foe!
Hungry men and women, no.
Let him fear the darksome night
But not daylight!

AZDAK. I think I understand you, woman.

GRUSHA (*suddenly and loudly*). I won't give him up. I've raised him, and he knows me.

[*Enter* SHAUWA *with the* CHILD.]

GOVERNOR'S WIFE. He's in rags!

GRUSHA. That's not true. But I wasn't given time to put his good shirt on.

GOVERNOR'S WIFE. He must have been in a pigsty.

GRUSHA (*furiously*). I'm not a pig, but there are some who are! Where did you leave your baby?

GOVERNOR'S WIFE. I'll show you, you vulgar creature! (*She is about to throw herself on* GRUSHA, *but is restrained by her lawyers.*) She's a criminal, she must be whipped. Immediately!

SECOND LAWYER (*holding his hand over her mouth*). Natella Abashwili, you promised . . . Your Honor, the plaintiff's nerves . . .

AZDAK. Plaintiff and defendant! The Court has listened to your case, and has come to no decision as to who the real mother is; therefore, I, the judge, am obliged to *choose* a mother for the child. I'll make a test. Shauwa, get a piece of chalk and draw a circle on the floor. (SHAUWA *does so.*) Now place the child in the center. (SHAUWA *puts* MICHAEL, *who smiles at* GRUSHA, *in the center of the circle.*) Stand near the circle, both of you. (*The* GOVERNOR'S WIFE *and* GRUSHA *step up to the circle.*) Now each of you take the child by one hand. (*They do so.*) The true mother is she who can pull the child out of the circle.

SECOND LAWYER (*quickly*). High Court of Justice, I object! The fate of the great Abashwili estates, which are tied to the child, as the heir, should not be made dependent on such a doubtful duel. In addition, my client does not command the strength of this person, who is accustomed to physical work.

AZDAK. She looks pretty well fed to me. Pull! (*The* GOVERNOR'S WIFE *pulls the* CHILD *out of the circle on her side;* GRUSHA *has let go and stands aghast.*) What's the matter with you? You didn't pull.

GRUSHA. I didn't hold on to him.

FIRST LAWYER (*congratulating the* GOVERNOR'S WIFE). What did I say! The ties of blood!

GRUSHA (*running to* AZDAK). Your Honor, I take back everything I said against you. I ask your forgiveness. But could I keep him till he can speak all the words? He knows a few.

AZDAK. Don't influence the Court. I bet you only know about twenty words yourself. All right, I'll make the test once more, just to be certain. (*The two women take up their positions again.*) Pull! (*Again* GRUSHA *lets go of the* CHILD.)

GRUSHA (*in despair*). I brought him up! Shall I also tear him to bits? I can't!

AZDAK (*rising*). And in this manner the Court has determined the true mother. (*To* GRUSHA.) Take your child and be off. I advise you not to stay in the city with him. (*To the* GOVERNOR'S WIFE.) And you disappear before I fine you for fraud. Your estates fall to the city. They'll be converted into a playground for the children. They need one, and I've decided it'll be called after me: Azdak's Garden.

[*The* GOVERNOR'S WIFE *has fainted and is carried out by the*

LAWYERS *and the* ADJUTANT. GRUSHA *stands motionless.* SHAUWA *leads the* CHILD *toward her.*]

Now I'll take off this judge's gown—it's got too hot for me. I'm not cut out for a hero. In token of farewell I invite you all to a little dance in the meadow outside. Oh, I'd almost forgotten something in my excitement . . . to sign the divorce decree. (*Using the judge's chair as a table, he writes something on a piece of paper, and prepares to leave. Dance music has started.*)

SHAUWA (*having read what is on the paper*). But that's not right. You've not divorced the old people. You've divorced Grusha!

AZDAK. Divorced the wrong couple? What a pity! And I never retract! If I did, how could we keep order in the land? (*To the old couple.*) I'll invite you to my party instead. You don't mind dancing with each other, do you? (*To* GRUSHA *and* SIMON.) I've got forty piasters coming from you.

SIMON (*pulling out his purse*). Cheap at the price, Your Honor. And many thanks.

AZDAK (*pocketing the cash*). I'll be needing this.

GRUSHA (*to* MICHAEL). So we'd better leave the city tonight, Michael? (*To* SIMON.) You like him?

SIMON. With my respects, I like him.

GRUSHA. Now I can tell you: I took him because on that Easter Sunday I got engaged to you. So he's a child of love. Michael, let's dance.

[*She dances with* MICHAEL, SIMON *dances with the* COOK, *the old couple with each other.* AZDAK *stands lost in thought. The dancers soon hide him from view. Occasionally he is seen, but less and less as more couples join the dance.*]

SINGER.

And after that evening Azdak vanished and was never seen again.
The people of Grusinia did not forget him but long remembered
The period of his judging as a brief golden age,
Almost an age of justice.

[*All the couples dance off.* AZDAK *has disappeared.*]

But you, you who have listened to the Story of the Chalk Circle,
Take note what men of old concluded:
That what there is shall go to those who are good for it,
Children to the motherly, that they prosper,
Carts to good drivers, that they be driven well,
The valley to the waterers, that it yield fruit.

CRITICAL COMMENTARY

No one cares whether they raise goats or grapes in Nuka, wherever that may be, but peasants are wonderful, especially when they are invented by Bertolt Brecht. They are even better after one has been shut in with Ibsen's and Pirandello's worriers. Gone are the Freudian blues, the exhausting introspections, the reductive obscurities, the clues that never lead to any good, and in their place are the fine, loose stories of Grusha and Azdak. Hannah Arendt guesses that Brecht was something of a peasant himself. His life (1898–1956) covered many horrors, but,

> his line "If my luck expires, I am lost" betrays an enormous calm and imperturbable certainty of self-reliance. . . . He never let himself be seduced by purely psychological considerations and always saw the comedy of a sentimentality which would like to measure the maelstrom of events with the yardstick of individual aspirations. It is not only psychological suicide, it is also comic, when the jobless man feels the international catastrophe of unemployment as a personal failure, or when people in the face of the catastrophe of war complain that they are no longer able to become well-rounded personalities. . . . (Peter Demetz, ed., *Brecht* [Twentieth Century Views], 1962, pp. 46–47.)

Peasants are also a good subject because we all know a good deal about them and are glad to cooperate in their creation. Peasants are earthy, shrewd, and goodhearted. They never fuss about themselves or the food or the accommodations. They have been around for a long time. The Watchman in *Agamemnon* came of peasant stock. They are clever in a straightforward, simple, innocent, human way. Their proverbs are better than our proverbs. In short, peasants easily and quickly become stage peasants. This of course relates them to characters like Barabas and Falstaff, the stage Jew and the stage coward. What "stage" really means in this context has been much discussed. One notices that Brecht's peasants, like Barabas and Falstaff, never actually get hurt. They live on a diet that makes Falstaff's look balanced; and they are reported to be halved and even quartered, but they seem to be naturally indestructible. Is this because they too are stage characters in a farcical comedy? Are the even stagier aristocrats "stagey" in the same way? They are so predictable, so paper-thin that they are ridiculous. Is this the point, that real aristocrats are ridiculous? Is the opposition in the play between peasants and aristocrats the basic one? Brecht himself gave some thought to this general subject, and he, or his critics, discussed it under the heading of "alienation" and the "A-effect." One of the effects involved is how we feel about "stage" characters, to what extent we are engaged or detached. Do we respond to the characters as if they were "real" people? Are they being sampled and demonstrated rather than lived? Is the effect here different from other plays where the full lives of the characters are of course not acted out either? If there is a difference, is it a result of the use of a story teller? Is his occasionally speeded-up scenario farcical like the breathtaking action in *The Jew of Malta*?

Brecht felt that answers to questions like these are properly answered on the stage, and clearly it takes great tact to catch and act the tone and mode of *The Caucasian Chalk Circle*. This is the point of Ronald Bryden's review of a recent production at Chichester, England (*The London Observer,* May 18, 1969):

> a straight-forward piece of sentimental story-telling, with lots of picturesque peasant jollity and little attempt to guide the performance into Brecht's style or moral pattern. There's no effort, for instance, to make the playing bring out the pleasure of the telling, as opposed to the story itself. The episode in which the fleeing kitchen-girl Grusha clambers with the baby she's rescued across a rotten rope-bridge is milked for excitement rather than the actress's skill in miming it. Heather Sears has the skill, all right, but by aiming at sincerity rather than artifice she makes the kitchen-girl a kind of wistful Cinderella rather than the comic maternal turnip Brecht created.

Do you think that Ronald Bryden has it quite right himself? Is not Grusha "sincere"? Is "turnip" the right word? What happens to the excitement if the actress merely mimes it? And is Grusha ever really in danger at any time? Bryden admired Topol's performance as Azdak: "Scalp shaven, grinning wolfishly, shooting keen brown glances from one woman to the other, his Azdak is not so much a character as an essay in a whole lost theatrical style, in which manner counts for more than detail and breadth more than realism." Does this sound right? Or is this portrayal of Azdak too simple?

Certainly when one starts to play around with the idea of peasants, one soon finds that it is not a simple subject after all. It spawns problems too. What is the relation between the peasant philosophy of live-and-let-live, the accommodation to life and to each other, the secret understanding of the poor, and just plain corruption? Are all peasants equally shrewd in the same way or is there among them a range of shrewdness? Is Grusha ever shrewd? Is Azdak shrewd or does he parody shrewdness?

Is the naive as complex as the ironic? Brecht is reported to have denounced people, Marxist or bourgeois, who try "to put the vital multiplicity, the innumerable shadings, the all-moving contradictions and absurdities into the same old slot." He equated the naive with the many-sided, and the many-sided with the concrete. Perhaps the most basic and the most appealing or seductive problem is the relation of simplicity to wisdom. Do Grusha and Azdak in their different ways possess a simplicity that gets to the heart of things? And what is the bearing on this of Brecht's remark that a "place swept clean is also an empty place" and the satirical proverb-matching between Simon and Azdak? Ronald Gray wonders about the problem in these sentences: Azdak "denies all the virtues, mocks at repentance and charity, ridicules courage, and, strangely enough, he gets our sympathy in the process." (Like Falstaff?) "Brecht persuades us not quite to believe in Grusha, to accept her as a creation of art, and to look beyond her to a reality which in part we create ourselves." (Peter Demetz, ed., *Brecht* [Twentieth Century Views], 1962, pp. 152, 155.) When we do so, is it daydreaming or a moral act?

Useful Criticism

Demetz, Peter, ed. *Brecht** (Twentieth Century Views). Englewood Cliffs, N.J.: Prentice-Hall, 1962.

Esslin, Martin. *Brecht: The Man and His Work.* Garden City, N.Y.: Doubleday, 1960.

Gray, Ronald. *Bertolt Brecht.* New York: Grove Press, 1961.

* Available in paperback.

THE GLASS MENAGERIE

Tennessee Williams

CHARACTERS

AMANDA WINGFIELD (the mother), a little woman of great but confused vitality clinging frantically to another time and place. Her characterization must be carefully created, not copied from type. She is not paranoiac, but her life is paranoia. There is much to admire in Amanda, and as much to love and pity as there is to laugh at. Certainly she has endurance and a kind of heroism, and though her foolishness makes her unwittingly cruel at times, there is tenderness in her slight person.

LAURA WINGFIELD (her daughter). Amanda, having failed to establish contact with reality, continues to live vitally in her illusions, but Laura's situation is even graver. A childhood illness has left her crippled, one leg slightly shorter than the other, and held in a brace. This defect need not be more than suggested on the stage. Stemming from this, Laura's separation increases till she is like a piece of her own glass collection, too exquisitely fragile to move from the shelf.

TOM WINGFIELD (her son and the narrator of the play). A poet with a job in a warehouse. His nature is not remorseless, but to escape from a trap he has to act without pity.

JIM O'CONNOR (the gentleman caller), a nice, ordinary, young man.

SCENE

An Alley in St. Louis.

TIME

Now and the Past.

Scene 1

The Wingfield apartment is in the rear of the building, one of those vast hive-like conglomerations of cellular living-units that flower as warty growths in overcrowded urban centers of lower middle-class population and are symptomatic of the impulse of this largest and fundamentally enslaved section of American society to avoid fluidity and differentiation and to exist and function as one interfused mass of automatism.

The apartment faces an alley and is entered by a fire-escape, a structure whose name is a touch of accidental poetic truth, for all of these huge buildings are always burning with the slow and implacable fires of human desperation. The fire-escape is included in the set—that is, the landing of it and steps descending from it.

The scene is memory and is therefore nonrealistic. Memory takes a lot of poetic license. It omits some details; others are exaggerated, according to the emotional value of the articles it touches, for memory is seated predominantly in the heart. The interior is therefore rather dim and poetic.

At the rise of the curtain, the audience is faced with the dark, grim rear wall of the Wingfield tenement. This building, which runs parallel to the footlights, is flanked on both sides by dark, narrow alleys which run into murky canyons of tangled clotheslines, garbage cans and the sinister latticework of neighboring fire-escapes. It is up and down these side alleys that exterior entrances and exits are made, during the play. At the end of TOM'S *opening commentary, the dark tenement wall slowly reveals (by means of a transparency) the interior of the ground floor Wingfield apartment.*

Downstage is the living room, which also serves as a sleeping room for LAURA, *the sofa unfolding to make her bed. Upstage, center, and divided by a wide arch or second proscenium with transparent faded portieres (or second curtain), is the dining room. In an old-fashioned what-*

not in the living room are seen scores of transparent glass animals. A blown-up photograph of the father hangs on the wall of the living room, facing the audience, to the left of the archway. It is the face of a very handsome young man in a doughboy's First World War cap. He is gallantly smiling, ineluctably smiling, as if to say, "I will be smiling forever."

The audience hears and sees the opening scene in the dining room through both the transparent fourth wall of the building and the transparent gauze portieres of the dining-room arch. It is during this revealing scene that the fourth wall slowly ascends, out of sight. This transparent exterior wall is not brought down again until the very end of the play, during TOM'S *final speech.*

The narrator is an undisguised convention of the play. He takes whatever license with dramatic convention as is convenient to his purposes.

TOM *enters dressed as a merchant sailor from alley, stage left, and strolls across the front of the stage to the fire-escape. There he stops and lights a cigarette. He addresses the audience.*

TOM. Yes, I have tricks in my pocket, I have things up my sleeve. But I am the opposite of a stage magician. He gives you illusion that has the appearance of truth. I give you truth in the pleasant disguise of illusion.

To begin with, I turn back time. I reverse it to that quaint period, the thirties, when the huge middle class of America was matriculating in a school for the blind. Their eyes had failed them, or they had failed their eyes, and so they were having their fingers pressed forcibly down on the fiery Braille alphabet of a dissolving economy.

In Spain there was revolution. Here there was only shouting and confusion.

In Spain there was Guernica. Here there were disturbances of labor, sometimes pretty violent, in otherwise peaceful cities such as Chicago, Cleveland, Saint Louis. . . .

This is the social background of the play. (*Music.*)

The play is memory.

Being a memory play, it is dimly lighted, it is sentimental, it is not realistic.

In memory everything seems to happen to music. That explains the fiddle in the wings.

I am the narrator of the play, and also a character in it.

The other characters are my mother, Amanda, my sister, Laura, and a gentleman caller who appears in the final scenes.

He is the most realistic character in the play, being an emissary from a world of reality that we were somehow set apart from.

But since I have a poet's weakness for symbols, I am using this character also as a symbol; he is the long delayed but always expected something that we live for.

There is a fifth character in the play who doesn't appear except in this larger-than-life-size photograph over the mantel.

This is our father who left us a long time ago.

He was a telephone man who fell in love with long distances; he gave up his job with the telephone company and skipped the light fantastic out of town. . . .

The last we heard of him was a picture post-card from Mazatlan, on the Pacific coast of Mexico, containing a message of two words—

"Hello—Good-bye!" and no address.

I think the rest of the play will explain itself. . . .

[AMANDA'*s voice becomes audible through the portieres.* LEGEND ON SCREEN: "OÙ SONT LES NEIGES?" [1] *He divides the portieres and enters the upstage area.* AMANDA *and* LAURA *are seated at a drop-leaf table. Eating is indicated by gestures without food or utensils.* AMANDA *faces the audience,* TOM *and* LAURA *are seated in profile. The interior has lit up softly and through the scrim we see* AMANDA *and* LAURA *seated at the table in the upstage area.*]

AMANDA (*calling*). Tom?

TOM. Yes, Mother.

AMANDA. We can't say grace until you come to the table!

TOM. Coming, Mother. (*He bows slightly and withdraws, reappearing a few moments later in his place at the table.*)

AMANDA (*to her son*). Honey, don't *push* with your *fingers.* If you have to push with something, the thing to push with is a crust of bread. And chew—chew! Animals have sections in their stomachs which enable them to digest food without mastication, but human beings are supposed to chew their food before they swallow it down. Eat food leisurely, son, and really enjoy it. A well-cooked meal has lots of delicate flavors that have to be held in the mouth for appreciation. So chew your food and give your salivary glands a chance to function!

[TOM *deliberately lays his imaginary fork down and pushes his chair back from the table.*]

TOM. I haven't enjoyed one bite of this dinner because of your constant directions on how to eat it. It's you that makes me rush through meals with your hawk-like attention to every bite I take. Sickening—spoils my appetite—all this discussion of—animals' secretion—salivary glands—mastication!

AMANDA (*lightly*). Temperament like a Metropolitan star! (*He rises and crosses downstage.*) You're not excused from the table.

TOM. I'm getting a cigarette.

AMANDA. You smoke too much.

[LAURA *rises.*]

LAURA. I'll bring in the blanc mange.

[1] "Where are the snows of yesteryear?"—the famous tribute to beautiful women written by the fifteenth-century lyric poet François Villon.

[*He remains standing with his cigarette by the portieres during the following.*]

AMANDA (*rising*). No, sister, no, sister—you be the lady this time and I'll be the darky.

LAURA. I'm already up.

AMANDA. Resume your seat, little sister—I want you to stay fresh and pretty—for gentlemen callers!

LAURA. I'm not expecting any gentlemen callers.

AMANDA (*crossing out to kitchenette. Airily*). Sometimes they come when they are least expected! Why, I remember one Sunday afternoon in Blue Mountain—(*Enters kitchenette.*)

TOM. I know what's coming!

LAURA. Yes. But let her tell it.

TOM. Again?

LAURA. She loves to tell it.

[AMANDA *returns with bowl of dessert.*]

AMANDA. One Sunday afternoon in Blue Mountain—your mother received—*seventeen!*—gentlemen callers! Why, sometimes there weren't chairs enough to accommodate them all. We had to send the nigger over to bring in folding chairs from the parish house.

TOM (*remaining at portieres*). How did you entertain those gentlemen callers?

AMANDA. I understood the art of conversation!

TOM. I bet you could talk.

AMANDA. Girls in those days *knew* how to talk, I can tell you.

TOM. Yes?

[IMAGE: AMANDA AS A GIRL ON A PORCH, GREETING CALLERS.]

AMANDA. They knew how to entertain their gentlemen callers. It wasn't enough for a girl to be possessed of a pretty face and a graceful figure—although I wasn't slighted in either respect. She also needed to have a nimble wit and a tongue to meet all occasions.

TOM. What did you talk about?

AMANDA. Things of importance going on in the world! Never anything coarse or common or vulgar. (*She addresses* TOM *as though he were seated in the vacant chair at the table though he remains by portieres. He plays this scene as though he held the book*) My callers were gentlemen—all! Among my callers were some of the most prominent young planters of the Mississippi Delta—planters and sons of planters! (TOM *motions for music and a spot of light on* AMANDA. *Her eyes lift, her face glows, her voice becomes rich and elegiac.* SCREEN LEGEND: "OÙ SONT LES NEIGES?")

There was young Champ Laughlin, who later became vice-president of the Delta Planters Bank.

Hadley Stevenson, who was drowned in Moon Lake and left his widow one hundred and fifty thousand in Government bonds.

There were the Cutrere brothers, Wesley and Bates. Bates was one of my bright particular beaux! He got in a quarrel with that wild Wainwright boy. They shot it out on the floor of Moon Lake Casino. Bates was shot through the stomach. Died in the ambulance on his way to Memphis. His widow was also well-provided for, came into eight or ten thousand acres, that's all. She married him on the rebound—never loved her—carried my picture on him the night he died!

And there was that boy that every girl in the Delta had set her cap for! That beautiful, brilliant young Fitzhugh boy from Greene County!

TOM. What did he leave his widow?

AMANDA. He never married! Gracious, you talk as though all of my old admirers had turned up their toes to the daisies!

TOM. Isn't this the first you've mentioned that still survives?

AMANDA. That Fitzhugh boy went North and made a fortune—came to be known as the Wolf of Wall Street! He had the Midas touch, whatever he touched turned to gold!

And I could have been Mrs. Duncan J. Fitzhugh, mind you! But—I picked your *father!*

LAURA (*rising*). Mother, let me clear the table.

AMANDA. No, dear, you go in front and study your typewriter chart. Or practice your shorthand a little. Stay fresh and pretty!—It's almost time for our gentlemen callers to start arriving. (*She flounces girlishly toward the kitchenette.*) How many do you suppose we're going to entertain this afternoon?

[TOM *throws down the paper and jumps up with a groan.*]

LAURA (*alone in the dining room*). I don't believe we're going to receive any, Mother.

AMANDA (*reappearing, airily*). What? No one—not one? You must be joking! (LAURA *nervously echoes her laugh. She slips in a fugitive manner through the half-open portieres and draws them gently behind her. A shaft of very clear light is thrown on her face against the faded tapestry of the curtains.* MUSIC: "THE GLASS MENAGERIE" UNDER FAINTLY. *Lightly.*) Not one gentleman caller? It can't be true! There must be a flood, there must have been a tornado!

LAURA. It isn't a flood, it's not a tornado, Mother. I'm just not popular like you were in Blue Mountain. . . . (TOM *utters another groan.* LAURA *glances at him with a faint, apologetic smile. Her voice catching a little.*) Mother's afraid I'm going to be an old maid.

[*The Scene Dims Out with "Glass Menagerie" Music.*]

Scene 2

LEGEND: "LAURA, HAVEN'T YOU EVER LIKED SOME BOY?"

On the dark stage the screen is lighted with the image of blue roses.

Gradually LAURA'S *figure becomes apparent and the screen goes out. The music subsides.*

LAURA *is seated in the delicate ivory chair at the small clawfoot table.*

She wears a dress of soft violet material for a kimono—her hair tied back from her forehead with a ribbon.

She is washing and polishing her collection of glass.

AMANDA *appears on the fire-escape steps. At the sound of her ascent,* LAURA *catches her breath, thrusts the bowl of ornaments away and seats herself stiffly before the diagram of the typewriter keyboard as though it held her spellbound.*

Something has happened to AMANDA. *It is written in her face as she climbs to the landing: a look that is grim and hopeless and a little absurd.*

She has on one of those cheap or imitation velvety-looking cloth coats with imitation fur collar. Her hat is five or six years old, one of those dreadful cloche hats that were worn in the late twenties, and she is clasping an enormous black patent-leather pocketbook with nickel clasps and initials. This is her full-dress outfit, the one she usually wears to the D.A.R.

Before entering she looks through the door.

She purses her lips, opens her eyes very wide, rolls them upward and shakes her head.

Then she slowly lets herself in the door. Seeing her mother's expression LAURA *touches her lips with a nervous gesture.*

LAURA. Hello, Mother, I was— (*She makes a nervous gesture toward the chart on the wall.* AMANDA *leans against the shut door and stares at* LAURA *with a martyred look.*)

AMANDA. Deception? Deception? (*She slowly removes her hat and gloves, continuing the sweet suffering stare. She lets the hat and gloves fall on the floor—a bit of acting.*)

LAURA (*shakily*). How was the D.A.R. meeting? (AMANDA *slowly opens her purse and removes a dainty white handkerchief which she shakes out delicately and delicately touches to her lips and nostrils.*) Didn't you go to the D.A.R. meeting, Mother?

AMANDA (*faintly, almost inaudibly*). —No.—No. (*Then more forcibly.*) I did not have the strength—to go to the D.A.R. In fact, I did not have the courage! I wanted to find a hole in the ground and hide myself in it forever! (*She crosses slowly to the wall and removes the diagram of the typewriter keyboard. She holds it in front of her for a second, staring at it sweetly and sorrowfully—then bites her lips and tears it in two pieces.*)

LAURA (*faintly*). Why did you do that, Mother? (AMANDA *repeats the same procedure with the chart of the Gregg Alphabet.*) Why are you—

AMANDA. Why? Why? How old are you, Laura?

LAURA. Mother, you know my age.

AMANDA. I thought that you were an adult; it seems that I was mistaken.

[*She crosses slowly to the sofa and sinks down and stares at* LAURA.]

LAURA. Please don't stare at me, Mother.

[AMANDA *closes her eyes and lowers her head. Count ten.*]

AMANDA. What are we going to do, what is going to become of us, what is the future?

[*Count ten.*]

LAURA. Has something happened, Mother? (AMANDA *draws a long breath and takes out the handkerchief again. Dabbing process.*) Mother, has—something happened?

AMANDA. I'll be all right in a minute, I'm just bewildered—(*Count five.*) —by life. . . .

LAURA. Mother, I wish that you would tell me what's happened!

AMANDA. As you know, I was supposed to be inducted into my office at the D.A.R. this afternoon. (IMAGE: A SWARM OF TYPEWRITERS.) But I stopped off at Rubicam's Business College to speak to your teachers about your having a cold and ask them what progress they thought you were making down there.

LAURA. Oh. . . .

AMANDA. I went to the typing instructor and introduced myself as your mother. She didn't know who you were. Wingfield, she said. We don't have any such student enrolled at the school!

I assured her she did, that you had been going to classes since early in January.

"I wonder," she said, "if you could be talking about that terribly shy little girl who dropped out of school after only a few days' attendance?"

"No," I said, "Laura, my daughter, has been going to school every day for the past six weeks!"

"Excuse me," she said. She took the attendance book out and there was your name, unmistakably printed, and all the dates you were absent until they decided that you had dropped out of school.

I still said, "No, there must have been some mistake! There must have been some mix-up in the records!"

And she said, "No—I remember her perfectly now. Her hands shook so that she couldn't hit the right keys! The first time we gave a speed-test, she broke down completely—was sick at the stomach and almost had to be carried into the wash-room! After that morning she never showed up any more. We phoned the house but never got any answer" —while I was working at Famous and Barr, I suppose, demonstrating those— Oh!

I felt so weak I could barely keep on my feet!

I had to sit down while they got me a glass of water!

Fifty dollars' tuition, all of our plans—my hopes and ambitions for you—just gone up the spout, just gone up the spout like that. (LAURA *draws a long breath and gets awkwardly to her feet. She crosses to the victrola and winds it up.*) What are you doing?

LAURA. Oh! (*She releases the handle and returns to her seat.*)

AMANDA. Laura, where have you been going when you've gone out pretending that you were going to business college?

LAURA. I've just been going out walking.

AMANDA. That's not true.

LAURA. It is. I just went walking.

AMANDA. Walking? Walking? In winter? Deliberately courting pneumonia in that light coat? Where did you walk to, Laura?

LAURA. All sorts of places—mostly in the park.

AMANDA. Even after you'd started catching that cold?

LAURA. It was the lesser of two evils, Mother. (IMAGE: WINTER SCENE IN PARK.) I couldn't go back up. I—threw up—on the floor!

AMANDA. From half past seven till after five every day you mean to tell me you walked around in the park, because you wanted to make me think that you were still going to Rubicam's Business College?

LAURA. It wasn't as bad as it sounds. I went inside places to get warmed up.

AMANDA. Inside where?

LAURA. I went in the art museum and the bird-houses at the Zoo. I visited the penguins every day! Sometimes I did without lunch and went to the movies. Lately I've been spending most of my afternoons in the Jewel-box, that big glass house where they raise the tropical flowers.

AMANDA. You did all this to deceive me, just for deception? (LAURA *looks down.*) Why?

LAURA. Mother, when you're disappointed, you get that awful suffering look on your face, like the picture of Jesus' mother in the museum!

AMANDA. Hush!

LAURA. I couldn't face it.

[*Pause. A whisper of strings.* LEGEND: "THE CRUST OF HUMILITY."]

AMANDA (*hopelessly fingering the huge pocketbook*). So what are we going to do the rest of our lives? Stay home and watch the parades go by? Amuse ourselves with the glass menagerie, darling? Eternally play those worn-out phonograph records your father left as a painful reminder of him?

We won't have a business career—we've given that up because it gave us nervous indigestion! (*Laughs wearily.*) What is there left but dependency all our lives? I know so well what becomes of unmarried women who aren't prepared to occupy a position. I've seen such pitiful cases in the South—barely tolerated spinsters living upon the grudging patronage of sister's husband or brother's wife!—stuck away in some little mouse-trap of a room—encouraged by one in-law to visit another—little birdlike women without any nest—eating the crust of humility all their life!

Is that the future that we've mapped out for ourselves?

I swear it's the only alternative I can think of!

It isn't a very pleasant alternative, is it?

Of course—some girls *do marry.* (LAURA *twists her hands nervously.*) Haven't you ever liked some boy?

LAURA. Yes. I liked one once. (*Rises.*) I came across his picture a while ago.

AMANDA (*with some interest*). He gave you his picture?

LAURA. No, it's in the year-book.

AMANDA (*disappointed*). Oh—a high-school boy.

[SCREEN IMAGE: JIM AS HIGH-SCHOOL HERO BEARING A SILVER CUP.]

LAURA. Yes. His name was Jim. (LAURA *lifts the heavy annual from the clawfoot table.*) Here he is in *The Pirates of Penzance.*

AMANDA (*absently*). The what?

LAURA. The operetta the senior class put on. He had a wonderful voice and we sat across the aisle from each other Mondays, Wednesdays and Fridays in the Aud. Here he is with the silver cup for debating! See his grin?

AMANDA (*absently*). He must have had a jolly disposition.

LAURA. He used to call me—Blue Roses.

[IMAGE: BLUE ROSES.]

AMANDA. Why did he call you such a name as that?

LAURA. When I had that attack of pleurosis—he asked me what was the matter when I came back. I said pleurosis—he thought that I said Blue Roses! So that's what he always called me after that. Whenever he saw me, he'd holler, "Hello, Blue Roses!" I didn't care for the girl that he went out with. Emily Meisenbach. Emily was the best-dressed girl at Soldan. She never struck me, though, as being sincere . . . It says in the Personal Section—they're engaged. That's—six years ago! They must be married by now.

AMANDA. Girls that aren't cut out for business careers usually wind up married to some nice man. (*Gets up with a spark of revival.*) Sister, that's what you'll do!

[LAURA *utters a startled, doubtful laugh. She reaches quickly for a piece of glass.*]

LAURA. But, Mother—

AMANDA. Yes? (*Crossing to photograph.*)

LAURA (*in a tone of frightened apology*). I'm—crippled!

[IMAGE: SCREEN.]

AMANDA. Nonsense! Laura, I've told you never, never to use that word. Why, you're not crippled, you just have a little defect—hardly noticeable, even! When people have some slight disadvantage like that, they cultivate other things to make up for it—develop charm—and vivacity—and—*charm!* That's all you have to do! (*She turns again to the photograph.*) One thing your father had *plenty of*—was *charm!*

[TOM *motions to the fiddle in the wings.*]

[*The Scene Fades Out with Music.*]

Scene 3

LEGEND ON SCREEN: "AFTER THE FIASCO—"

TOM *speaks from the fire-escape landing.*

TOM. After the fiasco at Rubicam's Business College, the idea of getting a gentleman caller for Laura began to play a more and more important part in Mother's calculations.

It became an obsession. Like some archetype of the universal unconscious, the image of the gentleman caller haunted our small apartment.

[IMAGE: YOUNG MAN AT DOOR WITH FLOWERS.]

An evening at home rarely passed without some allusion to this image, this spectre, this hope. . . .

Even when he wasn't mentioned, his presence hung in Mother's preoccupied look and in my sister's frightened, apologetic manner—hung like a sentence passed upon the Wingfields!

Mother was a woman of action as well as words.

She began to take the logical steps in the planned direction.

Late that winter and in the early spring—realizing that extra money would be needed to properly feather the nest and plume the bird—she conducted a vigorous campaign on the telephone, roping in subscribers to one of those magazines for matrons called *The Homemaker's Companion,* the type of journal that features the serialized sublimations of ladies of letters who think in terms of delicate cuplike breasts, slim, tapering waists, rich, creamy thighs, eyes like wood-smoke in autumn, fingers that soothe and caress like strains of music, bodies as powerful as Etruscan sculpture.

[SCREEN IMAGE: GLAMOR MAGAZINE COVER. AMANDA *enters with phone on long extension cord. She is spotted in the dim stage.*]

AMANDA. Ida Scott? This is Amanda Wingfield!

We *missed* you at the D.A.R. last Monday!

I said to myself: She's probably suffering with that sinus condition! How is that sinus condition?

Horrors! Heaven have mercy!—You're a Christian martyr, yes, that's what you are, a Christian martyr!

Well, I just now happened to notice that your subscription to the

Companion's about to expire! Yes, it expires with the next issue, honey! —just when that wonderful new serial by Bessie Mae Hopper is getting off to such an exciting start. Oh, honey, it's something that you can't miss! You remember how *Gone With the Wind* took everybody by storm? You simply couldn't go out if you hadn't read it. All everybody *talked* was Scarlett O'Hara. Well, this is a book that critics already compare to *Gone With the Wind.* It's the *Gone With the Wind* of the post-World War generation!—What?—Burning?—Oh, honey, don't let them burn, go take a look in the oven and I'll hold the wire! Heavens —I think she's hung up!

[*Dim Out.*]

[LEGEND ON SCREEN: "YOU THINK I'M IN LOVE WITH CONTINENTAL SHOEMAKERS?" *Before the stage is lighted, the violent voices of* TOM *and* AMANDA *are heard. They are quarreling behind the portieres. In front of them stands* LAURA *with clenched hands and panicky expression. A clear pool of light on her figure throughout this scene.*]

TOM. What in Christ's name am I—

AMANDA (*shrilly*). Don't you use that—

TOM. Supposed to do!

AMANDA. Expression! Not in my—

TOM. Ohhh!

AMANDA. Presence! Have you gone out of your senses?

TOM. I have, that's true, *driven* out!

AMANDA. What is the matter with you, you—big—big—IDIOT!

TOM. Look!—I've got *no thing,* no single thing—

AMANDA. Lower your voice!

TOM. In my life here that I can call my own! Everything is—

AMANDA. Stop that shouting!

TOM. Yesterday you confiscated my books! You had the nerve to—

AMANDA. I took that horrible novel back to the library—yes! That hideous book by that insane Mr. Lawrence. (TOM *laughs wildly.*) I cannot control the output of diseased minds or people who cater to them— (TOM *laughs still more wildly.*) BUT I WON'T ALLOW SUCH FILTH BROUGHT INTO MY HOUSE! No, no, no, no, no!

TOM. House, house! Who pays rent on it, who makes a slave of himself to—

AMANDA (*fairly screeching*). Don't you DARE to—

TOM. No, no, *I* mustn't say things! *I've* got to just—

AMANDA. Let me tell you—

TOM. I don't want to hear any more! (*He tears the portieres open. The upstage area is lit with a turgid smoky red glow.*)

[AMANDA'S *hair is in metal curlers and she wears a very old bathrobe, much too large for her slight figure, a relic of the faithless Mr. Wingfield. An upright typewriter and a wild disarray of manuscripts is on the dropleaf table. The quarrel was probably precipitated by* AMANDA*'s interruption of his creative labor. A chair lying overthrown on the floor. Their gesticulating shadows are cast on the ceiling by the fiery glow.*]

AMANDA. You *will* hear more, you—

TOM. No, I won't hear more, I'm going out!

AMANDA. You come right back in—

TOM. Out, out, out! Because I'm—

AMANDA. Come back here, Tom Wingfield! I'm not through talking to you!

TOM. Oh, go—

LAURA (*desperately*). —Tom!

AMANDA. You're going to listen, and no more insolence from you! I'm at the end of my patience!

[*He comes back toward her.*]

TOM. What do you think I'm at? Aren't I supposed to have any patience to reach the end of, Mother? I know, I know. It seems unimportant to you, what I'm *doing*—what I *want* to do—having a little *difference* between them! You don't think that—

AMANDA. I think you've been doing things that you're ashamed of. That's why you act like this. I don't believe that you go every night to the movies. Nobody goes to the movies night after night. Nobody in their right mind goes to the movies as often as you pretend to. People don't go to the movies at nearly midnight, and movies don't let out at two A.M. Come in stumbling. Muttering to yourself like a maniac! You get three hours' sleep and then go to work. Oh, I can picture the way you're doing down there. Moping, doping, because you're in no condition.

TOM (*wildly*). No, I'm in no condition!

AMANDA. What right have you got to jeopardize your job? Jeopardize the security of us all? How do you think we'd manage if you were—

TOM. Listen! You think I'm crazy *about the warehouse?* (*He bends fiercely toward her slight figure.*) You think I'm in love with the Continental Shoemakers? You think I want to spend fifty-five *years* down there in that—*celotex interior!* with—*fluorescent—tubes!* Look! I'd rather somebody picked up a crowbar and battered out my brains —than go back mornings! I *go!* Every time you come in yelling that God damn *"Rise and Shine!" "Rise and Shine!"* I say to myself, "How *lucky dead* people are!" But I get up. I *go!* For sixty-five dollars a month I give up all that I dream of doing and being ever! And you say self—*self's* all I ever think of. Why, listen, if self is what I thought of, Mother, I'd be where he is—GONE! (*Pointing to father's picture.*) As far as the system of transportation reaches! (*He starts past her. She grabs his arm.*) Don't grab at me, Mother!

AMANDA. Where are you going?

TOM. I'm going to the *movies!*

AMANDA. I don't believe that lie!

TOM (*crouching toward her, overtowering her tiny figure. She backs away, gasping*) I'm going to opium dens. Yes, opium dens, dens of vice and criminals' hang-outs, Mother. I've joined the Hogan gang,[2] I'm a hired assassin, I carry a tommy-gun in a violin case! I run a string of cat-houses in the Valley! They call me Killer, Killer Wingfield, I'm leading a double-life, a simple, honest warehouse worker by day, by night a dynamic *czar* of the *underworld, Mother.* I go to gambling casinos, I spin away fortunes on the roulette table! I wear a patch over one eye and a false mustache, sometimes I put on green whiskers. On those occasions they call me—*El Diablo!* Oh, I could tell you things to make you sleepless! My enemies plan to dynamite this place. They're going to blow us all sky-high some night! I'll be glad, very happy, and so will you! You'll go up, up on a broomstick, over Blue Mountain with seventeen gentlemen callers! You ugly—babbling old—*witch. . . .* (*He goes through a series of violent, clumsy movements, seizing his overcoat, lunging to the door, pulling it fiercely open. The women watch him, aghast. His arm catches in the sleeve of the coat as he struggles to pull it on. For a moment he is pinioned by the bulky garment. With an outraged groan he tears the coat off again, splitting the shoulder of it, and hurls it across the room. It strikes against the shelf of* LAURA*'s glass collection, there is a tinkle of shattering glass.* LAURA *cries out as if wounded.* MUSIC. LEGEND: "THE GLASS MENAGERIE.")

LAURA (*shrilly*). *My glass!*—menagerie. . . . (*She covers her face and turns away.*)

[*But* AMANDA *is still stunned and stupefied by the "ugly witch" so that she barely notices this occurrence. Now she recovers her speech.*]

AMANDA (*in an awful voice*). I won't speak to you—until you apologize!

[*She crosses through portieres and draws them together behind her.* TOM *is left with* LAURA. LAURA *clings weakly to the mantel with her face averted.* TOM *stares at her stupidly for a moment. Then he crosses to shelf. Drops awkwardly on his knees to collect the fallen glass, glancing at* LAURA *as if he would speak but couldn't.*]

[*"The Glass Menagerie" steals in as*
The Scene Dims Out.]

[2] "Dapper Danny" Hogan was the leader of the underworld in St. Paul, Minnesota, during the 1920's.

Scene 4

The interior is dark. Faint light in the alley.

A deep-voiced bell in a church is tolling the hour of five as the scene commences.

TOM *appears at the top of the alley. After each solemn boom of the bell in the tower, he shakes a little noise-maker or rattle as if to express the tiny spasm of man in contrast to the sustained power and dignity of the Almighty. This and the unsteadiness of his advance make it evident that he has been drinking.*

As he climbs the few steps to the fire-escape landing light steals up inside. LAURA *appears in night-dress, observing* TOM'*s empty bed in the front room.*

TOM *fishes in his pockets for door-key, removing a motley assortment of articles in the search, including a perfect shower of movie-ticket stubs and an empty bottle. At last he finds the key, but just as he is about to insert it, it slips from his fingers. He strikes a match and crouches below the door.*

TOM (*bitterly*). One crack—and it falls through!

[LAURA *opens the door.*]

LAURA. Tom, Tom, what are you doing?

TOM. Looking for a door-key.

LAURA. Where have you been all this time?

TOM. I have been to the movies.

LAURA. All this time at the movies?

TOM. There was a very long program. There was a Garbo picture and a Mickey Mouse and a travelogue and a newsreel and a preview of coming attractions. And there was an organ solo and a collection for the milk-fund—simultaneously—which ended up in a terrible fight between a fat lady and an usher!

LAURA (*innocently*). Did you have to stay through everything?

TOM. Of course! And, oh, I forgot! There was a big stage show! The headliner on this stage show was Malvolio the Magician. He performed wonderful tricks, many of them, such as pouring water back and forth between pitchers. First it turned to wine and then it turned to beer and then it turned to whiskey. I know it was whiskey it finally turned into because he needed somebody to come up out of the audience to help him, and I came up—both shows! It was Kentucky Straight Bourbon. A very generous fellow, he gave souvenirs. (*He pulls from his back pocket a shimmering rainbow-colored scarf.*) He gave me this. This is his magic scarf. You can have it, Laura. You wave it over a canary cage and you get a bowl of gold-fish. You wave it over the gold-fish bowl and they fly away canaries. . . . But the wonderfullest trick of all was the coffin trick. We nailed him into a coffin and he got out of the coffin without removing one nail. (*He has come inside.*) There is a trick that would come in handy for me—get me out of this 2 by 4 situation! (*Flops onto bed and starts removing shoes.*)

LAURA. Tom—Shhh!

TOM. What're you shushing me for?

LAURA. You'll wake up Mother.

TOM. Goody, goody! Pay 'er back for all those "Rise an' Shines." (*Lies down, groaning.*) You know it don't take much intelligence to get yourself into a nailed-up coffin, Laura. But who in hell ever got himself out of one without removing one nail?

[*As if in answer, the father's grinning photograph lights up.*]

[*Scene Dims Out.*]

[*Immediately following: The church bell is heard striking six. At the sixth stroke the alarm clock goes off in* AMANDA'*s room, and after a few moments we hear her calling: "Rise and Shine! Rise and Shine! Laura, go tell your brother to rise and shine!"*]

TOM (*sitting up slowly*). I'll rise—but I won't shine.

[*The light increases.*]

AMANDA. Laura, tell your brother his coffee is ready.

[LAURA *slips into front room.*]

LAURA. Tom!—It's nearly seven. Don't make Mother nervous. (*He stares at her stupidly. Beseechingly.*) Tom, speak to Mother this morning. Make up with her, apologize, speak to her!

TOM. She won't to me. It's her that started not speaking.

LAURA. If you just say you're sorry she'll start speaking.

TOM. Her not speaking—is that such a tragedy?

LAURA. Please—please!

AMANDA (*calling from kitchenette*). Laura, are you going to do what I asked you to do, or do I have to get dressed and go out myself?

LAURA. Going, going—soon as I get on my coat! (*She pulls on a shapeless felt hat with nervous, jerky movement, pleadingly glancing at* TOM. *Rushes awkwardly for coat. The coat is one of* AMANDA'*s, inaccurately made-over, the sleeves too short for* LAURA.) Butter and what else?

AMANDA (*entering upstage*). Just butter. Tell them to charge it.

LAURA. Mother, they make such faces when I do that.

AMANDA. Sticks and stones can break our bones, but the expression on Mr. Garfinkel's face won't harm us! Tell your brother his coffee is getting cold.

LAURA (*at door*). Do what I asked you, will you, will you, Tom?

[*He looks sullenly away.*]

AMANDA. Laura, go now or just don't go at all!

LAURA (*rushing out*). Going—going! (*A second later she cries out.* TOM *springs up and crosses to door.* AMANDA *rushes anxiously in.* TOM *opens the door.*)

TOM. Laura?

LAURA. I'm all right. I slipped, but I'm all right.

AMANDA (*peering anxiously after her*). If anyone breaks a leg on those fire-escape steps, the landlord ought to be sued for every cent he possesses! (*She shuts door. Remembers she isn't speaking and returns to room.*)

[*As* TOM *enters listlessly for his coffee, she turns her back to him and stands rigidly facing the window on the gloomy gray vault of the areaway. Its light on her face with its aged but childish features is cruelly sharp, satirical as a Daumier*[3] *print.* MUSIC UNDER: "AVE MARIA."

TOM *glances sheepishly but sullenly at her averted figure and slumps at the table. The coffee is scalding hot; he sips it and gasps and spits it back in the cup. At his gasp,* AMANDA *catches her breath and half turns. Then catches herself and turns back to window.*

TOM *blows on his coffee, glancing sideways at his mother. She clears her throat.* TOM *clears his. He starts to rise. Sinks back down again, scratches his head, clears his throat again.* AMANDA *coughs.* TOM *raises his cup in both hands to blow on it, his eyes staring over the rim of it at his mother for several moments. Then he slowly sets the cup down and awkwardly and hesitantly rises from the chair.*]

TOM (*hoarsely*). Mother. I—I apologize, Mother. (AMANDA *draws a quick, shuddering breath. Her face works grotesquely. She breaks into childlike tears.*) I'm sorry for what I said, for everything that I said, I didn't mean it.

AMANDA (*sobbingly*). My devotion has made me a witch and so I make myself hateful to my children!

TOM. *No,* you *don't.*

AMANDA. I worry so much, don't sleep, it makes me nervous!

TOM (*gently*). I understand that.

AMANDA. I've had to put up a solitary battle all these years. But you're my right-hand bower![4] Don't fall down, don't fail!

[3] Honoré Daumier (1808–1879) was a French caricaturist and painter. His famous lithographs hold the foibles of a bourgeois society up to ridicule.

[4] In the card games of euchre and five hundred, the highest card, the jack of trumps, is called the right bower.

TOM (*gently*). I'll try, Mother.

AMANDA (*with great enthusiasm*). Try and you will SUCCEED! (*The notion makes her breathless.*) Why, you—you're just *full* of natural endowments! Both my children—they're *unusual* children! Don't you think I know it? I'm so—*proud!* Happy and—feel I've—so much to be thankful for but—Promise me one thing, Son!

TOM. What, Mother?

AMANDA. Promise, Son, you'll never be a drunkard!

TOM (*turns to her grinning*). I will never be a drunkard, Mother.

AMANDA. That's what frightened me so, that you'd be drinking! Eat a bowl of Purina!

TOM. Just coffee, Mother.

AMANDA. Shredded wheat biscuit?

TOM. No. No, Mother, just coffee.

AMANDA. You can't put in a day's work on an empty stomach. You've got ten minutes—don't gulp! Drinking too-hot liquids makes cancer of the stomach. . . . Put cream in.

TOM. No, thank you.

AMANDA. To cool it.

TOM. No! No, thank you, I want it black.

AMANDA. I know, but it's not good for you. We have to do all that we can to build ourselves up. In these trying times we live in, all that we have to cling to is—each other. . . . That's why it's so important to—Tom, I—I sent out your sister so I could discuss something with you. If you hadn't spoken I would have spoken to you. (*Sits down.*)

TOM (*gently*). What is it, Mother, that you want to discuss?

AMANDA. *Laura!*

[TOM *puts his cup down slowly.* LEGEND ON SCREEN: "LAURA." MUSIC: "THE GLASS MENAGERIE."]

TOM. —Oh.—Laura. . . .

AMANDA (*touching his sleeve*). You know how Laura is. So quiet but—still water runs deep! She notices things and I think she—broods about them. (TOM *looks up.*) A few days ago I came in and she was crying.

TOM. What about?

AMANDA. You.

TOM. Me?

AMANDA. She has an idea that you're not happy here.

TOM. What gave her that idea?

AMANDA. What gives her any idea? However, you do act strangely. I—I'm not criticizing, understand *that!* I know your ambitions do not lie in the warehouse, that like everybody in the whole wide world—you've had to—make sacrifices, but—Tom—Tom—life's not easy, it calls for —Spartan endurance! There's so many things in my heart that I cannot describe to you! I've never told you but I—*loved* your father. . . .

TOM (*gently*). I know that, Mother.

AMANDA. And you—when I see you taking after his ways! Staying out late—and—well, you *had* been drinking the night you were in that—terrifying condition! Laura says that you hate the apartment and that you go out nights to get away from it! Is that true, Tom?

TOM. No. You say there's so much in your heart that you can't describe to me. That's true of me, too. There's so much in my heart that I can't describe to *you!* So let's respect each other's—

AMANDA. But, why—*why,* Tom—are you always so *restless?* Where do you *go* to, nights?

TOM. I—go to the movies.

AMANDA. Why do you go to the movies so much, Tom?

TOM. I go to the movies because—I like adventure. Adventure is something I don't have much of at work, so I go to the movies.

AMANDA. But, Tom, you go to the movies *entirely* too *much!*

TOM. I like a lot of adventure.

[AMANDA *looks baffled, then hurt. As the familiar inquisition resumes he becomes hard and impatient again.* AMANDA *slips back into her querulous attitude toward him.* IMAGE ON SCREEN: SAILING VESSEL WITH JOLLY ROGER.[5]]

AMANDA. Most young men find adventure in their careers.

TOM. Then most young men are not employed in a warehouse.

AMANDA. The world is full of young men employed in warehouses and offices and factories.

TOM. Do all of them find adventure in their careers?

AMANDA. They do or they do without it! Not everybody has a craze for adventure.

TOM. Man is by instinct a lover, a hunter, a fighter, and none of those instincts are given much play at the warehouse!

AMANDA. Man is by instinct! Don't quote instinct to me! Instinct is something that people have got away from! It belongs to animals! Christian adults don't want it!

TOM. What do Christian adults want, then, Mother?

AMANDA. Superior things! Things of the mind and the spirit! Only animals have to satisfy instincts! Surely your aims are somewhat higher than theirs! Than monkeys—pigs—

TOM. I reckon they're not.

AMANDA. You're joking! However, that isn't what I wanted to discuss.

TOM (*rising*). I haven't much time.

AMANDA (*pushing his shoulders*). Sit down.

TOM. You want me to punch in red at the warehouse, Mother?

AMANDA. You have five minutes. I want to talk about Laura.

[LEGEND: "PLANS AND PROVISIONS."]

[5] A black pirate flag with white skull and crossbones.

TOM. All right! What about Laura?

AMANDA. We have to be making some plans and provisions for her. She's older than you, two years, and nothing has happened. She just drifts along doing nothing. It frightens me terribly how she just drifts along.

TOM. I guess she's the type that people call home girls.

AMANDA. There's no such type, and if there is, it's a pity! That is unless the home is hers, with a husband!

TOM. What?

AMANDA. Oh, I can see the handwriting on the wall as plain as I see the nose in front of my face! It's terrifying!

More and more you remind me of your father! He was out all hours without explanation!—Then *left! Good-bye!*

And me with the bag to hold. I saw that letter you got from the Merchant Marine. I know what you're dreaming of. I'm not standing here blindfolded.

Very well, then. Then *do* it!

But not till there's somebody to take your place.

TOM. What do you mean?

AMANDA. I mean that as soon as Laura has got somebody to take care of her, married, a home of her own, independent—why, then you'll be free to go wherever you please, on land, on sea, whichever way the wind blows you!

But until that time you've got to look out for your sister. I don't say me because I'm old and don't matter! I say for your sister because she's young and dependent.

I put her in business college—a dismal failure! Frightened her so it made her sick at the stomach.

I took her over to the Young People's League at the church. Another fiasco. She spoke to nobody, nobody spoke to her. Now all she does is fool with those pieces of glass and play those worn-out records. What kind of a life is that for a girl to lead?

TOM. What can I do about it?

AMANDA. Overcome selfishness!

Self, self, self is all that you ever think of! (TOM *springs up and crosses to get his coat. It is ugly and bulky. He pulls on a cap with ear-muffs.*) Where is your muffler? Put your wool muffler on! (*He snatches it angrily from the closet and tosses it around his neck and pulls both ends tight.*) Tom! I haven't said what I had in mind to ask you.

TOM. I'm too late to—

AMANDA (*catching his arm—very importunately. Then shyly*). Down at the warehouse, aren't there some—nice young men?

TOM. No!

AMANDA. There *must* be—*some. . . .*

TOM. Mother—(*Gesture.*)

AMANDA. Find out one that's clean-living—doesn't drink and—ask him out for sister!

TOM. What?

AMANDA. For *sister!* To *meet!* Get *acquainted!*

TOM (*stamping to door*). Oh, my *go-osh!*

AMANDA. Will you? (*He opens door. Imploringly.*) Will you? (*He starts down.*) Will you? *Will* you, dear?

TOM (*calling back*): YES!

[AMANDA *closes the door hesitantly and with a troubled but faintly hopeful expression.* SCREEN IMAGE: GLAMOR MAGAZINE COVER. *Spot* AMANDA *at phone.*]

AMANDA. Ella Cartwright? This is Amanda Wingfield!

How are you, honey?

How is that kidney condition? (*Count five.*)

Horrors! (*Count five.*)

You're a Christian martyr, yes, honey, that's what you are, a Christian martyr!

Well, I just now happened to notice in my little red book that your subscription to the *Companion* has just run out! I knew that you wouldn't want to miss out on the wonderful serial starting in this new issue. It's by Bessie Mae Hopper, the first thing she's written since *Honeymoon for Three.*

Wasn't that a strange and interesting story? Well, this one is even lovelier, I believe. It has a sophisticated, society background. It's all about the horsey set on Long Island!

[*Fade Out.*]

Scene 5

LEGEND ON SCREEN: "ANNUNCIATION."[9] *Fade with music.*

It is early dusk of a spring evening. Supper has just been finished in the Wingfield apartment. AMANDA *and* LAURA *in light-colored dresses are removing dishes from the table, in the upstage area, which is shadowy, their movements formalized almost as a dance or ritual, their moving forms as pale and silent as moths.*

TOM, *in white shirt and trousers, rises from the table and crosses toward the fire-escape.*

AMANDA (*as he passes her*). Son, will you do me a favor?

TOM. What?

[9] The actual moment of the Incarnation, when the angel announced to the Virgin Mary that God the Son was to be born to her (Luke 1:26–28).

AMANDA. Comb your hair! You look so pretty when your hair is combed! (TOM *slouches on sofa with evening paper. Enormous caption "Franco Triumphs."*) There is only one respect in which I would like you to emulate your father.

TOM. What respect is that?

AMANDA. The care he always took of his appearance. He never allowed himself to look untidy. (*He throws down the paper and crosses to fire-escape.*) Where are you going?

TOM. I'm going out to smoke.

AMANDA. You smoke too much. A pack a day at fifteen cents a pack. How much would that amount to in a month? Thirty times fifteen is how much, Tom? Figure it out and you will be astounded at what you could save. Enough to give you a night-school course in accounting at Washington U! Just think what a wonderful thing that would be for you, Son! (TOM *is unmoved by the thought.*)

TOM. I'd rather smoke. (*He steps out on landing, letting the screen door slam.*)

AMANDA (*sharply*). I know! That's the tragedy of it. . . . (*Alone, she turns to look at her husband's picture.*)

[DANCE MUSIC: "ALL THE WORLD IS WAITING FOR THE SUNRISE!"]

TOM (*to the audience*). Across the valley from us was the Paradise Dance Hall. On evenings in spring the windows and doors were open and the music came outdoors. Sometimes the lights were turned out except for a large glass sphere that hung from the ceiling. It would turn slowly about and filter the dusk with delicate rainbow colors. Then the orchestra played a waltz or a tango, something that had a slow and sensuous rhythm. Couples would come outside, to the relative privacy of the alley. You could see them kissing behind ash-pits and telephone poles.

This was the compensation for lives that passed like mine, without any change or adventure.

Adventure and change were imminent in this year. They were waiting around the corner for all these kids.

Suspended in the mist over Berchtesgaden, caught in the folds of Chamberlain's umbrella—

In Spain there was Guernica!

But here there was only hot swing music and liquor, dance halls, bars, and movies, and sex that hung in the gloom like a chandelier and flooded the world with brief, descriptive rainbows. . . .

All the world was waiting for bombardments!

[AMANDA *turns from the picture and comes outside.*]

AMANDA (*sighing*). A fire-escape landing's a poor excuse for a porch. (*She spreads a newspaper on a step and sits down, gracefully and demurely as if she were settling into a swing on a Mississippi veranda.*) What are you looking at?

TOM. The moon.

AMANDA. Is there a moon this evening?

TOM. It's rising over Garfinkel's Delicatessen.

AMANDA. So it is! A little silver slipper of a moon. Have you made a wish on it yet?

TOM. Um-hum.

AMANDA. What did you wish for?

TOM. That's a secret.

AMANDA. A secret, huh? Well, I won't tell mine either. I will be just as mysterious as you.

TOM. I bet I can guess what yours is.

AMANDA. Is my head so transparent?

TOM. You're not a sphinx.

AMANDA. No, I don't have secrets. I'll tell you what I wished for on the moon. Success and happiness for my precious children! I wish for that whenever there's a moon, and when there isn't a moon, I wish for it, too.

TOM. I thought perhaps you wished for a gentleman caller.

AMANDA. Why do you say that?

TOM. Don't you remember asking me to fetch one?

AMANDA. I remember suggesting that it would be nice for your sister if you brought home some nice young man from the warehouse. I think that I've made that suggestion more than once.

TOM. Yes, you have made it repeatedly.

AMANDA. Well?

TOM. We are going to have one.

AMANDA. *What?*

TOM. A gentleman caller!

[THE ANNUNCIATION IS CELEBRATED WITH MUSIC. AMANDA *rises.* IMAGE ON SCREEN: CALLER WITH BOUQUET.]

AMANDA. You mean you have asked some nice young man to come over?

TOM. Yep. I've asked him to dinner.

AMANDA. You really did?

TOM. I did!

AMANDA. You did, and did he—*accept?*

TOM. He did!

AMANDA. Well, well—well, well! That's—lovely!

TOM. I thought that you would be pleased.

AMANDA. It's definite, then?

TOM. Very definite.

AMANDA. Soon?

TOM. Very soon.

AMANDA. For heaven's sake, stop putting on and tell me some things, will you?

TOM. What things do you want me to tell you?

AMANDA. *Naturally* I would like to know when he's *coming!*

TOM. He's coming tomorrow.

AMANDA. *Tomorrow?*

TOM. Yep. Tomorrow.

AMANDA. But, Tom!

TOM. Yes, Mother?

AMANDA. Tomorrow gives me no time!

TOM. Time for what?

AMANDA. Preparations! Why didn't you phone me at once, as soon as you asked him, the minute that he accepted? Then, don't you see, I could have been getting ready!

TOM. You don't have to make any fuss.

AMANDA. Oh, Tom, Tom, Tom, of course I have to make a fuss! I want things nice, not sloppy! Not thrown together. I'll certainly have to do some fast thinking, won't I?

TOM. I don't see why you have to think at all.

AMANDA. You just don't know. We can't have a gentleman caller in a pig-sty! All my wedding silver has to be polished, the monogrammed table linen ought to be laundered! The windows have to be washed and fresh curtains put up. And how about clothes? We have to *wear* something, don't we?

TOM. Mother, this boy is no one to make a fuss over!

AMANDA. Do you realize he's the first young man we've introduced to your sister?

It's terrible, dreadful, disgraceful that poor little sister has never received a single gentleman caller! Tom, come inside! (*She opens the screen door.*)

TOM. What for?

AMANDA. I want to ask you some things.

TOM. If you're going to make such a fuss, I'll call it off, I'll tell him not to come!

AMANDA. You certainly won't do anything of the kind. Nothing offends people worse than broken engagements. It simply means I'll have to work like a Turk! We won't be brilliant, but we will pass inspection. Come on inside. (TOM *follows, groaning.*) Sit down.

TOM. Any particular place you would like me to sit?

AMANDA. Thank heavens I've got that new sofa! I'm also making payments on a floor lamp I'll have sent out! And put the chintz covers on, they'll brighten things up! Of course I'd hoped to have these walls re-papered. . . . What is the young man's name?

TOM. His name is O'Connor.

AMANDA. That, of course, means fish—tomorrow is Friday! I'll have that salmon loaf—with Durkee's dressing! What does he do? He works at the warehouse?

TOM. Of course! How else would I—

AMANDA. Tom, he—doesn't drink?

TOM. Why do you ask me that?

AMANDA. Your father *did!*

TOM. Don't get started on that!

AMANDA. He *does* drink, then?

TOM. Not that I know of!

AMANDA. Make sure, be certain! The last thing I want for my daughter's a boy who drinks!

TOM. Aren't you being a little bit premature? Mr. O'Connor has not yet appeared on the scene!

AMANDA. But will tomorrow. To meet your sister, and what do I know about his character? Nothing! Old maids are better off than wives of drunkards!

TOM. Oh, my God!

AMANDA. Be still!

TOM (*leaning forward to whisper*). Lots of fellows meet girls whom they don't marry!

AMANDA. Oh, talk sensibly, Tom—and don't be sarcastic! (*She has gotten a hairbrush.*)

TOM. What are you doing?

AMANDA. I'm brushing that cow-lick down!

What is this young man's position at the warehouse?

TOM (*submitting grimly to the brush and the interrogation*). This young man's position is that of a shipping clerk, Mother.

AMANDA. Sounds to me like a fairly responsible job, the sort of a job *you* would be in if you just had more *get-up*.

What is his salary? Have you any idea?

TOM. I would judge it to be approximately eighty-five dollars a month.

AMANDA. Well—not princely, but—

TOM. Twenty more than I make.

AMANDA. Yes, how well I know! But for a family man, eighty-five dollars a month is not much more than you can just get by on. . . .

TOM. Yes, but Mr. O'Connor is not a family man.

AMANDA. He might be, mightn't he? Some time in the future?

TOM. I see. Plans and provisions.

AMANDA. You are the only young man that I know of who ignores the fact that the future becomes the present, the present the past, and the past turns into everlasting regret if you don't plan for it!

TOM. I will think that over and see what I can make of it.

AMANDA. Don't be supercilious with your mother! Tell me some more about this—what do you call him?

TOM. James D. O'Connor. The D. is for Delaney.

AMANDA. Irish on *both* sides! *Gracious!* And doesn't drink?

TOM. Shall I call him up and ask him right this minute?

AMANDA. The only way to find out about those things is to make discreet inquiries at the proper moment. When I was a girl in Blue Mountain and it was suspected that a young man drank, the girl whose attentions he had been receiving, if any girl *was*, would sometimes speak to the minister of his church, or rather her father would if her father was living, and sort of feel him out on the young man's character. That is the way such things are discreetly handled to keep a young woman from making a tragic mistake!

TOM. Then how did you happen to make a tragic mistake?

AMANDA. That innocent look of your father's had everyone fooled!

He *smiled*—the world was *enchanted!*

No girl can do worse than put herself at the mercy of a handsome appearance!

I hope that Mr. O'Connor is not too good-looking.

TOM. No, he's not too good-looking. He's covered with freckles and hasn't too much of a nose.

AMANDA. He's not right-down homely, though?

TOM. Not right-down homely. Just medium homely, I'd say.

AMANDA. Character's what to look for in a man.

TOM. That's what I've always said, Mother.

AMANDA. You've never said anything of the kind and I suspect you would never give it a thought.

TOM. Don't be so suspicious of me.

AMANDA. At least I hope he's the type that's up and coming.

TOM. I think he really goes in for self-improvement.

AMANDA. What reason have you to think so?

TOM. He goes to night school.

AMANDA (*beaming*). Splendid! What does he do, I mean study?

TOM. Radio engineering and public speaking!

AMANDA. Then he has visions of being advanced in the world!

Any young man who studies public speaking is aiming to have an executive job some day!

And radio engineering? A thing for the future!

Both of these facts are very illuminating. Those are the sort of things that a mother should know concerning any young man who comes to call on her daughter. Seriously or—not.

TOM. One little warning. He doesn't know about Laura. I didn't let on that we had dark ulterior motives. I just said, why don't you come and have dinner with us? He said okay and that was the whole conversation.

AMANDA. I bet it was! You're eloquent as an oyster.

However, he'll know about Laura when he gets here. When he sees how lovely and sweet and pretty she is, he'll thank his lucky stars he was asked to dinner.

TOM. Mother, you mustn't expect too much of Laura.

AMANDA. What do you mean?

TOM. Laura seems all those things to you and me because she's ours and we love her. We don't even notice she's crippled any more.

AMANDA. Don't say crippled! You know that I never allow that word to be used!

TOM. But face facts, Mother. She is and—that's not all—

AMANDA. What do you mean "not all"?

TOM. Laura is very different from other girls.

AMANDA. I think the difference is all to her advantage.

TOM. Not quite all—in the eyes of others—strangers—she's terribly shy and lives in a world of her own and those things make her seem a little peculiar to people outside the house.

AMANDA. Don't say peculiar.

TOM. Face the facts. She is.

[THE DANCE-HALL MUSIC CHANGES TO A TANGO THAT HAS A MINOR AND SOMEWHAT OMINOUS TONE.]

AMANDA. In what way is she peculiar—may I ask?

TOM (*gently*). She lives in a world of her own—a world of—little glass ornaments, Mother. . . . (*Gets up.* AMANDA *remains holding brush, looking at him, troubled.*) She plays old phonograph records and—that's about all— (*He glances at himself in the mirror and crosses to door.*)

AMANDA (*sharply*). Where are you going?

TOM. I'm going to the movies. (*Out screen door.*)

AMANDA. Not to the movies, every night to the movies! (*Follows quickly to screen door.*) I don't believe you always go to the movies! (*He is gone.* AMANDA *looks worriedly after him for a moment. Then vitality and optimism return and she turns from the door. Crossing to portieres.*) Laura! Laura! (LAURA *answers from kitchenette.*)

LAURA. Yes, Mother.

AMANDA. Let those dishes go and come in front! (LAURA *appears with dish towel. Gaily.*) Laura, come here and make a wish on the moon!

[SCREEN IMAGE: MOON.]

LAURA. (*entering*). Moon—moon?

AMANDA. A little silver slipper of a moon.

Look over your left shoulder, Laura, and make a wish! (LAURA *looks faintly puzzled as if called out of sleep.* AMANDA *seizes her shoulders and turns her at an angle by the door.*)

Now!

Now, darling, *wish!*

LAURA. What shall I wish for, Mother?

AMANDA (*her voice trembling and her eyes suddenly filling with tears*). Happiness! Good fortune!

[*The violin rises and the stage dims out.*]

[*The Curtain Falls.*]

Scene 6

IMAGE: HIGH SCHOOL HERO.

TOM. And so the following evening I brought Jim home to dinner. I had known Jim slightly in high school. In high school Jim was a hero. He had tremendous Irish good nature and vitality with the scrubbed and polished look of white chinaware. He seemed to move in a continual spotlight. He was a star in basketball, captain of the debating club, president of the senior class and the glee club and he sang the male lead in the annual light operas. He was always running or bounding, never just walking. He seemed always at the point of defeating the law of gravity. He was shooting with such velocity through his adolescence that you would logically expect him to arrive at nothing short of the White House by the time he was thirty. But Jim apparently ran into more interference after his graduation from Soldan. His speed had definitely slowed. Six years after he left high school he was holding a job that wasn't much better than mine. (IMAGE: CLERK.)

He was the only one at the warehouse with whom I was on friendly terms. I was valuable to him as someone who could remember his former glory, who had seen him win basketball games and the silver cup in debating. He knew of my secret practice of retiring to a cabinet of the washroom to work on poems when business was slack in the warehouse. He called me Shakespeare. And while the other boys in the warehouse regarded me with suspicious hostility, Jim took a humorous attitude toward me. Gradually his attitude affected the others, their hostility wore off and they also began to smile at me as people smile at an oddly fashioned dog who trots across their path at some distance.

I knew that Jim and Laura had known each other at Soldan, and I had heard Laura speak admiringly of his voice. I didn't know if Jim remembered her or not. In high school Laura had been as unobtrusive as Jim had been astonishing. If he did remember Laura, it was not as my sister, for when I asked him to dinner, he grinned and said, "You know, Shakespeare, I never thought of you as having folks!"

He was about to discover that I did. . . .

[LIGHT UP STAGE. LEGEND ON SCREEN: "THE ACCENT OF A COMING FOOT." *Friday evening. It is about five o'clock of a late spring evening which comes "scattering poems in the sky." A delicate lemony light is in the Wingfield apartment.* AMANDA *has worked like a Turk in preparation for the gentleman caller. The results are astonishing. The new floor lamp with its rose-silk shade is in place, a colored paper lantern conceals the broken light fixture in the ceiling, new billowing white curtains are at the windows, chintz covers are on chairs and sofa, a pair of new sofa pillows make their initial appearance. Open boxes and tissue paper are scattered on the floor.* LAURA *stands in the middle with lifted arms while* AMANDA *crouches before her, adjusting the hem of the new dress, devout and ritualistic. The dress is colored and designed by memory. The arrangement of* LAURA'S *hair is changed; it is softer and more becoming. A fragile, unearthly prettiness has come out in* LAURA: *she is like a piece of translucent glass touched by light, given a momentary radiance, not actual, not lasting.*]

AMANDA (*impatiently*). Why are you trembling?

LAURA. Mother, you've made me so nervous!

AMANDA. How have I made you nervous?

LAURA. By all this fuss! You make it seem so important!

AMANDA. I don't understand you, Laura. You couldn't be satisfied with just sitting home, and yet whenever I try to arrange something for you, you seem to resist it. (*She gets up.*)

Now take a look at yourself.

No, wait! Wait just a moment—I have an idea!

LAURA. What is it now?

[AMANDA *produces two powder puffs which she wraps in handkerchiefs and stuffs in* LAURA'S *bosom.*]

LAURA. Mother, what are you doing?

AMANDA. They call them "Gay Deceivers"!

LAURA. I won't wear them!

AMANDA. You will!

LAURA. Why should I?

AMANDA. Because, to be painfully honest, your chest is flat.

LAURA. You make it seem like we were setting a trap.

AMANDA. All pretty girls are a trap, a pretty trap, and men expect them to be. (LEGEND: "A PRETTY TRAP.")

Now look at yourself, young lady. This is the prettiest you will ever be!

I've got to fix myself now! You're going to be surprised by your mother's appearance! (*She crosses through portieres, humming gaily.*)

[LAURA *moves slowly to the long mirror and stares solemnly at herself. A wind blows the white curtains inward in a slow, graceful motion and with a faint, sorrowful sighing.*]

AMANDA (*off stage*). It isn't dark enough yet. (LAURA *turns slowly before the mirror with a troubled look.*)

[LEGEND ON SCREEN: "THIS IS MY SISTER: CELEBRATE HER WITH STRINGS!" MUSIC.]

AMANDA (*laughing, off*). I'm going to show you something. I'm going to make a spectacular appearance!

LAURA. What is it, Mother?

AMANDA. Possess your soul in patience—you will see!

Something I've resurrected from that old trunk! Styles haven't changed so terribly much after all. . . . (*She parts the portieres.*)

Now just look at your mother! (*She wears a girlish frock of yellowed voile with a blue silk sash. She carries a bunch of jonquils—the legend of her youth is nearly revived. Feverishly.*)

This is the dress in which I led the cotillion. Won the cakewalk twice at Sunset Hill, wore one spring to the Governor's ball in Jackson!

See how I sashayed around the ballroom, Laura? (*She raises her skirt and does a mincing step around the room.*)

I wore it on Sundays for my gentlemen callers! I had it on the day I met your father—

I had malaria fever all that spring. The change of climate from East Tennessee to the Delta—weakened resistance—I had a little temperature all the time—not enough to be serious—just enough to make me restless and giddy!—Invitations poured in—parties all over the Delta!—"Stay in bed," said Mother, "you have fever!"—but I just wouldn't.—I took quinine but kept on going, going!—Evenings, dances! —Afternoons, long, long rides! Picnics—lovely!—So lovely, that country in May.—All lacy with dogwood, literally flooded with jonquils! —That was the spring I had the craze for jonquils. Jonquils became an absolute obsession. Mother said, "Honey, there's no more room for jonquils." And still I kept on bringing in more jonquils. Whenever, wherever I saw them, I'd say, "Stop! Stop! I see jonquils!" I made the young men help me gather the jonquils! It was a joke, Amanda and her jonquils! Finally there were no more vases to hold them, every available space was filled with jonquils. No vases to hold them? All right, I'll hold them myself! And then I—(*She stops in front of the picture.* MUSIC.) met your father!

Malaria fever and jonquils and then—this—boy. . . . (*She switches on the rose-colored lamp.*)

I hope they get here before it starts to rain. (*She crosses upstage and places the jonquils in bowl on table.*)

I gave your brother a little extra change so he and Mr. O'Connor could take the service car home.

LAURA (*with altered look*). What did you say his name was?

AMANDA. O'Connor.

LAURA. What is his first name?

AMANDA. I don't remember. Oh, yes, I do. It was—Jim!

[LAURA *sways slightly and catches hold of a chair.* LEGEND ON SCREEN: "NOT JIM!"]

LAURA (*faintly*). Not—Jim!

AMANDA. Yes, that was it, it was Jim! I've never known a Jim that wasn't nice!

[MUSIC: OMINOUS.]

LAURA. Are you sure his name is Jim O'Connor?

AMANDA. Yes. Why?

LAURA. Is he the one that Tom used to know in high school?

AMANDA. He didn't say so. I think he just got to know him at the warehouse.

LAURA. There was a Jim O'Connor we both knew in high school—(*Then, with effort.*) If that is the one that Tom is bringing to dinner—you'll have to excuse me, I won't come to the table.

AMANDA. What sort of nonsense is this?

LAURA. You asked me once if I'd ever liked a boy. Don't you remember I showed you this boy's picture?

AMANDA. You mean the boy you showed me in the year book?

LAURA. Yes, that boy.

AMANDA. Laura, Laura, were you in love with that boy?

LAURA. I don't know, Mother. All I know is I couldn't sit at the table if it was him!

AMANDA. It won't be him! It isn't the least bit likely. But whether it is or not, you will come to the table. You will not be excused.

LAURA. I'll have to be, Mother.

AMANDA. I don't intend to humor your silliness, Laura. I've had too much from you and your brother, both!

So just sit down and compose yourself till they come. Tom has forgotten his key so you'll have to let them in, when they arrive.

LAURA (*panicky*). Oh, Mother—*you* answer the door!

AMANDA (*lightly*). I'll be in the kitchen—busy!

LAURA. Oh, Mother, please answer the door, don't make me do it!

AMANDA (*crossing into kitchenette*). I've got to fix the dressing for the salmon. Fuss, fuss—silliness!—over a gentleman caller!

[*Door swings shut.* LAURA *is left alone.* LEGEND: "TERROR!" *She utters a low moan and turns off the lamp—sits stiffly on the edge of the sofa, knotting her fingers together.* LEGEND ON SCREEN: "THE OPENING OF A DOOR!" TOM *and* JIM *appear on the fire-escape steps and climb to landing. Hearing their approach,* LAURA *rises with a panicky gesture. She retreats to the portieres. The doorbell.* LAURA *catches her breath and touches her throat. Low drums.*]

AMANDA (*calling*). Laura, sweetheart! The door!

[LAURA *stares at it without moving.*]

JIM. I think we just beat the rain.

TOM. Uh-huh. (*He rings again, nervously.* JIM *whistles and fishes for a cigarette.*)

AMANDA (*very, very gaily*). Laura, that is your brother and Mr. O'Connor! Will you let them in, darling?

[LAURA *crosses toward kitchenette door.*]

LAURA (*breathlessly*). Mother—you go to the door!

[AMANDA *steps out of kitchenette and stares furiously at* LAURA. *She points imperiously at the door.*]

LAURA. Please, please!

AMANDA (*in a fierce whisper*). What is the matter with you, you silly thing?

LAURA (*desperately*). Please, you answer it, *please!*

AMANDA. I told you I wasn't going to humor you, Laura. Why have you chosen this moment to lose your mind?

LAURA. Please, please, please, you go!

AMANDA. You'll have to go to the door because I can't!

LAURA (*despairingly*). I can't either!

AMANDA. Why?

LAURA. I'm *sick!*

AMANDA. I'm sick, too—of your nonsense! Why can't you and your brother be normal people? Fantastic whims and behavior! (TOM *gives a long ring.*)

Preposterous goings on! Can you give me one reason—(*Calls out lyrically.*) COMING! JUST ONE SECOND!—why you should be afraid to open a door? Now you answer it, Laura!

LAURA. Oh, oh, oh . . . (*She returns through the portieres. Darts to the victrola and winds it frantically and turns it on.*)

AMANDA. Laura Wingfield, you march right to that door!

LAURA. Yes—yes, Mother!

[*A faraway, scratchy rendition of "Dardanella" softens the air and gives her strength to move through it. She slips to the door and draws it cautiously open.* TOM *enters with the caller,* JIM O'CONNOR.]

TOM. Laura, this is Jim. Jim, this is my sister, Laura.

JIM (*stepping inside*). I didn't know that Shakespeare had a sister!

LAURA (*retreating stiff and trembling from the door*). How—how do you do?

JIM (*heartily extending his hand*). Okay!

[LAURA *touches it hesitantly with hers.*]

JIM. Your hand's *cold,* Laura!

LAURA. Yes, well—I've been playing the victrola. . . .

JIM. Must have been playing classical music on it! You ought to play a little hot swing music to warm you up!

LAURA. Excuse me—I haven't finished playing the victrola. . . .

[*She turns awkwardly and hurries into the front room. She pauses a second by the victrola. Then catches her breath and darts through the portieres like a frightened deer.*]

JIM (*grinning*). What was the matter?

TOM. Oh—with Laura? Laura is—terribly shy.

JIM. Shy, huh? It's unusual to meet a shy girl nowadays. I don't believe you ever mentioned you had a sister.

TOM. Well, now you know. I have one. Here is the *Post Dispatch.* You want a piece of it?

JIM. Uh-huh.

TOM. What piece? The comics?

JIM. Sports! (*Glances at it.*) Ole Dizzy Dean is on his bad behavior.

TOM (*disinterest*). Yeah? (*Lights cigarette and crosses back to fire-escape door.*)

JIM. Where are *you* going?

TOM. I'm going out on the terrace.

JIM (*goes after him*). You know, Shakespeare—I'm going to sell you a bill of goods!

TOM. What goods?

JIM. A course I'm taking.

TOM. Huh?

JIM. In public speaking! You and me, we're not the warehouse type.

TOM. Thanks—that's good news. But what has public speaking got to do with it?

JIM. It fits you for—executive positions!

TOM. Awww.

JIM. I tell you it's done a helluva lot for me.

[IMAGE: EXECUTIVE AT DESK.]

TOM. In what respect?

JIM. In every! Ask yourself what is the difference between you an' me and men in the office down front? Brains?—No!—Ability?—No! Then what? Just one little thing—

TOM. What is that one little thing?

JIM. Primarily it amounts to—social poise! Being able to square up to people and hold your own on any social level!

AMANDA (*off stage*). Tom?

TOM. Yes, Mother?

AMANDA. Is that you and Mr. O'Connor?

TOM. Yes, Mother.

AMANDA. Well, you just make yourselves comfortable in there.

TOM. Yes, Mother.

AMANDA. Ask Mr. O'Connor if he would like to wash his hands.

JIM. Aw, no—no—thank you—I took care of that at the warehouse. Tom—

TOM. Yes?

JIM. Mr. Mendoza was speaking to me about you.

TOM. Favorably?

JIM. What do you think?

TOM. Well—

JIM. You're going to be out of a job if you don't wake up.

TOM. I am waking up—

JIM. You show no signs.

TOM. The signs are interior.

[IMAGE ON SCREEN: THE SAILING VESSEL WITH JOLLY ROGER AGAIN.]

TOM. I'm planning to change. (*He leans over the rail speaking with quiet exhilaration. The incandescent marquees and signs of the first-run movie houses light his face from across the alley. He looks like a voyager.*) I'm right at the point of committing myself to a future that doesn't include the warehouse and Mr. Mendoza or even a night-school course in public speaking.

JIM. What are you gassing about?

TOM. I'm tired of the movies.

JIM. Movies!

TOM. Yes, movies! Look at them— (*A wave toward the marvels of Grand Avenue.*) All of those glamorous people—having adventures—hogging it all, gobbling the whole thing up! You know what happens? People go to the *movies* instead of *moving!* Hollywood characters are supposed to have all the adventures for everybody in America, while everybody in America sits in a dark room and watches them have them! Yes, until there's a war. That's when adventure becomes available to the masses! *Everyone's* dish, not only Gable's! Then the people in the dark room come out of the dark room to have some adventures themselves —Goody, goody!—It's our turn now, to go to the South Sea Islands— to make a safari—to be exotic, far-off!—But I'm not patient. I don't want to wait till then. I'm tired of the *movies* and I am *about* to *move!*

JIM (*incredulously*). Move?

TOM. Yes.

JIM. When?

TOM. Soon!

JIM. Where? Where?

[THEME THREE MUSIC SEEMS TO ANSWER THE QUESTION, WHILE TOM THINKS IT OVER. HE SEARCHES AMONG HIS POCKETS.]

TOM. I'm starting to boil inside. I know I seem dreamy, but inside—well, I'm boiling!—Whenever I pick up a shoe, I shudder a little thinking how short life is and what I am doing!—Whatever that means, I know it doesn't mean shoes—except as something to wear on a traveler's feet! (*Finds paper.*) Look—

JIM. What?

TOM. I'm a member.

JIM (*reading*). The Union of Merchant Seamen.

TOM. I paid my dues this month, instead of the light bill.

JIM. You will regret it when they turn the lights off.

TOM. I won't be here.

JIM. How about your mother?

TOM. I'm like my father. The bastard son of a bastard! See how he grins? And he's been absent going on sixteen years!

JIM. You're just talking, you drip. How does your mother feel about it?

TOM. Shhh!—Here comes Mother! Mother is not acquainted with my plans!

AMANDA (*enters portieres*). Where are you all?

TOM. On the terrace, Mother.

[*They start inside. She advances to them.* TOM *is distinctly shocked at her appearance. Even* JIM *blinks a little. He is making his first contact with girlish Southern vivacity and in spite of the night-school course in public speaking is somewhat thrown off the beam by the unexpected outlay of social charm. Certain responses are attempted by* JIM *but are swept aside by* AMANDA'*s gay laughter and chatter.* TOM *is embarrassed but after the first shock* JIM *reacts very warmly. Grins and chuckles, is altogether won over.* IMAGE: AMANDA AS A GIRL.]

AMANDA (*coyly smiling, shaking her girlish ringlets*). Well, well, well, so this is Mr. O'Connor. Introductions entirely unnecessary. I've heard so much about you from my boy. I finally said to him, Tom—good gracious!—why don't you bring this paragon to supper? I'd like to meet this nice young man at the warehouse!—Instead of just hearing him sing your praises so much!

I don't know why my son is so stand-offish—that's not Southern behavior!

Let's sit down and—I think we could stand a little more air in here! Tom, leave the door open. I felt a nice fresh breeze a moment ago. Where has it gone to?

Mmm, so warm already! And not quite summer, even. We're going to burn up when summer really gets started.

However, we're having—we're having a very light supper. I think light things are better fo' this time of year. The same as light clothes are. Light clothes an' light food are what warm weather calls fo'. You know our blood gets so thick during th' winter—it takes a while fo' us to *adjust* ou'selves!—when the season changes. . . .

It's come so quick this year. I wasn't prepared. All of a sudden—heavens! Already summer!—I ran to the trunk an' pulled out this light dress— Terribly old! Historical almost! But feels so good—so good an' co-ol, y' know. . . .

TOM. Mother—

AMANDA. Yes, honey?

TOM. How about—supper?

AMANDA. Honey, you go ask Sister if supper is ready! You know that Sister is in full charge of supper!

Tell her you hungry boys are waiting for it. (*To* JIM.) Have you met Laura?

JIM. She—

AMANDA. Let you in? Oh, good, you've met already! It's rare for a girl as sweet an' pretty as Laura to be domestic! But Laura is, thank heavens, not only pretty but also very domestic. I'm not at all. I never was a bit. I never could make a thing but angel-food cake. Well, in the

South we had so many servants. Gone, gone, gone. All vestige of gracious living! Gone completely! I wasn't prepared for what the future brought me. All of my gentlemen callers were sons of planters and so of course I assumed that I would be married to one and raise my family on a large piece of land with plenty of servants. But man proposes—and woman accepts the proposal!—To vary that old, old saying a little bit—I married no planter! I married a man who worked for the telephone company!—That gallantly smiling gentleman over there! (*Points to the picture.*) A telephone man who—fell in love with long-distance!—Now he travels and I don't even know where!—But what am I going on for about my—tribulations?

Tell me yours—I hope you don't have any!

Tom?

TOM (*returning*). Yes, Mother?

AMANDA. Is supper nearly ready?

TOM. It looks to me like supper is on the table.

AMANDA. Let me look— (*She rises prettily and looks through portieres.*) Oh, lovely!—But where is Sister?

TOM. Laura is not feeling well and she says that she thinks she'd better not come to the table.

AMANDA. What?—Nonsense!—Laura? Oh, Laura!

LAURA (*off stage, faintly*). Yes, Mother.

AMANDA. You really must come to the table. We won't be seated until you come to the table!

Come in, Mr. O'Connor. You sit over there, and I'll—

Laura? Laura Wingfield!

You're keeping us waiting, honey! We can't say grace until you come to the table!

[*The back door is pushed weakly open and* LAURA *comes in. She is obviously quite faint, her lips trembling, her eyes wide and staring. She moves unsteadily toward the table.* LEGEND: "TERROR!" *Outside a summer storm is coming abruptly. The white curtains billow inward at the windows and there is a sorrowful murmur and deep blue dusk.* LAURA *suddenly stumbles—she catches at a chair with a faint moan.*]

TOM. Laura!

AMANDA. Laura! (*There is a clap of thunder.* LEGEND: "AH!" *Despairingly.*) Why, Laura, you *are* sick, darling! Tom, help your sister into the living room, dear!

Sit in the living room, Laura—rest on the sofa.

Well! (*To the gentleman caller.*)

Standing over the hot stove made her ill!—I told her that it was just too warm this evening, but—(TOM *comes back in.* LAURA *is on the sofa.*)

Is Laura all right now?

TOM. Yes.

AMANDA. What *is* that? Rain? A nice cool rain has come up! (*She gives the gentleman caller a frightened look.*)

I think we may—have grace—now. . . . (TOM *looks at her stupidly.*)

Tom, honey—you say grace!

TOM. Oh . . .

"For these and all thy mercies—" (*They bow their heads,* AMANDA *stealing a nervous glance at* JIM. *In the living room* LAURA, *stretched on the sofa, clenches her hand to her lips, to hold back a shuddering sob.*)

God's Holy Name be praised—

[*The Scene Dims Out.*]

Scene 7

A Souvenir.

Half an hour later. Dinner is just being finished in the upstage area which is concealed by the drawn portieres.

As the curtain rises, LAURA *is still huddled upon the sofa, her feet drawn under her, her head resting on a pale blue pillow, her eyes wide and mysteriously watchful. The new floor lamp with its shade of rose-colored silk gives a soft, becoming light to her face, bringing out the fragile, unearthly prettiness which usually escapes attention. There is a steady murmur of rain, but it is slackening and stops soon after the scene begins; the air outside becomes pale and luminous as the moon breaks out.*

A moment after the curtain rises, the lights in both rooms flicker and go out.

JIM. Hey, there, Mr. Light Bulb!

[AMANDA *laughs nervously.* LEGEND: "SUSPENSION OF A PUBLIC SERVICE."]

AMANDA. Where was Moses when the lights went out? Ha-ha. Do you know the answer to that one, Mr. O'Connor?

JIM. No, Ma'am, what's the answer?

AMANDA. In the dark! (JIM *laughs appreciatively.*)

Everybody sit still. I'll light the candles. Isn't it lucky we have them on the table? Where's a match? Which of you gentlemen can provide a match?

JIM. Here.

AMANDA. Thank you, sir.

JIM. Not at all, Ma'am!

AMANDA. I guess the fuse has burnt out. Mr. O'Connor, can you tell a burnt-out fuse? I know I can't and Tom is a total loss when it comes to mechanics. (SOUND: GETTING UP: VOICES RECEDE A LITTLE TO KITCHENETTE.)

Oh, be careful you don't bump into something. We don't want our gentleman caller to break his neck. Now wouldn't that be a fine howdy-do?

JIM. Ha-ha! Where is the fuse-box?

AMANDA. Right here next to the stove. Can you see anything?

JIM. Just a minute.

AMANDA. Isn't electricity a mysterious thing?

Wasn't it Benjamin Franklin who tied a key to a kite?

We live in such a mysterious universe, don't we? Some people say that science clears up all the mysteries for us. In my opinion it only creates more!

Have you found it yet?

JIM. No Ma'am. All these fuses look okay to me.

AMANDA. Tom!

TOM. Yes, Mother?

AMANDA. That light bill I gave you several days ago. The one I told you we got the notices about?

[LEGEND: "HA!"]

TOM. Oh—Yeah.

AMANDA. You didn't neglect to pay it by any chance?

TOM. Why, I—

AMANDA. Didn't! I might have known it!

JIM. Shakespeare probably wrote a poem on that light bill, Mrs. Wingfield.

AMANDA. I might have known better than to trust him with it! There's such a high price for negligence in this world!

JIM. Maybe the poem will win a ten-dollar prize.

AMANDA. We'll just have to spend the remainder of the evening in the nineteenth century, before Mr. Edison made the Mazda lamp!

JIM. Candlelight is my favorite kind of light.

AMANDA. That shows you're romantic! But that's no excuse for Tom.

Well, we got through dinner. Very considerate of them to let us get through dinner before they plunged us into everlasting darkness, wasn't it, Mr. O'Connor?

JIM. Ha-ha!

AMANDA. Tom, as a penalty for your carelessness you can help me with the dishes.

JIM. Let me give you a hand.

AMANDA. Indeed you will not!

JIM. I ought to be good for something.

AMANDA. Good for something? (*Her tone is rhapsodic.*)

You? Why, Mr. O'Connor, nobody, *nobody's* given me this much entertainment in years—as you have!

JIM. Aw, now, Mrs. Wingfield!

AMANDA. I'm not exaggerating, not one bit! But Sister is all by her lonesome. You go keep her company in the parlor!

I'll give you this lovely old candelabrum that used to be on the altar at the church of the Heavenly Rest. It was melted a little out of shape when the church burnt down. Lightning struck it one spring. Gypsy Jones was holding a revival at the time and he intimated that the church was destroyed because the Episcopalians gave card parties.

JIM. Ha-ha!

AMANDA. And how about you coaxing Sister to drink a little wine? I think it would be good for her! Can you carry both at once?

JIM. Sure. I'm Superman!

AMANDA. Now, Thomas, get into this apron!

[*The door of kitchenette swings closed on* AMANDA'*s gay laughter; the flickering light approaches the portieres.* LAURA *sits up nervously as he enters. Her speech at first is low and breathless from the almost intolerable strain of being alone with a stranger.* THE LEGEND: "I DON'T SUPPOSE YOU REMEMBER ME AT ALL!" *In her first speeches in this scene, before* JIM'*s warmth overcomes her paralyzing shyness,* LAURA'*s voice is thin and breathless as though she has just run up a steep flight of stairs.* JIM'*s attitude is gently humorous. In playing this scene it should be stressed that while the incident is apparently unimportant, it is to* LAURA *the climax of her secret life.*]

JIM. Hello, there, Laura.

LAURA (*faintly*). Hello. (*She clears her throat.*)

JIM. How are you feeling now? Better?

LAURA. Yes. Yes, thank you.

JIM. This is for you. A little dandelion wine. (*He extends it toward her with extravagant gallantry.*)

LAURA. Thank you.

JIM. Drink it—but don't get drunk! (*He laughs heartily.* LAURA *takes the glass uncertainly; laughs shyly.*) Where shall I set the candles?

LAURA. Oh—oh, anywhere. . . .

JIM. How about here on the floor? Any objections?

LAURA. No.

JIM. I'll spread a newspaper under to catch the drippings. I like to sit on the floor. Mind if I do?

LAURA. Oh, no.

JIM. Give me a pillow?

LAURA. What?

JIM. A pillow!

LAURA. Oh . . . (*Hands him one quickly.*)

JIM. How about you? Don't you like to sit on the floor?

LAURA. Oh—yes.

JIM. Why don't you, then?

LAURA. I—will.

JIM. Take a pillow! (LAURA *does. Sits on the other side of the candelabrum.* JIM *crosses his legs and smiles engagingly at her.*) I can't hardly see you sitting way over there.

LAURA. I can—see you.

JIM. I know, but that's not fair, I'm in the limelight. (LAURA *moves her pillow closer.*) Good! Now I can see you! Comfortable?

LAURA. Yes.

JIM. So am I. Comfortable as a cow! Will you have some gum?

LAURA. No, thank you.

JIM. I think that I will indulge, with your permission. (*Musingly unwraps it and holds it up.*) Think of the fortune made by the guy that invented the first piece of chewing gum. Amazing, huh? The Wrigley Building is one of the sights of Chicago.—I saw it summer before last when I went up to the Century of Progress. Did you take in the Century of Progress?

LAURA. No, I didn't.

JIM. Well, it was quite a wonderful exposition. What impressed me most was the Hall of Science. Gives you an idea of what the future will be in America, even more wonderful than the present time is! (*Pause. Smiling at her.*) Your brother tells me you're shy. Is that right, Laura?

LAURA. I—don't know.

JIM. I judge you to be an old-fashioned type of girl. Well, I think that's a pretty good type to be. Hope you don't think I'm being too personal—do you?

LAURA (*hastily, out of embarrassment*). I believe I *will* take a piece of gum, if you—don't mind. (*Clearing her throat.*) Mr. O'Connor, have you—kept up with your singing?

JIM. Singing? Me?

LAURA. Yes. I remember what a beautiful voice you had.

JIM. When did you hear me sing?

[VOICE OFF STAGE IN THE PAUSE.]

VOICE (*off stage*).

O blow, ye winds, heigh-ho,
A-roving I will go!
I'm off to my love
With a boxing glove—
Ten thousand miles away!

JIM. You say you've heard me sing?

LAURA. Oh, yes! Yes, very often. . . . I—don't suppose—you remember me—at all?

JIM (*smiling doubtfully*). You know I have an idea I've seen you before. I had that idea soon as you opened the door. It seemed almost like I was about to remember your name. But the name that I started to call you—wasn't a name! And so I stopped myself before I said it.

LAURA. Wasn't it—Blue Roses?

JIM (*springs up. Grinning*). Blue Roses!—My gosh, yes—Blue Roses! That's what I had on my tongue when you opened the door!

Isn't it funny what tricks your memory plays? I didn't connect you with high school somehow or other.

But that's where it was; it was high school. I didn't even know you were Shakespeare's sister!

Gosh, I'm sorry.

LAURA. I didn't expect you to. You—barely knew me!

JIM. But we did have a speaking acquaintance, huh?

LAURA. Yes, we—spoke to each other.

JIM. When did you recognize me?

LAURA. Oh, right away!

JIM. Soon as I came in the door?

LAURA. When I heard your name I thought it was probably you. I knew that Tom used to know you a little in high school. So when you came in the door—

Well, then I was—sure.

JIM. Why didn't you *say* something, then?

LAURA (*breathlessly*). I didn't know what to say, I was—too surprised!

JIM. For goodness' sakes! You know, this sure is funny!

LAURA. Yes! Yes, isn't it, though. . . .

JIM. Didn't we have a class in something together?

LAURA. Yes, we did.

JIM. What class was that?

LAURA. It was—singing—Chorus!

JIM. Aw!

LAURA. I sat across the aisle from you in the Aud.

JIM. Aw.

LAURA. Mondays, Wednesdays and Fridays.

JIM. Now I remember—you always came in late.

LAURA. Yes, it was so hard for me, getting upstairs. I had that brace on my leg—it clumped so loud!

JIM. I never heard any clumping.

LAURA (*wincing at the recollection*). To me it sounded like—thunder!

JIM. Well, well, well, I never even noticed.

LAURA. And everybody was seated before I came in. I had to walk in front of all those people. My seat was in the back row. I had to go clumping all the way up the aisle with everyone watching!

JIM. You shouldn't have been self-conscious.

LAURA. I know, but I was. It was always such a relief when the singing started.

JIM. Aw, yes, I've placed you now! I used to call you Blue Roses. How was it that I got started calling you that?

LAURA. I was out of school a little while with pleurosis. When I came back you asked me what was the matter. I said I had pleurosis—you thought I said Blue Roses. That's what you always called me after that!

JIM. I hope you didn't mind.

LAURA. Oh, no—I liked it. You see, I wasn't acquainted with many—people. . . .

JIM. As I remember you sort of stuck by yourself.

LAURA. I—I—never have had much luck at—making friends.

JIM. I don't see why you wouldn't.

LAURA. Well, I—started out badly.

JIM. You mean being—

LAURA. Yes, it sort of—stood between me—

JIM. You shouldn't have let it!

LAURA. I know, but it did, and—

JIM. You were shy with people!

LAURA. I tried not to be but never could—

JIM. Overcome it?

LAURA. No, I—I never could!

JIM. I guess being shy is something you have to work out of kind of gradually.

LAURA (*sorrowfully*). Yes—I guess it—

JIM. Takes time!

LAURA. Yes.

JIM. People are not so dreadful when you know them. That's what you have to remember! And everybody has problems, not just you, but practically everybody has got some problems.

You think of yourself as having the only problems, as being the only one who is disappointed. But just look around you and you will see lots of people as disappointed as you are. For instance, I hoped when I was going to high school that I would be further along at this time, six years later, than I am now— You remember that wonderful write-up I had in *The Torch*?

LAURA. Yes! (*She rises and crosses to table.*)

JIM. It said I was bound to succeed in anything I went into! (LAURA *returns with the annual.*) Holy Jeez! *The Torch!* (*He accepts it reverently. They smile across it with mutual wonder.* LAURA *crouches beside him and they begin to turn through it.* LAURA*'s shyness is dissolving in his warmth.*)

LAURA. Here you are in *The Pirates of Penzance!*

JIM (*wistfully*). I sang the baritone lead in that operetta.

LAURA (*raptly*). So—*beautifully!*

JIM (*protesting*). Aw—

LAURA. Yes, yes—beautifully—beautifully!

JIM. You heard me?

LAURA. All three times!

JIM. No!

LAURA. Yes!

JIM. All three performances?

LAURA (*looking down*). Yes.

JIM. Why?

LAURA. I—wanted to ask you to—autograph my program.

JIM. Why didn't you ask me to?

LAURA. You were always surrounded by your own friends so much that I never had a chance to.

JIM. You should have just—

LAURA. Well, I—thought you might think I was—

JIM. Thought I might think you was—what?

LAURA. Oh—

JIM (*with reflective relish*). I was beleaguered by females in those days.

LAURA. You were terribly popular!

JIM. Yeah—

LAURA. You had such a—friendly way—

JIM. I was spoiled in high school.

LAURA. Everybody—liked you!

JIM. Including you?

LAURA. I—yes, I—I did, too— (*She gently closes the book in her lap.*)

JIM. Well, well, well!—Give me that program, Laura. (*She hands it to him. He signs it with a flourish.*) There you are—better late than never!

LAURA. Oh, I—what a—surprise!

JIM. My signature isn't worth very much right now.

But some day—maybe—it will increase in value!

Being disappointed is one thing and being discouraged is something else. I am disappointed but I am not discouraged.

I'm twenty-three years old.

How old are you?

LAURA. I'll be twenty-four in June.

JIM. That's not old age!

LAURA. No, but—

JIM. You finished high school?

LAURA (*with difficulty*). I didn't go back.

JIM. You mean you dropped out?

LAURA. I made bad grades in my final examinations. (*She rises and replaces the book and the program. Her voice strained.*) How is—Emily Meisenbach getting along?

JIM. Oh, that kraut-head!

LAURA. Why do you call her that?

JIM. That's what she was.

LAURA. You're not still—going with her?

JIM. I never see her.

LAURA. It said in the Personal Section that you were—engaged!

JIM. I know, but I wasn't impressed by that—propaganda!

LAURA. It wasn't—the truth?

JIM. Only in Emily's optimistic opinion!

LAURA. Oh—

[LEGEND: "WHAT HAVE YOU DONE SINCE HIGH SCHOOL?" JIM *lights a cigarette and leans indolently back on his elbows smiling at* LAURA *with a warmth and charm which lights her inwardly with altar candles. She remains by the table and turns in her hands a piece of glass to cover her tumult.*]

JIM (*after several reflective puffs on a cigarette*). What have you done since high school? (*She seems not to hear him.*) Huh? (LAURA *looks up.*) I said what have you done since high school, Laura?

LAURA. Nothing much.

JIM. You must have been doing something these six long years.

LAURA. Yes.

JIM. Well, then, such as what?

LAURA. I took a business course at business college—

JIM. How did that work out?

LAURA. Well, not very—well—I had to drop out, it gave me—indigestion—

[JIM *laughs gently.*]

JIM. What are you doing now?

LAURA. I don't do anything—much. Oh, please don't think I sit around doing nothing! My glass collection takes up a good deal of time. Glass is something you have to take good care of.

JIM. What did you say—about glass?

LAURA. Collection I said—I have one— (*She clears her throat and turns away again, acutely shy.*)

JIM (*abruptly*). You know what I judge to be the trouble with you?

Inferiority complex! Know what that is? That's what they call it when someone low-rates himself!

I understand it because I had it, too. Although my case was not so aggravated as yours seems to be. I had it until I took up public speaking, developed my voice, and learned that I had an aptitude for science. Before that time I never thought of myself as being outstanding in any way whatsoever!

Now I've never made a regular study of it, but I have a friend who says I can analyze people better than doctors that make a profession of it. I don't claim that to be necessarily true, but I can sure guess a person's psychology. Laura! (*Takes out his gum.*) Excuse me, Laura. I always take it out when the flavor is gone. I'll use this scrap of paper to wrap it in. I know how it is to get it stuck on a shoe.

Yep—that's what I judge to be your principal trouble. A lack of confidence in yourself as a person. You don't have the proper amount of faith in yourself. I'm basing that fact on a number of your remarks and also on certain observations I've made. For instance that clumping you thought was so awful in high school. You say that you even dreaded to walk into class. You see what you did? You dropped out of school, you gave up an education because of a clump, which as far as I know was practically non-existent! A little physical defect is what you have. Hardly noticeable even! Magnified thousands of times by imagination!

You know what my strong advice to you is? Think of yourself as *superior* in some way!

LAURA. In what way would I think?

JIM. Why, man alive, Laura! Just look about you a little. What do you see? A world full of common people! All of 'em born and all of 'em going to die!

Which of them has one-tenth of your good points! Or mine! Or anyone else's, as far as that goes—Gosh!

Everybody excels in some one thing. Some in many! (*Unconsciously glances at himself in the mirror.*)

All you've got to do is discover in *what!*

Take me, for instance. (*He adjusts his tie at the mirror.*)

My interest happens to lie in electro-dynamics. I'm taking a course in radio engineering at night school, Laura, on top of a fairly responsible job at the warehouse. I'm taking that course and studying public speaking.

LAURA. Ohhhh.

JIM. Because I believe in the future of television! (*Turning back to her.*)

I wish to be ready to go up right along with it. Therefore I'm planning to get in on the ground floor. In fact I've already made the right connections and all that remains is for the industry itself to get under way! Full steam—(*His eyes are starry.*)

Knowledge—Zzzzzp! *Money*—Zzzzzzp!—*Power!*

That's the cycle democracy is built on! (*His attitude is convincingly dynamic.* LAURA *stares at him, even her shyness eclipsed in her absolute wonder. He suddenly grins.*)

I guess you think I think a lot of myself!

LAURA. No—o-o-o, I—

JIM. Now how about you? Isn't there something you take more interest in than anything else?

LAURA. Well, I do—as I said—have my—glass collection—

[*A peal of girlish laughter from the kitchen.*]

JIM. I'm not right sure I know what you're talking about.
What kind of glass is it?

LAURA. Little articles of it, they're ornaments mostly!
Most of them are little animals made out of glass, the tiniest little animals in the world. Mother calls them a glass menagerie!
Here's an example of one, if you'd like to see it!
This one is one of the oldest. It's nearly thirteen. (MUSIC: "THE GLASS MENAGERIE." *He stretches out his hand.*) Oh, be careful—if you breathe, it breaks!

JIM. I'd better not take it. I'm pretty clumsy with things.

LAURA. Go on, I trust you with him! (*Places it in his palm.*)
There now—you're holding him gently!
Hold him over the light, he loves the light! You see how the light shines through him?

JIM. It sure does shine!

LAURA. I shouldn't be partial, but he is my favorite one.

JIM. What kind of a thing is this one supposed to be?

LAURA. Haven't you noticed the single horn on his forehead?

JIM. A unicorn, huh?

LAURA. Mmm-hmmm!

JIM. Unicorns, aren't they extinct in the modern world?

LAURA. I know!

JIM. Poor little fellow, he must feel sort of lonesome.

LAURA (*smiling*). Well, if he does he doesn't complain about it. He stays on a shelf with some horses that don't have horns and all of them seem to get along nicely together.

JIM. How do you know?

LAURA (*lightly*). I haven't heard any arguments among them!

JIM (*grinning*). No arguments, huh? Well, that's a pretty good sign! Where shall I set him?

LAURA. Put him on the table. They all like a change of scenery once in a while!

JIM (*stretching*). Well, well, well, well—
Look how big my shadow is when I stretch!

LAURA. Oh, oh, yes—it stretches across the ceiling!

JIM (*crossing to door*). I think it's stopped raining. (*Opens fire-escape door.*) Where does the music come from?

LAURA. From the Paradise Dance Hall across the alley.

JIM. How about cutting the rug a little, Miss Wingfield?

LAURA. Oh, I—

JIM. Or is your program filled up? Let me have a look at it. (*Grasps imaginary card.*) Why, every dance is taken! I'll just have to scratch some out. (WALTZ MUSIC: "LA GOLONDRINA.") Ahhh, a waltz! (*He executes some sweeping turns by himself then holds his arms toward* LAURA.)

LAURA (*breathlessly*). I—can't dance!

JIM. There you go, that inferiority stuff!

LAURA. I've never danced in my life!

JIM. Come on, try!

LAURA. Oh, but I'd step on you!

JIM. I'm not made out of glass.

LAURA. How—how—how do we start?

JIM. Just leave it to me. You hold your arms out a little.

LAURA. Like this?

JIM. A little bit higher. Right. Now don't tighten up, that's the main thing about it—relax.

LAURA (*laughing breathlessly*). It's hard not to.

JIM. Okay.

LAURA. I'm afraid you can't budge me.

JIM. What do you bet I can't. (*He swings her into motion.*)

LAURA. Goodness, yes, you can!

JIM. Let yourself go, now, Laura, just let yourself go.

LAURA. I'm—

JIM. Come on!

LAURA. Trying!

JIM. Not so stiff— Easy does it!

LAURA. I know but I'm—

JIM. Loosen th' backbone! There now, that's a lot better.

LAURA. Am I?

JIM. Lots, lots better! (*He moves her about the room in a clumsy waltz.*)

LAURA. Oh, my!

JIM. Ha-ha!

LAURA. Oh, my goodness!

JIM. Ha-ha-ha! (*They suddenly bump into the table.* JIM *stops.*) What did we hit on?

LAURA. Table.

JIM. Did something fall off it? I think—

LAURA. Yes.

JIM. I hope it wasn't the little glass horse with the horn!

LAURA. Yes.

JIM. Aw, aw, aw. Is it broken?

LAURA. Now it is just like all the other horses.

JIM. It's lost it's—

LAURA. Horn!

It doesn't matter. Maybe it's a blessing in disguise.

JIM. You'll never forgive me. I bet that that was your favorite piece of glass.

LAURA. I don't have favorites much. It's no tragedy, Freckles. Glass breaks so easily. No matter how careful you are. The traffic jars the shelves and things fall off them.

JIM. Still I'm awfully sorry that I was the cause.

LAURA (*smiling*). I'll just imagine he had an operation.

The horn was removed to make him feel less—freakish! (*They both laugh.*)

Now he will feel more at home with the other horses, the ones that don't have horns. . . .

JIM. Ha-ha, that's very funny! (*Suddenly serious.*)

I'm glad to see that you have a sense of humor.

You know—you're—well—very different!

Surprisingly different from anyone else I know! (*His voice becomes soft and hesitant with a genuine feeling.*)

Do you mind me telling you that? (LAURA *is abashed beyond speech.*) I mean it in a nice way. . . . (LAURA *nods shyly, looking away.*)

You make me feel sort of—I don't know how to put it!

I'm usually pretty good at expressing things, but—

This is something that I don't know how to say! (LAURA *touches her throat and clears it—turns the broken unicorn in her hands. Even softer.*) Has anyone ever told you that you were pretty? (PAUSE: MUSIC. LAURA *looks up slowly, with wonder, and shakes her head.*)

Well, you are! In a very different way from anyone else.

And all the nicer because of the difference, too. (*His voice becomes low and husky.* LAURA *turns away, nearly faint with the novelty of her emotions.*)

I wish that you were my sister. I'd teach you to have some confidence in yourself. The different people are not like other people, but being different is nothing to be ashamed of. Because other people are not such wonderful people. They're one hundred times one thousand. You're one times one! They walk all over the earth. You just stay here. They're common as--weeds, but—you—well, you're—*Blue Roses!* (IMAGE ON SCREEN: BLUE ROSES. MUSIC CHANGES.)

LAURA. But blue is wrong for—roses. . . .

JIM. It's right for you!—You're—pretty!

LAURA. In what respect am I pretty?

JIM. In all respects—believe me! Your eyes—your hair—are pretty! Your hands are pretty! (*He catches hold of her hand.*)

You think I'm making this up because I'm invited to dinner and have to be nice. Oh, I could do that! I could put on an act for you, Laura, and say lots of things without being very sincere. But this time I am. I'm talking to you sincerely. I happened to notice you had this inferiority complex that keeps you from feeling comfortable with people. Somebody needs to build your confidence up and make you proud instead of shy and turning away and—blushing—

Somebody—ought to—

Ought to—*kiss* you, Laura! (*His hand slips slowly up her arm to her shoulder,* MUSIC SWELLS TUMULTUOUSLY. *He suddenly turns her about and kisses her on the lips. When he releases her,* LAURA *sinks on the sofa with a bright, dazed look.* JIM *backs away and fishes in his pocket for a cigarette.* LEGEND ON SCREEN: "SOUVENIR.")

Stumble-john! (*He lights the cigarette, avoiding her look. There is a peal of girlish laughter from* AMANDA *in the kitchen.* LAURA *slowly raises and opens her hand. It still contains the little broken glass animal. She looks at it with a tender, bewildered expression.*)

Stumble-john!

I shouldn't have done that—That was way off the beam. You don't smoke, do you?

(*She looks up, smiling, not hearing the question. He sits beside her a little gingerly. She looks at him speechlessly—waiting. He coughs decorously and moves a little farther aside as he considers the situation and senses her feelings, dimly, with perturbation. Gently.*) Would you —care for a—mint? (*She doesn't seem to hear him but her look grows brighter even.*)

Peppermint—Life-Saver?

My pocket's a regular drug store—wherever I go. . . . (*He pops a mint in his mouth. Then gulps and decides to make a clean breast of it. He speaks slowly and gingerly.*)

Laura, you know, if I had a sister like you, I'd do the same thing as Tom. I'd bring out fellows and—introduce her to them. The right type of boys of a type to—appreciate her.

Only—well—he made a mistake about me.

Maybe I've got no call to be saying this. That may not have been the idea in having me over. But what if it was?

There's nothing wrong about that. The only trouble is that in my case—I'm not in a situation to—do the right thing.

I can't take down your number and say I'll phone.

I can't call up next week and—ask for a date.

I thought I had better explain the situation in case you—misunderstood it and—hurt your feelings. . . .

[*Pause. Slowly, very slowly,* LAURA*'s look changes, her eyes returning slowly from his to the ornament in her palm.* AMANDA *utters another gay laugh in the kitchen.*]

LAURA (*faintly*). You—won't—call again?

JIM. No, Laura, I can't. (*He rises from the sofa.*)

As I was just explaining, I've—got strings on me.

Laura, I've—been going steady!

I go out all of the time with a girl named Betty. She's a homegirl like you, and Catholic, and Irish, and in a great many ways we—get along fine.

I met her last summer on a moonlight boat trip up the river to Alton, on the *Majestic*.

Well—right away from the start it was—love! (LEGEND: LOVE! LAURA *sways slightly forward and grips the arm of the sofa. He fails to notice, now enrapt in his own comfortable being.*)

Being in love has made a new man of me! (*Leaning stiffly forward, clutching the arm of the sofa,* LAURA *struggles visibly with her storm. But* JIM *is oblivious, she is a long way off.*)

The power of love is really pretty tremendous!

Love is something that—changes the whole world, Laura! (*The storm abates a little and* LAURA *leans back. He notices her again.*)

It happened that Betty's aunt took sick, she got a wire and had to go to Centralia. So Tom—when he asked me to dinner—I naturally just accepted the invitation, not knowing that you—that he—that I—(*He stops awkwardly.*)

Huh—I'm a stumble-john! (*He flops back on the sofa. The holy candles in the altar of* LAURA'*s face have been snuffed out. There is a look of almost infinite desolation.* JIM *glances at her uneasily.*)

I wish that you would—say something. (*She bites her lip which was trembling and then bravely smiles. She opens her hand again on the broken glass ornament. Then she gently takes his hand and raises it level with her own. She carefully places the unicorn in the palm of his hand, then pushes his fingers closed upon it.*) What are you—doing that for? You want me to have him?—Laura? (*She nods.*) What for?

LAURA. A—souvenir. . . . (*She rises unsteadily and crouches beside the victrola to wind it up.* LEGEND ON SCREEN: "THINGS HAVE A WAY OF TURNING OUT SO BADLY!" OR IMAGE: "GENTLEMAN CALLER WAVING GOOD-BYE!—GAILY." *At this moment* AMANDA *rushes brightly back in the front room. She bears a pitcher of fruit punch in an old-fashioned cut-glass pitcher and a plate of macaroons. The plate has a gold border and poppies painted on it.*)

AMANDA. Well, well, well! Isn't the air delightful after the shower? I've made you children a little liquid refreshment. (*Turns gaily to the gentleman caller.*)

Jim, do you know that song about lemonade?

"Lemonade, lemonade
Made in the shade and stirred with a spade—
Good enough for any old maid!"

JIM (*uneasily*). Ha-ha! No—I never heard it.

AMANDA. Why, Laura! You look so serious!

JIM. We were having a serious conversation.

AMANDA. Good! Now you're better acquainted!

JIM (*uncertainly*). Ha-ha! Yes.

AMANDA. You modern young people are much more serious-minded than my generation. I was so gay as a girl!

JIM. You haven't changed, Mrs. Wingfield.

AMANDA. Tonight I'm rejuvenated! The gaiety of the occasion, Mr.

O'Connor! (*She tosses her head with a peal of laughter. Spills lemonade.*) Oooo! I'm baptizing myself!

JIM. Here—let me—

AMANDA (*setting the pitcher down*). There now. I discovered we had some maraschino cherries. I dumped them in, juice and all!

JIM. You shouldn't have gone to that trouble, Mrs. Wingfield.

AMANDA. Trouble, trouble? Why, it was loads of fun!

Didn't you hear me cutting up in the kitchen? I bet your ears were burning! I told Tom how outdone with him I was for keeping you to himself so long a time! He should have brought you over much, much sooner! Well, now that you've found your way, I want you to be a very frequent caller! Not just occasional but all the time.

Oh, we're going to have a lot of gay times together! I see them coming!

Mmm, just breathe that air! So fresh, and the moon's so pretty! I'll skip back out—I know where my place is when young folks are having a—serious conversation!

JIM. Oh, don't go out, Mrs. Wingfield. The fact of the matter is I've got to be going.

AMANDA. Going, now? You're joking! Why, it's only the shank of the evening, Mr. O'Connor!

JIM. Well, you know how it is.

AMANDA. You mean you're a young workingman and have to keep workingmen's hours. We'll let you off early tonight. But only on the condition that next time you stay later.

What's the best night for you? Isn't Saturday night the best night for you workingmen?

JIM. I have a couple of time-clocks to punch, Mrs Wingfield. One at morning, another one at night!

AMANDA. My, but you *are* ambitious! You work at night, too?

JIM. No, Ma'am, not work but—Betty! (*He crosses deliberately to pick up his hat. The band at the Paradise Dance Hall goes into a tender waltz.*)

AMANDA. Betty? Betty? Who's—Betty?

[*There is an ominous cracking sound in the sky.*]

JIM. Oh, just a girl. The girl I go steady with! (*He smiles charmingly. The sky falls.*)

[LEGEND: "THE SKY FALLS."]

AMANDA (*a long-drawn exhalation*). Ohhhh . . . Is it a serious romance, Mr. O'Connor?

JIM. We're going to be married the second Sunday in June.

AMANDA. Ohhhh—how nice!

Tom didn't mention that you were engaged to be married.

JIM. The cat's not out of the bag at the warehouse yet.

You know how they are. They call you Romeo and stuff like that.

(*He stops at the oval mirror to put on his hat. He carefully shapes the brim and the crown to give a discreetly dashing effect.*)

It's been a wonderful evening, Mrs. Wingfield. I guess this is what they mean by Southern hospitality.

AMANDA. It really wasn't anything at all.

JIM. I hope it don't seem like I'm rushing off. But I promised Betty I'd pick her up at the Wabash depot, an' by the time I get my jalopy down there her train'll be in. Some women are pretty upset if you keep 'em waiting.

AMANDA. Yes, I know—The tyranny of women! (*Extends her hand.*)

Good-bye, Mr. O'Connor.

I wish you luck—and happiness—and success! All three of them, and so does Laura!—Don't you, Laura?

LAURA. Yes!

JIM (*taking her hand*). Good-bye, Laura. I'm certainly going to treasure that souvenir. And don't you forget the good advice I gave you. (*Raises his voice to a cheery shout.*)

So long, Shakespeare!

Thanks again, ladies—Good night! (*He grins and ducks jauntily out. Still bravely grimacing,* AMANDA *closes the door on the gentleman caller. Then she turns back to the room with a puzzled expression. She and* LAURA *don't dare to face each other.* LAURA *crouches beside the victrola to wind it.*)

AMANDA (*faintly*). Things have a way of turning out so badly.

I don't believe that I would play the victrola.

Well, well—well—

Our gentleman caller was engaged to be married!

Tom!

TOM (*from back*). Yes, Mother?

AMANDA. Come in here a minute. I want to tell you something awfully funny.

TOM (*enters with macaroon and a glass of the lemonade*). Has the gentleman caller gotten away already?

AMANDA. The gentleman caller has made an early departure.

What a wonderful joke you played on us!

TOM. How do you mean?

AMANDA. You didn't mention that he was engaged to be married.

TOM. Jim? Engaged?

AMANDA. That's what he just informed us.

TOM. I'll be jiggered! I didn't know about that.

AMANDA. That seems very peculiar.

TOM. What's peculiar about it?

AMANDA. Didn't you call him your best friend down at the warehouse?

TOM. He is, but how did I know?

AMANDA. It seems extremely peculiar that you wouldn't know your best friend was going to be married!

TOM. The warehouse is where I work, not where I know things about people!

AMANDA. You don't know things anywhere! You live in a dream; you manufacture illusions! (*He crosses to door.*) Where are you going?

TOM. I'm going to the movies.

AMANDA. That's right, now that you've had us make such fools of ourselves. The effort, the preparations, all the expense! The new floor lamp, the rug, the clothes for Laura! All for what? To entertain some other girl's fiancé!

Go to the movies, go! Don't think about us, a mother deserted, an unmarried sister who's crippled and has no job! Don't let anything interfere with your selfish pleasure!

Just go, go, go—to the movies!

TOM. All right, I will! The more you shout about my selfishness to me the quicker I'll go, and I won't go to the movies!

AMANDA. Go, then! Then go to the moon—you selfish dreamer!

[TOM *smashes his glass on the floor. He plunges out on the fire-escape, slamming the door.* LAURA *screams—cut by door. Dance-hall music up.* TOM *goes to the rail and grips it desperately, lifting his face in the chill white moonlight penetrating the narrow abyss of the alley.* LEGEND ON SCREEN: "AND SO GOOD-BYE . . ." TOM'S *closing speech is timed with the interior pantomime. The interior scene is played as though viewed through soundproof glass.* AMANDA *appears to be making a comforting speech to* LAURA, *who is huddled upon the sofa. Now that we cannot hear the mother's speech, her silliness is gone and she has dignity and tragic beauty.* LAURA'*s dark hair hides her face until at the end of the speech she lifts it to smile at her mother.* AMANDA'*s gestures are slow and graceful, almost dancelike, as she comforts the daughter. At the end of her speech she glances a moment at the father's picture—then withdraws through the portieres. At close of* TOM'*s speech,* LAURA *blows out the candles, ending the play.*]

TOM. I didn't go to the moon, I went much further—for time is the longest distance between two places—

Not long after that I was fired for writing a poem on the lid of a shoe-box.

I left Saint Louis. I descended the steps of this fire-escape for a last time and followed, from then on, in my father's footsteps, attempting to find in motion what was lost in space—

I traveled around a great deal. The cities swept about me like dead leaves, leaves that were brightly colored but torn away from the branches.

I would have stopped, but I was pursued by something.

It always came upon me unawares, taking me altogether by surprise. Perhaps it was a familiar bit of music. Perhaps it was only a piece of transparent glass—

Perhaps I am walking along a street at night, in some strange city, before I have found companions. I pass the lighted window of a shop where perfume is sold. The window is filled with pieces of colored glass, tiny transparent bottles in delicate colors, like bits of a shattered rainbow.

Then all at once my sister touches my shoulder. I turn around and look into her eyes. . . .

Oh, Laura, Laura, I tried to leave you behind me, but I am more faithful than I intended to be!

I reach for a cigarette, I cross the street, I run into the movies or a bar, I buy a drink, I speak to the nearest stranger—anything that can blow your candles out! (LAURA *bends over the candles.*)—for nowadays the world is lit by lightning! Blow out your candles, Laura—and so good-bye. . . .

[*She blows the candles out.*]

[*The Scene Dissolves.*]

CRITICAL COMMENTARY

What is the subject of *The Glass Menagerie?* In his prefatory remarks, Tennessee Williams tells us to pay attention to the screen device, the music, the lighting, the set, the expressionistic stage business and properties. Discussions of the play have often implied that Williams' advice is the clue to the subject, almost the subject itself. The implication is apparent in the usual leading questions about the play: What effects are created each time there is off-stage music? What does the absent father's photograph contribute to the play? Why is Laura crippled, literally and metaphorically? What is implied by Tom's constant movie-going? What are the connotations of Blue Roses? What is symbolized by the opposition of the typewriter and the glass animals? And so on, until one rebels. There is something wrong with this approach. The answers are obvious, the play from this view is merely slick, and to analyze the obviously slick in a serious manner is to be had.

Since the action of the play is laid in the Thirties, perhaps the real subject is social and economic, the Depression. But again apparently not. The Thirties are dismissed as "quaint," and the Depression is spoken of in a distant, sophisticated way as being something like a middle-class reading problem ("Their eyes had failed them, or they had failed their eyes, and so they were having their fingers pressed forcibly down on the fiery Braille alphabet of a dissolving economy"). Of course the Wingfield family is depressed, struggling along in hand-me-downs on $65 a month in a lower middle-class tenement, but is it ever even implied that money would solve their peculiar problems? The still larger related issues of the time, the passing of the old South, the Spanish Civil War, Hitler, Munich—these are little more than unread headlines.

Williams also remarks that the "scene is memory and is therefore nonrealistic . . . for memory is seated predominantly in the heart. The interior is therefore rather dim and poetic." Perhaps the real subject, then, is the author's feeling about his past as he looks back from his own thirties. This is an appealing idea because in a sense it is everybody's subject and because the play does in fact echo Williams' own youthful life in the South. His real name is Tom, he began writing when he was young and persisted against his father's attempt to make him into a business man, he had a sister who was very shy and collected glass animals; but despite all this and all the talk about mood music, special lighting, and nostalgia, is nostalgia the central emotion of the play? And is not Tom-Tennessee's remorse at having deserted a helpless sister finally peripheral, almost tacked on?

The central emotion of the play seems to be closer to a cold, intense, frustrated anger. If that is true, would this be a fair description of *The Glass Menagerie:* A slightly old-fashioned middle-class ghetto play in which the characters are systematically castrated but are not allowed the modern relief of smashing things? The thing we would like to smash is obviously Amanda, and the right leading questions might therefore start like this: In what ways is Amanda evil? How does Mr. Williams set her up as the object of our anger? How is its full expression frustrated?

In trying to answer such questions, it may be tempting to equate Amanda with the South. Her romantic memories of her girlhood as a Southern belle are certainly important in the play, and even her speech seems more "Southern" than that of other characters. Her background, however, is larger than a region. She may have been formed, along with other good women of her kind, in the sentimental drama and fiction that accompanied the rise of the Protestant middle class. Here, for example, are some observations about the early eighteenth-century English sentimental drama. Do they apply to Amanda?

The sentimentalist plays a

> double game: he wants to think of himself as continuously virtuous, and he wants to get the job too. And these inconsistent desires require a continuous reinterpretation of every circumstance so as to emphasize the virtue and ignore the unscrupulousness. . . . By a necessary inconsistency, the sentimentalist can never admit to himself that his argument is a rationalization, or else it would fail in its designed effect: a clearing of his conscience and a conviction of his own sinlessness and altruism. Thus sentimental thinking is balanced delicately between hypocrisy and sincerity, simplicity and duplicity, self-consciousness and spontaneity. . . . The sentimentalist has been seen managing other people for the furthering of his own interest and theirs. . . . The sentimentalist clearly regards the person to be managed as his inferior, both in understanding and in virtue. Hence it is not surprising that sentimentalists often invoke the relationship between parent and child, with its similar indications of love and discipline . . . so the sentimentalist may play a game of spiritual coercion while seeming to exude nothing but love. . . . [There is usually] a scene where the less sentimental character has repented of his misdeeds and asked forgiveness of the more sentimental character. And in each of these cases, the character who has established a virtuous dominance has assured the other that his sins have been forgiven, and that he may now make a fresh start. . . . Usually in such scenes the repentant one admits he has been not only evil, but also stupid, ill-advised, and immature, whereas he now sees that the

sentimentalist is at once more sensible, more practical, and more virtuous. . . . Hence the value of the sinner to the sentimentalist . . . so long as the act of abasement is practiced with sufficient assiduity, the usually stuffy and prudish sentimentalist can forgive an amazing amount of wrongdoing. (Paul E. Parnell, "The Sentimental Mask," *PMLA,* 78, 1963, pp. 530–33.)

Useful Criticism

Donahue, Francis. *The Dramatic World of Tennessee Williams.* New York: Frederick Ungar, 1964.

Kernan, Alvin, ed. *The Modern American Theater: A Collection of Critical Essays.** Englewood Cliffs, N.J.: Prentice-Hall, 1967.

Nelson, Benjamin. *Tennessee Williams: The Man and His Work.* New York: Ivan Obolensky, 1961.

* Available in paperback.

HOUSE OF COWARDS

Dannie Abse

CHARACTERS

MR. HICKS
MRS. HICKS, his wife
GEORGE HICKS, their son
ALF JENKINS, a lodger
MISS CHANTRY, another lodger
SHEILA, George's fiancée
MR. JAY, a journalist
MR. NOTT, a stranger
SPIV

SYNOPSIS OF SCENES

ACT I
Living room of the Hicks family, one Thursday evening.

ACT II
Scene 1. *Street near a bridge, later that evening.*
Scene 2. *The same, just after 6.30 p.m. on Friday.*

ACT III
Living room of the Hicks family, later Friday evening.

ACT I

The scene is the living room of No. 1 Shelley Street, a corner house. Time, the present, one cold Thursday evening in February.

The furniture is old-fashioned and rather shabby. In the armchair nearest to the anthracite stove on the right sits Mr. Hicks, studying a chessboard under a standard lamp. He is a short, aggressive man of about sixty. As usual he is wearing two pullovers. His wife, a home-made woman, some six years younger than he, comes in through rear door right. Between this door and left wall is a window which overlooks the pavement and street outside. There is another door left leading to the hall. Just prior to her entering the room it would seem as if a van with loudspeaker is passing by in the street. At first the voice booming through the loudspeakers is distant, but soon becomes louder and intelligible, especially when Mrs. Hicks opens the window.

VOICE (*outside*). Four, five, six, seven. At seven o'clock. One, two, three, four, five, six, seven.

HICKS (*without looking up from the chessboard*). Close the window.

MRS. HICKS. But listen.

VOICE (*outside*). At Sunshine Hall tomorrow night. One, two, three, four, five, six, seven.

HICKS. We know all about that. We know the time. We know the place. Now close it. The draught. You'll set me off coughing.

MRS. HICKS. The van's going. That's twice it's been around here.

HICKS. Aye, and they'll be around again. It's a wonder Miss Chantry hasn't come down to tell us all about it. You'd think the Messiah was coming, listening to her. Do close it. It's a real arctic wind.

MRS. HICKS. I must say I'm a little confused. Miss Chantry says it's going to be a great religious meeting. Alf says it's political. And George says they're both wrong.

HICKS. Simpletons. All of them. Advertise dirt and they'd buy it. Dirt makes your face whiter. Mugs.

MRS. HICKS. I don't know, Bill. The whole town's excited, and it was in the news last night on television. They showed you a view of Sunshine Hall. Outside and in.

HICKS (*still staring at chessboard*). Mmmm.

MRS. HICKS. Aren't you pleased about George?

HICKS. Sheila's a nice girl only . . .

MRS. HICKS. Only what?

HICKS. Only they ought to have money behind them.

MRS. HICKS. Sheila earns her fair whack as a telephonist. And George won't always be a junior librarian.

HICKS. They need dough. I may not be able to work but I'm not a helpless invalid. Sheila's mother can't even take in boarders like us. If only I was in my prime. Remember before the war? Verity and Voce. Little Audrey laughed and laughed. Kid Berg. The Lambeth Walk. Oi! I remember. My old second-hand Morris Cowley. It was like a chorus girl, slow to start but when it got going! We soon lost that.

MRS. HICKS. I was carrying George that summer.

HICKS. Now don't get sentimental on me, Doris.

MRS. HICKS. I was thirty-seven. And having my first baby. We left it late, Bill.

HICKS. Damn it all, I had more business acumen than Dick Morrison had in his fat arse.

MRS. HICKS. If it hadn't been for your health, you would have done well, Bill. The war, bad luck, bad friends, bad health.

HICKS. I had ideas. The laundries. About the chain of laundries. Long time before anybody thought of Bendix.

MRS. HICKS. I know. I know.

HICKS. You don't know. That idea I had about barber shops. There was a future in that. An absolute future.

MRS. HICKS. The barber shops? I don't recall your idea about the barber shops.

HICKS. My health. That's what stopped me. I swear to God that's the truth. Anything else, any other version is a lie, jealousy, vicious gossip. (*Begins to cough.*) Where did I go wrong?

MRS. HICKS. It's time for your medicine. Leave it now. Leave it, Bill. It's not 'ealthy. God's been very kind really.

HICKS (*gasping*). Even now . . . I could pull out. Sixty-two, that's all I am.

MRS. HICKS (*pouring out medicine into a spoon*). Here, take this.

HICKS (*imploringly*). Doris, tell me. Couldn't I pull out? Take off again? Zoom?

MRS. HICKS. Of course you could. You know I know that. (*Bending over spoon.*) Careful now. Don't spill it.

HICKS (*taking medicine*). Vile taste. Doesn't seem to work as it used to . . . I'll be glad when the winter's over. Football on Saturdays. I miss watching the Baboons. TV isn't the same thing. What a team the Baboons used to have in the old days.

MRS. HICKS. All right, Bill?

HICKS. I'm all right. Course I'm all right. What are you looking at me like that for? Let me get on with this chess problem. (*Hands back spoon. Stares at chessboard and moves a piece.*)

MRS. HICKS. I sometimes think we don't get as much enjoyment out of things as we ought. I'm not unhappy. I'm not complaining. But it would be nice to get away for a holiday this year by the sea. Just not to have to do the cooking for a week. Not to have to make the beds. Not to have to do all the washing an' ironing an' polishing an' scrubbing. It's been years since we had a holiday. Wouldn't it be lovely to go somewhere nice an' warm. I dream sometimes of Italy. I've never been to Italy an' I don't know what Italy looks like but I *feel* I'm in Italy when I'm dreaming.

HICKS. Put a sock in it for God's sake.

MRS. HICKS. I hope George and Sheila will be very happy. I hope they love each other serenely I mean. You can start off so cheerful and confident on the journey. You get into the train singing. It goes off like, and years later you're still in the train only it's stopped at some derelict sidings and you're not singing any more. Everything rusts away, like, with the days. Where you are don' seem like a proper destination. You feel cheated but there's no return ticket. Still you 'ave to count your blessings, don't you? Oh Bill, I forgot to tell you. Mrs. Verney said a gent had been asking about us.

HICKS. What did he want? A room?

MRS. HICKS. He was a journalist.

HICKS. So what?

MRS. HICKS. This journalist is down from London to cover the Meeting at Sunshine Hall. He asked Mrs. Verney what family round here took in boarders so naturally she gave our names, like. Then this journalist creepy crawly fellow asks how many in our house and he writes down all our names. Mrs. Verney naturally told him about Mr. Mason 'aving a stroke.

HICKS. Naturally. She's a proper information bureau.

MRS. HICKS. And he writes down that too. Then he enquired if there was anything special about our house, like it having a yellow door or something and, of course, that baffled Mrs. Verney.

HICKS. What did old hag Verney say?

MRS. HICKS. Nothin' special, she says. It's No. 1 Shelley Street, a corner house, and then this journalist interrupts her and says that's a brilliant idea.

HICKS. What is?

MRS. HICKS. Our house being a corner house. It seemed to inspire him, Mrs. Verney said.

HICKS. I don't see . . .

MRS. HICKS. Nor I. Journalists are funny, you know.

[*Enter* MISS CHANTRY *from rear door right. She is a rather thin, angular, intense lady over forty.*]

MISS CHANTRY. I do hope I'm not disturbing you. I was going through some old papers of mine and look what I found, Mrs. Hicks. Oh, the dust which covers and buries the years. Would you like to see it? It's of Harry. Only the top half I'm afraid, and it's yellowing.

MRS. HICKS. Let me put my glasses on.

HICKS (*staring at chessboard*). Did you get a ticket for the Meeting, Miss Chantry?

MISS CHANTRY. No, no. But I'll get in.

MRS. HICKS (*looking at snapshot*). He was a handsome fellow. He looks younger than in the photograph you have in your room. And the cat? Was that his cat in the tree?

MISS CHANTRY. The lilac tree. It was one of my own cats. Felix the III. I wish you had a cat, Mrs. Hicks. I sometimes feel I need a cat around me like some people hunger for the sea.

MRS. HICKS. Look at this snap, Bill. Of Harry Wiggall. Didn't he have a

HICKS (*taking snapshot*). Ta. Mmm. I thought you said he was a tall man.

MISS CHANTRY. The bottom half is torn.

HICKS. Oh.

MISS CHANTRY. He's sitting down.

MRS. HICKS (*trying to save the situation*). Bill, you can certainly see the inner man, can't you?

HICKS. I can see the upper man.

MRS. HICKS. It's a very nice photo.

MISS CHANTRY. Oh, it doesn't flatter him. I wish he were alive now. To share with me the experience of the Meeting tomorrow night. Strange, isn't it? I mean the Meeting being *tomorrow* night. Thirty years to the day since poor Harry walked heart-high through the flames, into that impossible furnace. Still, all that's done and past.

HICKS. Yes, it's a nice photo all right. Thank you. (*Hands it back to* MISS CHANTRY.) Snapshots bring it all back, don't they. Oil the old memory. Stoke up the old fires.

MISS CHANTRY (*stiffly*). He was cremated alive, Mr. Hicks.

HICKS. I didn't mean. I'm sorry. I . . .

MISS CHANTRY. He was just my Harry.

[*Enter* GEORGE, *door left.* GEORGE HICKS *is half youth, half man, with a rather selfish, good-looking face. He is carrying a number of new books and an evening paper.*]

GEORGE. Did you hear it? The van with the megaphone. It's down the street now. All day in the library I've heard nothing except talk of the Speaker. Look at the evening paper. Headlines. Meeting, tomorrow night, at Sunshine Hall.

HICKS. I see you've got the books.

GEORGE. Yes, a new Daphne du Maurier for mum. A book of modern poems for you, Miss Chantry. And *Russian Kings of Chess.* (*Goes over towards his father.*) When I am ze white I win because I am ze white . . . (*Gives him book.*)

HICKS. And when I am ze black I win because I am Zorinonfilligoff.

GEORGE AND HICKS (*together*). Ha!

HICKS. What's this other book? By Frood? The Ego and the Penny?

GEORGE. Not penny. *Id*, Dad. *The Ego and the Id.*

[*Though the window is closed the voice through the megaphone can be heard distinctly.*]

VOICE (*outside*). Two, three, four, five, six, seven. Tomorrow night at Sunshine Hall. Hear the Speaker at Seven o'clock. One, two, three, (*Begins to fade.*) four, five, six, seven. One, two, three . . .

HICKS. Loud enough to wake the dead.

MISS CHANTRY. It's a miracle that the Speaker should come to our town. It's so exciting. The megaphone calling everybody to Sunshine Hall, tomorrow night.

HICKS. Like a damned Pied Piper.

GEORGE. Everybody I've met today is going. The whole town's up in the air. Like at the end of the war—on Victory Day. It's like that. And they've put up flags and bunting, and everyone seems happy.

MISS CHANTRY. Naturally.

GEORGE. Sincerely happy, not just faking it. It's as if they know that this Meeting really is significant.

HICKS. Mad, all of them. Up the ruddy greased pole.

GEORGE. You should go out and feel the mood of people, Dad.

HICKS. Huh!

GEORGE. Everybody greets you with a big "hello". Groups of people wave for no reason. Queues look as if they might suddenly start to sing like in an opera. It's cold out but the air is electric. When the Speaker arrives they'll be dancing in the streets.

HICKS. Going around saying things like that. It's like spreading good news when there is none. You make me want to scream.

GEORGE. That's because you assume that any public speaker is a phoney, every promise insincere.

MISS CHANTRY. Every programme uncertain or tepid or cynical or dishonest.

GEORGE. But the Speaker coming here. Why, that's more than one bargained for.

MRS. HICKS. I don't understand what you are all on about, but I want to cry suddenly. I don't feel unhappy but I just want to cry.

MISS CHANTRY. Once I saw something quite perfectly. I understood the pattern of all things in their entirety.

HICKS. A van goes by and they jump on to soapboxes.

MRS. HICKS. Go on, Miss Chantry, I think I understand.

MISS CHANTRY. It was like hearing a great voice. One single whispering voice. What that voice said, I don't remember—I can only recall understanding everything at the time, and feeling inexplicably jubilant, yet peaceful. I've forgotten what that voice said. I sometimes wonder whether I heard a voice at all. Maybe it was just my imagination, or maybe it was only a silly, pretty dream.

MRS. HICKS. No, no.

MISS CHANTRY. So I have to hear that voice again. I want to be happy like that again, in a way I cannot understand or communicate. That's why I'm looking forward to the Meeting. There will be a great religious revival.

GEORGE. It's not religious, Miss Chantry. It's nothing to do with religion. Not religion as you mean it, anyway.

MRS. HICKS. Alf says it's politics.

GEORGE. It's not political either. At least not in the way Alf thinks it is.

HICKS (*shouts*). Then what is it?

GEORGE. I . . . don't know.

HICKS. You don't know. He doesn't know. (*Laughs.*) He's been talking about how marvellous it all is—and he hasn't a clue. Oh, that's rich. (*Laughs uproariously.*)

GEORGE. It's . . . it's moral.

HICKS. Hear that? (*Laughs more.*) Moral. Not religious, not political (*Laughs.*) . . . but moral.

GEORGE (*testily*). I'm glad you find me amusing. I must be goin', Mum. I'm eating at Sheila's tonight, she'll be waiting, and I'm hungry.

MRS. HICKS. Take your scarf, it's in the hall.

[GEORGE *begins to exit.*]

HICKS. Moral. Did you hear what he said? (*Laughs.*) That's very comic.

[GEORGE *stops at the door, left.*]

That's very comic.

GEORGE. There's just a chance. There could be a different morality. Look at the mess. Dangers of radiation. Dangers of war.

[HICKS *begins to laugh again.*]

That's no laughing matter. STOP LAUGHING.

MRS. HICKS. Now, George.

GEORGE. He only thinks of himself. It's all self-interest. I'm all right, Jack, and blast everybody else. He of all people needs to hear the Speaker.

MRS. HICKS. Now, son.

GEORGE. Well, he does. When did he show you any consideration, any tenderness? I've never even seen him give you as much as a kiss. Not for years.

HICKS. That's enough.

GEORGE. On a birthday, or something, not so much as a hug, a kiss.

HICKS. Have you ever thought . . . have you ever considered . . . Why, grow up . . . Don't you think your mother might not want me to? You go off to your Sheila. You're just a kid. You don't know. Spending your money on a damned ring. I've been married thirty years. Thirty years and I know. The only Speaker that talks to me is money. M.O.N.E.Y.

GEORGE. Yes, money. You gave me plenty of that. You gave me a great start. No sacrifice too big for you. You're my father.

[*Exit* GEORGE.]

HICKS. I would have given him anything if I'd had it. There was no need for him to talk that way to me.

MISS CHANTRY. Supposing he doesn't turn up?

MRS. HICKS. Who?

MISS CHANTRY. The Speaker.

MRS. HICKS. Why, of course he'll turn up. It's been so widely advertised.

HICKS. Miss Chantry, if I had my health, a decent pair of lungs, I would have been right at the top. He and Sheila—why they'd be in gold clover. There was no need for him to say that to me.

MRS. HICKS. They wouldn't have hired the Hall if he wasn't going to turn up.

HICKS. I'm talking about important matters and you're blabbering on about this Meeting.

MISS CHANTRY. Mr. Hicks, you don't understand.

HICKS. You know so much like, because you go to church on Sundays and read modern poetry and *The Times* instead of the *Daily Star* like us.

MRS. HICKS. Really, Bill.

HICKS. Since I don't understand, since I'm so ignorant, let me ask you a question.

MISS CHANTRY. I don't profess to know so much, Mr. Hicks, but . . .

HICKS. But who put up the advertisements?

MISS CHANTRY. For the Meeting?

HICKS. Yes, go on. Tell me that, go on.

MISS CHANTRY. I don't know.

HICKS. Whose van was that going round with the megaphones?

MISS CHANTRY. I don't see . . .

HICKS. You don't see. You mean you don't know. Answer, go on Answer!

MISS CHANTRY. I don't know, but . . .

HICKS. Who hired the Hall for the Speaker?

MISS CHANTRY. I never thought.

HICKS. Isn't it time you thought? Who's behind it all?

MISS CHANTRY (*defeated*). I don't . . . know. (*Pause.*) You're destructive. Your husband is a bully and very destructive.

HICKS. Destructive? I'm destroyed. You've no inkling of the man I was. You don't realise how I've been dogged by bad luck.

MISS CHANTRY. Bad luck! Think how different it would have been for me if Harry hadn't gone into that fire. What we would have done, together. You shouldn't be sorry for yourself. At least you've got a son. Fire robbed me of my children.

[*Hurried exit rear door right.*]

HICKS (*calling after her*). That Meeting. It's all cooked up, that Meeting, (*Quietly to* MRS. HICKS.) for fools like her and George and Alf. Caw, that photo! Still, with her looks she couldn't be too choosy.

MRS. HICKS. I think Miss Chantry looks very nice. And she's got lovely hands—like a pianist's. Going into that fire, why Harry Wiggall was a hero.

[*The front door bell rings.* MRS. HICKS *rises to answer it but just then telephone rings also.*]

HICKS. Why is it the front door bell and the telephone always seem to ring at the same time?

MRS. HICKS (*picking up telephone*). Hello. Who? Mr. Mason? No, I'm sorry. Mr. Mason's dead. I said he's dead. He died a few weeks ago. Hello. No. Mr. Mason's dead. I said . . .

[*Front door bell rings again.*]

Just a minute, please. (*Holds hand over telephone.*) Answer the front door, Bill.

HICKS. The draught from the front door would start me off coughing.

MRS. HICKS. Hello, hello. Oh, they've rung off.

HICKS. Better answer the front door.

MRS. HICKS. Somebody asking for Mr. Mason, but the line wasn't very clear.

HICKS. Who'd be asking for Mason?

[MRS. HICKS *exits through door left to answer front door.*]

(*Singing quietly to himself.*) A pint of beer, a pint of beer, a Woodbine and a match. A fourpenny halfpenny walking stick to see the football . . . (*He stops abruptly.*) I wonder who'd be asking for Mason?

[MRS. HICKS *and* MR. JAY *enter. The latter is a tall man with a bony face. In every way he is rather larger than life. He owns a loud voice with an almost persistent chuckle in it. He is carrying a brand new suitcase.*]

HICKS (*puzzled*). What?

MRS. HICKS. He wishes to see you. It's Mr. . . .

JAY. Jay, Jay's the name. Bernard Jay of the *Daily Star*. You've heard of me perhaps? No matter. I must say you all must be very excited about it. More like a dream, isn't it? A million to one chance.

[*He puts his case down and goes over to shake hands with* MR. HICKS.]

HICKS. Excited?

MRS. HICKS. About what?

JAY. About the Speaker coming here.

HICKS. Oh, *that*. You want to see me, Mr. Jay?

MRS. HICKS. Is there anything wrong, sir?

JAY. Wrong! You have this marvellous luck—like finding a gold nugget in the garden, like having the right number turn up in roulette—and you ask if anything's wrong.

MRS. HICKS. I don't understand.

JAY. We're going to take pictures of you all. Everybody in this fortunate house, in this house of smiles and happiness. It'll be on the front page, magnificent. Yes, it's a great honour—having the Speaker coming here and it will be a great story. How do you feel about it, Mr. Hicks? I mean about the Speaker staying here?

MRS. HICKS. Well, George is very keen to hear him.

HICKS. Staying *here*. What do you mean, *here*?

JAY. Why, in your house, Mr. Hicks.

HICKS. Our 'ouse?

JAY. I'm not surprised you're overcome. No, no. It's remarkable. You see the Speaker never stays in an hotel. It's well known he always puts up with a humble family. Yes, he's a man of the people. A great man. You must be very proud. I hope you've prepared his room, Mrs. Hicks, because it's as natural as the sun rises in the morning and the sun sets in the evening that he will stay here.

HICKS. It would be damned unnatural, I'd say.

JAY. Your place is only five minutes from both the station and Sunshine Hall. And it's a corner house. You're very lucky. This is a wonderful day for the Hicks.

MRS. HICKS. We're very well situated. The shopping centre's only in the main road. It's very convenient and buses go up and down all the time. No. 3 is an excellent service. Besides, this house is very light. And we have hot water all the time. Our new Ideal boiler is a boon.

HICKS. Just a mo, Doris. We're not *selling* the house. True, we are five minutes from Sunshine Hall. But so are all the other people in Shelley Street or round the corner in Browning Way.

MRS. HICKS. It would be a great honour having the Speaker here. George thinks the world of him. We'd treat him as one of our own.

HICKS. Nobody would stand for that. You have to be blood of our blood to put up with that sort of treatment.

JAY. Anyway there'd be a lot of money coming your way as a result, Mr. Hicks. We intend to buy the serial rights.

HICKS. Serial rights—of what?

JAY. Your story. "The Speaker stayed in No. 1 Shelley Street." I'd write it, of course—but in your name.

HICKS. You mean like they do for a star footballer?

JAY. You'd get a four-figure fee. Well, here's the contract.

HICKS. Contract?

JAY. For the serial rights. Just sign here. My, you're fortunate, so very very fortunate.

HICKS (*reading*). One thousand nicker.

JAY. Course it's all null and void if he doesn't stay here. You'll see that in clause four.

MRS. HICKS. You think he will come?

HICKS. Just because we're five minutes from . . .

JAY. No, no. It's a corner house *and* you've got lodgers, haven't you?

HICKS. Miss Chantry and Alf. That's our total infantry since Mr. Mason's gone.

JAY. It's because of Mr. Mason that the Speaker will come to this house. Mr. Mason's stroke was a lucky stroke for you. (*Laughs and winks.*)

MRS. HICKS. Mr. Mason has passed on.

JAY. I know all about that. Yours is the only house round here that has had a death in it recently. The Speaker will know about that. The Speaker prefers corner houses. It's one of his quirks. Anyway, the *Daily Star* has sent the Speaker a telegram saying you expect him. On the ball, eh? They were trying to locate him when I left from London this morning.

HICKS. I want to believe you, Mr. Jay.

JAY. Wanting, why that's half the battle. I'm glad you'll co-operate. It's a great thing to meet folks who know which side their bread's buttered on. Yes, sign there, Mr. Hicks. (HICKS *signs and hands back contract.*) Thank you. By the way, may I leave this case here? I bought it in a shop near the station. A real bargain. I'll pick it up tomorrow.

MRS. HICKS. That phone call. The man who asked for Mr. Mason. Bill, do you think that could have been the Speaker's secretary?

JAY. Phone call? I didn't know about the 'phone. Still that's good. (*Winks.*) You're on the right beam, Mrs. Hicks. Brilliant. That's very good. I'll put that in. It's such a pleasure to meet people like you who think fast. The salt of England, that's what you are. (*Goes over to shake hands with* MR. HICKS.) You're the luckiest man in the world and the *Daily Star* has certainly made no mistake. I'll be going.

HICKS. Just a minute. When will the Speaker come? If he comes.

JAY. If he comes! Oh, you had me fooled for a minute. Yes, he's due to speak at seven, tomorrow evening. There's a train due in from London at 5.30 so I suppose he'll come straight round here.

HICKS. And if he doesn't stay here?

JAY. Away with such pessimism. Anyway what have you got to lose?

HICKS. That's right.

JAY. Even if it were a black day and he stayed in Swinburne Crescent—which he won't—well, the *Daily Star* would see you right. You'd figure in a news story and that would mean a fiver for you. But he will come. Everything's fixed. It's great news for you, isn't it? The *Daily Star* with its millions of readers is confident. "The Speaker stayed in No. 1 Shelley Street. An ordinary family prepares for the Speaker." Can't you see it? The photographers will come tomorrow. Well, good-bye again and bless you.

HICKS. Mr. Jay, you've left the Speaker's case.

JAY. The Speaker's case? My case, Mr. Hicks. Oh yes, yes. I see (*He winks.*) The case. What an idea. Splendid. He sent it on. Remember that. It's important. My, I certainly chose the right people, this time. It's been charming, Mrs. Hicks.

[*Exit* JAY, *door left.*]

HICKS. One thousand pounds. He's got to stay here.

MRS. HICKS. Won't George be excited when he hears about it? I must tell Miss Chantry at once. (*She goes towards door rear right, then stops doubtfully.*) Should I tell her, Bill?

HICKS. Why not?

MRS. HICKS. It's just that . . . Why should that journalist come here and say such things of such a nature to us?

HICKS. I know he sounded a sham.

MRS. HICKS. As if he was cooking up a story.

HICKS. Exactly. But sometimes you can't discount what people say merely because of the way they say it.

MRS. HICKS. That's a true word, Bill. A very true word.

HICKS. What I could do with a thousand pounds.

MRS. HICKS. Our photographs in the *Daily Star*. All the neighbours will see them.

HICKS. It must be true. Why should he make it all up? It's got to be true . . . I wouldn't blow it all in a week. No.

MRS. HICKS. He must be a very good man, the Speaker.

HICKS. I could give George the money when he gets married. Or I could spend next winter in the South of France. Cough, cough, cough, all the time. Or we could buy a car. Yes, a little car—not too heavy on petrol consumption. I can hardly walk when my chest plays me up.

MRS. HICKS. A car? Wouldn't that be a little extravagant?

HICKS. With a car, don't you see, I could do a job of work again. It's not dignified me sitting on my backside day in, day out. George bringing the money home and you collecting the rent, and fetching and carrying and cooking and washing up for strangers. It's degrading not working. With a car, I could start a private taxi service from the station. You always said they need more taxis waiting at the station. You don't know how boring it is, just sitting around the house, working at chess problems, doing the football pools, thinking of the past, hoping for nothing. What am I living for? This is a chance. The Speaker—why he's my chance to start again.

MRS. HICKS. It would be like a dream come true.

HICKS. And I know this town like the back of my hand. Every street in every district.

MRS. HICKS. You might earn enough to keep us.

HICKS. I'd learn when every train comes into the station. I'd go to work again (*Stands up.*) I'm going to work again. It's like a miracle. What's the matter with you?

MRS. HICKS. Bill, do you think that journalist was having us? I mean for a story. You know how they pick on individuals and then show their reactions to some important, dramatic event.

HICKS. I don't want to hear.

MRS. HICKS. That claptrap about Mason, and us being five minutes from Sunshine Hall.

HICKS. It's true, isn't it?

MRS. HICKS. No, Bill. I'm afraid it's too unlikely.

HICKS (*nods his head back and fore. Opens his mouth to speak but no words come. Then, at last, with difficulty says*). You . . . doubt . . . me? What are you trying to do? Destroy me?

MRS. HICKS. I don't doubt you.

HICKS. Are we five minutes from Sunshine Hall?

MRS. HICKS. Yes.

HICKS. And five minutes from the station?

MRS. HICKS. Yes.

HICKS. Is this a corner house or not?

MRS. HICKS. It is. It is.

HICKS. And isn't Mason dead?

MRS. HICKS. Quite right, Bill.

HICKS. And didn't the *Daily Star* send a telegram to the Speaker?

MRS. HICKS. Yes, yes.

HICKS. The Speaker *will* come here. Didn't you get a 'phone call saying he was coming?

MRS. HICKS. That's right, Bill. It was his secretary. He absolutely promised he was coming.

HICKS. And didn't the Speaker send his luggage on?

MRS. HICKS. That case?

HICKS. You don't believe me. Then open it.

MRS. HICKS. No, no.

HICKS (*shouting*). Open it.

MRS. HICKS. It's not ours, Bill.

HICKS. Open it, I say. You'll find proof in there.

MRS. HICKS. We won't bother. I'll just tell Miss Chantry the good news.

HICKS. Bring it HERE, I'll open it. Bring it *here*.

MRS. HICKS. Do you think you should? (*Brings case over to him.*) Perhaps it's better not to know.

HICKS. Now you'll see. Proof indisputable. (*He is about to open it but* MRS. HICKS *struggles to keep it closed.*)

MRS. HICKS. Bill, it doesn't matter what's inside. Listen to me. That call was from the Speaker's Secretary. He said, "There'll be room in No. 1 now Mr. Mason's dead."

[HICKS *forces case open.*]

HICKS. Why, there's nothing in it.

MRS. HICKS. That doesn't matter. Don't you want to believe he's coming here?

HICKS. It's empty.

MRS. HICKS. Are there any marks in it suggesting it belongs to any other person but the Speaker?

HICKS. No, no, that's true.

MRS. HICKS. Oh, Bill. (*Joyously.*) Think what we could do with a thousand pounds. I'll prepare his room at once.

HICKS. He sent on an empty case. Why shouldn't he send an empty case? A man like that has many quirks. The greater they are, the more peculiar they are.

MRS. HICKS. Of course.

HICKS. I'll be going to work again.

MRS. HICKS. That's right. Believe that, Bill.

HICKS. It'll be like old times.

MRS. HICKS (*going to door right and opening it*). Miss Chantry, I'll tell her the good news. (*Calls.*) Miss Chantry. Miss Chant—ry.

HICKS. We'll have a drink. We'll have a party. (*He goes to the sideboard and takes out a bottle and three glasses.*)

MRS. HICKS (*shouting*). Miss Chantry. Do come down. I wish she'd hurry. We'll tell Alf too, when he comes in.

HICKS. Everybody. We'll let everybody know. Some people are miserly with good news. Not me. Not the Hicks.

MRS. HICKS. We've been singled out, Bill, singled out. An honour.

HICKS. Certainly. I'm not a nobody any more. Me, I'm not going to be Mr. A. N. Other.

MRS. HICKS. We'll have everything nice and proper when he comes. Tasteful like. I could just clap hands.

HICKS. Clap hands, sweetheart. Stamp your feet. The Hicks are back again.

MRS. HICKS. We're over the top.

HICKS. And down the straight.

MRS. HICKS. We're first.

HICKS. We're home.

[MISS CHANTRY *enters.*]

Ah, my dear Miss Chantry, just in time for a little bit of what you fancy. (*Pours drinks out.*)

MISS CHANTRY. What's the matter?

MRS. HICKS (*taking up her glass*). Don't ask questions, dear. I'm so excited. I'll tell you all about it later. Don't let's spoil anything.

HICKS. To the Speaker.

MRS. HICKS. To the Speaker, God bless him.

MISS CHANTRY. To the Speaker?

HICKS. What a day. I could shout, I could sing, I could dance.

MISS CHANTRY. Perhaps it's because the Speaker's coming.

HICKS. He *is* coming.

MRS. HICKS. Yes, yes.

MISS CHANTRY. Mr. Hicks . . . (*Triumphantly.*) you've seen the truth at last. It makes me feel so good. You're not alone any more.

HICKS. Alone? ho, no, no, no. Not you. We're all fond of you here. (*Sings.*) A pint of beer, a pint of . . . Sing everybody, sing. Let yourself go.

MR. AND MRS. HICKS. A pint of beer, a pint of beer, a Woodbine and a match.

[HICKS *takes* MISS CHANTRY *by the hand and heavily dances with her as* MRS. HICKS *sings.*]

MRS. HICKS. a fourpenny halfpenny walking stick to see the football match. The ball was in the centre, the referee's whistle blew.

HICKS. Sing faster, Doris, faster, faster.

[MRS. HICKS *sings faster.* MR. HICKS *and* MISS CHANTRY *dance faster, and* MISS CHANTRY *is laughing.*]

MRS. HICKS. Pugh had his temper, and up the wing he flew. He passed the ball to Smith who didn't know what to do. He passed the ball to Stevens, and in the net it flew. Oh, yes we can, we beat West Ham. What was the score? Two nil, no more. Play up the Baboons in blue.

MISS CHANTRY. Oooh, I'm out of breath.

MRS. HICKS. Hurrah, hurrah.

HICKS (*stops dancing*). Hurrah.

MISS CHANTRY. Oh, Mr. Hicks, you *are* really.

HICKS. Funny, why I'm not out of breath at all. I'm like I used to be when I was young. I feel I could left up 'undredweights. I feel strong. I can't tell you 'ow I feel. (*Going over to* MRS. HICKS, *threateningly, who still has a glass in her hand.*) 'Ere, give me a kiss, darling. (*Tries to embrace her.*)

MRS. HICKS. Ha, ha, ha. Get away with you. Don't be soppy.

[HICKS *takes glass from her hand and deliberately, carefully, places it on to the floor, then with his heel crunches down on it.*]

MISS CHANTRY. Oooh!

MRS. HICKS. Ha, ha, ha.

MR. HICKS. Ha, ha, ha.

ALL TOGETHER. Ha, ha, ha, ha, ha, ha.

ACT II

Scene 1

Time, later that evening. Scene, a railway bridge not far from Shelley Street. The bridge is on a hump of a hill. The streets beyond, which lead to Sunshine Hall, are out of sight. In the rear, though, the top of a gasholder can be seen distantly. The upper parts of other structures, e.g. derelict looking warehouses, chimney stacks, etc., also loom up darkly from behind. In front the street curves from the left to the humped bridge and to the right is a lit lamppost which has a loudspeaker attached to it. Because the bridge is slanted from left to right, the left parapet of the bridge is clearly visible over which characters on stage can peer over to the railway lines that lie invisibly below and the other side of it.

As the curtain rises there is the sound off stage of a newsboy shouting.

VOICE OFF (*left*). *Echo. Evening Echo.* Special Edit-ion. News of the

Speaker. Special Edit-ion. *Echo*. Read all about it. New developments about the Meeting. Read all about it. Special Edit-ion.

[GEORGE *and* SHEILA *enter from left.* GEORGE *is reading a newspaper.*]

SHEILA. Well, what's it say?

GEORGE. Same as in the ordinary edition. Except that Sir Harold Tanner is definitely going to be the chairman.

SHEILA. Look George, on the lamppost there.

GEORGE. They've got those loudspeakers on every lamppost from here to Sunshine Hall for the overflow. The streets the other side of this bridge will be crowded with all those who can't get in tomorrow night. Sunshine Hall Square will be packed and the streets brimming probably all the way up to here. I don't expect many will be on the bridge though, because when the trains go under you won't be able to hear a thing.

SHEILA. It makes me afraid. People expect too much from the Speaker.

GEORGE. Well, he's the Speaker, isn't he? Why should he choose to speak here, of all places in England? A few minutes from here, why it's fabulous luck.

SHEILA. Your father must be the only person in town who's not chucking his hat up in the air. Even mother thinks she's going to throw away her crutches after he speaks.

GEORGE. I had a quarrel with Dad when I left this evening, Sheila.

SHEILA. Not about us.

GEORGE. No. About the Speaker. We've got to get into this Meeting. I don't want to hear him over one of those loudspeaker things. I'd like to be right in the middle of Sunshine Hall, right in the middle of history.

SHEILA. We'll both get in together.

GEORGE. It'll be very hard to get two tickets.

SHEILA. You wouldn't go without me?

GEORGE. No, no.

SHEILA. You don't sound very certain.

GEORGE. Course I'm certain. Two tickets or no tickets. Both of us or none of us.

SHEILA. You promise?

GEORGE. Of course. I wouldn't dream of going without you.

SHEILA. Your word of honour?

GEORGE. We're going to get married one day, Sheila. We're going to share everything, good and bad. I wouldn't go without you. I'd rather hear him speak from this bridge than go alone. Hearing him together, why it'll be like, I don't know . . . like something very pure, clean. Like snow before anybody walks over the snow to leave dirty brown holes on it.

SHEILA (*taking his hand*). Let's look over the bridge, George, and make a wish.

[*They walk over to the parapet. Distant noise of a train shunting, trucks clattering, a sad whistle.*]

SHEILA. Isn't it pretty, the lights and signals and things? And all them yellow windows there, decorating the dark. It looks awful during the day, but at night all the ugliness is gone.

GEORGE. Seems sort of empty, doesn't it? The way the moon leans over the railway lines, glinting on the empty railway lines. See what I mean?

SHEILA. February moon. Make a wish.

GEORGE. We'd better get moving. It's cold.

SHEILA. Drop the newspaper down, George.

GEORGE. What for?

SHEILA. Don't know. Just like to see it float down on to the railway lines.

GEORGE. You're not feeding the ducks.

SHEILA. Go on. Let it float down.

GEORGE. All right, litter louse. (*Drops newspaper over parapet.*)

SHEILA. Going . . . going . . . gone.

GEORGE. Come on.

SHEILA. What did you wish?

GEORGE. Me? Oh, you know. That we could be married soon. That the world was all right for everybody. Still, when the Speaker comes . . .

SHEILA. You know what I wished?

GEORGE. What did you wish, bunny?

SHEILA (*shyly*). I wished we were going away with each other, this week-end. Just the week-end together, now that we are engaged. You and me. Nobody else. In London. We could stay in one of them hotels in Bayswater or Russell Square or maybe even in the West End. We could sign our names in the register, Mr. and Mrs. Smith. I could turn my engagement ring over, you know. Wouldn't it be nice, George? To wake up together in the morning, have breakfast together. All these snatched kisses in doorways. This town is so small and people talk. We could get lost in London.

GEORGE (*doubtfully*). It would be nice only . . . Only there's plenty of time. We've got *years*.

SHEILA (*nods*). Anyway, I suppose it would cost a bit to go and stay in London.

GEORGE. It's not just that. In fact, I have £20 in my pocket.

SHEILA. Oh well, then, George, shall we?

GEORGE. On the other hand we ought to be sensible. We ought to save everything we've got. We ought . . . (*Gently.*) Would you really like to go, Sheila?

SHEILA. Yes, I would—but only if you really want to as well. Very much, if you want to.

GEORGE. Of course I want to. You know. I'm not made of stone. Only it will take another four months, four months easy, before I could save another twenty quid. And we're starting without a bean, without a single bean, love.

SHEILA (*half turning away*). Of course. Yes. Yes, I suppose so.

GEORGE. For heaven's sake any money I save is for both of us. It's not for *me,* it's for *us.*

SHEILA. One of your shoelaces is undone, George.

[*He looks down and ties it up. As he does so* MR. NOTT *enters from the right, the furthest side of the bridge. He is an insignificant man in a mackintosh.*]

MR. NOTT. Excuse me. I do beg your pardon. I'm so sorry. I just want to know if the London express has passed under the bridge.

GEORGE. No. (*Looking at his watch.*) It's not due for a quarter of an hour.

[MR. NOTT *goes over to the bridge and makes as if to climb on to the parapet.*]

SHEILA. George!

GEORGE. You can't do that.

NOTT. I'd have to climb up on to that parapet. I'd watch the train come, then I'd have to jump before that bellowing iron engine. Brr. In theory, simple. But in practice?

SHEILA. You would . . .

NOTT (*with back to them, looking over bridge*). It would be nothing, that's all. (*Swivels round to face them and almost shouts.*) Nothing, do you understand? No, that's impossible to understand. We have to fill our minds up with something.

GEORGE. You're not going to wait for the train?

NOTT. I don't know. I can imagine my blood hot under the wheels, my shriek the second before death, my limbs crunching under the iron monster, the noise a backbone makes broken in half.

SHEILA. I'm frightened, George.

GEORGE. Who are you?

NOTT. I used to think I was John Neely or Frank Dixon or Roy Morley.

SHEILA. Who are they?

NOTT. It depended on my mood. Yes, naturally, you're puzzled. It's unusual. Most deluded people imagine themselves to be much more grandiose. Some of my late colleagues imagined they were King Henry the Eighth or the Duke of Wellington or Lord Nelson—depending on what used to be their local pub, I suppose.

[*He laughs, but* GEORGE *and* SHEILA *just stare at him uneasily.*]

I was making a joke and it was in bad taste. Pray, excuse me.

SHEILA. Then you're from a mental hospital?

NOTT. I was, yes.

SHEILA. You escaped?

NOTT. No, no, no. I've been discharged. They purged me of every bizarre dream. My name is Nott. Nott like my father and his father before him. You're still puzzled. Of course, I haven't explained. I used to think I was Mr. Morley or Mr. Neely or Mr. Dixon. Ordinary people. Nothing special. I just wanted to be anybody but myself—that's how they explained it to me. Wanting to be someone else is half the trouble; when you *believe* yourself to be another person, however commonplace, that puts the lid on it. Psychotic delusions, yes. Still with insulin shocks, I became myself again. Plain Mr. Nott.

GEORGE. You're not from this town are you?

NOTT. No, I'm a stranger here. You see, I couldn't go back to Reading. Once you've been in for treatment your old neighbours regard you with some suspicion. It's worse than being a criminal. It doesn't matter how sane you are, they expect you to do funny things. I had a nice little business in Reading. Never mind. I thought it best to take a little holiday before starting somewhere new and I happen to have a friend in this town. I can see that you're still worried. It's hard to make others believe that I'm all right now. Perhaps I shouldn't try so hard.

GEORGE. If you're all right now, why do you want to throw yourself off the bridge?

NOTT. I explained it to you. I have no dreams left. They took them away from me one by one and now there's nothing left. (*Shouts.*) *Nothing.* No, no, I'm telling you a lie. I won't throw myself down there. I haven't the courage, anyway.

GEORGE. Did you say you have a friend living here?

NOTT. Chap by the name of Mason. I used to be friends with him years ago. He sent me a Christmas card every year. But now I've arrived here, I don't want to see him very much—though I did give him a ring, but I think I got the wrong number. Anyway it doesn't matter. There's plenty of time.

SHEILA. He doesn't mean that Mr. Mason who lived in your house?

GEORGE. It's a common name. There's something fishy about this story.

NOTT. I beg your pardon?

GEORGE. You didn't come here because of the Meeting tomorrow night?

NOTT. The Meeting? Oh, the Meeting. No, no. Lots of people seem to be talking about it. It doesn't concern me.

SHEILA. You should go along and hear the Speaker. It might make you feel happier.

GEORGE. Well, shouldn't we move on, Sheila?

SHEILA. Where are you going Mr. . . . er . . . ?

NOTT. Not Mr. Dixon. Alas, no. Not Mr. Morley or Mr. Neely either, more's the pity. No, no—it's not a pity. I'm very glad to be none those deluded people. You must forgive my contradictions. It's so h not to join the flight from reality. Now what were your asking—oh, yes, where am I going? Nowhere.

SHEILA. You're not going to stay here?

NOTT. I'm not going to jump in front of the London express, my dear, if that's what concerns you. I tremble merely thinking about it.

GEORGE. Come and have a drink with us. It's more cheerful in the pub. Better than watching the trains go by.

NOTT. Oh look, the lights have changed to green. That must mean the London express is on its way. If you don't mind I think I'll wait.

[*Enter* ALF JENKINS. *A dark-haired man with deep set eyes and a small red Welsh mouth. He walks over the bridge from the rear right towards them.*]

SHEILA. Here's Alf.

ALF. Ullo, ullo, my beauties. What are you doing by 'ere?

GEORGE. You're late tonight, Alf.

ALF. Just goin' 'ome. I expect your mam has a tidy bit for me to eat. Overtime. Trying to earn extra for the Meeting. Dew, the prices of the tickets. They're rocketing up. Becoming impossible, mun. There ought to be a shindy about it.

GEORGE. Mr. Nott, this is Alf Jenkins.

ALF. Evening.

[*Looks puzzled. Silently asks* GEORGE *who this man is*—GEORGE *shrugs his shoulders. Distant sound of megaphone attracts their attention.*]

VOICE OFF (*faintly*). Tomorrow night at Sunshine Hall. One, two, three, four, five . . .

MR. NOTT. What's that?

SHEILA. It's one of the vans again.

ALF. Five, six, seven. I'll be there, boy. I've been arguing with some of my mates. They was taking the mickey out of me. Darro, just because I went out an' wrote my protest on the wall.

GEORGE. Wrote on the wall?

ALF. Ay. They were pulling at me, see. Where will that get you, said they. Writing with chalk on the wall. That's my business, I said. Kids do that, they said. Kids write, John loves Joan. Bobby loves Betty. But I didn't write that, said I.

NOTT. What did you write, sir?

ALF. I just wrote "No". That's all. "No".

[GEORGE *and* SHEILA *laugh.*]

So they starts kidding me something considerable. Some people are very ignorant. No heart.

GEORGE. Well, what was the point in writing "No", Alf?

ALF. What was the point? You stand by there asking me what was the point? Why, you are venyer as ignorant as them. If we all thought a bit more, 'ad the will and courage to write "No" on the wall . . .

NOTT. Courage, yes courage.

ALF. Everyone of us marching in step and shoutin' "No. No", walking through the streets with banners with our terrible old "No" written on them, all together see, arms swingin', all yellin', with drums beatin' "No, no, no, no", why we'd change everything right away. Everything would be . . .

GEORGE. All right, Alf, don't get so excited.

ALF. Oh, it makes me want to cry like a baby. Anyway 'e's goin' to speak tomorrow night. 'E'll tell 'em all to say "No". To cry out "No" with all their might an' all their strength. And he'll tell them 'ow to say it and he'll be so persuasive and use words, words of gold mun, to convince them all, in a way I couldn't say. With truth and with poetry.

NOTT. It's a political meeting, is it?

GEORGE. No, no.

ALF. Of course it is. Everythin' is political. An' after the Speaker do speak, givin' out 'is panacea, why they'll never forget. The world will be different, boyo. It'll be what we want.

GEORGE. It's not political, Alf.

ALF. You're a child, George. Bless you, 'course it's political. Ay, well I better be gettin' on. Time waits, as they say. Your Ma will be waitin' for me. It was very nice to meet you, sir. I do hope I shall 'ave the pleasure . . .

SHEILA. Good night, Alf.

ALF. Ay, you're getting a pretty, Sheila. Night all.

[*Exit* ALF, *left.*]

GEORGE. Saying the Meeting is political. Just because he wants it to be political.

NOTT. Comes a day when our critical intelligence puts such faith under a microscope and finds it counterfeit. There is nothing there but a blurred fake that once—it seems now hardly possible—prompted us to action. The sense of endeavour all in vain, argument all in vain, yes, even integrity in vain. All past display, each affirmation, now appears trivial or irrelevant—symptoms merely of our deception. Self-deception. Then looking up from the microscope we must quit the room eventually and open the front door, though we are no longer the same people who hesitate in the porch. Now comes the challenge. We are out in the street, and we must turn left or right, or cross the road. The first unfair dilemma, the first all-important decision—and we are defeated hopelessly, for we have just learnt that all directions are an illusion. We are left with a taste in the head, and nowhere to go.

SHEILA. We better move on, George. Are you coming to the pub with us, Mr. Nott? We'll have to hurry or soon it will be closing time.

NOTT. Wait a minute. A train is coming. Would you mind very much if we waited till the train has passed?

GEORGE. It's getting late.

NOTT. I don't want to inconvenience you. And you have been very kind talking to me.

GEORGE. Are you sure . . . you are Mr. Nott? You're quite certain you haven't come down to address a meeting?

SHEILA. George!

NOTT. Just one train please. It'll only delay you a minute.

SHEILA. You don't intend jumping from that parapet?

NOTT. I told you. I haven't the spunk to do that. Please stay.

[NOTT *jumps on to the parapet.*]

SHEILA. Come down, Mr. Nott.

NOTT. Look, there it is in the distance. See the lights.

GEORGE. Mr. Nott. Mr. Nott, do come . . .

NOTT. The London express.

GEORGE. Quick, go and get Alf.

SHEILA. There isn't time. Do something, George.

NOTT. It's coming. It's coming.

GEORGE. Get off there. Get down you bloody fool. (*Pulls at his leg.*)

NOTT. If only I had the courage of Mr. Neely or Mr. Dixon or Mr. Morley.

GEORGE (*shouting*). The train will kill you.

NOTT (*shouting*). Let go of my leg. Let go.

SHEILA. Please, Mr. Nott. Please.

NOTT. I just have to shut my eyes and fall forward.

GEORGE (*yelling*). Come down. Come down.

[*The noise of the train becomes louder and louder and drowns the voices of* GEORGE *and* SHEILA *begging* MR. NOTT *to come down. As the train goes beneath bridge the noise is at its greatest volume. The noise of train gradually fades away. Silence.*]

NOTT. I told you I hadn't the courage.

[*He gets down from the parapet.* GEORGE *helps him.*]

SHEILA. You gave me a fright.

NOTT. Mr. Neely, Mr. Dixon, Mr. Morley—they weren't cowards. They could have done it. Not me. But Neely, Dixon or Morley didn't want to jump down. They weren't sane, you see. They didn't apprehend reality as it really is.

GEORGE. Come on, Mr. Nott. I need that drink.

NOTT. Thank you so much for waiting. There's so little natural courtesy about.

[*The three exit, leaving stage empty.*]

Scene 2

Scene as in Act Two, Scene 1. Time, Friday evening just after half past six.

On stage: George, Sheila, Mrs. Hicks, Mr. Nott, Alf Jenkins and Miss Chantry. Sound of distant military music.

GEORGE. When are they going to put those loudspeakers on? There's only twenty minutes to go.

MRS. HICKS. They'll be on soon, son.

SHEILA. Yes, stop worrying. They wouldn't have fixed up all those loudspeakers for nothing.

ALF. That band is playin' its 'eart out. Why don't they sing though? I like a good choir. All those people down there and no singin'. It makes me feel so lonely.

MRS. HICKS. Why didn't you bring one of your girl friends, Alf?

ALF. Oh, I could 'ave done. Plenty of girls would 'ave loved to come with me.

GEORGE. Now Alf, we're not in the mood to hear about your conquests again.

ALF. Are you suggestin' I couldn't 'ave brought a girl with me?

SHEILA. Of course he isn't, Alf.

ALF. There's not a bit of decent crumpet in this town that wouldn't give her left arm . . .

GEORGE. Oh, for Chrissake. Do we have to listen to him?

ALF. Only the girls I know aren't interested in politics. That's a masculine interest. That's why I came alone.

GEORGE. If he's not talking about politics it's sex.

MRS. HICKS. Now you two, stop bickering. Why is everybody so bad-tempered?

MISS CHANTRY. This isn't the time for vituperation and small mindedness. We are on the threshold of a divine revelation.

ALF. I'm not bickering, Mrs. Hicks. But your son's got a cheek. Just because he's engaged he thinks . . . why, there's very few that's as potent as me when they reach my age. I can tell you I'm better now than ever I was.

MISS CHANTRY. There are ladies present.

GEORGE. He can go on for hours like this.

ALF (*very annoyed*). Right again. I can go on for hours. That's a gift. A pure gift. Dew, I wish there were competitions for it.

[*Enter* MR. JAY *from left on his way to the Meeting.*]

MRS. HICKS. Oh, Mr. Jay. There you are. I thought you said the Speaker was going to stay with us.

JAY. So he will, Mrs. Hicks. Don't you worry now.

ALF. You go on an' tell that to poor Mr. 'icks—'cause 'e's broken up 'e is.

JAY. Oh, what a pessimist. He shouldn't be that way. Everything is going to be fine . . . What are you all so depressed for? Listen to the music. Soon the Speaker will be heard. You ought to be full of joy and thanksgiving.

MISS CHANTRY. Hear, hear.

ALF. That's right, no point in mopin', just because we couldn't get tickets.

GEORGE. You don't know how much I wanted to hear the Speaker.

JAY. You will hear him.

MRS. HICKS. My husband's heartbroken, Mr. Jay.

JAY. Heartbroken. Why, the Speaker will come straight to No. 1 Shelley Street straight after the Meeting. True I assumed he'd come before. But a minor mistake, a piffling error. As for your husband's future article, why it'll be a beauty. He'll be proud of it. The Night the Speaker Stayed at My House, by Bill Hicks.

NOTT. There is no Speaker. That's just a dream.

MISS CHANTRY. What on earth are you saying, Mr. Nott?

ALF. I've a good mind to clout you one, saying things like that. Who are you anyway?

GEORGE. Leave him alone, he's barmy.

MRS. HICKS. You really think the Speaker will come, after the Meeting, to our house?

JAY. No doubt about it. Exactly. I'll be around your house tonight, after the Meeting.

GEORGE. You haven't a spare ticket?

JAY. I'm *so* sorry. Just one press ticket, I'm afraid, but you'll hear well enough here.

SHEILA. Down there the streets are so thick, people are fainting.

GEORGE. Couldn't you get me in, with your influence? Please. I've waited so long to hear the Speaker.

ALF. And me. I 'ave too.

MISS CHANTRY. Nearly thirty years I've waited.

JAY. I'm sincerely sorry. It hurts me to see you distressed. But the loud-speaker . . . I'm sure it'll be very effective.

ALF. They're selling £1 tickets for sixteen quid. Put that in your paper. Dew, what a filthy racket. People who pay black market prices don't deserve to hear the Speaker's message.

SHEILA. They need to hear it, all the more.

ALF. Yes, afterwards it will be so different. Oh, you don't know, the social changes.

JAY. It's a great privilege. You ought to be all very happy. I'm excited myself. I've covered lots of highlights in my time—the Manchester United crash, the Boko Siamese twin story, the fatal end of Mike Hawthorn, and B. and K. visit, several top murder pieces—yes, but this; nothing like this. The most thrilling story since the Resurrection. I don't mean any disrespect. But that's what it is. One of the greats. Look at them all down there. The religious waiting confirmation of their religion. The political expecting a panacea, the sick expecting new health, the poor hoping for riches . . .

GEORGE. Listen, listen, the loudspeaker's on.

[*Hum of voices and crackling from the loudspeaker.*]

MISS CHANTRY. Oh, I think we ought to pray.

VOICE THROUGH LOUDSPEAKER. Good evening. Good evening. Ladies and gentlemen, good evening. This is your chairman, Sir Harold Tanner. For those of you unfortunate enough not to be inside Sunshine Hall, your attention please. The speech from the Speaker will be relayed at seven o'clock. We expect him to arrive at any moment.

JAY. I must hurry. See you later, all.

[*Exit* JAY, *hurrying over bridge to left.*]

VOICE THROUGH LOUDSPEAKER. We'll come back to you in seven minutes' time.

[*Invisible crowd distantly sings "Abide with me".*]

ALF. That's better, a bit of singing.

MISS CHANTRY. Isn't it exciting, Mrs. Hicks? My heart is thumping.

GEORGE. Well, this seems like it, Sheila.

MRS. HICKS. I hope Mr. Jay was right and he will come back afterwards.

[ALF *begins to sing. A procession passes across the stage. They are going to the meeting. They carry banners on which are written "The Speaker is Coming". At the end of the procession follows a spiv. The procession exits but he stays on stage.*]

SPIV. Oo wants a ticket? £3 ticket, dead in the centre with all the toffs. Oo's my darlin'? My very last ticket.

GEORGE. How much?

SPIV. For you, kid, £30.

ALF. Shocking.

SPIV. £29 then. I'm giving it away.

MRS. HICKS. Don't worry, George. We'll hear it all right.

SPIV. The Speech of the Century, 'oo wants it? Lissen, lissen (*To* GEORGE.) I'll give it you for £26; what about that then? I'm only making a quid on it.

GEORGE. £26. That's a hell of a lot.

SHEILA. Don't bother with him, George.

SPIV. I'm only makin' a quid I'm tellin' you. God make me blind if I'm tellin' a lie. Go on God blind me, blind me. There you are I can see.

ALF. Let's have a look at it.

SPIV. It's all right, cock, it's not forged. Do you want it or not? £25, there you are. That's charity that is.

ALF. I can't afford £25.

SPIV. Don't waste my time. What about you lady?

MISS CHANTRY. Please go away.

SPIV. What are you? A feminine suffragette or somethin'? Lissen' just £25 for the best seat in the house. You'll be sittin' next to the Archbishop of Canterbury, betcher.

MISS CHANTRY. You're asking for a large profit on a £3 ticket.

SPIV. £25 is nothing. Go out shopping an' what change will I get outa that? Do you want it lady?

MISS CHANTRY. You ought to be reported.

[*Enter* MAN, *from right.*]

SPIV. £25 only, Ladies and cocks. That's my last word an' this is my last ticket. Oo's the lucky geyser?

MAN. Hey. I'll give you £20.

SPIV. £20. Are you tryin' to cheat me?

MAN. Here four fivers. Take it or leave it.

SPIV. Allright allright allright. I'm cripplin' myself. Never mind. Be good to other people that's my motto.

MAN. One two three four.

SPIV. Fiveroos. Right. There you are. Enjoy yourself.

[*Exit* MAN.]

NOTT. Some people are stupid.

MRS. HICKS. It's nearly seven o'clock.

MISS CHANTRY. Why doesn't the loudspeaker go on?

GEORGE. I hope there won't be any hitches.

SPIV (*pulling out another ticket from his pocket*). Last ticket. Very last ticket.

GEORGE. You said the other one was your last ticket.

SPIV. This is me own ticket. 'Oo you tryin' to catch. Swear to you it's my last one. God blind me if it's not my last one. Go on, God, blind me, blind me.

MISS CHANTRY. You shouldn't tempt fate like that.

SPIV. There you are, vision sixty-sixty still. £18 for me last ticket. Fair enough?

GEORGE. £15.

SHEILA. George!

GEORGE. £15, I said.

SPIV. Let's see your money.

SHEILA. George, that's most of the money.

SPIV. I'm robbin' myself, but all right. Fifteen quid.

SHEILA. You can't, George. Why you wouldn't you couldn't.

SPIV. C'mon. I haven't got all day.

GEORGE. But Sheila, the Speaker, I want to go. I've got to go.

SHEILA. You promised . . .

MRS. HICKS. Don't be silly, George.

SHEILA. George, you promised, last night . . .

SPIV. You keep outa this, miss.

MRS. HICKS. You're not to spend all that money.

ALF. You'll hear it from the tannoid, mun.

MRS. HICKS. Your father'll go crazy.

SPIV. Lady, please, lady.

GEORGE. You wouldn't mind too much would you, Sheila?

SHEILA. Of course, I mind.

NOTT. You're wasting your money, George.

SPIV. He's barmy, round the twist saying things like that.

SHEILA. If you go, George, I'll never . . .

SPIV. I'll give you three before I double my price. One, two . . . Ah, ta.

SHEILA. George, oh George.

SPIV. Nah then. Oo wants balloons? (*Takes them out of his pocket.*) Red, white and blue balloons. Half a dollar each. Guaranteed not to bust.

[*Exit* SPIV.]

SPIV (*off*). Greet the Speaker with patriotic balloons.

MISS CHANTRY. Will you tell us what the Speaker looks like, George?

ALF. You'll be that close to him.

GEORGE. Sheila . . .

SHEILA. You talk about good conduct and morality, yet you break your promise.

GEORGE. Please, I've got to go, Sheila. Don't you understand?

SHEILA. You said it would be like snow before anybody walked across it. You!

GEORGE. Please, Sheila. I want to be in that Hall more than I want anything.

SHEILA. More than you want me?

GEORGE. Of course not. It's different. It's not the same question at all.

SHEILA. Why, that money could have taken us on holiday together.

GEORGE. Going to Sunshine Hall is more important than a holiday.

SHEILA. For you. Not for me. You said you wanted to save that twenty pounds. I thought how sensible perhaps, how responsible. I was an idiot to think that.

GEORGE. We'll have a holiday. There's plenty of time. I'll save up more. You'll go away.

SHEILA. Yes, I'll go away but not with you.

MRS. HICKS. So much money for that ticket, George. Sheila's right.

GEORGE. You keep out of this, Mum.

SHEILA. He promised me, Mrs. Hicks. He swore he wouldn't go on his own.

MRS. HICKS. Since you promised.

GEORGE. I've asked you to mind your own business.

[SHEILA *begins to exit.*]

GEORGE. Where're you going? Sheila, wait here. Sheila.

MRS. HICKS. Go after her, son.

GEORGE (*shouting after her*). Sheila, Sheila, try and understand.

NOTT. You could resell that ticket.

GEORGE. No. What are you all looking at me like that for? Damn it all, I'm going. It's once in a lifetime.

[*Exit* GEORGE.]

MRS. HICKS. Bring the Speaker back home, son.

NOTT. The damn fool.

MRS. HICKS. He's a good boy really. He's gone because of his father. That's the only reason. That's why he broke his promise.

NOTT. No. That's not true.

MRS. HICKS. I know my son better than you. I'm right, aren't I, Miss Chantry?

NOTT. I wish I could be fool enough to buy a ticket.

ALF. You don' 'ave to be a fool, Mister. All you need is money, an' the privileges that go with money.

MISS CHANTRY. Never mind. We'll hear him. That's all that counts. To hear his voice, that should be enough for any of us.

ALF. It's all wrong you know. People making profit on things like that. Oh, the Speaker certainly needed to come. Let's 'ope 'e hasn't left it too late.

MRS. HICKS. It's time. It's seven o'clock.

MISS CHANTRY. And there's the loudspeaker coming on.

ALF. 'Ow quiet the crowd are now. Listen . . .

VOICE OVER LOUDSPEAKER. Ladies and gentlemen. Your attention, please.

MRS. HICKS. That's Sir Harold Tanner.

ALF. This is it.

VOICE OVER LOUDSPEAKER. Citizens! I'm afraid we must apologise.

ALF. Now what's wrong?

VOICE OVER LOUDSPEAKER. Ladies and gentlemen, the Speaker has not arrived.

ALF. Do you hear that?

MISS CHANTRY. Not arrived?

MRS. HICKS. There's been some mistake.

VOICE OVER LOUDSPEAKER. Meantime I've asked one of the organisers to say a few words. Could we have your applause please? Your applause please? (*Silence.*)

ALF. They're stunned in the Hall.

MRS. HICKS. They're not even booing.

MISS CHANTRY. Shush.

SECOND VOICE OVER LOUDSPEAKER. Ladies and gentlemen. One, two, three, four, five, six, seven.

MASS VOICES OVER LOUDSPEAKER. Boo! Boo! Boo!

FIRST VOICE OVER LOUDSPEAKER. Please, citizens. Silence. Silence please.

SECOND VOICE OVER LOUDSPEAKER. And one, two, three, four, five, six, seven.

MRS. HICKS. What is he saying, Alf?

SECOND VOICE OVER LOUDSPEAKER. And seven, six, five, four, three, two, one.

ALF. They're not saying anything. The Speaker has not arrived.

SECOND VOICE OVER LOUDSPEAKER. And one, two, three——(*Loudspeaker crackles and then there's silence.*)

NOTT. It's broken down, the loudspeaker system has broken down.

MISS CHANTRY. We're going to miss the Speaker.

ALF. He hasn't turned up.

MRS. HICKS. Listen, the band has started to play again.

[*There is a faint sound of military music.*]

NOTT. He's not going to turn up. He never will turn up.

MRS. HICKS. I want to go home. I don't want to stay here any more.

ALF. He's got to turn up.

MRS. HICKS. Come home with me, Miss Chantry.

MISS CHANTRY. Never. Never. I want to weep.

NOTT. It's no use waiting here. There's no Speaker.

ALF. But it's impossible, mun. The advertisements. The announcements.

MRS. HICKS. I must go home. My husband's not well. Not at all well. He's very sick. He has a bad chest, you know. I must go right away.

[*Enter* GEORGE.]

MRS. HICKS. George. George. Take me home.

ALF. You're back quick.

GEORGE. Fifteen pounds down the drain. Look, it was a fraud.

NOTT. So was the Speaker, a fraud.

ALF. No, no. You're a liar. I've had enough of you.

NOTT. I tell the truth.

ALF. I'll give you one, you fascist.

MISS CHANTRY. He blasphemes. Hit him Alf, hit him hard.

[ALF *moves forward threateningly.*]

NOTT (*screams very rapidly*). One, two, three, four, five, six, seven, one, two, three, four, five . . .

MISS CHANTRY. Shut up. Shut up.

NOTT. One, two, three, four, five, six, seven, one, two, three, four, five . . .

GEORGE (*shouts*). Don't hurt him. Don't hurt him.

NOTT. six, seven, one, two, three, four . . .

[ALF *slaps him across the face.*]

NOTT. six, seven. Ha, ha, ha. Ha, ha, ha. Ha, ha, ha.

[NOTT *is suddenly quiet.* MISS CHANTRY *takes out a handkerchief and blows her nose.*]

MRS. HICKS. There, there, Miss Chantry.

MISS CHANTRY. Oh, Harry. Where are you, Harry?

GEORGE. Didn't Sheila come back?

NOTT. Dreams. Bloody dreams. Don't you think I want to believe there's a Speaker too? And you, (*To* GEORGE.) you're not in love with that girl, Sheila.

GEORGE. What?

NOTT. You merely want to escape from all this. Like the others. There are many ways to leave. I took another door, even less satisfactory. But if your heart had been genuinely touched, you would yearn for nothing, having all. There is no one so courageous as one who loves.

ALF. I wouldn't stand for that sort of talk, boy.

NOTT (*bullying*). And you, too.

ALF. Me?

NOTT. And you, (*Points to* MRS. HICKS.) and you, (*Points to* MISS CHANTRY.) all of you—you have no courage. No more than I had, or have. If you had, then everything would be so good—well, at least, better. You wouldn't have to search for any public orthodoxy, or build a cocoon of dreams, or any false structure to feel safe in, to lie in—there'd be just the green, cruel ordinary world that indisputably is, and you'd praise that difficult simplicity.

ALF. No.

NOTT. It's as if you say "no" out of habit.

[NOTT *turns to* MRS. HICKS *and* MISS CHANTRY.]

MRS. HICKS AND MISS CHANTRY. No, no, no. No.

[*They all look at* GEORGE.]

GEORGE (*hesitates, then as if upset nods his head slowly*). Yes.

ALF. I'm goin'. I'm not listening to 'im.

[*Some of the crowd come on to the bridge from the direction of Sunshine Hall muttering ad lib., e.g. "They made a proper Charlie out of us", "A real frost", etc.*]

MRS. HICKS. Are you coming, George?

[ALF *begins to exit.*]

NOTT. You all wanted to hear the Speaker, didn't you?

ALF. He's a nut.

MISS CHANTRY. I don't want to listen to that man any more.

[*The crowd on the bridge have begun to listen with interest to the proceedings.*]

NOTT. Come back. I'll tell you what the Speaker would have said. Come back and listen.

ALF (*turning back*). 'Ere boys, 'ere's a bloke what says he knows.

GEORGE. Leave him alone. Leave him be.

CROWD. Ya, ya.

NOTT. He'd say it's time we stopped deluding ourselves. It's time to accept.

ALF (*mockingly*). Hear, HEAR.

NOTT (*becoming more and more fantastic and rhetorical as his speech continues*). To accept even our own terror of ignorance, this here and now, this time, this earth, this most strange of meeting places.

ALF AND SEVERAL. Hear, HEAR. Hear, HEAR.

[*The crowd, interested, come closer to him to listen.* NOTT *continues his soapbox speech with his back to the audience. The faces and gestures of the crowd become more and more menacing as* NOTT *carries on with his oratory.*]

NOTT. We don't want any hysterical formulae for the future. We don't want "was" or "will be". We want "is".

ALF AND ALL THE CROWD. Hear, HEAR. Hear, HEAR. Hear, HEAR.

NOTT (*very phoney and theatrical*). I don't want to listen to another time's sad messages of "love", "obey", "War", "Peace", "Vote".

ALF AND ALL THE CROWD. Hear, hear. Hear, hear. Hear, hear. Hear, hear.

NOTT (*even more wildly*). No more tell me of the rose's waste. I see our eyes move into a different love. I see our heart forget the Night's infirmary.

ALF AND CROWD (*their rhythmical "hear-hears" now gradually begin to imitate the sound made by a train*). Hear-hear. Hear-hear. Hear-hear. Hear-hear. Hear-hear. Hear-hear.

NOTT (*raving*). What value is the grave bedecked with flowers.

CROWD (*during his speech*). Hear-hear. Hear-hear. Hear-hear. Hear-hear. Hear-hear.

NOTT (*making himself heard above the din*). Don't you know the Speaker is the fu-ture.

CROWD. Hear-hear. Hear-hear. Hear-hear. Hear-hear. Hear-hear. Hear-hear.

NOTT (*his voice almost drowned by the menacing chant*). Don't you know . . .

CROWD. Hear-hear. Hear-hear. Hear-hear. Hear-hear. Hear-hear. Hear-hear.

NOTT. Listen to me. Listen to . . .

CROWD. Hear-hear. Hear-hear. Hear-hear. Hear-hear. Hear-hear. Hear-hear. Hear-hear. (*etc.*)

[NOTT *puts his hands over his ears, terrified, as the chant of train-like "hear-hears" continues. Super-imposed now on the "hear-hears" is the actual sound of a train coming towards the bridge. With the engine's whistle this rises to a crescendo.* NOTT *falls down and all is silent.*]

NOTT (*quietly*). Don't you know that the Speaker is the future.

[*All on stage, feeling perhaps they've gone too far in baiting* NOTT, *exit quickly. Only* GEORGE *remains. He gently helps* NOTT *to his feet. Sympathetically he smiles at* NOTT, *nods his head, before beginning to exit.*]

ACT III

Scene as in Act One. Time, later Friday evening. On stage, MR. HICKS, GEORGE, ALF JENKINS *and* MISS CHANTRY. MR. HICKS *and* GEORGE *are playing a game of chess.*

HICKS (*turning round to* ALF). If that journalist comes here again I'll do him. He's got a nerve comin' here and promising all manner of things. They'd murder their own mothers for the sake of half a column.

GEORGE. Come on Dad, your move. You always go off on a tangent when you're losing.

ALF. If the Speaker had only come. I just fail to comprehend . . .

MISS CHANTRY. It was a mistake, that's all. We just have to wait, to keep faith. Perhaps it was our faith that was being tested? Like Job, in the Bible.

ALF. Oh Dew, she's got 'er sermon voice on again.

HICKS. What did you hope for anyway? I had a damn good reason for wanting the Speaker to turn up, none of this airy-fairy stuff.

MISS CHANTRY. I hoped for the dissipation of doubt. I hoped for evidence of my faith. I long for a revelation that would refresh us all. How arrogant of me. It was my pride that was speaking. All the same . . .

ALF. You're like that boyo on the bridge, Miss Chantry. A little bit daft. Screwy.

MISS CHANTRY. You don't have to be rude, Mr. Jenkins.

ALF. Well, don't go on like a religious broadcast. Only the other day I was saying to my mate at work, religion is the television of the masses. Religion is all right if you're religious, says he. It's not, I argues, it saps you. Look at all those priests that go round with skirts on. Shurrup Alf Jenkins, says he, my uncle's a priest. You better call 'im Auntie, says I, if he wears a skirt. No, he says, he's a real man. Garn, I bet 'e wears knickers I says. Why, if they behave like humans they get de-frocked. Mark that, mun. De-frocked, not de-trousered. That floored my pal. It really did.

MISS CHANTRY. You're highly irrelevant and absurd.

ALF. That bloke on the bridge was irrelevant and absurd. He made me tampin' mad. Where did 'e go to anyway?

GEORGE. He has a friend in the town. He went looking for him. I don't think he was so crazy. There was a lot of sense in what he said. I wish to hell I listened to him and stayed with Sheila instead of chasing moonbeams.

ALF. What did 'e know? No Speaker indeed. That ignorant sod.

HICKS. There!

GEORGE. You can't castle, Dad. My bishop's covering that square.

HICKS. Oh.

ALF. Somebody must know the way out. The Speaker would have told us.

MISS CHANTRY. The way out?

ALF. Yes. For me and millions of others whose work it is to put something by 'ere, fold something by there, minute in, minute out, only to have the monotony relieved by kicking a lever down once every half hour. I ask you—is such repetitive work fit for the dignity of human beings with brains and hearts and souls?

MISS CHANTRY. Someone has to do such work. Else where would we be?

HICKS. Automation! Auto-mat-ion!

GEORGE. Dad, are you playing or not?

ALF. Not even socialism is the answer. We're ruddy robots, that's what we are. Where's the satisfaction in working, looking at the telly, sleeping, doing boring work again an' 'aving a week or two holiday in Blackpool or Bridlington or Margate in the rain, and then going back to barren work? Where's the spiritual joy? Where's the system that do give an answer? What political party talks about the need of a man's mind, as well as the belly? Where's the flowerin' and the dancin' and the stampin' energy of joy? Where's the imaginative delight? Ay, we need the Speaker. We need a new political prophet. We need a new political philosophy. There was Karl Marx in the nineteenth century but now it's the mid-twentieth century and what's the answer?

MISS CHANTRY. Religion is the answer and the way. (*Goes to table and reads from book.*) "O my God . . ."

ALF. Oh Gawd!

MISS CHANTRY. "How does it happen in this poor old world that Thou art so great and yet nobody finds Thee, that Thou callest so loudly and nobody hears Thee, that Thou givest Thyself to everybody and nobody knows Thy name? Men flee from Thee and say they cannot find Thee; they turn their backs and say they cannot hear Thee." Yes, that's what my mother used to quote years and years ago. And now I, too, am one of the many who are deaf, blind and insensate.

ALF. Aw, for Ikey's sake give it a rest.

HICKS. There, mind your queen.

GEORGE. Check.

HICKS. Oh, my chest. It gets worse every day. (*He has a fit of coughing. Gasps. To* GEORGE.) Where's your mother?

MISS CHANTRY. She's having a little lie-down.

HICKS. I could do with something to eat.

GEORGE. Check.

HICKS. I know it's check. I know the rules. What are you going on about it for? I won't play with you if you boringly keep saying Check, Check, Check, Check. I can see the board. My chest is bad but my eyes are all right.

[*There is a ring from the front door bell.*]

GEORGE (*rising quickly, knocks over the board*). That's Sheila.

HICKS. Now look what you've done. You deliberately knocked the board over.

[GEORGE *exits hurriedly through door left.*]

(*To* ALF *and* MISS CHANTRY.) I was winning. That's why he did it. I was murdering him. That Check—I let him do that deliberately. He would have been mate in five moves. Knocking the board over. My God.

MISS CHANTRY. Harry used to say . . .

ALF. I don't care what your 'Arry Wiggle used to say. Wiggle—what an improbable name.

MISS CHANTRY. Really, Mr. Jenkins, you're becoming quite intolerable. No wonder women won't have anything to do with you.

ALF. I like that. I've just got to snap my fingers, sweetheart, and they come running. Do you know what they call me at work? The Welsh Don Juan.

[*Enter* MR. JAY *and* GEORGE.]

JAY. Hello everybody. What a fiasco! A sensation, the Speaker mistaking the date like that.

MISS CHANTRY. Mistake? I knew it was a mistake.

ALF. What 'appened. Tell me what 'appened.

JAY. He didn't turn up.

HICKS. I'll say he didn't turn up. You've got some explaining to do. Trample over people. No consideration.

[*Enter* MRS. HICKS *from door right.*]

Here's my wife. She'll tell you. She spent hours preparing that room.

GEORGE (*near door, left*). I'm going to look for Sheila.

JAY. You're not going to wait for the Speaker?

ALF. Who are you kidding?

JAY. Didn't you know? When the loudspeaker broke down, they announced that the Speaker had been unavoidably detained—but he would come tomorrow.

MRS. HICKS. Tomorrow?

JAY. Probably he'll turn up tonight. In this town. He might already be here. I wouldn't be surprised if he wasn't outside Sunshine Hall all the time.

ALF. Outside the 'All. Don't be so daft.

JAY. Temperamental. Great men are like that, you know. And I've done a great deal of research. It's compatible with his habits. I should know.

ALF. Doesn't sound as if 'e 'ad much consideration for people.

MISS CHANTRY. People! Look at them. Look at the circus they tried to make of it. The Black Market in tickets. The spivery and rowdyism. We weren't pure enough for him today. I understand. I understand very well. Let's hope we shan't all be so foolish tomorrow.

HICKS. You don't really think he's going to come tomorrow?

JAY. Of course: Why do you think I'm here?

GEORGE. Tell them all. Go on. Tell them there's no Speaker. Why lie? Why keep up the pretence?

MRS. HICKS. Don't be so rude to our guest, George.

GEORGE. You know, Dad. You were sceptical from the beginning. Tell them once and for all—and tell him to get out and to stop tormenting us with phoney promises.

HICKS. Now, not so hasty, lad. Maybe there's something in it. Mr. Jay here's from London. An educated man. A journalist who's a man of the world—and since he says—why George, please, think what it might mean to all of us.

GEORGE. Yesterday you were so sure.

HICKS. Earlier this evening *you* were sure.

GEORGE. . . . If Sheila comes, Mum, tell her I've gone to look for her. I'll only be five minutes.

JAY. Young generation walks out as Speaker is due.

GEORGE. Stop talking in generalisations and bloody silly headlines.

[*Exit* GEORGE.]

MRS. HICKS. I'm sorry, Mr. Jay.

JAY. Oh, I forgive him. He's young, he's earnest. A nice boy that, I like him.

[*Sound of* GEORGE *banging door forcibly, in a temper, off stage.*]

MISS CHANTRY. You bring good news, Mr. Jay.

JAY. Mr. Hicks. I make a prophecy. I don't say it lightly, mind you. I am weighing my words carefully. He won't come here tomorrow.

MISS CHANTRY. Oh.

HICKS. You're dead right for a change.

JAY. He'll come here *tonight.* So lift up your hearts, everybody. As I said, he's probably in the town already. He'll be here in this house *tonight.*

ALF. Are you trying to tell me . . . ?

MISS CHANTRY. Faith, faith, Mr. Jenkins.

JAY. I better start getting notes ready for your article, Mr. Hicks.

HICKS. I have a very bad chest. In the mornings I can hardly catch my breath, and at night I wake up, frightened.

JAY. Yes, I know. I'll get all that in.

HICKS. I'm not telling you that for any bloody article. I'm trying to say you shouldn't mislead a sick man like me.

JAY. Now I must know all about the people who live in this house. The boarders first. Could I have your curriculum vitae, sir?

ALF. Carriculum er? I 'aven't got one.

JAY. I just want information.

ALF. Information? That's what I do want.

JAY. Where were you born?

ALF. Mind your own bloody business.

MISS CHANTRY. Mr. Jenkins was born in South Wales. He's very crude.

ALF. I was born in Porthcawl in 1917, in the nude. All right Miss Chantry?

MRS. HICKS. Tell him about yourself, Alf. What's it matter anyway?

ALF. Aw, it's all silly, Mrs. Hicks.

JAY. What did your father do, Mr. Jenkins?

ALF. My Dad? He was killed in November 1918. The last bullet fired almost. Ay, the damn' idiot, getting mixed up in an imperialist war. Mam 'ad a sweet shop in Porthcawl. That's a seaside resort. Windy place. Sand dunes. Esplanade. Mam 'ad a cancer of the larynx when I was eleven an' I became an errand boy.

HICKS. I didn't know that, Alf.

ALF. Yes, I liked cycling, see. They let me ride a bicycle being an errand boy.

MISS CHANTRY. I expect you whistled all the time.

ALF. I 'ad an uncle in Treorchy. He got me a job there, in a bicycle shop. It was an 'appy time, that. 'Elping to sell Rudges and Raleighs, Royal Enfields, Humbers and Hudsons. Then there was the old B.S.A. and the Sunbeams and Hercules. Bicycles are not what they were, you know.

JAY. Could you bring me more up to date, Mr. Jenkins.

ALF. Mmm. I was just a boy, you know. Then bang came the depression and the Prince of Wales came down and says "Something must be done". People couldn't afford bicycles then. Eighteen years old and unemployed, so I came north but didn't 'ave the fare to go all the way, so stopped off here. Saturday it was. Beautiful sunset, I remember, an' I saw a flickin' ad in the paper for flippin' factory workers. Been 'ere ever since. I was a conchie during the war. I said "No" then an' I'm still saying "No".

JAY. Didn't you get married?

ALF. I said "no" to that too. I'm too fly for that boy. I never got trapped. Yes, it's all been one-night stands with me, boy, but there's been plenty of them. I'm still goin' strong.

JAY. I can't exactly put that in the paper. A story to touch the heart perhaps?

ALF. Well, if you want a sob story she's got one. Ask her about Mr. Wiggall.

MISS CHANTRY. I'd willingly co-operate, Mr. Jay, but not in front of all these people.

ALF. Give 'er a glass of gin an' you could fill up a Sunday newspaper.

MISS CHANTRY. Perhaps. Yes, perhaps I should like to tell you about Harry Wiggall and myself, Mr. Jay.

ALF. Not now, sweetheart. We all know it.

JAY. I don't. Please. Sit down. Tell me.

MISS CHANTRY. Mr. Wiggall and I were going to be married.

JAY. Yes?

MISS CHANTRY. It was a long time ago. There was family opposition. Harry's family weren't out of the top drawer. We, you see, were related to the Ross-Ruffels on my mother's side.

JAY. The Ross-Ruffels. Really?

MISS CHANTRY. I was only a gal of nineteen and my father thought he knew better. So we eloped, hoping of course my father would relent. We were very happy until Harry died in a fire, three months later.

JAY. A fire?

MISS CHANTRY. We were in the street, walking arm in arm. We turned a corner and there above a shop was a window with a woman and child shouting for help. The whole building was raging with straw coloured flames. On the pavement below, a group of people had gathered, but they didn't do anything and at that time the firemen hadn't arrived.

MRS. HICKS. Don't upset yourself again, Miss Chantry. Every time you tell it you get so upset.

MISS CHANTRY (*as if in a trance*). My Harry went into that Nebuchadnezzar's furnace. He went in like Shadrach, Meshach and Abed-nego. But no angel interceded. My darling ran back into the street ripping his clothes off. He wasn't a man any more. He was a human torch. I could smell his burning skin, the odour of charred meat. "Harry" I shouted, "Harry, Harry". Nobody did anything. "Help my Harry" I screamed, but nobody could do anything. I saw his eyes staring into my eyes. I'll never forget his eyes, never. The imploring, hopeless gaze.

MRS. HICKS. It's many years ago and it's time you put it out of your mind.

MISS CHANTRY (*suddenly screams*). Harry, Harry. For pity's sake. Don't leave me, Harry.

ALF. There, there, my dear.

MISS CHANTRY (*sobbing*). Oh, Harry, Harry. I love you so.

MRS. HICKS. Now Miss Chantry, I'll make you a nice cup of tea. Steady now.

MISS CHANTRY. I was only nineteen, Mrs. Hicks. Was it fair?

ALF (*suddenly to* MR. JAY). You said the Speaker was going to arrive. If he don't, mun, I'll break every bone in your body.

MRS. HICKS. Alf, Alf, what are you saying?

HICKS. It's half-past nine. It's getting late for a lodger to come.

JAY. Don't worry. Don't worry, I tell you.

MRS. HICKS. All right, Miss Chantry?

MISS CHANTRY. Thank you. I'm sorry.

ALF. You know. I once saw a girl getting on a bus. She was so beautiful. No lipstick, no make-up, no nothing, mun. She had a face like an angel. Big eyes, so sad and clear. I got on that bus though I wasn't going anywhere. I just wanted to look at her, longer. I never spoke to her or anything and when she got off I just went on to the terminus, then walked home. Me, the Welsh Don Juan.

JAY. What about you, Mrs. Hicks? Were you born here?

MRS. HICKS. Oh, yes, yes. I've lived here all my life.

JAY. And? Go on.

MRS. HICKS. Father was a schoolteacher, you know, but he went deaf. He couldn't work because of it. Like my poor husband. Mother had to help out.

HICKS. I'm not deaf. It's my chest.

MRS. HICKS. I worked as a secretary for Patterson and Son. Their offices are still near Sunshine Hall. I should have learnt languages.

HICKS. I know what's coming. Go on. Go on, tell all the world about Simon Mitchell.

MRS. HICKS. I was a pretty girl, you know, and Simon Mitchell did have a crush on me.

HICKS. That was *'undreds* of years ago.

MRS. HICKS. You be quiet. Surely you're not jealous now?

HICKS. Jealous? He was the lucky one.

MRS. HICKS. Simon went.

HICKS. To Italy.

MRS. HICKS. To Milan.

HICKS (*mimicking his wife's voice*). She could have got a job in Milan. (*Own voice.*) Don't be so stupid in front of everybody.

MRS. HICKS. I didn't learn Italian. I stayed behind. I wasn't a very practical person.

HICKS. Don't make such a fool of yourself in front of this . . . stranger.

MRS. HICKS. Yes, I was a silly girl. I dreamed of being a famous actress like Kay Francis, or Myrna Loy, and Norma Shearer, or Loretta Young.

JAY. You went on the stage, Mrs. Hicks?

MRS. HICKS. Oh dear, no. I got as far as the local drama group, that's all. That's where I met my husband—at one of their dances. I thought he looked a mixture of William Powell, Melvyn Douglas and Ronald Colman.

[JAY *looks at* HICK'*s face, astonished.*]

He didn't really. It was just that he wore a moustache in those days.

HICKS. And I thought she looked like Doris Karloff.

MISS CHANTRY. It takes me right back, you talking about Raleighs and Rudges and Sunbeams, Mr. Jenkins; I had a Raleigh myself when I was a gal.

ALF. Good bikes. Very good bikes, all of them.

MISS CHANTRY. It makes me think of a tune, I don't know why. Harry had a record. On one side was "I've got my Captain working for me now", and on the other, "You'd be surprised".

HICKS (*sings*). Da da di da da da da, da da di da da da da da, you'd be surprised.

MRS. HICKS. I remember that. (*Sings.*) Di di di, da, da da da, you'd be surprised.

HICKS (*sings*). I'm not much of a look-er, I'm not much of a lov-er, but when you get me in the dark, la la la di de de de da, you'd be surprised. (*Slaps his wife's bottom playfully.*)

MISS CHANTRY. You've got the words all wrong.

[MISS CHANTRY, MR. & MRS. HICKS, *sing all together.*]

ALF. I like a good choir, but, by damn, this!

[*They go on singing.*]

[*Ring on the front door bell. They stop singing and wait there not speaking for a moment, as if they just imagined that the bell had rung.* HICKS *stands up, looks towards the door; then sits down again, silently.*]

MRS. HICKS. I'll make some tea. Shall I make some tea?

HICKS. I would have won that game of chess, you know. George knocked the board over.

JAY. The bell rang.

ALF. I'd like to go back to Porthcawl one day.

HICKS. Yes, it would be nice to live by the sea.

ALF. It has a bit of a lighthouse an' a little harbour. They call it the slip. You can see the beach from there across the bay, and behind the beach the sand dunes, an' the fair.

JAY. I thought I heard the bell go. It's probably the Speaker.

HICKS. No, no. There was no bell.

MISS CHANTRY. Harry used to curl a lock of his hair round his index finger. It was a habit of his. Whenever I see a man do that I think of Harry.

[*Bell rings again.*]

JAY. Shall I open the door?

MRS. HICKS. That song, "You'd be surprised". Fancy you remembering that record, Miss Chantry.

MISS CHANTRY. And on the other side, "I've got my Captain working for me now".

[JAY *moves towards door left.*]

HICKS (*shouting*). You stay where you are, Mr. Jay.

ALF. I cut my foot on a piece of glass, bathing on that beach once. I was only a kid.

MRS. HICKS. That so, Alf? People shouldn't leave glass around.

JAY. It's the Speaker. At the door.

ALF. No, no.

HICKS. No. It can't be.

MISS CHANTRY. I'm afraid.

JAY. I'll let him in.

HICKS. There was no bell ringing.

ALF. He'll go away. Just hang on and he'll go.

JAY. Don't you want the Speaker to come?

HICKS. Of course. But there's no one at the door.

MISS CHANTRY. Of course we want the Speaker to come. And he's coming *tomorrow*.

[JAY *goes determinedly to the door left.*]

ALF. That's right, mun. Tomorrow.

HICKS. You're not to open that door.

[*Long pause.*]

MRS. HICKS. I'll go, Bill.

HICKS. Yes. Whatever you say.

[*Exit* MRS. HICKS *through door left.*]

MISS CHANTRY. I have a headache. A terrible headache. Whenever my mother had a headache she used to put eau-de-cologne on her forehead.

ALF. My foot. It was covered with blood. They had to put stitches in it, see.

HICKS. I'm getting old. It's terrible to get old.

JAY. I told you he'd come, Mr. Hicks. The *Daily Star* promised and there you are. I confess I was doubtful myself. I was just keeping up your spirits. But the *Star* must have found out his address and really sent that telegram.

MISS CHANTRY. It may only be Sheila.

ALF. Or George coming back. He said he'd only be a few minutes.

HICKS. No, George has got a key.

[*Enter* MRS. HICKS.]

MRS. HICKS. Come in please.

[*Enter* MR. NOTT.]

MRS. HICKS. He's looking for . . . Mr. Mason.

JAY (*triumphantly*). There, didn't I tell you? (*Shaken.*) Good Lord!

NOTT. Mrs. Hicks tells me he died. I didn't know.

HICKS. Yes, yes. Sudden. Poor Mason.

NOTT. I see we've all met before. (*To* HICKS.) Except you, sir. I er . . . didn't realise you were so near the station or I would have come earlier.

HICKS. It's a corner house. This place. No. 1 Shelley Street.

NOTT. Mmm. I like corner houses, they're so light.

JAY. I told you! (*Quietly.*) It frightens me.

ALF. But he's the barmy one, Bill. It's all wrong.

MISS CHANTRY. Alf, careful what you say.

NOTT. Oh . . . I don't mind. Poor Mr. Mason. I can hardly believe it.

JAY. I hope you have no objection to the Press? I er . . . I'm on the *Star*.

HICKS. Mason's dead, all right. This is the right house.

ALF. He's an impostor.

NOTT. I beg your pardon?

ALF. What's your name?

NOTT. Oh . . . Nott.

ALF. Are you sure?

NOTT. I sometimes used to call myself by other names.

JAY. Oh we understand, don't we, Mr. Hicks? You have to have several names. One must keep incognito.

NOTT. How understanding of you . . . all. When we were on the bridge, I feared you didn't like me.

MISS CHANTRY. You *are* the Speaker. All the time you lingered on the bridge whilst they waited for you to speak at Sunshine Hall.

NOTT. I don't follow you.

ALF. Are you the Speaker or no?

NOTT. The Speaker? Me?

HICKS. Of course he is. Jay said he'd come and here he is. Because of Mr. Mason he said, and it's true.

NOTT (*rising*). No, no. There's some mistake.

MISS CHANTRY. You saw that people weren't ready for you. You smelt the smell of corruption and kept your silence. I understand.

MRS. HICKS. And on the bridge you slapped his face.

ALF. He said there was no use waiting for the Speaker on the bridge.

NOTT. I must go.

HICKS. Naturally. He should know if he were going to speak or not.

JAY. I must get my photographer.

NOTT. Please. Please, everybody.

MISS CHANTRY. I thought it was too much to ask for: to hear the unhearable, to perceive that which cannot be perceived, to know that which cannot be known.

[MISS CHANTRY *goes down on her knees. Enter* GEORGE.]

ALF. Fancy. It was you, all the time.

HICKS. That contract, Mr. Jay. My God, I'll be able to work again.

MRS. HICKS. We were all afraid, but seeing you, we're not afraid any more.

NOTT. I must leave. I really must leave.

GEORGE. What's going on here?

NOTT. They think I'm the Speaker. I'm so unhappy.

GEORGE. The Speaker.

[GEORGE *begins to laugh, then as his laughter becomes a little out of control* MISS CHANTRY *rises.*]

What a joke . . . the Speaker.

MISS CHANTRY. What are you laughing at?

ALF. What's so funny?

MRS. HICKS. George!

HICKS (*shouts*). Stop laughing!

GEORGE. Laughing? Look!

ALF. What is it?

GEORGE (*opens his right hand*). The engagement ring. That's all. It's all off. Me and Sheila are through.

NOTT. I knew you shouldn't have bought that ticket. Well . . . good-bye.

JAY. Good-bye?

NOTT. Mr. Mason's dead. There's no point in staying here.

JAY. No point? Everybody's waiting for you, Mr. Speaker. We're all so happy. But, about the Meeting tomorrow, could I have a statement?

GEORGE. He's not the Speaker, you damn fool. He's just a man. A man called Nott.

NOTT. That's right. That's what I was trying to say.

GEORGE. Tell them about yourself.

NOTT. Mr. Mason and I. We met on a holiday once. We struck up a friendship. He told me if I ever was in this town I should call on him. I'm sorry.

HICKS. Sorry?

MISS CHANTRY. You're the Speaker.

NOTT. I can identify myself. Let me see. (*Pulls out papers from inside pocket.*) Here's my driving licence. You see my name? Nott. And here's a letter addressed to me. (*Gives it to* JAY.) It's from the Superintendent of a hospital. I was very ill. I still am ill, if you really want to know. They said I must take it easy for a while. I'm only convalescing.

JAY (*reading letter*). "Dear Mr. Nott, you certainly have made splendid progress and it was kind of you to write to us. Certainly, come back and chat with us any time you feel you want to. Remember, life is beautiful. All you need is courage. With very good wishes. Yours faithfully."

ALF. I said he was barmy.

JAY. It's signed R. S. Braybrook, M.D., D.P.M. A psychiatrist!

MISS CHANTRY. You're the Speaker. He's lying. Can't you see?

NOTT. I'm not.

MISS CHANTRY. I know you're the Speaker.

NOTT. You're deluded.

GEORGE. You've made a mistake, that's all, Miss Chantry.

MISS CHANTRY (*almost hysterical*). Say you're the Speaker. Tell them the truth. We've waited so long. Admit it, admit it.

NOTT. Please, control yourself.

MISS CHANTRY. You cruel bastard. (*Goes to attack him, both arms akimbo ready to strike.*)

NOTT. This woman. Keep her away from me.

MISS CHANTRY. You have the power and the glory. But you took Harry away from me.

[MISS CHANTRY *attacks* NOTT. GEORGE *and* ALF *intervene and hold her back.*]

(*Weeping.*) Let me get at him. The pig. The absolute, merciless swine.

NOTT. You should face up to the truth.

GEORGE. You better go.

NOTT. I'm very sorry about this.

[*Exit* MR. NOTT *through door left.*]

MISS CHANTRY (*screams*). Don't let him leave. Please. Please come back, come back.

ALF. Easy there, sweetheart, easy.

GEORGE. We all made an error, that's all, Miss Chantry. We put the wrong things first.

HICKS (*to* JAY). Now what have you got to say?

MISS CHANTRY (*sobs*). Face up to the truth. (*Covers her face with her hands.*)

JAY. It seems I was wrong. But here's five pounds, Mr. Hicks. You'll read about this . . .

HICKS. Get out.

MISS CHANTRY. Face up to the truth? I can face up to the truth.

MRS. HICKS. Of course you can, dear. Everything's going to be all right. Go upstairs and have a lie-down.

MISS CHANTRY. I'll tell you the truth. Harry Wiggall proposed to me.

MRS. HICKS. Not now, Miss Chantry. Later.

MISS CHANTRY. There was family opposition.

MRS. HICKS. I know, I know. They were wrong. Very wrong of them.

MISS CHANTRY. No, they were right.

ALF. Right?

MISS CHANTRY. You see my father knew. He knew Harry was a married man and had four children.

ALF. A married man. You never told us that.

MISS CHANTRY. My father presented me with the facts so, of course, I never saw him again—and later I left home. All Harry Wiggall and I had was one unsuccessful week-end.

MRS. HICKS. What about the fire?

MISS CHANTRY. There was no fire. I wished there had been a fire. He cheated me. He lied. When he dies, I hope the flames of hell burn him up. May they scorch his flesh. May he remain in perpetual torment as I have been all these years.

[*Exit through door rear right.*]

MRS. HICKS. Poor Miss Chantry.

ALF. Well, all the time she 'ad me fooled. Women, you can't trust them.

HICKS. Ah, you've no call to throw stones.

ALF. What do you mean? What are you driving at, Mr. Hicks?

HICKS. You and Don Juan. You've never been out with a woman in your life. All you like is boy scouts. Everybody in this house knows.

ALF. You've no right to say that. Just because you've never seen me with a bird. Just because I'm discreet. Hell!

MRS. HICKS. There, there, Bill.

HICKS. It's all very well to say "there, there" as if I were an infant. But do you realise what we've lost?

MRS. HICKS. What's it matter anyway?

HICKS. Matter? My taxi's gone, that's all. A chance to earn a dignified living.

MRS. HICKS. Even if you got the car you wouldn't have used it for a taxi. You would have sat right in that chair, and George would have driven the car around.

HICKS. What are you saying? My chest would have allowed me to do that. I like your cheek. You stupid . . .

MRS. HICKS. There's little wrong with your chest, you know that. The doctor has told you it's mainly nerves umpteen times. You know it was your brother who had bronchiectasis, not you. So what's the point in making a big song and dance about that car?

HICKS. My chest is bad. In the mornings I can hardly breathe. Nerves, rubbish. It's you who's got a nerve fabricating stories like that. Don't listen to 'er, Alf. Everybody knows about my chest. Isn't my chest bad, son? Go on tell them. Tell Alf all about my bronchiectasis. (*Coughs and gasps.*)

GEORGE. You know mother's right. Let's face up to the truth. All of us.

HICKS. You're an idiot too. No wonder Sheila threw you over.

GEORGE. Dad's chest is not so bad as he makes out, Alf. It was just an excuse for Dad not to work.

HICKS. Are you all mad?

GEORGE. That last job you had, when you stole the petty cash.

MRS. HICKS. Leave him alone, George. What's the use?

ALF. Stole, did you say? He should talk about me.

GEORGE. Why should we leave him alone? Sheila and I would be married now, instead of this mess, if he'd the courage to face up to things. You take in lodgers and I have to give you money, instead of being able to save enough to put down on a house. Life could be beautiful, that doctor said in the letter . . .

HICKS. I did my best. I couldn't help it. They just picked on me, that's all. That last firm, well they were foreigners mean as the devil. They asked for the petty cash to be whipped. They expected it to be. Others did, besides me.

GEORGE. And the job before that?

MRS. HICKS. What's the good, George?

GEORGE. The firm before that? Go on, tell Alf. Tell him, go on.

HICKS. You mean the glass merchant's. I'll tell him. I'll tell anybody. I have nothing to be ashamed of. It was the boss's son there. I was too clever, that was the trouble. I showed up the boss's son.

GEORGE. And before that job? What about the job before that, when you were a lorry driver? Tell Alf about that. Go on.

HICKS. I had one whiskey. Is that a crime? One whiskey. The lies they tell.

GEORGE. And before that, before that? At the cinema.

HICKS. When I was a cashier at a cinema? I didn't fiddle the books. I didn't Alf, I swear on my mother's grave I didn't.

GEORGE. And when you went out as a salesman for water-softeners?

HICKS. I never laid an 'and on that woman. I never did. (*Yelling.*) It's a lie. It's a lie. It's a lie.

GEORGE. And during the war? Tell them about when the bomb fell in Union Street. You hero. Go on tell them what you did.

HICKS (*coughing*). My chest. It's very bad this evening. I can hardly breathe. (*Gasps for breath.*) Oh, my God, I can hardly breathe.

[GEORGE *turns away.* ALF *looks embarrassed.*]

ALF. I must go up and tidy my room.

MRS. HICKS. You sit down, Alf.

[JAY *begins to exit left.*]

JAY. Terrible that man coming in here, upsetting you all. His name will be mud in the *Daily Star*. I give you my word.

HICKS. You . . . and the *Daily Star*. You're muck, that's what you are. And your paper.

JAY. The paper? Why, there's no need to abuse the *Daily Star*. It just reflects you, that's all. What you want: the glamour that you have not but would like, the violence you would indulge in, but dare not. It's your dreams in black and white, and if they seem cheap and sensational and sentimental, that's what they are.

GEORGE. That's not true. It leaves out too much. It's slanted.

JAY. Sometimes they go wrong. That's natural. I'm just employed by them and not responsible for everything. Anyway I believe in what I write.

HICKS. You're vile.

JAY. I wanted to be a serious writer once. When I was twenty. But that's a lot of crap when you have responsibilities as I have. The editor said, get a story of the Speaker, a personal story—nothing abstract. That's what I've tried to do. You'll read my piece and it'll be a good workmanlike job. That's something, you know. I'm not ashamed of that.

HICKS. You used us.

JAY. You wanted to be used. You only had to say "No" right at the beginning.

MRS. HICKS. Don't argue with him.

JAY. Funny thing is, at one time I really thought the Speaker was coming here.

HICKS. You and your lies about him liking corner houses and being five minutes from the station.

JAY. That could be true.

HICKS. You made it up.

JAY. I'm not certain about that.

HICKS. Get out, you're not worth fourpence halfpenny. (*Picks up suitcase and pushes it into Jay's arms.*) And take that with you.

JAY. Now, cheer up, Mr. Hicks. Nothing is worse than before I came. Be reasonable. I've done no harm. Look at the matter objectively. Everything will be all right. You'll see. I guarantee it. You'll look at things differently later. All of you. Yes, every one of you. Why, you'll feel the smiles form on your faces and the sun will be shining.

HICKS. Get out.

[*Exit* JAY *left.*]

Your son . . . he's a disgrace . . . to a father.

MRS. HICKS. There, Bill.

HICKS. I don't want him in the house. This is my 'ouse. He can go and live somewhere else.

ALF. Now Bill, you'll feel different tomorrow.

HICKS (*shouts at* GEORGE). Get out. Go and pack your bags.

MRS. HICKS. He didn't mean anything. He's just upset about his engagement. Naturally. Speak to your father, George.

HICKS. I don't want to hear his voice again.

MRS. HICKS. Tell him you're sorry, George. Go on.

ALF. Go on, George. Your old man's not so young any more.

MRS. HICKS (*yells*). What are you waiting for?

[*Pause.*]

GEORGE (*with his back to the others*). I'm sorry.

HICKS. That's not good enough.

MRS. HICKS. He said he was sorry. Now isn't that enough?

HICKS. Tell Alf you were telling lies. Or else get out.

MRS. HICKS. George, do as your father asks. Please.

GEORGE (*still not turning round*). I was telling lies.

HICKS. I've got a bad chest, haven't I? Bronchiectasis.

MRS. HICKS. Course you have. We all know.

HICKS. Otherwise I'd work myself to the bone.

MRS. HICKS. Yes, yes.

HICKS. I want to hear it from George.

MRS. HICKS. That's enough now.

HICKS (*shouting*). George has got to say it.

ALF. Go on, George.

GEORGE. I've said enough.

MRS. HICKS. George, for my sake, son.

GEORGE. He had bad luck that's all.

HICKS. And a bad chest.

GEORGE. A bad chest.

HICKS. What did I do?

MRS. HICKS. Please, dear.

GEORGE. You did your best. Nobody can do better than their best.

HICKS. And how did I do it?

GEORGE. By working day and night for us.

HICKS. And who did I think about all the time?

GEORGE. That's enough, Dad. That's enough.

HICKS (*raising his voice*). Who did I think about all the time?

GEORGE. About mam and me.

HICKS. And for whose sake was it that I did what I had to do?

GEORGE. For our sake.

HICKS. Was any sacrifice too great even with the 'andicap of my chest?

GEORGE. No sacrifice was too great.

HICKS. Did I keep back anything for myself?

GEORGE. No, you didn't. Nothing.

HICKS. What am I?

GEORGE. Someone I can respect.

HICKS. WHAT AM I?

GEORGE. You're the best father a son ever had.

HICKS. You heard what he said, Alf?

ALF. I heard him.

HICKS (*triumphantly*). The best father he said. The best father a son ever had.

MRS. HICKS (*goes over to* GEORGE *and takes his arm*). There, everything's all right.

HICKS. My chest feels easier. Yes.

ALF. You'll make up with Sheila, George boy. Just a tiff, that's all. Everything will look different in the morning. I tell you what mun. We'll make a foursome, this week-end, and go into the country. You and Sheila and me and . . . oh, well, I'll find a nice girl. You know how easy it is for me.

MRS. HICKS. Yes, Alf. The girls run after you.

[*Enter* MISS CHANTRY *from rear door right.*]

MISS CHANTRY. I don't know what I said before. I was so distraught and had such a headache. I fear I talked nonsense about my beloved Harry. Harry was wonderful. If it wasn't for that fire above a shop . . .

MRS. HICKS. We understand, dear.

MISS CHANTRY. He was a hero and died a hero's death.

HICKS. Yes, yes. It was a tragedy.

[*Pause.*]

GEORGE. Sheila will change her mind tomorrow. As you said, Alf, it was a tiff.

MRS. HICKS. Everything's all right now. Everything's back to normal.

HICKS. Come and have a game of chess, George. One before turning in.

GEORGE. All right.

MRS. HICKS. Are you going to football tomorrow, Alf?

[HICKS *and* GEORGE *set up chess pieces.*]

ALF. I don't know. Hull will murder them, see.

HICKS. When I'm white I win because I'm white.

GEORGE. And when I'm black I win because I'm Zorinonfilligoff.

GEORGE AND HICKS (*together*). Ha!

MISS CHANTRY. Listen, listen. Open the window, Alf.

ALF. By damn, I will.

VOICE OFF (*faintly*). Three, four, five, six, seven. Tomorrow night at Sunshine Hall. (*Getting louder.*) One, two, three, four, five, six, seven. Tomorrow the Speaker will speak at Sunshine Hall. (*Fainter.*) One, two, three, four . . .

MISS CHANTRY. You hear what they're saying. He's going to speak tomorrow at Sunshine Hall. I've been waiting for that all my life.

ALF. He'll tell them. He'll tell them to say "No".

HICKS. The journalist will be back. You'll see.

GEORGE. I'll get two tickets. Two or bust. Me and Sheila. I won't mess it up this time.

MRS. HICKS. It will be lovely tomorrow.

VOICE OFF (*faintly*). Tomorrow at Sunshine Hall. One, two, three, four, five, six, seven. At Sunshine Hall.

MRS. HICKS. The van's going.

HICKS. Close the window, Alf. My chest. It's a real arctic wind.

CRITICAL COMMENTARY

Of course it is not polite to say so, but isn't it true that other people are largely second-raters? In fact aren't they as transparent as textbook cases? There they sit, lazy, whining, self-indulgent, wrapped in cheap fantasies, a houseful of cowards, waiting for someone to bail them out—Lefty, the Gentleman Caller, Godot, the Speaker. No wonder the world is in a mess. What they need is simply enough courage to face the facts and enough character to make the proper choices.

Dannie Abse, fortunately, is one of us rather than one of the others. He was born in 1923 in Wales, an obviously disadvantaged place, and so he simply decided to go to London to medical school. Discovering that he wanted to write and that medicine is part alchemy, he made some more choices. Instead of copping out, taking to drink or pot, becoming a tiresome deadbeat writer or a rich, cynical specialist, he graduated, limited his practice, married a beautiful and intelligent young woman, had three fine children and wrote—a balanced account of his profession (*Medicine on Trial*), six volumes of poems (*Selected Poems,* Oxford, Eng., 1970, is the latest), and four plays so far.

It all seems clear enough. We happy, honest, uncomplicated few are in a position (we have even earned the right) to expose the others and to call them what they are: a house of cowards. And Abse's play of course does just that. The truth does indeed come out about everyone: the angular old maid, the hypochondriac father, the weak mother and son, the Welsh Don Juan, the naive girl friend, and the corrupted reporter. But the truth is offered to us in an unexpectedly complicated way. We are made to feel the pathos behind the desperate evasions of people trapped in a marginal existence, and there is something touching about their affection and tenderness for each other.

Even more important in the control of tone is the fact that the house of cowards is also a house of actors. This is perhaps the significance of the play's growth from Abse's 1957 poem "The Meeting" to its present theatrical form as the 1960 best English "Off-Broadway" play of the year. At any rate it is through the theatricality of the cowards that the author best controls our reactions. Take Miss Chantry for example. Any silly girl of nineteen can spend an unsuccessful week-end with a married man, but who, off the stage, can become such an absolute mistress of the cheap romantic and religious cliché? "Thirty years ago to the day since poor Harry walked heart-high through the flames. . . .

Fire robbed me of my children . . . My Harry went into that Nebuchadnezzar's furnace. He went in like Shadrach, Meshach and Abed-nego. But no angel interceded." There is not a word of truth in it. It is a work of theatrical art. Or take Mr. Hicks. He is more than a failure; he is a complete failure. There is something farcical about the sheer number of jobs he has lost and the speed and certainty with which he has been fired. And his splendid plans for the future—the string of laundries before automatic washers, the fleet of nonexistent taxi cabs—recall the stage dreams of alchemy. It is a role that W. C. Fields might have considered. In fact the cowards have spent so much time and care on their lies and the stage business that goes with them that they begin to resemble an old vaudeville troupe. When this happens, the truth is held at a distance or becomes somehow too complex for ordinary moral categories. After all, don't we all have our own routines and favorite family stories, fictions that both tell and hide the truth and give some style to existence? Something about the tone of the play can be learned from comparing George's apology to his father with Tom's apology to his mother in *The Glass Menagerie.* Are Abse's characters closer to Brecht's peasants than to Williams' psychological cripples?

Mr. Nott may be a special problem. Like Barabbas, he has so many theatrical assignments that he is hard to define. His treatment has cured him of his fantasies, and he can therefore be used both as a truth teller and as an embodiment of the cost of being cured. "All of you," he says, "you have no courage. . . . If you had, then everything would be so good—well, at least better. You wouldn't have to search for any public orthodoxy, or build a cocoon of dreams, or any false structure to feel safe in, to lie in—there'd be just the green, cruel ordinary world that indisputably is, and you'd praise that difficult simplicity." And then he becomes more and more rhetorical: "To accept even our own terror of ignorance, this here and now, this time, this earth, this most strange of meeting places." Perhaps there is hope even for Mr. Nott. Is he beginning to find a new act, a new identity, that of a good minor modern poet?

It is rewarding but not easy to translate the theatrical into a simpler language. Dannie Abse, echoing that earlier doctor, Anton Chekhov, warns us that his play,

> is not simply a play of ideas—if it is, then I have failed miserably and would have been better advised to write an essay. Rather I intended it to be about *people,* not only how such people make dreams, but how their dreams make them. . . . *House of Cowards* is concerned with a group of people in our time, in this country, who need to colour their unsatisfactory lives with gaudy dreams. They need, though, more than these private fictions. They also desperately yearn for the realisation of a public dream. They have, in short (like so many), messianic and utopian yearnings. For man,

I believe, has not only the need to see himself as good and generous but also ambiguously longs to exist with his fellow men, equally idealised, in a good and generous and beautiful world. These legitimate longings are sometimes exploited and therefore can be potentially dangerous; but, in themselves, pure, they are an optimistic symptom of the human condition—that's why I don't think *House of Cowards* is necessarily a pessimistic play, though in exploring public and private illusions I dare say it underlines the fact that "the song of a caged bird has only a reality of a huge weeping." (From the program for the performance at the Prince of Wales Theater, Cardiff, January, 1963)

Is this the play he wrote?

A 0
B 1
C 2
D 3
E 4
F 5
G 6
H 7
I 8
J 9